Cybersecurity

ALL-IN-ONE

by Joseph Steinberg; Kevin Beaver; Ted Coombs; and Ira Winkler

for **dummies**®

A Wiley Brand

Cybersecurity All-in-One For Dummies®

Published by: **John Wiley & Sons, Inc.,** 111 River Street, Hoboken, NJ 07030-5774, www.wiley.com

Copyright © 2023 by John Wiley & Sons, Inc., Hoboken, New Jersey

Media and software compilation copyright © 2023 by John Wiley & Sons, Inc. All rights reserved.

Published simultaneously in Canada

No part of this publication may be reproduced, stored in a retrieval system or transmitted in any form or by any means, electronic, mechanical, photocopying, recording, scanning or otherwise, except as permitted under Sections 107 or 108 of the 1976 United States Copyright Act, without the prior written permission of the Publisher. Requests to the Publisher for permission should be addressed to the Permissions Department, John Wiley & Sons, Inc., 111 River Street, Hoboken, NJ 07030, (201) 748-6011, fax (201) 748-6008, or online at http://www.wiley.com/go/permissions.

Trademarks: Wiley, For Dummies, the Dummies Man logo, Dummies.com, Making Everything Easier, and related trade dress are trademarks or registered trademarks of John Wiley & Sons, Inc. and may not be used without written permission. All other trademarks are the property of their respective owners. John Wiley & Sons, Inc. is not associated with any product or vendor mentioned in this book.

LIMIT OF LIABILITY/DISCLAIMER OF WARRANTY: WHILE THE PUBLISHER AND AUTHORS HAVE USED THEIR BEST EFFORTS IN PREPARING THIS WORK, THEY MAKE NO REPRESENTATIONS OR WARRANTIES WITH RESPECT TO THE ACCURACY OR COMPLETENESS OF THE CONTENTS OF THIS WORK AND SPECIFICALLY DISCLAIM ALL WARRANTIES, INCLUDING WITHOUT LIMITATION ANY IMPLIED WARRANTIES OF MERCHANTABILITY OR FITNESS FOR A PARTICULAR PURPOSE. NO WARRANTY MAY BE CREATED OR EXTENDED BY SALES REPRESENTATIVES, WRITTEN SALES MATERIALS OR PROMOTIONAL STATEMENTS FOR THIS WORK. THE FACT THAT AN ORGANIZATION, WEBSITE, OR PRODUCT IS REFERRED TO IN THIS WORK AS A CITATION AND/OR POTENTIAL SOURCE OF FURTHER INFORMATION DOES NOT MEAN THAT THE PUBLISHER AND AUTHORS ENDORSE THE INFORMATION OR SERVICES THE ORGANIZATION, WEBSITE, OR PRODUCT MAY PROVIDE OR RECOMMENDATIONS IT MAY MAKE. THIS WORK IS SOLD WITH THE UNDERSTANDING THAT THE PUBLISHER IS NOT ENGAGED IN RENDERING PROFESSIONAL SERVICES. THE ADVICE AND STRATEGIES CONTAINED HEREIN MAY NOT BE SUITABLE FOR YOUR SITUATION. YOU SHOULD CONSULT WITH A SPECIALIST WHERE APPROPRIATE. FURTHER, READERS SHOULD BE AWARE THAT WEBSITES LISTED IN THIS WORK MAY HAVE CHANGED OR DISAPPEARED BETWEEN WHEN THIS WORK WAS WRITTEN AND WHEN IT IS READ. NEITHER THE PUBLISHER NOR AUTHORS SHALL BE LIABLE FOR ANY LOSS OF PROFIT OR ANY OTHER COMMERCIAL DAMAGES, INCLUDING BUT NOT LIMITED TO SPECIAL, INCIDENTAL, CONSEQUENTIAL, OR OTHER DAMAGES.

For general information on our other products and services, please contact our Customer Care Department within the U.S. at 877-762-2974, outside the U.S. at 317-572-3993, or fax 317-572-4002. For technical support, please visit https://hub.wiley.com/community/support/dummies.

Wiley publishes in a variety of print and electronic formats and by print-on-demand. Some material included with standard print versions of this book may not be included in e-books or in print-on-demand. If this book refers to media such as a CD or DVD that is not included in the version you purchased, you may download this material at http://booksupport.wiley.com. For more information about Wiley products, visit www.wiley.com.

Library of Congress Control Number: 2022950725

ISBN 978-1-394-15285-8 (pbk); ISBN 978-1-394-15286-5 (ePDF); ISBN 978-1-394-15287-2 (epub)

SKY10076550_060324

Contents at a Glance

Table of Contents

Introduction

Computer and network security is a complex subject and an ever-moving target. Protecting your information means understanding the threats that are out there, and knowing how to defend against them. Whether you're securing a business network, cloud data, personal computer, or smart device, the techniques and tools outlined in *Cybersecurity All-in-One For Dummies* can help.

About This Book

Cybersecurity All-in-One For Dummies provides the guidance, instruction, and tools you need to protect your information from cyberthieves and other ne'er do wells.

The book describes common cyberattacks and how to defend against them. You also gain insight into the bad guys who perform the attacks. Leading cybersecurity experts detail the actions you can take to enhance your personal cybersecurity and that of your small or big business. You see how to protect your devices, and data stored on a network and on the cloud.

This book provides essential instructions for testing the security of your systems. And when you're ready to create and implement a security awareness program to help reduce potential damage caused by social engineering, physical, phishing, and other attacks, this book has got you covered.

A quick note: Sidebars (shaded boxes of text) provide details that may be of interest but are not crucial to understanding the topics being covered in the main text. Feel free to read them or skip them. You also can skip over paragraphs accompanied by the Technical Stuff icon, as text marked with this icon provides more detail about theory or other aspects of the topic covered in a section.

Foolish Assumptions

Here are some assumptions about you and why you're picking up this book:

» You want to secure your personal or business data and systems against cyberattack.

» You are an aspiring information technology (IT) or security professional, or you have some background in managing or working directly in the information security field.

» You're familiar with basic computer, network, and information security concepts and terms.

» You have access to a computer and a network on which to use these techniques and tools.

» You have the go-ahead from your employer or your client to perform the hacking techniques described in this book.

Disclaimer: This book is intended solely for information technology (IT) and information security professionals to test the security of their (or their clients') systems in an authorized fashion. If you choose to use the information in this book to hack or break into computer systems maliciously and without authorization, you're on your own. Neither the authors nor anyone else associated with this book shall be liable or responsible for any unethical or criminal choices that you might make and execute using the methodologies and tools that are described in this book.

Icons Used in This Book

REMEMBER

This important information merits repeating — and is worth remembering.

TECHNICAL STUFF

This icon flags information that is a little deeper or more conceptual than the main text. If you're in a hurry, feel free to skip these paragraphs.

TIP

This icon flags actions that can make life easier when you're working to secure your data and systems.

WARNING

Take heed of information flagged with this icon to save yourself from problems down the road.

Beyond the Book

In addition to the material in the print or e-book you're reading right now, this product comes with some access-anywhere goodies on the web. Check out the free Cheat Sheet for information on combatting social engineering attacks, selecting from password-cracking utilities, and creating a security awareness interview. To get this Cheat Sheet, simply go to www.dummies.com and search for "*Cybersecurity All-in-One For Dummies* Cheat Sheet" in the Search box.

Where to Go from Here

You don't have to read this book from cover to cover, but you can if you like! If you want to find information on a specific aspect of cybersecurity, take a look at the table of contents or index, and then turn to the chapter or section that interests you.

For example, if you want to understand the most common cybersecurity attacks and the people to defend against, turn to Book 1. If you're interested in enhancing your personal cybersecurity, see Book 2. To secure business data stored on your network and in the cloud, see Books 3 and 4. To test your business's vulnerability and increase security awareness throughout your organization, see Books 5 and 6.

No matter where you start, you'll find the information you need to secure the information stored on your personal and business devices, on networks and on the cloud. Good luck!

1

Cybersecurity Basics

Contents at a Glance

Chapter **1**

What Exactly Is Cybersecurity?

To improve your ability to keep yourself and your loved ones cybersecure, you need to understand what cybersecure means, what your goals should be vis-à-vis cybersecurity, and what exactly you're securing against.

While the answers to these questions may initially seem simple and straightforward, they aren't. As you see in this chapter, these answers can vary dramatically between people, company divisions, organizations, and even within the same entity at different times.

Cybersecurity Means Different Things to Different Folks

While *cybersecurity* may sound like a simple enough term to define, in actuality, from a practical standpoint, it means quite different things to different people in different situations, leading to extremely varied relevant policies, procedures, and practices. Individuals who want to protect their social media accounts from hacker takeovers, for example, are exceedingly unlikely to assume many of the approaches and technologies used by Pentagon workers to secure classified networks.

Typically, for example:

>> For **individuals,** *cybersecurity* means that their personal data is not accessible to anyone other than themselves and others they have authorized, and that their computing devices work properly and are free from malware.

>> For **small business owners,** *cybersecurity* may include ensuring that credit card data is properly protected and that standards for data security are properly implemented at point-of-sale registers.

>> For **firms conducting online business,** *cybersecurity* may include protecting servers that untrusted outsiders regularly interact with.

>> For **shared service providers,** *cybersecurity* may entail protecting numerous data centers that house numerous servers that, in turn, host many virtual servers belonging to many different organizations.

>> For **the government,** *cybersecurity* may include establishing different classifications of data, each with its own set of related laws, policies, procedures, and technologies.

REMEMBER

The bottom line is that while the word cybersecurity is easy to define, the practical expectations that enters people's minds when they hear the word vary quite a bit.

Technically speaking, cybersecurity is the subset of information security that addresses information and information systems that store and process data in electronic form, whereas *information security* encompasses the security of all forms of data (for example, securing a paper file and a filing cabinet).

That said, today, many people colloquially interchange the terms, often referring to aspects of information security that are technically not part of cybersecurity as being part of the latter. Such usage also results from the blending of the two in many situations. Technically speaking, for example, if someone writes down a password on a piece of paper and leaves the paper on a desk where other people can see the password instead of placing the paper in a safe deposit box or safe, that person has violated a principle of information security, not of cybersecurity, even though those actions may result in serious cybersecurity repercussions.

Cybersecurity Is a Constantly Moving Target

While the ultimate goal of cybersecurity may not change much over time, the policies, procedures, and technologies used to achieve it change dramatically as the years march on. Many approaches and technologies that were more than adequate to protect consumers' digital data in 1980, for example, are effectively worthless today, either because they're no longer practical to employ or because technological advances have rendered them obsolete or impotent.

While assembling a complete list of every advancement that the world has seen in recent decades and how such changes impact cybersecurity is effectively impossible, we can examine several key development areas and their impacts on the ever-evolving nature of cybersecurity: technological changes, economic model shifts, and outsourcing.

Technological changes

Technological changes tremendously impact cybersecurity. New risks come along with the new capabilities and conveniences that new offerings deliver. As the pact of technological advancement continues to increase, therefore, so does the pace of new cybersecurity risks. While the number of such risks created over the past few decades as the result of new offerings is astounding, the areas described in the following sections have yielded a disproportionate impact on cybersecurity.

Digital data

In the last few decades, dramatic changes have occurred in the technologies that exist, as well as who use such technologies, how they do so, and for what purposes. All of these factors impact cybersecurity.

Consider, for example, that when many of the people alive today were children, controlling access to data in a business environment simply meant that the data owner placed a physical file containing the information into a locked cabinet and gave the key to only people the owner recognized as being authorized personnel and only when they requested the key during business hours. For additional security, the data owner may have located the cabinet in an office that was locked after business hours and which itself was in a building that was also locked and alarmed.

Today, with the digital storage of information, however, simple filing and protection schemes have been replaced with complex technologies that must automatically authenticate users who seek the data from potentially any location at potentially any time, determine whether the users are authorized to access a particular element or set of data, and securely deliver the proper data — all while preventing any attacks against the system servicing data requests, any attacks against the data in transit, and any of the security controls protecting the both of them.

Furthermore, the transition from written communication to email and chat has moved tremendous amounts of sensitive information to Internet-connected servers. Likewise, society's move from film to digital photography and videography has increased the stakes for cybersecurity. Nearly every photograph and video taken today is stored electronically rather than on film and negatives — a situation that has enabled criminals situated anywhere to either steal people's images and leak them, hold people's valuable images ransom with ransomware, or use them to create turmoil in people's personal lives by creating fake profiles on dating sites, for example. The fact that movies and television shows are now stored and transmitted electronically has likewise allowed pirates to copy them and offer them to the masses — sometimes via malware-infested websites.

The Internet

The most significant technological advancement when it comes to cybersecurity impact has been the arrival of the Internet era, and, more specifically, the transformation of the Internet from a small network connecting researchers at a few universities to an enormous worldwide communication system utilized by a tremendous number of people, businesses, and organizations. In recent years, the Internet has also become the conduit for communication both by billions of smart devices and by people remotely connecting to industrial control systems. Just a few decades ago, it was unfathomable that hackers from across the globe could disrupt a business, manipulate an election, create a fuel shortage, pollute drinking water, or steal a billion dollars. Today, no knowledgeable person would dismiss any such possibilities.

Prior to the Internet era, it was extremely difficult for the average hacker to financially profit by hacking. The arrival of online banking and commerce in the 1990s, however, meant that hackers could directly steal money or goods and services — which meant that not only could hackers quickly and easily monetize their efforts, but unethical people had strong incentives to enter the world of cybercrime.

Cryptocurrency

Compounding those incentives severalfold has been the arrival and proliferation of cryptocurrency over the past decade, along with innovation that has dramatically magnified the potential return-on-investment for criminals involved in cyber-crime, simultaneously increasing their ability to earn money through cybercrime and improving their ability to hide while doing so. Criminals historically faced a challenge when receiving payments since the account from which they ultimately withdrew the money could often be tied to them. Cryptocurrency effectively elim-inated such risks.

In addition, not only has the dramatic rise in the value of cryptocurrencies held by criminals over the past few years enriched many crooks, providing evildoers with the resources to invest in enhancing their cyber-arsenals, but also the pub-lic's perception of cryptocurrency as a quick way to get rich has helped scammers perpetuate all sorts of social engineering–based cybercrimes related to cryptocur-rency investing.

Furthermore, the availability and global liquidity of cryptocurrency has helped criminals launder money obtained through the perpetration of all sorts of crimes.

Mobile workforces and ubiquitous access

Not that many years ago, in the pre-Internet era, it was impossible for hackers to access corporate systems remotely because corporate networks were not con-nected to any public networks, and often had no dial-in capabilities. Executives on the road would often call their assistants to check messages and obtain necessary data while they were remote. In later years they may have connected to corpo-rate networks via special dial-up connections using telephone-line–based private lines for extremely limited access to only one or two specific systems.

Connectivity to the Internet, of course, created risk, but initially most firewalls were set up in ways that did not allow people outside the organization to ini-tiate communications — so, short of firewall misconfigurations and/or bugs, most internal systems remained relatively isolated. The dawn of e-commerce and e-banking, of course, meant that certain production systems had to be reachable and addressable from the outside world, but employee networks, for example, usually remained generally isolated.

The arrival of remote access technologies — starting with services like Outlook Web Access and pcAnywhere, and evolving to full VPN and VPN-like access — has totally changed the game.

The dramatic reduction in the cost of cellular-based high-speed Internet access and the availability of mobile data plans supporting data limits sufficient enough to allow effective full-time use have dramatically reduced the need for utilizing public Wi-Fi connections. Risks that one might have deemed reasonable to take a few years ago in order to achieve various business aims have become unnecessary, and as such, policies and procedures regarding public Wi-Fi access must be updated.

Smart devices

Likewise, the arrival of smart devices and the *Internet of Things* (the universe of devices that are connected to the Internet, but that are not traditional computers) — whose proliferation and expansion are presently occurring at a startling rate — means that unhackable solid-state machines are being quickly replaced with devices that can potentially be controlled by hackers halfway around the world.

Globalization has also meant that cheap Internet of Things (IoT) devices can be ordered by consumers in one country from a supplier in another country halfway around the world — introducing without any oversight all sorts of unknown hardware into personal and corporate environments.

Big data

While big data is helping facilitate the creation of many cybersecurity technologies, it also creates opportunities for attackers. By correlating large amounts of information about the people working for an organization, for example, criminals can more easily than before identify ideal methods for social engineering their way into the organization or locate and exploit possible vulnerabilities in the organization's infrastructure. As a result, various organizations have been effectively forced to implement all sorts of controls to prevent the leaking of information, and the practices of many organizations have invited all sorts of accusations around data misuse and inappropriate protections from both employees and outsiders.

The COVID-19 pandemic

The COVID-19 pandemic served as a watershed moment in the history of cybersecurity. By forcing people to stay home in environments that are unprecedentedly isolated from one another, the novel coronavirus dramatically — and likely permanently — changed the way people in the Western world work, thereby yielding multiple, significant impacts on cybersecurity.

In the short term, the pandemic created all sorts of cybersecurity problems. Organizations that had no work-from-home infrastructures in place, or had such infrastructure but only for a limited portion of their employee populations, were suddenly faced with having to enable people to work from home — often without the ability to prepare users, policies, procedures, and technologies in advance. Many such businesses could not distribute laptops or security devices fast enough to prevent work stoppages, and as a result, relied on users to utilize their personal devices for work purposes without any additional security layers added.

Likewise, few organizations offered their employees separate Internet connections or separate routers for their remote workstations, so remote workers were nearly always sharing physical and logical networks with their other personal devices and possibly with their children who may have been gaming and/or attending virtual school. The security risks of doing such is discussed in detail in Book 2, Chapter 3.

Compounding COVID-19–inflicted cybersecurity problems was the fact that while many employers did provide some forms of endpoint security software, many did not, and even those that did rarely addressed any hardware-based risks. To this day, for example, many employers have no idea what router models their employees are using for remote access or when such devices were last updated.

Another major cybersecurity concern created by the pandemic has been that communications between employees shifted from conference rooms to remote meetings, opening the doors for hackers to disrupt communications or steal confidential information. The problems were so bad that a new term "zoom bombing" was coined in 2020 to refer to the practice of mischievous folks joining and wreaking havoc in virtual meetings to which they were never invited.

Of course, the fact that people who would otherwise work together in the same location are suddenly unable to communicate quickly in person has also opened the door for many social engineering attacks. For example, a CFO who receives an email from the boss asking that the company pay a certain party for services cannot verify the validity of the request as the CFO has done many times in the past by walking ten feet to the boss's office to confirm that the boss actually sent the message.

Likewise, people working in homes in which children are in virtual school, or quarantined, or simply living, often suffer from far more interruptions than they would had they been working in an office setting. Interruptions often lead to mistakes, and mistakes often lead to cybersecurity problems. The stress of remaining socially isolated for long periods of time also increases the odds of people making dangerous cybersecurity errors.

At a macro level, the sudden shift to work-at-home arrangements has meant that many cybersecurity professionals are increasingly overwhelmed, a problem further exacerbated by organizations having to reallocate resources — sometimes shifting both people and money from security projects to efforts to ensure continuity of operations.

And, of course, being confined to their homes has afforded many hackers more time to work on their crafts as well, perhaps contributing to the significant rise in the number of zero-day attacks and other newer forms of cybersecurity attacks seen since the pandemic's onset. Book 1, Chapter 2 dives into many of the common cyberattacks that are out there.

REMEMBER

Entire books have been written on the impact of technological advancement. The main point to understand is that technological advancement has had a significant impact on cybersecurity, making security harder to deliver and raising the stakes when parties fail to properly protect their assets. In addition, unforeseen developments, such as pandemics, can bring sudden, huge technological changes that carry with them tremendous cybersecurity dangers.

Social shifts

Various changes in the ways that humans behave and interact with one another have also had a major impact on cybersecurity. The Internet, for example, allows people from all over the world to interact in real-time. Of course, this real-time interaction also enables criminals all over the world to commit crimes remotely. But it also allows citizens of repressive countries and free countries to communicate, creating opportunities for dispelling the perpetual propaganda utilized as excuses for the failure of totalitarianism to produce quality of lives on par with the democratic world. At the same time, it also delivers to the cyberwarriors of governments at odds with one another the ability to launch attacks via the same network.

The conversion of various information management systems from paper to computer, from isolated to Internet-connected, and from accessible-only-in-the-office to accessible from any smartphone or computer has dramatically changed the equation when it comes to what information hackers can steal. And the COVID-19 pandemic has brought many of these issues to the forefront.

Furthermore, in many cases in which technological conversions were, for security reasons, not initially done, the pressure emanating from the expectations of modern people that every piece of data be available to them at all times from anywhere has forced such conversions to occur, creating additional opportunities for criminals. To the delight of hackers, many organizations that, in the past, wisely protected sensitive information by keeping it offline have simply lost the ability to enjoy such protections if they want to stay in business. No modern example portrays this as well as the sudden global shift to remote working arrangements in 2020.

Social media has also transformed the world of information — with people growing accustomed to sharing far more about themselves than ever before — often with audiences far larger than before as well. Today, due to the behavioral shift in this regard, it is trivial for evildoers from anywhere to assemble lists of a target's friends, professional colleagues, and relatives and to establish mechanisms for communication with all those people. Likewise, it is easier than ever before to find out what technologies a particular firm utilizes and for what purposes, discover people's travel schedules, and ascertain their opinions on various topics or their tastes in music and movies. The trend toward increased sharing continues. Most people remain blindly unaware of, and unconcerned with, how much information about them lives on Internet-connected machines and how much other information about them can be extrapolated from the aforementioned data.

All these changes have translated into a scary reality: Due to societal shifts, evildoers can easily launch much larger, more sophisticated social engineering attacks today than they could just a few years.

Economic model shifts

Connecting nearly the entire world has allowed the Internet to facilitate other trends with tremendous cybersecurity ramifications. Operational models that were once unthinkable, such as that of an American company utilizing a call center in India and a software development shop in the Philippines, have become the mainstay of many corporations. These changes, however, create cybersecurity risks of many kinds.

The last 20 years have seen a tremendous growth in the outsourcing of various tasks from locations in which they're more expensive to carry out to regions in which they can be accomplished at much lower costs. The notion that a company in the United States could rely primarily on computer programmers in India or in the Philippines or that entrepreneurs in New York seeking to have a logo made for their business could, shortly before going to bed, pay someone halfway around the globe $5.50 to create it and have the logo in their email inbox immediately upon waking up the next morning, would have sounded like economic science-fiction a generation ago. Today, it's not only common, but also in many cases, it is more common than any other method of achieving similar results.

Of course, many cybersecurity ramifications result from such transformations of how people do business.

Data being transmitted needs to be protected from destruction, modification, and theft, and globalization means that greater assurance is needed to ensure that back doors are not intentionally or inadvertently inserted into code. Greater protections are needed to prevent the theft of intellectual property and other forms of corporate espionage. Code developed in foreign countries, for example, may be at risk of having backdoors inserted by agents of their respective governments. Likewise, computer equipment may have backdoors inserted into hardware components — a problem the U.S. government is struggling with addressing as this book goes to print.

WARNING

Hackers no longer necessarily need to directly breach the organizations they seek to hack; they merely need to compromise one or more of the organizations' providers. And such providers may be far less careful with their information security and personnel practices than the ultimate target, or may be subject to manipulation by governments far less respectful of people's rights than are the powers-that-be in the ultimate targets' location.

Political shifts

As with advances in technology, political shifts have had tremendous cybersecurity repercussions, some of which seem to be permanent fixtures of news headlines. The combination of government power and mighty technology has often proven to be a costly one for ordinary people. If current trends continue, the impact on cybersecurity of various political shifts will continue to grow substantially in the foreseeable future.

Data collection

The proliferation of information online and the ability to attack machines all over the world have meant that governments can spy on citizens of their own countries and on the residents of other nations to an extent never before possible.

Furthermore, as more and more business, personal, and societal activities leave behind digital footprints, governments have much easier access to a much greater amount of information about their potential intelligence targets than they could acquire even at dramatically higher costs just a few years ago. Coupled with the relatively low cost of digital storage, advancing big data technologies, and the expected eventual impotence of many of today's encryption technologies due to the emergence of quantum computing and other cutting-edge developments, governments have a strong incentive to collect and store as much information as they can about as many people as they can, in case it is of use at some later date. It is more likely than not, for example, that hostile governments may have already begun compiling dossiers on the people who will eventually serve as president and vice president of the United States 25 years from now.

The long-term consequences of this phenomenon are, obviously, as of yet unknown, but one thing is clear: If businesses do not properly protect data, less-than-friendly nations are likely to obtain it and store it for use in either the short term, the long term, or both.

Election interference

A generation ago, for one nation to interfere in the elections of another was no trivial matter. Of course, such interference existed — it has occurred as long as there have been elections — but carrying out significant interference campaigns was expensive, resource-intensive, and extremely risky.

To spread misinformation and other propaganda, materials had to be printed and physically distributed or recorded and transmitted via radio, meaning that individual campaigns were likely to reach only small audiences. As such, the efficacy effects of such efforts were often quite low, and the risk of the party running the campaign being exposed was relatively high, and often carried with it the potential for severe repercussions.

Manipulating voter registration databases to prevent legitimate voters from voting and/or to allow bogus voters to vote was extremely difficult and entailed tremendous risks; someone "working on the inside" would likely have had to be nothing short of a traitor in order to have any real significant on election results. In a country such as the United States, in which voter registration databases are decentralized and managed on a county level, recruiting sufficient saboteurs to truly impact a major election would likely have been impossible, and the odds of getting caught while attempting to do so were likely extremely high.

Likewise, in the era of paper ballots cast in person and of manual vote counting, for a foreign power to manipulate actual vote counts on any large scale was impractical, if not impossible.

Today, however, the game has changed. A government can easily spread misinformation through social media at an extremely low cost. If it crafts a well-thought-out campaign, it can rely on other people to spread the misinformation — something that people could not do en masse in the era of radio recordings and printed pamphlets. The ability to reach many more people, at a much lower cost than ever before, has meant that more parties are able to interfere in political campaigns and can do so with more efficacy than in the past. Similarly, governments can spread misinformation to stir up civil discontent within their adversaries' nations and to spread hostility between ethnic and religious groups living in foreign lands.

Insecure mail-in ballots as used throughout the United States during the 2020 presidential election aggravated mistrust. And, with voter registration databases stored electronically and sometimes on servers that are at least indirectly connected to the Internet, records may be able to be added, modified, or deleted from halfway across the globe without detection. Even if such hacking is, in reality, impossible, the fact that many citizens today believe that it may be possible has led to an undermining of faith in elections, a phenomenon that we have witnessed in recent years and that has permeated throughout all levels of society. Even Jimmy Carter, a former president of the United States, expressed at one point that that he believed that full investigation into the 2016 presidential election would show that Donald Trump lost the election — despite there being absolutely no evidence whatsoever to support such a conclusion, even after a thorough FBI investigation into the matter. Statements and actions from the other side of the political aisle — including the terrible chaos at the U.S. Capitol after the 2020 presidential election — showed clearly that concerns about election integrity, and the perception that elections might be manipulatable through cyberattacks and other technology-based techniques, are bipartisan. It is also not hard to imagine that if online voting were ever to arrive, the potential for vote manipulation by foreign governments, criminals, and even political parties within the nation voting — and for removing the ballot auditability that exists today — would grow astronomically.

In an indication of how much concern is growing around potential election manipulation, consider that a decade ago, the United States did not consider election-related computer systems to be critical infrastructure, and did not directly provide federal funding to secure such systems. Today, most people understand that the need for cybersecurity in such areas is of paramount importance, and the policies and behavior of just a few years ago seems nothing short of crazy.

Hacktivism

Likewise, the spread of democracy since the collapse of the Soviet Union a generation ago, coupled with Internet-based interaction between people all over the globe, has ushered in the era of *hacktivism*. People are aware of the goings-on in more places than in the past. Hackers angry about some government policy or activity in some location may target that government or the citizens of the country over which it rules from places far away. Likewise, citizens of one country may target entities in another country with whose policies they disagree, or whose government they consider a national adversary.

Greater freedom

At the same time, repressed people are now more aware of the lifestyles of people in freer and more prosperous countries, a phenomenon that has both forced some governments to liberalize, and motivated others to implement cybersecurity-type controls to prevent using various Internet-based services.

Sanctions

Another political ramification of cybersecurity pertains to international sanctions: Rogue states subject to such sanctions have been able to use cybercrime of various forms to circumvent such sanctions.

For example, North Korea is believed to have spread malware that mines cryptocurrency for the totalitarian state to computers all over the world, thereby allowing the country to circumvent sanctions by obtaining liquid money that can easily be spent anywhere.

Thus, the failure by individuals to adequately secure their personal computers can directly impact political negotiations.

New balances of power

While the militaries of certain nations have long since grown more powerful than those of their adversaries — both the quality and quantity of weapons vary greatly between nations — when it comes to cybersecurity the balance of power is totally different.

While the quality of cyberweapons may vary between countries, the fact that launching cyberattacks costs little means that all militaries have an effectively unlimited supply of whatever weapons they use. In fact, in most cases, launching millions of cyberattacks costs little more than launching just one.

Also, unlike in the physical world in which any nation that bombed civilian homes in the territory of its adversary can reasonably expect to face a severe reprisal, rogue governments regularly hack with impunity people in other countries. Victims often are totally unaware that they have been compromised, rarely report such incidents to law enforcement, and certainly don't know whom to blame.

Even when a victim realizes that a breach has occurred and even when technical experts point to the attackers as the culprits, the states behind such attacks often enjoy plausible deniability (for example, they claim, "we didn't do it, maybe someone else within our country did it" or the like), preventing any government from publicly retaliating. In fact, the difficulty of ascertaining the source of cyberattacks coupled with the element of plausible deniability is a strong incentive for governments to use cyberattacks as a mechanism of proactively attacking an adversary, wreaking various forms of havoc without fear of significant reprisals.

Furthermore, the world of cybersecurity created a tremendous imbalance between attackers and defenders that works to the advantage of less powerful nations.

Governments that could never afford to launch huge barrages against an adversary in the physical world can easily do so in the world of cyber, where launching each attack costs next to nothing. As a result, attackers can afford to keep attacking until they succeed — and they need to breach systems only once to "succeed" — creating a tremendous problem for defenders who must shield their assets against every single attack. This imbalance has translated into a major advantage for attackers over defenders and has meant that even minor powers can successfully breach systems belonging to superpowers.

In fact, this imbalance contributes to the reason why cybersecurity breaches seem to occur so often, as many hackers simply keep attacking until they succeed. If an organization successfully defends against 10 million attacks but fails to stop the 10,000,001, it may suffer a severe breach and make the news. Reports of the breach likely won't even mention the fact that it has a 99.999999 percent success rate in protecting its data and that it successfully stopped attackers one million times in a row. Likewise, if a business installed 99.999 percent of the patches that it should have but neglected to fix a single known vulnerability, it's likely to suffer a breach due to the number of exploits available to criminals. Media outlets will point out the organization's failure to properly patch, overlooking its near perfect record in that area.

As such, the era of cybercrime has also changed the balance of power between criminals and law enforcement.

Criminals know that the odds of being caught and successfully prosecuted for a cybercrime are dramatically smaller than those for most other crimes, and that repeated failed attempts to carry out a cybercrime are not a recipe for certain arrest as they are for most other crimes. They are also aware that law enforcement agencies lack the resources to pursue the vast majority of cyber criminals. Tracking down, taking into custody, and successfully prosecuting someone stealing data from halfway across the world via numerous hops in many countries and a network of computers commandeered from law-abiding folks, for example, requires gathering and dedicating significantly more resources than does catching a thief who was recorded on camera while holding up in a store in a local police precinct. It is also far easier and more lucrative to launch cyberattacks against rich targets from a locale in which law enforcement can be "paid off" to look the other way, than it is to net the same reward via a physical robbery.

With the low cost of launching repeated attacks, the odds of eventual success in their favor, the odds of getting caught and punished miniscule, and the potential rewards growing with increased digitalization, criminals know that cybercrime pays, underscoring the reason that you need to protect yourself.

Looking at the Risks Cybersecurity Mitigates

People sometimes explain the reason that cybersecurity is important as being "because it prevent hackers from breaking into systems and stealing data and money." But such a description dramatically understates the role that cybersecurity plays in keeping the modern home, business, or even world running, and in keeping humans safe from physical harm.

In fact, the role of cybersecurity can be looked at from a variety of different vantage points, with each presenting a different set of goals. Of course the following lists aren't complete, but they should provide food for thought and underscore the importance of understanding how to cybersecure yourself and your loved ones.

The goal of cybersecurity: The CIA Triad

Cybersecurity professionals often explain that the goal of cybersecurity is to ensure the Confidentiality, Integrity, and Availability (CIA) of data, sometimes referred to as the CIA Triad, with the pun lovingly intended:

>> **Confidentiality** refers to ensuring that information isn't disclosed or in any other way made available to unauthorized entities (including people, organizations, or computer processes).

WARNING

Don't confuse confidentiality with privacy: Confidentiality is a subset of the realm of privacy. It deals specifically with protecting data from unauthorized viewers, whereas privacy in general encompasses much more.

Hackers that steal data undermine confidentiality.

>> **Integrity** refers to ensuring that data is both accurate and complete.

Accurate means, for example, that the data is never modified in any way by any unauthorized party or by a technical glitch. *Complete* refers to, for example, data that has had no portion of itself removed by any unauthorized party or technical glitch.

Integrity also includes ensuring *nonrepudiation,* meaning that data is created and handled in such a fashion that nobody can reasonably argue that the data is not authentic or is inaccurate.

Cyberattacks that intercept data and modify it before relaying it to its destination — sometimes known as *man-in-the-middle attacks* — undermine integrity.

>> **Availability** refers to ensuring that information, the systems used to store and process it, the communication mechanisms used to access and relay it, and all associated security controls function correctly to meet some specific benchmark (for example, 99.99 percent uptime). People outside of the cybersecurity field sometimes think of availability as a secondary aspect of information security after confidentiality and integrity. In fact, ensuring availability is an integral part of cybersecurity. Doing so, though, is sometimes more difficult than ensuring confidentiality or integrity. One reason that this is true is that maintaining availability often requires involving many more noncybersecurity professionals, leading to a "too many cooks in the kitchen" type challenge, especially in larger organizations. Distributed denial-of-service attacks attempt to undermine availability. Also, consider that attacks often use large numbers of stolen computer power and bandwidth to launch DDoS attacks, but responders who seek to ensure availability can only leverage the relatively small amount of resources that they can afford.

From a human perspective

The risks that cybersecurity addresses can also be thought of in terms better reflecting the human experience:

>> **Privacy risks:** Risks emanating from the potential loss of adequate control over, or misuse of, personal or other confidential information.

>> **Financial risks:** Risks of financial losses due to hacking. Financial losses can include both those that are direct — for example, the theft of money from someone's bank account by a hacker who hacked into the account — and those that are indirect, such as the loss of customers who no longer trust a small business after the latter suffers a security breach.

>> **Professional risks:** Risks to one's professional career that stem from breaches. Obviously, cybersecurity professionals are at risk for career damage if a breach occurs under their watch and is determined to have happened due to negligence, but other types of professionals can suffer career harm due to a breach as well. C-level executives can be fired, board members can be sued, and so on. Professional damage can also occur if hackers release private communications or data that shows someone in a bad light — for example, records that a person was disciplined for some inappropriate action, sent an email containing objectionable material, and so on.

>> **Business risks:** Risks to a business similar to the professional risks to an individual. Internal documents leaked after breach of Sony Pictures painted various the firm in a negative light vis-à-vis some of its compensation practices.

>> **Personal risks:** Many people store private information on their electronic devices, from explicit photos to records of participation in activities that may not be deemed respectable by members of their respective social circles. Such data can sometimes cause significant harm to personal relationships if it leaks. Likewise, stolen personal data can help criminals steal people's identities, which can result in all sorts of personal problems.

>> **Physical danger risks:** Cyberattacks on sewage treatment plants, utilities, and hospitals in recent years have shown clearly that the failure to maintain cybersecurity can lead to the endangering of human lives. For example, in 2020, a woman in Germany died while being transported between hospitals after the hospital at which she had been a patient was struck by ransomware. And in 2021, a lawsuit was filed arguing that a baby died as a result of medical mistakes made as she was born at a hospital in Alabama during system outages caused by a ransomware attack.

Chapter 2

Getting to Know Common Cyberattacks

Although many types of cyberattacks exist, this book focuses on those that are most likely to affect you or your business. The reality is, you're likely reading this book to learn about how to keep yourself cybersecure, not to learn about matters that have no impact on you, such as forms of attacks that are normally directed at espionage agencies, industrial equipment, or military armaments.

In this chapter, you find out about the different types of problems that cyberattackers can create through the use of attacks that commonly impact individuals and small businesses.

Attacks That Inflict Damage

Attackers launch some forms of cyberattacks with the intent to inflict damage to victims. The threat posed by such attacks is not that a criminal will directly steal your money or data, but that the attackers will inflict harm to you in some other specific manner — a manner that may ultimately translate into financial, military, political, physical, or other benefit to the attacker and (potentially) damage of some sort to the victim.

Types of attacks that inflict damage include

>> Denial-of-service (DoS) attacks

>> Distributed denial-of-service (DDoS) attacks

>> Botnets and zombies

>> Data destruction attacks

Denial-of-service (DoS) attacks

A *denial-of-service (DoS) attack* is one in which an attacker intentionally attempts to either partially cripple or totally paralyze a computer or computer network by flooding it with large amounts of requests or data, which overload the target and make it incapable of responding properly to legitimate requests.

In many cases, the requests sent by the attacker are each, on their own, legitimate — for example, a normal request to load a web page. In other cases, the requests aren't normal requests. Instead, they leverage knowledge of various protocols to send requests that optimize, or even magnify, the effect of the attack.

In any case, denial-of-service attacks work by overwhelming computer systems' central processing units (CPUs) and/or memory, utilizing all the available network communications bandwidth, and/or exhausting networking infrastructure resources such as routers.

Distributed denial-of-service (DDoS) attacks

A *distributed denial-of-service (DDoS) attack* is a DoS attack in which many individual computers or other connected devices across disparate regions simultaneously flood the target with requests. In recent years, nearly all major denial-of-service attacks have been distributed in nature — and some have involved the use of Internet-connected cameras and other devices as attack vehicles, rather than classic computers. Figure 2-1 illustrates the anatomy of a simple DDoS attack.

The goal of a DDoS attack is to knock the victim offline, and the motivation for doing so varies.

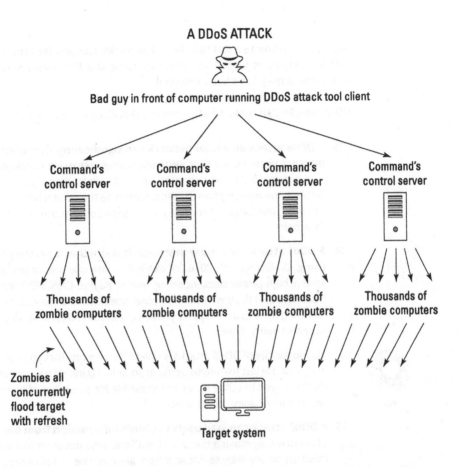

A DDoS ATTACK

Bad guy in front of computer running DDoS attack tool client

Command's control server

Command's control server

Command's control server

Command's control server

Thousands of zombie computers

Thousands of zombie computers

Thousands of zombie computers

Thousands of zombie computers

Zombies all concurrently flood target with refresh

Target system

FIGURE 2-1:
A DDoS attack.

Sometimes the goal is financial: Imagine, for example, the damage that may result to an online retailer's business if an unscrupulous competitor knocked the former's site offline during Black Friday weekend. Imagine a crook who shorts the stock of a major retailer of toys right before launching a DDoS attack against the retailer two weeks before Christmas.

DDoS attacks remain a serious and growing threat. Criminal enterprises even offer DDoS for hire services, which are advertised on the dark web as offering, for a fee, to "take your competitor's websites offline in a cost-effective manner."

In some cases, DDoS launchers may have political, rather than financial, motives. For example, corrupt politicians may seek to have their opponents' websites taken down during an election season, thereby reducing the competitors' abilities to spread messages and receive online campaign contributions. Hacktivists may also launch DDoS attacks in order to take down sites in the name of "justice" — for example, targeting law enforcement sites after an unarmed person is killed during an altercation with police.

In fact, according to a 2017 study by Kaspersky Lab and B2B International, almost half of companies worldwide that experienced a DDoS attack suspect that their competitors may have been involved.

DDoS attacks can impact individuals in three significant ways:

>> **A DDoS attack on a local network can significantly slow down all Internet access from that network.** Sometimes these attacks make connectivity so slow that connections to sites fail due to *session timeout* settings, meaning that the systems terminate the connections after seeing requests take longer to elicit responses than some maximum permissible threshold.

>> **A DDoS attack can render inaccessible a site that a person plans on using.** On October 21, 2016, for example, many users were unable to reach several high-profile sites, including Twitter, PayPal, CNN, HBO Now, The Guardian, and dozens of other popular sites, due to a massive DDoS attack launched against a third party providing various technical services for these sites and many more.

TIP

The possibility of DDoS attacks is one of the reasons that you should never wait until the last minute to perform an online banking transaction — the site that you need to utilize may be inaccessible for a number of reasons, one of which is an ongoing DDoS attack.

>> **A DDoS attack can lead users to obtain information from one site instead of another.** By making one site unavailable, Internet users looking for specific information are likely to obtain it from another site — a phenomenon that allows attackers to either spread misinformation or prevent people from hearing certain information or vantage points on important issues. As such, DDoS attacks can be used as an effective mechanism — at least over the short term — for censoring opposing points of view.

Botnets and zombies

Often, DDoS attacks use what are known as *botnets*. Botnets are a collection of compromised computers that belong to other parties, but that a hacker remotely controls and uses to perform tasks without the legitimate owners' knowledge.

Criminals who successfully infect one million computers with malware can, for example, potentially use those machines, known as *zombies*, to simultaneously make many requests from a single server or server farm in an attempt to overload the target with traffic.

Data destruction attacks

Sometimes attackers want to do more than take a party temporarily offline by overwhelming it with requests — they may want to damage the victim by destroying or corrupting the target's information and/or information systems. A criminal may seek to destroy a user's data through a *data destruction attack* — for example, if the user refuses to pay a ransomware ransom that the crook demands. Of course, all the reasons for launching DDoS attacks (see preceding section) are also reasons that a hacker may attempt to destroy someone's data as well.

Wiper attacks are advanced data destruction attacks in which a criminal uses malware to wipe the data on a victim's hard drive or SSD, in such a fashion that the data is difficult or impossible to recover.

To put it simply, unless the victim has backups, someone whose computer is wiped by a wiper is likely to lose access to all the data and software that was previously stored on the attacked device.

Is That Really You? Impersonation

One of the great dangers that the Internet creates is the ease with which mischievous parties can impersonate others. Prior to the Internet era, for example, criminals could not easily impersonate a bank or a store and convince people to hand over their money in exchange for some promised rate of interest or goods. Physically mailed letters and later telephone calls became the tools of scammers, but none of those earlier communication techniques ever came close to the power of the Internet to aid criminals attempting to impersonate law-abiding parties.

Creating a website that mimics the website of a bank, store, or government agency is quite simple and can sometimes be done within minutes. Criminals can find a near-endless supply of domain names that are close enough to those of legitimate parties to trick some folks into believing that a site that they are seeing is the real deal when it's not, giving crooks the typical first ingredient in the recipe for online impersonation.

WARNING

Sending an email that appears to have come from someone else is simple and allows criminals to perpetrate all sorts of crimes online.

Phishing

Phishing refers to an attempt to convince a person to take some action by impersonating a trustworthy party that reasonably may legitimately ask the user to take such action.

For example, a criminal may send an email that appears to have been sent by a major bank and that asks recipients to click on a link in order to reset their passwords due to a possible data breach. When users click the link, they are directed to a website that appears to belong to the bank, but is actually a replica run by the criminal. As such, the criminal uses the fraudulent website to collect usernames and passwords to the banking site.

WARNING

While phishing attacks have been around for many years, they show no signs of going away. Some experts believe that a majority of medium- and large-sized businesses in the United States now suffer some form of successful phishing attack every year.

Spear phishing

Spear phishing refers to phishing attacks that are designed and sent to target a specific person, business, or organization. If a criminal seeks to obtain credentials into a specific company's email system, for example, the attacker may send emails crafted specifically for particular targeted individuals within the organization. Often, criminals who spear phish research their targets online and leverage overshared information on social media in order to craft especially legitimate-sounding emails.

For example, the following type of email is typically a lot more convincing than, "Please login to the mail server and reset your password":

> *Hi, I am going to be getting on my flight in ten minutes. Can you please log in to the Exchange server and check when my meeting is? For some reason, I cannot get in. You can try to call me by phone first for security reasons, but if you miss me, just go ahead, check the information, and email it to me — as you know that I am getting on a flight that is about to take off.*

CEO fraud

CEO fraud is similar to spear phishing (see preceding section) in that it involves a criminal impersonating the CEO or other senior executive of a particular business, but the instructions provided by "the CEO" may be to take an action directly, not to log in to a system, and the goal may not be to capture usernames and passwords or the like.

The crook, for example, may send an email to the firm's CFO with instructions to issue a wire payment to a particular new vendor or to send all the organization's W2 forms for the year to a particular email address belonging to the firm's accountant.

CEO fraud often nets significant returns for criminals and makes employees who fall for the scams appear incompetent. As a result, people who fall prey to such scams are often fired from their jobs. CEO fraud increased during the COVID-19 pandemic as people worked from home and were unable to verify the veracity of communications with as much ease as they could prior to the arrival of the novel coronavirus.

Smishing

Smishing refers to cases of phishing in which the attackers deliver their messages via text messages (SMS) rather than email. The goal may be to capture usernames and passwords or to trick the user into installing malware.

Vishing

Vishing, or voice-based phishing, is phishing via POTS — that stands for "plain old telephone service." Yes, criminals use old, time-tested methods for scamming people. Today, most such calls are transmitted by Voice over Internet Protocol (VoIP) systems, but in the end, the scammers are calling people on regular telephones much the same way that scammers have been doing for decades.

Pharming

Pharming refers to attacks that present much like typical phishing attacks, but exploit different technical vulnerabilities in Internet-based routing in order to do so. Like phishing attacks, pharming attacks involve impersonating a trustworthy party that may legitimately ask the would-be victim to take some particular action. However, in pharming attacks, this is achieved not by tricking users into taking an action that brings them to a rogue clone of a legitimate website, but rather by poisoning routing tables and other network infrastructure so that any user who clicks a link to the legitimate website, or even enters the legitimate website's URL into a browser, will be routed to a criminal's clone.

Whaling: Going for the "big fish"

Whaling refers to spear phishing that targets high-profile business executives or government officials. (Yes, whales are mammals and not fish, but this is about phishing not fishing.) For more on spear phishing, see the section earlier in this chapter.

Messing around with Other People's Stuff: Tampering

Sometimes attackers don't want to disrupt an organization's normal activities, but instead seek to exploit those activities for financial gain. Often, crooks achieve such objectives by manipulating data in transit or as it resides on systems of their targets in a process known as *tampering*.

In a basic case of tampering with data in transit, for example, imagine that a user of online banking has instructed the bank to wire money to a particular account, but somehow a criminal intercepted the request and changed the relevant routing and account number to the criminal's own.

A criminal may also hack into a system and manipulate information for similar purposes. Using the previous example, imagine if a criminal changed the payment address associated with a particular payee so that when the Accounts Payable department makes an online payment, the funds are sent to the wrong destination (well, at least it is wrong in the eyes of the payer).

One can also imagine the impact of a criminal modifying an analyst's report about a particular stock before the report is issued to the public, with the criminal, of course, standing by to buy or sell stocks when the report is released in order to exploit the soon-to-be-reversed impact of the misinformation.

Captured in Transit: Interception

Interception occurs when attackers capture information in transit. In the context of cybersecurity, the transit is usually between computers or other electronic devices, but it could also be between a human and a device as well (such as capturing voice spoken to a voice recognition system). If the data isn't properly encrypted, the party intercepting it may be able to misuse it. And, of course, data captured directly from humans — such as the aforementioned voice recordings — often cannot be encrypted.

WARNING

Even properly encrypted data might be at risk. The protection afforded by today's encryption algorithms and mechanisms may be rendered worthless at some point in the future if vulnerabilities are discovered down the road, or as more powerful computers — especially quantum computers — arrive on the scene. As such, encrypted data that is intercepted may be secure from disclosure today, but may be stored and compromised in the future.

Man-in-the-middle attacks

One special type of interception is known as a *man-in-the-middle attack*. In this type of an attack, the interceptor proxies the data between the sender and recipient in an attempt to disguise the fact that the data is being intercepted. *Proxying* in such a case refers to the man-in-the-middle intercepting requests and then transmitting them (either in modified form or unmodified) to their original intended destinations and then receiving the responses from those destination and transmitting them (in modified form or unmodified) back to the sender. By employing proxying, the man-in-the-middle makes it difficult for senders to know that their communications are being intercepted because when they communicate with a server, they receive the responses they expect.

For example, a criminal may set up a bogus bank site (see the earlier "Phishing" section) and relay any information that anyone enters on the bogus site to the actual bank site so that the criminal can respond with the same information that the legitimate bank would have sent. Proxying of this sort not only helps criminals avoid detection — users who provide the crook with their password and then perform their normal online banking tasks may have no idea that anything abnormal occurred during the online banking session — but also helps the criminals ensure that they capture the right password. If a user enters an incorrect password, the criminal will know to prompt for the correct one.

Figure 2-2 shows the anatomy of a man-in-the-middle intercepting and relaying communications.

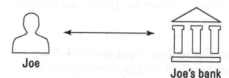

Man-in-the-middle attack
Joe wants to communicate with his bank

Joe   Joe's bank

But Bob's evil server is acting as a man-in-the-middle

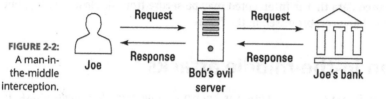

Request   Request

Response   Response

Joe   Bob's evil   Joe's bank
             server

FIGURE 2-2:
A man-in-
the-middle
interception.

Taking What Isn't Theirs: Data Theft

Many cyberattacks involve stealing the victim's data. An attacker may want to steal data belonging to individuals, businesses, or a government agency for one or more of many possible reasons.

People, businesses, nonprofits, and governments are all vulnerable to data theft.

Personal data theft

Criminals often try to steal people's data in the hope of finding items that they can monetize, including:

>> Data that can be used for identity theft or sold to identity thieves

>> Compromising photos or health-related data that may be sellable or used as part of extortion schemes

>> Information that is stolen and then erased from the user's machine that can be ransomed to the user

>> Password lists that can be used for breaching other systems

>> Confidential information about work-related matters that may be used to make illegal stock trades based on insider information

>> Information about upcoming travel plans that may be used to plan robberies of the victim's home

Business data theft

Criminals can use data stolen from businesses for a number of nefarious purposes:

>> **Making stock trades:** Similar to the criminals mentioned earlier in this chapter who tamper with data in order to manipulate financial markets, criminals may also seek to steal data in order to have advance knowledge of how a particular business's current and yet unreported quarter is going. They then use that insider information to illegally trade stocks or options, thereby potentially making a significant profit.

>> **Selling data to unscrupulous competitors:** Criminals who steal sales pipeline information, documents containing details of future products, or other sensitive information can sell that data to unscrupulous competitors or to unscrupulous employees working at competitors whose management may never find out how such employees suddenly improved their performance.

>> **Leaking data to the media:** Sensitive data can embarrass the victim and cause its stock to decline (perhaps after selling short some shares).

>> **Leaking data covered by privacy regulations:** The victim may be potentially fined.

>> **Recruiting employees:** By recruiting employees or selling the information to other firms looking to hire employees with similar skills or with knowledge of competitions' systems, criminals who steal emails and discover communication between employees that indicates that one or more employees are unhappy in their current positions can sell that information to parties looking to hire.

>> **Stealing and using intellectual property:** Parties that steal the source code for computer software may be able to avoid paying licensing fees to the software's rightful owner. Parties that steal design documents created by others after extensive research and development can easily save millions of dollars — and, sometimes, even billions of dollars — in research and development costs.

Data exfiltration

Data exfiltration is a somewhat complicated term for a simple concept, and refers to situations in which a party, through the use of malware or other automated means, or by manually issuing commands to a remote computer, causes data to be transferred without authorization from some information system or repository to somewhere else.

Anytime you hear of a data breach in which sensitive data has been copied by criminals, that is an example of data exfiltration. Depending on what data leaks and from whom, data exfiltration can easily harm the confidence of a business's customers, reduce trust in a government entity, undermine the confidentiality of proprietary information, and/or undermine national security.

Compromised credentials

Compromised credentials refers to account authentication information that someone else other than you is privy to, such as your username and/or password. Abusing compromised credentials almost always refers to situations in which a criminal uses a login and password combination that was obtained from one cybersecurity breach in order to gain unauthorized access to a system and carry out another cybersecurity breach. Such attacks with compromised credentials are common, as criminals know that people commonly reuse login username/ password combinations.

Likewise, use by a rogue employee of another employee's credentials for any nefarious purpose (and even for most non-nefarious purposes) is also an example of such an attack.

Forced policy violations

Any attack in which a user or device is forced to violate cybersecurity policies is considered a forced policy violation attack.

Cyberbombs That Sneak into Your Devices: Malware

Malware, or malicious software, is an all-encompassing term for software that intentionally inflicts damage on its users who typically have no idea that they are running it. Malware includes computer viruses, worms, Trojans, ransomware, scareware, spyware, cryptocurrency miners, adware, and other programs intended to exploit computer resources for nefarious purposes.

Viruses

Computer viruses are instances of malware that, when executed, replicate by inserting their own code into computer systems. Typically, the insertion is in data files (for example, as rogue macros within a Word document), the special portion of hard drives or solid state drives that contain the code and data used to boot a computer or disk (also known as *boot sectors*), or other computer programs.

Like biological viruses, computer viruses can spread like wildfire, but they cannot spread without having hosts to infect. Some computer viruses significantly impact the performance of their hosts, while others are, at least at times, hardly noticeable.

REMEMBER

While computer viruses still inflict tremendous damage worldwide, the majority of serious malware threats today arrive in the form of worms and Trojans.

Worms

Computer worms are stand-alone pieces of malware that replicate themselves without the need for hosts in order to spread. Worms often propagate over connections by exploiting security vulnerabilities on target computers and networks. Because they normally consume network bandwidth, worms can inflict harm even without modifying systems or stealing data. They can slow down network connections — and few people, if any, like to see their internal and Internet connections slow down.

Trojans

Trojans (appropriately named after the historical Trojan horse) is malware that is either disguised as nonmalicious software or hidden within a legitimate, nonmalicious application or piece of digital data.

Trojans are most often spread by some form of social engineering — for example, by tricking people into clicking on a link, installing an app, or running some email attachment. Unlike viruses and worms, Trojans typically don't self-propagate using technology — instead, they rely on the effort (or more accurately, the mistakes) of humans.

Ransomware

Ransomware is malware that demands that a ransom be paid to some criminal in exchange for the infected party not suffering some harm. Ransomware often encrypts user files and threatens to delete the encryption key if a ransom isn't paid within some relatively short period of time, but other forms of ransomware involve a criminal actually stealing user data and threatening to publish it online if a ransom is not paid.

Some ransomware actually steals the files from users' computers, rather than simply encrypting data, so as to ensure that users have no possible way to recover their data (for example, using an anti-ransomware utility) without paying the ransom.

Ransomware is most often delivered to victims as a Trojan or a virus, but has also been successfully spread by criminals who packaged it in a worm. In recent years sophisticated criminals have even crafted targeted ransomware campaigns that leverage knowledge about what data is most valuable to a particular target and how much that target can afford to pay in ransoms.

Figure 2-3 shows the ransom demand screen of WannaCry — a flavor of ransomware that inflicted at least hundreds of millions of dollars in damage (if not billions), after initially spreading in May 2017. Many security experts believe that the North Korean government or others working for it created WannaCry, which, within four days infected hundreds of thousands of computers in about 150 countries.

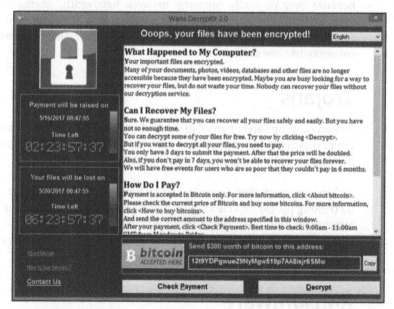

FIGURE 2-3: Ransomware demanding ransom.

Ransomware has emerged as one of the largest sources of financial losses due to cyberattacks for American businesses, as well as led to interruptions in the life of ordinary civilians. For example, in 2021, ransomware attacks on an American fuel pipeline operator led to shortages of gas and price increases, and attacks on a meat processing facility led to shortages of meat in some locations.

Scareware

Scareware is malware that scares people into taking some action. One common example is malware that scares people into buying security software. A message appears on a device that the device is infected with some virus that only a particular security package can remove, with a link to purchase that "security software." This topic is also explored in the discussion about fake malware later in this chapter.

Spyware

Spyware is software that surreptitiously, and without permission, collects information from a device. Spyware may capture a user's keystrokes (in which case it is called a *keylogger*), video from a video camera, audio from a microphone, screen images, and so on.

It is important to understand the difference between spyware and invasive programs. Some technologies that may technically be considered spyware if users had not been told that they were being tracked online are in use by legitimate businesses; they may be invasive, but they are not malware. This type of *nonspyware that also spies* includes beacons that check whether a user loaded a particular web page and tracking cookies installed by websites or apps. Some experts have argued that any software that tracks a smartphone's location while the app is not being actively used by the device's user also falls into the category of *nonspyware that also spies* — a definition that would include popular apps, such as Uber.

Cryptocurrency miners

Cryptocurrency miners, or cryptominers, are malware that, without any permission from devices' owners, commandeers infected devices' brainpower (its CPU cycles) to generate new units of a particular cryptocurrency (which the malware gives to the criminals operating the malware) by completing complex math problems that require significant processing power to solve.

The proliferation of cryptocurrency miners exploded in 2017 with the rise of cryptocurrency values. Even after price levels subsequently dropped, the miners are still ubiquitous as once criminals have invested in creating the miners, there is little cost in continuing to deploy them. Not surprisingly, as cryptocurrency prices began to rise again in 2019, new strains of cryptominers began to appear as well — some of which specifically target Android smartphones.

Many low-end cybercriminals favor using cryptominers. Even if each miner, on its own, pays the attacker very little, miners are easy to obtain and directly monetize cyberattacks without the need for extra steps (such as collecting a ransom) or the need for sophisticated command and control systems.

Adware

Adware is software that generates revenue for the party operating it by displaying online advertisements on a device. Adware may be malware — that is, installed and run without the permission of a device's owner — or it may be a legitimate component of software (for example, installed knowingly by users as part of some free, ad-supported package).

TIP

Some security professionals refer to the former as *adware malware,* and the latter as *adware.* Because no consensus exists, it's best to clarify which of the two is being discussed when you hear someone mention just the generic term adware.

Blended malware

Blended malware is malware that utilizes multiple types of malware technology as part of an attack — for example, combining features of Trojans, worms, and viruses.

Blended malware can be quite sophisticated and often stems from skilled attackers.

Zero-day malware

Zero-day malware is any malware that exploits a vulnerability not previously known to the public or to the vendor of the technology containing the vulnerability, and is, as such, often extremely potent.

Regularly creating zero-day malware requires significant resource and development. It's quite expensive and is often crafted by the cyber armies of nation states rather than by other hackers.

Commercial purveyors of zero-day malware have been known to charge over $1 million for a single exploit.

Fake malware on computers

Ironically, some attackers don't even bother to actually hack computers. Instead, they just send messages to would-be victims that the would-be victims' computers are infected and that to re-secure the device the intended victims must pay some fee or purchase some security software. Sometimes criminals are able to display messages to such an effect in a pop-up window, and sometimes they keep things simple, and just send the messages via email.

Fake malware on mobile devices

Fake malware may be even more common on mobile devices than on laptops and other computers. For various technical reasons, it is harder to hack mobile devices, so many criminals go for the "low hanging fruit" and just pretend to have compromised devices in order to get would-be victims to pay up. There are even flavors of "mobile device ransomware" that display ransomware-type demands without ever having encrypted anything on the mobile device.

Fake security subscription renewal notifications

A type of social-engineering attack that exploits people's desire to remain cyber-secure (included in the malware section because it is directly related to protection against malware), is fake "renewal notices" from anti-malware product vendors. Email that says one's security software subscription is expiring and asks users to click a link (don't do it!) or to otherwise submit payment for a renewal, can closely parallel their legitimate counterparts. This sort of attack has become extremely common during the COVID-19 pandemic era during which many people worked from home and, more often than ever before, were responsible for making sure they had current security software subscriptions.

Poisoned Web Service Attacks

Many different types of attacks leverage vulnerabilities in servers, and new weaknesses are constantly discovered, which is why cybersecurity professionals have full-time jobs keeping servers safe. Entire books — or even several series of books — can be written on such a topic, which is, obviously, beyond the scope of this work.

That said, it is important for you to understand the basic concepts of server-based attacks because some such attacks can directly impact you.

One such form of attack is a *poisoned web service attack,* or a *poisoned web page attack.* In this type of attack, an attacker hacks into a web server and inserts code onto it that causes it to attack users when they access a page or set of pages that the server is serving.

For example, a hacker may compromise the web server serving www.abc123.com and modify the home page that is served to users accessing the site so that the home page contains malware.

But a hacker does not even need to necessarily breach a system in order to poison web pages!

If a site that allows users to comment on posts isn't properly secured, for example, it may allow a user to add the text of various commands within a comment — commands that, if crafted properly, may be executed by users' browsers any time they load the page that displays the comment. A criminal can insert a command to run a script on the criminal's website, which can receive the authentication credentials of the user to the original site because it is called within the context of one of that site's web pages. Such an attack is known as *cross-site scripting,* and it continues to be a problem even after over a decade of being addressed.

Network Infrastructure Poisoning

As with web servers, many different types of attacks leverage vulnerabilities in network infrastructure, and new weaknesses are constantly discovered. The vast majority of this topic is beyond the scope of this book. That said, as is the case with poisoned web servers, you need to understand the basic concepts of server-based attacks because some such attacks can directly impact you. For example, criminals may exploit various weaknesses in order to add corrupt domain name system (DNS) data into a DNS server.

DNS is the directory of the Internet that translates human readable addresses into their numeric, computer-usable equivalents (IP addresses). For example, if you enter https://JosephSteinberg.com into your web browser, DNS directs your connection to an address taking the form of four numbers less than 256 and separated by periods, such as 104.18.45.53.

By inserting incorrect information into DNS tables, a criminal can cause a DNS server to return an incorrect IP address to a user's computer. Such an attack can easily result in a user's traffic being diverted to a computer of the attacker's choice instead of the user's intended destination. If the criminal sets up a phony bank site on the server to which traffic is being diverted, for example, and impersonates on that server a bank that the user was trying to reach, even a user who enters the bank URL into a browser (as opposed to just clicking on a link) may fall prey after being diverted to the bogus site. (This type of attack is known as *DNS poisoning* or *pharming.*)

REMEMBER

Network infrastructure attacks take many forms. Some seek to route people to the wrong destinations. Others seek to capture data, while others seek to effectuate denial-of-service conditions. The main point to understand is that the piping of the Internet is quite complex was not initially designed with security in mind, and is vulnerable to many forms of misuse.

Malvertising

Malvertising is an abbreviation of the words malicious advertising and refers to the use of online advertising as a vehicle to spread malware or to launch some other form of a cyberattack.

Because many websites display ads that are served and managed by third-party networks and that contain links to various other third parties, online advertisements are a great vehicle for attackers. Even companies that adequately secure their websites may not take proper precautions to ensure that they do not deliver problematic advertisements created by, and managed by, someone else.

As such, malvertising sometimes allows criminals to insert their content into reputable and high-profile websites with large numbers of visitors (something that would be difficult for crooks to achieve otherwise), many of whom may be security conscious and who would not have been exposed to the criminal's content had it been posted on a less reputable site.

Furthermore, because websites often earn money for their owners based on the number of people who click on various ads, website owners generally place ads on their sites in a manner that will attract users to the ads. As such, malvertising allows criminals to reach large audiences via a trusted site without having to hack anything.

Some malvertising requires users to click on the ads in order to become infected with malware; others do not require any user participation — users' devices are infected the moment the ad displays.

Drive-by downloads

Drive-by downloads is somewhat of a euphemism that refers to software that users download without understanding what they are doing. A drive-by download may occur, for example, if users download malware by going to a poisoned website that automatically sends the malware to the users' device when they open the site.

Drive-by downloads also include cases in which users know that they are downloading software, but is not aware of the full consequences of doing so. For example, if a user is presented with a web page that says that a security vulnerability is present on their computer and that tells the user to click on a button that says "Download to install a security patch," the user has provided authorization for the (malicious) download — but only because the user was tricked into believing that the nature of the download was far different than it truly is.

Stealing passwords

Criminals can steal passwords many different ways. Two common methods include

>> **Thefts of password databases:** If a criminal steals a password database from an online store, anyone whose password appears in the database is at risk of having their password compromised. If the store properly encrypted its passwords, it may take time for the criminal to perform what is known as a *hash attack,* but nonetheless, passwords — especially those that are likely to be tested early on — may still be at risk. To date, stealing passwords is the most common way that passwords are undermined.

>> **Social engineering attacks:** *Social engineering attacks* are attacks in which a criminal tricks people into doing something they would not have done had they realized that the person making the request was tricking them in some way. One example of stealing a password via social engineering is when a criminal pretends to be a member of the target's tech support department and tells the target that the target must reset a particular password to a particular value to have the associated account tested as is needed after the recovery from some breach, and the target obeys. (For more information, see the earlier section on phishing.)

>> **Credential attacks:** Credential attacks are attacks that seek to gain entry into a system by entering, without authorization, a valid username and password combination (or other authentication information as needed). These attacks fall into four primary categories:

- *Brute force:* Criminals use automated tools that try all possible passwords until they hit the correct one.

- *Dictionary attacks:* Criminals use automated tools to feed every word in the dictionary to a site until they hit the correct one.

- *Calculated attacks:* Criminals leverage information about a target to guess the target's password. Criminals may, for example, try someone's mother's family name because they can easily garner it for many people by looking at the most common last names of their Facebook friends or from posts on social media. (A Facebook post of "Happy Mother's Day to my wonderful mother!" that includes a user tag to a woman with a different last name than the user is a good giveaway.)

- *Blended attacks:* Some attacks leverage a mix of the preceding techniques — for example, utilizing a list of common last names, or performing a brute force attack technology that dramatically improves its efficiency by leveraging knowledge about how users often form passwords.

>> **Malware:** If crooks manage to get malware onto someone's device, it may capture passwords. (For more details, see the section on malware, earlier in this chapter.)

>> **Network sniffing:** If users transmit their password to a site without proper encryption while using a public Wi-Fi network, a criminal using the same network may be able to see that password in transit — as can potentially other criminals connected to networks along the path from the user to the site in question.

>> **Credential stuffing:** In credential stuffing, someone attempts to log in to one site using usernames and passwords combinations stolen from another site.

Exploiting Maintenance Difficulties

Maintaining computer systems is no trivial matter. Software vendors often release updates, many of which may impact other programs running on a machine. Yet, some patches are absolutely critical to be installed in a timely fashion because they fix bugs in software — bugs that may introduce exploitable security vulnerabilities. The conflict between security and following proper maintenance procedures is a never-ending battle — and security doesn't often win.

As a result, the vast majority of computers aren't kept up to date. Even people who do enable automatic updates on their devices may not be up to date — both because checks for updates are done periodically, not every second of every day, and because not all software offers automatic updating. Furthermore, sometimes updates to one piece of software introduce vulnerabilities into another piece of software running on the same device.

Advanced Attacks

If you listen to the news during a report of a major cyberbreach, you'll frequently hear commentators referring to advanced attacks. While some cyberattacks are clearly more complex than others and require greater technical prowess to launch, no specific, objective definition of an advanced attack exists. That said, from a subjective perspective, you may consider any attack that requires a significant investment in research and development to be successfully executed to be advanced. Of course, the definition of significant investment is also subjective. In some cases, R&D expenditures are so high and attacks are so sophisticated that there is near universal agreement that an attack was advanced. Some experts consider any zero-day attack to be advanced, but others disagree.

Advanced attacks may be opportunistic, targeted, or a combination of both.

Opportunistic attacks are attacks aimed at as many possible targets as possible in order to find some that are susceptible to the attack that was launched. The attacker doesn't have a list of predefined targets — the attacker's targets are effectively any and all reachable systems that are vulnerable to the launched attack. These attacks are similar to someone firing a massive shotgun in an area with many targets in the hope that one or more pellets will hit a target that it can penetrate.

Targeted attacks are attacks that target a specific party and typically involve utilizing a series of attack techniques until one eventually succeeds in penetrating into the target. Additional attacks may be launched subsequently in order to move around within the target's systems.

Opportunistic attacks

The goal of most opportunistic attacks is usually to make money — which is why the attackers don't care whose systems they breach; money is the same regardless of whose systems are breached in order to make it.

Furthermore, in many cases, opportunistic attackers may not care about hiding the fact that a breach occurred — especially after they've had time to monetize the breach, for example, by selling lists of passwords or credit card numbers that they stole.

While not all opportunistic attacks are advanced, some certainly are. Opportunistic attacks are quite different than targeted attacks.

Targeted attacks

When it comes to targeted attacks, successfully breaching any systems not on the target list isn't considered even a minor success.

For example, if a Russian operative is assigned the mission to hack into the Democratic and Republican parties' email systems and steal copies of all the email on the parties' email servers, the mission is going to be deemed a success only if the operative achieves those exact aims. If the operative manages to steal $1 million from an online bank using the same hacking techniques that were directed at the targets, it will not change a failure to breach the intended targets into even a small success. Likewise, if the goal of an attacker launching a targeted attack is to take down the website of a former employer the attacker had issues with, taking down other websites doesn't accomplish anything in the attacker's mind.

Because such attackers need to breach their targets no matter how well defended those parties may be, targeted attacks often utilize advanced attack methods — for example, exploiting vulnerabilities not known to the public or to the vendors who would need to fix them.

As you may surmise, advanced targeted attacks are typically carried out by parties with much greater technical prowess than those who carry out opportunistic attacks. Often, but not always, the goal of targeted attacks is to steal data undetected or to inflict serious damage — not to make money. After all, if one's goal is to make money, why expend resources targeting a well-defended site? Take an opportunistic approach and go after the most poorly defended, relevant sites.

Some advanced threats that are used in targeted attacks are described as *advanced persistent threats* (APTs):

>> **Advanced:** Uses advanced hacking techniques, likely with a major budget to support R&D

>> **Persistent:** Keeps trying different techniques to breach a targeted system and won't move on to target some other system just because the initial target is well protected

>> **Threat:** Has the potential to inflict serious damage

Blended (opportunistic and targeted) attacks

Another type of advanced attack is the opportunistic, semi-targeted attack. If criminals want to steal credit card numbers, for example, they may not care whether they successfully steal an equivalent number of active numbers from Best Buy, Walmart, or Barnes & Noble. All that the criminals likely care about is obtaining credit card numbers — from whom the numbers are pilfered isn't relevant.

At the same time, launching attacks against sites that don't have credit card data is a waste of the attacker's time and resources.

Some Technical Attack Techniques

While it is not necessary for most people to understand the details of how technical cyberattacks exploit system vulnerabilities, it is often interesting for people to understand the basic ideas behind popular methods utilized by hackers. The following sections outline some common ways of breaching and exploiting technical systems.

Rootkits

Rootkits are software toolsets that allow attackers to perform unauthorized activities at a privileged level on a compromised computer. ("Root" refers to the administrator account on UNIX systems.) Rootkits typically also contain features that seek to ensure that the attacker maintains access while that access remains secret from the authorized user or users of the compromised device.

Brute-force attacks

Brute-force attacks are simply attacks in which an attacker tries many possible values until the tools the attacker is using guess the correct value. A brute-force attack, for example, might consist of an attacker trying to log in to a user's account by trying every possible password combination until the attacker (or the attacker's brute-force attack tool, as the case may be) submits the correct one. Or the attacker may try different decryption keys until successfully decrypting an encrypted message.

Injection attacks

Injection attacks are attacks in which a system is expecting some sort of input from a user, but instead of submitting such input, an attacker submits malicious material such as code, which the receiving system then either executes or distributes to others to execute. Even though proper coding of applications can, at least in theory, prevent most forms of injection attacks, the reality is that many (if not most) systems remain vulnerable to such attacks, and as a result, injection attacks are an extremely commonly used tool within hacker arsenals.

Cross-site scripting

Cross-site scripting (XSS) is a specific type of injection attack in which an attacker adds malicious code into a legitimate website so that when a user visits the relevant website (via a web browser or app), the malicious code is delivered to the user's device and is executed there. The attacker is able to insert the malicious code into the legitimate server because the server allows users to submit material that will then be displayed to other users.

Online user forums and social media platforms are prime candidates for cross-site scripting attacks if they are not properly secured against such attacks. So are websites that allow users to comment on information such as a news article. For example, an XSS attack may occur if a hacker submits malicious code within a comment in such a fashion that when a subsequent user's browser tries to display the comment, it will end up executing the code.

SQL injection

SQL injection attacks are a specific type of injection attacks that exploit the way most computer systems store data, which is in relational databases that provide access to people and systems through the use of what is known as standard Structured Query Language (SQL) interfaces. When an attacker launches a SQL injection attack, the attacker simply submits data to the system that includes SQL commands rather than regular data. For example, if the system asks the user to submit a user ID in order to search on it, and the attacker, aware of the SQL command likely to be used by the system to its database in order to perform that search, instead submits a user ID that consists of code to both complete that command and to issue another command to display all records in the database, the system, if not protected against SQL injection, might do exactly what the attacker wants.

Even if the SQL injection attack does not fully work — and the system being attacked does not display the data — the system's response to the SQL injection attack may still reveal information about how it handles SQL injection, thereby providing the hacker with information about the system, the database, and the security mechanisms in place (or information as to what is not in place that should be).

Session hijacking

Session hijacking refers to situations in which an attacker takes over the communications session between two or more parties. For example, during an online baking session, if an attacker is able to come between the user and the user's bank in such a fashion that the bank continues its session with the attacker rather than with the legitimate user, that would be an example of a successful session hijacking attack.

In a session hijacking situation, the attacker effectively becomes the authenticated and authorized user as far as the other party is concerned, and the attacker can do anything on the relevant system that the legitimate user would have been authorized to do. Session hijacking often occurs when session management is mishandled by an application, especially in cases in which trust that communications are from a particular session with a particular user is established through technical mechanisms that should not be trusted for such purposes.

Malformed URL attacks

Malformed URL attacks are attacks in which an attacker crafts a URL that appears to link to a particular legitimate website, but because of special characters utilized within the URL text, actually does something nefarious. The attacker may then distribute the nefarious URL in email and text messages and/or by posting it within a comment on a blog or via other social media.

Another form of malformed URL attack is an attack in which an attacker crafts a URL that contains elements within it that will cause a system being accessed to malfunction.

Buffer overflow attacks

Buffer overflow attacks are attacks in which an attacker submits data to a system that exceeds the storage capacity of the memory buffer in which that data is supposed to be stored, thereby causing the system to overwrite other memory with the data the user submitted. Carefully crafted buffer overflow input by an attacker, for example, could overwrite memory space in which the system is storing commands that it will execute per the instructions of its authorized user — perhaps even replacing such commands with commands the attacker wants the system to execute.

Chapter **3**

The Bad Guys You Must Defend Against

Many centuries ago, the now world-famous Chinese military strategist and philosopher, Sun Tzu, wrote:

If you know the enemy and know yourself,

you need not fear the result of a hundred battles.

If you know yourself but not the enemy,

for every victory gained you will also suffer a defeat.

If you know neither the enemy nor yourself,

you will succumb in every battle.

As has been the case since ancient times, knowing your enemy is necessary in order to ensure that you can properly protect yourself.

Such wisdom remains true in the age of digital security. While Book 1, Chapter 2 covers many of the threats posed by cyber-enemies, this chapter covers the enemies themselves:

>> Who are they?

>> Why do they launch attacks?

>> How do they profit from attacks?

You also find out about nonmalicious attackers — both people and inanimate parties who can inflict serious damage even without any intent to do harm.

Bad Guys and Good Guys Are Relative Terms

Albert Einstein famously said that "everything is relative," and that concept certainly holds true when it comes to understanding who the "good" guys and "bad" guys are online. As someone seeking to defend yourself against cyberattacks, for example, you may view Russian hackers seeking to compromise your computer in order to use it to hack U.S. government sites as bad guys, but to patriotic Russian citizens, they may be heroes.

If you're an American enjoying free speech online and make posts promoting atheism, Christianity, Buddhism, or Judaism and an Iranian hacker hacks your computer, you'll likely consider the hacker to be a bad guy, but various members of the Iranian government and other fundamentalist Islamic groups may consider the hacker's actions to be a heroic attempt to stop the spread of blasphemous heresy.

In many cases, determining who is good and who is bad may be even more complicated and create deep divides between members of a single culture. For example, how would you view someone who breaks the law and infringes on the free speech of neo-Nazis by launching a crippling cyberattack against a neo-Nazi website that preaches hate? Or someone outside of law enforcement who illegally launches attacks against sites spreading child pornography, malware, or jihadist material that encourages people to kill Americans? Do you think that everyone you know would agree with you? Would U.S. courts agree?

Before answering, please consider that in the 1977 case, *National Socialist Party of America v. Village of Skokie*, the U.S. Supreme Court ruled that freedom of speech goes so far as to allow Nazis brandishing swastikas to march freely in a neighborhood in which many survivors of the Nazi Holocaust lived. Clearly, in the world of cyber, only the eye of the beholder can measure good and bad — and the eyes of different beholders can be quite different in such regards.

For the purposes of this book, therefore, you need to define who the good and bad guys are, and, as such, you should assume that the language in the book operates from your perspective as you seek to defend yourself digitally. Anyone seeking to harm your interests, for whatever reason, and regardless of what you perceive your interests to be, is, for the purposes of this book, bad.

Bad Guys Up to No Good

A group of potential attackers that is likely well-known to most people are the bad guys who are up to no good. This group consists of multiple types of attackers, with a diverse set of motivations and attack capabilities, who share one goal in common: They all seek to benefit themselves at the expense of others, including, potentially, you.

Bad guys up to no good include

>> Script kiddies

>> Kids who are not kiddies

>> Nations and states

>> Corporate spies

>> Criminals

>> Hacktivists

Script kiddies

The term *script kiddies* (sometimes shortened to skids or just kiddies) refers to people — often (but not always) young — who hack, but who are able to do so only because they know how to utilize scripts and/or programs developed by others to attack computer systems. These folks lack the technological sophistication needed in order to create their own tools or to hack without the assistance of others.

Kids who are not kiddies

While script kiddies are technologically unsophisticated (see preceding section), plenty of other kids are not. For many years, the caricature of a hacker has been a young, nerdy male interested in computers, who hacks from his parents' home or from a dorm room at college. In fact, the first crop of hackers targeting civilian systems included many technologically sophisticated kids interested in exploring or carrying out various mischievous tasks for bragging rights or due to curiosity.

While such attackers still exist, the percentage of attacks emanating from these attackers has dropped dramatically from a huge portion to a minute fraction of a percentage of all attacks.

Simply put, teenage hackers similar to those depicted in movies from the 1980s and 1990s may have been a significant force in the pre-commercial Internet era, but once hacking could deliver real money, expensive goods, and valuable, monetizable data, criminals seeking to profit joined the fray en masse. Furthermore, as the world grew increasingly reliant on data and more government and industrial systems were connected to the Internet, nation and states began to dramatically increase the resources that they allocated to cyber-operations from both espionage and military standpoints, further diluting the classic teenage hacker to a minute portion of today's cyberattackers.

Terrorists and other rogue groups

To date, terrorist groups and other parties intent on wreaking havoc and inflicting harm on innocent people have focused much of their online activities on brainwashing vulnerable people, recruiting members, and assembling supporters. There is little doubt, however, that such nefarious parties also understand the potential damage that can be inflicted by cyberattacks — and are actively building and seeking to exploit cyberattack capabilities — and that Western nations are beginning to react accordingly. In May 2019, for example, the Israeli military bombed a building in Gaza from which the Hamas terrorist organization — a group then receiving both financial aid and technology know-how from Iran — was allegedly launching cyberattacks against civilian targets.

Nations and states

Hacking by nations and states has received significant press coverage in recent years. The alleged hackings of the Democratic party email systems by Russian agents during the 2016 Presidential election campaign and the Republican party email system during the 2018 midterm elections are high profiles examples of nation state hacking.

That said, most nation and state cyberattacks are not nearly as high profile as those examples, do not receive media coverage, and do not target high profile targets. Often, they're not even discovered or known to anyone but the attackers!

Furthermore, in some countries, it is difficult, if not impossible, to distinguish between nation or state hacking and commercial espionage. Consider countries in which major companies are owned and operated by the government, for example. Are hackers from such companies nation or state hackers? Are such companies legitimate government targets, or is hacking them an example of corporate espionage?

Of course, nations and states that hack may also be seeking to impact public sentiment, policy decisions, and elections in other nations. Discussions of this topic have been aired via major media outlets on a regular basis since the 2016 presidential election. In fact, since then, accusations of foreign meddling in U.S. elections through the use of both cyber misinformation campaigns and hacking, only continue to grow.

Corporate spies

Unscrupulous companies sometimes utilize hacking as a way to gain competitive advantages or steal valuable intellectual property. The United States government, for example, has repetitively accused Chinese corporations of stealing the intellectual property of American businesses, costing Americans billions of dollars per year. Sometimes the process of stealing intellectual property involves hacking the home computers of employees at targeted companies with the hope that those employees will use their personal devices to connect to their employers' networks.

Criminals

Criminals have numerous reasons for launching various forms of cyberattacks:

>> **Stealing money directly:** Attacking to gain access to someone's online banking account and issue a wire transfer of money to themselves.

>> **Stealing credit card numbers, software, video, music files, and other goods:** Attacking to purchase goods or add bogus shipping instructions into a corporate system leading to products being shipped without payment ever being received by the shipper, and so on.

>> **Stealing corporate and individual data:** Attacking to obtain information that criminals can monetize in multiple ways (see the section "How Cybercriminals Monetize Their Actions," later in this chapter).

CHINESE FIRMS STEAL AMERICAN INTELLECTUAL PROPERTY

In May 2014, United States federal prosecutors charged five members of the People's Liberation Army (PLA) of China with hacking four U.S. businesses and one labor union as part of their service in Unit 61398, China's cyber-warrior unit. The allegedly hacked parties included Alcoa, Allegheny Technologies, SolarWorld, and Westinghouse, all of which are major suppliers of goods to utilities, and the United Steel Workers labor union.

While the full extent of the damage to American businesses caused by the hacking remains unknown to this day, SolarWorld claimed that as a result of confidential information stolen by the hackers, a Chinese competitor appeared to have gained access to SolarWorld's proprietary technology for making solar cells more efficient. This particular case illustrates the blurred lines between nation and state and corporate espionage when it comes to Communist nations and also highlights the difficulty in bringing hackers who participate in such attacks to justice; none of the indicted parties were ever tried, because none have left China to any jurisdiction that would extradite them to the United States.

Over the years, the type of criminals who commit online crimes has evolved from being strictly solo actors to a mix of amateurs and organized crime.

Hacktivists

Hacktivists are activists who use hacking to spread the message of their "cause" and to deliver justice to parties whom they feel aren't being otherwise punished for infractions that the activists view as crimes. Hacktivists include terrorists and rogue insiders.

Terrorists

Terrorists may hack for various purposes, including to

» Directly inflict damage (for example, by hacking a utility and shutting off power)

» Obtain information to use in plotting terrorist attacks (for example, hacking to find out when weapons are being transported between facilities and can be stolen)

» Finance terrorist operations (see the earlier section on criminals)

» Build credibility and invigorate supporters by demonstrating cyberattack prowess

Rogue insiders

Disgruntled employees, rogue contractors, and employees who have been financially incentivized by an unscrupulous party pose serious threats to businesses and their employees alike.

WARNING

Insiders intent on stealing data or inflicting harm are normally considered to be the most dangerous group of cyberattackers. They typically know far more than do any outsiders about what data and computer systems a company possesses, where those systems are located, how they are protected, and other information pertinent to the target systems and their potential vulnerabilities. Rogue insiders may target a business for one or more reasons:

>> They may seek to disrupt operations in order to lighten their own personal workloads or to help a competitor.

>> They may seek revenge for not receiving a promotion or bonus.

>> They may want to make another employee, or team of employees, look bad.

>> They may want to cause their employer financial harm.

>> They may plan on leaving and want to steal data that will be valuable in their next job or in their future endeavors.

Cyberattackers and Their Colored Hats

Cyberattackers are typically grouped based on their goals:

>> **Black hat hackers** have evil intent and hack in order to steal, manipulate, and/or destroy. When typical people think of a hacker, they are thinking of a black hat hacker.

>> **White hat hackers** are ethical hackers who hack in order to test, repair, and enhance the security of systems and networks. These folks are typically computer security experts who specialize in penetration testing, and who are hired by businesses and governments to find vulnerabilities in their IT systems. Hackers are considered to be white hat hackers only if they have explicit permission to hack from the owner of the systems that they are hacking.

>> **Gray hat hackers** are hackers who do not have the malicious intent of black hat hackers, but who, at least at times, act unethically or otherwise violate anti-hacking laws. Hackers who attempt to find vulnerabilities in a system

without the permission of the system's owner and who report their findings to the owner without inflicting any damage to any systems that they scan are acting as gray hat hackers. Gray hat hackers sometimes act as such to make money. For example, when they report vulnerabilities to system owners, they may offer to fix the problems if the owner pays them some consulting fees. Some of the hackers who many people consider to be black hat hackers are actually gray hats.

>> **Green hat hackers** are novices who seek to become experts. Where green hats fall within the white-gray-black spectrum may evolve over time, as does their level of experience.

>> **Blue hat hackers** are paid to test software for exploitable bugs before the software is released into the market.

For the purposes of this book, black and gray hat hackers are the hackers that should primarily concern you as you seek to cyberprotect yourself and your loved ones.

How Cybercriminals Monetize Their Actions

Many, but not all, cyberattackers seek to profit financially from their crimes. Cyberattackers can make money through cyberattacks in several ways:

>> Direct financial fraud

>> Indirect financial fraud

>> Ransomware

>> Cryptominers

Direct financial fraud

Hackers may seek to steal money directly through attacks. For example, hackers may install malware on people's computers to capture victims' online banking sessions and instruct the online banking server to send money to the criminals' accounts. Of course, criminals know that bank systems are often well-protected against such forms of fraud, so many have migrated to target less well-defended systems. For example, some criminals now focus more on capturing login credentials (usernames and passwords) to systems that store credits — for example, coffee shop apps that allow users to store prepaid card values — and steal the money effectively banked in such accounts by using it elsewhere in order to purchase goods and services. Furthermore, if criminals compromise accounts of users that have auto-refill capabilities configured, criminals can repetitively steal the value after each auto-reload. Likewise, criminals may seek to compromise people's frequent traveler accounts and transfer the points to other accounts, purchase goods, or obtain plane tickets and hotel rooms that they sell to other people for cash. Criminals can also steal credit card numbers and either use them or quickly sell them to other crooks who then use them to commit fraud.

REMEMBER

Direct is not a black-and-white concept; there are many shades of gray.

Indirect financial fraud

Sophisticated cybercriminals often avoid cybercrimes that entail direct financial fraud because these schemes often deliver relatively small dollar amounts, can be undermined by the compromised parties even after the fact (for example, by reversing fraudulent transactions or invalidating an order for goods made with stolen information), and create relatively significant risks of getting caught. Instead, they may seek to obtain data that they can monetize for indirect fraud. Several examples of such crimes include

>> Profiting off illegal trading of securities

>> Stealing credit card, debit card, or other payment-related information

>> Stealing goods

>> Stealing data

Profiting off illegal trading of securities

Cybercriminals can make fortunes through illegal trading of securities, such as stocks, bonds, and options, in several ways:

>> **Pump and dump:** Criminals hack a company and steal data, short the company's stock, and then leak the company's data online to cause the company's stock price to drop, at which point they buy the stock (to cover the short sale) at a lower price than they previously sold it.

>> **Bogus press releases and social media posts:** Criminals either buy or sell a company's stock and then release a bogus press release or otherwise spread fake news about a company by hacking into the company's marketing systems or social media accounts and issuing false bad or good news via the company's official channels.

>> **Insider information:** A criminal may seek to steal drafts of press releases from a public company's PR department in order to see whether any surprising quarterly earnings announcements will occur. If the crook finds that a company is going to announce much better numbers than expected by Wall Street, the criminal may purchase *call options* (options that give the crook the right to purchase the stock of the company at a certain price), which can skyrocket in value after such an announcement. Likewise, if a company is about to announce some bad news, the crook may short the company's stock or purchase *put options* (options that give the crook the right to sell the stock of the company at a certain price), which, for obvious reasons, can skyrocket in value if the market price of the associated stock drops.

Discussions of indirect financial fraud of the aforementioned types is not theoretical or the result of paranoid or conspiracy theories; criminals have already been caught engaging in precisely such behavior. These types of scams are often also less risky to criminals than directly stealing money, as it is difficult for regulators to detect such crimes as they happen, and it is nearly impossible for anyone to reverse any relevant transactions. For sophisticated cybercriminals, the lower risks of getting caught coupled with the relatively high chances of success translate into a potential gold mine.

Stealing credit card, debit card, and other payment-related information

As often appears in news reports, many criminals seek to steal credit card or debit card numbers. Thieves can use these numbers to purchase goods or services without paying. Some criminals tend to purchase electronic gift cards, software serial numbers, or other semi-liquid or liquid assets that they then resell for cash to unsuspecting people, while others purchase actual hard goods and services that they may have delivered to locations such as empty houses, where they can easily pick up the items.

Other criminals don't use the credit cards that they steal. Instead, they sell the numbers on the dark web (that is, portions of the Internet that can be accessed only when using technology that grants anonymity to those using it) to criminals who have the infrastructure to maximally exploit the credit cards quickly before people report fraud on the accounts and the cards are blocked.

Stealing goods

Besides the forms of theft of goods described in the preceding section, some criminals seek to find information about orders of high-value, small, liquid items, such as jewelry. In some cases, their goal is to steal the items when the items are delivered to the recipients rather than to create fraudulent transactions.

Stealing data

Some criminals steal data so they can use it to commit various financial crimes. Other criminals steal data to sell it to others or leak it to the public. Stolen data from a business, for example, may be extremely valuable to an unscrupulous competitor.

Ransomware

Ransomware is computer malware that prevents users from accessing their files until they pay a ransom to some criminal or criminal enterprise. This type of cyberattack alone has already netted criminals billions of dollars (yes, that is billions with a *b*) and endangered many lives as infected hospital computer systems became inaccessible to doctors. In fact, there are multiple cases known today in which ransomware may have directly contributed to a person dying prematurely or unnecessarily.

Ransomware remains a growing threat, with criminals constantly improving the technical capabilities and earning potential of their cyberweapons. Criminals are, for example, crafting ransomware that, in an effort to obtain larger returns on investment, infects a computer and attempts to search through connected networks and devices to find the most sensitive systems and data. Then, instead of kidnapping the data that it first encountered, the ransomware activates and prevents access to the most valuable information.

REMEMBER

Criminals understand that the more important the information is to its owner, the greater the likelihood that a victim will be willing to pay a ransom, and the higher the maximum ransom that will be willingly paid is likely to be.

Ransomware is growing increasingly stealthy and often avoids detection by antivirus software. Furthermore, the criminals who use ransomware are often launching targeted attacks against parties that they know have the ability to pay decent ransoms. Criminals know, for example, that the average American is far more likely to pay $200 for a ransom than the average person living in China. Likewise, they often target environments in which going offline has serious consequences — a hospital, for example, can't afford to be without its patient records system for any significant period of time.

Cryptominers

A cryptominer, in the context of malware, refers to software that usurps some of an infected computer's resources in order to use them to perform the complex mathematical calculations needed to create new units of cryptocurrency. The currency that is created is transferred to the criminal operating the cryptominer. Many modern day cryptominer malware variants utilize groups of infected machines working in concert to do the mining.

Because cryptominers create money for criminals without the need for any involvement by their human victims, cybercriminals, especially those who lack the sophistication to launch high-stakes targeted ransomware attacks, have increasingly gravitated to cryptominers as a quick way to monetize cyberattacks.

While the value of cryptocurrencies fluctuates wildly (at least as of the time of the writing of this chapter), some relatively unsophisticated cryptocurrency mining networks are believed to net their operators more than $30,000 per month.

Not All Dangers Come From Attackers: Dealing with Nonmalicious Threats

While some potential attackers are intent on benefiting at your expense, others have no intentions of inflicting harm. However, these parties can innocently inflict dangers that can be even greater than those posed by hostile actors.

Human error

Perhaps the greatest cybersecurity danger of all — whether for an individual, business, or government entity — is the possibility of human error. Nearly all major breaches covered in the media over the past decade were made possible, at least in part, because of some element of human error. In fact, human error is often necessary for the hostile actors to succeed with their attacks — a phenomenon about which they're well aware.

Humans: The Achilles' heel of cybersecurity

Why are humans so often the weak point in the cybersecurity chain — making the mistakes that enable massive breaches? The answer is quite simple.

Consider how much technology has advanced in recent years. Electronic devices that are ubiquitous today were the stuff of science-fiction books and movies just one or two generations ago. In many cases, technology has even surpassed predictions about the future — today's phones are much more powerful and convenient than Maxwell Smart's shoe-phone, and Dick Tracy's watch would not even be perceived as advanced enough to be a modern day toy when compared with devices that today cost under $100.

Security technology has also advanced dramatically over time. Every year multiple new products are launched, and many new, improved versions of existing technologies appear on the market. The intrusion detection technology of today, for example, is so much better than that of even one decade ago that even classifying them into the same category of product offering is questionable.

On the flip side, however, consider the human brain. It took tens of thousands of years for human brains to evolve from that of earlier species — no fundamental improvement takes place during a human lifetime, or even within centuries of generations coming and going. As such, security technology advances far more rapidly than the human mind.

Furthermore, advances in technology often translate into humans needing to interact with, and understand how to properly utilize a growing number of increasingly complex devices, systems, and software. Given human limitations, the chances of people making significant mistakes keep going up over time.

The increasing demand for brainpower that advancing technology places on people is observable even at a most basic level. How many passwords did your grandparents need to know when they were your age? How many did your parents need? How many do you need? And, how easily could remote hackers crack passwords and exploit them for gain in the era of your grandparents? Your parents? Yourself?

Add to the mix that many people today work from home — often at the same time during which their children attend school remotely from the same location — and the possibility of human errors made either due to interruptions mid-task, or due to the inability to speak in-person with a colleague, grow dramatically.

TIP

The bottom line: You must internalize that human error poses a great risk to your cybersecurity — and act accordingly.

Social engineering

In the context of information security, *social engineering* refers to the psychological manipulation of human beings into performing actions that they otherwise would not perform and which are usually detrimental to their interests.

Examples of social engineering include

>> Calling someone on the telephone and tricking that person into believing that the caller is a member of the IT department and requesting that the person reset their email password

>> Sending phishing emails (see Book 1, Chapter 2)

>> Sending CEO fraud emails (see Book 1, Chapter 2)

While the criminals launching social engineering attacks may be malicious in intent, the actual parties that create the vulnerability or inflict the damage typically do so without any intent to harm the target. In the first example, the user who resets their password believes that they are doing so to help the IT department repair email problems, not that they are allowing hackers into the mail system. Likewise, someone who falls prey to a phishing or CEO fraud scam is obviously not seeking to help the hacker who is attacking them.

Other forms of human error that undermine cybersecurity include people accidentally deleting information, accidentally misconfiguring systems, inadvertently infecting a computer with malware, mistakenly disabling security technologies, and other innocent errors that enable criminals to commit all sorts of mischievous acts.

WARNING

The bottom line is never to underestimate both the inevitability of, and power of, human mistakes — including your own. You will make mistakes — everyone does. So on important matters, always double-check to make sure that everything is the way it should be. It is better to check many times when there was, in fact, no social engineering attack, than to fail to check the one time that there was such an attack.

External disasters

As described in Book 1, Chapter 2, cybersecurity includes maintaining your data's confidentiality, integrity, and availability. One of the greatest risks to availability — which also creates secondhand risks to its confidentiality and integrity — is external disasters. These disasters fall into two categories: those that are naturally occurring, and those that are caused by humans.

Natural disasters

A large number of people live in areas prone to some degree to various forms of natural disasters. From hurricanes to tornados to floods to fires, nature can be brutal — and can corrupt, or even destroy, computers and the data that the machines house.

Continuity planning and disaster recovery are, therefore, taught as part of the certification process for cybersecurity professionals. The reality is that, statistically speaking, most people will encounter and experience at least one form of natural disaster at some point in their lives. As such, if you want to protect your systems and data, you must plan accordingly for such an eventuality. It is not surprising that organizations with proper continuity plans in place often fared far better than their unprepared counterparts when the COVID-19 pandemic hit and forced people to work from home.

A strategy of storing backups on hard drives at two different sites may be a poor strategy, for example, if both sites consist of basements located in homes within flood zones.

Pandemics

One particular form of natural disaster is a pandemic or other medical issue. As people around the world saw clearly in 2020, the arrival of a highly contagious disease can cause a sudden shutdown of many in-person working facilities and schools, and cause a sudden migration to online platforms — creating all sorts of cybersecurity-related issues.

Environmental problems caused by humans

Of course, nature is not the only party creating external problems. Humans can cause floods and fires, and these disasters can sometimes be worse than those that occur naturally. Furthermore, power outages and power spikes, protests and riots, strikes, terrorist attacks, and Internet failures and telecom disruptions can also impact the availability of data and systems.

Businesses that backed up their data from systems located in New York's World Trade Center to systems in the nearby World Financial Center learned the hard way after 9/11 the importance of keeping backups outside the vicinity of the corresponding systems, as the World Financial Center remained inaccessible for quite some time after the World Trade Center was destroyed.

Cyberwarriors and cyberspies

Modern-day governments often have tremendous armies of cyberwarriors at their disposal. Such teams often attempt to discover vulnerabilities in software products and systems to use them to attack and spy on adversaries, as well as to use as a law enforcement tool. Doing so, however, creates risks for individuals and businesses. Instead of reporting vulnerabilities to the relevant vendors, various government agencies often seek to keep the vulnerabilities secret — meaning that they leave their citizens, enterprises, and other government entities vulnerable to attack by adversaries who may discover the same vulnerability.

In addition, governments may use their teams of hackers to help fight crime — or, in some cases, abuse their cyber-resources to retain control over their citizens and preserve the ruling party's hold on power. Even in the United States, in the aftermath of 9/11, the government implemented various programs of mass data collection that impacted law-abiding U.S. citizens. If any of the databases that were assembled had been pilfered by foreign powers, U.S. citizens may have been put at risk of all sorts of cyberproblems.

The dangers of governments creating troves of data exploits are not theoretical. In recent years, several powerful cyberweapons believed to have been created by a U.S. government intelligence agency surfaced online, clearly having been stolen by someone whose interests were not aligned with those of the agency. To this day, it remains unclear whether those weapons were used against American interests by whoever stole them.

The impotent Fair Credit Reporting Act

Many Americans are familiar with the Fair Credit Reporting Act (FCRA), a set of laws initially passed nearly half a century ago and updated on multiple occasions. The FCRA regulates the collection and management of credit reports and the data used therein. The FCRA was established to ensure that people are treated fairly, and that credit-related information remains both accurate and private.

According to the Fair Credit Reporting Act, credit reporting bureaus must remove various forms of adverse information from people's credit reports after specific time frames elapse. If you don't pay a credit card bill on time while you're in college, for example, it's against the law for the late payment to be listed on your report and factored against you into your credit score when you apply for a mortgage two decades later. The law even allows people who declare bankruptcy in order to start over to have records of their bankruptcy removed. After all, what good would starting over be if a bankruptcy forever prevented someone from having a clean slate?

Today, however, various technology companies undermine the protections of the FCRA. How hard is it for a bank's loan officer to find online databases of court filings related to bankruptcies by doing a simple Google search and then looking into such databases for information relevant to a prospective borrower? Or to see whether any foreclosure records from any time are associated with a name matching that of someone seeking a loan? Doing either takes just seconds, and no laws prohibit such databases from including records old enough to be gone from credit reports, and, at least in the United States, none prohibit Google from showing links to such databases when someone searches on the name of someone involved with such activities decades earlier.

Expunged records are no longer really expunged

The justice system has various laws that, in many cases, allow young people to keep minor offenses off of their permanent criminal records. Likewise, our laws afford judges the ability to seal certain files and to expunge other forms of information from people's records. Such laws help people start over; it is not a secret that many wonderful, productive members of modern society may not have turned out as they did without these protections.

But what good are such laws if a prospective employer can find the supposedly purged information within seconds by doing a Google search on a candidate's name? Google returns results from local police blotters and court logs published in local newspapers that are now archived online. People who were cited for minor offenses and then had all the charges against them dropped can still suffer professional and personal repercussions decades later — even though they were never indicted, tried, or found guilty of any offense.

Social Security numbers

A generation ago, it was common to use Social Security numbers as college ID numbers. The world was so different back then that for privacy reasons, many schools even posted people's grades using Social Security numbers rather than using students' names! Yes, seriously.

Should all students who went to college in the 1970s, 1980s, or early 1990s really have their Social Security numbers exposed to the public because college materials that were created in the pre-web world have now been archived online and are indexed in some search engines? To make matters worse, some parties authenticate users by asking for the last four digits of people's phone numbers, which can often be found in a fraction of a second via a cleverly crafted Google or Bing search. If it is common knowledge that such information has been rendered insecure by previously acceptable behaviors, why does the government still utilize Social Security numbers and treat them as if they were still private?

Likewise, online archives of church, synagogue, and other community newsletters often contain birth announcements listing not only the name of the baby and the baby's parents, but the hospital in which the child was born, the date of birth, and the grandparents' names. How many security questions for a particular user of a computer system can be undermined by a crook finding just one such announcement? All of these examples show how advances in technology can undermine our privacy and cybersecurity — even legally undermining laws that have been established to protect us.

Social media platforms

One group of technology businesses that generate serious risks to cybersecurity are social media platforms. Cybercriminals increasingly scan social media — sometimes with automated tools — to find information that they can use against companies and their employees. Attackers then leverage the information that they find to craft all sorts of attacks, such as one involving the delivery of ransomware. For example, they may craft highly effective spear-phishing emails credible enough to trick employees into clicking on URLs to ransomware-delivering websites or into opening ransomware-infected attachments.

The number of virtual kidnapping scams — in which criminals contact the family of a person who is off the grid due to being on a flight or the like and demand a ransom in exchange for releasing the person they claim to have kidnapped — has skyrocketed in the era of social media, as criminals often can discern from looking at users' social media posts both when to act and whom to contact.

Google's all-knowing computers

One of the ways computer systems verify that people are who they claim to be is by asking questions to which few people other than the legitimate party would know the correct answers. In many cases, someone who can successfully answer "How much is your current mortgage payment?" and "Who was your seventh grade science teacher?" is more likely to be the authentic party than an impersonator.

But the all-knowing Google engine undermines such authentication. Many pieces of information that were difficult to obtain quickly just a few years ago can now be obtained almost instantaneously via a Google search. In many cases, the answers to security questions used by various websites to help authenticate users are, for criminals, "just one click away."

While more advanced sites may consider the answer to security questions to be wrong if entered more than a few seconds after the question is posed, most sites impose no such restrictions — meaning that anyone who knows how to use Google can undermine many modern authentication systems.

Mobile device location tracking

Likewise, Google itself can correlate all sorts of data that it obtains from phones running Android or its Maps and Waze applications — which likely means from the majority of people in the Western World. Of course, the providers of other apps that run on millions of phones and that have permission to access location data can do the same as well. Any party that tracks where a person is and for how long that person is there may have created a database that can be used for all sorts of nefarious purposes — including undermining knowledge-based authentication, facilitating social engineering attacks, undermining the confidentiality of secret projects, and so on. Even if the firm that creates the database has no malicious intent, rogue employees or hackers who gain access to, or steal, the database pose serious threats.

Such tracking also undermines privacy. Google knows, for example, who is regularly going into a chemotherapy facility, where people sleep (for most people, the time that they are asleep is the only time that their phones do not move at all for many hours) and who else is sleeping near them when they do, and various other information from which all sorts of sensitive extrapolations can be made.

Defending against These Attackers

REMEMBER

It is important to understand that there is no such thing as 100 percent cybersecurity. While people used to joke that you could get a 100 percent cybersecure computer by using a manual typewriter, even that was not true; if you used a manual typewriter instead of a computer, someone could potentially decipher what you would be typing by closely listening to the sounds of the letters striking paper, as each letter produces a slightly different sound when inking the page.

Rather than 100 percent cybersecurity, you must pursue *adequate cybersecurity*, which is defined by understanding what risks exist, which ones are adequately mitigated, and which ones persist.

Defenses that are adequate to shield against some risks and attackers are inadequate to protect against others. What may suffice for reasonably protecting a home computer, for example, may be wildly inadequate to shield an online banking server. The same is true of risks that are based on who uses a system: A cellphone used by the President of the United States to speak to advisors, for example, obviously requires better security than the cellphone used by the average sixth grader.

2

Personal Cybersecurity

Contents at a Glance

» Understanding how to protect against cyber risks

» Evaluating your current cybersecurity measures

» Taking a look at privacy

» Adopting best practices

Chapter **1**

Evaluating Your Current Cybersecurity Posture

The first step in improving your protection against cyberthreats is to understand exactly what it is that you need to protect. Only after you have a good grasp on that information can you evaluate what is actually needed to deliver adequate security and determine whether you have any gaps to address.

You must consider what data you have, from whom you must protect it, and how sensitive it is to you. What would happen if, for example, it were publicized on the Internet for the world to see? Then you can evaluate how much you're willing to spend — timewise and moneywise — on protecting it.

Don't be Achilles: Identifying Ways You May Be Less than Secure

One lesson to learn from the Greek hero Achilles is that if you suffer from a vulnerability, attackers may eventually exploit it to your detriment. As such, it is important to understand the various areas in which your current cybersecurity posture may be less than ideal so that you can figure out how to address any relevant issues, and thereby, ensure that you're adequately protected. You should, for example, inventory all items that could contain sensitive data, become launching pads for attacks, and so on.

Your home computer(s)

Your home computers may suffer from one or major types of potential problems relevant to cybersecurity:

- » **Breached:** A hacker may have penetrated your home computer and be able to use it much as you can — view its contents, use it to contact other machines, leverage it as a staging ground from which to attack other computers, phones, and smart devices and penetrate them, mine cryptocurrency, view data on your network, and so on.

- » **Malware:** Similar to the dangers created by human invaders, a computer-based attacker — that is *malware* — may be present on your home computer, enabling a criminal to use the computer much as you can — view the computer's contents, contact other electronic devices, mine cryptocurrency, and so on — as well as read data from your network traffic and to infect other computers on your network and outside of it.

- » **Shared computers:** When you share a computer with other people — including your significant other and/or your children — you expose your device to the risk that one or more of the other folks using it won't practice proper cyber-hygiene to the same level you do, and as a result, that person or people may expose the device to infection by malware or a breach by some hacker, or they may unintentionally inflict self-damage.

- » **Connections to other networks and storage applications:** If you connect your computer via a virtual private network (VPN) to other networks, such as the network at your place of employment, network-borne malware on those remote networks or hackers lurking on devices connected to those networks can potentially attack your network and your local devices as well. In some cases, similar risks may exist if you run applications that connect your computer to remote services, such as remote storage systems.

- » **Physical security risks:** As discussed in detail in Book 2, Chapter 2, the physical location of your computer may either increase or decrease the danger to it and its contents.

Your mobile devices

From an information security standpoint, mobile devices are inherently risky because they

>> Are constantly connected to the Internet, which is a highly insecure, public network on which many hackers are known to lurk, and over which nearly all cyberattacks take place

>> Often have significant amounts of confidential information stored on them

>> Are used to communicate with many people and systems, both of which are groups that include parties who aren't always trustworthy, via the Internet (which is also inherently not trustworthy)

>> Can receive inbound messages from parties with whom you have never interacted prior to receiving the messages in question, and some such parties may be up to no good

>> Often don't run full-blown security software due to resource limitations, or run security software that comes with the device and that you cannot manually upgrade or otherwise change if you find it doesn't meet your needs

>> Can easily be lost or stolen

>> Can easily be accidentally damaged or destroyed

>> Often connect to insecure and untrusted Wi-Fi networks

>> Are replaced on a regular basis, and are often not properly decommissioned when being disposed of

>> Are often traded in for upgraded devices — often without being properly decommissioned

Your Internet of Things (IoT) devices

The world of the connected computing has changed dramatically in recent years. Not that long ago, the only devices that were connected to the Internet were what people classically called computers — desktops, laptops, and servers that could be used for many different computing purposes. Today, however, we live in an entirely different world in which computers form only a small percentage of connected devices.

From smartphones to security cameras, refrigerators to cars, and coffeemakers to exercise equipment, numerous types of electronic devices now often have powerful computers embedded within them, and many of these computers are perpetually connected to the Internet.

The Internet of Things (IoT), as the ecosystem of connected devices is commonly known, has been growing exponentially over the past few years, yet the security of such devices is often, at best, inadequate. Many IoT devices do not contain security technology to secure themselves against breaches. Even those that do are often not properly configured to be secure. Hackers can exploit IoT devices to spy on you, steal your data, attack other systems and/or devices, launch denial-of-service attacks against networks or devices, and inflict various other forms of damage.

Your networking equipment

Networking equipment can be hacked to route traffic to bogus sites, capture data, launch attacks, block Internet access, and so on.

Your work environment

You may have sensitive data in your work environment — and you can be put at risk by colleagues at work as well. For example, if you bring any electronic devices to work, connect them to a network at work, and then bring those devices home and connect them to your home network, malware and other problems can potentially spread to your device from a device belonging to your employer or to any one or more of your colleagues using the same infrastructure and then later spread from your device to other machines on your home network.

Of course, the COVID-19 pandemic led to the blending of many work and home environments, and the cybersecurity effects of such developments have often been troubling.

Identifying Risks

To secure anything, you must know what it is that you're securing; securing an environment is difficult to do, if not impossible, to do if you do not know what is in that environment. (This concept is age-old wisdom; refer to the Sun Tzu quote at the beginning of Book 1, Chapter 3.)

To secure yourself, therefore, you must understand what assets you have — both those that are in digital formats and those in related physical formats — and what it is that you seek to protect. Those assets may or may not be in one location. In fact, some or all of them may be in locations that you cannot physically access. For example, you may have data stored in a cloud storage service such as Google Drive, Apple iCloud, or Microsoft OneDrive. You must also understand what risks you face to those assets.

UNDERSTANDING ENDPOINTS

An *endpoint* is any computer-enabled device that communicates with a network to which it is connected. Your laptop is an endpoint when it is connected to your home network; your smartphone is an endpoint both when it is connected via Wi-Fi to a network and when it is connected by a cellular connection such as 4G or 5G to the network of a cellular provider. Endpoints are called endpoints because they are at the end of a communication path. Internet-based communications may go through many "hops" to get to an endpoint, but at the endpoint they stop hopping.

All endpoints pose risks and must, therefore, be secured. Laptops, smartphones, tablets, and other computing devices should run security software, and IoT devices should be secured as necessary for whatever type of devices they may be.

Businesses often manage authorized endpoints centrally and may have centralized security systems that communicate with client software on the endpoints in order to enforce policies, detect anomalous activities, prevent data leaks, and stop attacks.

Individuals typically do not run such systems but should still ensure that all of the endpoints on their home networks are secured as described throughout this chapter and the rest of the book.

TIP

Inventorying such assets is usually pretty simple for individuals: Make a written list of all devices that you attach to your network. You can often get a list by logging into your router and looking at the Connected devices section. Of course, you may have some devices that you connect to your network only occasionally or that must be secured even though they do not attach to your network, so be sure to include those on your list as well.

Add to that list — in a separate section — all storage devices that you use, including external hard drives, flash drives, and memory cards, as well as any storage or computing services that you use from third parties. Write or print the list; forgetting even a single device can lead to problems.

Protecting against Risks

After you identify what you must protect (see preceding section), you must develop and implement appropriate safeguards for those items to keep them as secure as appropriate and limit the impact of a potential breach.

In the context of home users, protecting includes providing barriers to anyone seeking to access your digital and physical assets without proper authorization to do so, establishing (even informal) processes and procedures to protect your sensitive data, and creating backups of all configurations and basic system restore points.

Basic elements of protection for most individuals include

>> Perimeter defense

>> Firewall/router

>> Security software

>> Your physical computer(s) and any other endpoints

>> Backups

And part of learning how to protect against risks is knowing how to detect cyber-security events, respond to them appropriately, recover the affected devices, and improve defenses to reduce risk even more.

Perimeter defense

Defending your cyber-perimeter is essentially the digital equivalent of building a moat around a castle — attempting to stop anyone from entering except through authorized pathways while under the watchful eyes of guards.

You can build that digital moat by never connecting any computer directly to your Internet modem. Instead connect a firewall/router to the modem and connect computers to the firewall/router. (If your modem contains a firewall/router, then it serves both purposes; if your connection is to the firewall/router portion, not to the modem itself, that is okay.) Normally, the connections between firewalls and modems are wired — that is, are achieved using a physical network cable. In some cases both the modem and the firewall/router might even be contained within the same physical device.

Firewall/router

Modern routers used in home environments include firewalling capabilities that block most forms of inbound traffic when such traffic isn't generated as the result of activities initiated by devices protected by the firewall. That is, a firewall will block outsiders from trying to contact a computer inside your home, but it will not block a web server from responding if a computer inside your home requests a web page from the server. Routers use multiple technologies to achieve such protection.

One important technology of note is Network Address Translation (NAT), which allows computers on your home network to use Internet Protocol (IP) addresses that are invalid for use on the Internet, but can be used on private networks. To the Internet, all the devices on networks using NAT appear to use one address, which is the address of the firewall that is situated between them and the Internet and is handling the NAT function.

The following recommendations help your router/firewall protect you:

REMEMBER

» **Keep your router up to date.** Make sure to install all updates before initially putting your router into use and regularly check for new updates (unless your router has an auto-update feature, in which case you should leverage that feature).

   An unpatched vulnerability in your router can allow outsiders to enter your network.

» **Replace your router when it is no longer supported.** If the vendor is no longer providing support (including updates) for your router, it is probably time to replace it. Considering the lifecycle of such devices and the lifecycle of networking protocols, you may also benefit from improved performance by doing so.

» **Change the default administrative password on your firewall/router to a strong password that only you know.** Write the default and new passwords down, and put the paper on which you write them in a safe or safe deposit box. Do not store such passwords on devices that connect to that network. Practice logging into the router — and continue doing so on a regular basis so that you do not forget the relevant password.

» **Don't use the default name provided by your router for your Wi-Fi network name (its SSID).** Create a new name.

» **Configure your Wi-Fi network to use encryption of at least the WPA2 standard, and use WPA3 if possible.** These are the current standards at the time of the writing of this book.

» **Establish a password that any device is required to know to join your Wi-Fi network.** Make that password a strong one. For information on creating strong passwords that you can easily remember, see Book 2, Chapter 5.

» **If all your wireless devices know how to use the modern Wi-Fi 6 and/or Wi-Fi 5 wireless networking protocols, disable older Wi-Fi protocols that your router supports.** Disabling protocols such as 802.11b, 802.11g, and 802.11n may help improve performance and offers security benefits.

» **Enable MAC address filtering or make sure all members of your household know that nobody is to connect anything to the wired network**

without your permission. At least in theory, MAC address filtering prevents any device from connecting to the network if you do not previously configure the router to allow it to connect. Do not allow people to connect insecure devices to the network without first securing them.

» **Locate your wireless router centrally within your home.** Doing so will provide better signal for you and will also reduce the strength of the signal that you provide to people outside your home who may be seeking to piggyback onto your network. If you have a mesh routing system that comes with multiple access points, follow the relevant instructions regarding locating the devices.

» **Do not enable remote access to your router.** You want the router to be manageable only via connections from devices that it is protecting, not from the outside world. The convenience of remote management of a home firewall is rarely worth the increase in security risk created by enabling such a feature.

» **Maintain a current list of devices connected to your network.** Also include on that list devices that you allow to connect to your network but that are not currently connected.

» **For any guests for whom you want to give network access, turn on the guest network capability of the router and, as with the private network, activate encryption and require strong password.** Give guests access to that guest network and not to your primary network. The same applies for anyone else to whom you must give Internet access but whose security you do not fully trust, including family members, such as children.

» **If you're sufficiently technically knowledgeable to turn off DHCP and change the default IP address range used by the router for the internal network, do so.** Doing so interferes with some automated hacking tools and provides other security benefits. If you're not familiar with such concepts or don't have a clue what the aforementioned sentence means, simply ignore this paragraph. In this case, the security benefits of the recommendation are likely going to be outweighed by the problems that you may encounter due to the additional technical complexity that turning off DHCP and changing the default IP address range can create.

Security software

How should you use security software to protect yourself?

» Use security software on all your computers and mobile devices. The software should contain at least antivirus and personal device firewall capabilities.

- » Use antispam software on any device on which you read email.
- » Enable remote wipe on any and every mobile device.
- » Require a strong password to log in to any computer and mobile device.
- » Enable auto-updates whenever possible and keep your devices updated.

Your physical computer(s) and any other endpoints

To physically secure your computers and other endpoints:

- » **Control physical access to your computer and keep it in a safe location.** If anyone entering your home can get to a machine, for example, that device can be relatively easily stolen, used, or damaged without your knowledge.
- » **If possible, do not share your computer with family members.** If you must share your computer, create separate accounts for each family member and do not give any other users of the device administrative privileges on it.
- » **Do not rely on deleting data before throwing out, recycling, donating, or selling an old device.** Use a multiwipe erasure system for all hard drives and solid state drives. Ideally, remove the storage media from the computer before getting rid of the device — and physically destroy the storage media.

Also, keep in mind that that some computing devices that need to be secured might not be true "endpoints" in that they may have other devices connected to them. A smart home hub or smart wireless camera system, for example, may have smart devices and/or cameras connected to them using proprietary communication mechanisms; they still, of course, need to be properly secured.

Backups

Back up regularly. If you are not sure what "regularly" means in your case, the odds are pretty good that you are not backing up often enough.

For more on backups, see Book 3, Chapter 5.

Detecting

Detecting refers to implementing mechanisms by which you can detect cybersecurity events as quickly as possible after they commence. While most home users do not have the budget to purchase specialized products for the purpose of detection, that does not mean that the detection phase of security should be ignored.

Today, most personal computer security software has detection capabilities of various types. Make sure that every device that you manage has security software on it that looks for possible intrusions, for example. See Book 3, Chapter 3 for more details on detecting possible breaches.

Responding

Responding refers to acting in response to a cybersecurity incident. Most security software will automatically either act, or prompt users to act, if it detects potential problems. For more on responding, see Book 3, Chapter 4.

Recovering

Recovering refers to restoring an impacted computer, network, or device — and all of its relevant capabilities — to its fully functioning, proper state after a cybersecurity event occurs. See Book 3, Chapters 4, 6, and 7 for more on recovering.

REMEMBER

Ideally, a formal, written, simple and straightforward, prioritized plan for how to recover should be documented before it is needed. Most home users do not actually create one, but doing so can be extremely beneficial. In most home cases, such a plan will be less than one page long.

Improving

Shame on any of us if we do not learn from our own mistakes. Every cybersecurity incident offers lessons learned that can be put into action to reduce risk in the future.

Evaluating Your Current Security Measures

After you know what you need to protect and how to protect such items, you can determine the difference between what you need and what you currently have in place.

The following sections cover some things to consider. Not all of the following apply in every case:

Software

When it comes to software and cybersecurity, think about the following questions for each device:

>> Are all the software packages (including the operating system itself) on your computer legally obtained?

>> Were the software packages (including the operating system itself) obtained from reliable sources that always (or at least as close to always as is humanly possibly) provide legitimate versions?

>> Are all the software packages (including the operating system itself) currently supported by their respective vendors?

>> Are all the software packages (including the operating system itself) up-to-date?

>> Are all the software packages (including the operating system itself) set to automatically update?

>> Is security software on the device?

>> Is the security software configured to auto-update?

>> Is the security software up-to-date?

>> Does the security software include anti-malware technology — and is that capability fully enabled?

>> Are virus scans configured to run after every update is applied?

>> Does the software include firewall technology — and is that capability fully enabled?

>> Does the software include anti-spam technology — and is that capability fully enabled? If not, is other anti-spam software present, and is it running?

>> Does the software include remote lock and/or remote wipe technology — and is that capability fully enabled? If not, is other remote lock/remote wipe software present, and is it running?

>> Are all other aspects of the software enabled? If not, what is not?

>> Is backup software running that will back up the device as part of a backup strategy?

>> Is encryption enabled for at least all sensitive data stored on the device?

- » Are permissions properly set for the software — locking out people who may have access to the device, but who should not have access to the software?

- » Have permissions been set to prevent software from making changes to the computer that you may not want done (for example, is any software running with administrator privileges when it should not be)?

Of course, all these questions refer to software on a device that you use, but that you don't expose to use by untrusted, remote outsiders. If you have devices that are used as in the latter case — for example, a web server — you must address many other security issues, which are beyond the scope of this book.

Hardware

For all your hardware devices, consider the following questions:

- » Was the hardware obtained from a trusted party? (If you bought an IP-based camera directly from China via some online retailer than you never of heard of prior to making the purchase, for example, the answer to this question may not be yes.)

- » How sure are you of the answer to the previous question — and if you are highly confident, why are you so confident?

- » Is the hardware from a brand that the U.S. Government prohibits its own agencies from using because it does not trust that brand to be sufficiently secure from foreign spying or cyber risks?

- » Is all your hardware adequately protected from theft and damage (rain, electrical spikes, and so on) as it resides in its home location?

- » What protects your hardware when it travels?

- » Do you have an uninterruptible power supply or built-in battery protecting the device from a hard, sudden shut-off if power fails even momentarily?

- » Is all your hardware running the latest firmware — and did you download that firmware from a reliable source, such as the vendor's website or via an update initiated from within the device's configuration tool?

- » For routers (and firewalls), does your device meet the criteria listed as recommendations in the "Firewall/router" section earlier in this chapter?

- » Do you have a BIOS password, locking a device from use until a password is entered?

- » Have you disabled all wireless protocols that you do not need? If you're not using Bluetooth on a laptop, for example, turn off the Bluetooth radio, which not only improves security, but also helps your battery last longer.

Insurance

While cybersecurity insurance is often overlooked, especially by smaller businesses and individuals, it is a viable way of mitigating some cyber-risks. Depending on the particulars of your situation, purchasing a policy protecting against specific risks may make sense.

If you own a small business that may go bankrupt if a breach occurs, you will, of course, want to implement strong security. But, as security measures can never be 100 percent perfect and foolproof, purchasing a policy to cover catastrophic situations may be wise.

While cyber insurance used to be something that only large enterprises could obtain, in recent years, cybersecurity policies have started to become available to both individuals and small businesses.

Education

A little bit of education can go a long way in helping to prevent the people in your household (or other entity, as the case may be) from becoming the Achilles' heels of your cybersecurity. The following list covers some things to think about and discuss:

>> Do all you family members know what their rights and responsibilities are regarding vis-à-vis technology in the house, vis-à-vis connecting devices to the home network, and vis-à-vis allowing guest to connect to the home network (or the guest network)?

>> Have you taught your family members about the risks they need to be aware — for example, phishing emails. Do you have confidence that they "get it"?

>> Have you ensured that everyone in the family who uses devices knows about cybersecurity hygiene (for example, not clicking on links in emails)?

>> Have you ensured that everyone in the family who uses devices knows about password selection and protection?

>> Have you ensured that everyone in the family who uses social media grasps the risks associated with oversharing and understands what can and what can't be safely shared?

>> Have you ensured that everyone in the family understands the concept on thinking before acting?

Privacy 101

Technology threatens personal privacy in many ways: Ubiquitous cameras watch you on a regular basis, technology companies track your online behaviors via all sorts of technical methods, and mobile devices track your location.

While technology has certainly made the task of maintaining privacy far more challenging than doing so was just a few years ago, privacy is not dead. You can do many things to improve your level of privacy, even in the modern, connected era.

Think before you share

People often willingly overshare information when asked for it.

Consider the paperwork patients are given at a typical doctor's office in the United States that you have likely been asked to complete at more than one facility at your initial appointment with the doctor in question. While the answers to many of the questions are relevant and may contain information that is valuable for the doctor to know to properly evaluate and treat you, other portions are probably not. Many (if not most) such forms ask patients for their Social Security numbers. Such information was needed decades ago when medical insurance companies regularly used Social Security numbers as insurance ID numbers, but that dangerous practice has long since ended. Perhaps some facilities use the Social Security number to report your account to credit bureaus if you don't pay your bills, but in most cases, the reality is that the question is an unsafe vestige of the past, and you can leave the field blank.

REMEMBER

Even if you don't believe that a party asking you for personal data would ever abuse the information that it collected about you, as the number of parties that have private information about you increases, and as the quantity and quality of that data grows, the odds rise that you will suffer a privacy violation due to a data breach occurring somewhere.

If you want to improve your privacy, the first thing to do is to consider what information you may be disclosing about yourself and your loved ones before you disclose it. This is true when interacting with government agencies, corporations, medical facilities, and other individuals. If you do not need to provide private information, don't. All other factors being identical, the less private information that is "out there," and the fewer places it resides, the lower the risk to you of a privacy compromise.

Think before you post

Consider the implications of any social media post before making it — there could be adverse consequences of many sorts, including effectively compromising the privacy of information. For example, criminals can leverage shared information about a person's family relationships, place of employment, and interests as part of identity theft and to social engineer their way into your accounts.

WARNING

If, by choice or due to the negligent policies of a provider, you use your mother's birth or given name as a de facto password, make sure that you do not make it easy for criminals to find out that name by listing your mother as your mother on Facebook or by being friends on Facebook with many cousins whose last name is the same as your mother's family name. Often, people can obtain someone's mother's family name simply by selecting from another person's Facebook friends list the most common last name that is not the same as the account holder's name.

Sharing information about a person's children and their schedules may help facilitate all sorts of problems — including potentially kidnapping, break-ins into the person's home while the person is carpooling to work, or other harmful actions.

Sharing information related to medical activities may lead to disclosure of sensitive and private information. For example, photographs or location data placing a person at a particular medical facility may divulge that the person suffers from a condition that the facility is known to specialize in treating.

Sharing various types of information or images may impact a user's personal relationships and leak private information about such.

Sharing information or images may leak private information about potentially controversial activities in which a person has engaged — for example, consuming alcohol or using recreational drugs, using various weapons, participating in certain controversial organizations, and so on. Even disclosing that one was at a particular location at a certain time may inadvertently compromise the privacy of sensitive information.

REMEMBER

Also, keep in mind that the problem of oversharing is not limited to social networks. Oversharing information via chat, email, group chats, and so on is a serious modern day problem as well. Sometimes people do not realize that they are oversharing, and sometimes they accidentally paste the wrong data into emails or attach the wrong files to emails.

General privacy tips

In addition to thinking before you share, you can do a few other things to reduce your exposure to risks of oversharing:

>> **Use social media privacy settings.** In addition to not sharing private information (see preceding section), make sure that your privacy settings on social media are set to protect your data from viewing by members of the public — unless the post in question is intended for public consumption.

>> **But do not rely on them.** Nonetheless, never rely on social media security settings to ensure the privacy of information. Significant vulnerabilities that undermine the effectiveness of various platforms' security controls have been repetitively discovered.

>> **Keep private data out of the cloud unless you encrypt the data.** Never store private information in the cloud unless you encrypt it. Do not rely on the encryption provided by the cloud provider to ensure your privacy. If the provider is breached, in some cases the encryption can be undermined as well. So, if you must store sensitive information in the cloud, encrypt it yourself before uploading it — regardless of whatever encryption the cloud provider uses. There are applications available that simplify doing so for major cloud storage providers, such as by automatically encrypting and copying to the cloud any files placed in a special folder on your computer.

   Do not store private information in cloud applications designed for sharing and collaboration. For example, do not store a list of your passwords, photos of your driver's license or passport, or confidential medical information in a Google doc. This may seem obvious, but many people do so anyway.

>> **Leverage the privacy settings of a browser — or better yet, use Tor.** If you're using a web browser to access material that you don't want associated with you, at a minimum, turn on Private/Incognito Mode (which offers only partial protection), or, if possible, use a web browser like the Tor Browser Bundle (which contains obfuscated routing, default strong privacy settings, and various, preconfigured, privacy add-ons).

   If you do not take precautions when using a browser, you may be tracked. If you search for detailed information on a medical condition in a normal browser window, various parties will likely capitalize on that data. You have probably seen the effects of such tracking — for example, when ads appear on one web page related to something that you searched for on another.

>> **Do not publicize your real cellphone number.** Get a forwarding number from a service like Google Voice and, in general, give out that number rather than your actual cellphone number. Doing so helps protect against many risks — SIM swapping, spam, and so on.

>> **Store private materials offline.** Ideally, store highly sensitive materials offline, such as in a fireproof safe or in a bank safe deposit box. If you must store them electronically, store them on a computer with no network connection.

>> **Encrypt all private information.** Encrypt documents, images, videos, and so on. If you're not sure if something should be encrypted, it probably should.

>> **If you use online chat, use end-to-end encryption.** Assume that all your text messages sent via regular cellphone service (SMS messages) can potentially be read by outsiders. Ideally, do not share sensitive information in writing. If you must share some sensitive item in writing, encrypt the data.

TIP

The simplest way to encrypt data is to use a chat application that offers end-to-end encryption. *End-to-end* means that the messages are encrypted on your device and decrypted on the recipient's device and vice versa — with the provider effectively unable to decrypt the messages; as such, it takes far more effort by hackers who breach the provider's servers to read your messages if end-to-end encryption is utilized. (Sometimes, providers claim that hackers can't read such messages altogether, which isn't correct. for two reasons: 1. Hackers may be able to see the metadata — for example, with whom you chatted and when you did so, and 2. if hackers breach enough internal servers, they may be able to upload to the app store a poisoned version of the app containing a backdoor of some sort.) WhatsApp is probably the most popular chat application that uses end-to-end encryption.

>> **Practice proper cyberhygiene.** Because so much of the information that you want to keep private is stored in electronic form, practicing proper cyber-hygiene is critical to preserving privacy.

TURNING ON PRIVACY MODE

To turn on privacy mode:

- **Chrome:** Control + Shift-N or choose New incognito window from the menu

- **Firefox:** Control + Shift + P or choose New private window from the menu

- **Opera:** Control + Shift + N or choose New private window from the menu

- **Edge:** Control + Shift + P or choose New private window from the menu

- **Vivaldi:** Control + Shift + N or choose New private window from the menu

- **Safari:** Command + Shift + N or choose New private window from the File menu

- **Tor Browser Bundle:** Privacy Mode is on by default in this version of Firefox (and Tor enhances privacy as well)

Banking Online Safely

Eschewing online banking due to the security concerns that it creates is simply not practical for most people living in the modern age. Doing so would also increase the risks of other dangers that emanate from phone-based banking or from banking in person.

Fortunately, you don't have to give up the conveniences of online banking in order to stay secure. Here are some suggestions of what you can do to improve your security as you bank online:

>> **Your online banking password should be strong, unique, and committed to memory.** It should not be stored in a database, password manager, or anywhere else electronic. (If you want to write it down and keep the paper in a safe deposit box, that may be okay — but doing so is rarely necessary.)

>> **Choose a random Personal Identification Number (PIN) for your ATM card and/or phone identification.** Any PIN that you use for banking-related purposes should be unrelated to any information that you know. Don't use a PIN that you have used for some other purpose and don't establish any PINs or passwords based on the one you chose for your ATM card. Never write down your PIN. Never add it to any computer file. Never tell your PIN to anyone, including bank employees.

>> **Consider asking your bank for an ATM card that can't be used as a debit card.** While such cards may lack the ability to be used to buy goods and services, if you make your purchases using credit cards, you don't need the purchase feature on your ATM card. By preventing the card from being used as a debit card, you make it more likely that only someone who knows your PIN number can take money out of your account. Perhaps equally as important is that "crippled" ATM cards can also not be used by crooks to make fraudulent purchases.

REMEMBER

If your debit card is used fraudulently, you're out money and need to get it back. If your credit card is used fraudulently, you're not out any money unless an investigation reveals that you were the one doing the defrauding.

>> **Log in to online banking only from trusted devices that you control, that have security software on them, and that are kept up to date.**

>> **Log in to online banking only from secure networks that you trust.** If you're on the road, use your cellular provider's connection, not public Wi-Fi. Do not login to online banking or any other sensitive apps from locations in which communication providers are believed to target with malware devices connecting to their networks.

- >> **Log in to online banking using a web browser or the official app of the bank.** Never log in from a third-party app or an app obtained from anywhere other than the official app store for your device's platform.

- >> **Sign up for alerts from your bank.** You should configure to be alerted by text message and/or email any time a new payee is added, a withdrawal is made, and so on.

- >> **Use multifactor authentication and protect any device used for such authentication.** If you generate one-time passwords on your phone, for example, and your phone is stolen, your second factor becomes (at least temporarily) usable by the crook and not by you.

- >> **Do not allow your browser to store your online banking password.** Your online banking password should not be written down anywhere — certainly not in a system that will enter it on behalf of someone using a web browser.

- >> **Enter the URL of your bank every time you visit the bank on the web.** Never click links to it.

- >> **Ideally, use a separate computer for online banking than you use for online shopping, email access, and social media.** If that isn't possible or practical, use a different web browser — and be sure to keep that browser up to date.

TIP

As an extra precaution, you can configure your browser to remember the wrong password to a site so that if someone ever does get into your laptop or phone, that person will be less likely to successfully log into that site using your credentials.

- >> **Make sure to secure any devices from which you bank online.** That includes physically securing them (don't leave them on a table in a restaurant while going to the restroom), requiring a password to unlock them, and enabling remote wipe.

- >> **Monitor your account for unauthorized activity.**

Safely Using Smart Devices

Smart devices and the so-called Internet of Things create all sorts of cybersecurity risks. Here are some recommendations as to how to improve your security as you use such devices:

- >> **Make sure that none of your IoT devices create security risks in the event of a failure.** Never create a situation in which a smart lock prevents you from leaving a room during a fire, for example, or lets robbers into your house during a power outage or network failure.

>> **If possible, run your IoT devices on a separate network than your computers.** The IoT network should have a firewall protecting it.

>> **Keep all IoT devices up to date.** Hackers have exploited vulnerabilities in IoT devices to commandeer the devices and use them to carry out major attacks. If a device has a firmware auto-update capability, consider enabling it.

>> **Keep a full, current list of all devices connected to your network.** Also keep a list of all devices that are not currently connected but that are authorized to connect and sometimes do connect.

>> **If possible, disconnect devices when you're not using them.** If a device is offline, it is obviously not hackable by anyone not physically present at the device.

>> **Password-protect all devices.** Never maintain the default passwords that come with the devices. Each device should have a unique login and password.

>> **Check your devices' settings.** Many devices come with default setting values that are terrible from a security perspective.

>> **Keep your smartphone physically and digitally secure.** It likely runs apps with access to some or all of your devices.

>> **If possible, disable device features that you do not need.** Doing so reduces the relevant attack surface — that is, it reduces the number of potential points at which an unauthorized user can attempt to hack into the device — and simultaneously lowers the chances of the device exposing an exploitable software vulnerability.

Universal Plug and Play (UPnP) simplifies device setup, but it also makes it easier for hackers to discover devices and attack them for many reasons, including that many implementations of UPnP contain vulnerabilities, UPnP can sometimes allow malware to bypass firewall security routines, and UPnP can sometimes be exploited by hackers to run commands on routers.

>> **Do not connect your IoT devices to untrusted networks.**

Cryptocurrency Security 101

In simplified terms, *cryptocurrency* refers to "money" that is tracked using a ledger of accounts whose copies are distributed to *nodes* running the cryptocurrency network (which means numerous parties all over the world have copies of the ledger containing a list of all transactions that have ever occurred using that particular cryptocurrency). Most cryptocurrencies are managed not by a central party, but rather, by a majority consensus, with the definition of who is included in calculating the majority consensus varying by cryptocurrency.

The most well-known cryptocurrency is Bitcoin, which was also the first cryptocurrency to arrive on the scene. When someone owns a Bitcoin (or a fraction thereof), that information is stored in a ledger — not with the person's name, but with an address. For example, address 123 received one Bitcoin from address 321, which means that now address 123 has one Bitcoin.

The owner of the Bitcoin does not actually own anything; instead, the owner simply has control over the relevant Bitcoin address. In the previous example, the person who possesses the secret key needed to authorize any transactions made from address 321 controls any Bitcoins stored at that address.

While going into a discussion about the technology used by Bitcoin is beyond the scope of this book, one important security concern for people to be aware of is that when it comes to cryptocurrency, the secret key needed to perform transactions effectively defines ownership. If the owner of the Bitcoin at address 321 lost the key to that address, the owner would no longer be able to access the Bitcoin stored there, and would likely permanently lose whatever money was stored at that address.

Likewise, if someone else obtained the key for 321 and utilized it without authorization from the owner to transfer the Bitcoin to another address, that transaction would, in nearly all cases, be deemed valid, and the rightful owner will lose the Bitcoin.

REMEMBER

As such, it is critical to protect the secret keys associated with cryptocurrency holdings.

One way to do so is to store secret keys on a special hardware device called a hardware "wallet." Such a device keeps the keys offline so that no Internet-connected devices hold the keys anywhere where the keys could potentially be stolen by a hacker. When the rightful owner wants to perform a transaction with the cryptocurrency, the owner must connect the relevant hardware wallet to a computer (often by USB connection), and unlock the wallet (usually by using a passcode of some sort), in order to utilize the keys stored on the wallet.

REMEMBER

Note that hardware cryptocurrency wallets do not store cryptocurrency — they store keys used to authorize actions on particular cryptocurrency addresses on ledgers.

Also, keep in mind that when people store cryptocurrency at a cryptocurrency exchange, it is the exchange that stores the keys for the cryptocurrency. If the user's credentials to the exchange are stolen, the cryptocurrency may be stolen as well.

» Understanding the basics of physical security for data and electronic devices

» Identifying what needs protection

» Reducing physical security risks

Chapter **2**

Enhancing Physical Security

Y ou may be tempted to skip this chapter — after all, you are reading this book to learn about cybersecurity, not physical security.

But please don't.

Seriously.

Certain aspects of physical security are *essential* ingredients of any cybersecurity program, whether formal or informal. Without them, all of the policies, procedures, and technical defenses can prove to be worthless. In fact, just a few decades ago, the teams responsible for protecting computers and the data housed within them focused specifically on physical security. Locking a computer in a secured area accessible by only authorized personnel was often sufficient to protect it and its contents. Of course, the dawn of networks and the Internet era, coupled with the mass proliferation of computing devices, totally transformed the risks. Today, even computers locked in a physical location can still be accessed electronically by billions of people around the world. That said, the need for physical security is as important as ever.

This chapter covers elements of physical security that are necessary in order to implement and deliver proper cybersecurity. It covers the "what and why" that you need to know about physical security in order to keep yourself cybersecure. Ignoring the concepts discussed in this chapter may put you at risk of a data breach equivalent to, or even worse than, one carried out by hackers.

Understanding Why Physical Security Matters

Physical security means protecting something from unauthorized physical access, whether that access is by man or by nature. Keeping a computer locked in an office server closet, for example, to prevent people from tampering with it is an example of physical security.

The goal of physical security is to provide a safe environment for the people and assets of a person, family, or organization. Within the context of cybersecurity, the goal of physical security is to ensure that digital systems and data are not placed at risk because of the manner in which they're physically housed.

REMEMBER

Classified information contains secrets whose compromise can endanger American intelligence agents and operations, undermine diplomatic and military operations, and harm national security.

If you're storing highly sensitive classified files in your home, you had better know a lot more about information security than is taught in this book. Removing classified information from its proper storage location is often a serious crime.

Taking Inventory

Before you implement a physical security plan, you need to understand what it is that you have to secure. You likely possess more than one type of electronic device and have data that varies quite a bit in terms of the level of secrecy and sensitivity that you attach to it. Step 1 in implementing proper physical security is to understand what data and systems you have and determine what type of security level each one demands.

In all likelihood, your computer devices fall into two categories:

>> **Stationary devices,** such as a desktop computer sitting in your family room on which your teenagers play video games

>> **Mobile devices,** such as laptops, tablets, and cellphones

REMEMBER

Don't forget to inventory the equipment to which your devices are connected. When you inventory your devices, pay attention to networks and networking equipment. To what networks are stationary devices attached? How many networks are in place? Where do they connect to the outside world? Where is the relevant network equipment located? What mobile devices connect to wirelessly?

Stationary devices

Stationary devices, such as desktop computers, networking equipment, and many Internet of Things (IoT) devices, such as wired cameras, are devices that don't move from location to location on a regular basis.

These devices can, of course, still be stolen, damaged, or misused, and, therefore, must be adequately protected. Damage need not be intentionally inflicted — a server problem can occur when a person unknowingly unplugs an improperly secured server from its uninterruptible power supply in order to plug in another piece of equipment. As it is imperative to secure stationary devices in the locations in which they "live," you must inventory all such devices. Securing something that you do not know that you possess is difficult, if not impossible.

REMEMBER

In many cases, anyone who can physically access a computer or other electronic device can access all the data and programs on that device, regardless of security systems in place. The only question is how long it will take that party to gain the unauthorized access that it desires. Never mind that anyone who can access a device can physically damage it — whether by physically striking it, sending into it a huge power surge, dumping water on it, or setting it ablaze. In case you think that these scenarios are far-fetched, know that I have seen all four of these options utilized by people intent on damaging computers.

Mobile devices

Mobile devices are computerized devices that are frequently moved. Laptops, tablets, and smartphones are all mobile devices. In some ways mobile devices are inherently more secure than stationary devices — you likely always have your cellphone with you, so that device not sitting at home unwatched for long periods of time as a computer may be.

SMARTPHONES ARE A LOT MORE THAN SMART PHONES

The term *smartphone* is extremely misleading — the device in your pocket is a full-blown computer with more processing power than all the computers used to first put a man on the moon combined. It is only a smartphone in the same way that a Ferrari is a fast, horseless carriage — a technically correct description, but one that is highly misleading. Why do you call these devices smartphones — well, think of where you encountered your first smartphone.

Most people's first experience with a smartphone was when they upgraded from a regular cellphone — and they obtained the new devices from cellphone providers who (likely correctly) reasoned that people would be more likely to upgrade their cellphone to "smartphones" than to replace their cellphones with "pocket computers that have a phone app."

Smartphone is, as such, a marketing term. "Easily lost or stolen, and potentially hackable, pocket-sized computer with lots of sensitive information on it" provides a more accurate understanding.

That said, in reality, experience shows that portability dramatically increases the chances of an electronic device being lost or stolen. In fact, in some ways, mobile devices are the stuff of security professionals' nightmares. The "smartphone" in your pocket is constantly connected to an insecure network (the Internet), contains highly sensitive data, has access tokens to your email, social media, and a whole host of other important accounts, likely lacks security software of the sophistication that is on desktop computers, is frequently in locations in which it is likely to be stolen, is often out of sight, is taken on trips that cause you to deviate from your normal routine, and so on.

REMEMBER

Properly inventorying every mobile device so that you can properly secure all such devices is critical.

Locating Your Vulnerable Data

Review what data your devices house. Think of the worst-case consequences if an unauthorized person obtained your data or it leaked to the public on the Internet. No list of items to search for can possibly cover all possible scenarios, but here are some things to think about. Do you have

>> Private photos and videos

>> Recordings of your voice

>> Images of your handwriting (especially of your signature)

>> Financial records

>> Medical records

>> School-related documents

>> Password lists

>> Repositories of digital keys

>> Documents containing:

- Credit card numbers

- SSNs/EINs/taxpayer identification numbers

- Maiden names

- Codes to physical locks or other passcodes

- Correspondence with the IRS and state tax authorities

- Lawsuit-related information

- Employment-related information

- Mother's family name

- Birth dates

- Passport numbers

- Driver's license numbers

- Information about your vehicles

- Information about your former addresses

- Biometric data (fingerprints, retina scan, facial geometry, keyboard dynamics, and so on)

These items will need to be protected against cyberthreats, as described in multiple later chapters. But the data stores in which they reside also need to be protected physically, as described in the next section.

Creating and Executing a Physical Security Plan

In order to adequately physically protect your technology and data, you should not attempt to simply deploy various security controls on an ad hoc basis. Rather, it is far better to develop and implement a physical security plan — doing so, will help you avoid making costly mistakes.

In most cases, physically securing computing systems relies on applying a well-known established principal of crime prevention, known as Crime Prevention Through Environmental Design (CPTD), that states that you can reduce the likelihood of certain crimes being committed if you create a physical environment that allows legitimate users to feel secure, but makes ill-doers unconformable with actually carrying out any planned problematic activities.

Understanding this high-level concept can help you think about ways to keep your own systems and data safe. Three components of CPTD as they apply in general to preventing crime include access control, surveillance, and marking:

>> **Access control:** Limiting access to authorized parties, by using fences, monitored entrances and exits, proper landscaping, and so on makes it harder for criminals to penetrate a building or other facility, and increases the risk to crooks that they will be noticed, thus discouraging potential criminals from actually carrying out crimes.

>> **Surveillance:** Criminals often avoid committing crimes that are likely to be seen and recorded; as such, they gravitate away from environments that they know are well-watched. Cameras, guards, and motion-sensitive-lighting all discourage crime.

>> **Marking:** Criminals tend to avoid areas that are clearly marked as belonging to someone else — for example, through the use of fences and signs — as they do not want to stand out and be easily noticeable when committing crimes. Likewise, they avoid environments in which authorized parties are marked. Consider, for example, that an unauthorized person not wearing a post office uniform while walking around in an area marked "U.S. Postal Service Employees Only" is far more likely to be noticed and stopped than someone else walking in a similar unmarked environment belonging to a business that does not require uniforms.

TIP

You can apply these same principles in your own home — for example, placing a computer in a parent's home office sends a message to children, babysitters, and guests that the device is off limits, far stronger than the message would be delivered if the same machine were located in a family room or den. Likewise, curious babysitters or houseguests are far less likely to go into one's private home office without permission after being told not to if they are aware that the area is monitored with cameras.

You know your own environment. By applying these concepts you can improve the likelihood that unauthorized parties will not attempt to gain unauthorized access to your computers and data.

Implementing Physical Security

You can use many techniques and technologies to help secure an object or facility. How much physical security you implement for a device depends heavily on the purpose for which it is being used and what types of information it houses.

Here are some examples of methods of securing devices — based on your tolerance level for risk and your budget, you may choose variants of all, some, or none of these techniques:

>> **Locks:** For example, store devices in a locked room, with access to the room provided to only those people who need to use the device. In some environments, you may be able to utilize a smart lock to record or monitor all entrances and exits from the room. Another popular variant is to store laptops in a safe located in one's master bedroom or home office when the computers are not in use.

>> **Video cameras:** For example, consider having a video camera focused on the devices to see who accesses them and when they do so.

>> **Security guards:** Obviously, security guards are not a practical solution in most home environments, but human defenders do have a time and place. For example, consider posting guards inside the room where the device is located, outside the room, in halls around the entrance to the room, outside the building, and outside the perimeter fence.

>> **Alarms:** Alarms not only serve as a reactive force that scare away criminals who actually attempt to enter a home or office, they also serve as a strong deterrent, pushing many opportunistic evildoers to "look elsewhere" and target someone else.

>> **Perimeter security:** Traffic posts prevent people from crashing cars into a facility, and proper fences and walls prevent people from approaching a home or office building. You should note that most experts believe that a fence under 8 feet tall does not provide any significant security value when it comes to potential human intruders.

>> **Lighting:** Criminals tend to avoid well-lit places. Motion-triggered lighting is even more of a deterrent than static lighting. When lights go on suddenly, people in the area are more likely to turn and look at what just happened — and see the criminals just as they are illuminated.

>> **Environmental risk mitigation:** If you're in an area that is likely to be hit by floods, for example, ensure that computing resources are stationed somewhere not likely to flood. If such advice seems obvious, consider that residents of northern New Jersey lost telephone service after a storm in the late 1990s when telephone switching equipment flooded — because it was situated in the basement of a building standing next to a river. Having proper defenses against fires is another critical element of environmental risk mitigation.

>> **Backup power and contingencies for power failures:** Power failures impact not only your computers, but many security systems as well.

>> **Contingencies during renovations and other construction, and so forth:** The risks to data and computers during home renovations are often overlooked. Leaving your cellphone unattended when workers are routinely entering and exiting your home, for example, can be a recipe for a stolen device and/or the compromise of data on the device.

>> **Risks from backups:** Remember to protect backups of data with the same security precautions as you do the original copies of the data. Spending time and money protecting a computer with a safe and cameras because of the data on its hard drive, for example, is silly if you leave backups of that same data on portable hard drives stored on a family room shelf in plain sight of anyone visiting your home.

Of course, you should not consider the preceding list to be comprehensive. But, if you think about how you can apply each of these items to help keep your devices safe within the context of a CPTD approach, you will likely benefit from much greater odds against an "unfortunate incident" occurring than if you do not. (For more on CPTD, see the earlier section "Creating and Executing a Physical Security Plan.")

Security for Mobile Devices

TIP

Of course, mobile devices — that is, computers, tablets, smartphones, and other electronic devices that are moved from location to location on a regular basis — pose additional risks because these devices can be easily lost or stolen. As such, when it comes to mobile devices, one simple, yet critically important, physical security principle should be added: Keep your devices in sight or locked up.

Such advice may sound obvious; sadly, however, a tremendous number of devices are stolen each year when left unattended, so you can be sure that the advice is either not obvious or not followed — and, in either case, you want to internalize it and follow it.

In addition to watching over your phone, tablet, or laptop, you should enable location broadcasting, remotely triggerable alarms, and remote wipe — all of which can be invaluable at quickly reducing the risk posed if the device is lost or stolen. Some devices even offer a feature to photograph or video record anyone using a mobile device after the user flags it as stolen — which can not only help you locate the device, but can also help law enforcement catch any thieves involved in stealing it.

Realizing That Insiders Pose the Greatest Risks

According to most experts, the majority of information-security incidents involve insider threats — meaning that the biggest cyber risks to businesses are posed by their own employees. Likewise, if you share a home computer with family members who are less cyber-aware, they may pose the greatest risk to your cybersecurity. You may take great care of your machine and be diligent with cybersecurity every single day, but if your teen downloads malware-infected software onto the device on even a single occasion, you may be in for a nasty surprise.

One critical rule from "the old days" that rings true today — even though it is often dismissed as outdated due to the use of technologies such as encryption — is that anyone who can physically access a computer may be able to access the data on that computer.

REMEMBER

Anyone who can physically access a computer may be able to access the data on that computer.

This rule is true even if encryption is utilized, for at least two reasons: Someone who accesses your device may not be able to access your data, but that person can certainly destroy it and may even be able to access it due to one or more of the following reasons:

>> You may not have set up the encryption properly.

>> Your machine may have an exploitable vulnerability.

>> The encryption software may have a bug in it that undermines its ability to properly protect your secrets.

>> Someone may have obtained the password to decrypt.

>> Someone may be willing to copy your data and wait until computers are powerful enough to break your encryption. This is especially true today, as experts believe that in the not-so-distant future we will see the next generation of computers (known as quantum computers) that will be able to undermine most of today's encryption mechanisms.

WARNING

Here is the bottom line: If you do not want people to access data, not only should you secure it logically (for example, with encryption), you should also secure it physically in order to prevent them from obtaining a copy of the data, even in encrypted form.

On that note, if your computer contains files that you do not want your children to have access to, do not share your computer with your children. That may seem like obvious advice, but you would be amazed at how often it is ignored for financial reasons. (Why should I buy a second computer for my children when I already have a perfectly good computer at home?)

REMEMBER

Do not rely solely on digital security. Utilize a physical defense. While it is true that crafty, skilled children may be able to hack your computer across your LAN, the risks of such an attack occurring are miniscule compared with the temptation of a curious child who is actually using your computer. That said, ideally you should keep your most sensitive data and machines on a network physically isolated from the one that your children use.

creates security risks

>> **Understanding various types of risks created by — or made worse by — remote working**

>> **Learning how to address risks when working from home**

Chapter 3

Cybersecurity Considerations When Working from Home

I n early 2020, the spread of a new, deadly and highly contagious disease — COVID-19 — began to facilitate a worldwide change in the way many people work. For the first time in generations, the need to stop a global pandemic led to governments enforcing lockdowns that prohibited people from working together in offices. Unlike during all prior such lockdowns in human history, however, technological advances made over the past few decades meant that many people who would otherwise have been unable to work, could, in fact, continue to do their jobs — albeit remotely.

Naturally, the sudden transition of a tremendous number of in-office workers to remote workers, and on such short notice, translated into a whole host of cybersecurity challenges. In addition, while many business leaders initially thought that the remote-working phase would be short-lived, that was not to be the case. Remote working in some fashion is here to stay. This chapter discusses cybersecurity issues related specifically to working from home.

Network Security Concerns

A major cybersecurity concern with working remotely involves the networks from which remote employees access sensitive data. If those networks aren't properly secured, two really bad things can occur:

>> Someone may steal sensitive information — and neither the employee, nor the employer, may ever know that it happened.

>> Malware or a hacker may compromise some user's device and leapfrog from it to other corporate devices and networks — and, once inside corporate resources, wreak havoc in any one or more of many possible ways.

Why are remote-worker networks often unsafe?

Businesses often have much better firewalls than those offered in consumer products — and most remote workers are using consumer-grade routers and no additional firewalls. Should your employer really be trusting its cybersecurity to the router you bought for $19.99 on Black Friday five years ago? Likewise, most consumers have no idea how to configure their routers or firewalls, and utilize only basic options. Even when they are more sophisticated, people rarely deploy true intrusion detection systems and other security technologies at home. Such offerings are simply not available in inexpensive routers.

Businesses often have all sorts of security technologies deployed at their perimeters. An organization's firewalls, for example, may block certain types of outbound requests, and data loss prevention systems may stop emails that contain sensitive materials that appear to have been inadvertently attached to the messages. Remote workers rarely, if ever, have such security functionality available from their routers. On that note, how many employers even know what routers their employees are using when their employees work from home, never mind know if those routers have had their firmware kept up to date? Do managers of businesses really know if an employee working from home has properly conducted vulnerability scans?

Besides the issue of the router's patch level and firmware, how many employers have verified that their employees have properly secured their personal home-based Wi-Fi access points? And how many employers know who else is using the home network — and for what they are using it? Kids downloading games can easily infect computers with malware, and malware can spread via network connections.

While some have suggested that employers can utilize a full tunneling virtual private network (VPN) to address such risks — such a VPN would force all Internet traffic from the user to the employer's network and would route all Internet requests through the employer's security systems at the perimeter. Doing so is often highly risky as it essentially means that malware and other cyber-problems present on the employee's home network can potentially propagate to the employer's network. It also means that if something goes wrong with the employer's connectivity, the employee cannot work — even remotely.

How can you address such risks?

Ideally, your employer should provide you with a second router that connects to your home router — the second router would effectively form a separate work environment, with a different network segment, that is logically (somewhat) isolated from all of the other devices on the network.

If properly set up, the work network will be able to initiate outbound requests to the Internet, but your home network will not be able to initiate requests to the work network. One way to do this is shown in Figure 3-1. This type of configuration is better than using one router, but still not ideal as the work network can still communicate with the home network. While, in theory, there are ways to ensure that such a configuration is still secure, the opportunity increases for making configuration mistakes undermining security. Ideally, therefore, use two internal routers as shown Figure 3-2. It should be noted however, that deploying the third network segment as shown in Figure 3-2 can complicate printing and various other tasks, but as printers are inexpensive and do not take up a lot of space, ask your employer to supply you with a work-related printer.

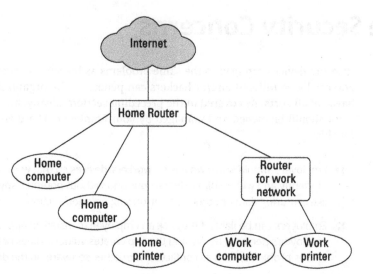

FIGURE 3-1: Network setup in which the work router communicates through the home router.

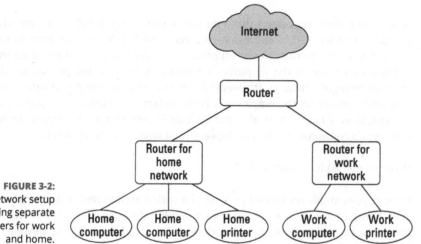

FIGURE 3-2:
Network setup
using separate
routers for work
and home.

TIP

In addition, because the work network router is supplied by your employer, your employer can select an appropriately equipped and remotely manageable device — and can keep it updated and patched.

Ideally, employees should also use computers owned by their employers — both for legal reasons (to prevent various privacy-related matters if private devices are used) and to prevent data leaks and prevent corporate data from ending up on computers that could be used by others and/or connected to insecure networks. In a perfect world, the only devices that ever connect to a work network are those owned by the employer.

Device Security Concerns

Insecure devices can lead to the same problems as insecure networks — data can potentially be pilfered and/or hackers can penetrate the organization and wreak havoc of all sorts. As covered in the preceding section, ideally, all devices used for work should be owned and managed by your employer. There are many reasons for this:

>> Employers should know what is on workers' devices so that workers can work efficiently and with minimal distractions and without potential spyware or the like capturing data or otherwise performing nefarious actions.

>> Employers can be liable if they ask an employee to install an app on the employee's personal device and the app creates vulnerabilities or otherwise causes problems, such as conflicting with other software on the device.

>> If an employee suddenly leaves the organization and has work-related data on a personal device, that data may remain intact and put the employer at risk intentionally or inadvertently. The same holds true of the device is stolen from the employee. Likewise, in a more extreme case, if an employee were to die, who knows where the employee's laptop containing sensitive work-related information will end up.

That said, issuing employer devices for employees to use from home is not always a practical possibility.

REMEMBER

In any case, all computing devices — whether laptops, tablets, and/or smartphones — need appropriate security software installed, enabled, and kept up to date. Such devices should also have the ability to be remotely wiped if lost or stolen, and all relevant data on them must be both encrypted and appropriately backed up.

Location Cybersecurity

The technology handing data is often considered to be the primary factor impacting the security of that data, but the reality is that other factors play at least as great a role. As described throughout this book, people themselves are a significant factor. Another important element is the location in which systems are used and data is accessed. This factor has dramatically increased in significance as a result of the migration from in office working to remote working, which means that location-based dangers are more important than ever to understand.

Shoulder surfing

One of the greatest risks created by employees working remotely to the security and privacy of employer data is actually a quite old-fashioned danger. If an employee works in a place in which other people or cameras can see sensitive information as it is displayed on the screen of the user's device, the confidentiality of the data may be compromised.

Such a problem is known colloquially as *shoulder surfing*. It is hardly a new concept, but it still remains a problem. Especially when large numbers of workers are expected to work outside of their usual professional workspaces. So, ideally, if you are going to work from home, do exactly that — work from *home* — and not from coffee shops, public parks, or the like.

Also, if possible, work in an environment that is configured in such a manner that your significant others and/or kids are not able to view sensitive information either. If need be, employers may even purchase furniture or equipment to help you ensure such privacy.

Eavesdropping

Similar risks apply in regard to voice communication — don't discuss sensitive information over the phone or other voice communication system from a location in which other people can hear you. This may sound obvious, but prior to the pandemic, I heard many sensitive work-related calls transpiring on buses to and from New York City, while the bus-riding employee was oblivious to the fact that they were compromising the privacy of information that was clearly intended not to become public.

TIP

When working from home, a simple sound machine that generates white background noise — such as those used by many psychologists and psychiatrists to prevent people in waiting rooms from hearing the conversations taking place in treatment rooms — can be of great assistance.

Theft

Home offices are rarely as well secured as professional office spaces, and public locations — such as parks, libraries, and coffee shops — are even less secure. Remote workers, therefore, often stand a greater chance of having a laptop stolen from them than do their counterparts whose devices never leave their normal at-work offices.

Human errors

It is important to understand that if people are repetitively interrupted, they are more likely to make mistakes than if that were not the case, and mistakes, of course, can easily lead to data leaks. If you are working remotely, create a workspace where you can keep disruptions to a minimum. Of course, remote working locations are often much more problematic than professional offices in such regard — especially during a pandemic when children are home all day and attend school virtually. So, seek to create a workspace in which you can work efficiently while staying focused and keeping data as private as is reasonably possible.

Video Conferencing Cybersecurity

As a result of the transition from in-office work to remote work that began in 2020 as a result of the COVID-19 pandemic, the use of video call and video conferencing technology has skyrocketed, with the number of people who regularly make work-related video calls from outside of their official places of work growing by orders of magnitude in just a short period of time. With the sudden and rapid adoption of such a transformative and unfamiliar technology comes risks, and, in the case of video conferencing, those risks include serious risks to information security and privacy.

Keep private stuff out of camera view

When you video conference, make sure you do not have any sensitive information or other private material on display in your camera's frame. Keep in mind that mirrors and reflective surfaces in frame can also allow people in a video conference to see materials that are technically out of the camera's view. If the preceding two points sound obvious, feel free to search online for how many significant cases are known of people not being careful as such.

TIP

Consider using a virtual background (preferably with a physical green screen) to keep inquisitive eyes focused on you rather than on background elements. At a minimum, utilize blur background features made available to you by your particular video conferencing tool.

WARNING

When participating in a video conference from home in which your camera and/or microphone are on (for even part of the time), make sure that any and all other people in the home are aware that you are engaging in such a session. Warn them that you are sharing your camera feed and microphone, and that if they speak near you or walk near you, they may be heard or seen by others. Sadly, there have been many embarrassing incidents in which people walked half naked into the field of view of someone else's video conference session.

Keep video conferences secure from unauthorized visitors

Video conferencing cybersecurity is about much more than just keeping sensitive data out of frame. In fact, the tremendous number of security violations that occurred during the earlier months of the COVID-19 pandemic — in which unauthorized parties regularly joined Zoom meetings and wreaked havoc — led to the creation and proliferation of a new term: *Zoom bombing*. To reduce the chances that your video communications will be Zoom bombed, consider the following advice:

» **Never use video conferencing for secret conversations.** No modern commercial video conferencing services are appropriate for truly secret conversations. Remember, video conferencing software, like all other software packages, may have exploitable vulnerabilities within it.

» **Password-protect your sessions.** If unauthorized users try to join your video calls without authorization, they will find doing so challenging, as without the password to your calls, they will not be able to easily join you.

» **Create a new room name for every meeting.** Some video call services allow you to use the same meeting room name over and over. Do not do so, as this makes it much easier for someone who obtains information about one of your calls to join another call.

» **Use a waiting room.** Many popular video-conferencing apps allow you to automatically redirect all participants into a virtual waiting room after they join the call. You, the host, get to decide who gets admitted from the waiting room into the actual call meeting room; you can usually either admit everyone in one shot, or select participants individually to admit into the session. You may also have the option of having pre-registered participants placed directly into the meeting room upon their joining the session, but forcing unknown parties seeking to join to wait for admission from the waiting room.

» **Lock your sessions.** Once all of the expected participants have joined a session, or after some period of time after the start of a session if some such folks have not joined, lock the session so that no additional parties can join.

» **"Throw the bums out."** Periodically scan the list of who is participating in your meeting. If you see anyone who does not belong, remove them immediately! Likewise, if an authorized participant is causing problems during a video call session, consider removing them as well. If you locked the session, you should only need to review the list of participants once — right after you lock the session. Of course, if you have cohosts, your locking may be undone by them, so make sure to scan the participant list periodically.

» **Disable private chatting.** If possible, disable the ability of participants to private message one another via the video conferencing app. If they want to chat, let them use their regular chat apps.

» **Do not allow general participants to share their screens.** Unless there is a need for a particular party in a virtual meeting to share their device's screen with other participants, either disable screen sharing altogether or set screen sharing to be available to only yourself, the host.

>> **Do not overshare meeting login information on social media.** When possible — and I know that it is not always possible — do not share on public social platforms any login details for meetings. Instead, if necessary, advertise about the meeting, but require people to sign up for it, check the list of registered participants, and email the relevant login information to the folks who both signed up and you want to attend. And, in any event, private meetings should *never* be announced on public social media.

Social Engineering Issues

People who work from home, in environments separate from those in which their colleagues do their own jobs, are more likely to fall for some types of social engineering attacks than are people who work together, in person, with their colleagues. People in distinct locations cannot as easily verify the authenticity of a request. A homebound CFO who receives a request from a CEO to issue a payment, for example, cannot simply walk to the office next door and ask the CEO in person if the request is legitimate.

In addition, as we saw during the early weeks of the COVID-19 pandemic, many businesses that were forced to suddenly convert to a remote work model did not have the chance to properly prepare for such a situation, and as a result, various technologies that they had in place in their professional offices to reduce the likelihood of users being exposed to social engineering attacks were not successfully extended to remote locations prior to the commencement of remote work.

REMEMBER

The most important element in a defense against social engineering attacks is to ensure that any and every remote worker understands that they are a target. People who internalize such a belief tend to act differently in situations that could lead to a data breach than do those who do not truly accept that reality. Of course, training and assessments can also help in this regard.

Regulatory Issues

The fact that people need to work remotely due to the rapid spreading of a dangerous virus does not negate the requirements of various laws and other regulations related to information security and privacy. Businesses subject to Europe's General Data Protection Regulation (GDPR), for example, still must ensure that remote working does not undermine efforts to protect the privacy of personal information. Likewise, the fact that a medical facility might have allowed its clerical staff to work remotely on tasks such as billing insurance companies for services, does not excuse it from compliance with the relevant data protection requirements of the Health Insurance Portability and Accountability Act of 1996 (HIPAA). U.S. Securities and Exchange Commission (SEC) rules still apply as well — so insider information cannot be allowed to leak, or otherwise be provided even to authorized parties at inappropriate times. The same holds true for other regulations and industry guidelines.

Make sure your remote working program is not going to get you or others into regulatory hot water.

» **Understanding the different types of data that need to be secured**

» **Securing your accounts from human error**

» **Being careful when connecting external storage media**

Chapter **4**

Securing Your Accounts

T he weakest link in the cybersecurity chain is almost always people, and the greatest threat to your own cybersecurity is likely yourself, with the members of your family being a close second. As such, all of the technology and technical knowledge in the world won't deliver much value if you don't also address various human shortcomings.

Realizing You're a Target

Perhaps the most significant first step in securing yourself digitally is to understand that you're a target and that nefarious parties have the desire to breach your computer systems, electronically accessible accounts, and anything else they can get their hands on.

Even if you already realize that you're a target, it is important that you truly internalize such a notion. People who believe that criminals want to breach their computers and phones act differently than people who do not appreciate this reality, and whose lack of skepticism sometimes leads them into trouble. There is a difference between knowing something in theory and truly believing it. If you want to stay secure you must convince yourself that you really are a target, not just simply understand that in theory you may be.

WARNING

Because your family members can also impact your digital security, they also need to be aware that they are potential targets. If your children take unwise risks online, they may inadvertently inflict harm not only on themselves, but upon you and other members of the family as well. In some cases, attackers have managed to attack people's employers via remote connections that were compromised because children misused computers on the same networks as computers that the employees were using for working remotely. Think about how dangerous such attacks can be and how much damage they can cause during an era in which large portions of the population work from home.

The threat posed by such attacks is usually not that a criminal will directly steal someone's money or data, but rather that some party will seek to harm the target in some other manner — a manner that may ultimately translate into some form of financial, military, political, or other benefit to the attacker and (potentially) damage of some sort to the victim. Often the damage is far greater than if the criminal were just seeking to "make a quick buck."

Securing Your External Accounts

Chapter 4 discusses how you can acquire your own technology products. But using these products isn't enough to keep you cybersecure as you, no doubt, have digital data of significant value that is stored outside of your own physical possession — that is, outside of data systems and data stores under your control.

In fact, data about every person living in the western world today is likely stored on computer systems belonging to many businesses, organizations, and governmental agencies. Sometimes those systems reside within the facilities of the organizations to which they belong, sometimes they're located at shared data centers, and sometimes the systems themselves are virtual machines rented from a third-party provider. Additionally, some such data may reside in cloud-based systems offered by a third party. Not always is the data (or every copy of the data) even located within the same country as the people who are the subjects of the data.

In any event, such data can be broken down and divided into many different categories, depending on which aspects of it a person is interested in. One way of examining the data for the purposes of discovering how to secure it, for example, is to group it according to the following scheme:

>> Accounts, and the data within them, that a user established and controls

>> Data belonging to organizations that a user has willingly and knowingly interacted with, but the user has no control over the data

>> Data in the possession of organizations that the user has never knowingly established a relationship with

Addressing the risks of each type of data requires a different strategy.

Securing Data Associated with User Accounts

When you bank online, shop online, use social media, or even simply browse the web, you provide all sorts of data to the parties that you interact with. When you establish and maintain an account with a bank, store, social media provider, or other online party, you gain control over significant amounts of data related to yourself that the party maintains on your behalf. Obviously, you can't fully control the security of that data because the data is not in your possession. That said, you should have a strong interest in protecting that data — and, in not undermining the protections for the data that the party hosting your account has established.

While every situation and account have unique attributes, certain strategies can help keep your data secure at third parties. Obviously, not all the ideas in the following sections apply to every situation, but applying the appropriate items from the menu to your various accounts and online behavior can dramatically improve your odds of remaining cybersecure.

Conduct business with reputable parties

There is nothing wrong with supporting small businesses — in fact, doing so is quite admirable. And, it is certainly true that many large firms have suffered serious security breaches. But if you search for the latest electronic gizmo, for example, and one store that you have never heard of is offering it at a substantial discount from the prices offered at all well-known stores, be wary. There may be a legitimate reason for the discount — or there may be a scam in the works.

WARNING

Always check the websites of stores that you're conducting business with to see whether something looks off — and beware if it does.

Use official apps and websites

Clones of official apps have been found in various app stores. If you install a banking, credit card, or shopping app for a particular company, make sure that you install the official app and not some malicious impersonator. Install apps only from reputable app stores, such as Google Play, Amazon AppStore, and Apple App Store.

Don't install software from untrusted parties

Malware that infects a computer can capture sensitive information from both other programs and web sessions running on the device. If a website is offering free copies of movies, software, or other items that normally cost money, not only may the offerings be stolen copies, but ask yourself how the operator is making money — it may be by distributing malware.

Don't root your phone

You may be tempted to *root* your phone (especially if your phone runs the Android operating system). *Rooting* is a process that allows you greater control over your device — but rooting also undermines various security capabilities, and may allow malware to capture sensitive information from other apps on the device, leading to account compromises.

Don't provide unnecessary sensitive information

Don't provide private information to anyone who doesn't need that particular data. For example, don't give your Social Security number to any online stores or doctors. While they often ask for it, they have no need for it.

REMEMBER

Keep in mind that the less information about you that a specific party has, the less data that can be compromised, and correlated, in case of a breach.

Use payment services that eliminate the need to share credit card numbers

Services like PayPal, Samsung Pay, Apple Pay, and so on let you make online payments without having to give vendors your actual credit card number. If a vendor is breached, the information about your account that is likely to be stolen is significantly less likely to lead to fraud (and, perhaps, even various forms of identity theft) than if actual credit card data were stored at the vendor. Moreover, major payment sites have armies of skilled information security professionals working to keep them safe that vendors accepting such payments can rarely, if ever, match.

TIP

In addition, many stores now accept such payments using near-field communication (NFC), which is another form of contactless communication between devices in which you hold your phone against or near a payment processing device to wirelessly make payment. Not only is such a payment scheme safer from a cybersecurity standpoint than handing credit cards to a clerk, but it also avoids exposing both payers and cashiers to the biological risks posed by passing cash or payment cards between potentially germ-infected people.

Use one-time, virtual credit card numbers when appropriate

Some financial institutions allow you to use an app (or website) to create disposable, one-time *virtual credit card numbers* that allow you to make a charge to a real credit card account (associated with the virtual number) without having to give the respective merchant your real credit card number. As seen in Figure 4-1, some virtual credit card systems also allow you to specify the maximum allowable charge size on a particular virtual card number at a figure much lower than it would be on the real corresponding card.

FIGURE 4-1:
A (slightly edited image of) a one-time credit card number generator.

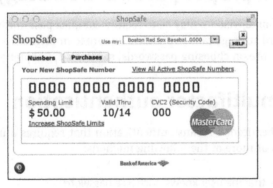

Securing Your Accounts

While creating one-time numbers takes time and effort, and, in fact, may be overkill when doing repeated deals with a reputable vendor in whose information-security practices you have confidence, virtual credit card numbers do offer benefits for defending against potential fraud and may be appropriately used when dealing with less familiar parties.

Besides minimizing the risk to yourself if a vendor turns out to be corrupt, virtual credit card numbers offer other security benefits. If criminals hack a vendor and steal your virtual credit card number that was previously used, not only can they not make charges with it, their attempts to do so may even help law enforcement track them down, as well as help relevant forensics teams identify the source of the credit card number data leak.

Monitor your accounts

TIP

You should regularly check your payment, banking, shopping, and other financial accounts for any unrecognized activities. Ideally, do this check by not only looking at online transaction logs, but also by checking relevant monthly statements (no matter whether such statements are physically delivered in the mail, sent to you electronically over email, displayed in apps, or posted on a web portal for you to download) for anything that does not belong.

Report suspicious activity ASAP

REMEMBER

The faster a case of fraud is reported to the parties responsible for addressing it, the greater the chance of reversing it, and of preventing further abuse of whatever materials were abused in order to commit it. Also, the sooner the fraud is reported, the greater the chance of catching the parties committing it. It is important, therefore, to quickly report potential cases of fraud and other forms of suspicious activity.

Employ a proper password strategy

While conventional wisdom may be to require complex passwords for all systems, such a password strategy fails in practice. Be sure to implement a proper password strategy. For more on choosing passwords, see Book 2, Chapter 5.

Utilize multifactor authentication

Multifactor authentication means authentication that requires a user to authenticate using two or more of the following methods:

» Something that the user knows, such as a password

» Something that the user is, such as a fingerprint

» Something that the user has, such as a hardware token

For extremely sensitive systems, you should use forms of authentication that are stronger than passwords alone. The following forms of authentication all have their places:

» **Biometrics,** which means using measurements of various human characteristics to identify people. Fingerprints, voiceprints, iris scans, facial structures, the speed at which people type different characters on a keyboard, and the like are all examples of features that differ between people, and that can be compared in order to distinguish between folks and establish someone's identity.

>> **Digital certificates,** which effectively prove to a system that a particular public key represents the presenter of the certificate. If the presenter of the certificate is able to decrypt messages encrypted with the public key in the certificate, it means that the presenter possesses the corresponding private key, which only the legitimate owner should have.

>> **One-time passwords,** or one-time tokens, generated by apps, read from a list of codes on a sheet of paper, or sent via SMS to your cellphone.

>> **Hardware tokens,** which are typically small electronic devices that either plug into a USB port, display a number that changes every minute or so, or allow users to enter a challenge number and receive a corresponding response number back. Today, smartphone apps perform such functions, allowing, at least theoretically, the smartphone to assume the role of a hardware token. Figure 4-2 shows you an example of using such an app to generate a one-time code for logging into Snapchat. (Note that smartphones can suffer from all sorts of security vulnerabilities that hardware tokens can't suffer from, so hardware tokens are still likely more appropriate for certain high-risk situations.)

>> **Knowledge-based authentication,** which is based on real knowledge, not simply answering questions with small numbers of possible answers that are often guessable like "What color was your first car?" Note that technically speaking, adding knowledge-based authentication questions to password authentication doesn't create multifactor authentication since both the password and the knowledge-based answer are examples of things that a user knows. However, doing so certainly does improve security when the questions are chosen properly.

TIP

Most financial institutions, social media companies, and major online retailers offer multifactor authentication — use it.

Also, note that while sending one-time passwords to users' smartphones via text messages theoretically verifies that a person logging in possesses the smartphone that the user is supposed to possess (something that the user has), various vulnerabilities undermine that supposition. It is potentially possible, for example, for a sophisticated criminal to intercept text messages even without possessing the relevant phone, or to hack into another chat application used for transmitting such codes.

FIGURE 4-2:
One-time password for Snapchat generated by the app Authy — an example of an app-generated multifactor authentication token.

Log out when you're finished

Don't rely on automatic timeouts, closing the browser, or shutting down a computer to log you out of accounts. Manually log out every time you're finished. Don't leave yourself logged in between sessions unless you're on a device that you know with — as close as possible to — certainty will remain secure.

Use your own computer or phone

You don't know how well others have secured any one of more of their devices — a particular computer may, for example, have malware on it that can capture your passwords and other sensitive information or that can hijack sessions and/or perform all sorts of other nefarious activities.

Furthermore, despite the fact that doing so is severely problematic, some applications and websites — to this day — cache data on endpoints that are used for accessing them. You don't want to leave other people souvenirs consisting of data from your sensitive sessions.

Lock your computer

Lock any computer that you use for accessing sensitive accounts, and keep it physically secure as well.

Use a separate, dedicated computer for sensitive tasks

Consider purchasing a special computer that you use for online banking and other sensitive tasks. For many people, a second computer isn't practical, but if it is, having such a machine — on which you never read email, access social media, browse the web, and so on — offers security benefits.

Use a separate, dedicated browser for sensitive web-based tasks

If you can't obtain a separate computer, at least use a separate browser for sensitive tasks. Don't use the same browser that you use for reading the news, accessing social media, checking out blog posts, and/or most other activities.

Secure your access devices

Every phone, laptop, tablet, and desktop used for accessing secure systems should have security software on it, and that security software should be configured to regularly scan applications when they're added, as well as to run periodic general scans. Also, make sure to keep the security software up to date — most antivirus technology products perform far better against newer strains of malware when they're kept up to date than they do when they're not.

Keep your devices up to date

Besides keeping your security software up to date, be sure to install operating system and program updates to reduce your exposure to vulnerabilities. Windows AutoUpdate and its equivalent on other platforms can simplify this task for you.

Don't perform sensitive tasks over public Wi-Fi

If you must perform a sensitive task while you're in a location where you don't have access to a secure, private network, do what you need to do over the cellular system, not over public Wi-Fi. Public Wi-Fi simply poses too many risks.

Never use public Wi-Fi in high-risk places

Don't connect any device from which you plan to perform sensitive tasks to a Wi-Fi network in areas that are prone to *digital poisoning* — that is, to the hacking of, or distribution of malware, to devices that connect to a network.

Hacker conferences and certain countries, such as China, that are known for performing cyberespionage are examples of areas that are likely to experience digital poisoning. Many cybersecurity professionals recommend keeping your primary computer and phone off and using a separate computer and phone when working in such environments. Such advice appeared in the media on a regular basis in the lead-up to the 2022 Winter Olympics in Beijing, during which both journalists covering the games, as well as athletes participating in them, discussed how they planned to address such concerns.

Access your accounts only in safe locations

Even if you're using a private network, don't type passwords to sensitive systems or perform other sensitive tasks while in a location where people can easily watch what you type and see your screen.

Use appropriate devices

Don't try to save money by using dangerous equipment. Do not, for example, purchase electronics directly from sellers overseas and install unbranded networking devices that are not certified by any U.S. authorities. Such devices could have poisoned hardware within them.

Set appropriate limits

Various online venues let you set limits — for example, how much money can be transferred out of a bank account, the largest charge that can be made on a credit card with the card not physically present (as in the case of online purchases), or the maximum amount of goods that you can purchase in one day.

TIP

Set these limits. Not only will they limit the damage if a criminal does breach your account, but in some cases, they may trigger fraud alerts in real time as a crook tries to use the cards, and thereby both prevent theft and increase the odds of law enforcement apprehending the relevant criminals.

Use alerts

If your bank, credit card provider, or a store that you frequent offers the ability to set up text or email alerts, you should seriously consider taking advantage of those services. Theoretically, it is ideal to have the issuer send you an alert every time activity occurs on your account. From a practical standpoint, however, if doing so would overwhelm you and cause you to ignore all the messages (as is the case for most people), consider asking to be notified when transactions are made over a certain dollar amount (which may be able to be set to different thresholds for different stores or accounts) or otherwise appear to the issuer to be potentially fraudulent.

Periodically check access device lists

Some websites and apps — especially those of financial institutions — allow you to check the list of devices that have accessed your account. Checking this list each time that you log in can help you identify potential security problems quickly.

Check last login info

After you log in to some websites and via some apps — especially those of financial institutions — you may be shown information as to when and from where you last successfully logged in prior to the current session. Whenever any entity shows you such information, take a quick glance. If something is amiss and a criminal recently logged in while pretending to be you, it may stand out like a sore thumb.

Respond appropriately to any fraud alerts

If you receive a phone call from a bank, credit card company, or store about potential fraud on your account, respond quickly. But do not do so by speaking with the party who called you. Instead, contact the outlet at a known valid number that is advertised on its website.

Never send sensitive information over an unencrypted connection

When you access websites, look for the padlock icon (see Figure 4-3), indicating that encrypted HTTPS is being used. Today, HTTPS is ubiquitous; even many websites that do not ask users to submit sensitive data utilize it. If you don't see the icon, unencrypted HTTP is being used. In such a case, don't provide sensitive information or log in.

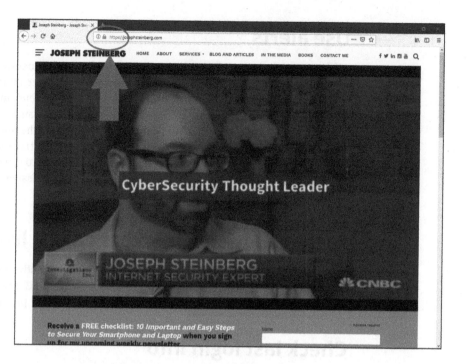

FIGURE 4-3:
A secure website.

TIP

The lack of a padlock on a site that is prompting for a login and password or handling financial transactions is a huge red flag that something is seriously amiss. However, contrary to what you've likely heard in the past, the presence of the lock doesn't necessarily mean that the site is safe.

Beware of social engineering attacks

In the context of cybersecurity, social engineering refers to the psychological manipulation by cyberattackers of their intended victims into performing actions that without such manipulation the targets would not perform or into divulging confidential information that they otherwise would not divulge. A huge portion of successful data breaches begin with social engineering attacks.

To help prevent yourself from falling prey to social engineering attacks, consider any and all emails, text messages, phone calls, or social media communications from all banks, credit card companies, healthcare providers, stores, and so on to be potentially fraudulent.

WARNING

Never click on links in any such correspondence. Always connect with such parties by entering the URL in the URL bar of the web browser.

Establish voice login passwords

Online access isn't the only path that a criminal can use to breach your accounts. Many crooks do reconnaissance online and subsequently social engineer their ways into people's accounts using old-fashioned phone calls to the relevant customer service departments at the target organizations.

TIP

To protect yourself and your accounts, establish voice login passwords for your accounts whenever possible — that is, set up passwords that must be given to customer service personnel in order for them to be able to provide any information from your accounts or to make changes to them. Many companies offer this capability, but relatively few people actually use it.

Protect your cellphone number

If you use strong authentication via text messages, ideally set up a forwarding phone number to your cellphone and use that number when giving out your cell number. Doing so reduces the chances that criminals will be able to intercept one-time passwords that are sent to your phone and also diminishes the chances of various other attacks succeeding.

For example, Google Voice allows you to establish a new phone number that forwards to your cellphone so that you can give out a number other than your real cellphone number and reserve the real number for use within the authentication process.

WARNING

If you use Google Voice or another free service, be sure to occasionally use the number for calls as well, as if you fail to do so, some providers may ultimately "reclaim" the number due to non-usage.

Don't click on links in emails or text messages

Clicking on links is one of the primary ways that people get diverted to fraudulent websites. If you click the link in the message shown in Figure 4-4, for example, you are brought to a phony LinkedIn login page that collects LinkedIn username and password combinations and provides them to criminals. Phishing emails and the like are examples of social engineering attacks, which are described earlier, in the section "Beware of social engineering attacks." Book 2, Chapter 6 shows how you can prevent social engineering attacks.

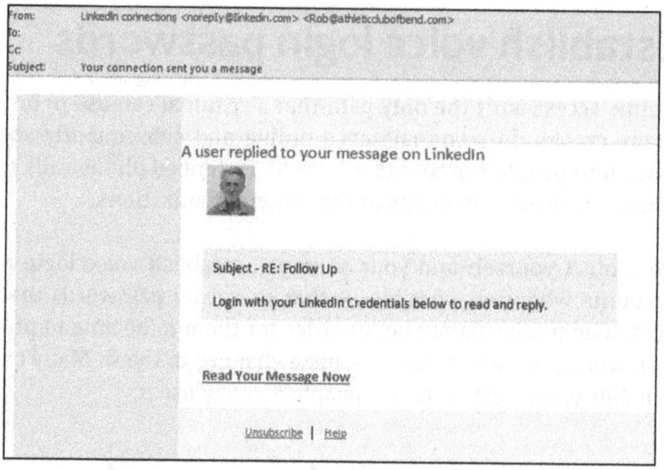

FIGURE 4-4:
Email with a link
to a phony page.

Securing Data with Parties You've Interacted With

When you interact online with a party, not all of the data related to your interaction is under your control. If you browse a website with typical web browser settings, that site may track your activity. Because many sites syndicate content from third parties — for example from advertising networks — sites may even be able to track your behavior on other sites.

To understand how this works, consider two different businesses with two different websites that are using the same advertising network. When the businesses add code to their discrete, separate sites, that code loads advertisements directly from the ad network. When a user visits the first site, the ad network may send a cookie to the user's device, which the same ad network can read back when the user visits the second site, since both sites cause the user to interact with the same ad network.

If you have an account on any sites that do such tracking and log in, all the sites utilizing the syndicated content may know your true identity and plenty of information about you — even though you never told them anything about yourself. Even if you don't have such an account or don't log in, profiles of your behavior may be established and used for marketing purposes, even without knowing who you are. (Of course, if you ever log in in the future to any site using the network, all the sites with the profiles may correlate them to your true identity.)

It is far more difficult to protect data about you that is in the possession of third parties but that is not under your control than it is to protect data in your accounts. That does not mean, however, that you're powerless. (Ironically, and sadly, most owners of such data likely do a better job protecting data about people than do the people themselves.)

TIP

Besides employing the strategies in the previous section, you may want to browse in private sessions. For example, by using a Tor browser — which, as shown in Figure 4-5, automatically routes all your Internet traffic through computers around the world before sending it to its destination — you make it difficult for third parties to track you. The image shown in the figure was generated using the Tor browser bundle running on a computer in New Jersey, USA, but because of Tor's security features, appears to the web server as if it were in the United Kingdom. The Tor browser bundle is free and comes with all sorts of privacy-related features enabled, including blocking cookies and canvas fingerprinting, an advanced form of tracking devices.

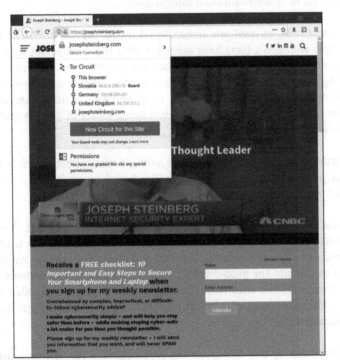

FIGURE 4-5:
A website as seen in a Tor browser, with the Tor circuit information button clicked so as to show how Tor is hiding the user's point of origin.

If Tor seems complicated, you can also utilize a reputable VPN service for similar purposes.

REMEMBER

By using browsing technology that makes it harder for sites to track you, they are less likely to establish as detailed profiles about you — and the less data about you that they have, the less data about you that can be stolen. Besides, you may not want those parties to build profiles about you in the first place.

WARNING

One technology that, despite its name, does not prevent tracking at anywhere near the level that do Tor or VPNs is the private mode offered by most web browsers. Unfortunately, despite its name, the private mode suffers from multiple serious weaknesses in this regard and does not come close to ensuring privacy.

Securing Data at Parties You Haven't Interacted With

Numerous entities likely maintain significant amounts of data about you, despite the fact that you've never knowingly interacted with them or otherwise authorized them to maintain such information.

For example, at least one major social media service builds de facto profiles for people who don't (yet) have accounts with the service, but who have been mentioned by others or who have interacted with sites that utilize various social widgets or other related technologies. The service can then use these profiles for marketing purposes — even, in some cases, without knowing the person's true identity, and without the person being aware of what is going on behind the scenes.

Furthermore, various information services that collect information from numerous public databases establish profiles based on such data — containing details that you may not even realize was available to the public.

Some genealogy sites utilize all sorts of public records and also allow people to update the information about other people. This ability can lead to situations in which all sorts of nonpublic information about you may be available to subscribers to the site (or people with free trial subscriptions) without your knowledge or consent. Such sites make finding people's mothers' maiden names or mothers' birthdays easy, which undermines the authentication schemes used by many organizations.

Besides family tree sites, various professional sites maintain information about folks' professional histories, publications, and so on. And, of course, credit bureaus maintain all sorts of information about your behavior with credit — such information is submitted to them by financial institutions, collection agencies, and so on.

While the Fair Credit Reporting Act may help you manage the information that the bureaus have about you, it can't help you remove negative information that appears in other venues, such as in old newspaper articles that are online. Besides the privacy implications of such, if any information in those articles provides the answer to challenge questions used for authentication, it can create security risks. In such cases, you may want to reach out to the provider of the data, explain the situation, and ask it to remove the data. In some cases, they will cooperate.

In addition, some businesses, such as insurance companies and pharmacies, maintain medical information about people. Typically, individuals have little control over such data. Of course, this type of data, which isn't under your complete control, can impact you. The bottom line is that many entities likely maintain significant amounts of data about you, even though you have never directly interacted with them.

It is the duty of such organizations to protect their data stores, but they do not always properly do so. As the Federal Trade Commission notes on its website, a data breach at the credit bureau Equifax, discovered in 2017, exposed the sensitive personal information of 143 million Americans.

The reality is that other than in the cases in which you can manually update records or request that they be updated, you can do little to protect the data in such scenarios.

Securing Data by Not Connecting Hardware with Unknown Pedigrees

While we have graduated from 720 kilobyte floppies to 2 terabyte USB drives, not much has changed conceptually since the 1980s in terms of the general danger of connecting data storage media with a questionable pedigree into a computer. If you connect a USB drive containing malware-infested files to your laptop, you may infect your laptop. Memory cards pose similar risks, as infected contents can lead to serious cybersecurity problems for any device into which the memory cards are inserted.

In addition, any time you connect a piece of hardware to a computer via a USB connection, you potentially enable communications between the two connected devices. Because of the way Plug and Play works, certain code on a USB device executes on a computer whenever the USB drive is first connected — and if that code is poisoned, you could be hacked as well.

The same holds true for other USB devices. Drivers are usually loaded upon connection, so a device with poisoned hardware or flash memory can create serious risk for any computer to which it is attached — and to any devices on the same network as that computer.

Furthermore, there are also dangerous USB devices designed to "fry" computers. Such devices charge themselves via the USB port, store the electricity in a capacitor, and then essentially fire it all out into the USB port in one big burst, permanently damaging electronics within the connected device in under a second.

Even phone chargers and the like can pose problems. Anything that connects to a USB port can potentially seek to communicate with the USB-port-enabled-device, and can potentially try to kill the USB-enabled device by overwhelming it with electricity.

When you travel, be sure to bring your chargers, USB drives, and memory cards.

» **Discovering how often you need to change passwords — or not**

» **Storing passwords**

» **Finding alternatives to passwords**

Chapter **5**

Passwords

Most people alive today are familiar with the concept of passwords and with the use of passwords in the realm of cybersecurity. Yet, there are so many misconceptions about passwords, and misinformation about passwords has spread like wildfire, often leading to people undermining their own security with poor password practices, sometimes even done in the name of improving cybersecurity.

In this chapter, you discover some best practices vis-à-vis passwords. These practices should help you both maximize your own security and maintain reasonable ease of use.

Passwords: The Primary Form of Authentication

Password authentication refers to the process of verifying the identity of users (whether human or computer process) by asking users to supply a password — that is, a previously agreed-upon secret piece of information — that ostensibly the party authenticating would only know if they were truly the party who it claimed to be. While the term "password" implies that the information consists of a single word, today's passwords can include combinations of characters that don't form words in any spoken or written language.

Despite the availability for decades of many other authentication approaches and technologies — many of which offer significant advantages over passwords — passwords remain de facto worldwide standard for authenticating people online. Repeated predictions of the demise of passwords have been proven untrue, and the number of passwords in use grows every day.

Because password authentication is so common and because so many data breaches have resulted in the compromise of password databases, the topic has received significant media attention, with reports often spreading various misleading information. Gaining a proper understanding of the realm of passwords is important if you want to be cybersecure.

Avoiding Simplistic Passwords

Passwords only secure systems if unauthorized parties can't easily guess them, or obtain them from other sources. Criminals often guess or otherwise obtain passwords by

>> **Guessing common passwords:** It's not a secret that 123456 and password are common passwords — data from recent breaches reveals that they are, in fact, among the most common passwords used on many systems (see the nearby sidebar)! Criminals exploit such sad reality and often attempt to breach accounts by using automated tools that feed systems passwords one at a time from lists of common passwords — and record when they have a hit. Sadly, those hits are often quite numerous.

>> **Launching dictionary attacks:** Because many people choose to use actual English words as passwords, some automated hacker tools simply feed all the words in the dictionary to a system one at a time. As with lists of common passwords, such attacks often achieve numerous hits.

>> **Using people's own information:** Sadly, many people use their own names or birthdays as passwords. It is quite simple for criminals to attempt to use such information as passwords.

>> **Credential stuffing:** *Credential stuffing* refers to when attackers take lists of usernames and passwords from one site — for example, from a site that was breached and whose username password database was subsequently posted online — and feed its entries to another system one at a time in order to see whether any of the login credentials from the first system work on the second. Because many people reuse username and password combinations between systems, credential stuffing is, generally speaking, quite effective.

TOP TEN COMMON PASSWORDS

In November 2021, the cybersecurity firm Bordpass released a list of the most common passwords that it claims to have assembled from over 4 terabytes of information about leaked passwords. Here are the top ten:

- 123456
- 123456789
- 12345
- qwerty
- password
- 12345678
- 111111
- 123123
- 1234567890
- 1234567

The researchers also found that a significant number of people still also use their own first names as passwords. "Charlie," for example, has been on the list of most common passwords for years and continues to be popular. In 2021, it still appeared as the ninth most popular password in the United Kingdom. As you can see, criminals benefit from the fact that, even in 2021, many people still use weak, easily guessable passwords.

Password Considerations

When you create passwords, keep in mind that, contrary to what you may have often heard from "experts," more complex isn't always better. Password strength should depend on how sensitive the data and system are that the password protects. The following sections discuss easily guessable passwords, complicated passwords, sensitive passwords, and password managers.

Easily guessable personal passwords

As alluded to earlier, criminals know that many people use the name or birth date of their significant other or pet as a password, so crooks often look at social media profiles and do Google searches in order to find likely passwords. They also use automated tools to feed lists of common names to targeted systems one by one, while watching to see whether the system being attacked accepts any of the names as a correct password.

Criminals who launch targeted attacks can exploit the vulnerability created by such personalized, yet easily guessable, passwords. However, the problem is much larger: Sometimes, reconnaissance is done through automated means — so, even opportunistic attackers can leverage such an approach.

Furthermore, because, by definition, a significant percentage of people have common names, the automated feeders of common names often achieve a significant number of hits.

Complicated passwords aren't always better

To address the problems inherent in weak passwords, many experts recommend using long, complex passwords — for example, containing both uppercase and lowercase letters, as well as numbers and special characters.

Using such passwords makes sense in theory, and if such a scheme is utilized to secure access to a small number of sensitive systems, it can work quite well. However, employing such a model for a larger number of passwords is likely to lead to problems that can undermine security:

>> Inappropriately reusing passwords

>> Writing down passwords in insecure locations

>> Selecting passwords with poor randomization and formatted using predictable patterns, such as using a capital for the first letter of a complicated password, followed by all lowercase characters, and then a number

Hence, in the real world, from a practical perspective, because the human mind can't remember many complex passwords, using significant numbers of complex passwords can create serious security risks.

According to *The Wall Street Journal*, Bill Burr, the author of NIST Special Publication 800-63 Appendix A (which discusses password complexity requirements), admitted shortly before the turn of the new decade that password complexity has failed in practice. He now recommends using passphrases, and not complex passwords, for authentication.

Passphrases are passwords consisting of entire phrases or phrase-length strings of characters, rather than of simply a word or a word-length group of characters. Sometimes passphrases even consist of complete sentences. Think of passphrases as long (usually at least 25 characters) but relatively easy to remember passwords.

Different levels of sensitivity

Not all types of data require the same level of password protection. For example, the government doesn't protect its unclassified systems the same way that it secures its top-secret information and infrastructure. In your mind or on paper, classify the systems for which you need secure access. Then informally classify the systems that you access and establish your own informal password policies accordingly.

On the basis of risk levels, feel free to employ different password strategies. Random passwords, passwords composed of multiple words possibly separated with numbers, passphrases, and even simple passwords each have their appropriate uses. Of course, multifactor authentication can, and should, help augment security when it's both appropriate and available.

TIP

Establishing a stronger password for online banking than for commenting on a blog on which you plan to comment only once in a blue moon makes sense. Likewise, your password to the blog should probably be stronger than the one used to access a free news site that requires you to log in but on which you never post anything and at which, if your account were compromised, the breach would have zero impact upon you.

Your most sensitive passwords may not be the ones you think

When classifying your passwords, keep in mind that while people often believe that their online banking and other financial system passwords are their most sensitive passwords, that is not always the case. Because many modern online systems allow people to reset their passwords after validating their identities through email messages sent to their previously known email addresses, criminals who gain access to someone's email account may be able to do a lot more than just read email without authorization: They may be able to reset that user's passwords to many systems, including to some financial institutions.

Likewise, many sites leverage social-media-based authentication capabilities — especially those provided by Facebook and Twitter — so a compromised password on a social media platform can lead to unauthorized parties gaining access to other systems as well, some of which may be quite a bit more sensitive in nature than a site on which you just share pictures.

TIP

If you change email addresses, remember to change the address associated with any account that uses email messages for authentication or for resetting passwords.

You can reuse passwords — sometimes

You may be surprised to read the following statement in a book teaching you how to stay cybersecure:

> *You don't need to use strong passwords for accounts that you create solely because a website requires a login, but that does not, from your perspective, protect anything of value.*

If you create an account in order to access free resources, for example, and you have nothing whatsoever of value stored within the account, and you don't mind getting a new account the next time you log in, you can even use a weak password — and use it again for other similar sites.

TIP

Essentially, think about it like this: If the requirement to register and log in is solely for the benefit of the site owner — to track users, market to them, and so on — and it doesn't matter one iota to you whether a criminal obtained the access credentials to your account and changed them, use a simple password. Doing so will preserve your memory for sites where password strength matters. Of course, if you use a password manager, you can use a stronger password for such sites.

Consider using a password manager

Alternatively, you can use a password manager tool, shown in Figure 5-1, to securely store your passwords. Password managers are software that help people manage passwords by generating, storing, and retrieving complex passwords. Password managers typically store all their data in encrypted formats and provide access to users only after authenticating them with either a strong password or multifactor authentication.

WARNING

Such technology is appropriate for general passwords, but not for the most sensitive ones. Various password managers have been hacked, and if something does go wrong you could have a nightmare on your hands. Remember, when you store passwords in a password manager you are "putting multiple eggs into one basket," and that password managers are also treasure chests for hackers and on their radars. As such, of course, be sure to properly secure any device that you use to access your password manager.

FIGURE 5-1:
A password
manager.

Norton Password Manager   + New Login   ▼   🔍 Search your vault   — □ ✕

Logins

🖼 Logins	**Logins**			☰▼
📇 Addresses	🖼 Amazon	JosephSteinberg	••••••••	👁 🗐 →
🗃 Wallet	🖼 JosephSteinberg.com	JosephSteinberg	••••••••	👁 🗐 →
🗒 Notes				
🏷 Tags				

✓Norton   ❓ ⚙   OPEN ••••

Many password managers are on the market. While all modern mainstream password managers utilize encryption to protect the sensitive data that they store, some store passwords locally (for example, in a database on your phone), while others store them in the cloud.

Many modern smartphones come equipped with a so-called *secure area* — a private, encrypted space that is *sandboxed*, or separated, into its own running environment. Ideally, any password information stored on a mobile device should be stored protected in the secure area (see Figure 5-2).

Data that is stored in the secure area is supposed to be rendered by the operating system to be inaccessible to a user unless that user enters the secure area, which usually requires running a secure area app and entering a special password or otherwise authenticating. Devices also typically display some special symbol somewhere on the screen when a user is working with data or an app located in the secure area.

REMEMBER

Remember, though, that operating systems are not perfect, and sometimes bugs do create exploitable vulnerabilities. So even if you do trust the secure area, keep in mind that its security is not 100 percent guaranteed.

Passwords

FIGURE 5-2:
Secure Folder,
the secure area
app provided by
Samsung for
its Android series
of phones, as
seen in the
Google Play Store.

Creating Memorable, Strong Passwords

The following list offers suggestions that may help you create strong passwords that are, for most people, far easier to remember than a seemingly random, unintelligible mix of letters, numbers, and symbols:

>> **Combine three or more unrelated words and proper nouns, with numbers separating them.** For example, laptop2william7cows is far easier to remember than 6ytBgv%j8P. In general, the longer the words you use within the password, the stronger the resulting password will be.

>> **If you must use a special character, add a special character before each number; you can even use the same character for all your passwords.** (If you use the same passwords as in the previous example and follow this advice, the password is laptop%2william%7cows.) In theory, reusing the same character may not be the best way to do things from a security standpoint, but doing so makes memorization much easier, and the security should still be good enough for purposes for which a password is suitable on its own anyway.

>> **Ideally, use at least one non-English word or proper name.** Choose a word or name that is familiar to you but that others are unlikely to guess. Don't use the name of your significant other, best friend, or pet.

>> **If you must use both capital and lowercase letters (or want to make your password even stronger), use capitals that always appear in a particular location throughout all your strong passwords.** Make sure, though, that you don't put them at the start of words because that location is where most people put them. For example, if you know that you always capitalize the second and third letter of the last word, then laptop2william7kALb isn't harder to remember than laptop2william7kalb.

Knowing When to Change Passwords

Conventional wisdom — as you have likely heard many times — is that it is ideal to change your password quite frequently. The American Association of Retired Persons (AARP), for example, until recently recommended on its website that people (including the disproportionately older folks who comprise its membership) "change critical passwords frequently, possibly every other week."

Theoretically, such an approach is correct — frequent changes reduce risks in several ways — but in reality, it's bad advice that you shouldn't follow.

If you have a bank account, mortgage, a couple credit cards, a phone bill, a high-speed Internet bill, utility bills, social media accounts, email accounts, and so on, you may easily be talking about a dozen or so critical passwords. Changing them every two weeks would mean 312 new critical passwords to remember within the span of every year — and you likely have many more passwords on top of that figure. For many people, changing important passwords every two weeks may mean learning a hundred new passwords every month.

Unless you have a phenomenal, photographic memory, how likely is it that you'll remember all such passwords? Or will you simply make your passwords weaker in order to facilitate remembering them after frequent changes?

The bottom line is that changing passwords often makes remembering them far more difficult, increasing the odds that you'll write them down and store them insecurely, select weaker passwords, and/or set your new passwords to be the same as old passwords with minute changes (for example, password2 to replace password1).

Passwords

REMEMBER

So, here is the reality: If you select strong, unique passwords to begin with and the sites where you've used them aren't believed to have been compromised, the cons of frequently changing the passwords outweigh the pros. Changing such passwords every few years may be a good idea. In reality, if a system alerts you of multiple failed attempts to log in to your account and you're not alerted of such activity, you can likely go for many years with no changes without exposing yourself to significant risk.

Of course, if you use a password manager that can reset passwords, you can configure it to reset them often. Commercial password-management systems are available that protect system administration access to sensitive financial systems by automatically resetting administrators' passwords every time they log on.

Changing Passwords after a Breach

If you receive notification from a business, organization, or government entity that it has suffered a security breach and that you should change your password, follow these tips:

>> Don't click any links in the message because most such messages are scams.

>> Visit the organization's website and official social media accounts to verify that such an announcement was actually made.

>> Pay attention to news stories to see whether reliable, mainstream media is reporting such a breach.

>> If the story checks out, go to the organization's website and make the change.

TIP

Do not change all your passwords after every breach you hear about on the evening news or read about online.

Ignore experts who "cry wolf" and tell you to change all your passwords after every single breach as a matter of "extra caution" or that it may not be necessary to change passwords, but that "it is better to be safe than sorry." If changing passwords is not necessary, doing so uses up your brainpower, time, and energy, and, whether you realize it or not, likely dissuades you from changing passwords if a situation arises in which you actually do need to make such changes.

After all, if after a breach you make unnecessary password changes and then find out that your friends who did not do so fared no worse than you, you may grow weary and ignore future warnings to change your password when doing so is actually necessary.

If you reuse passwords on sites where the passwords matter — which you should not be doing — and a password that is compromised somewhere is also used on other sites, be sure to change it at the other sites as well. In such a case, also take the opportunity when resetting passwords to switch to unique passwords for each of the sites.

Providing Passwords to Humans

On its website, the United States Federal Trade Commission (FTC) recommends the following:

> Don't share passwords on the phone, in texts, or by email. Legitimate companies will not send you messages asking for your password.

That sounds like good advice, and it would be, if it were not for one important fact: Legitimate businesses do ask you for passwords over the phone! So how do you know when it is safe to provide your password and when it is not?

Should you just check your caller ID? No. The sad reality is that crooks spoof caller IDs on a regular basis.

What you should do is never provide any sensitive information — including passwords, of course — over the phone unless you *initiated* the call with the party requesting the password and are sure that you called the legitimate party. It is far less risky, for example, to provide an account's phone-access password to a customer service representative who asks for it during a conversation initiated by you calling to the bank using the number printed on your ATM card than if someone calls you claiming to be from your bank and requests the same private information in order to "verify your identity."

Storing Passwords

Ideally, don't write down your passwords to sensitive systems or store them anywhere other than in your brain.

Storing passwords for your heirs

If you want to ensure that you have a copy of your most sensitive passwords (and perhaps any other passwords) written down somewhere — perhaps for your family in case something happens to you — write the passwords down and put the list in a safe deposit box or safe, and do not take the list out on a regular basis. Of course, if you want the list to be useful to your heirs, make sure to keep the list updated.

Some major technology providers, such as Facebook and Apple, also provide people with the ability to specify who should be given access to their accounts upon their deaths.

Storing general passwords

For less sensitive passwords, use a password manager or store them in an encrypted form on a strongly-secured computer or device. If you store your passwords on a phone, use the secure area. (For more on password managers and your phone's secure area, see the section "Consider using a password manager," earlier in this chapter.)

Transmitting Passwords

Theoretically, you should never email or text someone a password. So, what should you do if your child texts you from school saying that they forgot the password to their email, or the like?

TIP

Ideally, if you need to give someone a password, call that person and don't provide the password until you identify the other party by voice. If, for some reason, you must send a password in writing, choose to use an encrypted connection, which is offered by various chat tools. If no such tool is available, consider splitting the password and sending some via email and some via text.

Obviously, none of these methods are ideal ways to transmit passwords, but they certainly are better options than what so many people do, which is to simply text or email people passwords in clear text.

Discovering Alternatives to Passwords

On some occasions, you should take advantage of alternatives to password authentication. While there are many ways to authenticate people, a modern user is likely to encounter certain types:

» Biometric authentication

» SMS-based authentication

» App-based one-time passwords

» Hardware token authentication

» USB-based authentication

Biometric authentication

Biometric authentication refers to authenticating using some unique identifier of your physical person — for example, your fingerprint. Using biometrics — especially in combination with a password — can be a strong method of authentication, and it certainly has its place. Two popular forms used in the consumer market are fingerprints and iris-based authentication.

While using a fingerprint to unlock a phone is certainly convenient, and looking at the screen is even more convenient, in many cases, mandating that phones be unlocked only after a user provides a strong password actually provides better security.

Before using biometric authentication, consider the following points:

» **Your fingerprints are likely all over your phone.** You hold your phone with your fingers. How hard would it be for criminals who steal the phone to lift your prints and unlock the phone if you enable fingerprint based authentication using a phone's built-in fingerprint reader (see Figure 5-3)? If anything sensitive is on the device, it may be at risk. No, the average crook looking to make a quick buck selling your phone is unlikely to spend the time to unlock it — the crook will more than likely just wipe it — but if someone wants the data on your phone for whatever reason, and you used fingerprints to secure your device, you may have a serious problem on your hands (pun intended).

» **If your biometric information is captured, you can't reset it as you can a password.** Do you fully trust the parties to whom you're giving this information to properly protect it?

» **If your biometric information is on your phone or computer, what happens if malware somehow infects your device?** What happens if a server where you stored the same information is breached? Are you positive that all the data is properly encrypted and that the software on your device fully defended your biometric data from capture?

» **Masks create problems for facial recognition systems.** Most facial recognition systems will not work if a person is wearing a mask, as was required in many places during the COVID-19 pandemic.

- » **Cold weather creates problems.** Fingerprints can't be read even through smartphone-compatible gloves.

- » **Glasses, as worn by millions of people, pose challenges to iris scanners.** Some iris readers require users to take off their glasses in order to authenticate. If you use such authentication to secure a phone, you may have difficulty unlocking your phone when you're outdoors on a sunny day.

- » **Biometrics can undermine your rights.** If, for some reason, law enforcement wants to access the data on your biometric-protected phone or other computer system, it may be able to force you to provide your biometric authentication, even in countries like the United States where you have the right to remain silent and not provide a password. Likewise, the government may be able to obtain a warrant to collect your biometric data, which, unlike a password, you can't reset. Even if the data proves you innocent of whatever the government suspects you have done wrong, do you trust the government to properly secure the data over the long term? (These types of issues are in the process of being addressed by various courts, and the final results may vary by jurisdiction.)

- » **Impersonation is possible.** Some quasi-biometric authentication, such as the face recognition on some devices, can be tricked into believing that a person is present by playing to them a high-definition video of that person.

- » **Voice-based authentication is no longer trustworthy.** It has become possible for criminals to undermine voice-based authentication using what has become known as deep fake technology, which is technology that uses artificial intelligence to impersonate a person either in an audio recording or video recording. Criminals have already successfully stolen money using deep-faked audio.

FIGURE 5-3: A phone fingerprint sensor on a Samsung Galaxy S9 in an OtterBox case. Some phones have the reader on the front, while others, like the S9, have it on the back.

As such, biometrics have their place. Using a fingerprint to unlock features on your phone is certainly convenient but think before you proceed. Be certain that in your case the benefits outweigh the drawbacks.

SMS-based authentication

In *SMS (text message)-based authentication,* a code is sent to your cellphone. You then enter that code into a web or app to prove your identity. This type of authentication is, in itself, not considered secure enough for authentication when true multifactor authentication in required. Sophisticated criminals have ways of intercepting such passwords, and can sometimes even social-engineer phone companies in order to steal people's phone numbers, thereby, stealing their SMS messages. That said, SMS one-time passwords used in combination with a strong password are typically better than just using the password.

WARNING

Keep in mind, however, that, in most cases, one-time passwords are worthless as a security measure if you send them to a criminal's phishing website instead of a legitimate site. The criminal can replay them to the real site in real time.

App-based one-time passwords

One-time passwords generated with an app running on a phone or computer are a good addition to strong passwords, but they should not be used on their own. App-based one-time passwords are likely a more secure way to authenticate than SMS-based one-time passwords (see preceding section), but they can be inconvenient; if you get a new phone, for example, some one time password generation apps require you to reconfigure information at every one of the sites where you're using one-time passwords created by the generator app running on your smartphone. Even those that do not may require you to disable password generation on your old device in addition to enabling it on the new one.

As with SMS-based one-time passwords, if you send an app-generated one-time password to a criminal's phishing website instead of a legitimate site, the criminal can replay it to the corresponding real site in real time, undermining the security benefits of the one-time password in their entirety.

Hardware token authentication

Hardware tokens (see Figure 5-4) that generate new one-time passwords every x seconds are similar to the apps described in the preceding section with the major difference being that you need to carry a specialized device that generates the one-time codes. Some tokens can also function in other modes — for example, allowing for challenge-response types of authentication in which the site being logged into displays a challenge number that the user enters into the token in order to retrieve a corresponding response number that the user enters into the site in order to authenticate.

FIGURE 5-4:
An RSA SecureID brand one-time password generator hardware token.

Ocrho / Wikimedia Commons / Public domain

Although hardware token devices normally are more secure than one-time generator apps in that the former don't run on devices that can be infected by malware or taken over by criminals remotely, they can be inconvenient. They are also prone to getting lost, and are less likely to be quickly detected as missing as are phones. Many models are also not waterproof, leading to problems of such devices sometimes getting destroyed when people do their laundry after forgetting the devices in their pockets.

USB-based authentication

USB devices that contain authentication information — for example, digital certificates — can strengthen authentication. Care must be exercised, however, to use such devices only in combination with trusted machines — you don't want the device infected or destroyed by some rogue device, and you want to be sure that the machine obtaining the certificate, for example, doesn't transmit it to an unauthorized party.

Many modern USB-based devices offer all sorts of defenses against such attacks. Of course, you can connect USB devices only to devices and apps that support USB-based authentication. You also must carry the device with you and ensure that it doesn't get lost or damaged. And, as with other hardware keys, such devices are prone to being lost, and are not always waterproof.

Chapter 6

Preventing Social Engineering Attacks

Most, if not all, major breaches that have occurred in recent years have involved some element of social engineering. Do not let devious criminals trick you or your loved ones. In this chapter, you find out how to protect yourself.

Don't Trust Technology More than You Would People

Would you give your online banking password to a random stranger who asked for it after walking up to you in the street and telling you that they worked for your bank?

If the answer is no — which it certainly should be (and, if it is not, your security problems are much greater than just your cybersecurity) — you need to exercise the same lack of trust when it comes to technology. The fact that your computer shows you an email sent by some party that claims to be your bank instead of a random person approaching you on the street and making a similar claim is no reason to give that email your trust any more than you would give the stranger.

REMEMBER

Unless you are using an email security system that overcomes such issues with digital signatures and other security technologies, when you receive an email from someone, you are not actually receiving the email from that person. Your computer is simply telling you that another computer told it, based on what another computer told it, based on what another computer told it, and so on, that the person who is the "sender" actually sent you the included message.

In short, you don't give offers from strangers approaching you on the street the benefit of the doubt, so don't do so for offers communicated electronically — they may be even more risky.

Types of Social Engineering Attacks

Phishing attacks are one of the most common forms of social engineering attacks. (For more on phishing and social engineering, see Chapter 2.) Figure 6-1 shows you an example of a phishing email.

> ⚙ If there are problems with how this message is displayed, click here to view it in a web browser.
> From: Wells Fargo Online <atmarin@calpoly.edu>
> To: Recipients
> Cc
> Subject: Your Account Has Been Compromised.
>
> WELLS FARGO   wellsfargo.com
>
> **Your Account has been restricted, unlock**
>
> **Your account has been limited for security reason to keep your account safe note all your transaction will be monitored to enhance your security.**
>
> **To Unlock click on the below link and follow the security check Questions:**
>
> Go to http://www.welsfargo.com/secure
> **Answer the security questions carefully and correctly.**
> **After you answer all the security question has been answer you dont have to do anything.**
>
> **If you have questions about your account, please refer to the contact information on your statement. For questions about viewing your statements online, Wells Fargo C** https://www.wellsfargo.com/ **available 24 hours a day, 7 days a week. Call** privacy_security/fraud **2 or sign on to send a secure email.** Click to follow link
> wellsfargo.com | Fraud Information Center
>
> Please do not reply to this email directly. To ensure a prompt and secure response, sign on to email us.
>
> 213405-188-a5ed-117d3a1aa2-b28b65a2_5716fc7a_131b0-721

FIGURE 6-1:
A phishing email.

Phishing attacks sometimes utilize a technique called *pretexting* in which the criminal sending the phishing email fabricates a situation that both gains trust from targets as well as underscores the supposed need for the intended victims to act quickly. In the phishing email shown in Figure 6-1, note that the sender, impersonating Wells Fargo bank, included a link to the real Wells Fargo within the email, but failed to properly disguise the sending address.

Chapter 2 discusses common forms of social engineering attacks, including spear phishing emails, smishing, spear smishing, vishing, spear vishing, and CEO fraud. Additional types of social engineering attacks are popular as well:

>> **Baiting:** An attacker sends an email or chat message — or even makes a social media post that promises someone a reward in exchange for taking some action — for example, telling intended targets that if they complete a survey, they will receive a free item (see Figure 6-2). Or that if they perform such action, they will receive some free cryptocurrency. Sometimes such promises are real, but often they're not and are simply ways of incentivizing people to take a specific action that they would not take otherwise. Sometimes such scammers seek payment of a small shipping fee for the prize, sometimes they distribute malware, and sometimes they collect sensitive information. There is even malware that baits.

WARNING

Don't confuse baiting with *scambaiting*. The latter refers to a form of vigilantism in which people pretend to be gullible, would-be victims, and waste scammers' time and resources through repeated interactions, as well as (sometimes) collect intelligence about the scammer that can be turned over to law enforcement or published on the Internet to warn others of the scammer. I have sometimes led scammers on when they call by listening to their spiel and then giving them the FBI's New York office contact information for their requested follow-up call.

>> **Quid pro quo:** The attacker states that they need the person to take an action in order to render a service for the intended victim. For example, an attacker may pretend to be an IT support manager offering assistance to an employee in installing a new security software update. If the employee cooperates, the criminal walks the employee through the process of installing malware.

>> **Social media impersonation:** Some attackers impersonate people on social media in order to establish social media connections with their victims. The parties being impersonated may be real people or nonexistent entities. The scammers behind the impersonation shown in Figure 6-3 and many other such accounts frequently contact the people who follow the accounts, pretending to be the account owners, and request that the followers make various "investments."

>> **Tantalizing emails:** These emails attempt to trick people into running malware or clicking on poisoned links by exploiting their curiosity, sexual desires, and other characteristics.

>> **Tailgating:** *Tailgating* is a physical form of social engineering attack in which attackers accompany authorized personnel as they approach a doorway that they, but not the attackers, are authorized to pass and tricks them into letting the attackers pass with the authorized personnel. The attackers may pretend to be searching through a purse for an access card, claim to have forgotten their card, or may simply act social and follow the authorized party in.

>> **False alarms:** Raising false alarms can also social engineer people into allowing unauthorized people to do things that they should not be allowed to. Consider the case in which an attacker pulls the fire alarm inside a building and manages to enter normally secured areas through an emergency door that someone else used to quickly exit due to the so-called emergency.

>> **Water holing:** Water holing combines hacking and social engineering by exploiting the fact that people trust certain parties, so, for example, they may click on links when viewing that party's website even if they'd never click on links in an email or text message. Criminals may launch a watering hole attack by breaching the relevant site and inserting the poisoned links on it (or even depositing malware directly onto it).

>> **Virus hoaxes:** Criminals exploit the fact that people are concerned about cybersecurity, and likely pay undeserved attention to messages that they receive warning about a cyberdanger. Virus hoax emails may contain poisoned links, direct a user to download software, or instruct a user to contact IT support via some email address or web page. These attacks come in many flavors — some attacks distribute them as mass emails, while others send them in a highly targeted fashion.

Some people consider scareware that scares users into believing that they need to purchase some particular security software (as described in Chapter 2) to be a form of virus hoax. Others do not because scareware's "scaring" is done by malware that is already installed, not by a hoax message that pretends that malware is already installed.

>> **Technical failures:** Criminals can easily exploit humans' annoyance with technology problems to undermine various security technologies. For example, research I performed nearly two decades ago showed that if a criminal impersonates a website that normally displays a security image in a particular area, but in the fake copy, places a "broken image symbol," many users will not perceive danger, as they are accustomed to seeing broken-image symbols and associate them with technical failures rather than security risks. There is no reason to believe that over the years anything has changed for the significantly better in this regard.

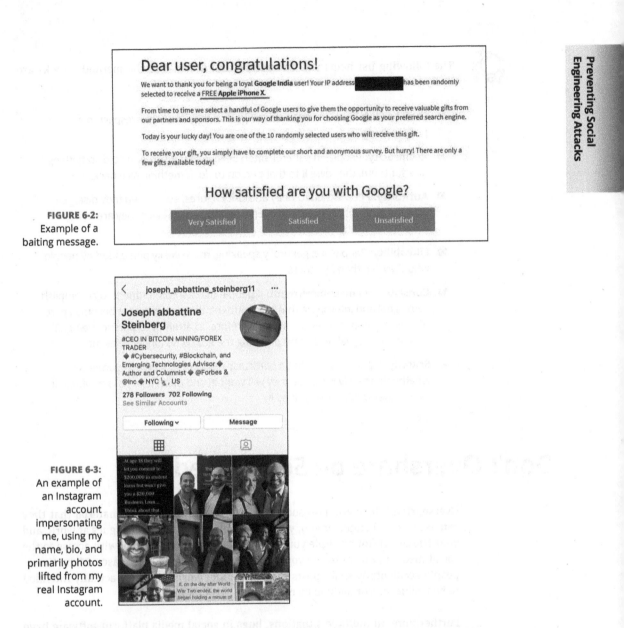

FIGURE 6-2:
Example of a
baiting message.

FIGURE 6-3:
An example of
an Instagram
account
impersonating
me, using my
name, bio, and
primarily photos
lifted from my
real Instagram
account.

Six Principles Social Engineers Exploit

Social psychologist Robert Beno Cialdini, in his 1984 work published by HarperCollins, *Influence: The Psychology of Persuasion*, explains six important, basic concepts that people seeking to influence others often leverage. Social engineers seeking to trick people often exploit these same six principles, so I provide a quick overview of them in the context of information security.

TIP

The following list helps you understand and internalize the methods crooks are likely to use to try to gain your trust:

>> **Social proof:** People tend to do things that they see other respectable people doing.

>> **Reciprocity:** People, in general, often believe that if someone did something nice for them, they owe it to that person to do something nice back.

>> **Authority:** People tend to obey authority figures, even when they disagree with the authority figures, and even when they think what they are being asked to do is objectionable.

>> **Likeability:** People are, generally speaking, more easily persuaded by people who they like than by others.

>> **Consistency and commitment:** If people make a commitment to accomplish some goal and internalize that commitment, that commitment becomes part of their self-image. They are likely, therefore, to attempt to pursue their goal even if the original reason for pursuing the goal is no longer relevant.

>> **Scarcity:** If people think that a particular resource is scarce, regardless of whether it actually is scarce, they will want it, and often take risks to obtain it, even if they don't actually need it.

Don't Overshare on Social Media

Oversharing information on social media arms criminals with material that they can use to social engineer you, your family members, your colleagues at work, and your friends. If, for example your privacy settings allow anyone with access to the social media platform to see your posted media, your risk increases. Many times, people accidentally share posts with the whole world that they actually intended to be visible and/or audible by only a small group of people.

Furthermore, in multiple situations, bugs in social media platform software have created vulnerabilities that allowed unauthorized parties to view media and posts that had privacy settings set to disallow such access.

Also, consider your privacy settings. Family-related material with privacy settings set to allow nonfamily members to view it may result in all sorts of privacy-related issues and leak the answers to various popular challenge questions used for authenticating users, such as "Where does your oldest sibling live?" or "What is your mother's maiden name?" And consider that romantic relationships can sour, too; there may be materials from previous relationships that you do not want a new partner to see, or vice versa.

A SOCIAL PLATFORM'S ENTIRE DATABASE LEAKS

While many major social media platforms have suffered from data-exposing security vulnerabilities, perhaps the greatest example of a mass data leak so far is the 2020 hacking of the American right-wing social media platform, Parler. In that leak, hackers copied essentially the entire contents of the platform and shared them online.

WARNING

Don't rely on social media privacy settings to protect truly confidential data. Some social media platforms allow for granular protection of posted items, while others do not. Certain items, if shared, may help criminals social engineer you or someone you know. This list isn't meant to be comprehensive. Rather, it's meant to illustrate examples to stimulate your thinking about the potential risks of what you intend to post on social media before you go ahead and post it.

REMEMBER

Numerous other types of social media posts than the ones I list in the following sections can help criminals orchestrate social engineering attacks. Think about potential consequences before you post and set your posts' privacy settings accordingly.

Your schedule and travel plans

Details of your schedule or someone else's schedule may provide criminals with information that may help them set up an attack. For example, if you post that you'll be attending an upcoming event, such as a wedding, you may provide criminals with the ability to *virtually kidnap* you or other attendees — never mind incentivizing others to target your home with a break-in attempt when the home is likely to be empty. (*Virtual kidnapping* refers to a criminal making a ransom demand in exchange for the same return of someone who the criminal claims to have kidnapped, but who in fact, the criminal has not kidnapped.)

Likewise, revealing that you'll be flying on a particular flight may provide criminals with the ability to virtually kidnap you or attempt CEO-type fraud against your colleagues. They may impersonate you and send an email saying that you're flying and may not be reachable by phone for confirmation of the instructions so just go ahead and follow them anyway.

WARNING

Avoid posting about a family member's vacation or trip, which may increase risks of virtual kidnapping (and of real physical dangers to that person or that person's belongings).

Financial information

Sharing a credit card number may lead to fraudulent charges, while posting a bank account number can lead to fraudulent bank activity.

In addition, don't reveal that you visited or interacted with a particular financial institution or the locations where you store your money — banks, crypto-exchange accounts, brokerages, and so forth. Doing so can increase the odds that criminals will attempt to social engineer their way into your accounts at the relevant financial institution(s). As such, such sharing may expose you to attempts to breach your accounts, as well as targeted phishing, vishing, and smishing attacks and all sorts of other social engineering scams.

Posting about potential investments, such as stocks, bonds, precious metals, or cryptocurrencies, can expose you to cyberattacks because criminals may assume that you have significant money to steal. In some cases, if you make posts encouraging people to investor to perform other forms of investment-related activities, you may also run afoul of rules laws or of regulations of the SEC, CFTC, or other government bodies. You may even also open the door to criminals who impersonate regulators and contact you to pay a fine for posting information inappropriately.

Personal information

For starters, avoid listing your family members in your Facebook profile's About section. That About section links to their Facebook profiles and explains to viewers the nature of the relevant family relationship with each party listed. By listing these relationships, you may leak all sorts of information that may be valuable for criminals. Not only will you possibly reveal your mother's maiden name (challenge question answer!), you may also provide clues about where you grew up. The information found in your profile also provides criminals with a list of people to social engineer or contact as part of a virtual kidnapping scam.

Also you should avoid sharing the following information on social media, as doing so can undermine your authentication questions and help criminals social engineer you or your family:

>> Your father's middle name

>> Your mother's birthday

>> Where you met your significant other

>> Your favorite vacation spot

>> The name of the first school that you attended

- » The street on which you grew up
- » The type, make, model, and/or color of your first car or someone else's
- » Your or others' favorite food or drink

WARNING

Despite many years of industry-wide understanding that challenge questions of this sort are generally not suitable to be asked as a means of authenticating people. In early 2022, as part of the authentication process in use by a major financial institution, I was still being asked for my mother's birthday. Go figure.

Likewise, never share your Social Security number as doing so may lead to identity theft.

Information about your children

WARNING

Sharing information about your children can not only set you up for attacks, but put your children at great risk of physical danger. For example, photos of your children may assist a kidnapper. The problem may be exacerbated if the images contain a timestamp and/or *geotagging* — that is, information about the location at which a photograph was taken.

Timestamps and geotagging do not need to be done per some technical specification to create risks. If it is clear from the images where your kids go to school, attend after-school activities, and so on, you may expose them to danger.

In addition, referring to the names of schools, camps, day care facilities, or other youth programs that your children or their friends attend may increase the risk of a pedophile, kidnapper, or other malevolent party targeting them. Such a post may also expose you to potential burglars because they'll know when you're likely not to be home. The risk can be made much worse if a clear pattern regarding your schedule and/or your children's schedule can be extrapolated from such posts. Also avoid posting about a child's school or camp trip. And, if you feel you must post about it, wait until your child is back home after completing the trip.

Information about your pets

As with your mother's maiden name, sharing your current pet's name or your first pet's name can set you or others who you know up for social engineering attacks because such information is often used as an answer to authentication questions.

Work information

Details about with which technologies you work with at your present job (or a previous job) may help criminals both scan for vulnerabilities in your employers' systems and social engineer your colleagues. Yet many people's profiles on profession-focused social media sites contain a wealth of information about the systems in use at their employers — sometimes even effectively disclosing the public what security systems the employer is using, and is considering for use in the future.

Possible cybersecurity issues

Many virus hoaxes and scams have gone viral — and inflicted far more damage than they should have — because criminals exploit people's fear of cyberattacks and leverage the likelihood that many people will share posts about cyber-risks, often without verifying the authenticity of such posts.

Crimes and minor infractions

Information about a moving violation or parking ticket that you received not only presents yourself in a less-than-the-best light, but can inadvertently provide prosecutors with the material that they need to convict you of the relevant offense. You may also give crooks the ability to social engineer you or others — they may pretending to be law enforcement, a court, or an attorney contacting you about the matter — perhaps even demanding that a fine be paid immediately in order to avoid an arrest.

In addition to helping criminals social engineer you in a fashion similar to the moving violation case, information about a crime that you or a loved one committed may harm you professionally and personally.

Medical or legal advice

If you offer medical or legal advice, people may be able to extrapolate that you or a loved one has a particular medical condition, or involved in a particular legal situation. And, if you offer incorrect advice, you could not only get yourself into hot water and legal troubles, but also contribute to unnecessary human suffering.

During the COVID-19 pandemic, social media platforms were regularly used to spread incorrect information — and this spread might have contributed both to increasing the number of coronavirus illnesses and deaths, and to prolonging the pandemic.

Your location

Your location or *check-in* on social media may not only increase the risk to yourself and your loved ones of physical danger, but may help criminals launch virtual kidnapping attacks and other social engineering scams.

In addition, an image of you in a place frequented by people of certain religious, sexual, political, cultural, or other affiliations can lead to criminals extrapolating information about you that may lead to all sorts of social engineering. Criminals are known, for example, to have virtually kidnapped a person who was in synagogue and unreachable on the Jewish holiday of Yom Kippur. They knew when and where the person would be walking to the temple, and called family members (at a time that they knew the person would be impossible to reach) claiming to have kidnapped the person. The family members fell for the virtual kidnapping scam because the details were right and they were unable to reach the "victim" by telephone in the middle of a synagogue service.

Your birthday

A happy birthday message to someone on social media may reveal the person's birthday. Folks who use fake birthdays on social media for security reasons have seen their precautions undermined in such a fashion by would be well-wishers.

Your "sins"

Anything that is "sin-like" may lead not only to professional or personal harm, but to extortion attempts as well as social engineering of yourself or others depicted in such posts or media. If in doubt, be careful. Something you post that may be questionable today might be considered nothing short of repugnant in the future; old posts cause people personal and professional harm on a regular basis.

Leaking Data by Sharing Information as Part of Viral Trends

From time to time, a *viral trend* occurs, in which many people share similar content. Posts about the ice bucket challenge, your favorite concerts, and something about you today and ten years ago are all examples of viral trends. Of course, future viral trends may have nothing to do with prior ones. Any type of post that spreads quickly to large numbers of people is said to have "gone viral."

WARNING

While participating may seem fun — and "what everyone else is doing" — be sure that you understand the potential consequences of doing so. For example, sharing information about the concerts that you attended and that you consider to be your favorites can reveal a lot about you — especially in combination with other profile data — and can expose you to all sorts of social engineering risks.

Identifying Fake Social Media Connections

Social media delivers many professional and personal benefits to its users, but it also creates amazing opportunities for criminals — many people have an innate desire to connect with others and are overly trusting of social media platforms. They assume that if, for example, Facebook sends a message that Joseph Steinberg has requested that they become his friend, that the real "Joseph Steinberg" has requested such — when, often, that is not the case.

Criminals know, for example, that by connecting with you on social media, they can gain access to all sorts of information about you, your family members, and your work colleagues — information that they can often exploit in order to impersonate you, a relative, or a colleague as part of criminal efforts to social engineer a path into business systems, steal money, or commit other crimes.

One technique that criminals often use to gain access to people's "private" Facebook, Instagram, or LinkedIn information is to create fake profiles — profiles of nonexistent people — and request to connect with real people, many of whom are likely to accept the relevant connection requests. Alternatively, scammers may set up accounts that impersonate real people — and which have profile photos and other materials lifted from the impersonated party's legitimate social media accounts.

How can you protect yourself from such scams? The following sections offer advice on how to quickly spot fake accounts — and how to avoid the possible repercussions of accepting connections from them.

REMEMBER

Keep in mind that none of the clues in the following sections operates in a vacuum or is absolute. The fact that a profile fails when tested against a particular rule, for example, doesn't automatically mean that it is bogus. But applying smart concepts such as the ones I list in the following sections should help you identify a significant percentage of fake accounts and save yourself from the problems that can ultimately result from accepting connection requests from them.

Photo

Many fake accounts use photos of attractive models, sometimes targeting men who have accounts that show photos of women and women whose accounts have photos of men. The pictures often appear to be stock photos, but sometimes are stolen from real users.

WARNING

If you receive a social media connection request from someone who you don't remember ever meeting and the picture is of this type, beware. If you're in doubt, you can load the image into Google's reverse image search and see where else it appears.

You can also search on the person's name (and, if appropriate, on LinkedIn) or title to see whether any other similar photos appear online. However, a crafty impersonator may upload images to several sites. Obviously, any profile without a photo of the account holder should raise red flags. Keep in mind, though, that some people do use emojis, caricatures, and so on as profile photos, especially on nonprofessional-oriented social media networks.

Verification

If an account appears to represent a public figure who you suspect is likely to be verified (meaning it has a blue check mark next to the user's account name to indicate that the account is the legitimate account of a public figure), but it is not verified, that is a likely sign that something is amiss. Likewise, it is unlikely that a verified account on a major social media platform is fake. However, there have been occasions on which verified accounts of such nature have been taken over temporarily by hackers.

Friends or connections in common

Fake people are unlikely to have many friends or connections in common with you, and fake folks usually will not even have many secondary connections (Friends of Friends, LinkedIn second level connections, and so on) in common with you either.

WARNING

Don't assume that an account is legitimate just because it has one or two connections in common with you; some of your connections may have fallen for a scam and connected with a fake person, and your contact's connecting with the fake account may be how the criminal found out about you in the first place. Even in such a scenario, the number of shared connections is likely to be relatively small as compared with a real, mutual connection, and the human relationship between the friends who did connect with the crook's profile may seem difficult to piece together.

TIP

You know your connections better than anyone else — exercise caution when someone's connection patterns don't make sense. You may want to think twice, for example, if people trying to connect with you seem to know nobody in the industry in which they work, but know three of your most gullible friends who live in three different countries and who do not know one another.

Relevant posts

Another huge red flag is when an account is not sharing material that it should be sharing based on the alleged identity of the account holder. If someone claims to be a columnist who currently writes for *Forbes*, for example, and attempts to but has never shared any posts of any articles that they wrote for *Forbes*, something is likely amiss.

Number of connections

A senior-level person, with many years of work experience, is likely to have many professional connections, especially on LinkedIn. The fewer connections that an account ostensibly belonging to a senior level person has on LinkedIn (the further it is from 500 or more), the more suspicious you should be.

Of course, every LinkedIn profile started with zero connections — so legitimate, new LinkedIn accounts may seems suspicious when they truly are not — but practical reality comes into play: How many of the real, senior-level people who are now contacting you didn't establish their LinkedIn accounts until recently? Of course, a small number of connections and a new LinkedIn account isn't abnormal for people who just started their first job or for people working in certain industries, in certain roles, and/or at certain companies — CIA secret agents don't post their career progress in their LinkedIn profiles — but if you work in those industries, you're likely aware of this fact already.

TIP

Contrast the number of connection with the age of an account and the number of posts it has interacted with or has shared — a person who has been on Facebook for a decade and who posts on a regular basis, for example, should have more than one or two friends.

Industry and location

Common sense applies vis-à-vis accounts purporting to represent people living in certain locations or working in certain industries. If, for example, you work in technology and have no pets and receive a LinkedIn connection request from a veterinarian living halfway across the world whom you have never met, something may be amiss. Likewise, if you receive a Facebook friend request from someone with whom you have nothing in common, beware.

WARNING

Don't assume that any claims made in a profile are necessarily accurate and that if you share a lot in common, the sender is definitely safe. Someone targeting you may have discerned your interests from information about you that is publicly available online.

Similar people

If you receive multiple requests from people with similar titles or who claim to work for the same company and you don't know the people and aren't actively doing some sort of deal with that company, beware. If those folks don't seem to be connected to anyone else at the company who you know actually works there, consider that a potential red flag as well.

REMEMBER

You can always call, text, or email real contacts and ask whether they see that person listed in a staff directory.

Duplicate contact

If you receive a Facebook friend request from a person who is already your Facebook friend, verify with that party that that person is switching accounts. In many cases, such requests come from scammers.

Contact details

Make sure the contact details make sense. Fake people are far less likely than real people to have email addresses at real businesses and rarely have email addresses at major corporations. They're unlikely to have physical addresses that show where they live and work, and, if such addresses are listed, they rarely correspond with actual property records or phone directory information that can easily be checked online.

Premium status

Historically, criminals avoided paying for paying for premium service for their scam accounts. Because LinkedIn charges tens of dollars per month for its Premium service, for example, some experts have suggested that Premium status is a good indicator that an account is real because a criminal is unlikely to pay so much money for an account.

While it may be true that most fake accounts don't have Premium status, some crooks do invest in obtaining Premium status in order to make their accounts seem more real — especially if they plan to use the accounts to engage in targeted attacks. In some cases, they are paying with stolen credit cards, so it doesn't cost them anything anyway. So, remain vigilant even if an account is showing the Premium icon.

TIP

Keep in mind that some Premium services, such as Twitter Blue, are relatively inexpensive, and criminals may be even more inclined to purchase such "authenticity" as a result.

LinkedIn endorsements

Fake people are not going to be endorsed by many real people. And the endorsers of fake accounts may be other fake accounts that seem suspicious as well.

Group activity

Fake profiles are less likely than real people to be members of closed groups that verify members when they join and are less likely to participate in meaningful discussions in both closed and open groups on Facebook or LinkedIn. If they are members of closed groups, those groups may have been created and managed by scammers and contain other fake profiles as well.

Fake folks may be members of many open groups — groups that were joined in order to access member lists and connect with other participants with "I see we are members of the same group, so let's connect" type messages.

WARNING

In any case, keep in mind that on any social platform that has groups, being members of the same group as someone else is not, in any way, a reason to accept a connection from that person.

Appropriate levels of relative usage

Real people who use LinkedIn or Facebook heavily enough to have joined many groups are more likely to have filled out all their profile information. A connection request from a person who is a member of many groups but has little profile information is suspicious. Likewise, an Instagram account with 20,000 followers but only two posted photos that seeks to follow your private account is suspicious for the same reason.

Human activities

Many fake accounts seem to list cliché-sounding information in their profiles, interests, and work experience sections, but contain few other details that seem to convey a true, real-life human experience.

Here are a few signs that things may not be what they seem:

>> On LinkedIn, the Recommendations, Volunteering Experience, and Education sections of a fake person may seem off.

>> On Facebook, a fake profile may seem to be cookie cutter and the posts generic enough in nature that millions of people could have made the same post.

>> On Twitter, they may be retweeting posts from others and never share their own opinions, comments, or other original material.

>> On Instagram the photos may be lifted from other accounts or appear to be stock photos — sometimes none of which include an image of the actual person who allegedly owns the accounts.

TIP

The content within a user's social media profile may provide terms and phrases that you can search for in Google along with the person's name to help you verify whether the account truly belongs to a human being whose identity the profile alleges to represent.

Likewise, if you perform a Google image search on someone's Instagram images and see that they belong to other people, something is amiss.

Cliché names

Some fake profiles seem to use common, flowing American names, such as Sally Smith, that both sound overly American and make performing a Google search for a particular person far more difficult than doing so would be for someone with an uncommon name.

TIP

More often than occurs in real life, but certainly not always, bogus profiles seem to use first and last names that start with the same letter. Perhaps, scammers just like the names or, for some reason, find them funny.

Poor contact information

If a social media profile contains absolutely no contact information that can be used to contact the person behind the profile via email, telephone, or on another social platform, beware.

Skill sets

If skill sets don't match someone's work or life experience, beware. Something may seem off when it comes to fake accounts. For example, if someone claims to have graduated with a degree in English from an Ivy League university, but makes serious grammatical errors throughout their profile, something may be amiss. Likewise, if someone claims to have two PhDs in mathematics, but claims to be working as a gym teacher, beware.

Spelling

Spelling errors are common on social media. However, something may be amiss if folks misspell their own name or the name of an employer, or makes errors of this nature on LinkedIn (a professionally oriented network).

Age of an account

Does the age of the account make sense considering to whom the account allegedly belongs? If you come across an active Instagram account belonging to some attractive person whom you met on a dating site, and the account has shared many photos, but all of the photos were uploaded within the last few weeks, ask yourself if it makes sense that the person in question did not post photos before that date. You may have encountered a *catfish* (a person with ill intent pretending to be someone they're not).

Suspicious career or life path

People who seem to have been promoted too often and too fast or who have held too many disparate senior positions, such as VP of Sales, then CTO, and then General Counsel, may be too good to be true.

Of course, real people have moved up the ladder quickly and some folks (including myself) have held a variety of different positions throughout the course of their careers, but scammers often overdo it when crafting the career progression or role diversity data of a bogus profile. People may shift from technical to managerial roles, for example, but it is extremely uncommon for someone to serve as a company's VP of Sales, then as its CTO, and then as its General Counsel — roles that require different skill sets, educational backgrounds, and potentially, different certifications and licenses.

TIP

If you find yourself saying to yourself "no way" when looking at someone's career path, you may be right.

DO YOU NEED TO AVOID FAKE CONNECTIONS?

It should be noted, however, that if you use an account to share material with the public — and not for personal use — that there may be no problem of connecting with "fake people." The issue of fake connections focuses on cases in which by connecting you expose some information to the party to whom you are connecting that it otherwise would not have been able to obtain from you.

Level or celebrity status

LinkedIn requests from people at far more senior professional levels than yourself can be a sign that something is amiss, as can Facebook friend requests from celebrities and others about whose connection request you're flattered to have received.

It is certainly tempting to want to accept such connections (which is, of course, why the people who create fake accounts often create such fake accounts), but think about it: If you just landed your first job out of college, do you really think the CEO of a major bank is suddenly interested in connecting with you out of the blue? Do you really think that Ms. Universe, whom you have never met, suddenly wants to be your friend?

In the case of Facebook, Instagram, and Twitter, be aware that most celebrity accounts are verified. If a request comes in from a celebrity, you should be able to quickly discern if the account sending it is the real deal.

Using Bogus Information

Some experts have suggested that you use bogus information as answers to common challenge questions. Someone — especially someone whose mother has a common last name as her maiden name — may establish a new, substitute "mother's maiden name" to be used for all sites that ask for such information as part of an authentication process. There is truth to the fact that such an approach somewhat helps reduce the risk of social engineering.

What such advice does in a much stronger fashion, however, is reveal how poor challenge questions are as a means of authenticating people. Asking one's mother's maiden name is effectively asking for a password while providing a hint that the password is a last name!

Likewise, because in the era of social media and online public records, finding out someone's birthday is relatively simple, some security experts recommend creating a second fake birthday for use online. Some even recommend using a phony birthday on social media, both to help prevent social engineering and make it harder for organizations and individuals to correlate one's social media profile and various public records.

While all these recommendations do carry weight, keep in mind that, in theory, there is no end to such logic — establishing a different phony birthday for every site with which one interacts offers stronger privacy protections than establishing just one phony birthday, for example. But how many "birthdays" can one remember? And besides, all using multiple fake birthdays does is effectively transform the authentication-using-birthday into an authentication using a second password — albeit one that is weak and has only 366 possible values.

TIP

In general, however, creating and utilizing one fake birthday, one fake mother's maiden name, and so on is probably worthwhile and doesn't require much additional brainpower and mindshare over using just the true one. Be sure, however, not to mislead any sites where providing accurate information is required by law (for example, when opening a credit card account).

Using Security Software

Besides providing the value of protecting your computer and your phone from hacking, various security software may reduce your exposure to social engineering attacks. Some software, for example, filters out many phishing attacks, while other software blocks many spam phone calls. While using such software is wise, don't rely on it. There is a danger that if few social engineering attacks make it through your technological defenses, you may be less vigilant when one does reach you — don't let that happen.

While smartphone providers have historically charged for some security features, over time they have seen the value to themselves of keeping their customers secure. Today, basic versions of security software, including technology to reduce spam calls and to scan apps for malware, are often provided at no charge along with smartphone cellular-data service. Premium offerings still exist and are often worthwhile to use.

General Cyberhygiene Can Help Prevent Social Engineering

Practicing good cyberhygiene in general can also help reduce your exposure to social engineering. If, as so commonly happened during the COVID-19 pandemic, your children, for example, have access to your computer but you encrypt all your data, have a separate login, and don't provide them with administrator access, your data on the machine may remain safe even if criminals social engineer their way into your child's account.

Likewise, not responding to suspicious emails or providing information to potential scammers who solicit it can help prevent all sorts of social engineering and technical attacks.

3

Securing a Business

Contents at a Glance

Chapter **1**

Securing Your Small Business

Nearly everything discussed in this book applies to both individuals and businesses. Small business owners and workers should be aware of some points that may not necessarily be important for individuals. This chapter discusses such cybersecurity issues.

One important note: Small businesses tend to frequently lack proper cybersecurity. This chapter isn't a comprehensive list of everything that every small business needs to know. Rather, it provides some cybersecurity "food for thought" for those running small businesses.

Making Sure Someone Is In Charge

Individuals at home are responsible for the security of their computers, but what happens when you have a network and multiple users? Somebody within the business needs to ultimately "own" responsibility for information security. That person may be you, the business owner, or someone else. But whoever is in charge must clearly understand that they are responsible.

REMEMBER

Confusion as to who within an organization is responsible for cybersecurity often leads to major cybersecurity headaches.

In many small businesses, the person in charge of information security will outsource some of the day-to-day activities that are involved with performing the cybersecurity function. Even so, that person is ultimately responsible for ensuring that necessary activities, such as installing security patches, happen — and happen on time. If a breach occurs, "I thought so-and-so was taking care of that security function" is not a valid excuse that will carry a lot of weight — although, sadly, you hear people trying to use it on a regular basis.

Watching Out for Employees

Employees, and the many cybersecurity risks that they create, can become major headaches for small businesses. Human errors are the No. 1 catalyst for data breaches. Even if you're reading this book and seeking to improve your cybersecurity knowledge and posture, your employees and coworkers may not have the same level of commitment as you do when it comes to protecting your data and systems.

As such, one of the most important things small business owners can do is to educate their employees. Education consists of essentially three necessary components:

- >> **Awareness of threats:** You must ensure that every employee working for the business understands that they, and the business as a whole, are targets. People who believe that criminals want to breach their computers, phones, and databases, or want to otherwise steal their data, act differently than people who have not internalized such realities. While formal, regular training is ideal, even a single, short conversation conducted when workers start, and refreshed with periodic reminders, can deliver significant value in this regard. For more about creating security awareness programs, see Book 6.

- >> **Basic information-security training:** All employees should understand certain basics of information security. They should, for example, know to avoid cyber-risky behavior, such as opening attachments and clicking on links found in unexpected email messages, downloading music or videos from questionable sources, inappropriately using public Wi-Fi, or buying products from unknown stores with too-good-to-be-true prices and no publicly known physical address.

  Numerous related training materials (often free) are available online. That said, never rely on training in itself to serve as the sole line of defense against any substantial human risk. Remember, we know with certainty that many people still do stupid things even after receiving clear training to the contrary.

Furthermore, training does nothing to address rogue employees who intentionally sabotage information security.

>> **Practice:** Information security training should not be theoretical. Employees should be given the opportunity to practice what they have learned — for example, by identifying and deleting/reporting a test phishing email. *Security Awareness For Dummies* by Ira Winkler (published by Wiley) covers how industry experts create and run phishing simulations as part of the comprehensive awareness programs they provide.

Incentivize employees

Just as you should hold employees accountable for their actions if things go amiss, you should also reward employees for performing their jobs in a cyber-secure fashion and acting with proper cyberhygiene. Positive reinforcement can go a long way and is almost always better received than negative reinforcement.

Furthermore, many organizations have successfully implemented reporting systems that allow employees to anonymously notify the relevant powers within the business of suspicious insider activities that may indicate a threat, as well as potential bugs in systems, that could lead to vulnerabilities. Such programs are common among larger businesses, but can also be of benefit to small companies and other organizations.

Avoid giving out the keys to the castle

There are countless stories of employees making mistakes that open the organizational "door" to hackers. Likewise, there have been numerus cases of disgruntled employees stealing data and/or sabotaging systems. The damage from such incidents can be catastrophic to a small business. Protect yourself and your business from these types of risks by setting up your information infrastructure to contain the damage if something does go amiss.

TIP

How can you do this? Give workers access to all the computer systems and data that they need in order to do their jobs with maximum performance, but do not give them access to anything else of a sensitive nature. Programmers shouldn't be able to access a business's payroll system, for example, and a comptroller doesn't need access to the version control system housing the source code of a company's proprietary software.

Limiting access can make a world of difference in terms of the scope of a data leak if an employee goes rogue. Many businesses have learned this lesson the hard way. Don't become one of them.

Give everyone separate credentials

Every employee accessing each and every system in use by the organization should have their own login credentials to that system. Do not share credentials!

Implementing such a scheme improves the ability to audit people's activities (which may be necessary if a data breach or other cybersecurity event happens) and also encourages people to better protect their passwords because they know that if the account is misused, management will address the matter with them personally rather than with a team. The knowledge that employees are going to be held accountable for their behavior for maintaining or compromising security can work wonders in a proactive sense.

Likewise, every person should have their own multifactor authentication capabilities — whether that be a physical token, a code generated on their smart-phone, and so on.

Restrict administrators

System administrators typically have superuser privileges — meaning that they may be able to access, read, delete, and modify other people's data. It is essential, therefore, that if you — the business owner — are not the only superuser, that you implement controls to monitor what an administrator does. For example, you can log administrator actions on a separate machine that the administrator does not have access to.

Allowing access from only a specific machine in a specific location — which is sometimes not possible due to business needs — is another approach, as it allows a camera to be aimed toward that machine to record everything that the administrator does.

Limit access to corporate accounts

Your business itself may have several of its own accounts. For example, it may have social media accounts — a Facebook page, Instagram account, and a Twitter account — customer support, email accounts, phone accounts, and other utility accounts.

REMEMBER

Grant access only to the people who absolutely need access to those accounts (see preceding section). Ideally, every one of the folks to whom you do give access should have *auditable access* — that is, it should be easy to determine who did what with the account.

Basic control and audibility are simple to achieve when it comes to Facebook Pages, for example, as you can own the Facebook Page for the business, while providing other people the ability to write to the page. In some other environments, however, granular controls aren't available and you will need to decide between providing multiple people logins to a social media account or having them submit content to a single person (perhaps, even you) who makes the relevant posts.

The challenge of providing every authorized user of corporate social media accounts with their own account to achieve both control and audibility is exacerbated by the fact that all sensitive accounts should be protected with multifactor authentication. (See Book 2, Chapter 4 for more on multifactor authentication.)

Some systems offer multifactor authentication capabilities that account for the fact that multiple independent users may need to be given auditable access to a single account. In some cases, however, systems that offer multifactor authentication capabilities do not blend well with multi-person environments. They may, for example, allow for only one cellphone number to which one-time passwords are sent via SMS. In such scenarios, you will need to decide whether to

>> **Use the multifactor authentication, but with a work-around.** For example, by using a VOIP number to receive the texts and configuring the VOIP number to forward the messages on to multiple parties via email (as is offered at no cost, for example, by Google Voice).

>> **Use the multifactor authentication with no work-around.** Configure the authorized users' devices not to need multifactor authentication for the activities that they perform.

>> **Use a form of multifactor authentication that does not need a work-around.** For example, one that allows multiple users to independently authenticate using different credentials and multifactor logins, and subsequently receive permission to act on the same account.

>> **Use a form of multifactor authentication that does not need a work-around, but does not multifactor separately for different users.** For example, allowing users to use separate initial authentication credentials, but use shared multifactor credentials such as by giving them a one-time code generator configured with the same seed (that is, configured to produce exactly the same one-time codes at exactly the same times).

>> **Not use the multifactor authentication, but instead rely solely on strong passwords.** This solution is not recommended.

>> **Find another work-around by modifying your processes, procedures, or technologies used to access such systems.**

>> **Utilize third-party products that overlay systems.** This is often the best option when available.

TIP

The last option is often the best option. Various content management systems, for example, allow themselves to be configured for multiple users, each with their own independent, strong authentication capabilities, and all such users have auditable access to a single social media account.

While larger enterprises almost always follow some variant of the last approach — both for management and security reasons — many small businesses tend to take the easy way out and simply not use strong, multifactor authentication in such cases. The cost of implementing proper security — both in terms of dollars and time — is usually quite low, so exploring third-party products should definitely be done before deciding to take another approach.

REMEMBER

The value of having proper security with auditability will become immediately clear if you ever have a disgruntled employee who had access to the company's social media accounts or if a happy and satisfied employee with such access is hacked.

Implement employee policies

Businesses of all sizes that have employees need an employee handbook that includes specific rules regarding employee usage of business technology systems and data. It is beyond the scope of this book to cover all elements of employee handbooks, but the following are examples of rules that businesses can implement to govern the use of company technology resources:

» Company's employees are expected to use technology responsibly, appropriately, and productively, as necessary to perform their professional responsibilities.

» The use of company devices, as well as company Internet access and email, as provided to employees by the company, are for job-related activities. Minimal personal use is acceptable provided that the employees using it as such does not violate any other rules described in this document and does not interfere with their work.

» Employees are responsible for any computer hardware and software provided by the company, including for the safeguarding of such items from theft, loss, or damage.

» Employees are responsible for their accounts provided by the company, including the safeguarding of access to the accounts.

» Employees are strictly prohibited from sharing any company-provided items used for authentication (passwords, hardware authentication devices, PINs, and so on) and are responsible for safeguarding such items.

» Employees are strictly prohibited from connecting any networking devices, such as routers, access points, range extenders, and so on, to company networks unless explicitly authorized to do so by the company's CEO. Likewise, employees are strictly prohibited from connecting any personal computers or electronic devices — including any Internet of Things (IoT) devices — to company networks other than to the Guest network, under the conditions stated explicitly in the Bring Your Own Device (BYOD) policy.

» Employees are responsible to make sure that security software is running on all company-provided devices. Company will provide such software, but it is beyond company's ability to check that such systems are always functioning as expected. Employees may not deactivate or otherwise cripple such security systems, and must promptly notify company's IT department if they suspect that any portion of the security systems may be compromised, nonfunctioning, or malfunctioning.

» Employees are responsible to make sure that security software is kept up to date. All company-issued devices come equipped with Auto-Update enabled; employees must not disable this feature.

» Likewise, employees are responsible for keeping their devices up to date with the latest operating system, driver, and application patches when vendors issue such patches. All company-issued devices come equipped with Auto-Update enabled; employees must not disable this feature.

» Performing any illegal activity — whether or not the act involved is a felony, a misdemeanor, or a violation of civil law — is strictly prohibited. This rule applies to federal law, state law, and local law in any area and at any time in which the employee is subject to such laws.

» Copyrighted materials belonging to any party other than the company or employee may not be stored or transmitted by the employee on company equipment without explicit written permission of the copyright holder. Material that the company has licensed may be transmitted as permitted by the relevant licenses.

» Sending mass unsolicited emails (spamming) is prohibited.

» The use of company resources to perform any task that is inconsistent with company's mission — even if such task is not technically illegal — is prohibited. This includes, but is not limited to, the accessing or transmitting sexually explicit material, vulgarities, hate speech, defamatory materials, discriminatory materials, images or description of violence, threats, cyberbullying, hacking-related material, stolen material, and so on.

» The previous rule shall not apply to employees whose job entails working with such material, only to the extent that is reasonably needed for them to perform the duties of their jobs. For example, personnel responsible for configuring the company's email filter may, without violating the preceding rule, email one another about adding to the filter configuration various terms related to hate speech and vulgarities.

» No company devices equipped with Wi-Fi or cellular communication capabilities may be turned on in China or Russia without explicit written permission from the company's CEO. Loaner devices will be made available for employees making trips to those regions. Any personal device turned on in those regions may not be connected to the Guest network (or any other company network).

» All use of public Wi-Fi with corporate devices must comply with the company's Public Wi-Fi policies. Ideally, companies should ban such use except in rare, specific types of cases.

» Employees must backup their computers by using the company's backup system as discussed in the company's backup policy.

» Employees may not copy or otherwise back up data from company devices to their personal computers, storage devices, or cloud-based repositories such as Dropbox, Google Drive, Box, or any other such services.

» Any and all passwords for any and all systems used as part of an employees' job must be unique and not reused on any other systems. All such passwords must consist of three or more words, at least one of which is not found in the English dictionary, joined together with numbers or special characters or meet all the following conditions:

- Contain eight characters or more with at least one uppercase character

- Contain at least one lowercase character

- Contain at least one number

- Not contain any words that can be found in an English dictionary

- Names of relatives, friends, or colleagues may not be used as part of any password

» Data may be taken out of the office for business purposes only and must be encrypted prior to removal. This rule applies whether the data is on hard drive, SSD, CD/DVD, USB drive, or on any other media or is transmitted over the Internet. It may not be taken out of the office by copying to employee cloud-storage accounts (such as Google Drive or Dropbox). Any and all data taken out of the business's infrastructure or infrastructure contracted for use by the business must be returned to the business (or at the company's sole discretion, destroyed) immediately after its remote use is complete or upon employee's termination of employment, whichever is sooner.

>> In the event of a breach or other cybersecurity event or of any natural or man-made disaster, no employees other than the company's officially designated spokesperson may speak to the media on behalf of the company.

>> No devices from any manufacturer that the FBI, the FCC, or other United States federal agencies have warned that they believe are potentially unsafe and/or that foreign governments are using to spy on Americans may be connected to any company network (including the guest network) or brought into the physical offices of the company. Nor should company data ever be stored or processed on such devices.

Enforce social media policies

Devising, implementing, and enforcing social media policies is important because inappropriate social media posts made by your employees (or yourself) can inflict all sorts of damage. They can leak sensitive information, violate compliance rules, and assist criminals to social engineer and attack your organization, expose your business to boycotts and/or lawsuits, and so on.

TIP

You want to make clear to all employees what is and is not acceptable use of social media. As part of the process of crafting the policies, consider consulting an attorney to make sure that you do not violate anyone's freedom of speech. You may also want to implement technology to ensure social media does not transform from a marketing platform into a nightmare.

Monitor employees

Regardless of whether or not they plan to actually monitor employees' usage of technology, companies should inform users that they have a right to do so. If an employee were to go rogue and steal data, for example, you do not want to have the admissibility of evidence challenged on the grounds that you had no right to monitor the employee. Furthermore, telling employees that they may be monitored reduces the likelihood of employees doing things that they are not supposed to do because they know that they may be monitored while doing such things. Of course, monitoring should be done only on employer-issued devices and networks. (This is discussed in more detail in the section on remote work that follows.)

Here is an example of text that you can provide to employees as part of an employee handbook or the like when they begin work:

Company, at its sole discretion, and without any further notice to employee, reserves the right to monitor, examine, review, record, collect, store, copy, transmit to others, and control any and all email and other electronic communications, files, and any and all other content, network activity including Internet use, transmitted by or through its technology systems or stored in its technology systems or systems, whether onsite or offsite. Such systems shall include systems that it owns and operates and systems that it leases, licenses, or to which it otherwise has any usage rights.

Furthermore, whether sent to an internal party, external party, or both, any and all email, text and/or other instant messages, voicemail, and/or any and all other electronic communications are considered to be Company's business records, and may be subject to discovery in the event of litigation and/or to disclosure based on warrants served upon company or requests from regulators and other parties.

Dealing with a Remote Workforce

While the concept of working remotely is not new, the number of people who actually work from home has skyrocketed since early 2020 when the novel coronavirus began to spread like wildfire throughout the world. The resulting COVID-19 pandemic has become, by far, the leading motivator for change vis-à-vis remote working. It quickly transformed the world from one in which nearly all people worked at locations chosen and administered by their employers, to one in which a significant percentage of the population worked solely from home. Even as people return to workplaces after the pandemic, many are still telecommuting from home some of the time.

While working remotely during a global pandemic may help people remain safe from invisible microscopic attackers, and may even offer various productivity and financial benefits to employers, the fact that remote workers must access important data and systems from geographically scattered environments not managed by their employers creates all sorts of cybersecurity concerns. Entire books could be written on such a topic — and probably will be. But for those who wish to learn what cybersecurity safeguards they can take while working from home, the following overview of some important ideas may prove useful.

Use work devices and separate work networks

If employees connect to employer networks, access employer systems, or work with employer data with their own personal devices, employers run serious risks of malware infections, data being stored in insecure locations, data being pilfered by nefarious parties, and all sorts of other cybersecurity nightmares. As such, if possible, all remote work should be done on computers and other types of computing devices that are owned by, managed by, and issued to employees by the employer.

Ideally, access to employer systems should also be conducted using Internet connections and networking equipment paid for and managed by the employer. And no personal devices should be connected. Employers might want to have the ability to remotely access such devices to monitor and/or wipe such devices in case they are lost or stolen. In many cases, however, such arrangements are either impractical or impossible, and as such, various other types of precautions should be taken.

If employees will be using their own Internet connections, for example, it is ideal that employers provide a network router to employees so that employees can connect that router to their home network routers, and thereby isolate the employer's equipment and data from the main network segment at home and all of its traffic.

TIP

While employees should not be connecting to employer networks with personal devices, if for some reason you or your employer choses to ignore such advice, at least make sure that any and all devices connecting to the employer network have up-to-date security software running on them. Employers should manage such software installations, and keep in mind that if any software an employer instructs an employee to install creates technical issues on the employee's personal device, the employer may be responsible to correct the problem.

WARNING

Of course, never, ever, attempt to monitor an employees' actions on their personal devices.

Set up virtual private networks

A virtual private network (VPN) provides remote workers with several significant benefits. It can prevent unauthorized parties from sharing any Internet connection back to the employer's network, and can prevent other parties connected to the same local network, as well as the Internet service provider for that connection, from seeing the contents of the VPN user's transmissions.

As such, a VPN from the separate network router to a special corporate remote-worker network (for those familiar with the term, this network would likely be a form of demilitarized zone [DMZ] — not fully trusted by the company, but yet not open to the public) may also ideal, especially if the user needs to use multiple corporate devices from the remote location, or in situations in which multiple employees may be working at that location. When network-to-network VPNs are not possible — or when only one user is using only one device — a connection directly from the user's remote corporate device may be appropriate.

In some cases, either type of VPN connection may actually be dangerous from a cybersecurity perspective, such as if an employer does not have the expertise or the capability to properly implement and supervise such a VPN. Even when no VPN is used, however, isolating work devices from any personal devices through the use of a separate network at the remote location (as described earlier) is ideal.

Of course, you can also subscribe to consumer-type VPN services, but these services are less ideal because these services do not connect the remote worker to the employer's infrastructure via a "secure tunnel" (think of a secured-by-encryption communication pathway over the insecure Internet); rather, they connect the employee to the VPN provider's systems over a secure tunnel and then communicate from the VPN provider's infrastructure to others on the Internet using potentially insecure transmissions.

WARNING

Employees should not connect their personal devices to an employer's VPN. Allowing people to connect as such is a recipe for a potential cybersecurity disaster.

Create standardized communication protocols

As discussed in Book 2, Chapter 3, ideally, an organization should create standardized policies, procedures, and technologies for any video calls or chatting, and security should weigh heavily as a factor when such decisions are made. Relevant policies should include configuration requirements, such as requiring that all video calls require a password in order for someone to gain access, that virtual "waiting rooms" be utilized to prevent anyone from attending a meeting until admitted by the host, and that only users properly authenticated and signed into the communication platform be admitted into any non-public meetings.

Use a known network

When working from home, make sure that any network to which you connect wirelessly is using encryption and a strong Wi-Fi key (WPA2 or better). The reason for such advice is not only to ensure that communications cannot be monitored between your devices and the Wi-Fi access point or router, but also to ensure that you are connecting to the correct access point or router in the first place.

Hackers can set up "evil twin networks" with the same name as your network, for example, and if you receive a better signal from the evil twin access point, your device may connect to it rather than the intended, legitimate access point. Utilizing Wi-Fi security reduces the likelihood of such a problematic connection occurring, as the hacker is unlikely to have established the same encryption key. (And if somehow an attacker has your key, you have bigger problems than just this connection.)

Determine how backups are handled

Make sure you have a plan in place — and properly implemented — for how remote workers' systems and data will be backed up. Backups should be performed, managed, and administered by the employer. Do not rely on employees to back up employer data. If for some reason, despite all of the information provided earlier in this chapter, you find yourself in a situation in which employees are using personal devices for working remotely, be absolutely sure as their employer not to back up any personal contents of such devices.

Be careful where you work remotely

Keep in mind that working from home is likely to be less secure than working at a normal professional work location, not only for technical reasons, but also due to the people often present in the respective areas. Simply put, besides technical issues, as discussed elsewhere in this book, working remotely creates major concerns about "shoulder surfing." Ideally, therefore, remote employees should be working strictly from home and other locations with strongly controlled human access, and not from coffee shops, airports, libraries, public parks, sidewalks, and/or restaurants.

Also, it should be noted that with workers situated in the safety of their homes, unauthorized outsiders are far more unlikely to see what appears on the display of the employee's computer or hear sensitive information conveyed by the employee during voice-based phone calls, many organizations are rightfully still uncomfortable with their employees' children or significant others knowing all sorts of information that remote workers may handle and expose during work-at-home sessions.

TIP

Using a noise machine, such as those intended to produce background noise to help people fall asleep, or those used by psychologists, psychiatrists, and social workers for years to prevent people in waiting rooms from hearing the conversations taking place in treatment rooms, can be used to reduce the likelihood of sensitive information being overheard.

In addition, privacy screens for laptops can reduce the likelihood of anyone being able to read what appears on the display. Such screens allow displayed contents to be seen clearly when someone looks directly at them, but not when someone looks from the side.

Be extra vigilant regarding social engineering

Would-be cyberattackers know that remote workers make good targets not only because of the technical cybersecurity limitations present at the vast majority of home-office sites, but because of human weaknesses as well.

Unlike their in-office counterparts, for example, people working remotely cannot simply walk down the hall and ask someone about a particular request allegedly made by that person and received in a chat message or email. Remote workers are also more likely than in-office workers to deviate from normal business hours for their work schedules. And such workers rarely benefit as much as do their in-office counterparts, from robust technology suites implemented to protect people from phishing and other social engineering attacks.

For those reasons as well as others, remote workers are believed by many to be more likely to be successfully social engineered by criminals than are otherwise similar people working in professional offices. Remote workers are more likely to open problematic emails, click on dangerous links, and/or otherwise inadvertently take action based on the request of a criminal. Think for a moment how likely you would be — if you were working remotely — to open a spear-phishing email made to look like it was sent by your boss with the subject, "Important Updates to Corporate Remote Working Policy."

As such, remote workers must be especially vigilant against social engineering attacks. To learn more about such attacks and how to defend against them, see Book 2, Chapter 6.

Considering Cybersecurity Insurance

While cybersecurity insurance may be overkill for most small businesses, if you believe that your business could suffer a catastrophic loss or even fail altogether if it were to be breached, you may want to consider buying insurance. If you do pursue this route, keep in mind that nearly all cybersecurity insurance policies have *carve outs*, or exclusions — so make sure that you understand exactly what is covered and what is not and for what amount of damage you are actually covered. If your business fails because you were breached, a policy that pays only to have an expert spend two hours restoring your data is not going to be worth much.

REMEMBER

Cybersecurity insurance is never a replacement for proper cybersecurity.

CYBERSECURITY INSURANCE IS NOW AVAILABLE TO BUSIENSSES OF ALL SIZES

For many years, cybersecurity insurance (also known as cyber liability insurance) policies were available primarily to large businesses. Today, however, that is not the case; various companies now offer policies to smaller businesses, and some even offer policies to individuals.

Before obtaining any policy, it is critical to understand what the policy covers and what it does not cover. Policies for smaller entities and individuals typically vary quite a bit from those of larger enterprises in such regard.

In any event, do not discount the value of cybersecurity insurance. If a situation ever arises in which you need to make a claim, you are likely to be extremely happy to have previously obtained a policy — to put it mildly.

In fact, to the contrary, insurers normally require that a business meet a certain standard of cybersecurity to purchase and maintain coverage. In some cases, the insurer may even refuse to pay a claim if it finds that the insured party was breached at least in part due to negligence on the insured's part or due to the failure of the breached party to adhere to certain standards or practices mandated by the relevant insurance policy.

Complying with Regulations and Compliance

Businesses may be bound by various laws, contractual obligations, and industry standards when it comes to cybersecurity. Your local Small Business Administration office may be able to provide you with guidance as to what regulations potentially impact you. Remember, though, that there is no substitute for hiring a properly trained lawyer experienced with this area of law to provide professional advice optimized for your particular situation.

The following sections provide examples of several such regulations, standards, and so on that often impact small businesses.

Protecting employee data

You're responsible for protecting sensitive information about your employees. If you don't properly protect this information, you could end up in hot water with government regulators, with your employees, or in the eyes of the public.

For physical files, you should, in general, protect records with at least *double-locking* — storing the paper files in a locked cabinet within a locked room (and not using the same key for both). For electronic files, the files should be stored encrypted within a password-protected folder, drive, or virtual drive. Such standards, however, may not be adequate in every particular situation, which is why you should check with an attorney.

REMEMBER

Keep in mind that failure to adequately protect employee information can have severe effects: If your business is breached and a criminal obtains private information about employees, the impacted employees and former employees can potentially sue you, and the government may fine you as well. Remediation costs may also be much higher than the costs of proactive prevention would have been. And, of course, the impact of bad publicity on the business's sales may also be catastrophic — sometimes even forcing a business to fail!

Remember, employee personnel records, W2 forms, Social Security numbers, I9 employment eligibility forms, home addresses and phone numbers, medical information including COVID-19 test results and/or vaccination records and any other health-related information that you may maintain, vacation records, family leave records, and so on are all potentially considered private.

TIP

In general, if you're unsure as to whether some information may be considered private, err on the side of caution and treat it as if it is private.

PCI DSS

Payment Card Industry Data Security Standard (PCI DSS) is an information security standard for organizations that handle major credit cards and their associated information. The standard has been updated and expanded multiple times; the most current version is Version 3.2.1, published in May 2018.

While all companies of all sizes that are subject to the PCI DSS standard must be compliant with it, PCI does take into effect the different levels of resources available to different sized businesses. PCI Compliance has effectively four different levels. To what level an organization must comply is normally based primarily on how many credit card transactions it processes per year. Other factors, such as how risky the payments are that the company receives, also weigh in. The different levels are

>> **PCI Level 4:** Standards for businesses that process fewer than 20,000 credit card transactions per year

>> **PCI Level 3:** Standards for businesses that process between 20,000 and 1,000,000 credit card transactions per year

>> **PCI Level 2:** Standards for businesses that process between 1,000,000 and 6,000,000 credit card transactions per year

>> **PCI Level 1:** Standards for businesses that process more than 6,000,000 credit card transactions per year

Exploring PCI in detail is beyond the scope of this book. Entire books have been written on the topic, and various organizations offer classes dedicated to the topic. If you operate a small business and process credit card payments or store credit card data for any other reason, be sure to engage someone knowledgeable in PCI to help guide you. In many cases, your credit card processors will be able to recommend a proper consultant or guide you themselves.

Breach disclosure laws

In recent years, various jurisdictions have enacted so-called *breach disclosure laws*, which require businesses to disclose to the public if they suspect that a breach may have endangered certain types of stored information. Breach disclosure laws vary quite a bit from jurisdiction to jurisdiction, but in some cases, they may apply even to the smallest of businesses.

REMEMBER

Be sure that you are aware of the laws that apply to your business. If, for some reason, you do suffer a breach, the last thing that you want is the government punishing you for not handling the breach properly. Remember: Many small businesses fail as the result of a breach; the government entering the fray only worsens your business's odds of surviving after a successful cyberattack.

The laws that apply to your business may include not only those of the jurisdiction within which you're physically located but the jurisdictions of the people you're handling information for.

GDPR

The *General Data Protection Regulation* (GDPR) is a European privacy regulation that went into effect in 2018 and applies to all businesses handling the consumer data of residents of the European Union, no matter the size, industry, or country of origin of the business and no matter whether the EU resident is physically located within the EU. It provides for stiff fines for businesses that do not properly protect private information belonging to EU residents. This regulation means that a small business in New York that sells an item to an EU resident located in New York may be subject to GDPR for information about the purchaser and, can, in theory, face stiff penalties if it fails to properly protect that person's data. For example, in July 2019, the United Kingdom's Information Commissioner's Office (ICO) announced that it intended to fine British Airways about $230 million and Marriott about $123 million for GDPR-related violations stemming from data breaches.

GDPR is complex. If you think that your business may be subject to GDPR, speak with an attorney who handles such matters.

TIP

Do not panic about GDPR. Even if a small business in the United States is technically subject to GDPR, it is unlikely that the EU will attempt to fine small American businesses that do not operate in Europe anytime soon; it has much bigger fish to fry. That said, do not ignore GDPR because eventually American small businesses may become targets for enforcement actions.

HIPAA

Federal law throughout the United States of America requires parties that house healthcare-related information to protect it in order to maintain the privacy of the individuals whose medical information appears in the data. The *Health Insurance Portability and Accountability Act* (HIPAA), which went into effect in 1996, provides for stiff penalties for improperly defending such information. Be sure to learn whether HIPAA applies to your business and, if so, ensure that you are properly protecting the data to which it applies according to industry standards or better. Many other jurisdictions around the world have regulations similar in concept to HIPAA.

Biometric data

If you utilize any forms of biometric authentication or for any other reason store biometric data, you may be subject to various privacy and security laws governing that data. Multiple states have already enacted laws in this regard, and others are likely to follow.

Anti-money laundering laws

Anti-money laundering laws seek to make it difficult for criminals to convert illegally obtained money into money that appears to have been legally obtained. While many anti-money laundering laws are applicable primarily to financial institutions, anyone utilizing cryptocurrency for performing transactions with unknown parties should be sure that their actions do not violate these laws.

International sanctions

Paying ransomware ransoms can sometimes in itself be a crime, especially in situations in which the criminals receiving the payments are under sanctions (meaning it is a federal crime to conduct any financial transactions with them). While, to date, people who have paid ransoms have not been prosecuted by the U.S. government for violating such laws, there are indications that tolerance for such violations may be waning.

Handling Internet Access

Small businesses face significant challenges related to Internet access and information systems that individuals rarely must think about, and must take various actions to prevent the emergence of various dangers. The following sections cover a few examples.

Segregate Internet access for personal devices

If you provide Internet access for visitors to your place of business, and/or for your employees to use with their personal smartphones and tablets while at work, implement this Internet access on a separate network from the network(s) used to run your business. Most modern routers offer such a capability, which is usually found somewhere in the configuration with a name like Guest network. (Likewise, as mentioned earlier in this chapter, remote home-based workers should be keeping their work and personal networks separate.)

Create bring your own device (BYOD) policies

If you allow employees to perform business activities on their own personal laptops or mobile devices, you need to create policies regarding such activity and implement technology to protect your data in such an environment.

WARNING

Don't rely on policies. If you don't enforce policies with technology, you could suffer a catastrophic theft of data if an employee goes rogue or makes a mistake.

In general, small businesses should not allow bring your own device (BYOD) — even if doing so is tempting. In the vast majority of cases when small businesses do allow employees to use their own devices for work-related activities, data remains improperly protected, and problems develop if an employee leaves the organization (especially if the employee leaves under less than optimal circumstances).

TIP

Many Android keyboards "learn" about a user's activities as the user types. While such learning helps improve spelling correction and word prediction, it also means that in many cases, sensitive corporate information may be learned on a personal device and remain as suggested content when a user types on it even after the employee leaves the employer.

If you do allow BYOD, be sure to set proper policies and procedures — both for usage and for decommissioning any company technology on such devices, as well as for removing any company data when an employee leaves. Develop a full mobile device security plan that includes remote wipe capabilities, enforces protection of passwords and other sensitive data, processes work-related data in an isolated area of the device that other apps can't access (a process known as *sandboxing*), installs, runs, and updates mobile-optimized security software, prohibits staff from using public Wi-Fi for sensitive work-related tasks, prohibits certain activities from the devices while corporate data is on them, and so on.

Properly handle inbound access

One of the biggest differences between individuals and businesses using the Internet is often the need of the business to provide inbound access for untrusted parties. Unknown parties must be able to initiate communications that result in communications with internal servers within your business.

For example, if a business offers products for sale online, it must allow untrusted parties to access its website to make purchases (see Figure 1-1). Those parties connect to the website, which must connect to payment systems and internal order tracking systems, even though they are untrusted. (Individuals typically do not have to allow any such inbound access to their computers.)

While small businesses can theoretically properly secure web servers, email servers, and so on, the reality is that few, if any, small businesses have the resources to adequately do so, unless they're in the cybersecurity business to begin with. As such, it is wise for small businesses to consider using third-party software and infrastructure, set up by an expert, and managed by experts, to host any systems used for inbound access. To do so, a business may assume any one or more of several approaches:

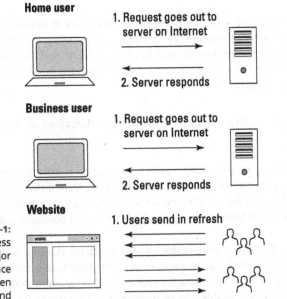

Home user

1. Request goes out to server on Internet

2. Server responds

Business user

1. Request goes out to server on Internet

2. Server responds

Website

1. Users send in refresh

2. Server responds

FIGURE 1-1: Inbound access is one major difference between businesses and individuals.

>> **Utilize a major retailer's website.** If you're selling items online, and sell only through the websites of major retailers, such as Amazon, Rakuten, and/or eBay, those sites serve as a major buffer between your business's systems and the outside world. The security armies at those companies defend their customer-facing systems from attacks. In many cases, such systems don't require small businesses to receive inbound communications, and when they do, the communications emanate from those retailers' systems, not from the public. Of course, many factors go into deciding whether to sell via a major retailer — online markets do take hefty commissions, for example. When you weigh the factors in making such a decision, keep the security advantages in mind.

>> **Utilize a third-party hosted retail platform.** In such a case, the third party manages most of the infrastructure and security for you, but you customize and manage the actual online store. Such a model does not offer quite the same level of isolation from outside users as does the preceding model, but it does offer much greater buffering against attacks than if you operate your own platform by yourself. Shopify is an example of a popular third-party platform.

>> **Operate your own platform, hosted by a third party that is also responsible for security.** This approach offers better protection than managing the security yourself, but it does not isolate your code from outsiders trying to find vulner-abilities and attack. It also places responsibility for the upkeep and security of the platform on you.

>> **Operate your own system hosted either internally or externally and use a managed services provider to manage your security.** In such a case, you're fully responsible for the security of the platform and infrastructure, but you're outsourcing much of the actual work required to satisfy that responsibility to a third party.

Other models and many variants of the models described in the preceding list exist as well.

While the models may step from easier to secure to harder to secure, they also step from less customizable to more customizable. In addition, while the earlier models may cost less for smaller businesses, the expense of the earlier models typically grows much faster than do the later ones as a business grows.

While using third-party providers does add some risks; the risk that a small business will be unable to properly implement and perpetually manage security is likely much greater than any security risk created by using a reliable third party. Of course, outsourcing anything to an unknown third party that you have done no due diligence on is extremely risky and is not recommended.

Protect against denial-of-service attacks

If you operate any Internet-facing sites as part of your business, make sure that you have security technology implemented to protect against denial-of-service (DoS) attacks. If you're selling via retailers, they likely have it already. If you're using a third-party cloud platform, the provider may supply it as well. If you're running the site on your own, you should obtain protection to ensure that someone can't easily take your site — and your business — offline. Various companies specialize in providing such protection.

Use https

If your business operates a website, be sure to install a valid TLS/SSL certificate so that users can communicate with it over a secure connection and know that the site actually belongs to your business.

Some security systems that protect against DoS attacks include a certificate as part of the package.

Use a VPN

As is discussed earlier in this chapter regarding home-based workers, if you intend to provide employees remote access to corporate systems, consider using a virtual private network (VPN) and multifactor authentication. In the case of remote access, the VPN should create an encrypted tunnel between your remote users and your business, not between users and a VPN provider. The tunnel both protects against people snooping on the communications between remote users and the business and also allows remote users to function as if they were in the company's offices, and utilize various business resources available only to insiders. Multifactor authentication is discussed in detail in Book 2, Chapter 4. Of course, if you use third-party, cloud-based systems, the relevant providers should already have security capabilities deployed that you can leverage — do so.

Run penetration tests

Individuals rarely run tests to see whether hackers can penetrate into their systems, and neither do most small businesses. Doing so, however, can be valuable — especially if you are deploying a new system of some sort or upgrading network infrastructure. See Book 5, Chapter 1 for more on penetration testing.

Be careful with IoT devices

Many businesses today utilize connected cameras, alarms, and so on. Be sure that someone is responsible for overseeing the security of these devices, which should be run on separate networks (or virtual segments) than any computers used to operate the business. Control access to these devices and do not allow employees to connect any unauthorized IoT devices to the business's networks. Ideally, purchase IoT devices only if they are made by a respectable manufacturer. Don't, for example, seek to get the least expensive connected cameras available online regardless of who made them and where they were made.

Use multiple network segments

Depending on the size and nature of your business, isolating various computers onto different network segments may be wise. A software development company, for example, should not have developers coding on the same network that the operations folks use to manage payroll and accounts payable. (As is discussed earlier in this chapter, the same holds true for remote home-based workers. Their personal and work networks should be separated.)

Be careful with payment cards

If you accept credit and/or debit cards — and are not selling via a major retailer's website — make sure to speak with your processor about various anti-fraud technology options that may be available to you. And make sure you comply with PCI DSS as discussed earlier in this chapter.

Managing Power Issues

Use an uninterruptable power supply (UPS) on all systems that you can't afford to have go down even momentarily. Do not overload UPSs — make sure they can handle the total load needed for all of the devices plugged into them. Also, make sure the power supplies can keep the systems up and running for longer than any expected outage. If you're selling various goods and services via online retail, for example, you may lose current sales and future sales, as well as suffer reputational harm, if your ability to sell goes offline even for a short period of time.

WARNING

Never let cleaning personnel enter the server closet unaccompanied — even for a moment. I personally witnessed a case in which a server actively and extensively used by dozens of people went down because an administrator allowed cleaning personnel to enter a server room unaccompanied only to find later that someone unplugged the relevant server from an uninterruptible power supply — a device that serves as both the entry point for power into the system as well as a battery backup — to plug in a vacuum cleaner.

LOCKING ALL NETWORKING EQUIPMENT AND SERVERS IN A VENTILATED CLOSET

You must control physical access to your systems and data if you want to protect them from unauthorized access. While individuals typically store computers in the open in their homes, businesses usually keep servers in locked racks or closets. You need to be sure, though, that any such rack or closet where you locate computer equipment is well ventilated, or your equipment may overheat and die. You may even need to install a small air conditioner in the closet if ventilation on its own does not sufficiently get rid of the heat generated by the equipment.

Chapter 2

Cybersecurity and Big Businesses

Many of the information security challenges facing large enterprises and small business are similar in nature. In fact, over the past decade, cloud-based offerings have brought to small businesses many well-protected systems sporting enterprise-class technologies, reducing some of the historical differences between firms of different sizes as far as the architecture of many major business systems is concerned. Of course, many security risks scale with enterprise size, but don't qualitatively differ based on the number of employees, partners, and customers that a business has, or based on the size of its information technology budget.

At the same time, however, bigger companies often face significant additional complications — sometimes involving orders of magnitude more complexity than the challenges facing small businesses. A large number of diverse systems spread across geographies and utilizing custom code, for example, often make securing a large enterprise quite difficult and complex — and such systems rarely if ever exist in the realm of small businesses.

Thankfully, however, larger firms tend to have significantly larger budgets to acquire defenses and defenders. Furthermore, despite the fact that all companies should, in theory, have formal information security programs, small business tend not to, while large businesses almost always do. This chapter explores some areas that disproportionately impact large companies.

Utilizing Technological Complexity

Large enterprises often have multiple offices and lines of business, many different information systems, complex business arrangements with partners and suppliers, and so on — all of which are reflected in much more complicated information infrastructure than typically exists in the case of smaller businesses. As such, large companies have a much larger *attack surface* — that is, they have many more potential points at which an attacker can attack them than do small businesses. The varied systems common in large business environments also usually mean that no individual, or even small number of people, can possibly be experts on all of them. Large firms use a blend of cloud and local systems, commercial-off-the-shelf and custom-built systems, numerous diverse technologies, complex network architectures, and so on — and their security teams must make sure that all of these work together in a secure fashion.

Managing Custom Systems

Large enterprises almost always have significant amounts of custom-built technology systems that are managed in-house. Depending on how they are deployed and utilized, these systems may require the same level of security patching that off-the-shelf software requires — which means that if security is to be maintained, internal folks and/or third-party contractors who helped build the systems need to manage the code from a security perspective, push out patches, and so on.

Furthermore, security teams must be involved with internal systems throughout the systems' entire life cycle — including phases such as initial investigation, analysis and requirements definition, design, development, integration and testing, acceptance and deployment, ongoing operations, and maintenance, evaluation, and disposal. They must also ensure that any third parties involved at any stages of system creation, implementation, or retirement and disposal adhere to proper security standards.

Simply put, security as an element of software development is a complicated and challenging matter. In fact, entire books have been written about delivering security during the software development life cycle, and various organizations even test competence levels and provide professional certifications in this area as well.

Continuity Planning and Disaster Recovery

While small businesses should have business continuity and disaster recovery plans (sometimes known as BCPs and DRPs) and should regularly test those plans as well, they typically have, at least from a formal perspective, rudimentary plans — at best. And that is being generous. In most cases, small businesses have no business continuity and disaster recovery plans other than identifying who will make decisions as to how to operate in the event of a disaster. Such a lack became obvious during the early days of the COVID-19 pandemic in 2020, during which many small businesses simply had to "wing it" as a result of having no plans as to what to do if employees could not make it to the office.

Large businesses, on the other hand, typically have much more formal plans in place — including detailed arrangements for resumption of work in case a facility becomes unavailable and so on. While many groups within large enterprises were hit hard by the COVID-19 pandemic's sudden work-at-home demands, many others were properly prepared and simply activated plans that they had already tested.

One point the COVID-19 pandemic should have made obvious to everyone, however, is that disasters do happen — and even serious disruptions can happen with far less warning than many folks might expect. Furthermore, hackers know that such disruptions, during which many businesses are flying by the seats of their pants and making all sorts of compromises when it comes to cybersecurity in order to ensure continuity of operations, are opportune times for hacking.

TIP

Prepare in advance. Remember, when it comes to cybersecurity, an ounce of prevention is worth many tons of cure.

Looking at Regulations

Large enterprises are often subject to many more regulations, laws, guidance, and industry standards than are small businesses. Besides all the issues that are described in the chapter on securing small businesses (Book 3, Chapter 1), for example, the following sections cover some other ones that may impact large enterprises.

Sarbanes Oxley

The Sarbanes Oxley Act of 2002, technically known as either the Public Company Accounting Reform and Investor Protection Act or the Corporate and Auditing

Accountability, Responsibility, and Transparency Act, established many rules intended to help protect investors in public companies. Many of its mandates, for example, are intended to improve the accuracy, objectivity, and reliability of corporate statements and disclosures and to create formal systems of internal checks and balances within companies. SOX, as it is often known, mandated stronger corporate governance rules, closed various accounting loopholes, strengthened protections for whistle-blowers, and created substantial penalties (including jail time) for corporate and executive malfeasance.

As its name implies, all publicly held American companies are subject to SOX, as are companies outside of the United States that have registered any equity or debt securities with the United States Securities and Exchange Commission (SEC). In addition, any third party, such as an accounting firm, that provides accounting or other financial services to companies regulated by SOX, is itself mandated to comply with SOX, regardless of its location.

SOX has many implications on information security — both directly and indirectly. Two sections of SOX effectively mandate that companies implement various information security protections:

» **Section 302** of SOX addresses the corporate responsibility to utilize controls to ensure that the firm produces accurate financial reports and requires companies to implement systems to prevent any unauthorized tampering with corporate data used to create such reports — whether the tampering is done by employees or external folks.

» **Section 404** is perhaps the most controversial portion of SOX and certainly, for many businesses, the most expensive with which to comply. This section makes corporate managers responsible to ensure that the company has adequate and effective internal control structures and requires that any relevant shortcomings be reported to the public. Section 404 makes management responsible to ensure that the corporation can properly protect its data processing systems and their contents and mandates that the firm must make all relevant data available to auditors, including information about any potential security breaches.

In addition to these two areas in which SOX plays a role, information security professionals are likely to deal with many other systems that companies have implemented in order to comply with other SOX requirements. Such systems need protection as well as they themselves must adhere to SOX, too.

SOX is complicated — and public companies normally employ people who are experts in the relevant requirements. Information security professionals are likely to interface with such folks.

Stricter PCI requirements

The PCI DSS standards for protecting credit card information (see Book 3, Chapter 1) include stricter mandates for larger companies (for example, those processing more credit card transactions) than for smaller firms. Also, keep in mind that from a practical perspective, larger firms are likely to have more processing terminals and more credit card data, as well as more diverse technology involved in their credit card processing processes — raising the stakes when it comes to PCI. Larger firms also face a greater risk of reputational damage: A violation of PCI DSS standards by a larger firm is far more likely to make the national news than if the same violation were made by a mom-and-pop shop.

Public company data disclosure rules

Public companies — that is, businesses owned by the public via their shares being listed on a stock exchange (or on various other public trading platforms) — are subject to numerous rules and regulations intended to protect the integrity of the markets.

One such requirement is that a company must release to the entire world at the same time various types of information that may impact the value of the company's shares. A publicly traded company cannot, for example, provide performance information to investment banks before disclosing exactly the same information to the media. In fact, anyone to whom a publicly traded company does release private (insider) information prior to the information's disclosure to the public at large — for example, the public company's accounting or law firms — is strictly prohibited from trading shares or any derivative based on that data. Illegally benefiting from such "insider information" is typically a felony — and even attempting to benefit as such can lead to a prison sentence in a federal penitentiary.

Because of the seriousness of protecting company data, large corporations often have all sorts of policies, procedures, and technologies in place to protect any data subject to such regulations — and to address situations in which some such data was inadvertently released.

Breach disclosures

Some breach disclosure rules exempt smaller businesses, but all require disclosures from large enterprises. Furthermore, large enterprises often have multiple departments that must interact and coordinate in order to release information about a breach — sometimes also involving external parties. Representatives of the marketing, investor relations, information technology, security, legal, and other departments, for example, may need to work together to coordinate the text of any release and may need to involve a third-party public relations firm and external counsel as well. Large enterprises also tend to have official spokespeople and media departments to which the press can address any questions.

Industry-specific regulators and rules

Various industry-specific rules and regulations tend to apply to larger firms more often than to small businesses. For example, the Nuclear Regulatory Commission (NRC), which is an independent federal agency that regulates nuclear power companies in the United States, regulates some major utilities, but few, if any, mom-and-pop shops will ever be subject to its regulations. Hence, only larger firms dedicate significant resources to ensuring compliance with its rules. In the world of NRC regulations, cybersecurity is an important element in governing various Supervisory Control and Data Acquisition systems (SCADA), which are computer-based control and management systems that speak to the controllers in components of a plant.

Likewise, with the exception of certain hedge funds and other financial operations, few small businesses are required to monitor and record all the social media interactions of their employees, the way major banks must do for certain workers.

As a result of industry specific regulations, many large businesses have various processes, policies, and technologies in place that yield data and systems requiring all sorts of information security involvement. Various states have also enacted breach disclosure rules. While such rules impact business of various sizes, they often place more onerous demands on larger organizations, as such firms are, in many cases, better equipped to quickly report breaches. It should be noted that in some cases, covering up a breach (or even *attempting* to cover up a breach) can expose an organization — and the individuals involved — to both civil and criminal liabilities.

Fiduciary responsibilities

While many small businesses don't have external shareholders to whom management or a board of directors may be fiduciarily responsible, most large corporations do have investors who may sue either or both parties if a cybersecurity breach harms the firm's value. Various laws require management and boards to ensure that systems are appropriately secured. In some cases, folks may even be able to be criminally charged if they were negligent. Even if senior executives are not charged after a breach, they may still suffer severe career and reputational damage for their failure to prevent it.

INSIDER TRADING AFTER A BREACH OCCURS AND BEFORE IT IS REPORTED

There have been instances in which, after a data breach occurred, but before it was reported to the public, executives of the breached entities have sold stock positions they held in the companies for which they worked. Such actions are not only reprehensible, they are often illegal as well, since advance knowledge of the breach is insider information not known to the public, and trading on such information is against the law.

One defense some executives have made for such behavior is that they were not personally aware of the relevant breach. While the public has the right to question the veracity of any such claims, it is certainly possible that a scenario could arise in which an executive honestly was unaware of the breach at the time the executive made a trade. For that reason and other reasons it is imperative that appropriate legal advice be obtained — not only immediately upon discovery of the breach vis-à-vis how to prevent potential issues related to accusations of insider trading, but also in advance in order to advise executives how to avoid such suspicions in the first place. (One method, for example, might be for executives who wish to sell stock to break up the position they which to sell into multiple subpositions and set up sales to occur automatically on a regular basis in order to liquidate those subpositions.)

Deep pockets

Because large enterprises have much deeper pockets than small businesses — in other words, they have a lot more money at their disposal — and because targeting mom-and-pop shops isn't usually as politically advantageous as targeting a large firm that exhibited some bad behavior, regulators tend to pursue compliance cases against large enterprises suspected of violations with much more gusto than they do against small businesses.

One exception to this rule is when it comes to cryptocurrency and other blockchain-related projects, as securities regulators have been increasingly targeting such operations in recent years even when such operations are relatively small.

Deeper Pockets — and Insured

Because larger organizations are more likely to have large amounts of cash and assets than small businesses, they make better targets for class action and various other forms of lawsuits than do mom-and-pop shops. Lawyers don't want to expend large amounts of time fighting a case if their target has no money with which to settle or may go bankrupt (and therefore not pay) in the case of a judgment. As a result, the odds that a larger enterprise will be targeted with a lawsuit if data leaks from it as a result of a breach are relatively high when compared with the odds that the same would happen to a much smaller business suffering a similar breach.

Considering Employees, Consultants, and Partners

Employees are often the weakest link in a business's security chain. Far more complex employment arrangements utilized by large enterprises — often involving unionized employees, non-unionized employees, directly hired contractors, contractors hired through firms, subcontractors, foreign workers in the United States, foreign employees outside of the United States, American employees outside the United States, and so on — threaten to make the problem even worse for larger business.

REMEMBER

Complexity of any sort increases the odds of people making mistakes.

With human errors being the No. 1 catalyst for data breaches, large enterprises must go beyond the human management processes and procedures of small businesses. They must, for example, establish and maintain streamlined processes for deciding who gets to access what and who can give authorization for what. They must establish simple processes for revoking permissions from diverse systems when employees leave, contractors complete their assignments, and so on.

Revoking access from departing parties is not as simple as many people might imagine. An employee of a large corporation might, for example, have access to multiple, unconnected data systems located in many different locations around the globe and that are managed by different teams from different departments. Identity and access management systems that centralize parts of the authentication and authorization processes can help, but many large enterprises still lack the totally comprehensive centralization necessary to make revoking access a single-step process. Cybersecurity professionals have often witnessed multiple situations in which accounts belonging to people who have left a large company have remained active for years after the individual left. Often, access was only terminated when the system itself was retired and shut down completely.

Dealing with internal politics

While all businesses with more than one employee have some element of politics, large businesses can suffer from conflicts between people and groups that are literally incentivized to perform in direct opposition to one another. For example, a business team may be rewarded if it delivers new product features earlier than a certain date — which it can do more easily if it skimps on security — while the information security team may be incentivized to delay the product release because it's incentivized to ensure that there are no security problems and not to get the product to market quickly.

REMEMBER

The only winners when there are conflicts between a firm's information security divisions and its business units are hackers.

Offering information security training

All employees should understand certain basics of information security. They should, for example, know to avoid cyber-risky behavior, such as opening attachments and clicking on links found in unexpected email messages, downloading music or videos from questionable sources, inappropriately using public Wi-Fi for sensitive tasks, or buying products from unknown stores with "too good to be true" prices and no publicly known physical address.

In large firms, however, most employees do not personally know most other employees. Such a situation opens the door for all sorts of social engineering attacks — bogus requests from management to send W2s, bogus requests from the IT department to reset passwords, and so on. Training and practice to make sure that such attacks cannot successfully achieve their aims are critical.

Today, it is also imperative that people be taught about deep fakes so that even if they hear the CEO's voice telling them to do something else, for example, they must not deviate from security protocols without verifying the authenticity of the request and authorization of its maker.

Replicated environments

Larger businesses often replicate environments not only in order to protect against outages, but also for maintenance purposes. As such, they often have three replicas for every major system in place: the production system (which may be replicated itself for redundancy purposes), a development environment, and a staging environment for running tests of code and patches.

REMEMBER

It is imperative not to mix these environments up. Never develop in the staging environment. And do not test in production before testing in staging. These may sound like obvious points, but deviations from such a scheme are still extremely common.

Looking at the Chief Information Security Officer's Role

While all businesses need someone within them to ultimately own responsibility for information security, larger enterprises often have large teams involved with information security and need someone who can oversee all the various aspects of information security management, as well as manage all the personnel involved in doing so. This person also represents the information security function to senior management — and sometimes to the board. Typically that person is the chief information security officer (CISO).

While the exact responsibilities of CISOs vary by industry, geography, company size, corporate structure, and pertinent regulations, most CISO roles share basic commonalities. In general, the CISO's role includes overseeing and assuming responsibility for all areas of information security. The following sections describe those areas.

Overall security program management

The CISO is responsible to oversee the company's security program from A to Z. This role includes not only establishing the information security policies for the enterprise, but everything needed to ensure that business objectives can be achieved with the desired level of risk management — something that requires performing risk assessments, for example, on a regular basis.

While, in theory, small businesses also have someone responsible for their entire security programs, in the case of large enterprises, the programs are usually much more formal, with orders of magnitude more moving parts. Such programs are also forever ongoing.

Test and measurement of the security program

The CISO is responsible to establish proper testing procedures and success metrics against which to measure the effectiveness of the information security plan and to make adjustments accordingly. Establishing proper security metrics is often far more complicated than one might initially assume, as defining "successful performance" when it comes to information security is not a straightforward matter.

Human risk management

The CISO is responsible for addressing various human risks as well. Screening employees before hiring them, defining roles and responsibilities, training employees, providing employees with appropriate user manuals and employee guides, providing employees with information security breach simulations and feedback, creating incentive programs, and so on all often involve the participation of the CISO's organization (along with human resources and other groups within the firm).

Information asset classification and control

This function of the CISO includes performing an inventory of informational assets, devising an appropriate classification system, classifying the assets, and then deciding what types of controls (at a business level) need to be in place to adequately secure the various classes and assets. Auditing and accountability should be included in the controls as well.

Security operations

Security operations means exactly what it sounds like. It is the business function that includes the real-time management of security, including the analysis of threats, and the monitoring of a company's technology assets (systems, networks, databases, and so on) and information security countermeasures, such as firewalls, whether hosted internally or externally, for anything that may be amiss. Operations personnel are also the folks who initially respond if they do find that something has potentially gone wrong.

Information security strategy

This role includes devising the forward-looking security strategy of the company to keep the firm secure as it heads into the future. Proactive planning and action are obviously a lot more comforting to shareholders than is reacting to attacks.

Identity and access management

This role deals with controlling access to informational assets based on business requirements, and includes identity management, authentication, authorization, and related monitoring. It includes all aspects of the company's password management policies and technologies, any and all multifactor authentication policies and systems, and any directory systems that store lists of people and groups and their permissions.

The CISO's identity and access management teams are responsible to give workers access to the systems needed to perform the workers' jobs and to revoke all such access when a worker leaves. Likewise, they manage partner access and all other external access.

Major corporations almost always utilize formal directory services systems of some sort — Microsoft's Active Directory, for example, is quite popular.

Data loss prevention

Data loss prevention includes policies, procedures, and technologies that prevent proprietary information from leaking. Leaks can happen accidentally — for example, a user may accidentally attach the wrong document to an email before sending the message — or through malice (for example, a disgruntled employee steals valuable intellectual property by copying it to a USB drive and taking the drive home just before resigning).

In recent years, some social media management functions have been moved into the data loss prevention group. After all, oversharing on social media often includes the de facto sharing by employees of information that businesses do not want going out onto publicly accessible social networks.

Fraud prevention

Some forms of fraud prevention may fall within the CISO's realm of responsibility. For example, if a company operates consumer-facing websites that sell products, the CISO may be responsible for minimizing the number of fraudulent transactions that are successfully completed using the websites.

Even when such responsibility doesn't fall within the purview of the CISO, the CISO is likely to be involved in the process, as anti-fraud systems and information security systems often mutually benefit from sharing information about suspicious users.

Besides dealing with combatting fraudulent transactions, the CISO may be responsible for implementing technologies to prevent rogue employees from perpetrating various types of schemes in order to steal money from the company — with the CISO usually focusing primarily on mechanisms that involve the use of computers.

Incident response plan

The CISO is responsible to develop and maintain the company's incident response plan. The plan should include not only the technical steps described in Book 3, Chapters 3 and 4, but also detail who speaks to the media, who clears messages with the media, who informs the public, who informs regulators, who consults with law enforcement, and so on. It should also detail the identities (specified by job description) and roles of all other decision-makers within the incident response process.

Disaster recovery and business continuity planning

This function includes managing disruptions of normal operations through contingency planning and the testing of all such plans. While large businesses often have a separate DR and BCP team, the CISO almost always plays a major role in these functions — if not owns them outright — for multiple reasons:

>> **Keeping systems and data available is part of the CISO's responsibility.** As such, there is little difference from a practical perspective if a system goes down because a DR and BC plan is ineffective or because a DDoS attack hit — if systems and data are not available, it is the CISO's problem.

>> **CISOs need to make sure that BCP and DR plans provide for recovery in such a manner that security is preserved.** This is especially true because it is often obvious from major media news stories when major corporations may need to activate their continuity plans, and hackers know that companies in recovery mode make ideal targets.

Compliance

The CISO is responsible to ensure that the company complies with all with legal and regulatory requirements, contractual obligations, and best practices accepted by the company as related to information security. Of course, compliance experts and attorneys may advise the CISO regarding such matters, but ultimately, it is the CISO's responsibility to ensure that all requirements related to information security are at least met, if not exceeded.

Investigations

If (and, sadly, when) an information security incident occurs, the folks working for the CISO in this capacity investigate what happened. In many cases, they'll be the same folks who coordinate investigations with law enforcement agencies, consulting firms, regulators, or third-party security companies. These teams must be skilled in forensics and in preserving evidence. It does little good to know that some rogue employee stole money or data, if, as a result of your own mishandling of digital evidence during your investigation, you can't prove in a court of law that that is the case.

Physical security

Ensuring that corporate informational assets are physically secure is part of the CISO's job. This includes not only systems and networking equipment, but the transport and storage of backups, disposal of decommissioned computers, and so on.

In some organizations, the CISO is also responsible for the physical security of buildings housing technology and for the people within them. Regardless of whether this is the case, the CISO is always responsible to work with those responsible to ensure that information systems and data stores are protected with properly secured facilities sporting adequate security perimeters and with appropriate access controls to sensitive areas on a need-to-access basis.

Security architecture

The CISO and the CISO's team are responsible to design and oversee the building and maintenance of the company's security architecture. Sometimes, of course, CISOs inherit pieces of the infrastructure, so the extent to which they get to design and build may vary. The CISO effectively decides what, where, how, and why various countermeasures are used, how to design network topology, DMZs, and segments, and so on.

Geopolitical risks

It is the CISO's responsibility to ensure that any geopolitical risks that could impact the security of the organization's data and systems are properly addressed by management. If the company is outsourcing software development to an area of the world under threat of violence, for example, the CISO must point out the risks of such to the CEO.

TIP

The CISO must weigh geopolitical risks when it comes to investing in security technology offered by overseas companies. Are there risks to receiving support? Is the company subject to the manipulation of a hostile foreign government? Are the company's products banned, or likely to be banned in the future, by the U.S. government for its own use?

Ensuring auditability of system administrators

It is the CISO's responsibility to ensure that all system administrators have their actions logged in such a fashion that their actions are auditable, and attributable to the parties who took them.

Cybersecurity insurance compliance

Most large companies have cybersecurity insurance. It is the CISO's job to make sure that the company meets all security requirements for coverage under the policies that are in effect, so that if something does go amiss and a claim is made, the firm will be covered.

Chapter **3**

Identifying a Security Breach

Despite valiant efforts to protect your computer systems and data, you may suffer some sort of breach. In fact, the odds that your data will — at some point — be somehow breached by someone are close to 100 percent. The only real question is whether the breach will take place on a device or network that you operate or one that is owned and operated by someone else.

Because you're ultimately responsible for maintaining your own computer systems, you need to be able to recognize the signs of a potential breach occurring of your equipment. If a hacker does manage to penetrate your systems, you need to terminate the attacker's access as quickly as possible. If your data has been manipulated or destroyed, you need to restore an accurate copy within a reasonable amount of time. If systems are malfunctioning, you need to stop them from performing inappropriate activities and get them back on track to deliver service as expected.

In this chapter, you learn about the typical symptoms of a breach. Armed with this knowledge, you can hopefully recognize if something is amiss so that you can take appropriate corrective actions, as discussed in the next chapter.

TIP

If you've already received notification from a third-party provider where you store data, or where others store data about you, that your data has been compromised or may have been compromised, see Book 3, Chapter 5.

Identifying Overt Breaches

The easiest breaches to identify are those in which the attacker announces to you that you've been breached and provides proof of that accomplishment. Three of the most common overt breaches are those involving ransomware, defacement, and claimed destruction.

Ransomware

Ransomware is a form of malware that encrypts or steals data on a user's device and demands a ransom in order to restore the data to the user's control (see Figure 3-1). Typically, ransomware includes an expiration date with a warning to the tune of "pay within x hours or the data will be destroyed forever!" (See Book 1, Chapter 2 for more on ransomware.)

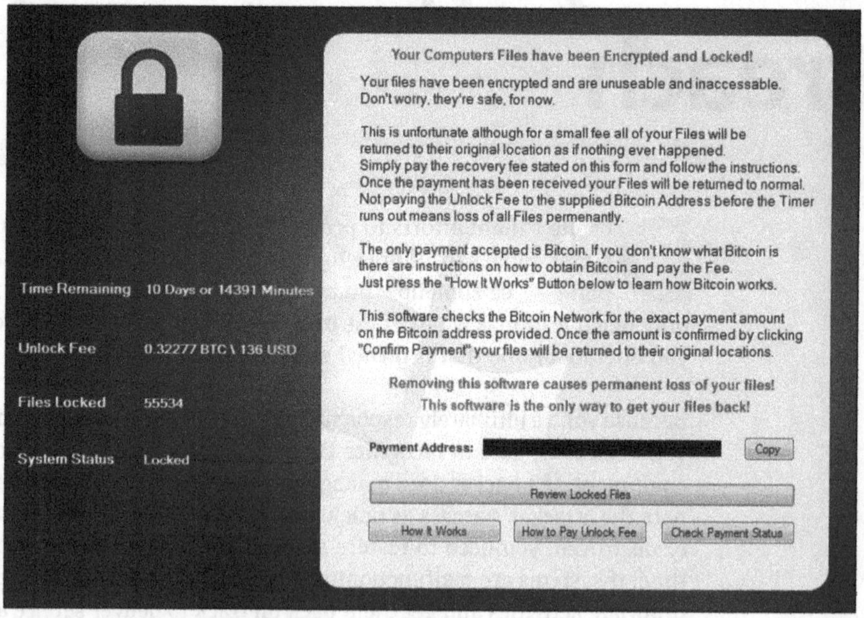

FIGURE 3-1: A ransomware screen from an overt infection.

Obviously, if your device presents you with such a demand and important files that should be accessible to you aren't available because they're missing or encrypted, you can be reasonably sure that you need to take corrective action.

Over the past few years, ransomware has become increasingly dominant as a weapon of choice by financially motivated cyberattackers, both in terms of opportunistic attacks and in terms of targeted attacks.

WARNING

One note: Some strains of bogus smartphone ransomware — yes, that is a real thing — display such messages but do not actually encrypt, destroy, or pilfer data. Before taking any corrective action — and certainly before paying any ransoms or ransom negotiation services — always check that ransomware is real.

Defacement

Defacement refers to breaches in which the attacker defaces the systems of the victim — for example, changing the target's website to display a message that the hacker hacked it (in an almost "virtual subway graffiti"-like sense) or a message of support for some cause, as is often the case with hacktivists (see Figure 3-2).

FIGURE 3-2: A defaced website (ostensibly by the hacker group known as the Syrian Electronic Army).

If you have a personal website and it's defaced or if you boot up your computer and it displays a `hacked by <some hacker>` message, you can be reasonably certain that you were breached and that you need to take corrective action. Of course, the breach may have occurred at the site hosting your site, and not on your local computer (see Book 3, Chapter 4).

Claimed destruction

Hackers can destroy data or programs, but so can technical failures or human errors. The fact that data has been deleted, therefore, doesn't necessarily mean that a system was breached. However, if some party claims responsibility, the odds that the problems are the result of a breach can skyrocket. (Although there have been instances in which parties falsely claimed responsibility for cyberattacks ostensibly in order to convince the public of their technical prowess.)

TIP

If someone contacts you, for example, and claims to have deleted a specific file or set of files that only a party with access to the system would know about, and those are the only files gone, you can be reasonably certain that the issue with which you are dealing is not a failure of hard disk sectors or solid-state disk chips.

Detecting Covert Breaches

While some breaches are obviously discernable to be breaches, many breaches are actually quite hard to detect. In fact, breaches are sometimes so hard to notice that various enterprises that spend tens of millions of dollars a year, or even hundreds of millions of dollars a year, on cybersecurity technology including systems that try to identify breaches have had breaches go undetected for significant periods of time — sometimes even for years! The following sections describe some symptoms that may indicate that your computer, tablet, or smartphone has been breached.

REMEMBER

Keep in mind that none of the following clues exists in a vacuum, nor does the presence of any individual symptom, on its own, provide a guarantee that something is amiss. Multiple reasons other than the occurrence of a breach may cause devices to act abnormally and to exhibit one or more of the ailments described in the following sections.

However, if a device suddenly seems to suffer from multiple suspicious behaviors or if the relevant issues develop just after you left the device unattended for some period of time in a public location, clicked on a link in an email or text message, downloaded and ran some software provided by a source with potentially deficient security practices, opened some questionable attachment, or did something else about which wisdom you now question, you may want to take corrective action, as described Book 3, Chapter 4.

REMEMBER

When considering the likelihood that a system was breached, always keep in mind relevant circumstances. If problems start occurring after an operating system auto-update, for example, the likely risk level is much lower than if the same symptoms start showing up right after you click on a link in a suspicious email message offering you $1,000,000 if you process a payment being sent from a Nigerian prince to someone in the United States. Always maintain a proper, "chilled" perspective and do not panic. If something did go amiss, you can still take action to minimize the damage. Panicking will not make matters better, and it certainly may lead you into making errors and making things worse.

Your device seems slower than before

Malware running on a computer, tablet, or smartphone often impacts the performance of the device in a noticeable fashion. Malware that transmits data can also sometimes slow down a device's connection to the Internet or even to internal networks.

REMEMBER

Keep in mind, however, that updates to a device's operating system or to various software packages can also adversely impact the device's performance, so don't panic if you notice that performance seems to be somewhat degraded just after you updated your operating system or installed a software upgrade from a trusted source. Likewise, if you fill up the memory on your device or install many processor and bandwidth intensive apps, performance is likely to suffer even without the presence of malware. Suspicious performance problems could be a matter of having opened too many applications and browser tab windows.

TIP

You can see what is running on a Windows PC by pressing Ctrl + Shift + Esc and checking out the Task Manager window that pops up. On a Mac, use the Activity Monitor, which you can access by clicking the magnifying glass on the right side of the menu bar on the top of the screen and starting to type Activity Monitor. After you type the first few characters, the name of the tool should display, at which point you can press Enter to run it.

On Android devices, one of the three buttons or swipe actions on the bottom of the screen will usually load up a list of active applications (exactly which button varies between devices).

Your Task Manager doesn't run

If you try to run Task Manager on Windows (see Figure 3-3) or Activity Monitor on a Mac (see preceding section) and the tool does not run, your computer may be infected with malware. Various strains of malware are known to impact the ability of these programs to operate.

Your Registry Editor doesn't run

If you try to run Registry Editor on Windows (for example, by typing **regedit** at the Run prompt) and it does not run, your computer may be infected with malware. Various strains of malware are known to impact the ability of the Registry Editor to execute.

Identifying a Security Breach

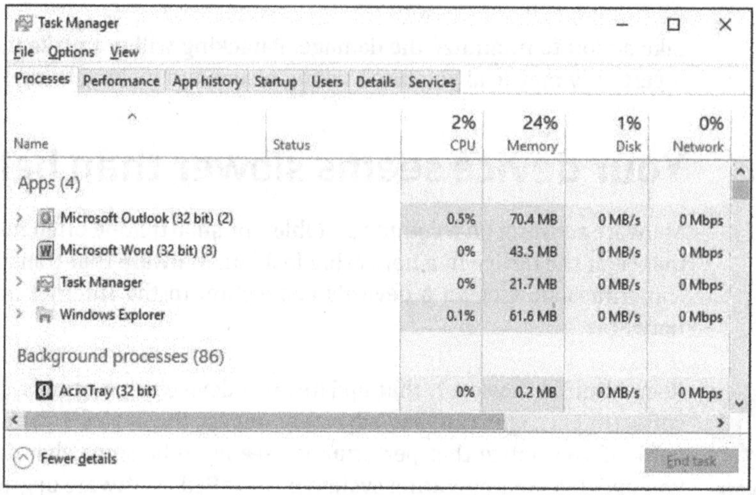

FIGURE 3-3:
The Microsoft
Windows Task
Manager.

WARNING

Note that you may receive a warning when running Registry Editor that it requires Administrator permissions. That warning is normal and not the sign of a problem. It also should remind you of the potentially serious consequences of making registry edits: Don't make any if you're not sure what you are doing. Technologists often consider making registry edits and edits to DNS servers as among the activities about which they most worry about making a mistake with potentially significant impact.

Your device starts suffering from latency issues

Latency refers to the time it takes for data to begin to travel after the instruction is issued to make it travel. If you're noticing delays that were not present before — especially if the delays seem significant — something may be amiss. Of course, you may also have a poor network connection, so check the network connection strength. If that connection is fine, it is still possible that your Internet provider or some other provider along the network path between yourself and the resources you are trying to access may be experiencing problems, and everything may be fine on your local device. However, if the latency issues appear from only one device or a particular set of devices and not from all devices connected to the same network and if rebooting the impacted device/s does not ameliorate the situation, your device/s may have been compromised.

TIP

If the device is using a wired network connection, be sure to test it with a new cable. If the problem goes away, the cause was likely a defective or damaged physical connection.

Your device starts suffering from communication and buffering issues

One highly visual symptom of communication-performance problems that can easily be discerned without much technical knowledge is if streaming videos seem to freeze while preloading future frames, or buffering, far more often than they did in the past (see Figure 3-4). Buffering is an annoyance that most folks experience from time to time. If buffering happens newly and regularly on a connection or device, this could indicate a compromised system. Determine whether the problem occurs only when the devices use a particular connection, and whether it occurs both wired and wirelessly. If the device is using a wired network connection, be sure to check any physical cables that may be causing network issues.

FIGURE 3-4:
An example of communication problems while streaming video. Note the viewable portion of the rotating circle in the middle of the video image.

REMEMBER

Note that communication performance problems can also be a sign that someone is *piggy-backing* on your Internet connection (in other words, someone is sharing your connection without your knowledge), which is also a type of breach.

Your device's settings have changed

If you notice that some of your device's settings have changed — and you're certain that you did not make the change — that may be a sign of problems. Of course, some software makes setting changes, too (especially on classic computers, as opposed to smartphones), so changes may have a legitimate source as well. Most software, however, does not make major changes without notifying you. If you see dramatic settings changes, beware.

Your device is sending or receiving strange email messages

If your friends or colleagues report receiving emails from you that you did not send to them, something is likely amiss — this is especially true if the messages appear to be spam. Likewise, if you're receiving emails that appear to be from people who claim to have never sent the relevant messages, you may have suffered a breach.

REMEMBER

Keep in mind, however, that many other reasons (including other kinds of attacks on systems other than your own devices and accounts) can lead to spam appearing to have emanated from you. For example, some hacked systems that compromise a list of contacts send emails to some of the parties in that list from other parties in the list, rather than always from the owner from whom the contact list was pilfered.

Your device is sending or receiving strange text messages

If your friends or colleagues report receiving text messages or other smartphone-type communications from you that you did not send to them, your smartphone may have been breached. Likewise, if you're receiving messages that appear to be from people who claim to have never sent the relevant messages, you may have suffered a breach. As before, there could be other explanations for such a situation, and it is possible that some other system or collection of systems are the actual victims who have been breached.

New software (including apps) is installed on your device — and you didn't install it

If new programs or apps suddenly appear on your device and you did not install them, something may be amiss. While, especially in the case of some portable devices, the manufacturer or relevant service provider may occasionally install certain types of apps without your knowledge, if new apps suddenly appear, you should always look into the matter. Of course, if you are using a corporate device that is centrally managed, the system administrators may have "pushed down" an app to you, so check with them.

Do a Google search on the apps and see what reliable tech sites say about them. If the apps are not showing up on other people's devices, you may have a serious issue on your hands.

REMEMBER

Keep in mind, however, that sometimes the installation routines of one program install other applications as well. It is relatively common, for example, for various programs that are offered for free to users in a limited-feature version to also install other programs that are comarketed alongside them. Normally, such installation programs ask for permission to install the additional programs, but such transparency is not mandated by law, and some applications do not afford users such choices.

REMEMBER

If you let someone else your computer, that person may have installed something (legitimate or illegitimate). Of course, if you have configured your device to never install auto-updates, and not to accept new apps from any providers associated with your account, then the presence of a new app that you, yourself, did not install should be even more concerning.

Your device's battery seems to drain more quickly than before

Malware running in the background uses battery power and can help drain the battery of laptops, smartphones, and tablets. Keep in mind, however, that the performance of rechargeable batteries can deteriorate over time due to repeated draining and charging. So, if your three-year-old laptop that you use every day does not seem to be holding a charge quite as well as it did three years prior, that may not be indicative of anything other than natures conforming to the laws of physics.

Your device seems to run hotter than before

Malware running the background uses CPU cycles and can cause a device to run physically hotter than before. You may hear internal cooling fans going on louder or more often than you usually do, or you may feel that the device is physically hotter to the touch.

File contents have been changed

If the contents of files have changed without you changing them and without you running any software that you expect would change them, something may be seriously amiss. Of course, if you let other people use your computer and gave them access to the files in question, before blaming malware or a hacker, be sure to check with the people you let use the computer whether they made any changes either on purpose or by accident.

Files are missing

If files seem to have disappeared without you deleting them and without you running any software that you expect might delete them, something may be seriously amiss. Of course, technical failures and human mistakes can also cause files to disappear — and, if you let someone else use your computer, that person may be the culprit.

Websites appear different than before

If someone has installed malware that is *proxying* on your device — that is, sitting between your browser and the Internet and relaying the communications between them (while reading all the contents of the communications and, perhaps, inserting various instructions of its own) — it may affect how some sites display and/or cause some sites, apps, or features within either or both, to malfunction.

Your Internet settings show a proxy, and you never set one up

If someone has configured your device to use their server as a proxy, that party may be attempting to read data sent to and from your device and may try to modify the contents of your session or even seek to hijack it altogether.

Some legitimate programs do configure Internet proxies — but such proxy information should show up when the software is installed and initially run, not suddenly after you click on a questionable link or download a program from a less-than-trustworthy source. (See Figure 3-5.)

FIGURE 3-5:
Internet
connections
configured to use
a proxy. If you do
not use a proxy
and suddenly one
appears listed in
your Internet
settings,
something is
likely amiss.

Some programs (or apps) stop working properly

If apps that you know used to work properly on your device suddenly stop functioning as expected, you may be experiencing a symptom of either proxying or malware interfering with the apps' functionality.

TIP

Of course, if such a problem develops immediately after you perform an operating system update, the update is a far more likely source of the issue than is something more sinister (assuming, of course, that you did not install the update after downloading it from a questionable source).

Security programs have turned off

If the security software that you normally run on your device has suddenly been disabled, removed, or configured to ignore certain problems, it may be a sign that a hacker (or malware) has penetrated your device and has turned off its defenses to prevent both the attacker's efforts from being blocked as well as to ensure that you do not receive warnings as the attacker carries out various additional nefarious activities.

An increased use of data or text messaging (SMS)

If you monitor your smartphone's data or SMS usage and see greater usage figures than you expect, especially if that increase begins right after some suspicious event, it may be a sign that malware is transmitting data from your device to other parties. You can even check your data usage per app — if one of them looks like it is using way too much data for the functionality that it provides, something may be amiss.

WARNING

If you installed the app from a third-party app store, you can try deleting the app and reinstalling it from a more trusted source. Keep in mind, however, that if malware is on your device, reinstalling the app may not always fix the problem, even if the app was the original source of the infection.

Increased network traffic

If you monitor your device's Wi-Fi or wired network usage and see greater levels of activity than you expect, especially if that increase begins right after some suspicious event, it may be a sign that malware is transmitting data from your device to other parties.

TIP

On some systems, you can even check your data usage per app — if one or more apps look like they are using way too much data for the functionality that they provide, something may be amiss. If you installed the app in question from a less-than-reliable source, you can try deleting the app and reinstalling it from a more trusted source — but if malware is present on your device, reinstalling the app that it brought to the device may not always fix the problem, even if the app was, in fact, the original source of the infection.

TIP

You can check how much data your computer is using — and even how much each program is using — by installing a bandwidth monitor program on the device in question.

Keep in mind that different types of apps can use wildly different amounts of bandwidth. An app used for sending email messages, for example, should usually be using no more than a tiny fraction of the bandwidth used by someone's Netflix app if that user streams and watches shows and/or movies on a regular basis.

Unusual open ports

Computers and other Internet-connected devices communicate using "ports" that can be thought of as numbered ports virtually lined up along the device as if they were piers along the coast. Communications for different applications typically enter the device via different ports. Ports are numbered, and most port numbers should always be *closed* — that is, not configured to allow communications in.

TIP

If ports that are not normally open on your computer are suddenly open and you did not just install software that could be using such ports, it is usually indicative of a problem. If you use Windows — especially if you understand a little about networking — you can use the built-in `netstat` command to determine which ports are open and what is connecting to your device.

Your device starts crashing

If your computer, tablet, or smartphone suddenly starts to crash on a much more frequent basis than in the past, malware may be running on it. Of course, if you just upgraded your operating system, installed or updated drivers for hardware components, or installed some significant new software package, that is a more likely source for the problem.

WARNING

If you are regularly seeing screens like the Blue Screen of Death (see Figure 3-6), or other screens indicating that your computer suffered a fatal error and must be restarted, you have a problem. It may be technical, or it may be due to corruption from malware or a hacker.

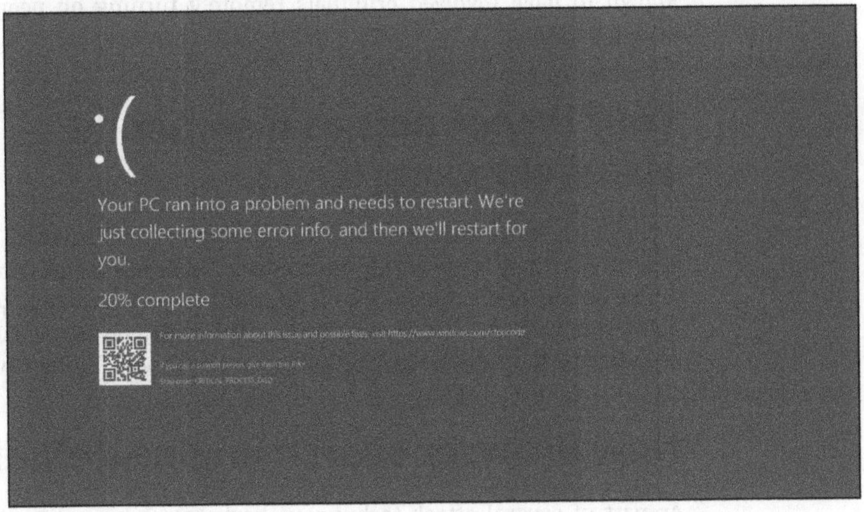

:(

Your PC ran into a problem and needs to restart. We're just collecting some error info, and then we'll restart for you.

20% complete

For more information about this issue and possible fixes, visit https://www.windows.com/stopcode

If you call a support person, give them this info:
Stop code: CRITICAL_PROCESS_DIED

FIGURE 3-6: The modern version of the notorious Blue Screen of Death that appears after a severe crash of a computer running Microsoft Windows 10.

Your cellphone bill shows unexpected charges up to here

Criminals are known to have exploited compromised smartphones in order to make expensive overseas phone calls on behalf of a remote party proxying through the device. Likewise, they can use a breached device to send SMS messages to international numbers and can ring up various other phone charges in other ways.

Unknown programs request access

Most security software for computers warns users when a program first attempts to access the Internet. If you receive such warnings and you don't recognize the program that is seeking access, or you recognize the program but can't understand why it would need to access the Internet (for example, Windows Calculator or Notepad), something may be amiss.

External devices power on unexpectedly

If one or more of your external input devices (including devices such as cameras, scanners, and microphones) seem to power on at unexpected times (for example, when you're not using them), it may indicate that malware or a hacker is communicating with them or otherwise using them. There are attacks that are known to have involved criminals remotely turning on people's cameras and spying on them.

Your device acts as if someone else were using it

Malicious actors sometimes take over computers and use them via remote access almost as if they were sitting in front of the device's keyboard. If you see your device acting as if someone else is in control — for example, you see the mouse pointer moving or keystrokes being entered while you're not using your mouse or keyboard — it may be a sign that someone else is actually controlling the machine.

New browser search engine default

As part of several attack techniques, hackers are known to change the default search engine used by people browsing the web. If your own browser's default search engine changed and you did not change it, something may be amiss. (To check if your search engine changed, check the list of default applications by searching for "default apps" in the Windows search box.)

Your device password has changed

If the password to your phone, tablet, or computer changed without you changing it, something is wrong, and the cause is likely something serious.

Pop-ups start appearing

WARNING

Various strains of malware produce pop-up windows asking the user to perform various actions (see Figure 3-7). If you're seeing pop-ups, beware. Such malware is common on laptops, but it exists for some smartphones as well.

Security Warning

Your Computer may be infected!!!

ZeuS.Zbot.aoaq is a new Trojan virus that steals banking passwords and financial account data.

Your antivrus can not block this threat and a comprehansive check-up is required in order to protect your personal data.

CALL NOW!!! 1-844-839-7975

FIGURE 3-7:
This pop-up window from adware malware attempts to scare people into purchasing bogus security software.

Keep in mind that pop-ups that appear when you're not using a web browser are a big red flag, as are pop-ups advising you to download and install "security software" or to visit websites of questionable repute. Pop-ups should never appear on an Android device.

New browser add-ons appear

You should be prompted before any browser add-on is installed. If a new add-on is installed without your knowledge, it likely indicates a problem. Some malware is delivered in poisoned versions of various browser toolbars.

New browser home page

As part of several attack techniques, hackers are known to change the home page of users' browsers. If your own browser's home page changed and you did not change it, something may be amiss.

Your email from the device is getting blocked by spam filters

If email that you send from the device in question used to be able to reach intended recipients with no problem, but is suddenly getting blocked by spam filters, it may be a sign that someone or something altered your email configuration in order to relay your messages through some server that is allowing an attacker to read, block, or even modify, your messages, and which other security systems are flagging as problematic. There are also other possible causes, however, so if you cannot find the source of the issue, you may want to check with your network administrator, email provider, or Internet provider.

Your device is attempting to access "bad" sites

If you use your computer, tablet, or smartphone on a network that blocks access to known problematic sites and networks (many businesses, organizations, and government entities have such technology on both their internal and bring-your-own-device [BYOD] networks) and you find out that your device was trying to access such sites without your knowledge, your device is likely compromised.

You're experiencing unusual service disruptions

If your smartphone seems to be suddenly dropping calls in locations with good cellular signal, or if you find your device unable to make calls altogether at times when you appear to have ostensibly good signal strength, something may be amiss.

TIP

If you hear strange noises during your phone conversations, something may also be amiss, and someone may even be listening in to, joining, or recording, your conversations.

Keep in mind that in most cases, the symptoms described here emanate from technical issues unrelated to a breach. However, in some cases, a breach is the reason for such ailments. So, if you noticed the relevant symptoms shortly after you took some action that you now question or regret, you may want to consider whether you need to take corrective action (see Book 3, Chapter 4).

Your device's language settings changed

People rarely change the language settings on their computers after performing the initial language setup procedure upon acquiring their devices or upon configuring a new keyboard, and few software packages change such settings either. So, if your computer is suddenly displaying menus and/or prompts in a foreign language or even has a language installed that you never installed, something is likely wrong.

You see unexplained activity on the device

If, on your device, you see emails in your Sent folder that you did not send, your device or email account was likely compromised. Likewise, if files that you're certain that you never downloaded appear in your Downloads folder, someone else may have downloaded them to your device.

You see unexplained online activity

If your social media account has social media posts that you're certain that neither you nor any app that you have authorized made, something is clearly amiss. It may be that your account was breached, and your devices are all secure, or it may be that one of your devices with access to the account was breached and became the conduit for the unauthorized access to your account.

The same is true if you see videos that you never ordered appearing in your previous rentals of a video streaming service, purchases that you never made appearing in your order history at an online retailer, and so on.

Your device suddenly restarts

While restarts are an integral part of many operating system updates, they should not happen suddenly outside the context of such updates. If your device is regularly rebooting without your approval, something is wrong. The only question is whether the problem emanates from a security breach or from some other issue.

TIP

It is generally a good idea to reboot your devices on a regular basis, as devices that are not rebooted for a long time are more likely to suffer from problems emanating from the repeated use of applications that do not properly release memory and other resources after completing their utilization of such resources.

You see signs of data breaches and/or leaks

Of course, if you know that some of your data has leaked, you should try to determine the source of the problem — and the process of checking obviously includes examining for signs of problems on all your smartphones, tablets, and computers.

You are routed to the wrong website

If you're sure that you typed in a correct URL, but were still routed to the wrong website, something is amiss. The problem may reflect a security breach elsewhere, but it could indicate that someone has compromised your device as well.

If the misrouting happens from only one or more particular devices, but not from others on the same network, the odds are that the devices in question were compromised. A hacker or malware could have configured poisoned routing tables on your device, for example. If you see that you are being incorrectly routed from multiple devices but only when they are connected to a particular network, or that a device that routes properly when connected to other networks routes improperly when connected to a particular network, networking equipment from that network, or a provider of routing services (such as DNS) to that network may have been compromised.

In any case, never perform any sensitive task (such as logging into a website) from a device that is routing you incorrectly. Even better, don't use the device at all (other than for debugging) until you figure out what is going on.

Your hard drive or SSD light never seems to turn off

If your hard drive or solid state drive (SSD) light remains on constantly, or near constantly, malware may be doing something to the drive. Of course, hard drive and SSD lights can come on for legitimate reasons when you are not actively using a computer — and, sometimes, a legitimate reason such as the system optimizing the disk in the background or performing a search for malware will cause the light to be on for quite some time — so don't panic if the light being on is the only sign that something might be amiss.

Other abnormal things happen

It is impossible to list all the possible symptoms that malware can cause a device to exhibit. So, if you keep in mind that parties are seeking to hack into your systems, and that anomalous behavior by your device may be a sign of problems, you increase your odds of noticing when something seems off — and, of properly responding to a breach if one does, in fact, occur.

Chapter **4**

Recovering from a Security Breach

OMG! It happened.

You've discovered that you've suffered a data breach.

Now what?

Read this chapter, which discusses how to respond in these types of situations.

An Ounce of Prevention Is Worth Many Tons of Response

REMEMBER

When it comes to recovering from a security breach, there simply is no substitute for adequate preparation. Simply put, no amount of post-breach expert actions can deliver the same level of protection as proper pre-breach prevention.

If you follow the various techniques described throughout this book about how to protect your electronic assets, you're likely to be in far better shape to recover from a breach than if you did not. Of course, preparation not only helps you reduce the risks of suffering a breach in the first place, but can also help you recover and help ensure that you can detect a breach if one occurs. Without proper preparation, you may not even be able to determine that a breach occurred, never mind contain the attack and stop it. (If you're unsure whether you've suffered a breach, see Book 3, Chapter 3.)

Stay Calm and Act Now with Wisdom

A normal human reaction to a cyber breach is to feel outraged, violated, and upset. It is also normal to experience some level of panic. To properly respond to a breach, however, you need to think logically and clearly and act in an orderly fashion. Spend a moment to tell yourself that everything will be all right, and that the type of cyberattack with which you are dealing is one that most successful people and businesses will likely have to deal with at some point (or at many points).

WARNING

Likewise, don't act irrationally. Do not attempt to fix your problem by doing a Google search for advice. Plenty of people online provide bad advice. Even worse, plenty of rogue websites with advice on removing malware and stopping attacks deposit malware on computers accessing them! Obviously, do not download security software or anything else from questionable sites.

Also, keep in mind that you need to act ASAP. Stop whatever else you're doing and focus on fixing the problem. Shut down any programs that you're using, save (and back up onto media that you will scan for malware before you reuse) any open documents and so on, and get to work on recovering from the breach.

REMEMBER

When a breach occurs, time usually works against you. The sooner that you stop someone from stealing your files, corrupting your data, or attacking additional devices on your network, the better off you will likely be.

Bring in a Pro

Ideally, you should bring in a cybersecurity professional to help you recover. While this book gives you good guidance, when it comes to technical skills, there is simply no substitute for the years of experience that a good pro has.

TIP

You should apply the same logic and seek professional help when faced with a serious computer and data crisis as you would if any of the following were true:

>> If you were seriously ill, you'd go to the doctor or hospital.

>> If you were arrested and charged with a crime, you'd hire a lawyer.

>> If the IRS sent you a letter that you're being audited, you'd hire an accountant.

Recovering from a Breach without a Pro's Help

TIP

If you do not have the ability to bring in a pro, the following steps are those that you should follow. These steps are essentially the ones most professionals follow:

1. Figure out what happened (or is happening).

2. Contain the attack.

3. Terminate and eliminate the attack.

Step 1: Figure out what happened or is happening

If possible, you want to figure out as much about the attack as possible so that you can respond accordingly. If an attacker is transferring files from your computer to another device, for example, you want to disconnect your device from the Internet ASAP.

That said, most home users do not have the technical skills to properly analyze and understand exactly what the nature of a particular attack may be — unless, of course, the attack is overt in nature (see Book 3, Chapter 3).

Gather as much information as you can about

>> What happened

>> What information systems and databases were hit

>> What could a criminal or other mischievous party do with the stolen material

>> What data and programs have been affected

WHEN AN ATTACK GOES UNDETECTED

The lack of expertise in this area by the average person should not be surprising. Most businesses that are breached, including many with their own information security professionals on staff, do not even discover that they have been successfully breached until months after the attackers began attacking! Some experts estimate that, on average, businesses do not discover non-overt information-security compromises until somewhere between six months and a year have elapsed since the initial breach occurred!

>> Who, besides yourself, may face risks because of the breach (this includes any potential implications for your employer)

>> What other parties (if any) need to be notified ASAP of the breach

REMEMBER

Do not spend a lot of time on this step — you need to take action, not just document — but the more information that you do have, the greater the chances that you will be able to prevent another similar attack in the future.

Step 2: Contain the attack

Cut off the attacker by isolating the attacker from the compromised devices. Containing may entail:

>> **Terminating all network connectivity ASAP:** To terminate network connectivity for all devices on a network, turn off your router by unplugging it. (*Note:* If you're in a business setting, this step is usually not possible.)

>> **Unplugging any Ethernet cables:** Understand, however, that a network-borne attack may have already spread to other devices on the network. If so, disconnect the network from the Internet and disconnect each device from your network until it is scanned for security problems.

>> **Turning off Wi-Fi on the infected device:** Again, a network-borne attack may have already spread to other devices on the network. If so, disconnect the network from the Internet and disconnect each device from your network by turning off Wi-Fi at the router and any access points, not just on the infected computer.

>> **Turning off cellular data:** In other words, put your device into airplane mode.

» **Turning off Bluetooth and NFC:** Bluetooth and NFC are both wireless communication technologies that work with devices that are in close physical proximity to one another. All such communications should be blocked if there is a possibility of infections spreading or hackers jumping from device to device.

» **Unplugging USB drives and other removable drives from the system:** *Note:* The drives may contain malware, so do not attach them to any other systems.

» **Revoking any access rights that the attacker is exploiting:** If you have a shared device and the attacker is using an account other than yours to which the attacker somehow gained authorized access, temporarily set that account to have no rights to do anything.

TIP

If, for some reason, you need Internet access from your device in order to get help cleaning it up, turn off all other devices on your network, to prevent any attacks from spreading over the network to your device. Keep in mind that such a scenario is far from ideal. You want to cut off the infected device from the rest of the world, not just sever the connections between it and your other devices.

Step 3: Terminate and eliminate the attack

Containing an attack (see preceding section) is not the same thing as terminating and eliminating an attack. Malware that was present on the infected device is still present after disconnecting the device from the Internet, for example, as are any vulnerabilities that a remote hacker or malware may have exploited in order to take control of your device. So, after containing the attack, it is important to clean up the system.

TERMINATING NETWORK CONNECTIVITY

While you can disconnect your Internet connection by physically unplugging from the router or network connection, you can also disable the connection on your device(s).

To terminate network connectivity on a Windows computer, follow these steps:

1. Type Network Connections in the Windows search box and select the View network connections option.

2. Right-click on the relevant connection (or connections one at a time) and then click on Disable.

The following sections describe some steps to follow at this point:

Boot the computer from a security software boot disk

While most modern users will not have a security software boot disk, if you do have one, boot from it. If you do not have one, please skip to the next section.

1. Remove all USB drives, DVDs, CDs, floppies (yes, some people still have them), and any other external drives from your computer.

2. Insert the boot disk into the CD/DVD drive.

3. Shut down your computer.

4. Wait ten seconds and push the power button to start your computer.

5. If you are using a Windows computer and it does not boot from the CD, turn the machine off, wait ten seconds, and restart it while pressing the BIOS-boot button (different computers use different buttons, but most use some F-key, such as F1 or F2) to go into the BIOS settings and set it to boot from the CD if a CD is present, before trying to boot from the hard drive.

6. Exit the BIOS and Reboot.

If you're using a Windows PC, boot the computer in Safe Mode. Safe Mode is a special mode of windows that allows only essential system services and programs to run when the system starts up. To do this, follow these steps:

1. Remove all USB drives, DVDs, CDs, floppies (yes, some people still have them), and any other external drives from your computer.

2. Shut down your computer.

3. Wait ten seconds and push the power button to start your computer.

4. While your computer is starting, press the F8 key repeatedly to display the Boot Options menu.

5. When the Boot Options menu appears, select the option to boot in Safe Mode.

If you're using a Mac, boot it with Safe Boot. MacOS does not provide the full equivalent of Safe Mode. Macs always boot with networking enabled. Its Safe Boot does boot cleaner than a normal boot. To Safe Boot, follow these steps:

1. Remove all USB drives, DVDs, CDs, floppies (yes, some people still have them), and any other external drives from your computer.

2. Shut down your computer.

3. **Wait ten seconds and push the power button to start your computer.**

4. **While your computer is starting, hold down the Shift key.**

TIP

Older Macs (macOS versions 6–9) boot into a special superuser mode without extensions if a user presses the hold key during reboot. The advice to boot with Safe Boot applies only to Macs running more recent operating systems.

Back up

Hopefully you can ignore this section, because you paid attention to the advice in the chapter on backups (Book 3, Chapter 5), but if you have not backed up your data recently, do so now. Of course, backing up a compromised device is not necessarily going to save all your data (because some may already be corrupted or missing), but if you do not already have a backup, do so now — ideally by copying your files to an external USB drive that you will not attach to any other devices until it is properly scanned by security software.

TIP

Do not back up a potentially compromised device to your usual backup data store — keep that drive disconnected from the potentially compromised equipment. Back up to some other media. And, of course, do not overwrite any other backups with the backup of the compromised device.

Delete junk (optional)

At this point, you may want to delete any files that you do not need, including any temporary files that have somehow become permanent (a list of such files appears in Book 3, Chapter 5).

Why do the deletion now?

Well, you should be doing periodic maintenance, and, if you are cleaning up your computer now, now is a good time. The less there is for security software to scan and analyze, the faster it will run. Also, some malware hides in temporary files, so deleting such files can also directly remove some malware.

For users of Windows 10 or Windows 11 computers, one easy way to delete temporary files is to use the built-in Disk Cleanup utility:

1. **In the search box on the taskbar, type** disk cleanup.

2. **Select Disk Cleanup from the list of results.**

3. **Select the drive you want to clean up and then click OK.**

4. **Select the file types to get rid of and then click OK.**

Run security software

Hopefully, you already have security software installed. If you don't, that may be the reason why you are dealing with the compromise in the first place! If you do have security software installed, run a full system scan. One important caveat: Security software running on a compromised device may itself be compromised or impotent against the relevant threat (after all, the security breach took place with the security software running), so, regardless of whether such a scan comes up clean, it may be wise to run the security software from a bootable CD or other read-only media, or, in cases of some products, from another computer on your home network.

Not all brands of security software catch all variants of malware. Security professionals doing a device "clean up" often run security software from multiple vendors.

If you are using a Mac and your Safe Boot includes Internet access, run the security software update routines prior to running the full scan.

Malware, or attackers, may add new files to a system, remove files, and modify files. They may also open communication ports. Security software should be able to address all of these scenarios. Pay attention to the reports issued by the security software after it runs. Keep track of exactly what it removed or repairs. This information may be important, if, for example, some programs do not work after the cleanup. (You may need to reinstall programs from which files were removed or from which malware-modified files malware was removed.) Email databases may need to be restored if malware was found within messages and the security software was unable to fully clean the mess up.

Security software report information may also be useful to a cybersecurity or IT professional if you end up hiring one at a later date. Also, the information in the report may provide you with clues as to where the attack started and what enabled it to happen, thereby also helping to guide you on preventing it from recurring.

Security Software often detects, and reports about, various non-attack material that may be undesirable due to their impact on privacy or potential to solicit a user with advertisements. You may, for example, see alerts that security software has detected tracking cookies or adware; neither is a serious problem, but you may want to remove adware if the ads bother you. In many cases you can pay to upgrade the software displaying the ads to a paid version that lacks ads. As far as recovering from an attack is concerned, these undesirable items are not a problem.

Sometimes, security software will inform you that you need to run an add-on in order to fully clean a system. Symantec, for example, offers its Norton Power Eraser, that it says "Eliminates deeply embedded and difficult-to-detect crimeware that traditional virus scanning doesn't always detect." If your security software informs you that you need to run such a scanner, you should do so, but make sure that you obtain it from the legitimate, official, original source. Also, never download or run any scanner of such a sort if you are told to do so not as the result of running security software. Plenty of rogue pop-ups will advise you similarly, but install malware if you download the relevant "security software."

Reinstall Damaged Software

There are experts who recommend uninstalling and reinstalling any software package that you know was affected by the attack, even if the security software fixed it. While doing so is not usually necessary, don't forget about this advice, as if you do detect any problems using the software after system recovery, you may need to go back and uninstall and reinstall.

Restart the system and run an updated security scan

For Windows computers, after you have cleaned the system, restart it in Safe Mode with networking using the procedure described above (but selecting Safe Mode with Networking rather than Safe Mode), run the security software, download all updates, and run the security software scan again. If there are no updates, then you do not need to rerun the security software.

If you are using a Mac, Safe Boot already included networking so there is no reason to repeat the scan. Install all relevant updates and patches. If any of your software has not been updated to its latest version and may contain vulnerabilities, fix this during the cleanup.

TIP

If you have the time to do so, run the security software full scan again after you have installed all the updates. There are several reasons for doing so, including the fact that you want it to check your system using its own most-up-to-date information on malware and other threats, as well as the fact that you want its heuristic analysis engine to have a baseline of what the system looks like with its latest updates.

Erase all potentially problematic System Restore points

System Restore is a useful tool, but it can also be dangerous. If a system creates a restore point when malware is running on a device, for example, restoring to that point will likely restore the malware! After cleaning up a system, therefore, be sure to erase all system restore points that may have been created when your system was compromised. If you are unsure if a restore point may be problematic, erase it. For most users, this means that it may be good to erase all system restore points. To do this:

1. **Type** "Restore Point" **in the Windows search bar and select the Create a restore point option . . . even those that's counterintuitive given your goal.**

2. **In the System Properties window, select the drive that's protected with restore points and click the Configure button.**

3. **Click the Delete button to the right of the words "Delete all restore points for this drive."**

4. **Click Continue in the dialog box that pops up.**

Restore modified settings

Some attackers and malware may modify various settings on your device. What page you see when you start your web browser — for example, your web browser home page — is one common item that malware commonly changes. It is important to change the browser page back to a safe page as the malware's starting page might lead to a page that reinstalls malware or performs some other nefarious task. The following sections walk you through the process for each browser.

REMEMBER

When using the phone or tablet versions of the browsers described in the following sections, the process will differ slightly, but should be simply discernable based on the instructions.

IN CHROME

To reset the Chrome browser:

1. **Click the three-dot menu icon in the top-right corner.**

2. **Click Settings.**

3. **Scroll down to the On Startup section and configure it accordingly.**

IN FIREFOX

To reset the Firefox browser:

1. Click the three-line menu icon in the top-right corner.

2. Click Options.

3. Click Home.

4. Configure the values in the New Windows and Tabs section accordingly.

IN SAFARI

To reset the Safari browser:

1. Click the Safari menu.

2. Click Preferences.

3. Select the General tab.

4. Scroll down to the Homepage field and configure it accordingly.

IN EDGE

To reset the Edge browser:

1. Click the three-dot menu icon in the top-right corner.

2. Click Settings.

3. Configure the Open Microsoft Edge with and Open new tabs with sections accordingly.

Rebuild the system

Sometimes it is easier, instead of following the aforementioned processes, to simply rebuild a system from scratch. In fact, because of the risk of security software missing some problem, or of user mistakes when performing the security cleanup, many experts recommend that, whenever possible, one should rebuild a system entirely after a breach.

Even if you plan to rebuild a system in response to a breach, it is still wise to run a security software scan prior to doing so as there are some rare forms of malware that can persist even after a restore (such as BIOS reprogramming malware, certain boot sector viruses, and so on), and to scan all devices on the same network as the compromised device at the time of the compromise or afterwards, so as to ensure that nothing bad can propagate back to the newly restored device.

Dealing with Stolen Information

If your computer, phone, or tablet was breached, it is possible that sensitive information on it was stolen. That data may be misused now or in the future, either by the party that stole it, or by another party to whom the original data thief sold or gave it.

As such, you should change any of your passwords that were stored on the device, for example, and check all accounts that were accessible from the device without logging in (due to your earlier setting of the device to "Remember Me" after a successful login) to ensure that nothing goes wrong. Obviously, if your passwords were stored in a strongly encrypted format the need to change them is less urgent than if they were stored in clear text or with weak encryption, but ideally, unless you are certain that the encryption will hold up for the long term, you should change them anyway.

TIP

If you suspect that information may have been taken that could be used to impersonate you, it may be wise also to initiate a credit freeze and file a police report. Keep a copy of the police report with you. If you are pulled over by a police officer who informs you that there is a warrant out for your arrest in some location where you have never been, for example, you will have proof that you filed a report that private information that could be used to steal your identity was stolen from you. Such a document may not prevent you from having problems entirely, but it certainly may make your situation better in such a scenario than it would be if you had no such proof.

If you believe that your credit or debit card information was stolen, contact the relevant party at the phone number printed on the back of your card, tell them that the number may have been compromised, and ask them to issue you a new card with a new number. Also check the account for any suspicious transactions.

Keep a log of every call you make, when you made it, with whom you spoke, and what occurred on the call. If the fact that information may have been stolen could impact other people you should, in most cases, notify them of what happened as well.

REMEMBER

The more sensitive that information is, the more important it is to take action and to take it quickly.

Here are some ways to think of information:

>> **Not private, but can help criminals with identity theft:**

- Names, address, and home telephone number.

- This type of information is really available to anyone who wants it, even without hacking you. (Consider that a generation ago this type of information was literally published in phone books and sent to every home that had a phone line.) That said, this type of information can be used in combination with other information to commit all sorts of crimes, especially if unsuspecting other people make mistakes (for example, by allowing someone with this information to open a library card without ever producing identification documents).

- Other public-record information: The price that you paid for your home, the names of your children, and so on. While this information is public record, a criminal correlating it with other information that may be lifted from your computer could create issues for you.

>> **Sensitive:** Email addresses, cellphone numbers, credit card account numbers without the CVC code, debit cards account numbers that require a PIN to use or without a CVC code, ATM card numbers, student ID numbers, passport numbers, complete birthdays including the year, and so on. These items create security risks when compromised — for example, a stolen email address may lead to sophisticated phishing attacks that leverage other information garnered from your computer, attempts at hacking into the account, spam emails, and so on. Also, this type of stolen information may be used by a criminal as part of identity theft and financial fraud crimes, but may require combining multiple pieces of information in order to create a serious risk.

>> **More sensitive:** Social Security numbers (or their foreign equivalents), passwords to online accounts, bank account numbers (when compromised by a potential criminal as opposed to when displayed on a check given to a trusted party), PINs, credit and debit card information with the CVC code, answers to challenge questions that you have used to secure accounts, and so on. These types of information can often be abused on their own.

Paying ransoms

If you have proper backups, you can remove ransomware the same way that you remove other malware. If any data gets lost in the process, you can restore it from backups.

If you have been hit with over ransomware and do not have proper backups, however, you may face a difficult decision. Obviously, it is not in the common interest for you to pay a ransom to a criminal in order get your data back, but in some cases, if your data is important to you, that may be the route that you need to go. In many cases, criminals will not even give you your data back if you do pay the ransom — so, by paying a ransom, you may not only waste money, but still suffer a permanent loss of your data. You will need to decide if you want to take that chance. (Hopefully, the information in the preceding few sentences will serve as a strong motivator for readers to back up proactively as discussed in Book 3, Chapter 5, rather than to rely on paying ransoms as a possible method of addressing ransomware attacks.)

The best defense for home users against the impact of ransomware is to back up and keep the backups disconnected from anything else!

REMEMBER

Before paying a ransom, consult an information security expert and a lawyer.

Consult a cybersecurity expert

TIP

Speaking with the cybersecurity expert is important, because some ransomware can be removed, and its effects undone, by various security tools. However, unless your security software tells you that it can undo the encryption done by ransomware, do not try to remove ransomware on your own once it has encrypted your data. Some advanced ransomware wipes the data permanently if it detects attempts to decrypt the data. Also, keep in mind that some advanced ransomware does not encrypt data, but rather removes it from the victim's device and only transmits it back if the ransom is paid. Such ransomware may be removable by security software, but security software cannot usually restore the data pilfered by the ransomware.

Consult a lawyer

Speaking with an attorney familiar with the relevant areas of law is important because, in some cases, paying a ransomware ransom can be a serious crime that could potentially land you in prison. Seriously!

While to date, the United States has not made it a crime to pay ransoms in general — although there are various ongoing efforts being made to influence legislators to enact such legislation — there are cases in which paying a ransom violates other laws.

For example, if criminals operating a particular ransomware system are under sanctions — meaning that it is a federal crime to conduct any financial transactions with them — it can be a felony to pay them a ransom in order to obtain access to your own data. While individuals have not, to date, been prosecuted by the U.S. government under such laws, at the end of the Trump administration's term, the federal government threatened to begin doing so, and regardless of who is in power, such enforcement is likely to become reality at some point in the not-so-distant future. After all, if sanctioned parties can easily become rich by perpetrating cybercrimes, and nobody is prosecuted for participating in the transactions that enrich them, what good are sanctions in the first place?

CYBER LIABILITY INSURANCE AND RANSOMS

Many cyber liability insurance policies cover ransomware ransom payments, and many do not. So, if you are securing an insurance policy in order to protect yourself against ransomware risks, make sure you have actually purchased an appropriate policy.

Also keep in mind that in some cases, paying a ransom may be illegal under federal law, or the laws of another jurisdiction. In such cases, an insurance company can potentially refuse to pay a ransom that it otherwise would have had to pay. As such, do not rely on cyber liability insurance to provide adequate protection from ransomware. Make sure you also act diligently to prevent problems.

Likewise, eventually, we may see prosecution of ransom payers under federal statues related to wire fraud and/or money laundering.

TIP

While the FBI generally officially recommends against paying ransoms, it is not the party that suffers the consequences of losing data when ransoms are not paid — the ransomware victims are. As such, many parties ignore the FBI's advice. Should the law mandate that ransoms not be paid, the FBI's instructions could potentially change from advice to a legal requirement.

Learning for the future

It is important to learn from breaches. If you can figure out what went wrong, and how a hacker managed to get into your systems (either directly or by using malware), you can institute de facto policies and procedures for yourself to prevent future such compromises. A cybersecurity professional may be able to help you vis-à-vis doing so.

Recovering When Your Data Is Compromised at a Third Party

Nearly all Internet users have received notification from a business or government entity (or both) that personal data was potentially compromised. How you address such a scenario depends on many factors, but the following sections tell you the essentials of what you need to know.

Reason the notice was sent

Multiple types of data breaches lead to organizations sending notifications. Not all of them represent the same level of risk to you, however. Notifications may be sent when a company has

>> Knowledge that an unencrypted database containing personal information was definitely stolen

>> Knowledge that an encrypted database containing personal information was definitely stolen

>> Detected unauthorized activity on a computing device housing your information

>> Detected unauthorized activity on a computing device, but not the one that houses your information (but on one connected to the same or logically connected network)

>> Detected the theft of credit or debit card numbers as can occur with a skimming device or the hacking of a point-of-sale credit card processing device

>> Discovered that there were, or may have been, improperly discarded computers, hard drives, or other storage media or paper-based information

>> Discovered that there was, or may have been, improperly distributed information, such as sensitive information sent to the wrong parties, unencrypted email sent to authorized parties, and so on

In all these cases, action may be warranted. But if a company notifies you that an unencrypted database of passwords including yours was stolen, the need to act is more urgent than if it detects unauthorized activity on a system on the same network as another machine containing only an encrypted version of your password.

Scams

Criminals see when a breach receives significant attention and often leverage the breach for their own nefarious purposes. One common technique is for crooks to send bogus emails impersonating the breached party. Those emails contain instructions for setting up credit monitoring or filing a claim for monetary compensation for the pain and inconvenience suffered due to the breach. Of course, the links in such messages point to phishing sites, sites that install malware, and other destinations to which you do not want to go.

Criminals also act quickly. In February 2015, for example, Better Business Bureaus across the United States started reporting complaints of emails impersonating Anthem, Inc., less than one day after the health insurance company announced that it had suffered a breach.

Passwords

One of the types of breaches most commonly reported in the mass media involves the theft of password databases. Modern password authentication systems are designed to provide some protection in case of a breach. Passwords are usually stored in a *hashed format*, meaning that they are stored with one-way encryption. When you enter your password during an attempt to log in, what you type is hashed and then compared with the relevant hash value stored in the password database. As such, your actual password is not stored anywhere and is not present in the password database. If a hacker steals a password database, therefore, the hacker does not immediately obtain your password.

At least that is how things are supposed to work.

In reality, however, not all authentication systems are implemented perfectly; hashed password databases have multiple exploitable weaknesses, some of which can help criminals decipher passwords even when they're hashed. For example, if a criminal looks at the database and sees that the hashed password for many people is the same, it is likely to be a common password (maybe even "password"), which often can be cracked quickly. There are defenses against such attacks, but many authentication systems do not use them.

As such, if you are notified by a company that it has been breached and that an encrypted version of your password was stolen, you should probably reset the password. You don't need to panic, though. In most cases, your password was likely protected by the hashing (unless you selected a common, weak password, which, of course, you should not have). If, for some reason, you have reused the compromised password on other sites that you don't want unauthorized parties to log in on as you, you should reset your password there as well and don't reuse the new password this time!

REMEMBER

Keep in mind that every so often hash functions are rendered obsolete and vulnerable. So, if a party is using outdated software, the hashed versions of passwords may be far less secure than necessary.

Payment card information

If your credit card information or debit card information may have been compromised, take the following measures:

>> **Leverage credit monitoring services.** Breached firms often give those people potentially affected by the relevant breaches a free year or two of credit monitoring. While one should never rely on such services to provide full protection against identity theft, using such services does have benefit. Being that the cost to you is only a few minutes of time to set up an account, you should probably do so.

>> **Monitor your credit reports.** If you see any new accounts that you did not open, immediately contact the party involved. Remember, when it comes to fraud, the earlier that you report a problem, the less aggravation you are likely to suffer from it.

>> **Set up text alerts.** If your card issuer offers the capability to set up text alerts, use the feature. That way, you'll be notified when charges are made and can act quickly if something appears to be amiss.

>> **Check your monthly statements.** Make sure that you continue to receive your account's statements as you did before and that they are not being misdirected to someone else.

>> **Switch to e-statements.** If possible, set up your account to receive electronic monthly statements rather than physical statements and make sure that you receive an email and/or text message when each and every statement is issued. Of course, be sure to properly protect the email account and smartphone to which such messages are sent.

Government-issued documents

If your passport, driver's license, or other government-issued identity document has been compromised, you should contact the agency that issued the relevant document and ask how you should proceed. Document everything that you're told, including details as to who told you what, and when they did so. Keep a log of all calls that you make and what transpired on those calls.

You should also check online on the agency's website to see whether it offers instructions for such scenarios. In some cases, agencies will advise you to replace the document, which may necessitate a physical visit to an agency office. In other cases, the agency will advise you to do nothing, but will tag your account so that if the document is used for identification at other government agencies, those checking the ID will know to be extra vigilant (which, in itself, might be a reason to replace the document so that you do not encounter any extra aggravation when using it as ID).

School or employer-issued documents

If your school or employer ID information is compromised, you should immediately notify the issuer. Not only could the compromised information be used to social engineer your school or employer, but it may potentially be used to obtain sensitive information about you from either one, or to otherwise get you into trouble.

Social media accounts

If any of your social media accounts is compromised, immediately contact the relevant social media provider. All major platforms have mechanisms to address stolen accounts because all major platforms have had to deal with stolen accounts numerous times. Keep in mind that you may be asked to provide government ID to prove your identity as part of the account recovery process.

In such a situation, it is also often a good idea to warn people with whom you are connected on the compromised social media platform of the potential misuse of your account. If you make fully public posts on the platform housing the compromised account, you may wish to notify the public at large.

You can notify people via your non-compromised social media accounts that the compromised account has been compromised, so that if the party that took over the accounts attempts to perpetrate a scam using the account (such as by posting some request for money or the like), fewer people will fall prey. You can also use email, texting, or the phone to contact individual parties who may be put at risk.

Chapter **5**

Backing Up

While backing up your data sounds like a simple concept — and it is — actually implementing an efficient and effective backup routine is a bit more complicated. To properly back up, not only do you need to know about your backup options, but you also need to think about many other details, such as the location of your backups, encryption, passwords, and boot disks. In this chapter, you find out about all those backup details and more.

Backing Up Is a Must

In the context of cybersecurity, *backing up* refers to creating an extra copy, or extra copies, of data (that may consist of data, programs, or other computer files) in case the original is damaged, lost, or destroyed.

Backing up is one of the most important defenses against the loss of data, and, eventually, it's likely to save you from serious aggravation, as nearly everyone, if not everyone, will, at some point, want to access data to which they no longer have access.

In fact, such scenarios occur on a regular basis. Sometimes, they're the result of human error, such as a person inadvertently deleting a file or misplacing a computer or storage device. Sometimes, they're the result of a technical failure, such as a hard drive dying or an electronic device falling into water. And sometimes, they're the result of ransomware attacks or other hostile hacker action. And when it comes to ransomware, an ounce of prevention — having all of your valuable data backed up and ready to restore in an efficient manner — is often worth many tons of cure.

Sadly, many people believe that they back up all their data only to find out when something goes wrong that they do not have proper backups. Don't let that happen to you. Be sure to back up on a regular basis — often enough that if you had to restore from a backup, you would not panic. In general, if you're in doubt as to whether or not you are backing up often enough, you aren't.

TIP

Do not think of backups as being there for you if you ever lose data. Think of them being there for you *when* you lose data. At some point, essentially every person who uses electronic devices on a regular basis will lose data.

Backing Up Data from Apps and Online Accounts

While most of this chapter focuses on backing up data that resides on your laptop or other local computer data store, it is also important to back up data that resides not within your own "infrastructure," but which other parties house for you as a result of using their systems.

REMEMBER

If you store any data in the cloud or use a third-party service to host any of your systems or data, the party that owns the physical and/or virtual systems on which your data resides may or may not back it up — often without your knowledge or approval. If you store data on a Google Drive, for example, you have absolutely no control over how many copies Google makes of your data. Likewise, if you use a third-party service such as Facebook, any data that you upload to the social media giant's servers — regardless of the privacy settings you set for the uploads (or possibly even if you deleted them) — may be backed up by Facebook to as many backups as the firm so desires, in as many different locations as the firm desires.

In some cases, third-party backups resemble drive backups. While the provider has your data backed up, only you — the party who "owns" the data — can actually read it in an unencrypted form from the backup. In other cases, however, the backed-up data is available to anyone who has access to the backup.

That said, most major third parties have robust redundant infrastructure and backup systems in place, meaning that the odds that data stored on their infrastructure will remain available to users is extremely high when compared with data in most people's homes. However, risks still remain.

SMS texts

Your cellular service provider may provide backup capabilities for your SMS text messages, and your phone's operating system may provide general device backup features that include all SMS messages within the backups. If not, or if you choose not to use such backups, various apps can be downloaded from Google Play and Apple App Store that provide such features specifically.

Social media

Every major social media platform allows you to download all of your respective social media account's data. While many people seem to think that there is no reason to back up such data (after all, they reason, the social media provider does its own backups of all account data), there are actually good reasons to do so.

First, if your social media account were somehow breached and taken over by a hacker, and that hacker deleted material from the account, you may have difficulty getting the material back — even if you successfully regain access to the account. This is true even if the social media provider actually has a backup in its possession of your original data; remember, restoring your data is not its highest priority.

Second, there is no guarantee that social media providers will remain in business forever. People are fickle, and while certain mainstay platforms may seem now to be "too big to fail," that is most definitely not the case. Not that many years ago, MySpace was the dominant platform, with few people knowing about something called "The Face Book." How things have changed!

And while MySpace is still around in some form, Friendster, which had over 100 million users, and Yik Yak, which had a valuation of over $400 million, have vanished, taking with them to the history books any access to the data that they once held for people. Also gone are Google Plus and Vine, and while the companies that last operated them still exist as tech giants (Vine was acquired by Twitter), the platforms are dead and the material that was on them is no longer easily accessible.

Third, a social media provider itself may be hacked, or otherwise go offline. Not that long ago, the right-wing social media network, Parler, for example, went offline completely for a period of many months. People who wanted to access their accounts could not do so.

While the exact mechanisms of backing up data vary between platforms, there is typically a function within the settings or help menus called Download Account Data or something of the like. You should periodically use it.

WhatsApp

WhatsApp, which was acquired by Facebook (now known as Meta) in 2014, is arguably the world's most popular tool for communication; its operator claims that the tool has more than 2 billion users worldwide.

To back up your Android device's WhatsApp data, go into the Settings menu in the top-right corner of your screen, tap Chats, tap Chat Backup, and either tap BACKUP to manually back up, or configure the appropriate settings for periodic automatic backups. On Apple devices, you can reach the Chat Backup feature by tapping Settings at the bottom-right corner of the screen, tapping Chats, and then tapping Chat Backup.

Google Photos

If you use Google Photos, you can also separately configure Google to sync copies of your photos and videos on your phone to storage space in the cloud (Google Drive). To do so, click your profile photo that appears in the top-right corner of the screen in the Google Photos app, click Photos Settings, click Backup & Sync, and turn on the feature accordingly.

Other apps

Many other apps offer backup capabilities. Look through the app's settings options, or check help forums online, if you have difficulty finding such features.

TIP

If you back up app data and store the backups on your laptop's local hard disk or solid state drive (SSD), and then back up that laptop drive as described in the following sections, you will have copies of your app backups within your laptop backups. If you typically use apps on a smartphone, ideally don't back up to only that device.

Backing Up Data on Smartphones

Both Google and Apple offer automatic syncing of data; using such a feature keeps a copy of your most recent data and also simplifies transferring your data when you upgrade to a new phone. Such syncing, however, also means that if you delete data, the deletions also sync. As such, you should still back up.

Android

Android provides two ways to back up your data and apps: automatic backups and by backing up manually.

Automatic backups

On Android versions 9 and later you can easily set up automatic backups as follows:

1. Tap the Google One app to open it.
2. Tap Storage.
3. In the device backup section, tap "Set up data backup."
4. Tap "Manage backup."
5. Set up what you want backed up, and how often, etc.

Depending on your phone's current configuration, you may receive additional instructions (such as to update a Google app necessary for the backups to run). If you do, follow such instructions. You may also be asked to allow Google apps to have access permissions needed to run the backups. Once your first backup has run you will see "On" listed below the data types that have been backed up.

Manual backups

You can run manual backups on Android at any point simply by opening the Settings app, tapping System, and then tapping Backup. Some Android phone manufacturers have slightly different menu schemes, so just search through the menus for the Backup or Backup Now option.

Apple

Apple offers several built-in ways to back up your iPhone (or other iOS device).

Backing up to iCloud

To back up your device to iCloud, run the Settings app, and tap your name at the top of the screen. You will then see an option for iCloud — tap it. You will then see a switch to turn on automatic backups to iCloud as well as a button to immediately launch a manual backup.

Backing up using iTunes

Apple lets you backup your Apple device to a Windows PC or to a Mac.

To back up on Windows:

1. **Run iTunes**

2. **Connect your device to your computer. (On modern Apple devices this is normally done using a USB to lighting cable — the USB side goes into the computer and the Lighting side goes into the Apple device.)**

   iTunes will start. If you have configured your device to require a password to unlock it this is when you will be prompted to enter it.

3. **Find where your device is displayed as an icon in iTunes and select it.**

4. **Click Summary.**

   Optionally (but you know what you should do) turn on "Encrypt local backup" and create a password to protect your backup.

5. **Click Back Up Now.**

To back up on a Mac:

1. **On modern Macs running the macOS Catalina operating system or later, open a Finder window.**

   Note: If you are using a Mac running an older version of macOS (macOS-Mojave or earlier) you will first need to open iTunes, then follow Steps 2–4 that follow.

2. **Connect your device to your Mac using a USB to lighting cable and enter your device password if prompted.**

3. **Select the icon for your iPhone as seen on your computer.**

   Optionally (but you know what you should do) turn on "Encrypt local backup" and create a password to protect your backup.

4. **Click Back Up Now.**

Conducting Cryptocurrency Backups

Because cryptocurrency is tracked on a ledger and not stored in a bank, backing up cryptocurrency involves backing up the private keys used to control the addresses in the ledger at which one has cryptocurrency, not backing up the cryptocurrency itself. Often, for security reasons, keys are not maintained electronically. They're printed on paper and stored in a bank vault or fireproof safe.

For those who use hardware wallets to store the keys to their cryptocurrency, the backup for the wallet device is often a *recovery seed*, which is a list of words that allows the device to re-create the keys needed for the relevant addresses. It is generally accepted that, for security reasons, the list of words should be written down on paper and stored in a bank vault and/or safe — not stored electronically.

REMEMBER

In most cases, anyone who obtains either aforementioned form of backup can easily transfer to themselves all of the related cryptocurrency — in which case you would likely have no way to recover what was taken.

Backing Up Passwords

Anytime that you back up lists of passwords, make sure to do so in a secure manner. For important passwords that do not change often and are not likely to be needed on an urgent basis, consider making no digital records of them at all. Instead, write them down on a piece of paper and put that paper in a bank safe deposit box.

Looking at the Different Types of Backups

Backups of your data can be categorized in many different ways. One important way of distinguishing various types of backups from one another is based on what is actually being backed up when a backup process runs. The following sections look at the different types of backups based on that approach.

Full backups of systems

A *full system backup* is a backup of an entire system, including the operating system, programs/apps, settings, and data. The term applies whether the device being backed up is a smartphone or a massive server in a data center.

Technically speaking, a full system backup includes a backup of all drives attached to a system, not just those mounted inside of it — although if some drives are attached to the system only from time to time and are not needed for the primary use of the system, some might exclude the contents of such drives from full system backups, especially if they're attached to other systems, or are backed up as part of the backup of other systems. For most home users, however, a full system backup means exactly what it sounds like: Backing up everything.

A full system backup is sometimes known as a *system image* because it essentially contains an image of the system as it existed at a particular point in time. If a device that you have an image of fails, you should be able to use the system image to re-create the entire system as it was at the time that the backup was made. When you use the rebuilt system, it should function exactly as the previous system did at the time of the backup.

WARNING

Full system backups typically do *not* include backing up any material that is accessible to a system via a network share. So, if your computer has a network drive mounted as N:, for example, a full system backup run on the device may not include the data you have stored on N:.

TIP

Full system backups are the form of backup that typically is fastest to restore an entire system from, but they take longer to create than other forms of backup. They also usually require more storage space.

One important caveat: Because a system backup includes settings, hardware drivers, and so on, restoring from a system image does not always work well if you restore to a different device than the one that was originally backed up. If you imaged a laptop that runs Windows 7 as its operating system, for example, and then acquired a newer device intended to run Windows 11, which has different hardware in it, a restored system image of the first device may not work well on the newer device. The reverse is even more likely to be true: If you keep an old computer in your closet "just in case" and that just-in-case situation turns into reality, your attempts to restore the image from a newer machine to the older machine may fail fully or in part.

TIP

System images are sometimes referred to as *ghosts* (with ghost also being the verb for creating such images), especially among techies. The name originates from one of the original disk cloning software packages for PCs.

WARNING

It is important to note that some backup software packages offer "full system backups" that do not truly image everything on a system. Always read the "fine print" when software provides information about a backup option.

Original system images

One special case of system images is the original system image, also known as a *factory image*.

Many modern computing devices, whether laptops, tablets, or smartphones, come equipped with a factory image that can be restored. This means that when you acquire the device, it comes with an image of the original configuration that you receive — including the operating system, all the original software, and all the default settings — stored in a hidden partition or other storage mechanism not normally accessible to users.

At any point in time, you can perform a *factory reset* and set your device to look identical to the way that it did when it was new. When you do so, the device restores from the hidden image.

WARNING

Three important caveats:

>> Some computers allow users to manually overwrite factory images if they so desire. It is highly recommended that you not do so. If you need more storage space, obtain it elsewhere.

>> Some devices overwrite the factory reset image with new images in the event of certain operating system upgrades.

>> If you factory reset a computer, all security updates installed since the factory image was originally created will not be present on the restored device. Be sure to update your system ASAP after restoring and before going online for any other purpose!

Later system images

Some systems also create periodic images that you can restore from without having to go back to the original factory settings. Windows 10 and Windows 11, for example, have such capabilities built in.

WARNING

Never restore from an image unless you know that any problems that developed and caused you to need to restore did so after that image was made.

Original installation media

Original installation media is for programs that you acquire and install after you purchased your device. If software came on a DVD, CD, or USB drive, saving the physical media that it came on allows you to reinstall the software in case of a problem.

WARNING

Keep in mind, however, that if any updates for the software were issued and installed subsequent to the original installation, you will need to redownload and reinstall the updates. Doing so may happen automatically upon reinstallation, or it may require manual effort.

Downloaded software

If you've acquired programs since you purchased your device, it's likely that some or all of them were delivered to you via digital download.

When software is delivered as a download, the downloader does not receive a physical copy. However, if you received software via a download, you can store a copy of the installation file that you downloaded on one or more of many different types of media, such as a thumb drive or a CD or DVD. Alternatively, you can store the copy on a hard drive, but be sure to back up that drive if it is part of your computer infrastructure.

In addition, some stores that sell downloadable software maintain copies of the software for you in a *virtual locker* so that you can download it at a later date. Such "backups" are useful, but be sure that you know how long the store will maintain the product in your locker. Some people have had serious problems because they relied on such "backups" only to find out that the software was not available to them at the time that they needed it.

TIP

For music and video files, the vendor's retention period is often theoretically forever, or at least as long as the material is available to purchase by others. For software, as new versions are released and old versions are *sunsetted* (the technical term for a software vendor phasing out and, ultimately, terminating support for an obsolete version of its software), the retention period may be far shorter.

Full backups of data

An alternative to performing a full backup of the entire system is to perform a full backup of the data on the system, but not of software and the operating system. (Configuration settings for both the operating system and various installed programs are often stored in data folders and included in such backups.) Performing a full data backup allows users to restore all of their data in one shot if something goes wrong. Depending on the tool used to perform the backup, users may be able to restore a subset of the data as well — for example, by choosing to restore only one particular file that they accidentally deleted.

REMEMBER

Restoring from a full data backup will not restore applications. If a system has to be rebuilt entirely, recovering from full backups of data likely requires prior restorations to factory settings (or a later image of the computer) and reinstallation of all software. That is certainly more tedious than simply restoring from a system image. At the same time, it is also far more portable. The recovery can usually be done without any problems on many devices that vary quite a bit from the original device. Reduce the likelihood of your restored system suffering a security breach by updating the reinstalled software with the latest patches immediately after the relevant installations.

Incremental backups

Incremental backups are backups made after a full backup and that contain copies of only the portion of data (or, in the case of a system backup, the portion of the entire system) that has changed since the preceding backup (full or incremental) was run.

Incremental backups normally run much faster than full backups because, on most systems, the vast majority of data files do not change on a regular basis. For the same reason, incremental backups also use less storage space than do full backups.

To recover data, however, restoration must be done from the last full backup plus all the incremental backups performed since that last full backup.

TIP

If you decide to use incremental backups, consider limiting the number of such backups that you create after a full backup. For example, if you did only one full backup on the first day of the calendar month and performed incremental backups on all subsequent days until the next month began, then if something went wrong on the last day of the month, you would potentially need to restore from as many as 30 backups in order to recover your files.

Many people (and many businesses as well) choose to do full system backups on one of the days of the weekend and then do incremental backups during each other day of the week, thereby finding a happy medium between the efficiency gains during the backup process and the potential for a tedious recovering process.

Differential backups

Differential backups contain all the files that changed since the last full backup. (They are similar to the first in a series incremental backups run after a full backup.) A series of differential backups therefore requires more time to run and uses more storage space than incremental backups, but less than the same number of full backups. Recovering from differential backups can be faster and simpler than doing so from incremental backups because a restore needs to be done from only the last full backup and last differential backup.

If you decide to use differential backups, consider how many backups you should be making before making the next full backup. If the differential backup starts to grow quite large, there will not be much performance gains while making the backup, and any restoration will take far longer than if done from just a full backup.

Many people (and many businesses as well) choose to do full system backups on one of the days of the weekend, and then do differential backups during each other day of the week.

Mixed backups

Incremental and differential backups are made in conjunction with full backups, as shown in Table 5-1.

A Comparison of Full, Incremental, and Differential Backups

	Full Backup	Incremental Backup	Differential Backup
Backup #1	All data	—	—
Backup #2	All data	Changes from Backup #1	Changes from Backup #1
Backup #3	All data	Changes from Backup #2	Changes from Backup #1

Do not mix incremental and differential backups within the same backup scheme, as doing so can create complexity and lead to confusion and costly mistakes.

Continuous backups

Continuous backups refers to backups that run continuously. Every time that a change is made to data (or to a system and data), a backup of that change is made.

Continuous backups are great in case of a hard drive failure in the primary system — the backup is available and up-to-date — but do little in the case of a malware infection or data destruction, as the malware typically propagates to the backup as soon as it infects the primary system.

One exception are complex backup systems that log each backup action and have the ability to reverse them. These backups can undo problematic portions of backups to the point that they occurred.

TIP

The process of continuously backing up is sometimes known as *syncing* (or *synchronizing*). You may see it described as such on your electronic devices or within various software packages.

Partial backups

Partial backups are backups of a portion of data. As opposed to full backups, partial backups do not back up all elements of data from a system. If a system were to be completely hosed, for example, you would have no way to fully recover all of its data contents from partial backups made earlier of that system.

Partial backups can be implemented in a full incremental-like model in which the first backup in a series includes all the elements that are part of the set included in the partial backup, and subsequent backups in the series include only items from that set that have changed.

Partial backups can also be implemented as always full-like — in which case, all elements of the set included in the partial backup are backed up each time, regardless of whether or not they have changed since the last backup.

REMEMBER

Partial backups are not intended to be full backups in case of a malware attack or the like. They are useful, however, in other situations, such as one in which a particular set of files needs to be backed up separately due to the needs of a particular individual or group or due to the sensitivity of the material. For example, while the IT department may do full and incremental backups of all files on a shared network drive, the accountants who need constant access to a particular set of spreadsheets stored on that drive — and would be unable to work if those files become inaccessible — may set up their own backups of just those files. They can use their backups if something goes wrong when they are on the road or working from home on the weekend, without the need to bother members of the technical support department to work unnecessarily on a Sunday.

Folder backups

Folder backups are similar to partial backups in situations where the set of items being backed up is a particular folder. While backup tools can facilitate folder backups, to the chagrin of many cybersecurity professionals and IT departments, many users perform such backups in an ad hoc fashion by manually making a copy of hard drive (or SSD) folders to USB drives at the end of each workday and consider such backups to be sufficient protection in case of problems.

Theoretically, of course, such backups work and can be used to recover from many problems. Reality dictates, however, that ad hoc backup procedures almost never result in proper backups: People forget on some days to back up or do not back up because they're hurried, neglect to back up some materials that they should have backed up, store the backups on insecure devices in insecure locations, or lose the devices on which the backups are stored — you get the idea!

If you want to be sure that you have proper backups when you need them — and, at some point, you are likely to need them — do not rely on ad hoc folder backups.

Never back up a folder onto the same drive as the original folder resides. If the drive fails, you will lose both the primary source of data as well as the backup copy.

TIP

Drive backups

A *drive backup* is similar to a folder backup, but for situations where an entire drive is being backed up instead of only a folder. Ad hoc backups of drives do afford some protection, but rarely deliver sufficient protection against risks of losing data.

Never store the backup of a drive on the same drive as the one being backed up. If the drive fails, you will lose the primary source of data and the backup copy.

WARNING

Virtual drive backups

One special case of drive backup is that in which a person or organization uses an encrypted virtual drive. For example, users may store their files within a BitLocker drive on Windows. BitLocker is a utility built in to many versions of Windows that allows users to create a *virtual drive* that appears as any other drive to the user when it is in use, but appears as one giant encrypted file when not in use. To access the drive, the user must unlock it, normally by entering a password.

Backing up such drives is often accomplished by simply including the encrypted file within the full, incremental, folder, or drive backup. As such, all contents of the encrypted drive are copied without being referred to by name and remain inaccessible to anyone who does not know how to open the encrypted drive. Many backup tools offer drive backups in addition to more structured forms of backup.

TIP

Some software packages refer to the creation of an image of an entire disk as *cloning*.

While such a scheme protects the contents of the encrypted drive as they live in backups by using the same encryption as was used for the primary copies, note several caveats:

>> **Even if one small change was made to a single file within the virtual drive, the entire encrypted file will be changed.** As such, a 1KB change could easily lead to an incremental backup having to back up an entire 1TB file.

>> **The backup is useless for recovery unless someone knows how to unlock the encrypted drive.** While encryption may be a good defense mechanism against unauthorized parties snooping on sensitive files in the backup, it also means that the backup is not, on its own, fully usable for recovery. It is not hard to imagine problems developing as a result — for example, if someone attempting to utilize a backup several years after it was originally made forgets the access code, or if the person who created a backup is unavailable at the time that someone needs to restore from it.

>> **As with all encrypted data, there is a risk that as computers become more powerful — and, especially, as quantum computing takes hold — today's encryption may not offer sufficient protection against brute force attacks.** While production systems will, no doubt, be upgraded with better encryption capabilities over time (as they already have been since the 56-bit encryption of the 1990s), backups that were made with old encryption technology and keys may become vulnerable to decryption by unauthorized parties. Hence, encryption may not forever protect your sensitive data contained in backups. You must store such backups in a secure location or destroy them when they are no longer needed.

Exclusions

Some files and folders do not need to be backed up unless you are imaging a disk (in which case the image must looks exactly like the disk). Operating system paging files and other temporary files that serve no purpose if a system is restored, for example, need not be backed up.

The following are examples of some such files and folders that you can exclude from backups on a Windows 10 machine. If you're using backup software, the software likely comes with a built-in list of default exclusions that may resemble this list:

>> **The Recycle Bin,** which effectively temporarily backs up deleted files in case users change their minds about deleting them

- » **Browser caches,** which are temporary Internet files from web browsers, such as Microsoft Edge or Internet Explorer, Firefox, Chrome, Vivaldi, or Opera

- » **Temporary folders,** which are often called Temp or temp and reside in c:\, in the user directory, or in the data directory of software

- » **Temporary files,** which are usually named *.tmp or *.temp

- » **Operating system swap files,** such as pagefile.sys

- » **Operating system hibernation-mode system image information,** such as hyberfil.sys

- » **Backups** (unless you want to back up your backups), such as Windows File History

- » **Operating system files backed up during an operating system upgrade,** as usually found in C:\Windows.old on Windows computers that have had their operating systems upgraded

- » **Microsoft Outlook cache files (*.ost),** but Outlook local data stores (*.pst) should be backed up (in fact, in many cases, they may be the most critical files in a backup)

- » **Performance log files** in directories called PerfLogs

- » **Junk files** that users create as personal temporary files to hold information, such as a text file in which users type a phone number that someone dictated to them, but that the users have since entered into their smartphone directory

To conserve storage space, some backup engines will also back up only one copy of an identical file that appears in two places instead creating two "links" to the contents of that file in the backup. Sometimes such a feature appears as an option in an Exclusions settings section.

In-app backups

Some applications have built-in backup capabilities that protect you from losing your work if your computer crashes, power fails, or you don't have battery power left.

One such program is Microsoft Word, which offers users the ability to configure how often files should be saved for AutoRecover. For most people, this feature is quite valuable.

While the mechanism of configuring AutoRecover varies between some versions of Word, in most modern versions, the process is the following or something similar: Choose File ⇨ Options ⇨ Save and configure the options according to your taste.

In-app backups usually take just seconds to configure, normally run without your being actively involved, and can save you a lot of aggravation. In almost all cases, you should enable the feature if it exists.

Figuring Out How Often You Should Backup

No simple one-size-fits-all rule applies as to how often you should backup your system and data. In general, you want to ensure that you never lose enough work that it would cause you significant heartache.

Performing a full backup every day requires the most amount of storage space for backups and also takes the most time to run. However, doing so means that more total copies of data are available — so, if a backup were to go bad at the same time as the primary data store, less data is likely to be lost — and fewer backups are required to perform a system or data restoration.

Performing a full backup everyday may be feasible for many individuals, especially those who can run the backups after work hours or while they are asleep at night. Such a strategy offers the best protection. With storage prices plummeting in recent years, the cost of doing so, which was once prohibitive for most individuals, is now affordable to most folks.

Some people and organizations choose to perform a weekly full backup and couple that backup with daily incremental or differential backups. The former strategy provides the fastest backup routine; the latter offers the faster recovery routine and reduces the number of backups needed in order to perform a restore to a maximum of two instead of seven.

In addition, consider using manual backups or an automated in-app backup scheme if you are working on important materials during the day. Using the in-app automated backups in Word, for example, can protect you from losing hours of work if your computer crashes. Likewise, copying documents to a second location can prevent losing significant work if your hard drive or SSD fails.

For apps that do not have in-app-auto-backup capabilities, some folks have suggested periodically using the Windows or Mac Send menu option to send to themselves via email copies of files that they are working on. While doing so is clearly not a formal backup strategy, it does provide a way of backing up work during the day between regular backups and often does so offsite, ensuring that if one's computer were to die suddenly, an entire day's worth of work would not be lost.

TIP

In general, if you are not sure if you are backing up often enough, you probably aren't.

Exploring Backup Tools

You can use multiple types of tools to create, manage, and restore from backups. Tools can automate various types of backups, for example, or can manage the process of a perpetual syncing backup. Backup tools come in wide variety of price ranges, depending on their robustness and scalability.

Backup software

Backup software is software designed specifically to run and manage backups and restorations from backups. You can find multiple vendors of such software, with exact features varying between products and between the platforms that they support (for example, features may vary between Windows and Mac versions of the same backup software package). Some offerings are intended for home users, some for large enterprises, and others for pretty much every level in between.

You can use backup software to manually or automatically backup — that is, you can configure it to backup specific systems, data, drives, or folders at specific times, using different backup models, such as full, incremental, and so on.

WARNING

Backups can run only if a machine is on. So, be sure that your device to be backed up is on at those times! (Some backup software can be configured in cases of a missed backup to run the backup the next time that the device is booted or is idle.)

TIP

Backup software can take some time to set up, but after you do so, it can often make the process of creating proper backups much easier than any other method of backing up.

Ideally, you should configure your systems to automatically back up at specific times to make sure that you actually back up and don't neglect doing so while you do any of the many things that come up in life.

WARNING

Do not confuse these manual and automatic options with manual and automated task copying.

If you just worked on some important project or spent many hours creating some new work on your computer, however, you may want to kick off an extra manual backup to protect your work and the time that you invested in it.

TIP

Beware of bogus backup software! Unscrupulous parties offer free backup software that contains malware of various severity, ranging from annoying adware to data-stealing infectors. Make sure that you obtain your backup software (as well as any other software that you use) from a reliable source.

Drive-specific backup software

Some external hard drives and solid state devices come with built-in backup software. Such software is often extremely intuitive and easy to use, and users may find it the most convenient way to set up their backup routines.

WARNING

Three caveats, however:

>> Remember not to leave the drive connected to the system holding the primary data store.

>> If you use drive-specific versions of backup software, you may need to purchase all your backup drives from the same manufacturer in order not to complicate backup and restore procedures.

>> Drive-specific software is less likely to support newer technologies as they emerge from other vendors than is general backup software.

Windows Backup

Windows comes equipped with basic backup software built in. The software sports several features, and, for many people, may be sufficient. Using Windows Backup is certainly better than not backing up at all.

Depending on if your Windows computer is running good ol' Windows 10 or the more up-to-date Windows 11, you can find backup settings by:

>> Clicking on the Start menu in Windows 10 and selecting Update & Security ⇨ Backup.

>> Clicking on the Start menu on your Windows 11 computer and selecting Settings ⇨ Accounts ⇨ Windows backup.

Additionally, a Windows File Backup utility automatically backs up files as you modify them. You can access its configuration options via the Control Panel File History option. If you have plenty of disk space and work efficiently, make sure that your files are backed up quite often.

For more on restoring files from Windows File History, see Book 3, Chapter 6.

Smartphone/tablet backup

Many devices come equipped with the ability to automatically sync your data to the cloud — a process that allows you to restore the data to a new device if your device is lost or stolen. Even devices that do not have this feature built in almost always can run software that effectively delivers these features for a specific folder tree or drive.

Using the sync feature provides great protection, but it also means that your data is sitting *in the cloud* — which, simply means that it is on someone else's computer — and potentially accessible to both the cloud-service provider (in the case of most smartphones, the provider would be Apple or Google), as well as to any government agencies that demand access to the relevant data while armed with a warrant, rogue insiders, or hackers who manage to somehow obtain access to it.

As discussed earlier, syncing also typically means that if you delete something on your device, it gets deleted from the synced copy (which means syncing is not sufficient on its own as a means of backing up).

REMEMBER

Even if you haven't committed any crimes, the government may still demand your data as part of data collection procedures related to crimes committed by other people. Even if you trust the government not to abuse your data, the government itself has had several breaches and data leaks, so you have good reason not to trust it to adequately protect your information from being stolen by other parties who may abuse it.

Before you decide whether or not to use the sync, think about the pros and cons.

Manual file or folder copying backups

Manual backups are exactly what they sound like: backups performed manually, often by people copying files, folders, or both from their primary hard drive (or solid-state drive) to a network folder or thumb drive.

WARNING

Manual backups have their purpose, but using them on their own is not usually a good backup strategy. People inevitably do not perform such backups as frequently as they should, do not properly store such backups, and often do not back up all the items they should be storing copies of.

Automated task file or folder copying backups

Automated-task backups are essentially manual backups on steroids; they are manual backups that are run by a computer automatically instead of by people manually kicking them off. While automating the backup process reduces the risk of forgetting to back up or not backing up due to someone being hurried, file and folder copying is still risky because if some sensitive information is, for some reason, not stored in the proper folder, it may not be backed up.

One possible exception is the case of virtual drives. If users automate the process of copying of the file containing the entire drive on which they store all of their data files, such backups may be sufficient. For most home users, however, setting up an automated copying routine is not a practical solution. Using backup software is a far simpler, and better, option.

Creating a Boot Disk

If you ever need to re-create your system, you will need the ability to boot the computer, so as part of the backup process, you should create a boot table disk. For most smartphones and tablets, creating a boot disk is not an issue because resetting the device to factory settings will make it bootable.

Such simplicity is not, however, always the case with computers, so when you perform your first backup you should ideally make a bootable disk that you know is safe to boot from (in other words, no malware and so on). Most backup software packages will walk you through this process, and some computer manufacturers will do the same on your initial startup of the system. Various security software packages are distributed on bootable CDs, DVDs, and/or USB drives as well.

Knowing Where to Back Up

For backups to have any value, they must be properly stored so they can be quickly and easily accessed when needed. Furthermore, improper storage of backups can severely undermine the security of information contained within the backups. You've probably heard stories of unencrypted backup tapes that contained sensitive information on them getting lost or stolen.

That said, there is not a one-size-fits-all approach to proper storage of backups. You can back up in different places, which results in different storage locations.

Local storage

Storing a *local copy* of your backup — meaning somewhere near a home computer or readily accessible to the owner of a smartphone, tablet, or laptop — is a good idea. If you accidentally delete a file, you can quickly restore it from the backup.

REMEMBER

That said, you should never keep all your backups local. If you store your backups in your house, for example, and your house were to be severely damaged in a natural disaster, you could simultaneously lose your primary data store (for example, your home computer) and your backups.

Backups should always be stored in a secure location — not on a bookshelf. A fireproof and waterproof safe bolted down to the floor or fastened to the wall are two good options.

Also, keep in mind that hard drives and other magnetic media are less likely to survive certain disasters than solid-state drives, thumb drives, and other devices containing memory chips.

Offsite storage

Because one of the purposes of backing up is to have the ability to preserve data (and systems) even if your primary copy is destroyed, you want to have at least one backup *offsite* — meaning in a different location than your primary data store.

Opinions differ as to how far away from the primary store the backup should be kept. Essentially, the general rule is to keep the backups far away enough that a natural disaster that severely impacts the primary site would not impact the secondary.

TIP

Some people store a backup copy of their data in a fireproof and waterproof bag inside a safe deposit box. Bank safes typically survive natural disasters, so even if the bank is relatively close to the primary site, the backup is likely to survive even if it cannot be retrieved for several days.

Cloud

Backing up the cloud offers the benefits of offsite storage. If you lose all your equipment and systems to a natural disaster, for example, a copy of your data will almost always still exist in the cloud. Also, from a practical standpoint, the odds are that the information-security team at any major provider of cloud storage has much greater knowledge of how to keep data secure than do most individuals and have at their disposal tools that the average person cannot afford to purchase or license.

At the same time, cloud-based backup has its drawbacks.

When using cloud-based backup, you are relying on a third-party to protect your data. While that party may have more knowledge and better tools at its disposal, its primary concern is not you. If a breach occurs, for example, and large customers are impacted, its priorities may lie in addressing their concerns before addressing yours. Also, major sites are often major targets for hackers because they know that such sites contain a treasure trove of data, far greater than what they may be able to lift from your home PC. Of course, if the government serves the cloud provider a warrant, law enforcement agents may obtain copies of your backups — even, in some cases, if the warrant was served because it has demonstrated probable cause only that someone else (and not you) committed a crime.

That said, for most people, cloud-based backup makes sense, with the pros outweighing the cons, especially if you encrypt your backups, thereby making their contents inaccessible to the cloud provider.

REMEMBER

When it comes to computers, *cloud* really means "someone else's computers." Anytime you store sensitive data, including sensitive data within in backups, in the cloud, you're really storing it on some physical computer belonging to someone else. The cloud provider may offer better security than you can offer yourself, but do not expect that your using the cloud will somehow magically eliminate cybersecurity risks.

Network storage

Backing up to a network drive offers a blend of features from several of the prior locations for storing backups.

Like a local backup, a network backup is normally readily available, but perhaps at a slightly lower speed.

Like an offsite backup, if the network server on which the backup is located is offsite, the backup is protected from site problems at the primary data's site. Unlike offsite backup, however, unless you know for sure that the files are offsite, they may be in the same facility as the primary data.

Like cloud backup, network based backup can be restored to other devices on your network. Unlike cloud backup, it may be accessible to only devices on the same private network (which, may be a problem, or, in some situations, a good thing from a security standpoint).

Also, network storage is often implemented with redundant disks and with automatic backups, offering better protection of your data that many other storage options.

TIP

If you use network storage for backups, make sure that whatever mechanism you are using to run the backup (for example, backup software) has the proper network permissions to write to the storage. In many cases, you may need to configure a login and password.

Mixing locations

There is no reason to only back up to one location. From the perspective of restoring data quickly, the more places that you have your data securely backed up, the better. In fact, different locations provider different types of protection optimized for different situations.

Keeping one copy local so that you can quickly restore a file that you accidentally delete, as well as maintaining a backup in the cloud in case of natural disaster, for example, makes sense for many people.

Keep in mind, however, that if you do store backups in multiple locations you need to make sure all the locations are secure. If you can't be sure about the security of some form of backup, beware and do not back up there just because "the more backups, the better."

TIP

As different backup locations provide different strengths and weaknesses, utilizing multiple backup locations can protect you better against more risks than using just one site.

Knowing Where Not to Store Backups

Never, ever, store backups attached to your computer or network, unless you have another backup that you are willing to recover in case of a malware attack. Ransomware that infects your computer and renders the files on it inaccessible to you may do the same to your attached backup.

WARNING

After backing up, never leave backup hard drives or solid-state drives connected to the systems or networks that they are backing up. Any malware that infects the primary system can spread to the backups as well. Removing your backup from being connected to the material that it is backing up can make all the difference between quickly recovering from a ransomware attack and having to pay an expensive ransom to a criminal.

If you back up to write-once, read-many-times-type media, which is most commonly found today in the form of CD-Rs and DVD-Rs, it is safe to leave the backup in an attached drive after you have finalized the backup recording and set the disk to read-only.

TIP

Always consider the environment and weather patterns when deciding where to store backups. You might be amazed at how many people have lost data after storing hard drives on the floor of basements that were prone to flooding.

Encrypting Backups

Backups can easily become a weak point in the data protection security chain. People who are diligent about protecting their personal information, and organizations that are careful to do the same with their confidential and proprietary information, often fail to afford the same level of protection to the exact same data when it resides in backups rather than in its primary location.

How often do you hear news stories, for example, of sensitive data put at risk because it was present in an unencrypted form on backups tapes that were lost or stolen?

TIP

In general, if you're not sure if you should encrypt your backup, you probably should.

Be sure to encrypt your backups if they contain any sensitive information, which, in most cases, they do. After all, if data is important enough to be backed up, the odds are pretty good that at least some of it is sensitive and should be encrypted.

Just be sure to properly protect the password needed to unlock the backups. Remember, it may be a while before you actually need to use the backups, so do not rely on your memory, unless you practice using that password on a regular basis to test the backups.

TIP

From a practical standpoint, many professional system administrators who deal with multiple backups every day have never seen a backup that did not need to be encrypted.

Also, keep in mind that if encryption methods used to protect backups go obsolete, the backups should be replaced with backups re-encrypted with better encryption. This issue is likely going to become a major headache for many organizations as quantum computing matures.

Testing Backups

Many folks have thought that they had proper backups only to discover at the time that they needed to restore that the backups were corrupted. Hence, testing backups is critical.

While, theoretically, you should test every backup that you make and test that every single item within the backup can be restored, such a scheme is impractical for most people. Do, however, test the first backup that you make with any software, check the auto-recover files the first time that you use Word, and so on.

Some backup software comes with the capability to *verify* backups — that is, after making a backup, it checks that the original data and data in the backups match. Running such verification after making a backup adds significant time to the backup process, but is well worth running if you can do so because it helps ensure that nothing was improperly recorded or otherwise became corrupted during the backup process.

WARNING

If you do not test that your backups actually work, you may be in for a terribly nasty surprise if you ever do need to restore from them.

Disposing of Backups

People and organizations often store backups for long periods of time — sometimes preserving materials for so long that the encryption used to protect the sensitive data on backup media is no longer sufficient to adequately protect the information from prying eyes.

As such, it is imperative that, from time to time, you either destroy your backups or re-create them.

REMEMBER

Both hardware and software formats change over time. If you backed up to tapes in the 1980s, to Bernoulli Boxes in the early 1990s, or to Zip drives in the late 1990s, you may have difficulty restoring from the backups today because you may have problems obtaining the necessary hardware, compatible drivers, and other software needed to read the backups on a modern computer.

Likewise, if you backed up data along with various DOS programs or early Windows 16-bit executables needed to process the contents of those backups, you may be unable to restore from the backups to many modern machines that may be unable to run the executables. Obviously, if you did a full system image of a machine 20 years ago, you are going to have difficulty restoring from the image today (you may be able to do so using virtual machines — something well beyond the technical skill level of most users).

Even some older versions of data files may not work easily. Word documents from the mid-1990s, for example, which can be infected with various forms of malware, do not open in modern versions of Word unless a user enables such access, which may be difficult or impossible to do in certain corporate environments. Files formats utilized specifically by software that has long since disappeared entirely from the market may be even harder to open.

As such, old backups may not have much value to you anyway. So, once a backup is no longer valuable or once its data protection may be at risk of compromise, get rid of it.

How should you dispose of the backup tapes, disks, and so on? Can you just throw them in the trash?

No. Do not. Doing so can totally undermine the security of the data in the backups.

Instead, utilize one of the following methods:

>> **Overwriting:** Various software programs will write over every sector of the storage media several times (the actual number of times depends on the security level that the user specifies), making subsequent recovery of data from the decommissioned media difficult, if not impossible.

>> **Degaussing:** Various devices containing strong magnets can be used to physically render data on magnetic media (such as hard drives and floppy disks) inaccessible by exposing the media to a strong magnetic field.

>> **Incineration:** Burning storage media in a high-temperature fire is often enough to destroy it. Do not attempt this on your own. If you want to pursue such a method, find a professional with experience. The incineration process varies based on the type of media involved.

>> **Shredding:** Cutting the media into tiny pieces. Ideally, such media should be totally pulverized into dust. In any case, shredding using an old-fashioned shredder that cuts media into strips is generally not considered secure disposal of media that has not been previously overwritten or degaussed.

TIP

Do not underestimate the importance of properly storing and disposing of backups. Serious data leaks have resulted from backup media that was lost after being stored for quite some time.

Chapter **6**

Resetting Your Device

B ook 3, Chapter 5 talks about backing up and why backing up is a critical component of any and every cybersecurity plan. The odds are close to 100 percent that, at some point, you will lose access to some file to which you still need access, and restoring from a backup will be a "lifesaver." This chapter discusses resetting your computer and teach you what you need to know to successfully reset your device so that it's (almost) as good as new.

Exploring Two Types of Resets

Sometimes, the easiest way to restore — and to help ensure that none of the problems that forced you to restore in the first place remain — is to start over by resetting your device to factory settings and reinstalling your apps and copying your data files from a backup.

However, even resets that are called "factory resets" often do not really set the device back to an identical state as that in which it came; some significant changes that have been made in the ensuing time will not be undone. For example, in many cases, if the BIOS of a device was updated since the device was acquired, a "factory reset" will not reset the BIOS back to its original state. And, as is discussed later, if any updates that were downloaded also updated the "factory image" used for restoration to factory settings, the restored computer will have those updates as well.

From a security perspective, this is important to understand, for at least two important reasons:

>> Any malware that infects the BIOS may not be removed by a factory reset.

>> If you have physical installation media (for example, a CD or DVD) for any software that you installed on the device previously, and you plan to install it again from such media and download and install updates to that software online after installing the version on the media, you must keep in mind that in some rare cases the versions on the media may not be compatible with the BIOS that is now in the device, and the installations could potentially fail.

TIP

Some forms of malware can survive a factory reset. So, if your device was infected with malware, be sure to address that problem even if you plan to reset your device. Or consult with an expert.

In addition, there will likely be times when your device crashes — that is, it becomes unresponsive and stops functioning normally. Such occasions can be scary for many nontechnical users, who assume that they may lose their data. Performing the proper type of reset in such occasions, however, is quite simple and will almost always preserve the user's files (although files currently being worked on may be preserved as they were last saved).

Resets come in two major flavors — soft and hard. It is critical to know the difference between them before you use either type.

Soft resets

A *soft reset* is the equivalent of physically turning a device off and then turning it back on. A soft reset does *not* wipe programs, data, or malware, and does not reset most previously set configuration elements.

TIP

One common use of soft resets is to restart a device if it crashes and becomes unresponsive. It can also be useful after a Blue Screen of Death-type of crash.

Older devices

Most modern computing devices have a soft reset capability, but some older devices do not. In such devices, however, the battery is often removable, so removing the battery and cutting off all power to the device (in other words, make sure to unplug it from the "mains") achieves the same desired effect.

Windows computers

Most Windows computers can be soft reset by holding down the Power button (for ten seconds or so) to do a shutdown. Holding down the button cuts off power to the computer from both the battery and any connected AC adapters/mains (even if the battery is connected and fully charged) and shuts it down.

TIP

After the device shuts down, wait ten seconds and press the Power button once to restart the computer. It will restart even if you don't wait the ten seconds, but waiting the ten seconds reduces the risks of rare electrical damage that occur from turning a device off and then on. (At a high level, and oversimplified, the damage occurs from an overload of electrical current if you send new current into the device while some of the current that was previously there before it was turned off has not fully left the scene because it was stored within capacitors and present even for a few seconds after being unplugged.)

Mac computers

Various models of Mac computers can be soft reset through different means:

» Hold down the Power button for about five seconds, and the Mac should shut down completely. Let go of the Power button, wait a few seconds, and press it once again, and the Mac should reboot. On some Macs pressing and holding the Power button may display a menu, in which case you should press R for Reboot and reboot directly, rather than shutting down and restarting the device.

» Press and hold the Control + ⌘ key together with the Power button.

» Press and hold the TouchID button until the Mac reboots.

Android devices

The way to soft reset an Android device varies between manufacturers. One of the following methods is likely to work:

» Press and hold the Power button until you see a shutdown/restart menu and then press Restart. (Or press Power Off, wait a few seconds, and then press the Power button again to turn the phone back on.)

» Press and hold the Power button. If no menu appears, keep holding the Power button for 2 minutes. At some point the phone should turn off — when it does, wait 10 seconds and turn it back on.

» If you have a removable battery, remove it, wait ten seconds, put it back in, and turn on the phone.

iPhones

The way to soft reset an iPhone varies based on the model. In general, one of the following methods will work:

>> Press and release the Volume Up button, then press and release the Volume Down button, and then press and hold the Side button (the Power button) until the Apple logo appears on the screen. Wait for the device to reboot.

>> Press and hold the Power button. While still holding it, press and hold the Volume Down button. When a Slide To Power Off prompt and slider appears on the screen, slide the slider to the right and turn the device off. Wait ten seconds and press the Power button to turn it back on.

>> Press and hold the Power button, and, while still doing so, press and hold the Volume Down button. Continue to hold both buttons as the iPhone powers off and back on. Release both buttons when the Apple logo appears on the screen and wait for the device to reboot.

WARNING

If you are using some versions of the iPhone X, following this option for performing a soft reset could end up calling emergency services (911 in the United States) because holding these particular buttons for longer than five seconds may be preprogrammed to issue an SOS signal from the device.

Hard resets

Hard resets reset a device to its factory image or to something similar. (For more on factory image, see Book 3, Chapter 5.)

If you want to recover to the original factory image — to effectively reset your device to the way it was when it was new — you need to follow the instructions for your particular device.

WARNING

Hard resets are almost always irreversible. Once you run a hard reset and a device is set back to its factory settings, you typically cannot undo the reset. Anything that you previously installed on the device (other than BIOS updates and the like as discussed earlier in this chapter), and any data that you stored on it is likely gone forever. (Advanced tools may, in some cases, be able to recover some of the material, but such recoveries are often incomplete, and, in many cases, impossible altogether.) As such, do not run a hard reset until you are sure that you have backups of all the material that you need on the device that you are hard resetting.

Also keep in mind the following:

» In some cases, a factory reset will not reset your device to the way it was when it was new because during operating system updates, the recovery image was updated as well. Factory resetting such a device will set the device to the way the device would have looked (or quite similar to the way it would have looked) when it was new had you purchased it with the new operating system.

» After performing a factory reset, one or more (or possibly all) patches and other security updates that you have installed on the device may be gone — meaning that your device is more likely than not vulnerable to various compromises. So, immediately after restoring you should run the operating system update process (repetitively — until it finds no needed updates) as well as the update process for any security software (also repetitively until it finds no needed updates). Only after those steps have been completed should you begin to install other software or perform any other online activities.

Resetting a Windows device

Your Windows device likely offers one or more ways to reset it. The following sections describe two ways to reset a Windows 10 or Windows 11 device.

WINDOWS 10 METHOD

1. In the Start menu, click on Settings.
2. In Windows Settings, click on Update and Security.

   The Windows Update screen appears.
3. Click on Recovery in the menu on the left side of the Window.
4. Click on the Get Started button in the Reset this PC section at the top of the window.

WINDOWS 11 METHOD

1. In the Start menu, click on Settings.
2. Select System from the menu on the left and click Recovery.

   The Windows Update screen appears.

3. **Click the Reset PC button in the Reset this PC bar.**

Windows 10 and Windows 11 work the same from this point forward. Windows offers you two choices. Both remove programs and apps and reset settings to their defaults:

- **Keep my files:** Selecting this option leaves your data files intact (as long as they are stored in data folders).

- **Remove everything:** Selecting this option removes all your data files along with the apps and programs (this is the factory reset option).

4. **Select either reset option.**

TIP

If you're performing a full reset because your system was infected by malware or your data files may otherwise have been corrupted, ideally select Remove everything and restore your data files from a clean backup.

If you select to remove your files along with everything else, Windows presents you with two choices:

- **Just remove my files:** Selecting this option erases your files, but does not perform any drive cleaning. This means that someone who gains access to the drive may be able to recover the data that was in the files — in full or in part — even after the files are deleted by the rest. This option runs relatively quickly.

- **Remove files and clean the drive:** Selecting this option not only removes all your data files, it wipes the drive — that is, writes over every 1 or 0 in your file — to dramatically reduce the likelihood that anyone in the future could recover any data from the deleted files. Cleaning a drive is time-consuming; if you select this option the restore can take much longer than if you select the first option.

TIP

If you are resetting the system so that you can use a clean system after recovering from a malware infection, there is no reason to clean the drive. If you are wiping it before giving it to someone else, fully cleaning the drive is a good idea. (In fact, some would argue that you should wipe the entire drive with even better wiping technology than is provided through the reset option discussed in this chapter.)

At this point, you may receive a warning message. If your computer originally had a different operating system and was upgraded to Window 10 or Windows 11, resetting the system will remove the recovery files created during the upgrade that allow you to downgrade back to the previously running operating system — meaning that if you reset the system, you will have a Windows 10 or Windows 11 computer that cannot be easily downgraded to another operating system. In most cases, this warning is not a significant issue — Windows 10 is very mature and Windows 11 is relatively mature, and few people who upgrade to either version as of the data of this book's publishing choose to downgrade.

Of course, if you are resetting the system because it is not working properly after you performed an upgrade to Windows 10 or Windows 11, do not proceed with the reset. Downgrade it to the older version of Windows using the relevant tool.

You then will see a final warning message that tells you that the computer is ready to reset — and which communicates what that means. Read what it says. If you do not want any of the things that it says will happen to happen, do not proceed.

5. **When you are ready to proceed, click on the Reset button.**

You can probably go out for coffee. A reset takes quite some time, especially if you chose to clean your drive.

6. **After a while, if you receive a prompt asking you whether you want to continue to Windows 10 or Windows 11 or to perform troubleshooting, click on Continue.**

METHOD 2

If you're *locked out* of your computer, meaning that it boots to a login screen, but you cannot log in — for example, if a hacker changed your password — you can still factory reset the machine:

1. **Boot your PC.**

2. **When the login screen appears, click on the Power icon in the bottom right-hand corner.**

You are prompted with several choices. Do not click on them yet.

3. **Without clicking any choices, first hold down the Shift key and then click on Restart.**

A special menu appears.

4. **Click on Troubleshoot.**

5. **Select Reset This PC.**

6. **Select Remove Everything.**

WARNING

Read the warnings, and understand what the consequences of running a hard reset are before you run it. This reset is likely irreversible.

Resetting a modern Android device

Modern Android devices come equipped with a Factory Reset feature, although the exact location of the activation option for it varies based on the device's manufacturer and operating system version.

I show you several examples of how to activate a hard reset on several popular devices. Other devices are likely to have similar options.

SAMSUNG GALAXY SERIES RUNNING ANDROID 13

On popular Samsung Galaxy phones running Android version 13 (the latest version of Android as of this writing), you can access the factory reset option by following these instructions:

1. Run the Settings app.
2. From the main Settings menu, click on General Management.
3. Click on Reset.
4. Click on Factory Data Reset.
5. Follow the instructions presented with the relevant warning.

SAMSUNG TABLETS RUNNING ANDROID 13

The popular Samsung series of tablets have menu structures for hard-resetting that are similar to those used for the Galaxy series, although with a different look and feel.

1. Run the Settings app.
2. From the main Settings menu, click on General Management.
3. In the General Management menu, click on Reset.
4. Click on Factory Data Reset.
5. Follow the instructions at the warning to continue.

Resetting a Mac

Before you hard reset a Mac, you should perform the following steps:

1. Sign out of iTunes.
2. De-authorize any apps that are locked to your Mac.

Sign out of them so that you can relog-in from the newly restored device, which those systems may see as if it were a different device.

3. **Sign out of Messages.**

4. **Sign out of iCloud.**

   You can do this in the System Preferences app. You will need to put in your password.

While a hard reset will work without the preceding three steps, performing the steps can prevent various problems when you restore.

After you're signed out of iTunes, Messages, and iCloud:

1. **Restart your Mac in Recovery Mode by restarting your Mac and holding down the Command and R keys while it reboots.**

   You may be presented with a screen asking you in what language you want to continue. If you are, select your preferred language.

2. **Run the Disk Utility.**

3. **In the Disk Utility screen, select your device's main volume and click on Unmount then Erase.**

4. **Erase any other disks in the device.**

5. **Exit the Disk Utility by clicking Quit Disk Utility in the Disk Utility menu.**

6. **Click on Reinstall macOS and follow the steps to reinstall the operating system onto the primary disk within your Mac.**

Resetting an iPhone

To hard reset a modern iPhone:

1. **Run the Settings app and choose General ⇨ Reset ⇨ Erase All Content and Settings.**

2. **If you're asked for your Apple ID and Password to confirm the erasure, enter them.**

3. **When you see a warning and a red Erase iPhone (or iPad) button, click on it.**

Rebuilding Your Device after a Hard Reset

After you hard reset a device, you should

>> Install all security updates

>> Install all the programs and apps that you use on the device — and any relevant updates

>> Restore your data from a backup

WARNING

After you restore a device, any updates or configuration changes you made in order to address security concerns are likely gone. Make sure to have a list of such changes prior to the reset so that you have a plan of action in place when you restore.

Chapter 7

Restoring from Backups

Backing up is a critical component of any and every cybersecurity plan. After you reset a device to its factory settings as part of the recovery process (see Book 3, Chapter 6), you can restore your data and programs so that your device will function as normal.

Because most people do not have to restore from backups regularly and because restoration is typically done after something "bad" happened that forced the restoration to be necessary, many folks first experience the process of restoring from backups when they are quite stressed. As such, people are prone to making mistakes during restoration, which can lead to data being lost forever. Fortunately, this chapter shows you how to restore.

You Will Need to Restore

The odds are close to 100 percent that, at some point, you will lose access to some file to which you still need access, and restoring from a backup will be a lifesaver. But restoring is not necessarily simple. You need to contemplate various factors before performing a restoration. Proper planning and execution can make the difference between recovering from lost data and losing even more data.

TIP

Restoring from backups is not as simple as many people think. Take the time to read this chapter before you perform a restore.

Wait! Do Not Restore Yet!

You noticed that some data that you want to access is missing. You noticed that a file is corrupted. You noticed that some program is not running properly. So, you should restore from a backup, right? Wait!

WARNING

Restoring without knowing why the problem occurred in the first place may be dangerous. For example, if you have a malware infection on your computer, restoring while the malware is still present won't remove the threat, and, depending on the type of malware and backup, may lead to the files in your backup becoming corrupted as well. If the malware corrupts the primary data store, you may lose your data and have nowhere from which to restore it!

For example, people who tried to restore data from backups on external hard drives have lost data to ransomware. The moment the external drive was connected to the infected computer, the ransomware spread to the backup and encrypted it as well!

WARNING

Malware can spread to cloud-based storage as well. Merely having the backup in the cloud is not a reason to restore before knowing what happened.

Even in the case of backups that are on read-only media, which malware cannot infect, attempting to restore before neutralizing the threat posed by the infection can waste time and potentially give the malware access to more data to steal.

Before you restore from any backups, make sure to diagnose the source of the problem that is causing you the need to restore. If you accidentally deleted a file, for example, and know that the problem occurred due to your own human error, by all means go ahead and restore. But if you're unsure what happened, apply the techniques described in Book 3, Chapters 3 and 4 to figure out what you need to do to make your computer safe and secure prior to restoring from the backup.

Restoring Data to Apps

As discussed in Book 3, Chapter 5, many apps and social media accounts provide their own backup and restore mechanisms. Typically the restore functions can be found in the same places within the apps' respective configuration settings as the backups.

In any event, if, when making your backups, you took note of where the restore functions are and wrote that information down, you should be in good shape to go. If not, look on the support pages for that app.

Restoring from Full Backups of Systems

A *full system backup* is a backup of an entire system, including the operating system, programs/apps, settings, and data. The term applies whether the device being backed up is a smartphone or a massive server in a data center.

As such, the restoration process recreates a system that is effectively identical to the one that was backed up at the time that it was backed up. (This is not totally true in the absolute sense — the system clock will show a different time than the original system, for example — but it is true for the purposes of learning about system restoration.)

Restoring to the computing device that was originally backed up

System restoration from a system image works best when systems are restored to the same computing device from which the original backup was made. If your system was infected with malware, for example, and you restore to the same device from an image created before the malware infection took place, the system should work well. (Of course, you would lose any work and other updates done since that time, so hopefully you backed them up using one of the methods in Book 3, Chapter 5.)

WARNING

Full system restores are often irreversible. And if a restore fails, as can happen if a backup is corrupted or for any one or more of a number of reasons including some discussed in the next section, you could have a system that is unusable in its present form. Be absolutely sure that you want to run a full system restore before you actually run one.

Restoring from a full system backup is likely the fastest way to restore an entire system, but the process can take dramatically longer than restoring just a few files that were corrupted. It is also far more likely to lead to accidentally erasing settings or data created since the last backup. As such, use a full system restore only when one is truly needed.

TIP

If you accidentally delete a bunch of files or even folders, do not perform a full system restore. Just restore those files from a backup using one of the techniques described later in this chapter.

Restoring from Backups

Restoring to a different device than the one that was originally backed up

REMEMBER

System restoration from an image often won't work on a system with totally different hardware components than the system that was originally imaged. In general, the more different a system is from the system that was imaged, the more problems that you may encounter.

Some of those problems may autocorrect. If you restore a system with drivers for one video card to a system with another video card, for example, the restored system should realize that the wrong drivers are installed and simply not use them. Instead, it defaults to the operating system's built-in drivers and allows you to install the drivers for the correct card (or, in some cases, automatically download them or prompt you to do so).

Some problems may not autocorrect. For example, if the computer that was backed up used a standard USB-connected keyboard and mouse and the device to which you are restoring uses some proprietary keyboard that connects differently, it may not work at all after the restore; you may need to attach a USB keyboard to the system to download and install the drivers for your proprietary keyboard. Such situations are becoming increasingly rare due to both standardization and improvements in modern operating systems, but they do exist.

Some problems may not be correctable. If you try to restore the system image of a Mac to a computer designed to run Windows, for example, it won't work.

TIP

Some backup software packages allow you to configure a restore to either install separate drivers or search for drivers that match the hardware to which the restoration is being done to replace those found in the backup that are unsuitable. If you have such a feature and have difficulty restoring without it, you may want to try it.

A full system backup may or may not include a backup of all content on all drives attached to a system, not just those mounted inside of it. (Theoretically, all such drives should be included in a system image, but the term *system image* is often used to mean an image of the internal hard drives and SSDs.)

TIP

If a device for which you have an image fails, you should be able to use the system image to re-create the entire system as it was at the time that the backup was made. When you use the rebuilt system, it should function exactly as the previous system did at the time of the backup.

Original system images

If you want to recover to the original factory image of a system prior to restoring your data and programs, see Book 3, Chapter 6, which is dedicated to performing such restorations.

After performing such a factory reset, one or more (or possibly all) patches and other security updates that you have installed on the device may be gone. Your device is likely vulnerable to various compromises. Immediately after restoring, you should, therefore, run the operating system update process (repetitively until it finds no needed updates) as well as the update process for any security software (also repetitively until it finds no needed updates).

Only after those steps are completed should you install other software, restore your data, or perform any other online activities.

Later system images

Before you restore from any system image, you must ascertain that whatever problem occurred that necessitated the restoration will not remain, or be restored, during the restoration. If your computer was infected with ransomware, for example, and you remove the malware with security software, but need to restore the criminally encrypted files from a backup, you do not want to end up restoring the ransomware along with the data.

If you know for certain that an image was made prior to the arrival of the problem, go ahead and use it. If in doubt, if possible, restore to an extra device and scan it with security software prior to performing the actual restoration. If you do not have an extra device to which you can restore and are unsure as to whether the backup is infected, you may want to hire a professional to take a look.

Installing security software

After you restore from a system image (whether factory settings or a later image), the first thing that you should do is check whether security software is installed. If it is not, install it. Either way, make sure to run the auto-updates until the software no longer needs updates.

TIP

Install security software before attempting to do anything online or read email. If you do not have security software in place before you perform such tasks, performing them could lead to a security breach of your device.

If you have the security software on CD, DVD, or USB drive, install it from there. If you created a USB drive or other disk with the security software on it, you can install it from there. If not, copy the security software to the hard drive from wherever you have it and run it.

Original installation media

For programs that you acquire and install after you purchased your device, you can reinstall them after you restore the original system image or even a later image that was created before the software was installed.

TIP

If you reinstall software from a CD, DVD, or USB drive any updates to the software that were released after the CD, DVD, or USB drive image was created will not be installed. Be sure to either configure your program to auto-update or manually download and install such updates. In some cases, software installation routines may also ask you whether you want them to automatically perform a check for updates immediately upon the completion of the installation. In general, answering affirmatively is a wise idea.

Downloaded software

The way that you reinstall programs that you previously purchased and installed at some point after you purchased your device depends on where the software is located:

>> **If you have a copy of the software on a thumb drive,** you can reinstall from the drive by connecting it into your device, copying the files to your hard drive, and running the install.

TIP

If there is any possibility that the thumb drive is infected with malware — for example, you're restoring due to a malware infection and may have inserted the thumb drive into your infected computer at some point in the past — make sure to scan it with security software before you run or copy anything from it. Do so from a device with security software running that will prevent infections from spreading upon connection from the drive to the machine being used for scanning.

>> **If you copied the software to a DVD, USB drive, or CD,** you can install from that disc. Make sure to install all necessary updates.

>> **If the purchased software can be redownloaded from a virtual locker,** do so. In some cases, software that is redownloaded will have been automatically upgraded to the latest release. In other cases, it will be the same version as you originally purchased, so make sure to install updates.

>> **If the software is downloadable from its original source** (public domain software, trialware that you activate with a code, and so on), feel free to redownload it. In some cases — for example, if newer versions require paying an upgrade fee — you may need to download the version that you had previously. In any case, make sure to install all updates for the version that you do install.

Restoring from full backups of data

In many cases, it makes sense to restore all the data on a device:

>> **After a restore from a factory image:** After restoring from a factory image and reinstalling all necessary software, your device will still have none (or almost none) of your data on it, so you need to restore all your data.

>> **After certain malware attacks:** Some malware modifies and/or corrupts files. To ensure that all your files are as they should be, after an infection, restore all your data from a backup. Of course, this assumes that you have a recent enough backup from which to do so without losing any work.

>> **After a hard drive failure:** If a hard drive fails, in full or in part, you will want to move your files to another drive. If you have a separate drive for data than for the operating system and programs — as many people do — performing a full restore of data is the easiest way to restore.

>> **When transitioning to a new, similar device:** Restoring from a backup is an easy way to ensure that you put all your data files onto the new device. Because some programs store settings in user data folders, copying the files directly or performing a selective restoration from a backup is usually a better way to go. But as people sometimes inadvertently leave out files when using such a technique, full restorations are sometimes used.

>> **After accidental deletions:** People occasionally accidentally delete large portions of their data files. One easy way to restore everything and not worry about whether everything is "back to the way that it should be" is to do a full restore of all data.

Unlike restoring from a full system backup, restoring from a full data backup won't restore applications. If a system has to be rebuilt entirely, recovering from full backups of data likely requires prior restorations to factory settings (or a later image of the computer) and reinstallation of all software.

TIP

The multi-step process of restoring from a factory image and then reinstalling applications and restoring data may seem more tedious than simply restoring from a more recent system image, but it also usually proves to be far more portable. Recovery can usually be done on devices that vary quite a bit from the original device, using images of those devices (or onto a new device), followed by the reinstallation of programs and the restoration of data.

Restoring from Incremental Backups

Incremental backups are backups made after a full backup and contain copies of only the portion of the contents being backed up that have changed since the preceding backup (full or incremental) was run.

TIP

Some simplistic backup software products use incremental and differential backups internally, but hide the internal workings from users. All users do is select which files or file types to restore and, if appropriate, which versions of those files, and the system works like magic hiding the merging of data from multiple backups into the resulting restoration.

Incremental backups of data

In many cases of home users, *incremental backup* refers to incremental backups of data. To recover data that was backed up using an incremental backup scheme requires multiple steps:

1. A restoration must be done from the last full data backup.

2. After that restoration is complete, restoration must be performed from each incremental backup performed since that last full backup.

Failing to include any of the incremental backups necessary in Step 2 may lead to corrupt data, missing data, data being present that should not be, or inconsistent data.

WARNING

Most modern backup software will warn (or prevent) you if you try to skip any incremental backups during an incremental restoration. Such software, however, sometimes does not, however, tell you if you're missing the final backup or backups in a series.

Incremental backups of systems

Incremental system backups are essentially updates to system images (or partial system images in the case of partial backups) that bring the image up to date as of the data that the backup was made. The incremental system backup contains copies of only the portion of the system that changed since the preceding backup (full or incremental) was successfully run.

To restore from an incremental backup of a system:

1. **A restoration must be done from the last full system backup.**

2. **After that restoration is complete, restoration must be performed from each incremental backup performed since that system image was created.**

Failing to include any of the incremental backups necessary in Step 2 may lead to corrupt of missing programs, data, operating system components, and incompatibility issues between software. Most modern backup software will warn (or prevent) you if you try to skip various incremental backups during a restore from an incremental backup. They often do not, however, tell you if you're missing the final backup or backups in a series.

Differential backups

Differential backups contain all the files that changed since the last full backup was successfully run. (They are similar to the first in a series incremental backups run after a full backup.)

TIP

While creating a series of differential backups usually takes more time than creating a series of incremental backups, restoring from differential backups is usually much simpler and faster.

To recover from a differential backup:

1. **Perform a restoration from the last full system backup.**

2. **After that restoration is complete, perform a restoration from the most recent differential backup.**

Be sure to restore from the last differential backup and not from any other differential backup.

Restoring from Backups

TIP

Many backup systems won't warn you if you attempt to restore from a differential backup other than the latest one. Be sure to double-check before restoring that you're using the latest one!

Table 7-1 shows the comparative restoration processes from full, incremental, and differential backups.

TABLE 7-1   **Restoration Processes**

	Full Backup	Incremental Backup	Differential Backup
After Backup #1	Restore from Backup #1	Restore from Backup #1 (Full)	Restore from Backup #1 (Full)
After Backup #2	Restore from Backup #2	Restore from Backups #1 and #2	Restore from Backups #1 and #2
After Backup #3	Restore from Backup #3	Restore from Backups #1, #2, and #3	Restore from Backups #1 and #3
After Backup #4	Restore from Backup #4	Restore from Backups #1, #2, #3, and #4	Restore from Backups #1 and #4

Continuous backups

Some continuous backups are ideal for performing system restore. Similar to a system image, they allow you to restore a system to the way that it looked at a certain point in time. Others are terrible for performing restores because they allow restoration to only the most recent version of the system, which often suffers from the need to be rebuilt in the first place.

In fact, the normal use of continuous backups is to address equipment failures, such as a hard drive suddenly going caput — not the rebuilding of systems after a security incident. Furthermore, because continuous backups constantly propagate material from the device being backed up to the backup, any malware that was present on the primary system may be present on the backup.

Partial backups

Partial backups are backups of a portion of data. Likewise, partial backups are not intended to be full backups in case of a malware attack or the like. They are useful, however, in other situations, and you should be aware of how to restore from them.

If you have a particular set of files that are extremely sensitive and need to be backed up and stored separately from the rest of your system, you may use a partial backup for that data. If something happens and you need to rebuild a system or restore the sensitive data, you will need that separate partial backup from which to do the restore.

Digital private keys that provide access to cryptocurrency, email encryption/ decryption capabilities, and so on, for example, are often stored on such backups along with images of extremely sensitive documents.

Often, partial backups of sensitive data are performed to USB drives (or, in cases of less up-to-date environments, writeable DVDs, CDs, or even floppy disks!) that are then locked in safes or safe deposit boxes. Restoring from the backup would, in such cases, demand that the restorer obtain the physical USB drive (or other form of media), which could mean a delay in restoration. If the need to restore arises at 6 p.m. Friday, for example, and the drive is in a safe deposit box that is not available until 9 a.m. Monday, the desired material may remain inaccessible to the user for almost three days.

REMEMBER

Make sure that you store your partial backups in a manner that will allow you to access the backed-up data when you need it.

Another common scenario for specialized partial backups is when a network-based backup is used — especially within a small business — and users need to ensure that they have a backup of certain material in case of technical problems while traveling. Such backups should never be made without proper authorization. If permission has been obtained and a backup has been created, a user on the road who suffers a technical problem that requires restoration of data can do the restore by copying the files from the USB drive or other form of media (after, presumably, decrypting the files using a strong password or some form of multi-factor authentication).

Folder backups

Folder backups are similar to partial backups because the set of items being backed up is a particular folder. If you performed a folder backup using a backup tool, you can restore it using the techniques described in the preceding section.

The restore process is different if, however, you created the relevant backup by simply copying a folder or set of folders to an external drive (hard drive, SSDs, USB drive, or network drive). Theoretically, you simply copy the backup copy of the folder or folders to the location of the original folder. However, doing so will potentially overwrite the contents of the primary folder, so any changes made since the backup will be lost.

Drive backups

A *drive backup* is similar to a folder backup, but an entire drive is backed up instead of a folder. If you backed up a drive with backup software, you can restore it via that software. If you backed up a drive by copying the contents of the drive somewhere else, you will need to manually copy them back. Such a restore may not work perfectly, however. Hidden and system files may not be restored, so a bootable drive backed up and restored in such a fashion may not remain bootable.

Virtual-drive backups

If you backed up an encrypted virtual drive, such as a BitLocker drive that you mount on your computer, you can restore the entire drive in one shot or restore individual files and folders from the drive.

Restoring the entire virtual drive

To restore the entire virtual drive in one shot, make sure the existing copy of the drive is not mounted (you will probably get an error message if you try to restore it while it is mounted, but do not rely on that). The easiest way to do so is to boot your computer and not mount any Bitlocker drives.

If your computer is booted already and the drive is mounted, simply dismount it:

1. **Choose Startup ➪ This PC.**

2. **Locate the mounted Bitlocker drive.**

   The drive appears with an icon of a lock indicating that it is encrypted.

3. **Right-click on the drive and select Eject.**

   Once the drive is dismounted, it disappears from the This PC list of drives.

After the drive is unmounted, copy the backup copy of the drive to the primary drive location and replace the file containing the drive.

You can then unlock and mount the drive.

Restoring files and/or folders from the virtual drive

To restore individual files or folders from the virtual drive, mount the backup as a separate virtual drive and copy the files and folders from the backup to the primary as if you were copying files between any two drives.

Ideally, you should back up the backup of the virtual drive before mounting it and copying files and/or folders from it and mount it read-only when you mount it.

Always unmount the backup drive after copying files to the primary. Leaving it mounted — which inherently means that two copies of a large portion of your file system are in use at the same time — can lead to human mistakes.

Dealing with Deletions

One of the problems of restoring from any restore that does not entirely overwrite your data with a new copy is that the restore may not restore deletions.

For example, if after making a full backup, you delete a file, create ten new files, modify two data files, and then perform an incremental backup, the incremental backup may or may not record the deletion. If you restore from the full backup and then restore from the incremental, the restore from the incremental should delete the file, add the ten new files, and modify the two files to the newer version. In some cases, however, the file that you previously deleted may remain because some backup tools do not properly account for deletions.

Even when this problem happens, it is not usually critical. You just want to be aware of it. Of course, if you've deleted sensitive files in the past, you should check whether a restoration restored them to your computer. (If you intend to permanently and totally destroy a file or set of files, you should also remove it/them from your backups.)

Excluding Files and Folders

Some files and folders should not be restored during a restoration. In truth, they should not have been backed up in the first place unless you imaged a disk, but in many cases, people do back them up anyway.

The following are examples of some such files and folders that can be excluded from typical restorations done on a Windows 10 machine. If you're using backup software, the software likely excluded these files when creating the backup. If you are copying files manually, you may have backed them up.

>> Contents of the Recycle Bin

>> Browser caches (temporary Internet files from web browsers, such as Microsoft Edge or Internet Explorer, Firefox, Chrome, Vivaldi, or Opera)

>> Temporary folders (often called Temp or tem and reside in C:\, in the user directory, or in the data directory of software

>> Temporary files (usually files named *.tmp or *.temp)

>> Operating system swap files (pagefile.sys)

>> Operating system hibernation-mode system image information (hyberfil.sys)

>> Backups (unless you want to back up your backups) such as Windows File History backup

>> Operating system files backed up during an operating system upgrade (usually found in C:\Windows.old on Windows computers that have had their operating systems upgraded)

>> Microsoft Outlook cache files (*.ost — note that Outlook local data stores [*.pst] should be backed up; in fact, in many cases they may be the most critical files in a backup)

>> Performance log files in directories called PerfLogs

>> Junk files that users create as personal temporary files to hold information (for example, a text file in which users type a phone number that someone dictated to them, but which the users have since entered into their smartphone directory)

IN-APP BACKUPS

Some applications have built-in backup capabilities that protect you from losing your work if your computer crashes, power fails and you don't have battery power left, and other mishaps.

Some such applications will automatically prompt you to restore documents that would otherwise have been lost due to a system crash or the like. When you start Microsoft Word after an abnormal shutdown of the application, for example, it provides a list of documents that can be autorecovered — sometimes even offering multiple versions of the same document.

Understanding Archives

The term *archive* has multiple meanings in the world of information technology. The following sections describe the relevant meanings.

Multiple files stored within one file

Sometimes multiple files can be stored within a single file. This concept was addressed with the concept of virtual drives earlier in this chapter and in Book 3, Chapter 4. However, storing multiple files within one file does not necessitate the creation of virtual drives.

You may have seen files with the extension .ZIP, for example. *ZIP files*, as such files are called, are effectively containers that hold one or more compressed files. Storing multiple files in such a container allows for far easier transfer of files (a single ZIP file attached to an email is far easier to manage than 50 small individual files). It also reduces the amount (sometimes significantly) of disk space and Internet bandwidth necessary to store and move the files.

There are other forms of ZIP files that have the file extension .ZIPx. These files have been compressed with even more advanced compression mechanisms than standard .ZIP files, but are not able to be opened by many computers unless special software is installed in addition to the operating system. In addition to ZIP files, there are many other forms of compressed containers of files, and the files containing them have many different extensions, but ZIP is — by far — the type most people will encounter the most often.

If you need to restore files from a ZIP or similar archive, you can either extract all the files from the archive to your primary source, or you can open the archive and copy the individual files to your primary location as you would with any files found in any other folder.

Archive files come in many different formats. Some appear automatically as folders within Windows and Mac file systems and their contents as files and folders within folders. Others require special software to be viewed and extracted from.

Old live data

Sometimes old data is moved off of primary systems and stored elsewhere. Storing old data can improve performance. For example, if a search of all email items means searching through 25 years' worth of messages, the search will take far longer than a search through just the last 3 years. If nearly all relevant results will always be within the last few years, the older emails can be moved to a separate archive where you can access and search them separately if need be.

If you use archiving, factor that in when restoring data. You want to ensure that archives are restored to archives and that you don't accidentally restore archives to the primary data stores.

Also, keep in mind that even if you believe that data is not needed on a regular basis, you may be subject to regulations regarding its storage and safety. There are two primary aspects to this point. First, never delete an archive just because you have restored from it. Some data may be required to be retained for certain periods of time or even, in some cases, indefinitely, and the archive may have been created for that reason. Second, certain data may be subject to security and privacy regulations for as long as it is stored and wherever it is stored — sometimes restoring old data can bring with it security and privacy requirements.

Old versions of files, folders, or backups

The term *archives* is also sometimes used to refer to old versions of files, folders, and backups even if those files are stored on the primary data store. Someone who has ten versions of a contract, for example, that were executed at different points in time, may keep all the Word versions of these documents in an Archive folder. Archiving of this sort can be done for any one or more of many reasons. One common rationale is to avoid accidentally using an old version of a document when the current version should be used.

If you're archiving, factor that in when restoring data. Restore all the archives to their proper locations. You may see multiple copies of the same file being restored; don't assume that that is an error.

Restoring Using Backup Tools

Restoring using backup software is similar to the process of backing up using backup software. To restore using the backup software that was utilized to create the backups from which you are restoring, run the software (in some cases, you may need to install the software onto the machine, rather than run it from a CD or the like) and select Restore.

When you restore, make sure that you select the correct backup version to restore from.

WARNING

Beware of malware masquerading as bogus restoration prompts! Various forms of malware present bogus prompts advising you that your hard drive has suffered some sort of malfunction and that you must run a restore routing to repair data. Only run restores from software that you obtained from a reliable source and that you know that you can trust!

Many modern backup software packages hide the approach used to back up — full, differential, incremental, and so on — from users and instead allow users to pick which version of files they want to restore.

If you're restoring using the specialized backup and recovery software that came with an external hard drive or solid-state device that you use to back up your device, attach the drive, run the software (unless it runs automatically), and follow the prompt to restore.

Such software is usually simple to use; restoration typically works like a simplified version of that done using other backup software (see preceding section).

REMEMBER

Disconnect the drive from the system after performing the restore!

Restoring from a Windows backup

To restore from a Windows backup to the original locations from which the data was backed up, follow these steps:

1. **On a Windows 10 device, choose Start ⇨ Settings ⇨ Update & Security ⇨ Backup. On a Windows 11 device, open the Control Panel and select System and Security ⇨ Backup and Restore.**

2. **Click Restore files from a current backup.**

   If your device doesn't provide a link, click the Select another backup to restore files from link to guide it to the right place.

3. **In the File System viewer, browse through different versions of your folders and files or type and search for the name of the file you're looking for.**

4. **Select what you want to restore.**

5. **Click Restore.**

Restoring to a system restore point

Microsoft Windows allows you to restore your system to the way it looked at a specific time at which the system was imaged by the operating system:

1. **Click the Start button and select Settings.**

2. **Choose Control Panel ⇨ System and Maintenance ⇨ Backup and Restore.**

3. **Click Restore My Files to restore your files or Restore All Users' Files to restore all users' files (assuming that you have permissions to do so).**

Restoring from a smartphone/tablet backup

Many portable devices come equipped with the ability to automatically sync your data to the cloud, which allows you to restore the data to a new device if your device is lost or stolen. Even devices that do not have such a feature built in almost always can run software that effectively delivers such features for a specific folder tree or drive.

When you start an Android device for the first time after a factory reset, you may be prompted if you want to restore your data. If you are, restoring is pretty straightforward. Answer yes. While the exact routines may vary between devices and manufacturers, other forms of restore generally follow some flavor of the following process:

To restore contacts from an SD card:

1. **Open the Contacts App.**

   If there is an import feature, select it and jump to Step 4.

2. **Select Settings from the main menu (or click the Settings icon).**

   If you aren't displaying all contacts, you may need to click the Display menu and select All Contacts.

3. **Select Import/Export Contacts (or, if that option is not available, select Manage Contacts and then select Import Contacts on the next screen).**

4. **Select Import from SD Card.**

5. **Review the file name for the backup of the Contact list then click OK.**

   Contacts are often backed up (or exported to) VCF files.

To restore media (pictures, videos, and audio files) from an SD card:

1. **Using File Manager, open the SD card.**

2. **Click to turn on check boxes next to the file or files that you want to restore.**

3. **To copy files to the phone's memory, go to the menu and select Copy ⇨ Internal Storage.**

4. **Select the folder to which you want to copy the files or create the folder and move into it.**

5. **Select Copy Here.**

Restoring from manual file or folder copying backups

To restore from a manual file or folder copy, just copy the file or folder from the backup to the main data store. (If you are overwriting a file or folder, you may receive a warning from the operating system.)

REMEMBER

Disconnect the media on which the backup is located from the main store when you are done.

Utilizing third-party backups of data hosted at third parties

If you utilized the backup capabilities of a third-party provider at which you store data in the cloud or whose cloud-based services you utilize, you may be able to restore your relevant data through an interface provided by the third-party provider.

If you use a third-party cloud-based-service provider and you have not performed backups, you may still be able to restore data. Contact your provider. The provider itself may have backed up the data without notifying you.

TIP

While you should never rely on your cloud service provider performing backups that you did not order, if you are in a jam and contact the provider, you may (or may not) be pleasantly surprised to find out that they do have backups from which you can restore.

Returning Backups to Their Proper Locations

After you restore from a physical backup, you need to return it to its proper location for several reasons:

>> You do not want it to be misplaced if you ever need it again.

>> You do not want it to be stolen.

>> You want to ensure that you do not undermine any storage strategies and procedures intended to keep backups in different locations than the data stores that they back up.

Network storage

Ideally, when restoring from a network-based backup, you should mount the network drive as read-only to prevent possible corruptions of the backup. Furthermore, be sure to disconnect from the network data store once you are done performing the restoration.

TIP

Make sure that whatever mechanism you are using to run the restore (for example, backup software) has the proper network permissions to write to the primary data storage location.

Restoring from a combination of locations

There is no reason to back up to only one location. Restoration, however, typically will utilize backups from only one location at a time. If you do need to restore from backups that are physically situated at more than one location, be extremely careful not to restore the wrong versions of files as some of the files may exist on multiple backups.

Restoring to Non-Original Locations

When it comes to restoring data, some folks choose to restore to locations other than original locations, test the restored data, and then copy or move it to the original locations. Such a strategy reduces the likelihood of writing over good data with bad data, and is recommended when practical and possible.

You can make a bad day worse if you lose some of your data and discover that your backup of the data is corrupted. If you then restore from that backup over your original data and thereby corrupt it, you lose even more of your data.

Never Leave Your Backups Connected

WARNING

After restoring, never leave backup hard drives or solid-state drives connected to the systems or networks that they are backing up. Any future malware infections that attack the primary system can spread to the backups as well. Removing your backup from being connected to the material that it is backing up can make all the difference between quickly recovering from a ransomware attack and having to pay an expensive ransom to a criminal.

If you back up to write-once read-many-times media, such as CD-Rs, it is theoretically safe to leave the backup in an attached drive after you finalize the restoration, but you still should not do so. You want the backup to be readily available in its proper location in case you ever need it in the future.

Restoring from Encrypted Backups

Restoring from encrypted backups is essentially the same as restoring from non-encrypted backups except that you need to unlock the backups prior to restoration.

Backups that are protected by a password obviously need the proper password to be entered. Backups protected by certificates or other more advanced forms of encryption may require that a user possess a physical item or digital certificate in order to restore. In most cases, security conscious home users protect their backups with passwords. If you do so (and you should), do not forget your password.

Testing Backups

Many folks have thought that they had proper backups only to discover when they needed to restore that the backups were corrupted. Hence, testing backups is critical.

While theoretically you should test every backup that you make and test every single item within the backup can be restored, such a scheme is impractical for most people. But do test the first backup that you make with any software, check the auto-recover files the first time that you use Word, and so on.

Some backup software comes with the capability to verify backups — that is, after making a backup, it checks that the original data and data in the backups matches. Running such verification after making a backup adds significant time to the backup process. However, it's well worth running if you can do so because it helps ensure that nothing was improperly recorded or otherwise corrupted during the backup process.

Restoring Cryptocurrency

Restoring cryptocurrency after it is erased from a computer or some other device it was stored on is totally different than any of the restore processes described in this chapter.

Technically speaking, cryptocurrency is tracked on a ledger, not stored anywhere, so the restoration is not done to restore the actual cryptocurrency, but rather to restore the private keys needed in order to control the address (or addresses) within the respective ledger (or ledgers) at which the cryptocurrency is "stored."

Hopefully, if you lost the device on which your cryptocurrency is stored, you have the keys printed on paper that is stored in a safe or safe deposit box. Obtain the paper, and you have your keys. Just don't leave the paper lying around; put it back into the secure location ASAP. (If you keep the paper in a safe deposit box, consider performing the restoration technique at the bank so that you never take the paper out of the safe deposit box area.)

If you store cryptocurrency at an exchange, you can restore your credentials to the exchange through whatever means the exchange allows. Ideally, if you properly backed up your passwords to a secure location, you can just obtain and use them.

WHAT IS A DIGITAL WALLET?

The term digital wallets as applied to cryptocurrency is misleading — you store digital keys, not cryptocurrency, in a digital wallet. The name digital keyring would have been far more accurate and less confusing, but apparently, because people are used to storing money in wallets, and think of cryptocurrency as forms of money, the term "digital wallet" has stuck.

For those who use hardware wallets to store the keys to their cryptocurrency, the backup for the wallet device is often a *recovery seed*, which is a list of words that allows the device to re-create the keys needed for the relevant addresses. It is generally accepted that the list of words should be written down on paper and stored in a bank vault and/or safe, not stored electronically.

Booting from a Boot Disk

If you ever need to boot from a boot disk that you created (as might be necessary during a system reset and restore process), boot your system, go into the BIOS settings, and set the boot order to start with the disk from which you want to boot. Then restart the system.

WARNING

When you have booted, be sure to change the system back to boot from the internal hard drive or SSD first rather than the USB drive. Leaving a system with a configuration to boot first from a USB drive is a security risk on multiple accounts; anyone who has physical access to the device can potentially (intentionally or inadvertently) infect it with malware, for example, by installing an infected USB drive and booting from it.

4

Securing the Cloud

Contents at a Glance

Chapter **1**

Clouds Aren't Bulletproof

All the great innovators have been known to "have their head in the clouds." Now it's your turn. Cloud computing is one of the greatest innovations of modern computing since the Internet, but with all its many benefits come certain responsibilities. One *vital* responsibility is the management of security. You can think of clouds as Infrastructure Elsewhere, but the security of all infrastructure must be managed. In this chapter, I spell out the basics of getting to know your business so that you can best create a security plan, which is the first step toward optimal application and data security when using clouds.

REMEMBER

For the most part, whenever later chapters mention clouds, these indicate public clouds, like AWS and Google Cloud.

A word to the wise: When the responsibility for cloud security falls in your lap, don't panic. You'll soon find out that, with the right plan and the right tools, the task can be easily managed. To get started, you have to get to know your business. You may *think* you know it, but in order to provide truly successful security, you have to know it *in detail,* beyond just knowing the name of the person manning the front desk.

Knowing Your Business

It's great to know exactly what your business sells, whether it's widgets or services, but when it comes to cybersecurity, you need to know your business a bit more intimately. This new insight into how your business runs not only allows you to create a rock-solid security plan but also may help you innovate by better understanding how things get done. One of the first steps is knowing what you want to protect.

Discovering the company jewels

It's time to gather your first thoughts about cloud security into an actionable strategy, by understanding which assets you're trying to protect. This becomes the most important part of your plan. Depending on the size of your company, the strategies will start to differ. If you're thinking that cloud security doesn't differ much from everyday cybersecurity, you're absolutely correct. Getting cloud security right means you have a plan for all your cyberassets — wherever they live and operate.

TIP

Create an inventory of all your assets. The section "Building Your Team," later in this chapter, offers suggestions for creating the right team. It's best to rely on them when creating an inventory of assets rather than try to noodle it out yourself.

Initiating your plan

Small companies can start their plan in a spreadsheet. You could probably get away with using a simple yellow legal pad, but then it's not so easy to share with others, and *that* is the part of the plan that comes next. Create a spreadsheet or database if you're more comfortable with it and start to list all applications used by your company. (It's easier said than done!) Many departments use applications that are hidden from the IT department. These *siloes* are towers of applications and data that are cut off from the other parts of the company — for example, accounting applications that are in use only by Accounting or sales tracking applications used only by Sales. This single exercise can be an eye-opener. You may look at the list and think, "Who is watching all this stuff?" That's why you start here.

REMEMBER

All your applications are creating and using data. Each application on your list should also include information about the kinds of data it creates or uses.

Automating the discovery process

Larger organizations might use automated discovery applications that can help you create a basic list of applications, networks, and data. This is a particularly important first step when migrating to the cloud. For example, Amazon Web Services (AWS, for short) has an application called the AWS Application Discovery Service. (More about that service in the next sections.)

AWS Discovery Service

The AWS Discovery Service collects and documents information about the applications in use within your company and then stores that information in an AWS Migration Hub. This vital data can then be exported into Excel or certain AWS analysis tools. This is the data that underlies your ultimate cloud security plan!

TIP

AWS also has APIs (application programming interfaces) that allow you to store performance data about each of these applications. (Save room for storing the risk level information covered later in this chapter.)

There are two ways to gather information using the AWS Discovery Service:

>> **Agentless:** This system collects data by gathering it from your VMWare application. If you have not deployed virtual machines at this point in your migration to the cloud, this system won't be useful. If you choose AWS as your cloud service provider, you'll find that AWS and VMWare are intricately interconnected.

>> **Agent-based:** Deploy this application on each of your servers, both physical and virtual. The system then collects a variety of information, including the number of applications currently running on the server, the network connections, the performance metrics, as well as a listing other processes currently running.

Google Cloud Discovery Service

This particular discovery service is built into the Google Cloud. If you've already gotten started using the Google Cloud for your applications, you can make use of instance metadata, which is great for obtaining information on elements such as an application's IP address, the machine type, and other network information.

The project metadata collected by the Google Cloud Discovery Service tracks the same kind of information but includes applications that may still be running in your (physical) data center. When you're ready to tackle collecting instance and project metadata, check out the following link to Google documentation on storing and retrieving this kind of information:

https://cloud.google.com/compute/docs/metadata/overview

Knowing Your SLA Agreements with Service Providers

A *service level agreement*, also known as an SLA, spells out the performance and reliability levels promised to you by your cloud service provider. Though performance isn't technically part of cloud security, it's part of the overall availability of your applications and data. Your company's IT department likely has SLA agreements in place with the departments it serves. These SLA agreements depend on the cloud service providers doing their part, and they give you an idea of what they promise. For example, you can't promise 99.99 percent uptime if the cloud service provider offers only 99.5 percent. Some SLA agreements might also include references to the security they provide.

REMEMBER

One main benefit of using the cloud is that some of the security responsibility for your applications is handled by the cloud service provider. This normally includes physical security and some, but not all, antimalware security. They may additionally offer security services for hire.

Here are links to the many SLA agreements offered by some of the top clouds. Though this list is by no means complete, it gives you an idea of what's being offered and what you might expect from the cloud service provider you select or have selected:

>> **Amazon:** https://aws.amazon.com/legal/service-level-agreements

>> **Google:** https://cloud.google.com/terms/sla

>> **Oracle:** www.oracle.com/cloud/sla

These service level agreements cover issues such as guaranteed uptime, disk operation efficiency, domain name system (DNS) integrity, email delivery, and more. Most of these are guaranteed at levels approaching 100 percent. Because nothing is perfect, they usually guarantee 99.99 percent or 99.95 percent for the unforeseen failures that can and do happen, but don't lose sleep over it. Statistically, you're safe with these services.

Where is the security?

One promise that's hard to track down in a cloud service provider's SLA is one concerning security. Security isn't guaranteed — just implied. Cloud service providers protect your data and applications to the limit of their ability, including issues such as physical security and some degree of malware detection by a 24/7 network operations center.

Because security is a shared responsibility, you often find that, in discussions about their security, cloud service providers talk about how they can help you create a secure cloud experience. Many of them have tools for these tasks:

>> Encrypting data

>> Monitoring for malware attack

>> Remediating catastrophic failure

Some of the applications that perform these tasks are third-party products and services that interoperate with the cloud service provider. You generally find the partner companies listed on the cloud service provider's website.

TIP

Explore the security and service offerings of companies that are partnering with your selected cloud service provider. These companies are usually certified and provide a seamless software experience.

Knowing your part

When it comes to cloud security, the ball is primarily in your court. It's up to you to decide whether you have the company resources needed in order to provide the necessary security services. You can also choose to contract with a third-party service provider. They generally offer security monitoring and in some cases also provide applications for identity and login management.

TIP

Consider using an artificial intelligence (AI) security framework. See *Cloud Security For Dummies* by Ted Coombs (published by Wiley) for more detail about how using artificial intelligence for IT operations (AIOps, for short) can help you integrate your cloud security into your overall cybersecurity using big data to recognize data intrusions and speed up resolutions.

Building Your Team

One part of security planning that's often overlooked involves the important step of building a security team. The people on the team don't need to be security or cloud experts, but they need to understand the kinds of applications and data that your company is running in the cloud. Your success depends largely on putting together the right team, so this section talks about putting together that team.

Finding the right people

It's true that data security issues normally cross boundaries within a company: Different departments or groups run different applications, have different security requirements, and possibly follow some different legal data protection requirements. For cloud computing environments, this is even more true — cloud computing not only spans the various parts of your company but is also, in most cases, hosted outside of your company's data center. This increases the responsibility of managing the security of the various parts of your cloud environment.

The people you want on your team will help build your security plan and later make sure that it's implemented within their neck of the woods. Because these team members will work closely with the people using the cloud applications and associated data, it often becomes their responsibility to do the housekeeping to make sure their coworkers are following the best security practices. They don't just wander around looking for "sticky notes" with passwords stuck to monitors — they educate, they do some of the policing, and they further the objectives of the plan they help create. This strategy spreads the responsibility for cloud security throughout the entire company.

Including stakeholders

When talking about stakeholders, you might have a tendency to look around the room during a meeting to spot people you think may be interested in being responsible for cloud security. Choosing the right stakeholders is a bit of an art. Getting the right people on your team is important for maximum success. There are a number of stakeholders you might not have imagined that can be involved when using cloud services, including these:

>> **Cloud service providers:** These are the companies providing the actual cloud services, such as Infrastructure as a Service (IaaS), Software as a Service (SaaS), and Platforms as a Service (PaaS).

>> **Cloud carriers:** These are the telecom companies providing access to the cloud services. They are often forgotten but are quickly remembered whenever their systems fail. Cloud service providers can promise you 99.99 percent uptime, but if the cloud carrier fails, the promise is moot.

>> **Cloud brokers:** These companies provide value added services on top of cloud service providers. You can think of them as packagers. They're important because the value added services they provide can cover areas such as security and identity management applications.

>> **Cloud auditors:** This one is exactly what it sounds like — third-party services that audit your systems to make sure you're complying either with items such as your SLA agreements or with regulations safeguarding your data.

>> **Cloud consumers:** This one consists of you and the people in your company. You and your company's end users are an important part of developing your security plan.

TIP

Find a contact, within the organization, from each of the various cloud service providers you use and make them part of your team.

When selecting company stakeholders, you might be tempted to choose only department heads to be on your security team. In many situations, they are not the people most familiar with the applications and how they're used. For example, department heads might not know which external applications are being accessed via an API, and they may not be up to speed on the level of security involved in managing the credentials used to gain access to the API.

Find the people who are using the applications and data — the *actual* stakeholders, in other words — and put them on your team. This strategy does two things:

>> It involves the people most likely to be impacted in creating and knowing the security plan. That way, it's not handed down to them in a memo that gets "filed." Instead, they have a personal stake in making the plan work.

>> It lets the employees who are most familiar with the applications and data they use every day know who needs what level of access to which applications.

TIP

Hold group meetings (Zoom is just one option) and select your stakeholder team members based on their level of interest, excitement, and knowledge.

Creating a Risk Management Plan

After you've put together your team, it's time to get to work. After the obligatory icebreaker "What's your name, which department do you work in, and where's your favorite lunch restaurant?" the real work of creating a security plan starts.

You can't begin protecting something when you don't know what you're protecting and how much protection it needs. Not all applications and data are created equal. Some may require access limitations to only a few people and need special encrypted communications, whereas others may require a simple username and password for access. Get started by creating a simple diagram, as shown in Figure 1-1, that will give you an idea of where your risks may be lurking. This section covers some of the basic strategies for creating a risk management plan.

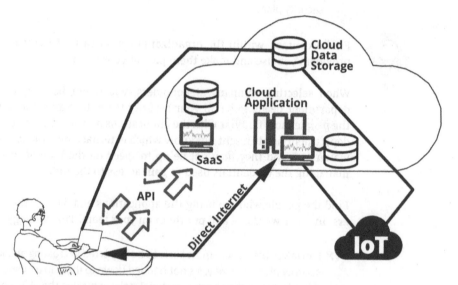

FIGURE 1-1: Map applications, APIs, data storage, and IoT devices.

Identifying the risks

If your relatively small business is looking to document the security risks you're facing, you can probably start with just a simple spreadsheet. If you have many assets, you might consider either having your developers put together a database application or use one of the commercial asset management applications.

REMEMBER

Asset management applications differ from configuration management database applications. Although they can overlap in some areas, their focus is quite different. Asset management applications deal with *assets* — anything that has value, in other words (admittedly, a fairly broad definition). A configuration management program manages configuration items, or CIs — those items one uses to successfully complete the much narrower task of delivering an IT service. So, CIs are assets, but not all assets are CIs. An asset might be a knowledge base, but not be important enough to be managed as part of an IT service. Configuration management database applications (also known as CMDBs) are cooler than asset management programs because they track how various systems interoperate with one another. When it comes to risk management, knowing how stuff works together is the key.

Most configuration management systems (CMSes) can generate a service map showing dependencies between systems. It's pretty cool.

For now, put together a list of the assets that are critical to your operation. You can worry later about what kind of software program manages them.

To get started, list all your assets, including these:

>> Cloud data storage

>> Local data storage

>> Cloud applications

>> Local applications

>> Data repositories accessed via APIs

>> Computers, mobile devices, IoT devices

>> Other compute devices

When documenting your assets list, it helps to list the location where each device might be found. This includes specifying whether it's a local physical location or in the cloud. (And, if it's in the cloud, be sure to say which one.)

Assessing the consequences of disaster

No one wants to think about consequences, but in order to prepare for eventual catastrophes, you must know what potential events might occur. Carefully think about the risk involved for each asset. Ask yourself questions such as, "If this device were compromised, or destroyed by malicious hackers, what would do I stand to lose?" Put this assessed risk into a column or database field.

Assigning a numeric value to the potential risk allows you to create some useful visuals, as covered later in this chapter.

Pointing fingers at the right people

After you have an idea of the risk involved with each asset, you should assign that risk to the team member best capable of managing that risk. Spell out the roles and responsibilities involved with managing the risk.

TIP

Don't dump all the responsibilities on one person, or even on a couple of people. Spread them out so that no one gets overwhelmed, particularly if things start going wrong. You don't want one person trying to manage a potential catastrophe.

Create a role-based responsibility matrix. That term sounds like a mouthful, but it's simply a list of responsibilities, a description that lays out both what's involved in the responsibility and who's assigned to manage it. They may also have people on staff who ultimately take on the assigned tasks.

REMEMBER

Perhaps the most important step in creating the plan is to figure out how not to fail. Think of the things you need to do to prevent, to the best of your ability, bad things from happening. Perhaps this strategy involves limiting data access or ensuring that access occurs only by way of an encrypted tunnel.

Disaster planning

If all the steps you take to avoid disaster are successful, you might never need to implement contingency plans — but you should have such plans on hand anyway. What will you do if the nightmare becomes real and you're faced with a situation such as a ransomware attack, where all your data is locked up and the bad guys are asking for millions in Bitcoin? Maybe a hot backup with different security protocols running in the background that you can quickly switch to can do the trick. Maybe not. The thing is, you simply have to be creative in coming up with a solution that you know will work, given your particular circumstances.

REMEMBER

Keep in mind the old saying "No risk, no reward." Risk is something that should be managed — few things come without risk.

In your risk assessment plan, meet with the stakeholders and talk about the information you've put together so far and decide how much risk you can actually live with. The first solution you suggest — a hot backup, for example — may be too expensive or too much work to be feasible, but stakeholders need to be aware that, without it, there is higher risk. And neither is it the case that a shutdown is all you have to deal with. Customer trust can fly out the window if all their personal financial details are released to the world, or at least to the world of people trying to exploit it.

REMEMBER

Managing risk isn't a one-time endeavor. It's a challenge that you have to constantly focus on because risks change. New exploits are created. Staff turnover can create new risks if the new hires are uneducated in the security procedures you've put in place.

When Security Is Your Responsibility

When you finally have worked out the details of your cloud security plan, you still have to put that plan into action. Being responsible for cloud security is a bit like being a circus ringmaster: You're sure to have irons in many fires at a time, and a bit of juggling may be going on.

REMEMBER

Your security plan is not a dead document. It's meant to be enhanced, revised, and ignored on weekends. (Okay, maybe not the last one.) Revisit the plan often to make sure that your asset list is up to date and that you have an accurate understanding of the risk level of your various assets.

Determining which assets to protect

As suggested earlier in this chapter, you can break out a spreadsheet and creating an application to track your applications by entering them into the spreadsheet, but in the end it's probably more cost effective to just use an automated asset tracking tool. These tools allow you to keep your list of assets up to date daily — something you probably couldn't do manually, or at least wouldn't want to.

These are the assets you track:

>> Software applications

>> Computer hardware, including mobile devices

>> Networks, both hardware and software based

>> Internet of Things devices or other technology devices

Using an automation tool

An *IT asset management* tool (also known as an ITAM because everything IT needs its own acronym) is a software tool that allows you to track all your company's technology assets. It's a bit like the spreadsheet describes earlier in this chapter — but one on steroids.

ITAM tools track detailed information such as the purchase price, maintenance costs, repair costs, and device manufacturer. This is important information, particularly as part of a disaster recovery plan.

You have to know where everything is at any given moment. Because people are the greatest threat to security, you want to know where all those employee laptops and mobile devices are and what condition they're in. Do they have the latest security patches? Are all the licenses up to date? Are passwords being changed regularly?

Contractual information is also tracked in an ITAM tool. You can track warranty information, licenses, support agreements, and any terms and conditions for use, particularly for software assets.

Letting ITAM help you comply

Many companies must work within different security compliance regulations. For example, SOC 2 compliance can give your company an edge when working with sensitive customer information. (For more on SOC 2, see the nearby sidebar, "SOC 2 in a nutshell.")

SOC 2 IN A NUTSHELL

SOC 2, the number-2 variety of system organizational control, is a best practices audit to make sure that your business-to-business (B2B) services are secure and trustworthy. Becoming SOC 2 certified lets the businesses you work with know that they can depend on you to secure their information. The trust service criteria include the ones described here:

- **Security:** Securing access to information
- **Availability:** Making sure your systems are up at least 99 percent of the time.
- **Process Integrity:** Maintaining data change authorization
- **Confidentiality:** Keeping sensitive information safe
- **Privacy:** Securing data lifecycle management

Becoming SOC 2 compliant isn't an overnight process. It can take up to a year to get your policies and procedures in place to guarantee the level of security SOC 2 requires. This is more than just a piece of paper: When you do business with a company that is SOC 2 certified, you can have a high degree of confidence that its leaders have done the hard work of making sure your data remains safe.

Applications designed to manage and protect your company's assets

Spreadsheets and databases can be great risk assessment tools for smaller business, but if you have a larger company with many assets, you may want to get started immediately using an automation tool to automatically discover your assets, and update your CMDB or asset tracking system, and then manage assets with greater visibility. You can also find applications that will assist you in discovering vulnerabilities in the overall *attack surface* — all the points an attacker might gain entry into your system — and alert you to fixes or, in the case of AI deep learning systems, will automatically repair the problem before it even rears its ugly head.

This list details a few of the major applications, to get you started:

» **Qualsys** (www.qualys.com): Here's a company offering a whole suite of applications for asset tracking, cloud and IT security, and regulation compliance. The (free) asset tracking app does global IT asset inventory and discovery. Its goal is to make everything visible. Qualsys also offers several applications for threat detection, a CMDB for configuration item tracking, an inventory of digital certificates, and a cloud security monitoring app, among others. The cloud security monitoring app continuously monitors cloud assets and resources for misconfigurations and nonstandard deployments.

» **Ivanti** (www.ivanti.com): With Ivanti's tools, you can use AI to discover problems with your cloud assets. In fact, you can automagically discover and fix problems before they even become an issue. That's the great thing about deep learning and AI; Ivanti tools comb through massive amounts of data in order to spot things that are acting out of the ordinary and then either alert you or automatically fix the problems. This is the essential use of AIOps.

» **Tanium Asset** (www.tanium.com/products/tanium-asset): Visibility is a vital part of managing complicated cloud environments. Automating asset discovery and being able to see your assets and how they're performing is critical to efficiency and success. The Tanium Asset application is up to the task, even feeding real-time information to your CMDB so that you have the most up to date configuration information available.

» **Tenable.io** (www.tenable.com/products/tenable-io): Tenable is a risk-based vulnerability management SaaS application. As such, it gives you a view of where vulnerabilities might exist and the risks they pose. After scanning your entire network, it can suggest ways for you to shore up weak points. It also integrates with a CMDB — without having to use scanners or agents. Their vulnerability assessment can provide information as short-lived resources scale up and down, something often missed during normal vulnerability scans.

» **Detectify** (https://detectify.com): This suggestion isn't an asset management application per se, but it still helps you protect one of your most important assets. One point of weakness for many companies is the website. Though this isn't the number-one asset weakness, it's likely number two — and it's public-facing. One thing you can do to test your website for vulnerabilities is to *penetration-test* it (known as *pen-testing*). Many software applications out there can assist you with this process — Detectify is one of the better apps out there. It scans your public-facing websites, looking for vulnerabilities, and offers suggestions on how to overcome them.

Knowing your possible threat level

When figuring out the risk for each of your assets, set up a standardized threat-level metric that works for you. You can also use the standard shown in Table 1-1, if it's easier.

TABLE 1-1   **Risk Levels**

Risk Level	Asset Type
Low	Public data, such as an informational website
Low	Easily recoverable systems that contain no confidential information or critical services and are not networked to higher -risk networks
Low	Runs noncritical services
Medium	Contains confidential or internal-use-only data
Medium	Network-connected to other medium risk networks
Medium	Provides important services or information important to business operations, but not enough to stop or severely damage the business
High	Contains secret, financial, personally identifying information
High	Contains data restricted by compliance regulations, such as medical records or financial and credit card information
High	Provides business-critical services
High	Networked to other high-risk networks.

REMEMBER It's easy to overlook systems, servers, or devices that may not contain any confidential information or critical services themselves but are networked to systems that are higher risk and contain risky information. The seemingly low-risk system may act as a gateway for unauthorized access to the higher-risk information.

TIP

Different regions of the world have varying restrictions on privacy and different compliance regulations. The European Union is a good example of an area with higher privacy regulations and "the right to be forgotten." Companies that maintain public information, like Google for instance, are required to remove private information at the request of the person to which it refers. In other words, if you don't want to appear in a search, you can have that searchable information removed, maintaining your privacy.

Van Gogh with it (paint a picture of your scenario)

A picture is worth a thousand words. Making your risk assessment simple to read and easily understood by those responsible for protecting systems is best done with a heatmap.

A *heatmap,* with colors from green to red, allows you to quickly assess the risk and dangers involved with each possible security breach or system failure. Figure 1-2 gives you an idea of the color scheme you might use in creating a heatmap. Even here with the scenarios laid out, you can see that the deep red (shown in the printed book as dark gray) is reserved for only the riskiest scenarios and represents a lower percentage of overall risk.

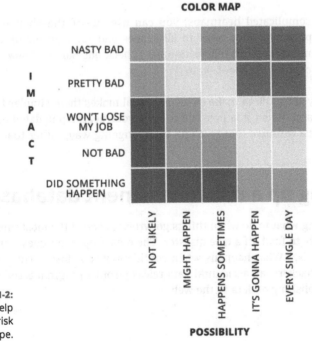

FIGURE 1-2:
Color maps help
visualize your risk
landscape.

Giving each color a numeric value allows you to do things like sort your spreadsheet based on overall risk. You can see in Figure 1-3 that the values show the highest risk quickly and easily. Giving each risk a numeric value also allows you to export this data to other applications that will help evaluate and monitor your risk.

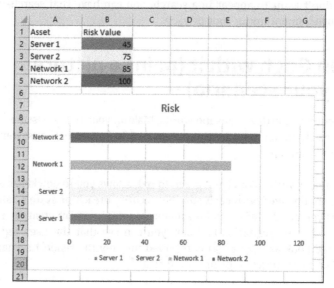

FIGURE 1-3:
Simple
spreadsheet
heatmap shows
the highest risk.

TIP

For more complicated heatmaps, you can use an off-the-shelf heatmap generation application. They come in all shapes and sizes, including ones you can integrate into a map for geopositioning. (Check out Balbix at `www.balbix.com/ insights/cyber-risk-heat-map/`.)

Whatever you can do to make concepts visual makes them simpler for your team to understand. When it is possible to have your heatmap updated automatically, you'll have a resource that is useful in an ongoing way, rather than just a planning tool.

Setting up a risk assessment database

Determining what to do when things go wrong is one of the most important steps you can take to fend off a true disaster. The most important question you need an answer for is, "What happens when confidentiality is lost?" This loss might be caused by hackers, an accidental data release from a program error, or the inadvertent publishing of data to the web.

TIP

More damage is done by trying to cover up a data breach than by the breach itself. It's a difficult task to own up to this kind of security failure, but it's the right thing to do.

Confidential data loss

You should make a plan to deal with confidentiality loss, even though it may seem like trying to close the barn doors after the horses have escaped. The loss will have generated an impact that might be felt for a long time. The good news is that if you work to shore up your security after a failure, trust can be rebuilt. Rarely do companies go out of business for this kind of a security breach. If the information was of a personal nature, it may be more difficult for people to secure a new credit card, protect themselves from identity theft, or prevent bad actors from trying to steal money from their bank accounts.

Integrity loss

Whenever critical infrastructure has been compromised, whether it's a server or a network, it temporarily loses its ability to host services and data in a trusted manner. Luckily, this is the simplest problem of all to overcome.

Make sure you have applied all the security patches and increased security on the devices that were involved in the breach. Recover any lost data from backups. Monitor the regenerated system or systems like crazy. Be aware that some of the data that may have been compromised can contain information that makes it easier for a hacker to gain access to the newly regenerated system.

Data access loss

Many scenarios can lead to data loss. Data theft might have occurred, or data may have been encrypted during a ransomware attack, or the data storage device may have been attacked or simply failed. Part of the risk assessment must include the plan for dealing with these kinds of catastrophic losses and a plan to recover from them.

Data access loss can also be temporary, caused by network failure such as the one caused when the cloud computing company, Fastly, went down. That failure took down some of the largest Internet businesses for an hour in June of 2021.

Access to data can also be lost to a software failure such as the database management system's failure to respond or the hardware hosting the data failing or degrading. Hackers can also block access to data through exploits such as denial of service (DoS) attacks.

When you build the risk assessment database, you want to track fields such as these:

>> The prospect that the negative event will occur

>> The possibility of a confidentiality breach

>> The impact of integrity loss

>> The impact of loss of availability

With each of these items, you should include the *security level* (high, medium or low) and the *mitigation plan* — in other words, instructions for what to do when things go wrong and you haven't had your morning coffee yet.

TIP

The good news is that much of the hard work of developing a cloud security framework has already been done for you by somebody else. You can make free use of the following established frameworks:

>> **NIST risk management framework:** https://csrc.nist.gov/Projects/risk-management

>> **CSA CCM framework:** https://cloudsecurityalliance.org/research/cloud-controls-matrix

>> **ISO 27017/18 framework:** www.iso27001security.com/html/27017.html

>> **ISO 27701 framework:** www.iso.org/standard/71670.html (Privacy information management)

Avoiding Security Work with the Help of the Cloud

Using a cloud for your applications or data storage doesn't completely free you from the duties of cybersecurity, but it does move *some* of the responsibility to the cloud service provider. This section talks about what those responsibilities are and how you can best work with your cloud service provider to implement the best security plan.

Having someone else ensure physical security

Physical security in a data center can be a costly and time-consuming headache. Badges, biometrics, physical barriers, and closed circuit camera systems are all part of the physical security you may need to maintain around your server equipment. Okay, you might have your server in a repurposed utility closet with a cooling fan, but if you're serious about protecting direct access to the server, you need a great deal of infrastructure, continued maintenance, and personnel to manage it all.

By the way, that server running in the closet just may have data on it that you'd rather not let out into the wild. Part of the risk analysis will reveal just how much protection you should have around this device and deciding whether the data and applications should live in the cloud is part of that assessment.

One benefit of using the cloud for your services and data storage is that the cloud service provider is ultimately responsible for maintaining physical security around the hardware hosting your stuff.

Making sure providers have controls to separate customer data

Cloud service providers generally host many customers on the same hardware. This is known as multitenancy. When malware infects one tenant, it may allow access to the hypervisor that controls the virtual machines on the device, potentially allowing unauthorized access to other virtual machines belonging to other cloud customers. There is no simple fix other than to guard against malware. It's important to understand that multitenancy is one of the risks of doing business in the cloud.

Recognizing that cloud service providers can offer better security

Let me give you an example — here are some of the things Amazon Web Services does to guarantee the security of your applications and data:

>> **Geographic site selection** to reduce risk from natural disasters such as earthquakes, hurricanes, and flooding

>> **Multiple data centers** that provide a redundant backup and failover mechanism

>> **Services** such as business continuity plans and pandemic responses

>> **Restricting physical access** to approved employees and contractors

>> **Monitoring and logging all data center access** as well as providing security guards, CCTV cameras, and sensor-intrusion detection systems

>> **Monitoring data centers** for fire, water leaks, climate and temperature, and electric power with backup

>> **Carrying out security and risk review** internally and by third-party companies to evaluate ongoing security risks

As you can see, these measures are more than most businesses — even large businesses — will want to take on by themselves. You literally rent all this security when you begin using a cloud service provider.

REMEMBER

These measures aren't unique to AWS. All major cloud service providers have these kinds of security measures in place. Some of them even surpass these measures with antipersonnel plants, such as creeping juniper and other noxious or thorny plants, around the building, antitank barriers that can be raised by security, and even oxygen-free server rooms.

Chapter **2**

Getting Down to Business

C hapter 1 of Book 4 sets the stage for your cloud security rollout. Armed with a plan, you can now get busy with the details of securing your private and cloud computing environments. In this chapter, you gain an understanding of your responsibilities when using the cloud, learn about the various services offered by cloud service providers, see how security is shared between you and the cloud service provider, and manage your environment by restricting access and managing the plethora of connected devices.

Cloud security can be easily overlooked or taken for granted. A few years ago, pro wrestling fans woke up to find out that their personal information had been exploited when the WWE data stored on an Amazon Web Services server had been hacked. The personal information of over 3 million fans was leaked. Though hackers gained access through an apparent database vulnerability, the hack may never have happened if the WWE had been better prepared. You must understand your part in the world of cloud security — and collecting the information into systems that give you an overview of your environment is one of the most important steps you can take. Without this overview, security planning is like slogging through mud.

Negotiating the Shared Responsibility Model

Each cloud service provider adheres to a model of shared security (also called *shared responsibility*). This model outlines which security areas they're responsible for and what areas are your responsibility. This differs, depending on which cloud service provider you decide to go with, or in some cases your company may use multiple cloud service providers.

REMEMBER

Different departments in a larger company commonly set up their own cloud computing environments, which is often the easiest way to gain access to applications unique to their department or a quick-and-easy way to set up remote data storage. These departments likely fail to consider the security responsibilities they've taken on when they set up their cloud service. It then becomes the responsibility of the person in charge of cloud security to check the shared responsibility between your company and the cloud service provider.

The responsibility varies depending on the type of service you're making use of. These service types are covered in greater detail later in this chapter. Table 2-1 gives you an idea of how responsibilities are different, depending on the service. Read further to learn the details of Software as a Service (SaaS), Platforms as a Service (PaaS), and Infrastructure as a Service (IaaS).

Coloring inside the lines

You must pay attention to the details of how your data security is shared with a cloud service provider. Much of the security is your responsibility. "Coloring inside the lines" (see the section heading) means that you should use a guide to make sure you're following industry best practices. You can use an industry standard guide that can be downloaded for free. Here are a couple different downloads:

» **CIS Controls Cloud Companion Guide:** (www.cisecurity.org/white-papers/cis-controls-cloud-companion-guide)

This document highlights some of the basic service models covered later in this chapter.

» **NIST Cybersecurity Framework Policy Template Guide:** (www.cisecurity.org/wp-content/uploads/2020/07/NIST-CSF-Policy-Template-Guide-2020-0720-1.pdf)

The NIST Cybersecurity Framework is the industry standard you will want to follow for your IT security.

TABLE 2-1   **Responsibilities per Service**

Responsibility	SaaS	PaaS	IaaS	Your Business
Devices	YOU	YOU	YOU	YOU
Data	YOU	YOU	YOU	YOU
Identity accounting*	YOU/ THEM	YOU/ THEM	YOU	YOU
Computer applications	THEM	YOU/ THEM	YOU	YOU
Virtual networks	THEM	YOU/ THEM	YOU	YOU
Operating systems	THEM	THEM	YOU	YOU
Physical servers	THEM	THEM	THEM	YOU
Physical networks	THEM	THEM	THEM	YOU
Physical data center	THEM	THEM		YOU

Some cloud service providers offer identity accounting services as an add-on or via a third party.

TIP

Make sure all your security keys are secure and up to date. These are the keys that are the foundation of your encryption, and it's the encryption that keeps your data safe, whether stored or in transit to and from the cloud. Book 4, Chapter 6 goes into more detail about managing your keys.

Learning what to expect from a data center

When you contract services from a cloud service provider, it will have one or more data centers that provide various kinds of security. Because that security policy essentially becomes yours, you should review it carefully. Here are some items that call for special attention:

>> **Physical security:** Basic physical security for a data center first involves ensuring that there are only a few access points. That means the building generally has no windows and few doors and that the few doors that exist are manned by security guards who monitor the number of people entering and leaving. The people passing through security machines usually need to enter some type of digital access information, whether it's a security card or biometric information such as a handprint, fingerprint, retinal scan, or facial ID. In some cases, a *man trap* is used. A person enters a door, sometimes

unlocked by a security guard watching on a camera, entering a small space (sally port), and a second door must then be unlocked, either by a guard or some other form of biometric like a handprint or eye scan.

>> **Virtual security:** Virtual security is best known as malware detection. Just as you might do this kind of virus and malware checking on your own personal computer, data centers have a huge responsibility to check data for tampering and malware when it resides in, or is transferred in and out of, its data center. This real-time monitoring of data provides good but not perfect security, because new exploits are created every minute.

Data centers must also monitor attempts to gain unauthorized access by hacking network connections and public-facing devices. Firewalls, port scanners, and AI-based network analysis tools are used to monitor against attack. *Honeypots* are caches of fake data serving no purpose other than to alert network administrators if someone accesses them.

>> **Redundancy:** Knowing that things break or fail, data centers must have redundant systems, whether it's in the form of data storage devices or items such as cooling systems. Servers generate a lot of heat and quickly fail if cooling systems go down. Another type of infrastructure that must be redundant is the physical Internet connection, whether it's a fiber bundle, T3 line, or any other connection to the outside world. It happens that trunk lines are cut accidentally by crews digging in the street, which is often the cause of massive Internet outages. Network systems must be ready to route traffic over backup lines when this happens.

>> **Power continuity:** Emergency generators and battery backup systems can provide continuous electricity during a power outage. Many large data centers have more than one redundant power system in the event of an emergency. There is one caveat to this — power to the servers may remain turned on with backup power, but your connection to the servers may disappear because of power outages locally at your facility or with Internet service providers that connect you to cloud services.

>> **Disaster preparedness:** Storms, floods, earthquakes, volcanic eruptions, tsunamis, hurricanes, tornadoes, and fires — oh, my! These events certainly happen, and data centers must be prepared to withstand any of these or have a backup site that's ready to take over if the site is lost or severely damaged. Some data centers are built to withstand nuclear warheads.

REMEMBER

Though every precaution might be taken, disastrous situations transcend any human ability to keep your services live. The best anyone can do is make sure that plans are in place to manage the likely disasters. These preparations can be costly and cumbersome and beyond what your company could possibly manage on its own within onsite data centers, so putting your resources in the cloud is often the best choice to avoid disasters.

Taking responsibility for your 75 percent

You cannot run away from the fact that, in the long run, you're the one responsible for your data security. Though shared responsibility is great, and a benefit of using the cloud, you can't just relax, thinking that half your job is done. (See the matrix diagram of these responsibilities later in this chapter, in Figure 2-1.)

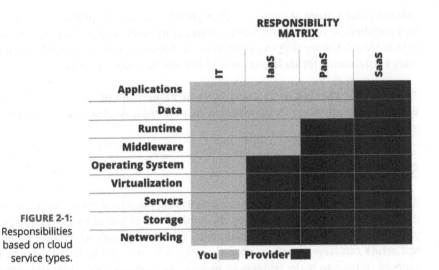

RESPONSIBILITY MATRIX

FIGURE 2-1:
Responsibilities based on cloud service types.

SaaS, PaaS, IaaS, AaaA!

The IT world is full of acronyms and abbreviations, and cloud computing is no different. All the services seem to have a double *a* in the middle of their name — perhaps a clue that what follows next is that this service involves cloud computing.

SaaS

SaaS, or Software as a Service, is a popular way to use software applications hosted in the cloud rather than on your desktop or even your local data center. Chances are high that your company uses some of the popular ones, like Salesforce for tracking customers and sales leads, Dropbox for saving and sharing files, Shopify for ecommerce, or Zoom — which needs no explanation.

The advantage of using SaaS is that the service provider — usually, a software vendor hosting its application using a cloud service provider — takes responsibility for updates and delivery. This is helpful because IT departments trying to roll out software updates to individual computers can be a major pain.

It's also great for the software company because changes can be made quickly, and if security issues pop up, they can be dealt with immediately. This definitely fits the agile model of software development: *Release often*. The other benefit is that these software vendors usually take advantage of the cloud's ability to distribute applications geographically nearest to where they are being used, known as *edge computing* or *edge delivery*.

Another great feature of using a SaaS application is that the problem of how various members of your organization can access the same application and the same data is solved. Connecting to applications in the cloud does away with older and more cumbersome technologies such as Remote Desktop connections.

REMEMBER

The world has changed in so many ways. Working from home is now the norm. Working from anywhere in the world is also common. SaaS solves the complexity of shared applications.

SaaS security

When setting the risk assessment of using SaaS applications, you want to consider the types of data being handled by the application. If you're using Google Docs, you might be writing classified documents. When using SaaS accounting systems, bad actors can have access to your financial info and customer list, and to the vendors you use to make widgets or provide your services. Consider the security needs of each application.

Though the security responsibility ultimately falls on you, SaaS providers usually take on the responsibility of managing user login identification. But back to you now. Persuading your fellow employees to use strong passwords that are changed frequently and are unique to the application is no simple task. Consider implementing a password manager, a type of vault that stores the passwords unique to each application. That way, if one password is hacked, the attackers don't have carte blanche to every single one of your accounts.

One technology that is sometimes used is single sign on (SSO). Systems such as Imprivata (www.imprivata.com/) allow users to use one set of credentials to access many applications without having to maintain a different user ID and password for each one.

WARNING

Don't think that just because companies are huge, they must somehow follow awesome security practices that are sure to keep your identity safe. In 2020, Zoom announced that 500,000 user passwords had been stolen and put up for sale. Though having hackers attend your Zoom meetings for you might appear to be an easy way out of all your commitments, it does little for corporate security.

PaaS

PaaS, or Platforms as a Service, is a cloud-based service that allows software developers to easily write code using tools provided by the PaaS service provider in a virtualized environment. This means that the applications you use are shared only with the people on your development team. It's a bit like having your own server, except that the server is virtual and may actually be on the same machine as other virtual servers.

PaaS servers generally provide development tools, storage, databases, and, of course, the operating system for which you might be developing — normally, either Linux or Windows. This is a slick idea because your developer can be using a Windows machine and be connected to a virtualized Linux platforms for development.

Here are some benefits of using PaaS:

>> Able to develop from anywhere

>> Can easily include developers from around the world

>> Able to provide a highly secure development environment

>> Rapidly scalable

PaaS security

The PaaS provider handles most of the security, and it's not unlike all other forms of cloud or standard IT security, where authentication of the user is the key to guard against unauthorized access to your development environment. When you reach the point of selecting a PaaS provider, take the time to see what types of authorization they require. Most of them are username- and password-based. Check to see the level of complexity they require in a password and whether they offer two-factor authentication, biometrics, or other security measures. Because these services are generally provided via a web-based environment, the whole login process is encrypted using secure sockets layer (SSL) protocol.

When you're satisfied that the level of security provided by the PaaS provider is sufficient, your developers will be in a position to focus on application security, making certain that the programs they develop can withstand hacking attempts.

IaaS

IaaS, or Infrastructure as a Service, provides computing resources, networking, and data storage on demand. Not only can you get started almost immediately with as much or as little infrastructure as you need, it's generally also provided on a pay-as-you-go basis. This makes using cloud-based servers and networking affordable for even the smallest company.

In the old days (before some of you were even out of grade school), you could conceivably rent a server or co-locate a machine in a data center, but you were responsible for nearly 100 percent of the security and if you needed more capacity, it was a long-and-involved process to get another server up and running. Virtualization changed all that, and now infrastructure providers can quickly spin up a new server for you and —when you no longer need it — make it go away.

TIP

When you need access to underlying hardware, it's possible to take advantage of BMaaS (no, that's not a joke). Bare Metal as a Service has all the benefits of cloud computing, such as pay-as-you-go, but additionally gives you hardware access. Of course, you lose some of the benefits of virtualization with this option.

IaaS security

Sometimes, you need more security than is generally provided by a typical IaaS environment. This is when you might want to look into a *logical network*, a virtualized network that appears to the end user like a hardware network. it gives you the ability to create a private network within a public cloud. This level of security may be required in order to meet compliance requirements or simply to provide higher-level security for your high-risk data or applications.

Larger cloud service providers will have tools for creating virtual private clouds. These services allow you to

>> Set your own IP address

>> Create subnets

>> Configure routing tables

Amazon Web Services (AWS), for example, even allows you to store your data on its Simple Storage Service (Amazon S3) and then restrict access so that it's only accessible by applications from within your virtual private cloud.

FaaS

When you create functionality on infrastructure managed by the cloud service provider, this is Function as a Service, or FaaS. It's also known as *serverless computing*, which is a shortcut way to build functionality without the hassles of an IaaS environment. The cloud service provider takes care of everything else, and all you have to do is provide the functionality. When it comes to simplicity and scalability, FaaS is the way to go.

SaaS, PaaS, IaaS, FaaS responsibilities

To easily see how each service type stacks up when it comes to who takes responsibility for managing the individual components, such as applications, servers, and networking, check out Figure 2-1.

REMEMBER

The responsibility for security ultimately falls on you, whether you provide it or make sure someone else is adequately providing it.

Managing Your Environment

The first and most important step in managing your environment involves cataloging your assets to best protect them. In a large organization, finding all the assets and maintaining an accurate and current inventory is no simple undertaking. You need to use a discovery tool along with a log management tool, usually required for most scenarios involving compliance requirements.

There are two basic types of discovery tools:

>> **Active:** These software programs ping devices on the network to see whether they're connected. Some active discovery tools log in to the devices to catalog applications being run on the devices. One downside to using an active discovery tool is that it can be bandwidth intensive. In other words, it can slow your network with its constant pinging and possibly returning application inventories. It also requires a bit of complicated security to allow traffic in both directions between devices and the discovery tool.

>> **Passive:** These software applications act as listeners, waiting for devices to send information about themselves known as *system logs,* or *syslogs.* This approach uses far less bandwidth and is easier to configure for firewall security. Using log management software to return syslog data allows both

active or live data as well as archival logs to be used for identifying connected devices. The downside of using a passive discovery tool is that each device must be able to send syslog data, and not all devices are configured to do that — particularly, IoT devices.

Here are some discovery tools:

LogicMonitor: www.logicmonitor.com/ (Active)

Spiceworks: www.spiceworks.com (Passive)

OpenNMS: www.opennms.com (Passive)

TIP

I also want to mention DHCP (Dynamic Host Configuration Protocol) logging, which can track the devices trying to log on to your network. DHCP is the network program that hands out IP addresses to devices that aren't configured to have dedicated IP addresses. Auditing tools are available to track DHCP access and, most importantly, changes over time. This way, you or an AI can determine, when possible, that you might be under attack. You can find many of these tools — select one depending on the operating system you require.

Restricting access

Allowing only authorized access to each one of your assets is one of your greatest responsibilities in a shared security model, such as the one you share with your cloud service provider. Book 4, Chapter 4 covers restricting access and authentication in considerable detail.

Briefly, data has associated risks that range from "Whatever — who really cares?" to "If that ever gets out, we're dead." You must take the time to manage who has access to data at each level. Applications are a bit like people in this regard. When applications create data that needs to be restricted — or merely have access to restricted data — they may prove tempting targets for potential attacks.

Make certain that machines with restricted data are networked in a way that prevents access at lower restriction levels. Data access restriction is like the multi-headed monster, Hydra: You cut off one head, and more pop up.

REMEMBER

People are the weakest link in the security chain. Making sure your coworkers use strong passwords and practice safe computing practices is your concern.

Assessing supply chain risk

Restricting access to data and resources for employees of your company is only part of the task. Managing risk and controlling logins to those third parties, vendors, and suppliers who also need access to your data is known as supply chain security risk management.

Depending on how your company does business, this supply chain can include a global and diverse set of service providers. This situation is common now for companies supporting lean development, where a great many of your company's services may be outsourced.

For example, you may have hired programmers from around the world using one of the popular freelancing sites. You've probably done some research or testing to find out what skills they have, but you don't really know who they are or what risks they might pose. They might not even be risks personally, but the site itself might have a weak security infrastructure, or the system might be vulnerable because of a previous hack.

Security risks exist not only within the freelancing market — medium and even large businesses on which you rely may also have weak IT security. In fact, the larger the size of the third-party vendor, the greater the risk landscape.

REMEMBER

Don't make some of the common mistakes of assessing the risk of third parties only when you first contract their services. These risks change over time and should be evaluated on an ongoing basis. People change, and corporations change a lot! Another common mistake is ignoring the small guy. Normally, a great deal of focus is placed on your top suppliers, meaning that the individual freelancers are often forgotten. It's true that it's more work, but every person matters when it comes to evaluating security risks. Sometimes the risks of supply chains often seem to outweigh their usefulness. Of course, only an IT manager sees it this way.

You must consider three main risks in the management of supply chain security:

>> **Data leaks:** Data can leak from both internal and external sources. Data leakage occurs when your private or confidential information is unintentionally released to the public, such as on the Internet. This can happen intentionally when someone steals and exposes your data, or unintentionally due largely to configuration errors. For example, someone checks their account on your web page, and the data of thousands of users suddenly appears.

>> **Supply chain breaches:** Hackers gain entry into part of your supply chain and cause havoc. In some cases, malware can be installed in your products during the manufacturing process. The idea is that the malware, entered in a

less-secure process causes further damage farther down the supply chain, kind of like a time bomb.

>> **Malware attacks:** Recently, the worst kind of malware attack has been ransomware — someone encrypts or blocks access to your data and then demands a payment to release it back to you.

Managing virtual devices

As if tracking physical devices weren't complicated enough, in the increasingly complex environment created by mobile devices, and IoT thingies there is an even more labyrinthine environment — that of virtual devices. A program called a *hypervisor* creates virtual devices, most often servers, with specific operating systems and software ready to go the minute they're spun up (created).

One complex part of tracking virtual devices is that they tend to be ephemeral. They are spun up when needed and then disappear (they're destroyed) when they aren't. Not all virtual devices are ephemeral, and some store and use sensitive data. Obviously, knowing where these devices exist and the risks they pose is important.

Other virtual devices include virtual networks and even virtual clouds. Virtual clouds are usually private clouds hosted within a public cloud.

Application auditing

After you've used one of the discovery tools that shows you a list of devices connected to your network, you should catalog the applications that run on them. Cataloging applications allows you to control application versions, software patches (covered later in this chapter), the types of data and risk levels associated with each application, types of users (roles) that are allowed access to the applications, and (finally) license expirations. Many of the discovery tools manage this task for you, not only letting you know which machines are connected but also polling the device to discover which applications are running on them. This strategy sometimes includes information such as installation dates and version numbers.

Many stand-alone asset discovery applications have been discontinued in favor of smarter applications that use artificial intelligence to track the data flowing through these applications, looking for situations that fall outside of an expected range and alerting you to problems before they even happen. (The acronym here is AIOps, which is short for *artificial intelligence for IT operations.*)

HERDING CATS (MANAGING THE GROWING CHAOS)

One thing you can expect in any technological environment is that it will grow and become more chaotic. This statement is true for so many reasons. One is that the number and types of devices connecting to your network and using data expands every day. Though everyone knows that mobile phones and Internet-connected smart speakers are just one of those ways, now smart glasses, which have gotten a slow start, have started to mature, creating a whole new device type that connects to your cloud applications and uses your data. Also, a new wave of security devices and remote video cameras is on the forefront.

One company at the forefront of providing security at the device level is Deep Instinct, a firm that uses deep learning and other AI techniques to predict potential threats and prevent them on mobile devices. Check out Deep Instinct at www.deepinstinct.com.

Managing Security for Devices Not Under Your Control

Often, certain devices that store and manage important information aren't connected to your company network. These devices generally don't appear in automated asset discovery systems because they don't send log data to a log management program or use DHCP to log in to a network. You can easily overlook these kinds of devices. Some of them appear in the supply chain mentioned earlier in this chapter.

Inventorying devices

Manually inventorying these devices can be critical to your company's information security. Most larger companies put bar code plaques on devices for tracking. Though most of these are for the physical inventory of assets, you can take advantage of those bar codes and manage devices that way. Use these physical tags to tie your devices to a risk management system where more detailed digital tags describe things such as the risk associated with this machine, owner information (and risks about the owner), the expected physical location of the device, and much more. If this sounds like something you would want to pursue, check out www.myassettag.com.

TIP

Use asset inventories when managing periodic device risk assessments. Don't get caught doing one and then never doing them again.

REMEMBER

When you use the cloud, the servers in the cloud aren't under your control. The good news is that when data is stored in the cloud, it isn't as vulnerable to attack as it might be when stored locally. Humans are easy prey for all sorts of social engineering attacks that allow breaches in local security. This is not a flaw shared by data stored in the cloud, which tends to have more robust security.

Using a CASB solution

A *clouds asset security broker* (CASB, for short) brokers transactions between your users and the cloud. It can be implemented in either hardware or software, and locally or in the cloud. Unlike firewalls that control basic access, a CASB offers fine-grained control over access and can discover unusual user activity. They are used to

>> Manage cloud security risk

>> Comply with privacy restrictions

>> Enforce local security restrictions

A CASB is particularly good at managing security across diverse cloud environments in a unified way. It provides visibility into what is taking place that may be evading your attempts at management. This statement is particularly true when departments are using unsanctioned applications, creating a situation known as shadow IT. Though shadow IT is common in large organizations, it poses a security risk. Using a CASB solution helps you manage those risks.

You can choose from various methods for employing a CASB solution:

>> **Using an API:** With this option, your choices are limited to what's allowed by your SaaS provider.

>> **Using a forward proxy:** Forward proxies grab data headed to an application in the cloud and forward it to the CASB for checking before forwarding it to the application. This can be tricky in situations where there's a fluid number and/or types of devices.

>> **Using a reverse proxy:** Here, data is directed to a federated identity system that manages a user's identity across multiple identification systems and then sent on to the SaaS application. This method is the most versatile of the options listed here.

One of the easiest CASB solutions to use is Netskope, which follows the data-centric approach of following data wherever it goes. Check it out at www .netskope.com.

REMEMBER

Many CASB solutions are on the market. You need to figure out which one meets your needs and your budget. For example, Netskope isn't the cheapest option on the market, but it gets high marks from Gartner, Inc., a leading global research and advisory firm.

Applying Security Patches

This might seem to be a no-brainer but applying security patches in a timely manner is often the most overlooked part of securing your applications, whether they're running in the cloud, in your data center, or on individual compute devices. Yes, your phone (unless it's a flip phone) is a compute device and needs security patching.

And of course, you know what's coming — there's an app for that! Yes, rather than try to manually manage all your security patches or, worse just blowing off this task, you can use a patch management application.

What you're replacing when you use a patch management application is the chaos that's created whenever you rely on each different software application to update itself. Half the time they don't, or else you don't have it configured correctly or the phone wasn't plugged in or the computer was turned off or the Internet went down. Avoid all that nonsense. Make life easier and use one of the following applications:

>> **GFILanGuard:** This application is good for businesses running machines with different operating systems. It has releases for Windows, Mac, and Linux, and it updates more than 80 different applications.

>> **ManageEngine Patch Manager Plus:** This excellent business patch management tool has Windows, Mac, and Linux versions. More than 350 applications are covered by this program, and it's free for up to 20 computers and 5 servers.

>> **Chocolatey:** Admittedly, it's Windows-only, but this software updates more than 7,000 different programs. For a Windows shop, this is a must-have program, even if it is a bit work intensive.

WARNING

Poorly configured patch management software can trip you up by letting you download the wrong security patches or older patches that have been superseded.

Looking Ahead

Now that all your devices and applications are secure, the next chapter begins the discussion of data and how you secure it. After all, that's the heart of any cybersecurity strategy, though you can find some exceptions that prove the rule. Devices connected to and in control of factory equipment, medical devices, and utility command-and-control systems deal with more than just data as such and hacking them can have serious repercussions. For example, in 2021 Colonial Pipeline was hacked by a ransomware attack, shutting down oil delivery in its four main pipelines serving the eastern and southeastern United States. Millions of dollars in cryptocurrency were paid to regain control of these services.

In the case of Colonial Pipeline, according to the company's CEO, hackers exploited an unused, and probably forgotten, virtual private network (VPN). You can see how accessing a VPN that likely wasn't listed as an asset that needed to be protected yet was networked to high-risk assets was the weak point in their cyberdefense system. It's not clear how the hacker got the credentials to exploit the VPN, but it's likely that social engineering was involved. This is where someone pretending to be a trusted person convinces someone else to grant them access. That's why a robust user access system is critical.

The Colonial Pipeline hack is a perfect example of the security issues discussed in this chapter. This lone exploit not only cost Colonial tens of millions of dollars but also impacted the national security and economy of the United States. And all because of old VPN — it's certainly something to think about.

Chapter **3**

Developing Secure Software

C loud security often focuses on user authentication and not enough on other security holes, such as the ones that often remain during software application development. This chapter covers issues in secure software development and how it impacts cloud security. Simplistically, cloud security involves people, applications, data handling, and hardware. Though there are many ways to build secure software, this chapter begins by focusing on DevOps and DataOps, two methodologies for application development that not only increase development speed but also offer built-in ways to ensure the security of applications and how they handle data.

Turbocharging Development

Technology and IT requirements to manage cloud security are increasing every day. Even though the rapid growth of technology, like tentacles into every part of our human lives, continues to increase at breakneck speed, we need to find ways to bring it to heel. One of the challenges we face when trying to enforce security and governance is finding the balance between enforcing security and promoting agility.

Often overlooked, application development contains one of the great risks in computing and in particular cloud computing. IT development struggled to find just the right path forward in finding the right balance between planning, developing, testing, and implementing code and the ability to be agile. This path forward is known as *DevOps*, which are the guiding principles applied to code development that allow for agility *and* maintain order and control.

DevOps uses principles and tools that maintain software code in repositories that make developers check in code and check out code, a little like checking your coat at a theater or museum. One benefit of this process, which you don't get when you do a coat-check, is that you can roll back code in the event of a failure. To stick with the same analogy, if you check out your coat and spill a drink on it, you can simply trash that coat, go back to where you initially stored it, and get your coat back again — as though nothing had happened.

These are some of the other features of DevOps:

» Encapsulated and reusable code

» Agility

» Distributed development (when developers are in different geographical locations)

» Automated testing (particularly important for cloud security)

These features, among others, have made DevOps now the go-to way professionals use to develop applications. These principles — ones that revolutionized software development — are now being applied directly to how we use and develop with data. After all, when you develop applications, the chances are high that they will operate against a dataset.

No more waterfalls

The agile method of software development bypasses a lengthy planning process where you have everything thought out before the first line of code is written, as in the *waterfall* model, a methodology dating back to 1956. In fact, the waterfall model often includes the step of first writing the program in pseudocode and later translating it into whichever programming language you've opted to use. The *agile method*, however, starts the developer writing code immediately after the requirements have been developed and a simple plan laid out. (See Figure 3-1.)

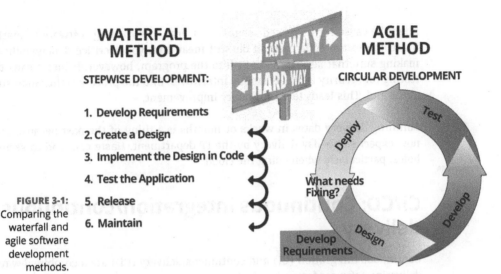

WATERFALL METHOD

STEPWISE DEVELOPMENT:

1. Develop Requirements
2. Create a Design
3. Implement the Design in Code
4. Test the Application
5. Release
6. Maintain

AGILE METHOD

CIRCULAR DEVELOPMENT

EASY WAY
HARD WAY

Test
Deploy
Develop
Design
What needs Fixing?
Develop Requirements

FIGURE 3-1: Comparing the waterfall and agile software development methods.

Agility is gained by putting applications quickly into the customer's hands and then letting the customer "bang on it" and then figuring out where it needs to be fixed or enhanced and then having the developer get busy again on the next version. Whew! This strategy became quite popular when web development started. Nonprofessional programmers just started banging out code because everyone wanted a web page immediately, and the programmers could then finesse the code as needed. It soon became clear that this was a faster and easier way to get things done.

Agile development depends on these components:

>> Incremental code delivery

>> Team collaboration

>> Continual planning

>> Continual testing (which increases cloud security)

>> Continued learning

Development for data analytics has all the same challenges, and so it benefits from this same circular development pattern of designing, delivering incremental code releases, and testing on the fly.

Older methodologies just aren't up to the task of meeting 21st century requirements. To meet these growing needs, making the switch to the agile method of software development is a no-brainer. Agility comes with continuous delivery, planning, learning, and improvement. You might think that revving up the speed might be cause for increased security concerns, not rushing software to market. Switching to the agile method doesn't mean that you sacrifice dependability or making sure that security is built into the program, however. It just means that testing for security issues is simply interwoven into the process rather than stuck at the end. This leads to evolutionary improvement.

REMEMBER

Fulfilling delivery dates in weeks or months is a thing of the past because users now expect same-day delivery by the IT department. Haste can lead to security holes, particularly when using the cloud.

CI/CD: Continuous integration/continuous delivery

Continuous integration (CI) and continuous delivery (CD) are a combined way of delivering software faster, in which one or more programmers check their changes into a central code repository several times a day.

When code has been checked in, it triggers an automated testing process. This rapid test is quickly delivered, sometimes in less than 10 minutes, so that the developer can make any necessary corrections and then continue with development.

Shifting left and adding security in development

The concept of shift-left comes from the waterfall method, where security considerations were part of the testing that was scheduled just before a final release. Once the product was released, development teams normally collected user error reports. Edits to the code were completed and saved in a pre-release version until a large software update release was planned. Rather than benefit from small, incremental fixes and updates, users often had to wait months or even years for fixes. Figure 3-2 shows the linear and cumbersome steps in the waterfall method. Moving the testing phase into the coding step so that they are both done continuously is "shifting it left."

Tackling security sooner rather than later

Shifting testing left means that security also moves left in the overall pipeline of software development. Addressing the operational parts of software development, such as applications running in the cloud, should come earlier rather than later. You may have heard this old saying:

"He who fails to plan is planning to fail."

Linear Left to Right Waterfall Method

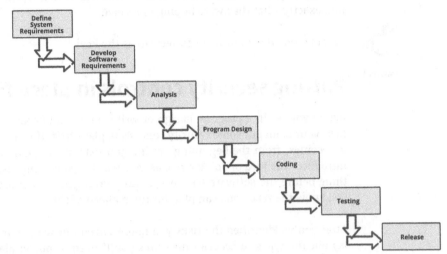

FIGURE 3-2:
Moving testing into coding essentially moves it left.

This quote has been attributed to both Winston Churchill and Benjamin Franklin. Both were smart enough to come up with the phrase and, regardless of who originally said it, what was said was absolutely correct. By shifting left the planning for security, you get to prepare much earlier in the development process for issues related to running your application in the public cloud.

TIP

Don't bolt on security — make security a planned part of development.

Making security part of the development plan early on will save you headaches later. You won't achieve truly secure software by simply throwing tools at the problem — it takes a comprehensive plan that covers every part of the development cycle, from inception to release.

Because all software is different, there is no clear picture of what must be done, because security concerns differ based on what the program is intended to do, the level of security needed to protect its data, and the risk associated with flaws in the program. Step one: Build a team that extends throughout your organization. You hear this advice time and time again because, in today's world, the division lines between an IT department and other company departments or groups has nearly disappeared, or, more accurately, the lines have become more intertwined. In the past, during the development phase, you would talk to the customer, ascertain their needs, create a plan, have the customer sign off on the plan, write the program, and then deliver the program. Development teams now include the stakeholders. They remain an integral part of the process because continuous delivery requires continuous input and feedback. This way, the program evolves into exactly what they were hoping to receive.

REMEMBER

Organizational commitment to security is the key!

Putting security controls in place first

Before you begin a program design or write one word of code, it's a good idea to have your team put some security controls in place first. If you start with security, it becomes, from the beginning, an integral part of the plan. Book 4, Chapter 1 introduces the idea of doing a risk assessment for your company. Doing the same thing before the software has been written gives you a clear path forward. Once you know the risks, you can plan for them ahead of time.

After you've identified the risks you might encounter with your application, you lay out the types of security measures you'll need to put in place to secure the application. This might include straight encryption or the use of encrypted communication tunnels or special measures to protect memory so that the application, running in the public cloud where it might share hardware with other applications, is protected.

Your team should include all the people who might have a say in how security is managed. In larger companies this may include a compliance team that's responsible for making sure the applications comply with government and industry security regulations. You can see how setting out a plan to meet compliance is easier on the front end than trying to shoehorn it in later.

Circling back

A continuous delivery cycle is circular, such that most of the development phases are repeated. Part of that cycle should be to review the security plan and the details your team has put together and then make certain they have all been accomplished for each cycle. Don't make a plan and then never check to see whether it was followed.

TIP

Make a simple spreadsheet of the steps to meet each of the risk factors and review this list during each testing phase. To make this task easier, you can automate security testing with the help of DevSecOps. (More on that topic in the next section.)

Implementing DevSecOps

Tools to automate security testing can be used to not only speed up the process but also make it more efficient by checking each of the requirements you've laid out in your plan. Here are some of the programs that can help you make sure that your applications are following best practices:

>> **Microsoft Azure Advisor** (https://azure.microsoft.com/en-us/services/advisor): It's like having a best practices expert in your pocket. This application allows you to focus on the critical operations that will ultimately save you time and money. Prioritize your efforts by picking which changes to make now and which you can put off until later.

>> **Prisma Cloud** (www.paloaltonetworks.com/prisma/cloud): Using a shared dashboard with your entire development team, this application scans servers and VMs in in order to secure applications, data, and infrastructure. Great for developers because it integrates with most popular development IDEs.

>> **Gauntlt** (http://gauntlt.org): This tool helps facilitate testing and communication between the groups involved in the development process. Communication between everyone involved is critical to success.

>> **Veracode** (www.veracode.com): You definitely want an application that scans your code to look for security holes. Veracode has a suite of applications for testing that target static analysis, software composition, vendor analysis (for testing third-party applications), and web application scanning.

Automating Testing during Development

With a rapid development cycle, you need the advantages of automated code testing. Manual code testing simply takes too long. You will pay dearly in person-hours to save a few dollars on a good testing application. Rest assured that adding automated testing allows you to be thorough while maintaining an efficient development cycle that doesn't impact your development schedule. Not doing the testing, or trying to do it manually, will likely have a significant negative impact on your schedule, particularly if you have to go back and fix errors in your code that are found later during a software audit, or worse, after release.

REMEMBER

Software audits have long been a necessary part of the development cycle, but if you're finding significant problems in the audit, you likely have done no automated testing along the way.

Using static and dynamic code analysis

Static code analysis automates what in the past would have been a manual code review. What you're looking for is weakness in the code that can lead to vulnerabilities that can and probably will be exploited by hackers. This strategy is particularly important when your code is running in the cloud, where it has a large potential threat landscape.

Static code analysis happens early in the development cycle. This catches potential code weaknesses early so that they aren't overlooked later. Also, when you're releasing code as quickly as possible, you want these errors caught early and fixed.

TIP

Static code analysis helps you comply with industry standards or government oversight by checking the code for specific flaws.

Dynamic code analysis happens later in the development phase, when a program is unit-tested. Most applications are built of component parts, or units, which are individually tested. Though this type of code analysis catches many types of problems, it often overlooks the kinds of errors normally caught by static code analysis.

TECHNICAL STUFF

The big difference between static and dynamic code analysis is that static code analysis finds fundamental flaws in the code that will cause crashes — the ones you might find in a manual code review such as memory leaks and more — but doesn't catch problems when code doesn't do what you expect functionally. That is the job of dynamic code analysis. Dynamic code analysis shows how an application responds in real life to user input.

The value of using a static code analyzer is threefold:

>> **Speed:** Automated code reviews are significantly faster than manual reviews.

>> **Depth:** Static code analyzers can check every single code path.

>> **Accuracy:** Automating code review takes out the chance of human error.

These are a some of the more popular static software testing tools:

>> **Sonarqube** (www.sonarqube.org/): This application is open-sourced software developed by SonarSource. It performs continuous inspection of your code, detecting bugs and security vulnerabilities in more than 20 different programming languages.

>> **Coverity** (www.synopsys.com/): An excellent, scalable static software code analysis tool. Not only does it find vulnerabilities in your code but also

manages risk by ensuring that your apps comply with all security and coding standards.

Here are a couple of the popular dynamic software testing tools to check out as well:

>> **Accunetic** (www.acunetix.com/): This application automates testing of web applications. It discovers your applications, scans them for vulnerabilities, and then lets you know the exact lines of code that are causing the issues.

>> **Netsparker** (www.netsparker.com/): This tool scans your discovered applications for vulnerabilities and even assigns tasks to developers for code repair when vulnerabilities are found.

Taking steps in automation

Automating software testing is a bit like teaching a child: You start with the simple concepts first. Beginning with simple tasks, such as checking database interactions, helps you be thorough and efficient, taking care of the easy fixes first and then moving on to more difficult challenges.

REMEMBER

Include all repetitive tasks in your automation. It's the mundane and boring tasks that are often either overlooked or prone to error because humans eventually screw up while performing the same action again and again. Taking repetitive tasks into account not only saves you a great deal of time but also increases the likelihood of finding security flaws.

Combing through large amounts of data is another area that cries out for automation. Doing it manually is time consuming, often repetitive, and prone to human error. This is an area where automated testing procedures truly excel.

Once your application reaches a release stage — something you should expect to happen often in a continuous delivery cycle — you use automated tools to check for security flaws not caught throughout the development process. Because many applications are now web-based, check out tools such as the ones described in this list:

>> **Burp Suite** (https://portswigger.net): A very popular suite of testing tools. Check out the CI/CD driver in the Enterprise Edition. The suite has a huge library of add-ons. A bit on the expensive side but worth it.

>> **OWASP Zap** (https://owasp.org/www-project-zap): A free set of testing tools that has many of the features of Burp Suite and more.

Leveraging software composition analysis

Software applications are now rarely written completely from scratch. The idea of code reusability has reached a level of maturity to allow applications to now be developed using many third-party components and code written by freelance coders, as shown in Figure 3-3. Software composition analysis (SCA) will:

- » Search your code for the use of any open-source components.
- » Checks open-source components to make sure that they comply with license requirements.
- » Verifies the quality of the component's code.
- » Evaluates the software security of the component.

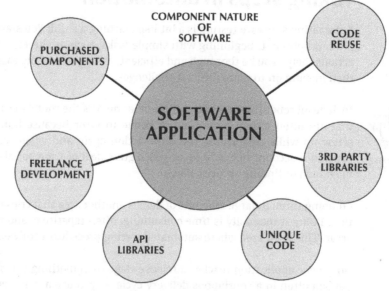

FIGURE 3-3:
Software is made up of various components.

Security holes in open-source code

Open-source code has become part of almost every modern web application. Libraries such as Bootstrap (used to make applications mobile-ready) are often used, and JavaScript component libraries like jQuery and jQueryUI are almost must-have items. No one develops these components from scratch. Visual components that display elements such as buttons and icons are also common with libraries like FontAwesome.

Though it makes perfect sense to use as many labor-saving components as possible, each one you add presents a possible security hole. The components just mentioned are less likely to contain security flaws because they have been tried and tested in millions of websites. Other open-source component libraries may not have been as thoroughly vetted as these.

Have a Plan B. Depending on the size of a particular open-source development community, vulnerabilities may take considerable time to correct. This is particularly true when direct support of a component is unavailable and you must either rely on your own programmers to fix the problem or wait for community developers to come to the rescue.

TIP

Check out license types of the open-source software you're using, to ensure compliance with its license. (Some licenses require that you release your source code to the public.) Check to see that your security profile allows that kind of release. Software composition analysis will discover your licenses.

Synopsis (www.synopsis.com) is a popular software composition analysis tool. This tool checks your package managers used in software development, source code, binary files of compiled applications, container images and any other types of files on which your application relies. It checks these components against the National Vulnerability Database found at nvd.nist.gov.

Dependency tracking

Dependency tracking is an automated tool that performs component analysis. This relies on a *software bill of materials* (BOM), which is a list of all components that make up a software package. (It's not unlike a dinner recipe.) This idea was originally created to bring about software transparency. The BOM plugs into your DevSecOps monitoring system for continuous monitoring of the components and then spits out any problems it finds. This gives you the power of continuous delivery, continuous insight, and continuous transparency.

Security holes and how to plug them

Plugging potential holes or security flaws begins with an understanding of how much open-source and third-party-developed software is being used in your applications. Many companies have a longstanding policy about the use of open-source software, based on the need for support. It was understood that privately developed applications came with support — either free or pay. Open-source applications tended to come with community support and may not be as reliable as privately written, closed source applications.

Develop an audit to determine and document the use of open-source components in your software. This can help send up flags if or when security flaws are discovered in a component. You can then swap out the component for a fixed version or choose to replace it with one that's more secure.

REMEMBER

The decision to use open-source components should be part of your security plan when you first begin your application plan. Weigh any vulnerabilities these components may have against your risk tolerance.

TIP

Using GitHub (https://github.com) as your source code repository helps, because the site makes vulnerability searches through code in the repository and alerts you to any issues. For tips on how to extract data from GitHub and load it into your cloud-based data warehouse, check out this description of Snowflake at https://github.tosnowflake.com.

Proving the job has been done right

These are the two most important reasons for making sure your security measures have been effective:

>> You don't want people hacking your system.

>> You may have to provide proof of your success in order to be in compliance with security and privacy regulations.

Your cloud service provider maintains logs of what occurs in your environment. It's up to you to do something with that information. Automating the monitoring process is always the best way to go.

Logging and monitoring

One of the most common ways of monitoring security is logging who has had access to your cloud environment. This type of monitoring is still fairly new to many cloud service providers — therefore, their expertise in this area is a factor to consider when selecting a cloud service provider.

What you need are some tools to do the monitoring. Certain cloud service providers can route event information and allow you to build some basic security policies that will monitor events. If you're using AWS for your cloud service provider, check out the AWS CloudTrail, CloudWatch, and GuardDuty apps. They can get you started on monitoring your security.

You may opt to use a third-party monitoring tool like DynaTrace, at www.dynatrace.com. This particular application monitors metrics, and logs, in addition to user experience data. In an agent-based system, all you need to do is install the OneAgent component. This AI-based engine alerts you when problems are found and directs you to the root cause.

Another way to monitor security is to route your event traffic to a big data security analysis system such as Splunk for further analysis. Splunk (`www.splunk.com`), a leader in cybersecurity products, claims that it can help companies reduce data breaches by 70 percent.

REMEMBER

Not monitoring your cloud environment means you're operating with zero visibility into potential problems. Waiting for disasters to happen is the wrong approach.

Ensuring data accountability, data assurance, and data dependability

The job of a data analyst is complex and has largely been a manual one involving data integration, the assembling of data pipelines assemblage, testing, managing production development and, of course, creating documentation. This level of demand creates slow processes that are time consuming and forever error prone. This makes it difficult to keep up with user demand and same-day expectations.

Beyond simply keeping up with demand, you also have the increased burden of showing that you're doing it right. To accomplish this, there must be *change control* (making a trackable list of the changes you've made) and an audit trail of who was responsible for the changes providing accountability, assurance, and dependability.

In addition to an audit trail, a key requirement for assurance and dependability is testing. Testing at every stage before code is moved into the software repository provides positive assurance. In this way, your code base serves as your source of truth.

With the increased burden that comes with complexity, meeting user expectations, increased governance, and increased testing, the only way forward is to do more with less. One way to accomplish that is to free data teams from the tasks that provide no direct value (drudgery, in other words).

As with many IT challenges, the answer to complex testing is automation. Testing is an example of a laborious and mundane task that needs to be automated. Without automation, the task of testing would be not only a laborious chore, often overlooked, but also one that is prone to errors and would definitely take too much time in a DataOps delivery schedule.

Once your data has been tested to eliminate as many future problems as possible, it then behooves you to include automated monitoring to catch problems before the user does. These systems check the quality of your production data, analytics processes, and new code releases.

Consider using a tool such as Aunalytics (www.aunalytics.com) to automate your data validation and monitoring. FirstEigen (https://firsteigen.com) uses AI to perform data quality testing. As a machine learning tool, its ability to spot errors and data use habits grows over time.

You can automate tasks like traceability and issue tracking with continuous code releases. Automating the day-to-day tasks of testing and monitoring increases the efficiency and agility of the entire data analytics process.

In addition to freeing your team from mind-numbing tasks, automation has a direct impact on the TCO — or total cost of ownership — which includes the ongoing cost of maintaining your code.

A popular DataOps tool that seems to have all the functionality you'll need — and more — is DataKitchen (https://datakitchen.io). This is an enterprise-level DataOps platform that automates end-to-end data workflows to help you coordinate your data analytics teams, people, projects, and testing.

Running Your Applications

Once you've developed an application that actually runs in the cloud, you need to host it there. You have lots to consider when deciding which hosting provider to choose. Cost is usually factor number one, followed closely by the number and kinds of services that are provided by the cloud service provider.

In addition to cost and services, think about where the company has servers around the world. If you have an international customer base using your application, you'll want to make sure that the cloud service provider has servers where your customers live, if for no other reason than connection speed and network lag time considerations.

Because the choice you make is one you will likely live with for years to come, and one that may impact your business competitively, you need to select a provider that you believe will have longevity, flexibility, and the ability to develop new services that will support your application over time.

Another approach to consider is one where you develop your application to run on more than a single provider, known as a cloud agnostic approach. (More on that in the next section.)

Taking advantage of cloud agnostic integration

More than 80 percent of companies that use cloud services use more than one cloud service provider. When developing applications that run in the cloud, one important consideration is being able to run your application in more than one cloud environment — being cloud agnostic, in other words. Cloud agnosticism is similar to the old days of Java programming, when the idea of write once, run anywhere first became a reality.

Even if your company uses only a single cloud service provider, developing applications that will run on several platforms without changing the code ensures that you don't get stuck with a single-provider scenario. Though it seems that some of the larger cloud service providers are too big to fail, anything can happen. If for no other reason than price comparison, you want the ability to either make the switch or add cloud service providers. There are hundreds of different cloud service providers, but AWS, Google, Alibaba, and Microsoft control over 50 percent of the market.

Another reason you might choose a cloud agnostic approach is to avoid situations where one cloud service provider runs into technical difficulties. It happens to the best of them. In certain huge outages, trunk lines have been accidentally disrupted during excavations. Other providers, such as Nirvanix in 2013, simply went out of business and gave their customers a couple of weeks to migrate. Imagine how much simpler things would be if the applications hosted there could simply begin running on a different provider. There is probably no greater concern for most companies than reliability.

TIP

Track when cloud services are up and down by using Downdetector (https://downdetector.com).

Cloud service providers are more than just hosting sites. Part of what makes them attractive as services are the applications that are part of the offering. You may decide that the applications of another vendor are preferable to what you're getting now, and you may want to switch to take advantage of new services. Or, when services go bad (see the later section "Understanding That No Cloud Is Perfect"), you may need to switch to another provider to avoid catastrophe.

In any case, you want to position your company to take advantage of the flexibility of a cloud agnostic approach. Companies that have been taking advantage of a cloud infrastructure for years may not have had the advantage of creating applications with a cloud agnostic strategy and may now be stuck with vendor lock-in.

Recognizing the down sides of cloud agnostic development

So, with all the upside of a cloud agnostic approach, the downside is that the initial development cost increases because more aspects must be taken into consideration. There may be a learning curve for the developers and team when incorporating some of the newer technologies. Moving from a monolithic development strategy to a more distributed and manageable microservices model is one that requires a new way of thinking about design and an understanding of the underlying technologies.

Feature specificity — the unique features one cloud offers over another — can become an issue impacting your decision to use more than one cloud service provider. When one of the providers offers a solution not offered by others, or when the solution is so much better in one cloud service provider than what the others provide, it may be difficult to move away from a service you enjoy. This is particularly true when selecting cloud-provided database management systems. Some of them are easier, faster, and more powerful than others.

Experience is also a consideration. Quite often a development team will have experience working with a particular cloud service provider and be expert at developing in line with their unique set of tools and specifications. Moving outside their comfort zone might be too high of a cost or risk. Go with what you know might be the best strategy in this case.

TIP

Create a pros-versus-cons assessment when considering a cloud agnostic approach before starting development. You may want to select only a few platforms to support, because it's virtually impossible to write code that runs on all of them equally well. Select the platforms that provide these features:

>> Reliability, dependability, and durability

>> Services you need

>> Global coverage

>> Security (of course!)

>> The right price

>> Ease of use

Developing a matrix of the cloud service providers and how they stack up in these various areas makes it easier to select the right ones to develop for.

Getting started down the cloud agnostic path

There are several different methods and technologies to consider when choosing to develop your application with a cloud agnostic approach. Make sure you follow good methodologies to achieve the best outcome. Here's a look at the basic approaches:

>> **Automate like crazy:** This chapter has laid out the advantage of a DevOps approach to development. Using a continuous delivery strategy requires that many of the steps along the way need to be automated.

   Cloud agnosticism means that the workload in a DevOps development cycle will increase, because you must make certain that the code you develop runs equally well on the platforms you want to support.

>> **Design using a microservice modules approach:** Gone are the days when every application had a monolithic architecture. Applications can now be developed using a microservice architecture, where functionality is broken into small units, or modules. This style of architecture structures an application into a form that is

   • Easily maintained

   • Easily tested

   • Structured around business functions

   • Developed by a team that has responsibility for that module

   This architectural style enables the delivery of complex applications in a component form that fits well into a continuous delivery environment. Elements of an application are broken down into units based on their function. Having a team responsible for a specific microservice unit makes them easier to develop, maintain, and test. It also makes for great code reuse.

REMEMBER

   When building an application as cloud agnostic, you can more easily manage the application when it's broken into smaller units. When moving between cloud services, you might find it easier to match services to microservice modules.

>> **Use a service mesh:** As your application becomes more complex as the number of microservices grow, you'll want to employ *a service mesh* — a dedicated infrastructure layer that enables service-to-service communications using a proxy. Service mesh applications enable more than simple interservice communications — they also enable security, observability, workflow, and more.

   Istio (https://istio.io) is an open-source service mesh that layers over the top of applications, providing communications, load balancing, traffic behavior, and automatic metrics, logs, and traces. Istio runs on top of Kubernetes (https://kubernetes.io), an open-source container-orchestration system.

>> **Containerize:** Containers are lightweight and stand-alone executable software packages that let you run applications in a virtual environment that includes all of the system tools, libraries and application settings necessary to run. One of the more popular container applications, Docker (www.docker.com) does exactly that, making it simple to move a Docker container from one cloud to another. It's easy to see how using Docker containers would simplify the development of a cloud agnostic application.

Docker containers are different from virtual machines because Docker containers do not virtualize the machine and rather share the operating system kernel with other applications. Having said that, it's important to know that Docker containers are well isolated, so they present a low risk when sharing the OS with other containers.

REMEMBER

The goal of cloud agnostic development is to make it easy to move your application from one cloud type to another with a minimum amount of effort.

This is just a brief introduction into technologies that each requires a book. The idea and technologies are still new and maturing. There is no single sure way to make sure your applications are cloud agnostic. Employing some (or all) of these technologies, such as containerization and a service mesh, moves your application into the next level of capabilities and increases the ability to manage a complex, or even distributed, application.

Like DevOps but for Data

Data stored in the cloud is definitely an important consideration in cloud security, but there is another, and maybe more important, factor: the development of those data analytics capabilities that make use of that data on a daily basis. Data simply stored away is useless, whereas today's companies are more data-driven than ever.

As with software development, your data analytics team also faces a growing demand to provide insights from your data with increased speed and efficiency and without sacrificing security. To achieve the same kinds of development speed, you can borrow from the proven ability of DevOps to get the job done quickly and efficiently.

The principles of DevOps applied to data are known as *DataOps*, short for *data operations*. Though the principles are similar, allowing for factors such as check-in and check-out of data, and evolutionary, continuous delivery, DataOps is more than DevOps applied to data. The principles are similar, but the challenges met by

DataOps are somewhat different. The important aspects of DataOps that mirror what you see in DevOps includes things such as agile code development, version control systems, and automated testing.

A DataOps application development environment generally involves the use of a pipeline that manages the various development steps in this agile and rapid delivery scheme. One tool you might consider using to manage the huge amounts of data involved is Genie (`https://netflix.github.io/genie`), a federated big data orchestration-and-execution engine developed by Netflix and released as open source. Another large and complex business, Airbnb, developed Apache Airflow, a workflow tool that was also released as open source: `http://airflow.apache.org`.

The agility of the DevOps principles transfers well to the concept of DataOps. This enables faster results when developing applications for data analysis. Companies are demanding immediate access to insight from the data it owns. Efficiency and reliability in providing those insights is the goal.

Source code control using a source code control system such as Git (`https://git-scm.com`) allows you to check in and check out code. This not only allows multiple developers in various locations to work together but also gives you the ability to roll back code — and it creates an automatic audit trail of development. Git also allows for *branching* your code, which allows for different versions of an application to be created that stem from an "original" version of the code. In the world of DataOps, this also means creating a new branch of data. The data used in this manner allows for similar features such as rollback of data and audit trails. With branched data, you can create a development sandbox for trying things out rather than jumping right in to work on production data.

Earlier sections in this chapter cover writing reusable and maintainable code. Creating modularized code in the form of microservices gives you an application that is easily maintainable and easily testable. You can think of this concept as building a car: Over time, cars have become more complex and at the same time more modular, with parts easily plugged in. This arrangement has made cars easier to troubleshoot and repair and has also lowered their overall cost. Modularized code development is much the same as a car: Cars have idiot lights that alert you to problems and easily point repair people in the right direction. Well-written code does exactly the same thing.

Branching data, in much the same way as code through version control systems, has revolutionized development. You no longer need to operate on production data nor on copies that quickly become stale and outdated. In the past, creating feature branches of data was difficult because of the size and complexity of large datasets. They call it big data for a reason! DataOps takes a different approach by building, changing, and destroying environments automatically, a concept taken from virtualization.

The version control system provides the type of audit trail most governance requires. Because governance is part of the initial development plan, a DataOps development plan employs *privacy by design* (software development with privacy in mind) and *governance by design* (keeping governance requirements at the forefront while creating your applications). When changes are made to a data project, every modification is tested for security and code errors.

TIP

Automate or die! Keeping up with the competition in a rapidly changing environment requires that you automate. It's not really a choice.

Automated testing allows you to scale development. Scalability is one of the key benefits of DataOps or DevOps or any of the Ops. Part of the process of continuous delivery and delivery, automating your application testing greatly increases the speed with which you can release new code. "Greatly increase" is a bit of an understatement, though: When it comes to testing, if it's not done in an automated fashion, it's likely to be overlooked, which leads to the desperate situation of "hope" projects, where you release a project and just hope it works.

The ability to rapidly test code and data is one of the limiting factors to growth. There is no reason not to implement an automated testing tool that can catch most of, if not all, the errors. Rapid testing and deployment enable large, data-heavy companies to code and deploy updates at a rate commensurate with industry demands.

Testing, 1-2-3

Testing occurs in both the innovation pipeline (where data is fixed and code changes) and the value pipeline (where code is fixed and data changes). Testing in the innovation pipeline validates that the code is producing the expected results. Testing in the value pipeline is looking for *outliers* — data that falls outside the statistical norm. For this reason, both code and data tests are required to continuously monitor the health of the data application.

Data analytics is not just an exercise. In the real world, data drives critical business decisions. DataOps requires that data returned from a data product be valid for decision-making.

REMEMBER

Automated testing of data can lead to greater assurance and quality.

Is this thing working?

In addition to testing, monitoring after release is important. With monitoring, errors that were uncaught previously may be caught, or new errors in the data will be caught by the monitoring system. This way, errors are quickly caught — hopefully, before they cause a problem — and corrected. (Dynatrace, at www.dynatrace.com, has an all-in-one system monitoring tool that works well in a DataOps environment.)

If you're building data applications, you may also want to build an application that can spot outliers in your data as an alert mechanism.

Working well with others

DataOps has a core principle that collaboration is the key to success. Collaboration between members of a team and across disciplines leads to creative solutions and better results. Including the end user in your discussions is important because this person has the best idea of what they need from a data project. Also, feeling heard, they will be much happier along the path to the end result.

Developing in isolation leads to problems such as heroism (trying to do it all yourself) and poorly understood (or an inability to meet) changing requirements. After all, DataOps embraces change. In a simple example, when operations team members discuss how a project impacts them and then data scientists (concerned, as always, with accuracy) add their feedback, the iterative nature of agile development allows for a continually improved end-product and happier end users. This is also how governance and agility are kept in balance.

Modern data development should lead to the idea of creating data products rather than simply developing for a single need. These products and data pipelines can be simply reused, either as is or modified through the principles of inheritance borrowing from object-oriented programming. When certain aspects of a pipeline are reusable, they can be refined into a new data product in a fraction of the time it took to create the original product. The result is also more reliable and better trusted.

Baking in trust

Beyond creating better security, DataOps also increases user trust in the data on which your business relies daily. Data analytics provides the insights that businesses rely on to make important decisions. Nothing is worse than trying to use data that is full of errors. The resulting insights from that kind of data are simply wrong — in other words, useless.

Not only is user trust at stake in managing your data correctly, but government oversight also requires that the data be reliable. The big balancing act is to provide better data reliability without sacrificing efficiency and speed.

Developing in a cycle where testing is an integrated part increases the chance that errors are caught early and more often. (Take another look at Figure 3-1 to see how testing is part of the DevOps development cycle.)

Part of developing trust is making all the stakeholders part of your testing plan. After the users of the data understand what has been tested, they feel ownership in the quality of the data. (This is especially true if their input was requested in developing a test plan.)

REMEMBER

Data changes. Users will trust it until they can't, so data testing and monitoring must remain a continuous effort.

DevSecOps for DataOps

There are so many Ops it's sometimes hard to keep them all straight. DataSecOps is the extension of DevSecOps for the data analytics world. The DevOps philosophy proposes that you create a working relationship between all stakeholders while developing applications and that they continue working closely together during the cycles of continuous delivery resulting in well-tested and secure applications. This same idea is applied to the applications developed by data scientists and data analysts that bring forth the insight from the terabytes of data your business has collected and stored over the years. Figure 3-4 shows how teams of data engineers, heads of security, governance, risk, and compliance as well as data stewards and data owners work collaboratively to bring about secure data analytics applications.

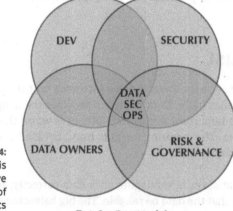

FIGURE 3-4:
DataSecOps is the collaborative method of data analytics development.

DataSecOps Model

REMEMBER

Having all the stakeholders, security, and development teams working together is the key to making this streamlined DevOps-like method of development efficient and secure.

DataSecOps provides a development environment that is

>> **Agile:** Developed in a rapid, almost ad hoc, manner by related teams.

>> **Democratized:** Data is touched by a large number of people throughout the organization, each with a say in how it's used. They all should have security in mind.

Security considerations are part of the data analytics development cycle. Automated testing is an important part of this cycle, and that is a perfect place in the cycle to review security concerns.

As with DevOps, your teams should make a list of security concerns when the project is first conceived and then revisit these during each release cycle. For example, if data is sensitive or is governed by regulations, these should be reviewed to make certain that they're taken into consideration. This process makes security an integrated part of the analytics development rather than something cobbled on later.

REMEMBER

Make security an integrated part of your DataOps development cycle.

Considering data security

Perhaps the most obvious data security consideration is establishing who has access to the data being used for analytics. Ask questions like these:

>> Have you restricted access to only those people who have legitimate authority to view the data?

>> Has the data been modified in such a manner that private data is either obscured or not included in the dataset being examined?

>> Will my analytics reveal confidential information to the wrong people?

Guessing isn't the way forward. Knowing about your data beforehand can save you a considerable amount of time and headaches.

As with many IT challenges, the answer is automation. Testing is an example of a laborious and mundane task that needs to be automated. Once your data has been tested to eliminate as many future problems as possible, it's then a great idea to include automated monitoring to catch issues before the user does. These systems check the quality of your production data, analytics processes, and new code releases.

TIP

Catch data errors in testing before the customer or end user finds them.

You can automate traceability and issue tracking with continuous code releases. Automating the day-to-day tasks of testing and monitoring increases the efficiency and agility of the entire data analytics process.

In addition to freeing your team from mind-numbing tasks, automation has a direct impact on the TCO — total cost of ownership — which includes the ongoing cost of maintaining your code.

Ending data siloes

Data that ends up in a data warehouse is generally subjected to some level of security that sometimes makes it difficult or impossible for users in the same organization to integrate data between datasets. Business units protecting access to their data often create new privacy silos. This is particularly true of data stored across multiple cloud storage environments. It's common for departments to create their own cloud resources and then store their data there, away from both the prying eyes of others as well as the company data analytics teams. This causes a frustrating duplication of data and effort, as well as increasing the security risks involved exponentially. One way around this quandary is the development of a data store — a shop of sorts, not a storage location. A data store is a database of all your data, where it lives, a description of the data, and in some cases, data analytics that have already been performed. In some cases, it is important to query and analyze data that is located in multiple applications and locations.

TIP

You may consider using a product such as the Starburst Analytics Engine (www.starburst.io) to simplify querying data that is distributed throughout many applications and storage locations. It makes access to distributed data fast and easy and works well within a DataOps environment.

Developing your data store

A data store is a company-wide marketplace for data. It can take on many forms, but in essence it's simply a shopping list of datasets. This is far from a silly idea. The shopping list (or a menu, if you like that analogy better) describes the dataset using metadata. This datastore is how you overcome data siloes where only a small group of people have access to specific data. Now, anyone in the company with the proper access can gain new insights by viewing data published by other departments or groups within the company.

Part of the metadata that describes the data also specifies the security level of the people who can access the data. To make the data available to the greatest number of people, the data is often scrubbed or modified to obscure the sensitive data while continuing to offer important elements useful in data analytics. For example (and, yes, this is a silly example, but it can give you a broad idea), the HR department releases a dataset describing all the company employees but with personal information obscured. The people responsible for facility parking can use the data to do capacity planning by viewing how many people drive cars to work, or perhaps even what kinds of cars so that they can figure out how many electric charging stations will be needed to accommodate employee needs. Without access to employee personal information, financial data, or salary data, the facilities team still has a useful dataset they didn't have to create for themselves by sending out a company-wide email asking people for their auto information, duplicating data that may already exist and creating a siloed dataset.

Another example, along the same lines, is an analytics assignment to figure out how far people commute to work each day. This can include employee addresses, which may be accessible only to people with specific authorization to view that level of sensitive data. A security review of the data, as part of the DataSecOps development cycle, considers that the data be further anonymized by eliminating employee names or street numbers while still providing fairly accurate distance information.

ELEMENTS OF A GOOD DATA STORE

A good data store clearly describes the dataset. Part of that description should specify whether it's a static dataset that was created in the past and contains no live data. It should include the date the set was created, by whom, and who maintains responsibility for the dataset.

The data store should clearly specify the security access levels required for access to the data. If this is done in a clearly coded manner, access can be granted in an automated fashion, speeding up access to the data. This also makes it clear to data scientists what level of confidentiality their users must have in order to review the analytics they create. For instance, their analytics might review competitive business analysis that would harm the company if released to the wrong people.

Where the data is stored is another element a good data store must have in its description of a dataset. It should tell potential users of the data whether it's stored locally or in the cloud. When describing the data storage, the type of DBMS should also be mentioned to make querying the data simpler. This is also important if you're integrating data from multiple datasets that might be stored on multiple clouds and data storage types.

A more real-world example is a hospital looking at the types of gallbladder opera-tions performed each year. To get this information, hospital reps need to have access to patient records governed by HIPAA regulations. Security analysts work-ing with the data analytics team can continuously review this analytics project to make sure that all HIPAA guidelines are being followed during the development of this project. The data could provide invaluable insight while protecting patient privacy.

Meeting the Challenges of DataSecOps

Securing application development keeps hackers from breaking into your applica-tion to steal data. Securing data analytics is a bit more direct because it means not handing data directly to the hackers.

Securing applications is a bit more straightforward because network operations can monitor who has access to an application and can shut down access to unau-thorized users. Data is a bit more static, and therefore monitoring access to the data is more challenging. It can easily go undetected. The FBI recently announced that foreign interests have had access to confidential government data stores for years. A group known as Advanced Persistent Threat 16 (APT16) has been stealing data since at least 2011. At the same time, foreign interests had access to the Office of Personnel Management, stealing highly sensitive data of millions of govern-ment workers, even including records of CIA agents working secretly in the field. There is no clear evidence that this group and others are not still camped out on servers full of sensitive data.

REMEMBER

Data breaches can go undetected for years.

A challenge for security teams in general, whether protecting data storage, appli-cations, or any other type of security, is that the bad guys tend to outspend the good guys. The value of stolen information is so great that the resources applied to obtain it are extraordinary. This isn't a call to throw up your hands and give up. It's more of a call to create better data security measures.

Increased data security can have a dampening effect on the use of data. No one wants to use data that is difficult or impossible to access because of the secu-rity measures placed on it. People want fast-and-secure access to data that pro-vides important insights. This might be the single greatest challenge of the teams involved in DataSecOps.

Selecting the appropriate privacy-enhancing technology is one of the more tech-nical challenges within DataSecOps. Overprotecting data — making it difficult to access, or so anonymized or obscured that the end result is meaningless — is always a danger. The trick is finding a balance between overprotecting and under-protecting your data. This is definitely one of those collaborative discussions your team will need to have when building your data store.

DataSecOps borrows the underlying principles of all the Ops methodologies. Good DataSecOps are

>> **Agile:** This term means continuous delivery and continuous security.

>> **Collaborative:** All stakeholders, security professionals, developers, and data scientists need to be involved.

>> **Security-embedded:** Security isn't tacked on at the end but rather is an integral part of development and tested at each release cycle.

>> **Staged:** Separation of development into stages, similar to what's done in a software development project, needs to be encouraged. This keeps testing from being done on production environments where faulty software can wreak havoc.

REMEMBER

When developing a DataSecOps strategy, it's important to focus on your most sensitive data. Chapter 1 talks about creating a risk assessment to understand where the greatest risks lie within your data, whether stored locally or in the cloud. That's great advice to follow.

When developing your data store, include a clear picture of who created/owns the dataset, when it was created, and perhaps why it was created, and then, if you don't think you'll ever need it again, get rid of it. Old, stale data can become a huge security risk. Don't be a data hoarder.

Establish clear policies about who has access to specific data or types of data. You can do this in a role-based policy matrix to make determining who has access to what data, at which levels (for example, read-only), and under what conditions. Conditions might include annual tax filings or an HR audit. This is specific to your business and the types of data it collects and uses. The goal is to be crystal-clear so that you can avoid lengthy approval processes that slow access to critical data.

REMEMBER

You must include freelancers and contractors when checking for data access restrictions. Don't forget about them!

A successful DataSecOps environment provides for rapid access to data without sacrificing quality or security. Clarity and collaboration can take you a long way toward that goal.

TIP

If you're ready to make your move into DataSecOps, it helps to use a ready-made platform. This is still a new methodology, so not many players are in the market. Here are a couple to start with:

>> **Satori:** https://satoricyber.com

>> **Exate:** www.exate.com

DataSecOps is sure to mature quickly, which means lots of additional products becoming available. The need for security in development and in DataOps only becomes more critical with time.

Understanding That No Cloud Is Perfect

When you depend on software written by someone else, you increase your risk factor. The number of applications in use in a typical cloud environment is multitudinous. (Yeah, that's a word.) This chapter covers what it takes to write secure software. This is what happens when things go wrong in someone else's development.

Although this chapter covers cloud security, Microsoft warned thousands of cloud customers about exposed databases. Security researchers were able to discover keys that allowed access to Microsoft's Cosmos DB databases. To change the keys, the customers had to modify their own keys. This was merely a hassle in this case and disaster was averted.

It was reported that there was no evidence the flaw had been exploited, but the potential for a monstrous data leak was there for thousands of companies using their cloud database service. The team that found the exploit called it ChaosDB, because it certainly had the potential to have inflicted chaos. Many companies have abandoned local databases for the benefits of using a cloud-based DBMS.

The discovered flaw was not in the database software itself, but rather through a visualization tool called Jupyter Notebook, which ended up being enabled in Cosmos by default. The flaw gave enough access to the database to allow for a complete database wipe or changing individual records. This points out that the sheer complexity of the software used for analysis, and the applications that make use of cloud databases have the potential for great harm when security flaws are exploitable.

The company that discovered the security flaw, Wiz (www.wiz.io/#), has its own cloud security software that identifies high-risk attack vectors without the use of agents. It can track security across several of the top cloud services by scanning all your virtual machine layers and containers, either active or offline, and looking for possible exploits.

Chapter **4**

Restricting Access

Restricting access to data is one of the important (and perhaps stunningly obvious) parts of cloud security. This chapter delves into that topic, but also introduces the basics of compliance because, though not limited to access restrictions, most of the compliance requirements deal heavily with who has access to which types of data.

Protecting data with user access restriction has been around since the first days of computers, when users had to log in to a mainframe over a hardwired dumb terminal. There isn't much new to the idea of user validation, but how it's done in the 21st century is quite different. This next section goes into detail in determining the types of access restrictions you should set for your data and corresponding applications.

Determining the Level of Access Required

Properly configuring your resources so that only authorized people have access can be a complicated matter. The reason it isn't as straightforward as it seems is that there may be no clear idea of how sensitive data might be and what kinds of people should have access.

Some basic principles can help you along, but much of what you need to determine is subjective — until it involves compliance regulations, which is covered in some detail later in this chapter. You should begin by knowing who is capable of legitimately accessing your data. Sadly, it's often difficult to know when people are accessing your data without authorization and, what's even worse, this kind of a breach can go on for *long* periods. Someone masquerading as a legitimate user may be able to fly under the radar and gain full access to your data.

Artificial intelligence is improving at recognizing patterns of use. This is one way it's possible to figure out when someone's user credentials have been stolen and are being used by hackers. For example, knowing what times someone normally logs in and out helps AI tracking logins to spot outliers. Someone logging in during the middle of the night may be an unauthorized user, and a good AI system throws up flags alerting network administrators that a hack may be in progress.

Catching flies with honey

One possible way to know when your account has been hacked is by way of a *honeypot*, when you put fake and recognizable data online for a hacker to steal, which may allow you to spot a breach when someone starts accessing the fake resource. Honeypots are most often used to catch someone who has gained unauthorized access to your data by using someone's credentials, which is why it's being mentioned as a tool in the section on user authentication.

A honeypot can be a database table, an entire database, or even an entire virtual server. Honeypots are categorized by the types of "bait" you offer:

>> **High interaction:** Uses virtual machines with a full set of services to keep your actual data as isolated as possible

>> **Low interaction:** Uses a virtual machine with a limited set of services, such as a DBMS

>> **Canary:** A cloud-based honeypot

A pure honeypot involves setting up a physical server, but this is costly and a more dangerous type of lure because, once someone has accessed a physical server, they likely have access to your network and other servers.

The cloud honeypot has some distinct advantages over more traditional hardware and VM honeypots. They can be easily placed geographically in high-risk areas to lure hackers. The geographical location is easily moved. Also, the cost of setting up a cloud honeypot is low, for a couple of reasons: First, no physical hardware is involved and new instances can be spun up in seconds. Second, cloud resources generally cost very little when not being used, and, hopefully, your honeypot isn't getting slammed with usage.

REMEMBER

Honeypots are one of the oldest tricks in the book. However, luring hackers into your network, whether local or part of your cloud setup, is a dangerous game. Hackers have become more sophisticated and, once on your network, have powerful tools to discover vulnerabilities in your system. Honeypots are still used today because they are cheap, easy to set up and sometimes catch the less skillful hacker.

Honeypots can also include fake data, fake documents and fake accounts that throw up red flags when accessed.

Determining roles

Stepping away from catching the bad guys for a minute, it's important to figure out how to grant access to the people who need it. One of the first steps you should take is to create a list of roles. You can think of roles as job titles, something one or more people might carry.

Rather than grant access to individuals, you grant access to a role. Figure 4-1 shows a typical role-based security system.

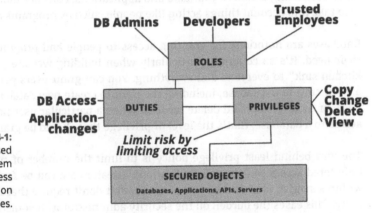

FIGURE 4-1:
A role-based security system grants access based on responsibilities.

Auditing user requirements

Tracking user requirements is one of those things that should be done regularly, as requirements change over time. Identity access management (IAM) is a set of policies and technologies that manage user identities and control access to all your cloud resources. In addition to third-party providers, major cloud service providers employ an IAM. It has been said that this is the system that protects a company's crown jewels. Because access management is no simple matter, you need to find the system that works best for you and balances expense, agility, and flexibility.

TIP

One thing you might consider is employing your configuration management database (CMDB) to help you track and audit the requirements users have for access. A good CMDB system not only tracks devices, data, and applications but can also track users and their interactions with the other components.

REMEMBER

Careful planning and preparation can simplify the task of identity auditing. Carefully tag user roles. Once tagged, make sure that you have clear and auditable policies for why a role should have access, when, and where. Most importantly, a person can have multiple roles, and roles can change over time. You need systems like those in a CMDB to help you track users and the roles they have.

Understanding Least Privilege Policy

Least privilege policy essentially states that you should grant no unneeded privileges. It's kind of a bare minimum policy that restricts anyone from gaining access beyond their absolute need.

TIP

When restricting access to your data and applications, consider more than people. Also take into account things acting like people, such as programs and processes.

Databases are notorious for granting access to people and programs far beyond their need. It's so common, particularly when building websites, to grant "the kitchen sink" to everyone and everything. You can grant users permission to do a lot of stuff to a database, including the right to create new databases, delete old ones, or modify, add, and delete records. When a particular user needs only read access to a database, that's the level of privilege that should be granted.

The idea behind least privilege policy is to limit the number of roles that have unfettered access to data and applications. Greater care can be focused on users within sensitive roles and less on accounts that don't require that level of sensitivity. This eases the burden on the security administrator. If someone does compromise one of these lower-level accounts, they aren't granted access to sensitive data or given the ability to do any harm.

REMEMBER

It's not always a human hacker directly attempting to access one of your systems. Malware can be devious and unrelenting at attempts to worm its way in.

When looking at the sensitivity of your data, you might be tempted to think, "Who cares about how many socks I keep in inventory?" Perhaps no one really cares but you. If you no longer had access to your inventory information, though, how would it impact your business? Would you be able to continue selling socks? Would it slow you down or require you to take a physical inventory? Many exploits care little about the information and care more about its value to the owners. That's why ransomware attacks work so well: Hackers encrypt your data and ask for payment to decrypt it. It's best to limit the possibility of attacks in the first place.

Granting just-in-time privileges

Granting access to your systems doesn't have to be a one-and-done kind of deal. You can grant access on an as-needed basis. For instance, if someone needs root access to a server to perform an administrative task, you can grant root permission for as long as it takes to perform the task and then restrict privileges, once again, to only what is needed.

You can limit the ability to perform actions based on date and time. This way, no one can perform these actions except during a particular window of time. For instance, AWS allows the ability to restrict actions to specific periods by setting these values in its identity and access management (IAM) policies.

The need-to-know strategy

The idea of least privilege may seem to be straightforward on the surface. In fact, it's a simple idea: If someone doesn't need to know something, or access something, don't allow it. But it gets far more complicated than that.

An example of a complicated scenario is a DevOps team that releases code in a continuous development environment. The team regularly changes databases, updates applications, and pokes around in general in some sensitive areas. Figuring out who needs what access and when can be a complicated task.

TIP

Avoid creating roles with unlimited privileges (*God roles*). Though it's tempting to just grant access to everything all at once, this is the most dangerous type of role, and if exploited, it can be devastating.

Granting access to trusted employees

When building your identity management system to manage the principles of least privilege, start with your employees. Consider the roles each of them plays within your organization. Don't get sucked into the idea that just because someone's pay grade is higher, they need more access. It just makes them a bigger

Restricting Access

target for hackers. For example, you might want to give the CEO every one of the privileges, but in fact the CEO may need zero privileges. Other people/roles are responsible for supplying decision information, and therefore the CEO has zero need to have privileges that grant access to your data.

In large enterprises, consider segmenting your identity privileges. Because someone has rights over one database doesn't mean they should have the same rights over another department's database, or even someone else's database within the same department. Creating a more fine-grained set of privileges limits risk should access be exploited.

With many companies relying more on remote work environments, employee access must be managed even more carefully. The trend to remote work has been a boon to hackers. It has also created a larger access landscape. More tools and applications are being used to get the job done remotely where they were once used directly on a desktop with local network access to resources and data.

Restricting access to contractors

When you're faced with a scenario where you've just hired a contractor on UpWork or one of the other freelancing sites and they've given you a list of privileges they require to get the job done, take a step back before blindly handing over those privileges. You don't know these people — and though they may be trustworthy beyond belief, you have no idea what types of security measures they have in place to protect access. If *they* are hacked, *you* are hacked.

Chances are good that there are trusted employees that manage contractors and freelancers. Consider giving them the privileges for tasks like the release of source code. Let freelance developers write code and release it into a sandbox until it's time to release the code. (See Figure 4-2.) Then grant the employee the privilege in the source code control system to release code into production. This extra step can save you a lot of grief.

The same idea is true for changes to databases. Book 4, Chapter 3 introduces the idea of creating copies of data for development using DataOps. The GIT source code control system has this ability to quickly and easily create copies of data so that you aren't risking direct access to your production data. You might also consider working with sample data. This is particularly true when your data contains sensitive data, or when access to the data is restricted by governance policies.

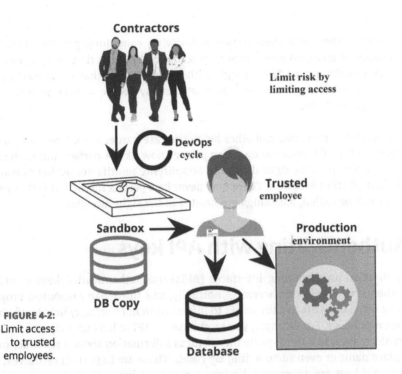

FIGURE 4-2:
Limit access
to trusted
employees.

Implementing Authentication

Authentication is, if not the heart of cloud security, certainly at least one of the chambers of the heart. Controlling who has access to your systems is the most direct and basic form of security. The days of simple user ID and password authentication are no longer sufficient, and so authentication has become a more complex task, beginning with multifactor authentication.

Multifactor authentication (Or, who's calling me now?)

Multifactor authentication is covered in greater detail later in this book, but, as an introduction, this term means asking for a third or even fourth form of authentication beyond simply knowing a user ID and password. In some cases, systems send an email or text message with a code to validate that you have access to a trusted system, such as a known device like a cellphone or access to the email account. This system isn't perfect, of course, because if your account has been hacked, it's possible that the hacker has access to these systems as well.

Another method of authentication is knowing something private, such as the questions often asked when setting up accounts, like your first pet's name or your father's middle name. The struggle with this method is that social media phishing has made it almost useless because so many people answer all those stupid Facebook questions.

Fingerprints, iris scans, and other biometrics are harder to fool, but not impossible. Even Face ID, common on many phones now, is not perfect. But such strategies are a step in the right direction. Simplifying multifactor authentication will aid in its further adoption. There may never be a perfect method of authentication that can't be fooled, but things are headed in the right direction.

Authenticating with API keys

Application programming interfaces (APIs) use authentication keys in order to authenticate application access — normally, to a third-party resource. Programmers often use APIs to gain access to information not normally held by the application provider. For example, you might use an API to look up a zip code. Sending an API request to a third-party then returns information about a zip code, such as a place name or even surrounding zip codes. These are important resources, but if your API keys are discovered, hackers can gain access to these resources — or to the resources you might provide. A good key management system helps manage your API keys.

Using Firebase authentication

Software developers need the ability to include authentication in the applications they build. One such system, known as Firebase, provides a software development kit (SDK) that you can use to authenticate users to your apps.

Firebase supports authentication by using these methods:

>> Email and passwords

>> Phone numbers

>> Federated ID providers such as Google, Facebook, and Twitter. (A federated ID links a person's identity across different identity management systems in a form of single sign-on technology.)

Firebase integrates with industry standard authentication methods such as OpenID Connect and OAuth. (More on OAuth in the next section.)

WARNING

OpenID was an idea to allow people to use the same ID to sign in to different sites. The problem is that, after a hacker knows your credentials, they can then log into multiple sites. This idea has now come and gone. A newer version of OpenID was developed as a part of OAuth.

Employing OAuth

OAuth, or Open Authorization, isn't exactly an authentication system — it's really an authorization framework that provides a system where, once you've logged in to an application that knows who you are, you can then grant authorization to another application and never have to give the "other" application your user ID and password. OAuth uses access tokens sent to third-party services without ever revealing a user's credentials.

The advantage of using OAuth is that it limits how many people know your user access credentials. Once you've logged into one place, you can authorize other places using an OAuth access token either temporarily, or in some cases, for recurring access. Additionally, applications using OAuth tokens don't need to maintain a user account database, increasing security.

Google and Facebook authentication methods

Google has a smartphone app known as Authenticator, which provides two-factor authentication by displaying a code that resets regularly. The benefit of using Authenticator is that it needs no network connectivity to create the code; a two-factor system that sends an SMS message does. Authenticator works by creating a code on both your phone and the server at the same time using a hacker-proof algorithm authenticating you as a valid user.

Facebook, rather than use the Google method, has an authentication system built directly into its cellphone app. When you try to log in to Facebook from a desktop that isn't recognized, you may be asked to access your mobile account and use the Facebook app to send an authorization message. This method does require network connectivity to work.

Introducing the Alphabet Soup of Compliance

Companies that collect sensitive information — whether it's financial, credit, or health information — must comply with regulations. This statement is even more true when dealing with international restrictions such as the European Union (EU) privacy regulations.

Global compliance

Cloud computing has made it cost effective to do business online, anywhere in the world. Of course, some physical limitations still exist, such as product fulfillment, but a larger hurdle for many businesses is meeting the demands of global compliance.

The International Standards Organization (ISO) defines compliance this way:

"The state where an organization is meeting all its obligations and commitments."

There are compliance standards when it comes to cybersecurity — many of them, in fact. This list describes some of the best known:

>> **PCI DSS:** One of the best-known compliance regulations for most businesses, the Payment Card Industry Data Security Standard regulates how credit card and credit cardholder information is kept private.

>> **GDPR:** Failing to meet the requirements of this regulation, the EU's General Data Protection Regulation, can come with some heavy fines.

>> **HIPAA:** The Health Insurance and Portability and Accountability Act of 1996 protects the privacy of your health records.

>> **POPI:** The Protection of Personal Information Act is South Africa's own, personal set of information protection regulations.

>> **FERPA:** The Family Education and Rights Privacy Act is the set of compliance regulations that pertain to protecting the private information of students.

WARNING

Don't think that you can comply and forget it later, like a bad date. Security compliance is an ongoing process that will involve your constant attention (as long you both shall live).

CYBERSPACE

Curious where the term *cybersecurity* came from? Essentially, it means to protect *cyberspace,* which is a word that was used to describe the Internet in its very early days. The term *cyberspace* was first used by the science fiction author William Gibson, in 1982, in his short story "Burning Chrome" and then again in his novel *Neuromancer.*

Complying with PCI

One of the common compliance regulations relates to protecting credit card information. Commerce today is done primarily by credit card, whether personal or corporate. The health of our very economy now depends on the security of credit card information. Because of this, PCI compliance is one of the most stringent sets of regulations.

Complying with PCI is a complex task. PCI compliance that has as its goal the protection of credit card details generally requires meeting these 12 requirements:

>> Build and maintain a firewall to protect cardholder data.

>> Use passwords and security parameters that exceed vendor default values.

>> Protect stored cardholder data.

>> Encrypt credit card transaction data as it passes over public networks. *Hint:* The Internet is a public network.

>> Employ antimalware software.

>> Be certain that applications you build are secure. (See Book 4, Chapter 3.)

>> Limit access to cardholder data.

>> Assign a unique identity to anyone with computer access.

>> Restrict physical access to cardholder data. (Try that with your teenager!)

>> Monitor and track all access to network and cardholder data.

>> Test security systems and processes regularly.

>> Establish a security policy for employees and contractors.

Each one of these 12 requirements has many detailed subrequirements. Meeting the PCI requirement is no simple task, and many companies have chosen to have companies that specialize in credit card data manage their transactions rather than bear the cost and risk. Even those companies are much stricter now about

Restricting Access

how clients communicate with them. Using a third-party vendor to process credit card transactions saves a great deal of overhead and hassle. Rather than try to store your customer's credit card information and set yourself up for a terrible data breach, it can make sense to make this process someone else's problem for the small percentage they charge for the service.

One of the largest-ever credit card detail breaches happened in 2017 when Equifax was hacked, which led to the release of the private information of 143 million people along with credit card details of just over 200,000 individuals. More recently, Capital One was breached in 2019, revealing the credit card details of more than 100,000 of its customers. Capital One is the fifth largest credit card issuer. ("What's in your wallet?") Over the years, hundreds of millions of credit card details have been revealed by way of hacks. Many of those details are then sold over the dark web, an off-the-beaten path area of the Internet not accessible using standard web browsers.

Complying with GDPR

Businesses doing business within or with EU companies are required to comply with the GDPR (https://gdpr.eu/). Failing to do so can result in some stiff fines.

The goal of the GDPR is to protect the privacy rights of its citizens, residents, and even its visitors. This requirement is placed on businesses within, and operating outside, the EU and is enforced via treaties.

The GDPR goes beyond financial transactions. If you're offering any goods or services to people in the EU, then the GDPR requires that you comply. You can get started doing this by first gaining permission to use someone's private information. Permission is part of the way there.

TIP

Maintaining an EU-happy privacy policy on your website helps you comply with the GDPR.

As with many security issues, always do an impact assessment. Figure out what happens if the data you're using is released into the wild during a breach. If your answer is "It's bad," it behooves you to take extra steps to protect the data. This begins with encryption.

Encryption isn't the great fix-all that everyone wants it to be, but it keeps out the wannabe hackers. Always make sure your communications have end-to-end encryption. Use a TLS (formerly SSL) certificate with your website, and this happens automagically. These certificates ensure that users are communicating with the right website and not some random hacker. The encrypted form of web communications protocol HTTPS takes over from them and sets up end-to-end encryption.

Though the buck stops with you, it's your responsibility to make sure that any of your contractors or vendors who have access to your private customer data also comply with the requirements of the GDPR. This includes the cloud provider you've selected. If you use cloud-based services, such as an email provider, that service also has to comply with the GDPR when doing business with EU customers.

One of the more unusual hoops you need to jump through to comply with the GDPR is to appoint a representative in the EU. This doesn't apply if you're just occasionally processing the personal data of EU folks. As long as you're not processing tons of information, you might be able to skip this step. The question to ask yourself is whether the release of the information will impact the rights and freedoms of people in the EU.

You need to know what to do if there's ever a data breach involving the private information of EU residents. (Moving to Russia is not an option.) If you're using strong encryption for your communications, this goes a long way in mitigating any fines for negligent handling of data, and in some cases avoiding some of the reporting requirements.

Using your best efforts to comply with the spirit of these requirements should keep you from being scrutinized by EU regulators.

HIPAA compliance

If you've been to the doctor's office or hospital lately, you've likely had to sign a document informing you that the doctor or hospital must comply with HIPAA regulations. If your organization is health-related and must comply with HIPAA, you should take this regulation seriously because fines for failures to comply can be serious. In fact, even if you didn't know of a breach or, using reasonable diligence, should have known of a breach, you can still be fined for each occurrence. One breach can lead to multiple violations, one for each record that was released. For example, if a laptop is lost or stolen containing private data that has a thousand records stored on it and that data is released, you could get fined for a thousand violations. Serious stuff. Paying attention matters, though, because, if you can show you've taken reasonable measures, you might be forgiven and slip by without fines.

Here are some steps you need to follow to comply with HIPAA:

» **Put someone in charge of your HIPAA security.** At least a single point of contact is required. You can give them a cool title, like HIPAA security officer.

» **Know the rules.** Basically, you can't release private information covered under HIPAA without permission of the person whose information you're storing. There are exceptions but getting permission is the easiest way to be safe.

» **Know what rights people have.** HIPAA grants rights to people regarding their personal information. Essentially, a person can control what information is released or specify who receives that information (an insurance company or a specialist medical provider). Rather than stand at the nurse's station for everyone to hear, individuals can request privacy.

» **Put it in writing.** It's *vital* to put your HIPAA policies in writing. Failure to do this constitutes willful neglect, and that's bad. You need to have policies regarding privacy or notification of a breach, for instance — thus, the paper you sign at the doctor's office.

» **Make some forms.** Part of putting it in writing means you've created forms that meet the HIPAA guidelines. All these are available from HIPAA websites. It's nothing you have to create from scratch. Don't feel you can simply have a piece of paper that says, "Mum's the word. Sign here." A sample can be found here: www.southernute-nsn.gov/wp-content/uploads/sites/15/2020/06/AAOS-HIPAA-Notice-of-Privacy-Practices-2013.pdf.

» **Execute associate agreements.** This is one aspect where cloud security definitely plays a role. When you store private data in the cloud, you must have a signed agreement with the cloud provider. This also pertains to their subcontractors. A cloud storage provider that handles HIPAA-compliant data will most likely have those in place.

» **Complete a risk assessment of your hardware.** A solid assessment of the security risks involving all your hardware has been and always will be an essential first step in implementing your cloud security policy. Your risk assessment should be done regularly and be well-documented. Be diligent. In today's mobile world, it's easy to overlook hardware that may allow access to your HIPAA-controlled data.

» **Put in administrative, technical, and physical safeguards.** No system is perfect, and there may be occasional unintentional disclosures. But you can get off the hook without a fine if you can show that you've done a reasonable job of putting the right safeguards in place. Following the cloud security guidelines in this book will help!

- >> **Implement training.** Who doesn't like a day off from work to eat doughnuts and watch PowerPoint slides? New employees must receive training within a reasonable amount of time from their hire date or else you risk the wrath of the HIPAA compliance folks if one of your employees suddenly decides to post private medical data on Facebook. If they were trained, it's not so bad for you, because you did your part. (In training sites Krispy Kreme doughnuts are usually appreciated.)

- >> **Respond quickly to breaches and violations.** This requirement should be true of all your security measures.

- >> **Report breaches within 60 days.** You must let people know if you've unintentionally disclosed their private data.

TIP

Each state maintains their own requirements for breach notification. For a spreadsheet of the requirements by state, check out `https://iapp.org/resources/article/state-data-breach-notification-chart/`.

Complying with HIPAA can seem tough, but if you take reasonable precautions to protect private data and document all your efforts carefully, you should be able to avoid fines and hassles and maybe even disclosures.

Government compliance

When your company works with the U.S. federal government, you must meet compliance standards as well, depending on the level of confidentiality or secrecy of the data. It's way beyond the scope of this book, however, to cover all those guidelines. It's good to meet at least the most basic compliance guideline published by the National Institute of Standards and Technology (NIST) known as NIST 800-171 (`https://csrc.nist.gov/publications/detail/sp/800-171/rev-2/final`). This covers unclassified but controlled data.

You'll be happy to know that complying with NIST 800-171 requires no outside audit of your organization. You can self-report compliance. These are the three basic compliance requirements:

- >> **Create a security plan.** The plan should cover a description of your overall IT environment, including all cloud resources you use. You can easily overlook these when creating documentation of your physical plant. Make sure your plan describes all interconnections your system has with the outside world. You also need to specify which measures you'll take in case of a security breach.

- >> **Document exceptions.** You need to document any reasons that your company might fail to meet reasonable security measures to protect private data. Along with your list of exceptions, you need a plan for how you'll make those failures right. You can't just say, "We've got problems, and we'll fix them." Also, document what you actually did to remediate the exceptions.

» **Give yourself a score.** NIST 800-171 has an assessment methodology you need to follow when giving yourself a score, and then that score is stored in a federal database, allowing you to show compliance so that you can get certain government contracts.

Compliance in general

Draw seven letters from your favorite word game and chances are high that you can spell one or more acronyms of compliance requirements. There are international, federal, state, and local compliance regulations and guidelines. In a nutshell, put someone in charge, give them a fancy title, give them a filing cabinet large enough to hold all the paperwork, make a security plan, document everything, store it in the filing cabinet (locked, of course), and train everyone.

TIP

Your cloud security measures must comply with the requirements of all the various information security and privacy guidelines. Your cloud provider can most likely guide you in documenting your cloud security compliance.

Maintaining Compliance and CSPM

As with all security measures, it's not enough to simply make all the efforts once and then sit on your laurels and say, "Job well done." All security measures must be revisited regularly, from minute by minute for complex network infrastructure to weekly or monthly for smaller organizations working with data that may not be as sensitive.

When your organization handles private data that is covered by one or more compliance regulations, you will likely submit to a regular audit of your security. In a smaller organization, you may be able to squeak by with making a list of the processes, infrastructure and security measures that are regularly audited and then check them regularly to verify that they're still in compliance. Larger companies need to use tools to help validate compliance, which makes verification and reporting easier.

TIP

Cloudcheckr (`https://cloudcheckr.com`) is an enterprise-level tool that can handle the heavy lifting of compliance. This tool works across various cloud infrastructure designs. In addition to assisting you with compliance, the Cloudcheckr CMX platform performs tasks such as asset management and resource utilization.

CSPM, or cloud security posture management, automates the task of locating and fixing security problems across cloud infrastructures. The risk identification handles IaaS (Infrastructure as a Service), SaaS (Software as a Service), and PaaS (Platform as a Service) cloud services.

The complexity of cloud services means that, for a medium- to large-size business, the cloud services you connect with and disconnect from can number in the thousands each day. This type of complexity is what makes clouds extremely useful but also makes them even more difficult to make secure.

The reason clouds are particularly difficult to secure is that they have no perimeter, such as a local- or wide-area network might have. In those cases, you can simply throw up firewalls to keep out the unwanted. With clouds, you don't have that delimited barrier to protect.

With the complexity of cloud connections and services, there is just no way you could ever hope to protect your cloud services manually, even with a network operations center working 24 hours a day. It's simply impossible, or at the very least unfeasible.

REMEMBER

You can't protect what you can't see.

Visibility is the key to good cybersecurity. Working across many clouds of various types and brands makes visibility *difficult*. In fact, it makes trying to protect your cloud infrastructure a bit like groping in the dark. Another thing that makes visibility difficult when working with clouds is that the cloud is merely the platform on which innumerable technologies operate and new ones are popping up every day. Keeping abreast of the new services and how you might protect them is an onerous task.

Visibility is also more than just an overview of the programs running on cloud platforms. Trying to oversee an environment with thousands of users connecting and disconnecting from multiple devices and platforms is worse than air traffic control at Dallas/Fort Worth International Airport. Each one of those users is a security risk.

A CSPM application automatically discovers entities as they connect and disconnect. This includes applications as well as users. As the entities are discovered, the system can see when they are operating within their security guidelines and when they are outliers in the system. That information then gets passed on to network operators.

Discovering and remediating threats with CSPM applications

Threats are a bit like a rat infestation: Once you're infested with rats, it's difficult to find them even though they seem everywhere. Cloud security threats are like rat infestations for a number of reasons. First, we tend to invite them in. A high percentage of threats occur because we've misconfigured something. Human error is responsible for most of the weaknesses we bake into our cybersystems.

Another reason that cloud security threats are like a rat infestation is that they gnaw away at the good infrastructure until catastrophic failures occur. It doesn't take the entire system to be overcome, only the weak spots. Once they're in, rats or hackers, it's game over. It's then hard to get rid of them and the damage is done.

In larger enterprises, infrastructure management has been automated in code, a process known as IaC (Infrastructure as Code). That means instructions on managing infrastructure are written as code instructions, which can be the source of many errors and security holes. CSPM systems are designed to find and correct the misconfigurations that plague complex systems.

A good cloud security and posture management application monitors and helps prevent disaster by using these methods:

>> Prevention

>> Detection

>> Response

>> Prediction

Prevention involves setting up safeguards against both intentional and unintentional breaches. Intentional breaches are what you might think they are — hackers trying to break into your systems, looking for those vulnerabilities they usually find with enough determination. This is the focus of most cloud security applications.

When preventing breaches, you should also be looking toward the unintentional breach — when human error reveals private information in places that are easily accessed, even by people not trying to hack your systems. The history of cybersecurity is full of examples where, on one fateful day, a company somehow manages to accidentally start displaying all its customer information on the web for everyone to view.

CSPM systems work to avoid intentional as well as unintentional breaches by providing clear and simple visibility over even the most complex cloud infrastructures. Detecting security problems from alerts is what a good CSPM system does well. When security holes are easily detected, they are easily fixed. Part of the benefit of using a unified system to manage the cloud security posture is avoiding *alert fatigue*, which happens when security alerts start popping up from multiple systems and become overwhelming, kind of like crickets. One cricket is kind of fun to hear at night — tens of thousands becomes an overwhelming drone. The same thing happens with security alerts. This causes many important alerts to be overlooked.

CSPM systems generally employ AI to sort through alerts. This enables alerts to be combined from multiple sources into a single alert. AI-enabled CSPM systems can then either recommend responses to specific threats or be automated to handle them on their own through prewritten automation scripts set up to solve issues as they happen.

The AI then becomes predictive, letting you know when the systems are ripe for a breach, spotting all the small risks that later turn into big risks.

TIP

Using AI to predict security failures allows them to be corrected before they actually occur. You're then being proactive instead of reactive, and though you might lose hero status for solving problems, you'll be known for not allowing them to occur in the first place.

Automating Compliance

Earlier in this chapter, you can see how complying with regulations that work to protect private information can be difficult to manage. A good CSPM system goes a long way in managing your compliance across complicated cloud environments.

Because many of the corrective actions to security problems can be automated within your CSPM application, you can self-correct when compliance begins to wander from the guidelines. Being able to do this in an automated fashion reduces the manpower required to oversee a large cloud-first system. Automated threat detection works tirelessly around the clock with reduced risk of operator failure.

Integrating with DevOps

Your developers use DevSecOps to secure applications before they're released. The CSPM system provides monitoring after an application has been released and reports security issues with released applications back to the DevOps team for correction. In a perfect world, security risks are caught during the continuous testing that happens before each release. Coding errors do happen, however, and catching them quickly and efficiently is important when it comes to establishing trust in the software. You don't want the end user catching the problem or, worse, having this be the cause of a security breach.

WARNING

When CSPM systems detect misconfigurations, they are corrected in the runtime environment and not in the IaC instructions. That means that configuration changes to the virtual environment are not saved when the runtime ceases to exist. The IaC (Infrastructure as Code) instructions are not changed. To make sure that the same misconfigurations don't occur each time an application is launched, they must be corrected within the IaC. This strategy maintains the instructions in the IaC as the single source of truth.

Companies like Sysdig (https://sysdig.com) have added CSPM modules into their DevOps applications. This module lets you write rules for accessing cloud infrastructure. One nice feature is that this module monitors cloud utilization that turns off cloud resources when they aren't being used. Running only the services you need reduces the overall security risk. This Sysdig module works together with the Sysdig open-source Falco security platform for Kubernetes (https://falco.org) and the threat detection system donated to the Cloud Native Computing Foundation (www.cncf.io).

Controlling Access to the Cloud

Controlling access to cloud resources is perhaps the single most important facet of cloud security. Misconfigurations of cloud access control have been responsible for some of the largest data breaches in history. Cloud service providers generally offer an access control system that allows individuals access to cloud resources in a controlled manner. (For more on role-based permissions, see Book 4, Chapter 3.)

TIP

Use logging tools to discover when cloud access permissions have been misconfigured. Many logging tools will report errors alerting network administrators that a problem exists. Error logs are often the first indication that something's gone wrong.

You may choose to go beyond the capabilities of the cloud access system of your cloud provider for greater flexibility as well as uniformity across multiple cloud environments. This is done with a Cloud Access Security Broker. More on that option in the next section.

Using a cloud access security broker (CASB)

Cloud access security brokers (CASBs) enable companies to develop policies beyond those set by the cloud provider. You can do this to make sure that your cloud environment security policies fall in line with your on-premises (local) security policies. It also allows you to catch security problems that may have fallen through the cracks with traditional or in-house security systems. You can see where the CASB system fits into your IT infrastructure as a whole by checking out Figure 4-3.

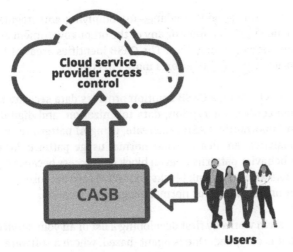

FIGURE 4-3: The CASB system sits between your users and your cloud access control system.

Using a CASB can be revealing. When it comes to visibility, you might be shocked at what a CASB can reveal. You might believe that your corporate cloud usage is at one level, only to find that it's ten times or even a hundred times the usage level you'd imagined. One of the original uses for the CASB was to eliminate or at least greatly reduce shadow IT systems (computing environments operating outside the purview of the IT department), the bane of all cybersecurity officers. The use of a CASB has become essential to enterprises operating complex cloud environments.

CASB products have various offerings, but most of them offer a range of basic services, such as

>> Data loss prevention

>> Sharing and collaboration controls

>> Configuration audits

>> Virus and malware detection

>> SSO (single sign-on) and IAM (identity access management) integration

>> Governance risk assessment

Risk assessment of cloud apps is an important feature of a CASB. Monitoring access to cloud applications provides the kind of visibility into your cloud app usage that enables intelligent decisions about when to throttle or stop app usage due to risk. This kind of decision is usually done manually by a security team, but they need the information provided by the CASB to make intelligent decisions.

A CASB system can provide guidance in complying with regulations, either the ones mentioned in this chapter or any of the other government and industry compliance regulations you may face. The CASB identifies areas of high risk that will help you focus your security efforts more effectively.

In addition to visibility, a CASB solution provides data security measures such as collaboration control, encryption, data tokenization, and digital rights management. Most importantly, CASB can create, using AI pattern recognition and entity behavior analytics, an idea of what normal usage patterns look like and report anomalous behavior patterns or even block user access because of outlier patterns. It's a little like when the bank blocks your ATM card because of an unusually large purchase or one outside your normal geographic location.

The CASB system works by first developing a list of all your services. There are two ways this list is compiled. One is agent-based, where a software agent constantly searches for connected resources. This is the more difficult type of discovery system to employ. The second is agentless, which doesn't rely on a hardware or software device constantly scanning; instead, the system registers users and devices when a user attempts a login to the device or application. It's a type of on-demand service that makes use of the machine's (or virtual machine's) native services.

TIP

Agentless CASB systems may be easier to employ in the cloud because of their increased ability to operate in high-density virtual server environments.

Bitglass (www.bitglass.com) is a multimode CASB that allows protection of data at rest as well as data being accessed. Most security systems only offer to protect data at rest. Bitglass uses a reverse proxy to provide agentless CASB services.

Middleware protection systems

CASB systems are one part of the overall cloud security software plan. Other *middleware* applications (those that sit between applications and system software) provide additional security services. For full security coverage, you should consider using a secure web gateway and a data loss prevention system.

Employing a secure web gateway (SWG)

The web has grown over the years as the foundation of application development. Web development has outstripped traditional desktop application development because there is no need to distribute it. Changes made to web applications impact everyone immediately, without the need for downloads. Built-in encryption also secures applications end-to-end. A secure web gateway protects users and applications from external and internal threats.

The Fortinet SWG (www.fortinet.com) provides services like these:

>> URL filtering

>> Data loss prevention

>> Malware protection

An SWG sits between users and your web server and acts as a security filtering device. It directs connection requests based on your company security policy. Checking certificate validity and deep SSL/TLS inspection can keep web communications safe from people trying to redirect web traffic or spoof a website. It also blocks malware from entering your network when users initiate web traffic.

Come up with use policies that allow you to restrict access to inappropriate websites, enforce security policies, and protect against unauthorized data transfers. Secure web gateways are often used alongside VPNs when employees are accessing applications while working remotely.

Data loss prevention (DLP) systems

Data loss prevention (DLP) systems inspect network traffic, leaving your systems looking for sensitive data, such as social security numbers, credit card information, medical information, or intellectual property. Traffic that is carrying unauthorized data is then terminated to protect from data loss.

TIP

DLP systems can run as stand-alone software applications or are often embedded in commercial secure web gateway applications.

Using a Firewall as a Service (FWaaS)

Firewalls have been protecting networks from the early days of the Internet. Once, the Internet was the wild, wild west of development — until hackers saw the opportunities and simple vulnerabilities afforded by Internet access through network ports. Almost overnight that came to a halt, when almost all Internet traffic was forced to use Port 80, the World Wide Web port. This was the dawn of the web-based Internet application, as nearly every other application was shut down except for email and FTP and a few others.

Now that networks incorporate one or more clouds, protecting networks has become more difficult, and it created the need for a firewall that can protect cloud resources. With a shared responsibility for security between your company and the cloud provider, it's up to you to add the additional security not provided by the cloud.

An FWaaS runs in the cloud and performs all the same basic services you might expect from a traditional hardware or software firewall running on your local network such as packet filtering, IPSec VPN, SSL/TLS support, and IP mapping.

Additionally, FWaaS services can

>> Aggregate the network traffic from both cloud and onsite networks

>> Enforce uniform security policies across a diverse network

>> Give you more visibility and control over your network

>> Identify malware

When the firewall inspects the header of each data packet trying to enter your network, it does an intelligent discovery of the source of the packet using deep packet inspection (DPI) and alerts network operators to seemingly innocuous but dangerous traffic. Some FWaaS systems incorporate AI learning systems that have the capability to spot never-before-seen malware.

Because of the agile nature of today's network and cloud infrastructure, installing traditional firewalls no longer makes sense. Employing cloud-based firewall systems makes good security and financial sense.

Secure Access Service Edge (SASE)

Secure Access Service Edge (SASE) is a model for networking and network security that is the combination of wide-area networking, CASB, FWaaS, and the implementation of Zero Trust policies that delivers services based on these factors:

>> Identity of the entity

>> Real-time context

>> Your company's security policies

>> Compliance restrictions

>> Risk assessment

According to Gartner, a leading technology research and consulting company, SASE provides unprecedented integration. This integration includes a number of different entities, including users, groups of users, departments, divisions, applications, toasters and refrigerators, and other IoT devices, no matter where they are located — locally or out on the edge of the cloud where you deliver services. SASE identifies users and devices and then applies zero-trust and policy-based security to traffic between applications and users.

Many solutions exist for implementing SASE. Lookout (www.lookout.com) has an application designed for remote workers that provides end-to-end security between remote workers and the cloud. It provides some of the following features:

>> Dynamic access control

>> Visibility into endpoints, users, cloud apps, and data

>> Protects data at rest or in motion

>> Policy control, threat identification, and investigation

Using an SASE solution such as this creates an environment like one that has a perimeter, such as a local- or wide-area network, except that this includes diverse cloud infrastructure and mobile workers from a large array of devices. This is known as a *software-defined wide-area network* (SDWAN).

You might also take a look at Netskope www.netskope.com/, one of the market leaders in the CASB marketplace.

Identifying user behavior

One way that risk is mitigated in a SASE solution is by using AI to understand user behavior and identifying possible risk at every endpoint. This is different from traditional cybersecurity, which tends to provide security through deep scans comparing results against malware profiles. Because malware changes by the minute, the databases of malware information are quickly outdated, making them nearly useless. With AI, it's like having a grade school teacher at the head of the class with their back turned. The teacher hears talking and immediately knows who is speaking, based on previous behavior. There's no need for the ubiquitous question of "Who's talking?"

Combine anomalous user behavior with app, device, and network threat detection, and you have a powerful security barrier. Having it all combined into a single solution means that you avoid the risk of overlooking security policies between multiple security software applications. A single and consistent solution operates seamlessly over many different cloud types and networks.

Carrying out forensic investigations

After an attack, network security operations need telemetry data, logs, and running audits to find the source of the attack and harden the network against future attacks.

Hackers almost always leave footprints, and progress toward eliminating attacks is possible only when you have the right information from all your network-connected devices.

REMEMBER

When you consider the amount of money companies spend on network security, hackers funded by criminals spend considerably more to defeat it.

Using a managed service provider

You may be using some or all the technologies that make up the SASE framework. An option to doing it all yourself is to outsource this complicated task to a managed service provider. AT&T (www.att.com) offers a SASE-managed service provider plan. Using this plan allows you to

>> Reach your security goals faster

>> Enable scaling

>> Outsource expensive and manpower-intensive 24/7 monitoring

>> Take advantage of the security solutions and expertise of a large company

You can choose to have a managed service provider like AT&T fully manage or co-manage your SDWAN.

Getting Certified

It doesn't do much good to spend time, money, and effort on developing rock-solid network security if the people you do business with have not taken a similar path. But how do you know? One way is by achieving a network security certification. When you have such a certification, other businesses will know that you've jumped through all the hoops and dotted all the i's. It also makes it easier, particularly if your company must comply with security regulations, to know exactly what level of security your vendors or partner companies might have.

ISO 27001 Compliance

ISO/IEC 27001 is an international standard of managing information security. You can voluntarily choose to have your organization certified as compliant with this recognized standard. As with most certifications, publishing your compliance means that other organizations trust your security efforts in protecting not only your own data but theirs as well. See Figure 4-4.

Businesses that carry ISO 27001 certification make themselves better suited to be trusted business partners.

Business A carries ISO 27001.

Business B trusts Business A with private data.

FIGURE 4-4:
Certification leads to better B2B information security trust.

When your business is larger than a few desks by the window, you can limit which parts of your organization carry an ISO 27001 certification. It's not necessary that every part of the business comply with the standard. It can be limited to a single business unit.

SOC 2 compliance

The SOC 2 certification (short for System and Organization Controls 2 certification, as opposed to the System and Organization Controls 1 certification) was created by the American Institute of CPAs (AICPA). Figure 4-5 shows the five pillars of SOC 2 certification. Each auditing company provides its own certification logo upon successful certification that your company can then proudly display.

Privacy   **Security**

SOC2
certification

Confidentiality   **Availability**

**Processing
integrity**

FIGURE 4-5:
The five
pillars of SOC 2
certification.

Certifying security

SOC 2 audits make certain your business complies with reasonable levels of access security. Auditors check for

>> Protection against system abuse

>> Protection against data theft or unauthorized deletion

>> Software security

>> Methods to protect against unauthorized information disclosure

Implementing the tools of an SASE-compliant network enables your company to meet the requirements of SOC 2 security compliance. The tools auditors look for include intrusion detection, access controls, and firewalls — traditional as well as Firewalls as a Service when your company employs complex cloud environments.

Certifying availability

Data centers have been certifying availability for many years. You often see promises of 99.999 percent uptime. The services your company provides need to be able to guarantee uptime (availability) by having in place all the right service level agreements — contracts that guarantee availability and the infrastructure necessary to make all that happen. The infrastructure can include disaster recovery, failover plans, and security incident response teams.

Availability simply means you can get to the programs you need; it doesn't mean the applications run well or run bug-free. That is handled by the next SOC 2 pillar.

Certifying processing integrity

Do your applications deliver as promised? You need to show that they operate accurately and securely, and that data handling meets expected standards. If your development team uses a good DevOps and DataOps model, chances are high that your applications will meet the standards required for SOC 2 certification.

REMEMBER Being able to show that your applications are operating securely via monitoring is important for both compliance and certification.

Certifying confidentiality

When access to data is restricted to a person or group of people, it's considered confidential. The levels of confidentiality you need depend completely on the nature of the data. Governments maintain standards of confidentiality for government data, the same as you will be expected to maintain standards of confidentiality. Book 4, Chapter 1 goes into more detail about applying risk assessments to data release.

Not all confidential data can be found in a database. Your company maintains all sorts of confidential information from internally protected business plans, intellectual property, and accounting data. Certification checks to see how this type of information is being protected.

Certifying privacy

Personal information and its collection, distribution, and use should be carefully controlled within your company. Some government compliance regulations, such as those in the EU, demand careful control over private data. At the very least, your public-facing website should have a privacy policy, and your company should be careful to honor it.

Certification will likely involve the Generally Accepted Privacy Principles, or GAPP. You can download a document describing those guidelines here:

www.michigan.gov/documents/dmb/GAPP_2009_327570_7.pdf

PCI certification

PCI certification audits your use and protection of credit card data. When your company stores credit card data, auditors ensure that you're using best practices for security and dissemination. This includes firewalls, encryption, and antimalware at its most basic levels.

Your monitoring system must ensure that only authorized people have access to credit card information. Even customers who make use of credit card processing systems must ensure a level of PCI compliance. (For more on PCI compliance, see "Complying with PCI" earlier in this chapter.)

There are four levels of PCI compliance:

>> Level 1: Greater than 6 million credit card transactions a year

>> Level 2: Between 1 million and 6 million credit card transactions a year

>> Level 3: 20,000 to 1 million transactions a year

>> Level 4: Greater than 20,000 transactions a year

The highest levels of PCI compliance require annual security audits and quarterly scans by an approved scanning vendor (ASV). Lower levels must submit to an annual assessment and quarterly scans.

This chapter covers compliance and certification when dealing with complex cloud systems securely. Following the guidelines of compliance, whether your company is required to comply with regulations or not, goes a long way toward ensuring that your company is well protected against data theft and loss. Knowing which resources your company uses and where they are helps you gain visibility into your network.

Chapter **5**

Implementing Zero Trust

M ore than any other framework or technology, the zero trust framework embodies all that is important in defending your network from people trying to break in. For example, DataOps is a good way to build security into your development, and AIOps is an intelligent way to monitor your network from unusual activity, from either attempted security breaches or hardware failures. But *zero trust* is a more fundamental approach than either of those because it has at its core the idea that people should never be given more security privileges than they need. That means managing access to applications, devices, virtual machines, networks, and data in such a way that everyone must first be

» Authenticated

» Validated

» Continually checked for validation

Managing access is critically important in protecting your resources, no matter where they exist.

REMEMBER

Making the Shift from Perimeter Security

Perimeter security, which is the idea that you can protect your digital assets behind a firewall, no longer applies. It's the difference between trying to protect a herd of corralled horses compared to a flock of birds. Zero trust protection is like making the switch from the ancient ways of protecting cities by throwing up a high wall with guards to putting everyone in body armor: Every resource becomes "personally" responsible for its own security. That isn't to say that the security necessarily needs to be built-in; it only means that you have to make certain that anyone trying to access has full trust and permission. By default, no one is trusted. So imagine the old city walls and the people at the gate shouting downward, "Who goes there?"

The old-time perimeter that was protected was usually the company network (or networks). Great pains were taken, and at great expense, to make sure it was difficult to get into the network if you didn't belong there. Once you were in, it was carte blanche. This was like standing in line at a night club and waiting for the bouncer to decide whether you were allowed to enter. Once you were in, you were golden and it was party time.

John Kindervag, a cybersecurity guru, came up with the idea of the zero trust framework, built on the much older idea that you should start by trusting no one and grant allowance from that point.

For about 70 years, applications were either unprotected or merely required a user ID and password, so most IT technology today uses that scheme of authentication. The oldest applications didn't even need passwords — if you could get into the network via a terminal of some sort with a user ID and password, then the applications you found there were available for use.

Enter cloud technology. Now the perimeter no longer surrounded all your digital assets. They were off in some nebulous place where they may or may not be protected by the cloud service provider. In your shared trust model, some of the responsibility for security was yours and some belonged to the cloud service provider. On top of that, every cloud had its own policies, applications, and procedures — making a unified approach difficult. Yes, user IDs and passwords were required in order to gain access to the cloud, creating several or several hundred little perimeters, depending on the size of your company (okay, maybe thousands), that had to be protected. The need for a unified security policy was born out of that chaos.

Examining the Foundations of Zero Trust Philosophy

The primary idea or philosophy behind zero trust is that cybersecurity protections should move from perimeter security (like firewalls) to the resources themselves. To implement this kind of security, you have to ensure, at minimum, that you have five features in place. The next few sections examine each feature individually.

Two-way authentication

Communication between users and resources requires that you have policy based authentication with each connection. To do this, both parties need a way to authenticate each other. (In other words, you have to know who's on the other end of the line.)

WARNING

Applications that use third-party single sign-on providers to provide authentication tokens don't meet the standards of the zero trust philosophy.

Using more than a single means to authenticate someone — traditionally, a user ID and password — increases the likelihood that the person on the other end is who they say they are. Yet user IDs and passwords are stolen every day around the world, making them next to useless for serious authentication. Using more than one method of authentication is known as *multifactor authentication*. That term isn't as commonly used as the more specific terms that detail how many forms of authentication are required, such as two-factor authentication or three-factor authentication. Here are some types of authentication:

>> User ID and password

>> Biometrics, such as fingerprints or retinal scans

>> Other biometrics, such as facial recognition and voice ID

>> One-time keys from physical fobs or RFID chips, also known as *token authentication*

>> One-time keys *(tokens)* from software applications like Authenticator

>> Telephony, such as SMS text message or a phone call

Implementing multifactor authentication requires that you use at least any two of these authentication methods, as shown in Figure 5-1. There are other weird authentication methods, such as your typing style. (Yes, some apps actually claim that they can recognize you from how you type on a keyboard.) Some claim to know you merely by seeing your ear.

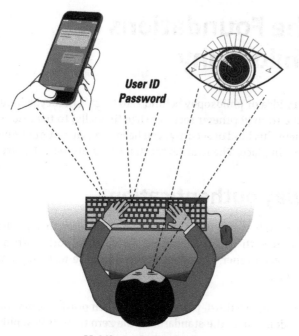

User ID
Password

Multifactor Authentication

FIGURE 5-1:
Using more
than one type of
authentication
increases
security.

Many web applications now require that you enter a user ID and password, use a login method from a third party that has OAuth (an access delegation standard) for authentication, and additionally require that you receive a text message with a code that you then enter into a web form.

Multifactor authentication can increase security and provide more options for authentication in different situations. However, authentication must take place between the two communicating entities.

Endpoint device management

People are involved in communication, but the actual communication channel is between two devices, as shown in Figure 5-2. It's up to the hardware devices to establish secure communications, including authentication. This sets up a pattern of trust that doesn't end with the authenticated folks trying to communicate; you also need to know that the hardware you're using to communicate has not been compromised.

Endpoint device management relies on a verifiable hardware root of trust in each device. Following the zero trust principle that security is at the endpoint and not in the network or out on the periphery, each device continually checks its health status by uploading log files to a central monitoring system, such as an AIOps AI monitoring system. In this case, the monitoring system becomes the source of trust for each endpoint.

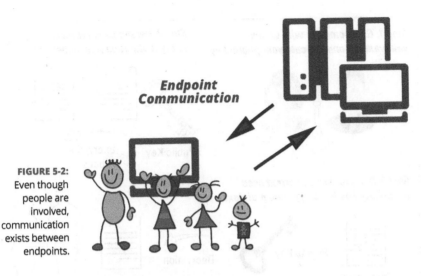

**Endpoint
Communication**

FIGURE 5-2:
Even though
people are
involved,
communication
exists between
endpoints.

End-to-end encryption

End-to-end encryption is a method of communication where the information is encoded in such a way that only the users on each side of the communication can decipher it. This keeps snoopers from reading the communications you send.

Using the web, which has been the de facto operating environment of the Internet since the 1990s, in combination with firewalls (first introduced to reduce the number of ports on which software could communicate), encryption has also become the way most information is processed before being sent out onto the net. Most modern web browsers now warn you when you're communicating with a server and not using encryption.

Public key/private key encryption

There is a point of truth where you know that a connection can be trusted when using encryption across the Internet: Web servers need an SSL/TLS certificate issued by a certificate authority (CA). These are purchased from the same registrars where you purchase domain names and are installed on your server. The certificate authority verifies websites so that you know who you're communicating with — hopefully, preventing a type of attack known as *spoofing*, where nefarious actors pretend to be something they are not. This is a key part of the type of encryption commonly used on the web, called *public key cryptography*. Using pairs of keys, public and private, information that's encrypted with a public key can only be decrypted using the associated private key. They are mathematically paired. (See Figure 5-3 for the story of public key/private key cryptography. Tissues not included.) This is a huge topic, but this resource can quickly bring you up to speed: www.dtos-mu.com/understanding-the-basics-of-public-key-cryptography.

FIGURE 5-3:
The happy story of public key/ private key cryptography.

Step 1: Give someone with whom you want to communicate your public key

Step 2: Person uses the key to encrypt plaintext into ciphertext

Public Key   Encryption Process

Step 3: Recipient of ciphertext uses the private key to decrypt into plaintext

Ciphertext   Private Key   Decryption   Plaintext

A scary bit about email

By default, email communications aren't encrypted. As your email travels across the network as open text, hackers using sniffing tools can read it — unless, as is the case with Gmail, the communication path between your device and your email server is encrypted using end-to-end encryption. Here are some facts you should know about who has access to your email:

>> Did you give your kids access to your phone so that they can play games? Adding that game could have added spyware, keyloggers, or other malware on your device — potentially granting malicious individuals access to your email.

>> Your network administrator may be able to read email as it's being sent or read it in your inbox.

>> Your Internet service provider (ISP) can read any data you send and receive traveling unencrypted.

>> Your email service provider can read your email.

This is really only half the list because the same is true for the recipient of your email. Anyone who has access to their machine can read the email you sent and so on.

Policy based access

Writing a policy is exactly how it sounds: You create rules that become policy in the same way your business creates rules about everything from parking to break time. These rules become policy. When it comes to making rules about who can and can't access your cloud resources, policy based access is considered the most flexible access control system. It has these characteristics — it is

>> **Flexible:** When policies are built of multiple rules, you can modify them, making access flexible.

>> **Scalable:** You can add new rules to your policies as needed (to include new resources, for example).

>> **Compliance friendly:** Regulatory agencies love to be able to see exactly who and how you've decided to let people access your systems.

>> **Makes your distributed workforce happy:** The new work-from-home trend has created some new security challenges. In a policy based system, you can design access rules that take working from home into account.

A brief look at the strategies that came before policy based access should convince you that, in situations where you need fine-grained access control, policy based access is the way to go.

>> **RBAC:** Role based access control (RBAC) looks at roles rather than policies when assigning privileges. The challenge of role based access is that of *role explosion*, where security managers are handling thousands of roles for hundreds of users. It becomes a bit of a management nightmare.

>> **ABAC:** Attribute based access control (ABAC) allows for Boolean logic to create logical combinations such as "if an accountant" and "if has payroll privileges" and not "risk level high." These attribute rules can become quite fine-grained, such as traffic must come from a specific IP address and only during certain hours of the day. These rules can be assigned to users, actions, resources, or environments. As with the complexity of role based access, managing the attributes and rules can also become extremely complicated.

Another problem with ABAC access is that IT security folks need to know how to write rules using an older and more difficult XACML language. This can increase the queue time for allowing someone access to a critical system.

>> **PBAC:** Policy based access control (PBAC) is generic to the application using it — it's written in natural language. A policy might say, "Accountants can access the accounting system." The accounting system will have a server back-end and a web based user interface. The theory behind using natural

language is that it frees you from using a programmer to create access policies. Business managers can define their own access policies in real time, down to the document level.

Access policies can be ephemeral and apply only during specific periods.

TIP

Involving people with an average skill level in the process broadens the responsibility for security and fits with the mindset of making stakeholders more responsible for the day-to-day workings of their systems and data.

» Because policies can be fine-grained, they can include the broadest range of users: employees, suppliers, freelancers, collaborators — whomever. Because each of these groups of people can be assigned roles as well as risk levels or any number of attributes, what you have is a scalable and flexible access control system. (If only refrigerators had that kind of access control, you could assign roles, such as cook and snacker. Then you could grant access based on weight or cholesterol numbers or connect to the Fitbit and allow access only after so many steps — and then only to the fruit drawer.)

REMEMBER

Just because PBAC can be excessively fine-grained doesn't mean that it has to be. It completely depends on how coarse you want to make the rules.

A PBAC system creates policies for Segregation of Duties (SOD, also referred to as separation of duties). SOD is a basic building block of risk management. The idea is that the responsibility for a resource is shared among more than one role. The example often given is one of responsibility for nuclear weapons, where the launch keys and launch codes are shared among several people to avoid the dangers of personal vendetta, coercion, extortion, and human error. A good example of this strategy is the fairly recent announcement in Hawaii of an inbound missile attack sent over the public alert system. Many people were scared. It turns out that this one was sent because of human error.

To find out more about how you can implement PBAC, check out the plainID website at www.plainid.com. You'll find that the Policy Manager application allows for visibility into access privileges at both the user and resource levels.

Accountability

When bad things happen — and they will — the basic premise of zero trust means that when said bad things happen, someone is to blame or will be held accountable. Devices as well as people must be trusted, and therefore can also be held accountable. Accountability is determined by monitoring applications that perhaps didn't catch the security breach before it happened, but you can be certain that it's gathering after-the-fact information about who-did-what-to-whom.

Logs are a first layer of accountability. Once considered a nuisance because they would just grow until the hard drive was full and then need to be deleted, logs are now considered big data and are archived in cloud storage for use by AI as a way to predict the next problem.

TIP

Accountability systems go a long way toward satisfying some of the most stringent compliancy requirements.

Guarding against external threats with SIEM

SIEM is a combination of security information management (SIM) and security event management (SEM) that provides tracking of security information and event tracking for the purpose of auditing and compliance. This discussion of SIEM appears in this chapter on zero trust because two of its hallmarks are accountability and security. Zero trust implementations require both.

In addition to providing accountability, this AI-based solution (similar to AIOps) uses machine learning to recognize anomalies in user behavior, detect threats, and provide incident response. It can also automate many of the more mundane security tasks.

One way SIEM falls short is that it tends to be rule-based and good only for spotting real-time threats. Many modern threats have become far more sophisticated and require a more nuanced approach, using machine learning to spot attacks previously unknown.

Protecting against internal threats with UEBA

Similar to SIEM, user and entity behavior analytics systems (UEBA) can spot anomalies in both user and device behaviors using machine learning, statistics, and algorithms. UEBA focuses on insider threats, designed to focus on user analytics rather than on external security threats.

Behavioral analytics could almost be called a biometric security system. Though it's possible to snag a person's login credentials, it's almost impossible to perfectly mimic their behavioral patterns after they're logged in. For example, a person may always first download the company's daily newsletter and then read Scott Adams' *Dilbert* page before reading their email. This is the same way credit card companies spot fraud. If you use your card only to grocery shop and suddenly you're buying chocolates in Belgium, a red flag goes up. UEBA can spot nuanced attacks that can take months or years to implement using a risk scoring system.

TIP

Implementing both SIEM and UEBA into your zero-trust-based systems can provide the maximum amount of threat intelligence while also serving as an advanced accountability application.

Least privilege

The principle of least privilege is the foundation of zero trust. (It's known by other names, such as the principle of least authority or the principle of minimal privilege.) In a nutshell, it means that you grant privileges only when someone absolutely needs them in order to accomplish some task and has also earned the privilege based on having a risk profile that matches the data or resource to which you're granting access.

Least privilege applies to more than just people: It also applies to applications, processes, files, and systems. For example, an application that needs access to sensitive data may not always need that access. Granting access to sensitive data all the time puts the application at a higher security risk because, if an unauthorized person gains control of that application, it has access to sensitive data all the time. Restricting when the application is able to access sensitive data means you have reduced the amount of time during which the application poses a security risk. You can even make plans to increase security around the application during times it accesses the sensitive or private data. To increase the security of the application temporarily, you can reduce the privileges of others to access the application for a specified period, as shown in Figure 5-4.

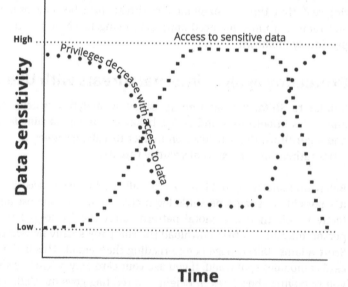

FIGURE 5-4: Privileges decrease as access to sensitive data increases.

Network access control and beyond

Network Access Control (NAC), sometimes called Network Admission Control, is a set of protocols that, as its name suggests, controls the access to a network by implementing policies that limit where a user can connect and, once connected, what they can connect with.

A computer attempting to connect must first satisfy policies such as these:

>> Level of antivirus protection

>> Software update and version levels

>> Configuration settings

NAC can be either agent based or agentless. In an agent based solution, the software agent, installed locally, checks to see whether the computer meets the required policies. If the computer doesn't stack up, the agent allows the computer to connect to resources that help it meet the requirements. For example, the computer might be directed to a software update or to new antivirus databases. Once the policy is met, the agent then allows the computer to connect to the network or to resources within the network, depending on the type of NAC system that has been implemented. An agentless NAC system does primarily the same thing except, rather than rely on a preinstalled agent to report on whether the endpoint meets the policy, the system relies on other scanning and network information software to gather the information.

There are two basic types of NAC systems: pre-admission and post-admission. Pre-admission agents check adherence to policies — antivirus levels, for example — before allowing someone on the network. Post-admission policies check for user behavior after connecting to the network.

Here's the bad news: NAC is a perimeter safeguard strategy and isn't designed to protect cloud resources. This chapter covers NAC in order to point companies that are already using this older strategy in a slightly different direction while employing the same ideas.

This new approach uses a *cloud access security broker (CASB)*, a system that can be implemented as a cloud-hosted solution, installed locally as software or as a hardware device. It's designed to protect SaaS, PaaS, and IaaS cloud environments. A CASB, like NAC, is based on policies. If you're already using NAC or another policy based system, you can extend those policies to the cloud using a CASB system. You can see in Figure 5-5 that, although the NAC is set to control local resources using policies, similar policies can be used to protect access to cloud resources using the CASB.

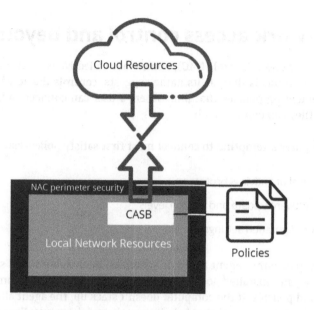

FIGURE 5-5:
The NAC and CASB systems can have the same policies when it comes to controlling access.

Cloud Resources

NAC perimeter security

CASB

Local Network Resources

Policies

Many implementations of cloud access security systems are based on policy control. Not all of them are known as CASB systems — here are some examples:

>> **McAfee's MVISION Cloud:** www.mcafee.com/enterprise/en-us/ products/mvision-cloud.html

>> **Aruba ClearPass:** www.arubanetworks.com/products/security/ network-access-control/secure-access

REMEMBER

You need to think beyond perimeter security to make sure your cloud resources are protected.

CSPM risk automation

Cloud security posture management (CSPM) is an automated system for identifying and handling cloud-based security threats. The goal of CSPM is to prevent breaches, detect security flaws, respond to any of these occurrences, and, most of all, figure out where such occurrences may occur next. CSPM handles threats in all the major cloud environments, including SaaS, PaaS, and IaaS. CSPM provides services such as these:

>> Incident response

>> Compliance monitoring

>> DevOps integration

CSPM excels at providing incident response across many cloud configurations, right down to the container level.

REMEMBER

Both intentional and unintentional risks are out there, with unintentional risks responsible for as much as 90 percent of all breaches.

Unintentional risk — accidentally leaving the barn door open, in other words — is responsible for the greatest number of security incidents, far greater than those caused by hackers attempting to break through your security. That isn't to say that determined people aren't out there looking for your mistakes to exploit them.

It's possible to monitor misconfigurations, often caused by malformed Infrastructure as Code (IaC) configuration files, for potential configuration errors. CSPM is capable of monitoring these and other configurations across multiple cloud environments simultaneously and provides visibility in a single console.

Dealing with Zero Trust Challenges

Zero trust is a challenging goal. It's likely to be a multiyear endeavor unless your business is just getting started and you have no legacy systems to design around. In that case, implementing zero trust is a bit more straightforward — you simply choose resources that are designed with zero trust in mind. But things are rarely that simple.

REMEMBER

Engage the greatest percentage of employees and educate them on the principles of zero trust and why it's important. You need their support in implementing the strategies that bring about a zero trust environment.

Zero trust is a bit like taking away the little jar next to the snacks where you expect employees to pay their fair share. Zero trust is more like the vending machine that requires you to pay first, receive snacks after. Though it may not seem like the friendliest approach, it's the safest in a world where people are trying to steal more than your breakroom snacks. The following sections offer several ideas to help implement zero trust in a going concern.

Choose a roadmap

Many roads lead to Rome, and many different paths lead to implementing the zero trust framework. For example, the Cybersecurity and Infrastructure Security Agency (CISA, at www.cisa.gov) has been developing a plan known as the zero trust maturity model. (These are the people responsible for securing resources in the .gov domain.) Though their model offers guidance, a lot of the heavy lifting is still up to you. Even the introduction to the maturity-model documentation states, "This document is not meant to be a robust set of guidance toward zero trust."

Another set of documentation, this time from the National Institute of Standards and Technology (NIST), sets forth the essentials of building a zero trust architecture (ZTA) and then warns that implementing zero trust will take years. It defines zero trust this way:

> Zero trust provides a collection of concepts and ideas designed to minimize uncertainty in enforcing accurate, least privilege per-request access decisions in information systems and services in the face of a network viewed as compromised. ZTA is an enterprise's cybersecurity plan that uses zero trust concepts and encompasses component relationships, workflow planning, and access policies. Therefore, a zero trust enterprise is the network infrastructure (physical and virtual) and operational policies that are in place for an enterprise as a product of a ZTA plan.

To read the entire publication, go to https://csrc.nist.gov/publications/detail/sp/800-207/final.

Take a simple, step-by-step approach

Implementing zero trust can be overwhelming. Giving yourself a step-by-step process for implementing it gives you a clear idea of what needs to be done next. Here are some steps to get you started:

1. **Figure out what needs protecting.**

   Refer to the risk assessment you may have created earlier, while reading Book 4, Chapter 1. It gives you a clear picture of what you need to protect, including the items described in this list:

   - *Critical applications:* These are applications that if they went down would cripple your business, even in the short term.

   - *Critical data:* This is data your company relies on or, if released, corrupted, or locked in the case of ransomware, would hurt your business. It also includes data protected by privacy regulations such as credit card or health data.

   - *Assets:* This includes critical points of entry into the systems that make your company work — for example, hospital equipment, manufacturing equipment, or critical infrastructure such as dams and power grids.

- *Services:* These are the IT services critical to your business, such as Domain Name System, or DNS (Facebook recently learned how critical this one is), Dynamic Host Control Protocol, or DHCP, which assigns IP addresses, and many other devices critical to your business.

Some of these assets have no way to implement zero trust. In these cases, you need to build your own perimeter around each one of them.

2. Map the data flow pattern.

Being able to easily see how applications interact makes it easier to protect them. Create a map that shows how data flows between them. There are templates you can use to make this step easy. See Figure 5-6 for a simple, fairly no-nonsense, data flow map. From this you can form an idea of how to construct a data flow map that is meaningful for you and your team.

3. Create a segmented network.

This next step depends on completion of the first two. You must first know what you're trying to protect. Second, you need to know how the data flows between the various parts of the applications and devices you're trying to protect.

Because so many of the applications in use aren't zero-trust-ready, you need to build a zero trust network that connects them. Of course, this starts with protecting your network with a high-end firewall — one that acts as a gateway and also lets you compartmentalize your network. Compartmentalizing is done by creating subnets (mini networks within a greater network). Zero trust can then be applied to who and how these subnets are accessed. Essentially, you have created wrappers around each of your applications using this approach. This type of segmentation can be set up to protect virtual machines, containers, and bare metal servers.

4. Architect your access policies.

This next step involves creating a set of policies based on the Kipling method. Rudyard Kipling was no cybersecurity guru, but he did once write a poem that is believed to be the foundation of the questions What, Why, When, How, Where, and Who. Kipling's poem "I Keep Six Honest Serving Men" was published in the children's storybook *Just So Stories* in 1902 (available on Amazon). It's a poem about curiosity, and that's exactly what you need as a foundation to zero trust. It's important to ask the right questions when creating access policies.

Here's the poem:

Keep Six Honest Serving Men

I keep six honest serving-men

(They taught me all I knew);

Their names are What and Why and When

And How and Where and Who.

I send them over land and sea,

I send them east and west;

But after they have worked for me,

I give them all a rest.

I let them rest from nine till five,

For I am busy then,

As well as breakfast, lunch, and tea,

For they are hungry men.

But different folk have different views;

I know a person small

She keeps ten million serving-men,

Who get no rest at all!

She sends em abroad on her own affairs,

From the second she opens her eyes

One million Hows, Two million Wheres,

And seven million Whys!

—Rudyard Kipling

Creating these policies by asking questions results in a resource access policy list. These policies should answer the following Kiplingesque questions:

- *What* applications access resources within the protected network segment?

- *Why* is the protected resource being accessed?

- *When* is the resource accessed?

- *How* is the resource being accessed?

- *Where* is the data going?

- *Who* needs to access a resource?

Answering these questions results in policies that result in fine-grained control over application communications within your network. Asking yourself these questions when developing zero trust policies and procedures or when implementing new security strategies will put you on a sure path to success.

Malware breaches occur as a result of policies that allow access. You need to play close attention to who is allowed rather than on who is not allowed.

5. **Monitor and maintain the network.**

This final step includes reviewing all logs (internal and external) from the base physical and data link layers network layers all the way through the network application layer, focusing on the operational aspects of zero trust. Because zero trust is an iterative process, inspecting and logging all traffic provides valuable insights into how to improve the network over time.

Once you have completed the five-step methodology for implementing a zero trust network for your first protect surface, you can expand to iteratively move other data, applications, assets, or services from your legacy network to a zero trust network in a way that's cost-effective and nondisruptive.

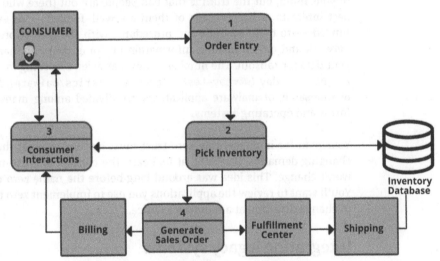

FIGURE 5-6:
Sample data flow
pattern shows
how simple this
process can be.

Keep in mind some challenges you face in implementing zero trust

Because zero trust is a framework, and a little loosey-goosey at best, there is no single correct way to implement it, and no application lets you just set it and forget it. So, challenges lie ahead. Here are some of them:

>> The inevitability of change

>> Legacy systems integration

>> Full visibility

- >> The lack of complete solutions

- >> The lack of business collaboration

- >> Zero trust agility requirements

- >> Multiple zero trust standards

- >> The responsibility to build the right team

The next few sections look at each challenge in some detail.

Dealing with change

Everything changes, and you're literally working against people who are working against you. This is a thought that you more than likely would love to put out of your mind, but the truth is that bad people are out there who don't have your best interests at heart. Many of them are well-funded — or even government funded — to build systems and procedures with the goal of breaking into your network and either stealing information or doing dastardly harm, like holding your data for ransom. The number of novel attacks, according to AV Test, is about 450,000 per day (www.av-test.org/en/statistics/malware). These hundreds of thousands of malware applications are divided among many different platforms and operating systems.

Your plan for implementing zero trust must be fluid to meet the continued and changing demands. Basically, at its heart, the concept of trust-no-one probably won't change. This idea was around long before the name zero trust adopted it. You'll want to review the applications you use to implement zero trust and be able to change direction at a moment's notice.

Integrating legacy systems

One of the difficulties in any large IT environment is backward compatibility. This isn't just a software idea, where new releases must work with older ones — it also has to do with hardware, networking, and people. Yes, legacy people exist. Don't become one. Be adaptive.

Older resources relied on the concept of *implicit trust*, which means that you trust without question. Nobody has to prove that they're worthy of trust — you just trust them. It's that "goes without saying" problem that has you looking at zero trust today.

Review your older software systems — there is a chance your larger mainframes still run COBOL applications. Then ask yourself how you'll implement modern zero trust applications into something that may or may not still eat cards. (This isn't just a reference to old-timey business machines. Research organizations still rely on many legacy FORTRAN applications running on older machines held together with duct tape.)

You then must ask yourself a question that's difficult to answer: Is implementing zero trust in a legacy environment — which might mean recoding old applications or replacing old hardware — worth it? It's not likely that the new infrastructure will be zero-trust-capable. For one thing, the huge financial and labor intensive undertaking must be considered. Second, on the other side, does continuing to run old applications pose too large a security risk? There are no easy answers. You just have to be ready to face these difficult questions.

The solution in part is to make a burrito. Yes, wrap a big tortilla around the whole thing to hide what's inside. Seriously, putting a software wrapper around the entire project to create some semblance of security is about your only option if you need to keep the program running and it's considered high risk.

WARNING

Some legacy systems aren't necessarily old; they just hide potential security flaws. One example is the P2P infrastructure embedded in Windows 10 to implement Windows Update.

Creating full visibility

To implement zero trust, you can't have any chinks in the armor. A *chink* is a hole. To ensure that there are no holes, you have to check everything — shadow IT operations, any cloud environments, mobile devices, and even the card scanner that lets people in the door. Getting to 100 percent visibility, even with some of the most awesome discovery tools on the market, is not a simple task for a moderately large organization.

One challenge of implementing zero trust is deciding when something is good enough. It's similar to data center guarantees: No one guarantees 100 percent uptime. It's always 99.999 percent or something similarly obscure. When Facebook went down for five hours in October of 2021, you have to ask yourself whether it fell into the 99.999 percent guaranteed uptime. Of course, it didn't — it was human error. Or was it?

Building DIY solutions

A challenge in implementing zero trust when using the cloud is that it wasn't truly designed with zero trust in mind. It doesn't lend itself to segmentation by default. In a perfect world, your applications should have zero trust built in. Migrating existing applications that have been protected by perimeter security to the cloud doesn't cut it. Do-it-yourself solutions will have to account for the legacy systems you need to protect using barrier network security in a segmented network environment.

Many companies need to comply with industry or government compliance regulations. To be certain you'll make it through the audit with your DIY zero trust implementation, your environment needs to include these items:

>> **Logs:** These are definitely a key part of accountability, containing as they do the information needed by AI systems looking for unusual activity.

>> **Policy based access control systems:** These are necessary to keep fine-grained control over the access to your resources, both in the cloud and local.

>> **Encryption:** This one is truly a foundational requirement for today's information security. Use public key infrastructure (PKI) with valid digital certificates.

>> **Malware threat updates from third-party security experts:** These feed you threat intelligence and the most current information on malware.

>> **A security information and event management (SIEM) system:** This gathers the data you need for postmortem analysis of security issues. It also aids AI systems in spotting problems before or as they happen.

Zero trust and the cloud: Using a third-party solution

Citrix (www.citrix.com) has an application that helps wrap your cloud environments in a zero trust security layer, allowing your remote workers to access your network without the hassle of using a VPN.

Citrix Secure Private Access gives you zero trust access to your network and applications without connecting user endpoints directly to the network. This system uses adaptive authentication to monitor user activity after they're logged in. It monitors the security based on the role of the user, the security of the device, and the location of the request. This goes beyond simple multifactor authentication. Based on the role of the user, you can control what kind of functions they can perform such as printing or copy-and-paste, further protecting the unauthorized transfer of information.

Enabling business collaboration

Collaboration is the key when implementing zero trust. It goes partly back to the visibility issue. You must collaborate in-house to make sure you have the maximum amount of visibility. This is also true for vendors and collaborators that also log in to your network and applications. Any one of them can become a weak link, and their risk should be evaluated accordingly.

REMEMBER

Making sure your vendors accessing your systems are security certified goes a long way toward reducing risk and supporting compliance.

Making zero trust agile

Most successful zero trust implementations are those that have been zero-trust-happy from the first day they were created. Trying to make them compliant later by shoehorning in legacy systems is difficult at best and impossible in the worst case scenario.

One benefit of agility is that it can change on the fly. Before agile systems became the norm, change was plodding, full of red tape, costly, and interminable, and it often ended in failure. Agile systems may still fail, but they do so in small and easily correctible ways. With continuous development and integration, you can build zero trust principles into your applications as they're being developed and tested.

REMEMBER

Zero trust is more of a goal than a destination. You don't have to achieve zero trust immediately. Just make sure that, in this fast-paced world of change, you evaluate the changes you're making with zero trust principles as a guide.

Building the right team

Following the agile strategy for team-building — including all the right stakeholders and giving them an environment where communication becomes not only simple but also powerful — empowers your team. If you were able to follow that nasty run-on sentence, you can see that what you want to do is make sure that all employees and partners involved in a project are educated in, and onboard with, the principles that guide zero trust. If you find that your team members aren't trusting one another, that's a good thing.

» Instituting cloud security validation and multifactor authentication

» Handling hardware security modules

» Working with key management services

» Exploring crypto service gateways

Chapter **6**

Using Cloud Security Services

The number of cloud security services increases daily with the ever-changing cloud landscape. It's almost impossible to keep up with all of them. If you've done your homework, you know what the risks are and you know where your vulnerabilities lie. Next comes the job of figuring out the cost effectiveness of either providing the services you need in-house or visiting the marketplace for solutions.

Though you may be responsible for providing security for your cloud environment — particularly, your data — you aren't required to have at your fingertips all the capabilities you need. Keep your business goals in mind. Unless your business is cloud security, it's sometimes best to leave that task to people who eat, live, and breathe cloud security. They have the equipment, the expertise, and the skilled workforce to do the job — and they tend to keep up with changes in the industry because that's their business.

You can pick and choose from a broad array of services to ensure your cloud and local data security as well as help you meet compliance regulations.

Customizing Your Data Protection

Managed data protection services offer specialized security protection for your data. This differs from most generalized information security services in that they focus specifically on protecting one of your most important assets: your data. These services help you meet some of the following demands:

>> Maintaining security in a rapidly changing security landscape

>> Assessing data for risk levels to help you prioritize data security

>> Managing user data interaction to overcome accidental or purposeful data corruption or breaches

>> Managing compliance regulation conformity

WARNING

When flexibility goes up, security levels go down. This is one of the basic truths about using cloud services. Those providing much greater flexibility make security more challenging.

One typical solution is offered by Cloudrise (`https://cloudrise.com`). It automates data protection and privacy solutions, security for business applications, and visualization tools with rapid incident response and report.

Validating Your Cloud

One huge challenge for businesses is to keep pace with the burgeoning number of cloud resource types offered to users every single day. The continual release of new products and resources by cloud providers makes it a difficult task for a business to validate and certify each of these new changes.

Prancer (`www.prancer.io`) helps you keep up with this heavy requirement by doing the heavy lifting of maintaining your security compliance throughout your entire cloud environment. These folks will even work directly with your development team to see that security is enforced in your DevSecOps group writing Infrastructure as Code (IaC) configurations. (It's these misconfigurations that pose a huge risk to your organization if not managed well.)

Using its static code analyzer, Prancer uses Policy as Code to enforce the security of your IaC and live cloud resources by performing policy checks for compliance using the more important compliance regulations or even your own custom company-security policies.

Multifactor authentication

Multifactor authentication (MFA) has become one of the de facto ways to authenticate users logging in to company resources — particularly, cloud SaaS applications. You're required to further authenticate your identity established by a user ID and password by responding to a phone call or text message or by entering a one-time passcode.

One popular MFA system is the SurePassID (https://surepassid.com). Here's a list of some of its features:

>> Hybrid and on-premise deployment

>> Offline desktop login with two-factor authentication (2FA)

>> Firewall configurations that include network pathing and replication schemes

>> User login and logout audits

The system integrates with your existing security information and event management (SIEM) system and helps you comply with some of the most stringent compliance regulations.

WARNING

SMS one-time passwords are vulnerable to man-in-the-middle attacks and are thus no longer compliant with multifactor authentication. Because messages sent by SMS have become insecure, passcodes sent by SMS can no longer be trusted.

One-time passwords

One-time passwords (OTPs) are randomly generated passwords that are used only a single time. This type of password system overcomes the vulnerability of passwords that have already been breached, passwords that are weak and easily discoverable, and passwords that have been stolen. These one-time passwords, known as *tokens*, come in one of four types:

>> **Soft:** Delivered using a mobile phone app

>> **Hard:** Delivered using a key fob

>> **On-demand:** Delivered by SMS and email

>> **FIDO U2F:** Inserted as a fob into a USB port

   The canine-sounding acronym stands for Fast IDentity Online Universal 2nd Factor.

SOFT TOKENS

An example of a soft token is the application Google Authenticator. After downloading this app to your phone, you can add applications that use this type of 2FA. Once added, they continually update your app with new tokens that are created using the keys of each application.

Some applications, such as Facebook, have their own authentication OTP generator. Suppose that you've elected to use two-factor authentication in Facebook. To be able to log in to Facebook from a new device, you have to use the Facebook mobile app to get a new code from the code generator found on the Facebook menu. Only after entering the code located there into the device requesting 2FA do you then authenticate the new device.

Mobile phones are fairly ubiquitous — in fact, by this point it's probably more correct to say that many techies can't live without them. This makes using soft tokens from an app pretty simple. The codes generated by the app are time-based and therefore don't require a connection to the Internet to create codes. Being *time-based* means that the passwords expire quickly — usually, every 30 seconds. This feature protects you from password replay attacks, where passwords are intercepted by a hacker and later used to access private resources such as a bank account or network login.

Here are the downsides to using this technology:

>> Mobile devices can be stolen, and if someone manages to slip past your device's security PIN, they then also have access to your two-factor authentication code generator.

>> Phishing attacks may intercept your code in a fake request and then use your code within the 30-second time frame to log in and authenticate as you.

>> Mobile phones are still vulnerable to attacks that can allow snooping of your phone activity.

HARD TOKENS

Hard tokens are small digital fobs (shown in Figure 6-1) that are often placed on keyrings to prevent them from getting lost. This device generates a one-time password from a cryptographic seed also shared with the server. The advantage over a soft token is that a hard token isn't connected to a network that can be attacked. Instead, it's air gapped and stand-alone. (Something is considered "air gapped" when it is not connected to an insecure network; it's a measure used to protect devices from external attack.)

Brett_Hondow / Pixabay

FIGURE 6-1:
Fobs, often placed on keyrings, provide one-time tokens without the need for a mobile phone.

These little devices are power-friendly with batteries lasting up to about seven years.

These are the downsides of hard tokens:

>> **Expense:** The little devices aren't cheap.

>> **Administration:** Someone needs to physically hand out the device and keep track of who has them.

>> **Easily lost or stolen:** Even though putting them on a key ring helps keep track of these small tokens, keys are also lost. Of course, if found it's useless without knowing your user ID and password.

Though these seem like perfect little devices, they're still vulnerable to man-in-the-middle attacks because you still need to enter the code it generates into an application. When codes are generated, they expire after a short period of time. If an attacker intercepts your code, they could immediately use it to impersonate you. Saving the code for later use fails. Intercepted codes are the weak link. The passcode is secure right up to the moment where it needs to be used. Still, hard tokens are the standard of the industry, even after decades of use.

ON-DEMAND TOKENS

Soft tokens and hard tokens each have their uses. A simpler system, on-demand tokens, is useful for occasions where you may need to authenticate someone only during their first login. These tokens are sent via either SMS message or email. The advantage of using an on-demand token is that, in addition to authenticating the person, you've authenticated one of their contact methods.

Once a user has logged in with a user ID and password — often, for the first time — the application they're logging in to sends them a random code that it generates on its own. This code is then sent either to the user's SMS mobile phone number (if they entered a mobile phone number) or to their email (which is standard info to ask for when someone signs up for a transaction). These codes aren't time-based, like the other two methods described. Instead, the user has a set period in which to enter the code into the application before it expires. The expiration tends to be longer than other types of token generators because you have all sorts of issues to consider, such as network lag and the time it takes an email to be delivered (and then located in the spam folder where it inevitably ends up).

Some of the benefits of using on-demand tokens include the fact that it's simple and inexpensive and requires no administration, like a hard token — and it can be used without a smartphone. (SMS messages can be received on phones with older technology.) On-demand tokens depend on the fact that there is no shared secret between the device and the server that can be exploited. The server simply sends random values. The number of digits sent varies on the level of assurance your system needs.

The downside of using on-demand tokens is that they just aren't all that secure. Too many people and systems are involved in the creation and delivery of the code that usually isn't delivered cryptographically. They also aren't recommended for systems that require regulation compliance, because the codes are easily stolen and simply receiving an email doesn't authenticate an individual, because fake email addresses are far too simple to set up. Instead, the National Institute of Standards and Technology (NIST) suggests that you use push notifications (in-app pop-up messages) to a device that makes certain the user is in possession of the device.

FIDO U2F TOKENS

You probably know about the little USB fobs that wireless keyboards use. FIDO U2F tokens look just like those. What they do is provide a token automagically when you attempt a login at a site that supports this technology. After you've entered your user ID and password, you press a button on the USB device and, like magic, you're authenticated.

Of all the token types, this one is the most secure. It uses public key cryptography to create a client-server real-time challenge-response between the client (your web browser) and the server. It protects against

>> **Phishing:** No codes to type so phishing isn't a thing.

>> **Session hijacking:** Keeping criminals from stealing a session id or session cookie because these are not relied on for authentication.

>> **Man-in-the-middle attacks:** Avoids the ability to intercept your network traffic because the server will detect anomalies in the response and deny transmission.

>> **Malware attacks:** Malware can't fake the encrypted challenge-response.

Also, if you lose the little guy, it has no identifying information on it to reveal who might own the device. It works only with sites where you've already registered.

One interesting feature about this type of security is that the protocol allows for two devices to be registered to every account. This means that if you lose one device, you're not totally locked out of your account.

The FIDO U2F token method is often used as the primary authentication method. Once authentication has been achieved and you have trusted devices, soft tokens can be used. If they should ever fail or become lost or stolen, you can then reuse the FIDO USB device to authenticate your account on a new device.

Here are some of the downsides to FIDO U2F:

>> **Cost:** They can cost upward of $20 each.

>> **Support:** It's still a new technology, so it doesn't have widespread industry support yet.

>> **Size:** It's tiny (not even the size of a keyring fob), so it's easily lost.

>> **Dependability:** USB ports weren't designed for daily devices to be inserted and removed, so this type of port can experience degradation over time.

>> **Mobile support:** It isn't fully supported for mobile phones. (See the note below about Yubikeys.)

When it comes to mobile phones, which have no USB ports, you can still use FIDO U2F. TapID Mobile Account Security lets you tap NFC-enabled phones the same way you might use a card to make a payment. This solution isn't quite ready for prime time, though.

A popular solution is offered by Yubiko www.yubico.com/. Their Yubikeys work fantastic and come in a variety of form factors including mobile Lightning connectors.

Managing file transfers

When data is moved from one place to another, whether it's sent via an application or an email or by FTP or another file transfer mechanism (data in motion), it's at considerable risk. You should feel that risk in your bones, the same as when you were a child and feared monsters under your bed. When you got up and headed into the next room with your parents, you felt at risk until you got there. Your company faces file transfer risks when it moves sensitive data within the company, to vendors, and to partners that need the data.

Most cloud solutions have a mechanism for sending data in an encrypted form to and from the users or other devices. Secure file transfer is a topic you rarely hear mentioned, for that reason. It just works. But sometimes you need to go beyond just sending and receiving data. This is when you need some forensic evidence of a transfer, or the transfer needs to be tracked to make absolutely certain it was successful. Also, there may be occurrences when you need a level of encryption or safety beyond that offered by the standard SSL/TLS processes.

To solve this complex data-in-motion problem, you need to use a secure file transfer mechanism. One of the companies offering this service is Progress (www.ipswitch.com), with its MOVEit Managed File Transfer application. This SaaS program offers compliant and secure file transfer of sensitive data.

Progress also offers a secure File Transfer Protocol (sFTP) server known as WinSock FTP (WS_FTP). WS_FTP was one of the first widely distributed FTP applications on the Internet. Though not as popular as it once was, FTP in general is still used today after 50 years. There is still a need for secure file transfer, but these services have largely moved to the cloud. ExaVault (www.exavault.com) has just such a cloud FTP platform.

Data in motion and file transfer have largely been replaced by simpler file transfer mechanisms — Secure Sockets Layer (SSL)/Transport Layer Security (TSL), for example, which is used by most cloud providers for security in their data connections. MediaFire (www.mediafire.com), a popular cloud storage and file sharing application, uses this type of secure transfer made simple with a drag-and-drop interface, as shown in Figure 6-2.

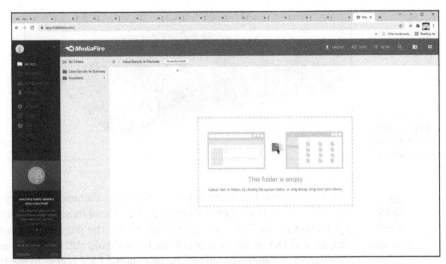

FIGURE 6-2:
A simple drag-and-drop interface lets you move and share files using built-in SSL/TLS security.

HSM: Hardware Security Modules for the Big Kids

A hardware security module (HSM) is a physical computing device that safeguards and manages digital keys and performs encryption and decryption functions for digital signatures as well as strong authentication and other cryptographic functions. These modules traditionally come in the form of a plug-in card or an external device that attaches directly to a computer or network server. A hardware security module contains one or more secure cryptoprocessor chips for fast cryptographic processing. This replaces servers with math cards that weren't designed for this kind of heavy math computing. An HSM is a smarter solution and is much more scalable than building server farms for the purpose of cryptography.

The secret behind HSMs is that they have been hardened and made tamper resistant to such an extent that they can be trusted to protect your company's most sensitive data by cryptographically storing private keys. (See Figure 6-3.) These modules are thus able to perform a variety of cryptographic functions, including generating, managing, and storing the keys used for public/private key encryption and for digitally signing documents and code.

Here are the typical functions of an HSM:

>> Key storage

>> Key exchange

>> Encryption

FIGURE 6-3:
A typical HSM,
with tamper-
resistant tape.

REMEMBER

An HSM contains special cryptographic hardware that uses a security-focused operating system tested to a standard set up in the Federal Information Processing Standard publication 140-2 (FIPS 140-2 certified, to use the jargon of the security industry.) Despite that fact, network access to an HSM should still be limited and controlled. In a zero trust environment, almost no one should have access to the HSM.

Looking at HSM cryptography

Cryptographic keys are strings of random letters and numbers. Because computers aren't really designed to create random strings, you need special processes to generate strings that are truly random. An HSM has this special cryptographic chip that excels at generating this level of randomness that results in strong, random keys.

The HSM hardware is designed to perform mathematical processes for developing random keys at scale. This requires that the cryptographic chips be capable of amazing math performance, generating in the millions of digital signatures per second. Hardware devices such as the Futurex HSM (www.futurex.com) have some of the fastest processing speeds. Another company to look at is Cryptomathic (www.cryptomathic.com.) It provides an array of key management products with functionality such as

>> The ability to route data to hardware security modules

>> Key management in a bring-your-own-key (BYOK) scenario, where enterprises choose to create and manage their own keys

>> Digital signing credentials management

Managing keys with an HSM

HSMs are purpose-built for the protection and management of cryptographic keys. Organizations that make heavy use of cryptography because of the amount of encryption they use generally make use of multiple HSMs.

REMEMBER

Cryptographic keys are used for encrypting data, digitally signing documents, and even signing code developed by your developers. This ensures that signed code has not been changed and that you know who the author is — without a doubt.

Key management systems are designed to control access to these keys and update keys when needed, all within the security policies set by the corporation. Many of these security policies will be dictated by security compliance regulations. With an HSM managing keys, you can be assured that they're safe and at the same time easily managed.

REMEMBER

Following a zero trust policy means that only the most trusted individuals should have access to the HSM. Remember that they become the weak link because they are the system's only true vulnerability.

In keeping with the highest level of security, an HSM also maintains a full audit as well as log traces. This enables a forensic investigation in the unlikely event that the device is somehow compromised.

A little bit about keys

HSMs are designed to generate and store both symmetric and asymmetric keys. The difference between the two is simple. *Symmetric* encryption has a single, private key. It might seem a little like a password, but it's more than that — it's the key used to encrypt the data and, consequently, you'd use the same key to decrypt it.

This same kind of cryptography was used as far back as ancient Sparta in 600 BCE, when messages were sent using a leather strip that was meaningless unless you had a special stick that revealed the message when you wrapped the leather strap around it. (See Figure 6-4.) Later, Julius Caesar made use of a substitution cypher requiring that you knew which letters were switched with others in order to understand the message. It was about 1500 years later when Giovan Battista Bellaso came up with the first encryption key. (It's an excellent trivia question for nerds.)

The problem with symmetric encryption is that both the encryptor and the decryptor need the same key, which means it has to be transferred between them. Some of the greatest old spy novels of days gone by included the subterfuge used to transfer symmetric keys. Advances were made in encryption right up to 1997, when the Data Encryption Standard (DES) encryption that had been used since the 1970s was finally cracked.

FIGURE 6-4:
A scytale revealed
a message when
leather was
wrapped around
a specially
designed stick.

Twenty years before DES was cracked, a pair of crypto researchers — Whitfield Diffie and Martin Hellman — published a paper that laid out the idea of an encryption pair of keys then known as the Diffie-Hellman key. This was the basis for asymmetric cryptography. In 2000, the AES Advanced Encryption Standard became the gold standard. But it's still a symmetric key. This type of key is commonly used to encrypt data where there's no need for anyone other than the person who encrypted it to be able to do so.

Asymmetric encryption uses a public key to encrypt data that can be decrypted only by someone who has the corresponding private key. This strategy is particularly important in a world like the Internet where data must be sent encrypted, without both user and sender needing to have the private key. Encrypting data in motion is a perfect use for asymmetric encryption.

TIP

Your private key can also be used to encrypt data that can be decrypted using the public key, something that brings about non-repudiation, proving the sender is who they say they are.

Bitcoin and other cryptocurrency

Yet another type of encryption is elliptic curve cryptography (ECC), an advanced type of public key cryptography that can make use of shorter keys without a resulting decrease in security. This type of algorithm is used to encrypt blockchains that form the distributed storage mechanisms of cryptocurrencies like Bitcoin. Because knowing the key to your Bitcoin is necessary to unlocking its value, these keys must be securely stored, and an HSM is the perfect place to store them. Cryptocurrency is generally stored in an electronic wallet compatible with the type of currency you're storing, and this wallet can then be stored on the HSM.

Building in tamper resistance

An HSM isn't worth much if you can tamper with it. It's not impossible to break in, but most of them have certain safeguards and after-the-fact detection, including

>> Visible tampering indications

>> Tampering logs to provide forensic evidence

>> Alert systems to notify automated security systems or system administrators

An HSM can take additional measures beyond the physical detection, logging, or alerting that can make an attack on an HSM more difficult (automatically deleting the keys it's protecting when tampering is detected, for example). Of course, such measures can prove to be a problem if use of these keys is critical to your business continuity. You don't want to lock yourself out of your own systems.

To manage high-throughput cryptography, which is compute-intensive, HSMs are equipped with secure cryptoprocessor chips that also work to prevent tampering and bus probing by encrypting bus traffic. (The bus is the hardware equipment over which data travels, so this device protects against anyone trying to read the data by physically connecting to the hardware.) The secure cryptoprocessor will likely have its own tamper resistant packaging (the term used is *potting*) that makes it less necessary for the rest of the HSM to have tamper resistance. It's like breaking into the box just to find a brick. Physical tamper evidence is usually a type of tape, easily torn, indicating that someone has tried to tamper with the item. It's the same way your spouse knows that you were the last one to use the plastic wrap — the evidence is obvious.

Using HSMs to manage your own keys

Managing your own keys is the most secure way to maintain cryptographic keys. Entrusting them to a third party is asking for trouble and may even be a no-no for some regulation compliance.

Most HSMs have a single purpose — managing secret keys. With tamper systems ready to zero out a key if tampering is detected, you'll want a secure backup of your keys. HSM units can securely back up the keys they manage in order to secure portable devices, such as secure smart cards.

TIP

IDFactors (https://idfactors.com) makes trusted smart card equipment suitable for backing up the keys stored in your HSM.

Meeting financial data security requirements with HSMs

Financial data is some of the most sensitive data you can create. It forms the backbone of the US economy, and a failure caused by a cryptohack can lead to global financial devastation. This description is more than a fairytale: On June 19, 2011, the Mt. Gox cryptocurrency exchange in Japan was hacked. More than 2600 Bitcoins were transferred when the Mt. Gox auditor credentials were stolen. At today's prices, that's almost $162 million. The second time Mt. Gox was hacked, in 2014, was even worse. At the time, it was responsible for about 70 percent of all the Bitcoin trades in the world. It was later learned that around 750,000 Bitcoins were stolen. Today, that amount would be $47 billion. These are late-2021 prices.

The cryptoexchange hacks are some of the most amazing examples of financial crime, but you don't need to steal billions to create significant financial consequences. If nothing else, when banks are hacked — and don't forget that a great deal of a bank's transactions are now digital — confidence in the institution is lost and major depositors often leave for another bank. For this reason, financial data security is heavily regulated. Equipment such as HSMs are generally certified to international standards or the US FIPS 140-2 standard. This level of certification ensures that the equipment can withstand even the most aggressive attacks and gives bank officials and depositors the assurance they need.

DNSSEC

One of the underlying security technologies is one you really don't have to pay much attention to because it's built into the foundations of the Internet. The Domain Name Service (DNS) is the system that uses aliases (URLs) to stand for numeric IP addresses. Being able to modify these aliases to change which IP addresses they point to is an area of Internet security that has been addressed using cryptography. For example, OpenDNSSEC makes use of an HSM to manage its cryptographic keys. (For more on OpenDNSSEC, see the next section.)

DNS has been one of the weak links in Internet security and is often the root cause of many devastating exploits. Familiarize yourself with this critical piece of IT infrastructure because its security (or lack thereof) is of critical importance to you. DNS translates domain names into IP addresses with the help of domain registries.

Many of these registries sign their zone files — the primary file that matches URLs with IP addresses — with a cryptographic key and then store the keys in an HSM. Before this level of security was employed, DNS wasn't secure — many exploits used to breach security were made possible by hackers spoofing DNS.

Work began on a solution to the DNS security problem back in the 1990s. The result, deployed in early 2007, is known as the DNS Security Extensions (DNSSEC). DNSSEC uses digital signatures to secure authentication in DNS communications. Every DNS zone has its own key pair (public and private). Using PKI (public key infrastructure), the two components of DNS (the zone server and the resolver) use these keys to authenticate one another. HSMs are used by certificate authorities (CAs) and domain registration authorities to generate, store, and manage key pairs.

There are two components to DNSSEC:

>> **Data origin authentication:** This involves making sure the information is actually from the authorized zone. If authentication fails, the resolver assumes that there is an attack and disregards the attempt.

>> **Data integrity protection:** This involves making certain that the data wasn't changed en route. This is possible because the data is signed and can be verified using a key.

DNS resolving is done using a tree-structured layer of zones with a root zone at the top. Each zone is signed with the root zone signature the most trusted, or *trust anchor*. Each layer is then subsequently signed creating a layering of trust.

TECHNICAL
STUFF

The top five DNS attacks use DNS tunneling, ransomware, distributed denial of service (DDoS), identity reconnaissance, and DNS service vulnerability exploits.

OpenDNSSEC

OpenDNSSEC (www.opendnssec.org) is an open-source application that maintains your DNSSEC keys and the signing of zones. It works by taking unsigned zones and adding the necessary digital signatures and other DNSSEC records. Once this information has been added to the zone, it's then sent on to the authoritative name servers managing that zone.

The data flow in the OpenDNSSEC system is shown in Figure 6-5.

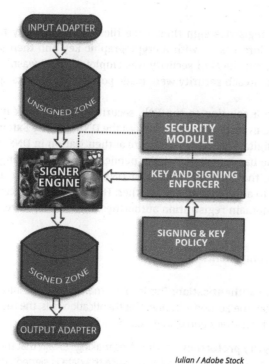

FIGURE 6-5: OpenDNSSEC flow diagram.

Iulian / Adobe Stock

Evaluating HSM products

When selecting an HSM, you want to make sure they work, no matter which cloud service provider you're using. You want to look for an HSM that is secure, fast, and scalable. Because of the limited marketplace, you have only a few HSM vendors to choose from. These are the best known:

- » **nShield:** www.entrust.com/digital-security/hsm/products/nshield-hsms/nshield-connect

- » **Thales Group:** https://cpl.thalesgroup.com/encryption/hardware-security-modules

- » **PKI Solutions:** www.pkisolutions.com

Thales Group is the brains behind the SafeNet Luna SA HSM, shown in Figure 6-3.

The devices themselves are pretty simple boxes. You may want to select an HSM because of the associated software capabilities. For example, the nShield monitor and nShield Remote Administration products connect HSMs and remotely monitor the HSM for performance and uptime. An HSM also helps you do infrastructure planning by showing you load trends and usage statistics. As an additional level of security, the HSM also reports on tamper events, warnings, and alerts.

The Remote Administration application allows you to administer the HSM via a secure interface. This way, you aren't tied physically to the device, and you can administer it remotely.

Looking at cloud HSMs

An alternative to using a hardware HSM is to employ a cloud HSM. Some of the major cloud providers such as Google and AWS allow you to host your HSM in the cloud, freeing you from the responsibility of managing the device. In the case of Google Cloud and AWS, you can host your encryption keys and complete your other cryptographic operations using a cluster of FIPS 140-2 Level 3 certified HSMs.

Here are some benefits of using a cloud HSM:

>> Increased security

>> Scalability

>> Reduced management requirements

>> The reassurance that comes from not having your device in a vulnerable building

HSM solutions certainly aren't the cheapest way to go, but for large corporations that rely on the highest level of security or for those that manage secret and private information that must be protected by cryptographic means, HSMs are currently the ultimate solution.

There are not that many HSM providers. Here are a couple:

>> nShield offers an HSM as a SaaS application.

>> The Thales Group offers its Luna Cloud HSM.

KMS: Key Management Services for Everyone Else

If going the HSM route or even using a cloud-hosted HSM is more than you need for managing your keys, you have an alternative, known as *key management services KMS*. Encrypting keys give those who have access to them direct access to private and privileged data. They're a bit like super passwords, but more, because these keys have the ability to unlock things that are deeply locked away.

TIP

Definitely consider a key management service if you have any investment in cryptocurrencies. You can store your wallet credentials there as a means of protecting your investment.

SSH compliance

SSH keys can provide access to your critical assets. The Secure Shell (SSH), part of the Linux operating system and all its variants, was originally created in 1995 and became an Internet standard in 2006. SSH became the standard way to access remote systems securely. This public key cryptography key pair is the most common way users authenticate themselves when logging in to remote servers.

The increased level of authentication provided by SSH overcomes the weaknesses of standard username-and-password combinations, which are generally plagued by poor password maintenance and behavior. In an SSH authentication system, you can use passwords as a second authentication factor, giving you two-factor authentication.

TIP

Recent research suggests that longer strings of unusual words form better passwords than shorter strings of numbers, letters, and special characters.

The first step in setting yourself up for SSH access is generating your own set of keys, both the public one and the private one that you give to no one and protect at all costs. You then post your public key in the system to which you want to log in. It becomes part of your user account and, if your public key is ever made public, it matters little to you because it can't be used in any meaningful way.

When you first create your SSH key pair, you're given a few choices. One is whether to protect your keys with a password. This extra level of protection is helpful but not foolproof. Another is the type of key format you want to use — RSA or ECDSA. RSA (based on the RSA algorithm) is the older format and remains fairly strong. The newer form, ECDSA (short for Elliptic Curve Digital Signature Algorithm) uses, as its name implies, an elliptical curve encryption like the one used to protect Bitcoin. Whether you choose RSA (the old standard) or the newer ECDSA, you have the option of choosing the length of your key.

There are trade-offs to key length. Longer keys are far more secure than shorter ones, but the trade-off is that when you use the key to encrypt or decrypt something, it does take somewhat longer.

REMEMBER

Your system administrators, when protecting your systems with SSH key authentication, should disable standard password login capability.

Once you have set up your system to allow access using only an SSH key, you then need to make sure your SSH logins are logged for the purpose of auditing and compliance regulations. Keep zero trust in mind when limiting access to individuals based on need and risk.

SSH audit logs are important for their ability to feed data to applications like those in an AIOps-managed system, as shown in Figure 6-6. These applications use AI to spot potential user security issues. For example, it spots unauthorized actions taken by a user and takes further action to deny further access, revoking their authorization until you can investigate the incident. Audit logs are also a requirement of most compliance regulations.

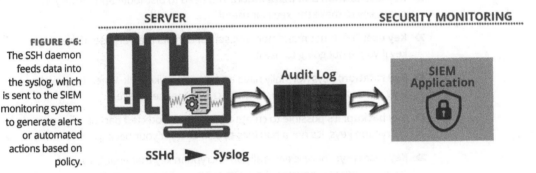

FIGURE 6-6: The SSH daemon feeds data into the syslog, which is sent to the SIEM monitoring system to generate alerts or automated actions based on policy.

When using AWS, the SSH audit trail is performed by Amazon's CloudTrail application. This tracks which users accessed which encryption keys, which resources they were used for, and when they were used.

The AWS KMS (Key Management System) can be integrated with other AWS services so that you can encrypt things such as data at rest. This is done using envelope encryption, where a data key is employed to encrypt the data and then that key is then encrypted by a KMS key that is then stored in the AWS KMS application.

There are a couple of different KMS key resources you can create with AWS:

>> **Automatically create an AWS-managed KMS key.** Permissions for the resource are managed by the AWS service for which it was created.

>> **Manage the KMS key yourself.** This type of key gives you maximum control over the permissions and the key lifecycle.

The encryption-key lifecycle

Encryption keys are like salmon: They have a complicated and detailed lifecycle. As you may know, salmon begin their lives as young fry that flow downstream to the ocean, where they grow up in a saltwater environment. As adults, they swim back upstream. If they aren't eaten by bears or other predators, they lay eggs, fertilize them, and then . . . are eaten by more bears. Encryption-key lifecycles are even more complicated. Not all the following lifecycle stages are mandatory:

>> **Key generation:** This one is mandatory because this is when the key is made.

>> **Key registration:** You must register your key.

>> **Key storage:** Unless you have a photographic memory and don't mind typing 2048 characters, you should store the key.

>> **Key distribution and installation:** You need to distribute and install your public key to make the key pair useful.

>> **Key use:** This is not mandatory but sort of defeats the purpose of creating a key if you're not going to use it.

>> **Key rotation:** Keys normally have an expiration, like milk. When they expire, they are destroyed and new keys are created in their place.

>> **Key backup:** It's possible to create a password-protected backup of your encryption keys. It's not a bad idea to also encrypt your backup.

>> **Key recovery:** There is generally an encryption key that enables you to restore another production key. Without it, you're just not getting the encrypted data back.

>> **Key revocation:** This optional lifecycle stage doesn't actually destroy the key. It's simply a message to users of a particular key that it's no longer valid.

>> **Key suspension:** Suspending a key means removing it from memory so that the key isn't written to disk during a memory write. The key can still be used later.

>> **Key destruction:** This permanently destroys the key — just like that salmon being eaten by a bear.

TIP

Key management can be complicated and require several layers of encryption and keys. StrongSalt (www.strongsalt.com) has an Encryption as a Service (EaaS) offering that allows you to have a keyless and decentralized management system.

Setting Up Crypto Service Gateways

A *crypto service gateway* (CSG) is a middleware application that acts like a router for encryption service requests. You can think of it as Cryptography as a Service. Each request is routed to the HSM or crypto service module best suited to handle the request. Having a centralized service over HSMs that, to everyone's misfortune, have been distributed silo fashion throughout an organization makes good sense. It shortens the time and effort it takes to make policy decisions, such as which encryption standard you'll use. (Standards do change, and when you want to change to keep up with the Joneses, you'll want an easy way to do it.)

A CSG also makes auditing a cinch. More compliance security audits are required each year. Having a centralized system creating visibility throughout your cryptographic environment saves you considerable time and money. This is particularly important in financial institutions, where encryption is a normal part of all transactions.

With a CSG, you'd be able to

>> Seamlessly use HSMs from different vendors

>> Easily scale your organization because HSM management is centralized

>> Deliver cryptographic applications to production in shorter times

>> Enable load share between HSMs

>> Establish centralized and simplified audit mechanisms

The CSG doesn't actually do any key management. It acts to redirect requests for crypto services. Key management will still be done in your HSM or KMS systems.

REMEMBER

Cryptomathic, a major player in the security field, makes a CSG system: www. cryptomathic.com/products/key-management/crypto-service-gateway.

TIP

5

Testing Your Security

Contents at a Glance

Chapter **1**

Introduction to Vulnerability and Penetration Testing

This book is about testing your computers and networks for security vulnerabilities and plugging the holes you find before the bad guys get a chance to exploit them.

Straightening Out the Terminology

Everyone has heard of hackers and malicious users. Many people have even suffered the consequences of their criminal actions. Who are these people, and why do you need to know about them? The next few sections give you the lowdown on these attackers.

REMEMBER

This book uses the following terminology:

>> **Hackers** (or *external attackers)* try to compromise computers, sensitive information, and even entire networks for ill-gotten gains — usually from the outside — as unauthorized users. Hackers go for almost any system they think they can compromise. Some prefer prestigious, well-protected systems, but hacking into anyone's system increases an attacker's status in hacker circles.

>> **Malicious users** (*external* or *internal attackers, often called black-hat hackers)* try to compromise computers and sensitive information from the outside (such as customers or business partners) or the inside as authorized and trusted users. Malicious users go for systems that they believe they can compromise for ill-gotten gains or revenge, because they may have access or knowledge of a system that gives them a leg up.

Malicious attackers are, generally speaking, both hackers and malicious users. For the sake of simplicity, this book refers to both as *hackers* and specify *hacker* or *malicious user* only as needed to differentiate and drill down further into their unique tools, techniques, and ways of thinking.

>> **Ethical hackers** (or *good guys),* often referred to as white-hat hackers or penetration testers, hack systems to discover vulnerabilities to protect against unauthorized access, abuse, and misuse. Information security researchers, consultants, and internal staff fall into this category.

Hacker

Hacker has two meanings:

>> Traditionally, hackers like to tinker with software or electronic systems. Hackers enjoy exploring and learning how computer systems operate. They love discovering new ways to work — both mechanically and electronically.

>> Over the years, *hacker* has taken on a new meaning: someone who maliciously breaks into systems for personal gain. Technically, these criminals are *crackers* (criminal hackers). These "crackers" break into — or crack — systems with malicious intent. They seek fame, intellectual property, profit, or even revenge. They modify, delete, and steal critical information, and they spread ransomware and take entire networks offline, often bringing large corporations and government agencies to their knees.

WARNING

Don't get me started on how pop culture and the media have hijacked the word *hack,* from *life hacking* to so-called election meddling. Marketers, politicians, and media strategists know that the average person doesn't understand the term *hacking,* so many of them use it however they desire to achieve their goals. Don't be distracted.

The good-guy *(white-hat)* hackers don't like being lumped in the same category as the bad-guy *(black-hat)* hackers. (In case you're curious, the *white hat* and *black hat* come from old Western TV shows in which the good guys wore white cowboy hats and the bad guys wore black cowboy hats.) *Gray-hat* hackers are a bit of both. Whatever the case, the word *hacker* often has a negative connotation.

Many malicious hackers claim that they don't cause damage but help others for the greater good of society. Yeah, whatever. Malicious hackers are electronic miscreants and deserve the consequences of their actions.

Be careful not to confuse criminal hackers with security researchers. Researchers not only hack aboveboard and develop the amazing tools that we get to use in our work, but they also (usually) take responsible steps to disclose their findings and publish their code. Unfortunately, there is a war going on against legitimate information security research, and the tools and techniques are often questioned by government agencies. Some people are even forced to remove these tools from their websites.

Malicious user

A malicious user — meaning a rogue employee, contractor, intern, or other user who abuses their trusted privileges — is a common term in security circles and in headlines about information breaches. The issue isn't necessarily users hacking internal systems but users who abuse the computer access privileges they've been given. Users ferret through critical database systems to glean sensitive information, email confidential client information to the competition or elsewhere to the cloud to save for later, or delete sensitive files from servers that they probably didn't need to have access to in the first place.

Sometimes, an innocent (or ignorant) insider whose intent isn't malicious still causes security problems by moving, deleting, or corrupting sensitive information. Even an innocent fat finger on the keyboard can have dire consequences in the business world. Think about all the ransomware infections affecting businesses around the world. All it takes is one click by a careless user for your entire network to be affected.

Malicious users are often the worst enemies of IT and information security professionals because they know exactly where to go to get the goods and don't need to be computer-savvy to compromise sensitive information. These users have the access they need, and management trusts them — often without question.

SECURITY TESTING CERTIFICATIONS

If you perform vulnerability and penetration tests and want to add another certification to your credentials, you may want to consider becoming a Certified Ethical Hacker (C|EH) through a certification program by EC-Council. See www.eccouncil.org for more information. Like Certified Information Systems Security Professional (CISSP), the C|EH certification is a well-known, respected certification in the industry, accredited by the American National Standards Institute (ANSI 17024).

Other options include the SANS Global Information Assurance Certification (GIAC) program, IACRB Certified Penetration Tester (CPT), and the Offensive Security Certified Professional (OSCP) program, a hands-on security testing certification. All too often, people who perform this type of work don't have the proper hands-on experience with the tools and techniques to do it well; certifications help address this issue. See www.giac.org, www.iacertification.org, and www.offensive-security.com for more information.

Recognizing How Malicious Attackers Beget Ethical Hackers

You need protection from hacker shenanigans. You have to become as savvy as the guys who are trying to attack your systems. A true IT or security professional possesses the skills, mindset, and tools of a hacker but is trustworthy. They perform hacks as security tests against systems based on how hackers think and work and make tireless efforts to protect the organizations' network and information assets.

REMEMBER

Ethical hacking (otherwise known as vulnerability and penetration testing) involves the same tools, tricks, and techniques that criminal hackers use, with one major difference: It's performed with the target's permission in a professional setting. The intent of this testing is to discover vulnerabilities from a malicious attacker's viewpoint to better secure systems. Vulnerability and penetration testing is part of an overall information risk management program that allows for ongoing security improvements. This security testing can also ensure that vendors' claims about the security of their products are legitimate.

Vulnerability and penetration testing versus auditing

Many people confuse security testing via vulnerability and penetration testing with security auditing, but *big* differences exist in the objectives. Security auditing involves comparing a company's security policies (or compliance requirements) with what's actually taking place. The intent of security auditing is to validate that security controls exist, typically by using a risk-based approach. Auditing often involves reviewing business processes, and in some cases, it isn't as technical. Some security audits, in fact, can be as basic as security checklists that simply serve to meet a specific compliance requirement.

REMEMBER

Not all audits are high-level, but many of the ones I've seen — especially those involving compliance with the Payment Card Industry Data Security Standard (PCI DSS) and the Health Insurance Portability and Accountability Act (HIPAA) — are quite simplistic. Often, these audits are performed by people who have no technical security experience — or, worse, work outside IT altogether!

Conversely, security assessments based on ethical hacking focus on vulnerabilities that can be exploited. This testing approach validates that security controls *don't* exist or are ineffectual. This formal vulnerability and penetration testing can be both highly technical and nontechnical, and although it involves the use of formal methodology, it tends to be a bit less structured than formal auditing. Where auditing is required (such as for SSAE 18 SOC reports and the ISO 27001 certification) in your organization, you might consider integrating the vulnerability and penetration testing techniques outlined in this book into your IT/security audit program. You might actually be required to do so. Auditing and vulnerability and penetration testing complement one another really well.

Policy considerations

If you choose to make vulnerability and penetration testing an important part of your business's information risk management program, you need to have a documented security testing policy. Such a policy outlines who's doing the testing, the general type of testing that's performed, and how often the testing takes place. Specific procedures for carrying out your security tests could outline the methodologies covered in this book. You should also consider creating security standards documented along with your policy that outline the specific security testing tools used and the specific people performing the testing. You could establish standard testing dates, such as once per quarter for external systems and biannual tests for internal systems — whatever works for your business.

Compliance and regulatory concerns

Your own internal policies may dictate how management views security testing, but you also need to consider the state, federal, and international laws and regulations that affect your business. In particular, the Digital Millennium Copyright Act (DMCA) sends chills down the spines of legitimate researchers. See www.eff.org/issues/dmca for everything that the DMCA has to offer.

Many federal laws and regulations in the United States — such as the Health Insurance Portability and Accountability Act (HIPAA) and the associated Health Information Technology for Economic and Clinical Health (HITECH) Act, Gramm-Leach-Bliley Act (GLBA), North American Electric Reliability Corporation (NERC) Critical Infrastructure Protection (CIP) requirements, and the Payment Card Industry Data Security Standard (PCI DSS) — require strong security controls and consistent security assessments. There's also the Cybersecurity Maturity Model Certification (CMMC). CMMC is a follow-on to NIST Special Publication 800-171 Protecting Controlled Unclassified Information in Nonfederal Systems and Organizations. This certification is intended to ensure that the U.S. Department of Defense's (DoD's) Defense Industrial Base (DIB) of suppliers/contractors are adequately protecting the DOD's information assets.

Related international laws — such as the Canadian Personal Information Protection and Electronic Documents Act (PIPEDA), the European Union's General Data Protection Regulation (GDPR), and Japan's Personal Information Protection Act (JPIPA) — are no different. Incorporating your security tests into these compliance requirements is a great way to meet state and federal regulations and to beef up your overall information security and privacy program.

Understanding the Need to Hack Your Own Systems

To catch a thief, you must think like a thief. That adage is the basis of vulnerability and penetration testing. Knowing your enemy is critical. The law of averages works against security. With the increased number of hackers and their expanding knowledge and the growing number of system vulnerabilities and other unknowns, all computer systems and applications are likely to be hacked or compromised somehow. Protecting your systems from the bad guys — not just addressing general security best practices — is critical. When you know hacker tricks, you find out how vulnerable your systems really are and can take the necessary steps to make them secure.

Hacking preys on weak security practices and both disclosed and undisclosed vulnerabilities. More and more research, such as the annual Verizon Data Breach Investigations Report (www.verizon.com/business/resources/reports/dbir/), shows that long-standing, *known* vulnerabilities are continually being targeted. Firewalls, advanced endpoint security, security incident and event management

(SIEM), and other fancy (and expensive) security technologies often create a false feeling of safety. Attacking your own systems to discover vulnerabilities — especially the low-hanging fruit that gets so many people into trouble — helps you go beyond security products to make them even more secure. Vulnerability and penetration testing is a proven method for greatly hardening your systems from attack. If you don't identify weaknesses, it's only a matter of time before the vulnerabilities are exploited.

As hackers expand their knowledge, so should you. You must think like them and work like them to protect your systems from them. As a security professional, you must know the activities that the bad guys carry out, as well as how to stop their efforts. Knowing what to look for and how to use that information helps you thwart their efforts.

TIP

You don't have to protect your systems from *everything*. You can't. The only protection against everything is unplugging your computer systems and locking them away so no one can touch them — not even you and especially not your users. But doing so is not the best approach to security, and it's certainly not good for business! What's important is protecting your systems from known vulnerabilities and common attacks — the 20 percent of the issues that create 80 percent of the risks, which happen to be some of the most overlooked weaknesses in most organizations.

Anticipating all the possible vulnerabilities you'll have in your systems and business processes is impossible. You certainly can't plan for all types of attacks — especially the unknown ones. But the more combinations you try and the more often you test whole systems instead of individual units, the better your chances are of discovering vulnerabilities that affect your information systems in their entirety.

Don't take your security testing too far, though; hardening your systems from unlikely (or even *less* likely) attacks makes little sense and will probably get in the way of doing business.

REMEMBER

Your overall goals for security testing are to

>> Prioritize your systems so that you can focus your efforts on what matters.

>> Test your systems in a nondestructive fashion.

>> Enumerate vulnerabilities and, if necessary, prove to management that business risks exist.

>> Apply results to address the vulnerabilities and better secure your systems.

Understanding the Dangers Your Systems Face

It's one thing to know generally that your systems are under fire from hackers around the world and malicious users around the office; it's another to understand specific potential attacks against your systems. This section discusses some well-known attacks but is by no means a comprehensive listing.

Many security vulnerabilities aren't critical by themselves, but exploiting several vulnerabilities at the same time can take its toll on a system or network environment. A default Windows operating system (OS) configuration, a weak SQL Server administrator password, or a mission-critical workstation running on a wireless network may not be a major security concern by itself. But someone who exploits all three of these vulnerabilities simultaneously could enable unauthorized remote access and disclose sensitive information (among other things).

REMEMBER

Complexity is the enemy of security.

Vulnerabilities and attacks have grown enormously in recent years because of virtualization, cloud computing, and even social media. These three things alone add immeasurable complexity to your environment. On top of that, with the new ways of the world and so many people working from home, the complexities have grown exponentially.

Nontechnical attacks

Exploits that involve manipulating people — your users and even you — are often the greatest vulnerability. Humans are trusting by nature, which can lead to social engineering exploits. *Social engineering* is exploiting the trusting nature of human beings to gain information — often via email phishing — for malicious purposes. With dramatic increases in the size of the remote workforce, social engineering has become an even greater threat, especially with more personal devices being used that are likely much less secure. Check out Book 5, Chapter 6 for more information about social engineering and how to guard your systems and users against it.

Other common, effective attacks against information systems are physical. Hackers break into buildings, computer rooms, or other areas that contain critical information or property to steal computers, servers, and other valuable equipment. Physical attacks can also include *dumpster diving* — rummaging through trash cans and bins for intellectual property, passwords, network diagrams, and other information.

Network infrastructure attacks

Attacks on network infrastructures can be easy to accomplish because many networks can be reached from anywhere in the world via the Internet. Examples of network infrastructure attacks include the following:

>> Connecting to a network through an unsecured wireless access point attached behind a firewall

>> Exploiting weaknesses in network protocols, such as File Transfer Protocol (FTP) and Secure Sockets Layer (SSL)

>> Flooding a network with too many requests, creating denial of service (DoS) for legitimate requests

>> Installing a network analyzer on a network segment and capturing packets that travel across it, revealing confidential information in cleartext

Operating system attacks

Hacking an OS is a preferred method of the bad guys. OS attacks make up a large portion of attacks simply because every computer has an operating system. They are susceptible to many well-known exploits, including vulnerabilities that remain unpatched years later.

Occasionally, some OSes that tend to be more secure out of the box — such as the old-but-still-out-there Novell NetWare, OpenBSD, and IBM Series i — are attacked, and vulnerabilities turn up. But hackers tend to prefer attacking Windows, Linux, and macOS because they're more widely used.

Here are some examples of attacks on operating systems:

>> Exploiting missing patches

>> Attacking built-in authentication systems

>> Breaking file system security

>> Installing ransomware to lock down the system to extort money or other assets

>> Cracking passwords and weak encryption implementations

Application and other specialized attacks

Applications take a lot of hits by hackers. Web applications and mobile apps, which are probably the most popular means of attack, are often beaten down. The following are examples of application attacks and related exploits that are often present on business networks:

>> Websites and applications are everywhere. Thanks to what's called *shadow IT*, in which people in various areas of the business run and manage their own technology, website applications are in every corner of the internal network and out in the cloud. Unfortunately, many IT and security professionals are unaware of the presence of shadow IT and the risks it creates.

>> Mobile apps face increasing attacks, given their popularity in business settings. There are also rogue apps discovered on the app stores that can create challenges in your environment.

>> Unsecured files containing sensitive information are scattered across workstation and server shares as well as out into the cloud in places like Microsoft OneDrive and Google Drive. Database systems also contain numerous vulnerabilities that malicious users can exploit.

Following the Security Assessment Principles

Security professionals must carry out the same attacks against computer systems, physical controls, and people that malicious hackers do. (I introduce those attacks in the preceding section.) A security professional's intent, however, is to highlight any associated weaknesses. Parts 2 through 5 of this book cover how you might proceed with these attacks in detail, along with specific countermeasures you can implement against attacks on your business.

To ensure that security testing is performed adequately and professionally, every security professional needs to follow a few basic tenets. The following sections introduce the important principles.

WARNING

If you don't heed these principles, bad things could happen. I've seen them ignored or forgotten by IT departments while planning and executing security tests. The results weren't positive; trust me.

Working ethically

The word *ethical* in this context means working with high professional morals and values. Whether you're performing security tests against your own systems or for someone who has hired you, everything you do must be aboveboard in support of the company's goals, with no hidden agenda — just professionalism. Being ethical also means reporting all your findings, whether or not they may create political backlash. Don't laugh; on numerous occasions, I've witnessed people brushing off security vulnerability findings because they didn't want to rock the boat or to deal with difficult executives or vendors.

Trustworthiness is the ultimate tenet. It's also the best way to get (and keep) people on your side in support of your security program. Misusing information and power is forbidden; that's what the bad guys do, so let them be the ones who pay a fine or go to prison because of their poor choices.

Respecting privacy

Treat the information you gather with respect. All information you obtain during your testing — from web application flaws to clear text email passwords to personally identifiable information (PII) and beyond — must be kept private. Nothing good can come of snooping into confidential corporate information or employees' or customers' private lives.

TIP

Involve others in your process. Employ a peer review or similar oversight system that can help build trust and support for your security assessment projects.

Not crashing your systems

One of the biggest mistakes I've seen people make when trying to test their own systems is inadvertently crashing the systems they're trying to keep running. Crashing systems doesn't happen as often as it used to given the resiliency of today's systems, but poor planning and timing can have negative consequences.

Although you're not likely to do so, you can create DoS conditions on your systems when testing. Running too many tests too quickly can cause system lockups, data corruption, reboots, and similar problems, especially when you're testing older servers and web applications. (I should know; I've done it!) Don't assume that a network or specific host can handle the beating that network tools and vulnerability scanners can dish out.

You can even accidentally create accounts or lock users out of the network without realizing the consequences. Proceed with caution and common sense. Either way, be it you or someone else, these weaknesses likely exist on your network, and it's better that you discover them first!

TIP

Most vulnerability scanners can control how many requests are sent to each system simultaneously. These settings are especially handy when you need to run the tests on production systems during regular business hours. Don't be afraid to throttle back your scans. Completing your testing will take longer, but throttling back may save you a lot of grief if an unstable system is present.

Using the Vulnerability and Penetration Testing Process

As with practically any IT or security project, you need to plan security testing. It's been said that action without planning is the root of every failure. Strategic and tactical issues in vulnerability and penetration testing need to be determined and agreed on in advance. To ensure the success of your efforts, spend time planning for any amount of testing, from a simple OS password-cracking test against a few servers to a penetration test of a complex web environment.

WARNING

If you choose to hire a "reformed" hacker to work with you during your testing or to obtain an independent perspective, be careful. The sidebar "Thinking about hiring a *reformed* hacker?" offers some food for thought.

THINKING ABOUT HIRING A *REFORMED* HACKER?

Former hackers — I'm referring to the malicious hackers who have hacked into computer systems in the past and ended up serving time in prison — can be very good at what they do. No doubt, some of them are very smart. Many people swear by hiring reformed hackers to do their testing. Others compare this practice to hiring the proverbial fox to guard the henhouse. If you're thinking about bringing in a former (un)ethical hacker to test your systems, consider these issues:

- Do you want to reward malicious behavior with your organization's business?

- A hacker who claims to be reformed isn't necessarily. They could have deep-rooted psychological issues or character flaws that you're going to have to contend with. *Buyer, beware!*

- Information gathered and accessed during security assessments is some of the most sensitive information your organization possesses. If this information gets into the wrong hands, even ten years down the road, it could be used against you. Some hackers and reformed criminals hang out in tight social groups. You may not want your information to be shared in such circles.

That said, everyone deserves a chance to explain what happened in the past. Zero tolerance is senseless. Listen to the hacker's story, and use common-sense discretion about whether you trust the person to help you. The supposed black-hat hacker may have been a gray-hat hacker or a misguided white-hat hacker who would fit well in your organization. It's your call. Just be prepared to defend your decision when the time comes.

Formulating your plan

Getting approval for security testing is essential. Make sure that what you're doing is known and visible — at least to the decision-makers. Obtaining sponsorship of the project is the first step. This is how your testing objectives are defined. Sponsorship could come from your manager, an executive, your client, or even yourself if you're the boss. You need someone to back you up and sign off on your plan. Otherwise, your testing may be called off unexpectedly if someone (including third parties such as cloud service and hosting providers) claims that you were never authorized to perform the tests. Worse, you could be fired or charged with criminal activity.

The authorization can be as simple as an internal memo or an email from your boss when you perform these tests on your own systems. If you're testing for a client, have a signed contract stating the client's support and authorization. Get written approval of this sponsorship before you ever start working to ensure that none of your time or effort is wasted. This documentation is your "Get Out of Jail Free" card if anyone — such as your Internet service provider (ISP), cloud service provider, or a related vendor — questions what you're doing or if the authorities come calling. Don't laugh — it wouldn't be the first time it has happened.

One slip can crash your systems, which isn't necessarily what anyone wants. You need a detailed plan, but you don't need volumes of testing procedures that make the plan overly complex. A well-defined scope includes the following information:

>> **Specific systems to be tested:** When selecting systems to test, start with the most critical systems and processes or the ones that you suspect are the most vulnerable. You could test server OS passwords, test an Internet-facing web application, or attempt social engineering via phishing before drilling down

into all your systems. Another consideration is whether to test computer systems that are being used by employees who are working from home. Unless they are connected to the corporate environment over a VPN or are otherwise remotely accessible, you might not even be able to reach them. Furthermore, what are the ramifications of testing computers — especially personal systems — that are running on a home network? Are there medical devices, specific software, or Internet of Things systems that might be disrupted? Thinking all of this through with all the right people is imperative.

>> **Risks involved:** Have a contingency plan for your security testing process in case something goes awry. Suppose that you're assessing your firewall or a web application, and you take it down. This situation can cause system unavailability, which can reduce system performance or employee productivity. Worse, it might cause data integrity loss, loss of data itself, and even bad publicity. It'll most certainly tick off a person or two and make you look bad. All of these can create business risks.

Handle social engineering and DoS attacks carefully. Determine how they might affect the people and systems you test.

>> **Dates when the tests will be performed and overall timeline:** Determining when the tests are to be performed is something you must think long and hard about. Decide whether to perform tests during normal business hours, or late at night or early in the morning so that production systems aren't affected. Involve others to make sure that they approve of your timing.

You may get pushback and suffer DoS-related consequences, but the best approach is an unlimited attack, in which any type of test is possible at any time of day. The bad guys aren't breaking into your systems within a limited scope so why should you? Some exceptions to this approach are performing all-out DoS attacks, social engineering, and physical security tests.

TIP

>> **Whether you intend to be detected:** One of your goals may be to perform the tests without being detected. You might perform your tests on remote systems or on a remote office and don't want the users to be aware of what you're doing. Otherwise, the users or IT staff may catch on to you and be on their best behavior instead of their normal behavior.

>> **Whether to leave security controls enabled:** An important, yet often overlooked, issue is whether to leave enabled security controls such as firewalls, intrusion prevention systems (IPSes), and web application firewalls (WAFs) so that they block scans and exploit attempts. Leaving these controls enabled provides a real-world picture of where things stand. Disabling these controls, essentially allowlisting (or whitelisting) your source IP addresses, enables you to identify a greater number of vulnerabilities.

Many people want to leave their security controls enabled. After all, that approach can make them look better, because many security checks will likely be blocked. To me, this defense-in-depth approach is great, but it can create a serious false sense of security and doesn't paint the entire picture of an organization's overall security posture. There's no right or wrong answer. Just make sure that everyone is on board with what is being tested and what the final outcomes and report represent.

>> **Knowledge of the systems before testing:** You don't need extensive knowledge of the systems you're testing — just basic understanding, which protects both you and the tested systems. Understanding the systems you're testing shouldn't be difficult if you're testing your own in-house systems. If you're testing a client's systems, you may have to dig deeper. Only one or two clients have asked me for a fully blind assessment.

Most IT managers and others who are responsible for security may be scared of blind assessments, which can take more time, cost more, and be less effective. Base the type of test you perform on the organization's or client's needs.

>> **Actions to take when a major vulnerability is discovered:** Don't stop after you find one or two security holes; keep going to see what else you can discover. I'm not saying that you should keep testing until the end of time or until you crash all your systems; ain't nobody got time for that! Instead, simply pursue the path you're going down until you can't hack it any longer (pun intended). If you haven't found any vulnerabilities, you haven't looked hard enough. Vulnerabilities are there. If you uncover something big such as a weak password or SQL injection on an external system, you need to share that information with the key players (developers, database administrators, IT managers, and so on) as soon as possible to plug the hole before it's exploited.

>> **The specific deliverables:** Deliverables may include vulnerability scanner reports and your own distilled report outlining important vulnerabilities to address, along with recommendations and countermeasures to implement.

Selecting tools

As in any project, if you don't have the right tools for your security testing, you'll have difficulty accomplishing the task effectively. Having said that, just because you use the right tools doesn't mean that you'll discover all the right vulnerabilities. Experience counts.

TIP

Know the limitations of your tools. Many vulnerability scanners and testing tools generate false positives and negatives (incorrectly identifying vulnerabilities). Others skip vulnerabilities. In certain situations, such as testing web applications, you have to run multiple vulnerability scanners to find all the vulnerabilities.

Many tools focus on specific tests, and no tool can test for everything. For the same reason that you wouldn't drive a nail with a screwdriver, don't use a port scanner to uncover specific network vulnerabilities or a wireless network analyzer to test a web application. You need a set of specific tools for the task. The more (and better) tools you have, the easier your security testing efforts will be.

Make sure that you're using tools like these for your tasks:

>> To crack passwords, you need cracking tools such as Ophcrack and Proactive Password Auditor.

>> For an in-depth analysis of a web application, a web vulnerability scanner (such as Acunetix Web Vulnerability Scanner or Probely) is more appropriate than a network analyzer (such as Wireshark or OmniPeek).

The capabilities of many security and hacking tools are misunderstood. This mis-understanding has cast a negative light on otherwise excellent and legitimate tools; even government agencies around the world are talking about making them illegal. Part of this misunderstanding is due to the complexity of some of these security testing tools, but it's largely based in ignorance and the desire for control. Whichever tools you use, familiarize yourself with them before you start using them. That way, you're prepared to use the tools in the ways that they're intended to be used. Here are ways to do that:

>> Read the readme and/or online help files and FAQs (frequently asked questions).

>> Study the user guides.

>> Use the tools in a lab or test environment.

>> Watch tutorial videos on YouTube (if you can bear the poor production of most of them).

>> Consider formal classroom training from the security-tool vendor or another third-party training provider, if available.

Look for these characteristics in tools for security testing:

>> Adequate documentation

>> Detailed reports on discovered vulnerabilities, including how they might be exploited and fixed

>> General industry acceptance

>> Availability of updates and responsiveness of technical support

>> High-level reports that can be presented to managers or nontechnical types (especially important in today's audit- and compliance-driven world)

These features can save you a ton of time and effort when you're performing your tests and writing your final reports.

SAMPLE SECURITY TESTING TOOLS

When selecting the right security tool for the task, ask around. Get advice from your colleagues and from other people via Google, LinkedIn, and YouTube. Hundreds, if not thousands, of tools are available for security tests. Following are some commercial, freeware, and open-source security tools to consider:

- Acunetix Web Vulnerability Scanner
- Cain & Abel
- Burp Suite
- CommView for WiFi
- Elcomsoft System Recovery
- LUCY
- ManageEngine Firewall Analyzer
- Metasploit
- Nessus
- NetScanTools Pro
- Netsparker
- OmniPeek
- Proactive Password Auditor
- Probely
- Qualys
- SoftPerfect Network Scanner

I discuss these tools and many others in Parts 2 through 5 in connection with specific tests. The appendix contains a more comprehensive list of these tools for your reference.

Executing the plan

Good security testing takes persistence. Time and patience are important. Also, be careful when you're performing your tests. A criminal on your network or a seemingly benign employee looking over your shoulder may watch what's going on and use this information against you or your business.

Making sure that no hackers are on your systems before you start isn't practical. Just be sure to keep everything as quiet and private as possible, especially when you're transmitting and storing test results. If possible, encrypt any emails and files that contain sensitive test information or share them via a cloud-based file sharing service.

You're on a reconnaissance mission. Harness as much information as possible about your organization and systems — much as malicious hackers do. Start with a broad view and narrow your focus. Follow these steps:

1. **Search the Internet for your organization's name, its computer and network system names, and its IP addresses.**

   Google is a great place to start.

2. **Narrow your scope, targeting the specific systems you're testing.**

   Whether you're assessing physical security structures or web applications, a casual assessment can turn up a lot of information about your systems.

3. **Further narrow your focus by performing scans and other detailed tests to uncover vulnerabilities on your systems.**

4. **Perform the attacks and exploit any vulnerabilities you find (if that's what you choose to do).**

Check out Book 5, Chapters 4 and 5 for information and tips on this process.

Evaluating results

Assess your results to see what you've uncovered, assuming that the vulnerabilities haven't been made obvious before now. Knowledge counts. Your skill in evaluating the results and correlating the specific vulnerabilities discovered will get better with practice. You'll end up knowing your systems much better than anyone else does, which will make the evaluation process much simpler moving forward.

TIP

Submit a formal report to management or to your client outlining your results and any recommendations you need to share. Keep these parties in the loop to show that your efforts and their money are well spent.

Moving on

When you finish your security tests, you (or your client) will still need to implement your recommendations to make sure that the systems are secure. Otherwise, all the time, money, and effort spent on testing goes to waste.

REMEMBER

New security vulnerabilities continually appear. Information systems change and are becoming more complex. New security vulnerabilities and exploits are being uncovered. Vulnerability scanners and related testing tools get better. Security tests provide a snapshot of the security posture of your systems. At any time, everything can change, especially after you upgrade software, add computer systems, or apply patches. This situation underscores the need to keep your tools updated — before each use, if possible. Plan to test regularly and consistently (such as monthly, quarterly, or biannually).

Chapter 2

Cracking the Hacker Mindset

Before you start assessing the security of your systems, it's good to know a few things about the people you're up against. Many security product vendors and security professionals claim that you should protect all of your systems from the bad guys — both internal and external. But what does this mean? How do you know how these people think and execute their attacks?

Knowing what hackers and malicious users want helps you understand how they work. Understanding how they work helps you look at your information systems in a whole new way. This chapter describes the challenges that you face from the people who actually do the misdeeds, as well as their motivations and methods. This understanding better prepares you for your security tests.

What You're Up Against

Thanks to sensationalism in the media, public perception of *hacker* has transformed from a harmless tinkerer to a malicious criminal. Nevertheless, hackers often state that the public misunderstands them, which is mostly true. It's easy to prejudge — or misjudge — what you don't understand. Unfortunately, many hacker stereotypes are based on misunderstanding rather than fact, and that misunderstanding fuels a continued debate.

Hackers can be classified by both their abilities and their underlying motivations. Some are skilled, and their motivations are benign; they're merely seeking more knowledge. Still, other hackers may have malicious intent and seek some form of personal, political, or economic gain. Unfortunately, the negative aspects of hacking usually overshadow the positive aspects and promote the negative stereotypes.

Historically, hackers hacked for the pursuit of knowledge and the thrill of the challenge. *Script kiddies* (hacker wannabes with limited skills) aside, traditional hackers are adventurous and innovative thinkers who are always devising new ways to exploit computer vulnerabilities. (For more on script kiddies, see the section "Who Breaks into Computer Systems" later in this chapter.) Hackers see what others often overlook. They're very inquisitive and have good situational awareness. They wonder what would happen if a cable was unplugged, a switch was flipped, or lines of code were changed in a program. They do these things and then notice what happens.

When they were growing up, hackers' rivals were monsters and villains on video-game screens. Now hackers see their electronic foes as only that: *electronic*. Criminal hackers who perform malicious acts don't really think about the fact that human beings are behind the firewalls, web applications, and computer systems they're attacking. They ignore the fact that their actions often affect those human beings in negative ways, such as jeopardizing their job security and putting their personal safety at risk. Government-backed hacking? Well, that's a different story, as those hackers are making calculated decisions to do these things.

On the flip side, the odds are good that you have at least an employee, contractor, intern, or consultant who intends to compromise sensitive information on your network for malicious purposes. These people don't hack in the way that people normally suppose. Instead, they root around in files on server shares; delve into databases they know they shouldn't be in; and sometimes steal, modify, and delete sensitive information to which they have access. This behavior can be very hard to detect, especially given the widespread belief among management that users can and should be trusted to do the right things. This activity is perpetuated if these users passed their criminal background and credit checks before they were hired. Past behavior is often the best predictor of future behavior, but just because someone has had a clean record and authorization to access sensitive systems doesn't mean that they won't do anything bad. Criminal behavior has to start somewhere!

REMEMBER

As negative as breaking into computer systems often can be, hackers and researchers play key roles in the advancement of technology. In a world without these people, the odds are good that the latest network and cloud controls, endpoint security, or vulnerability scanning and exploit tools would likely be different — if they existed at all. Such a world might not be bad, but technology does keep security professionals employed and the field moving forward. Unfortunately, the technical security solutions can't ward off all malicious attacks and unauthorized use because hackers and (sometimes) malicious users are usually a few steps ahead of the technology designed to protect against their wayward actions. Or the people in charge of these technologies are so distracted that they miss the obvious.

However you view the stereotypical hacker or malicious user, one thing is certain: Somebody will always try to take down your computer systems and compromise information by poking and prodding where they shouldn't — through denial of service (DoS) attacks or by creating and launching malware, especially ransomware. You must take the appropriate steps to protect your systems against this kind of intrusion.

THINKING LIKE THE BAD GUYS

Malicious attackers often think and work like thieves, kidnappers, and other organized criminals you hear about in the news every day. The smart ones devise ways to fly under the radar and exploit even the smallest weaknesses that lead them to their targets. Following are examples of how hackers and malicious users think and work. This list isn't intended to highlight specific exploits covered in this book or tests that the book recommends that you carry out, but it demonstrates the context and approach of a malicious mindset:

- **Evading an intrusion prevention system** by changing the MAC or IP address every few minutes (or packets) to get farther into a network without being blocked.

- **Exploiting a physical security weakness** by being aware of offices that have already been cleaned by the cleaning crew and are unoccupied (and, thus, easy to access with little chance of getting caught). For example, such a weakness might be made obvious by the fact that the office blinds are opened, and the curtains are pulled shut in the early morning.

- **Bypassing web access controls** by elevating their privileges via a vulnerable web page, the application's login mechanism, or a vulnerable password reset process.

- **Using unauthorized software that would otherwise be blocked at the firewall** by changing the default TCP port on which it runs.

(continued)

(continued)

- **Setting up a wireless "evil twin"** near a local Wi-Fi hotspot to entice unsuspecting Internet surfers onto a rogue network, where their information can be captured and easily manipulated.

- **Using an overly trusting colleague's user ID and password** to gain access to sensitive information that they'd otherwise be highly unlikely to obtain and that could then be used for ill-gotten gains.

- **Unplugging the power cord or Ethernet connection to a networked security camera** that monitors access to the computer room or other sensitive areas and subsequently gaining unmonitored system access.

- **Performing SQL injection or password cracking against a website** via a neighbor's unprotected wireless network to hide the malicious user's own identity.

Malicious hackers operate in countless ways, and this list presents only a small number of the techniques hackers may use. IT and security professionals need to think and work this way to find security vulnerabilities that may not otherwise be uncovered.

Who Breaks into Computer Systems

Computer hackers have been around for decades. Since the Internet became widely used in the 1990s, the mainstream public has started to hear more about hacking. Certain hackers, such as John Draper (also known as Captain Crunch) and Kevin Mitnick, are well known. Many more unknown hackers are looking to make names for themselves, and they're the ones you have to look out for.

In a world of black and white, describing the typical hacker is easy. The historical stereotype of a hacker is an antisocial, pimply teenage boy. But the world has many shades of gray, and many types of people do the hacking. Hackers are unique people, so a profile is hard to outline. The best broad description of hackers is that all hackers *aren't* equal. Each hacker has unique motives, methods, and skills.

Hacker skill levels

Hacker skill levels fall into three general categories:

>> **Script kiddies:** These hackers are computer novices who take advantage of the exploit tools, vulnerability scanners, and documentation available free on the Internet but who don't have any real knowledge of what's going on

behind the scenes. They know just enough to cause you headaches but typically are very sloppy in their actions, leaving all sorts of digital fingerprints behind. Even though these guys are often the stereotypical hackers that you hear about in the news media, they need only minimal skills to carry out their attacks.

>> **Criminal hackers:** Sometimes referred to as *crackers,* these hackers are skilled criminal experts who write some of the hacking tools, including the scripts and other programs that the script kiddies and security professionals use. These folks also write malware to carry out their exploits from the other side of the world. They can break into networks and computers and cover their tracks. They can even make it look as though someone else hacked their victims' systems. Sometimes, people with ill intent may not be doing what's considered to be hacking; nevertheless, they're abusing their privileges or somehow gaining unauthorized access.

Advanced hackers are often members of collectives that prefer to remain nameless. These hackers are very secretive, sharing information with their subordinates (lower-ranked hackers in the collectives) only when they deem those subordinates to be worthy. Typically, for lower-ranked hackers to be considered worthy, they must possess unique information or take the ganglike approach by proving themselves through a high-profile hack. These hackers are some of your worst enemies in IT. (Okay, maybe they're not as bad as untrained and careless users, but they're close. They do go hand in hand, after all!) By understanding criminal hacker behavior, you're simply being proactive, finding problems before they become problems.

>> **Security researchers:** These people are highly technical, publicly (or some-what publicly) known security experts who not only monitor and track computer, network, and application vulnerabilities, but they also write tools and other code to exploit them. If these guys didn't exist, security profession-als wouldn't have much in the way of open-source and even certain commer-cial security testing tools.

TIP

Consider following security researchers via their personal or company blogs, Twitter feeds, and articles. You also can review Kevin Beaver's blog, Principle Logic (www.principlelogic.com). Following the progress of these security researchers helps you stay up to date on vulnerabilities, as well as the latest, greatest security tools.

REMEMBER

Hackers can be good (*white hat*) and bad (*black hat*) hackers. *Gray hat* hackers are a little bit of both. There are also *blue-hat* hackers, outsiders who are hired to find security flaws in client systems. Blue-hat hackers are more recently referred to as purple-hat hackers.

A study from the Black Hat security conference found that everyday IT professionals even engage in malicious and criminal activity against others. And people wonder why IT doesn't get the respect it deserves!

Regardless of age and complexion, hackers possess curiosity, bravado, and often very sharp minds.

Hacker motivations

Perhaps more important than a hacker's skill level is their motivation. The following groups of hackers have different motivations:

>> **Hacktivists:** These hackers try to disseminate political or social messages through their work. A hacktivist wants to raise public awareness of an issue but wants to remain anonymous. In many situations, these hackers try to take you down if you express a view that's contrary to theirs. Examples of hacktivism are the websites that were defaced by the "Free Kevin" messages that promoted freeing Kevin Mitnick, who was in prison for his famous hacking escapades. Other cases of hacktivism include messages about legalized drugs, antiwar protests, wealth envy, big corporations, and just about any other social and political issue you can think of.

>> **Terrorists:** Terrorists (both organized and unorganized and often backed by government agencies) attack corporate or government computers and public utility infrastructures such as power grids and air-traffic control towers. They crash critical systems, steal classified data, and/or expose the personal information of government employees. Countries take the threats that these terrorists pose so seriously that many mandate information security controls in crucial industries, such as the power industry, to protect essential systems from these attacks.

>> **Hackers for hire:** These hackers are often (but not always) part of organized crime on the Internet. Many of these hackers hire out themselves or their ransomware and DoS-creating botnets for money — lots of it!

REMEMBER

Criminal hackers are in the minority, so don't think that you're up against millions of these villains. Like the email spam kings of the world, many members of collectives prefer to remain nameless; the nefarious acts are carried out by a small number of criminals. Many other hackers just love to tinker and only seek knowledge of how computer systems work. One of your greatest threats works inside your building and has an access badge to the building, a network account, and hair on top, so don't discount the insider threat.

Why They Do It

Hackers hack because they can. Period. Okay, the reason goes a little deeper. Hacking is a hobby for some hackers; they hack just to see what they can and can't break into, usually testing only their own systems. These folks aren't the ones addressed in this book. Instead, this book focuses on those hackers who are obsessive about gaining notoriety or defeating computer systems and those who have criminal intentions.

Many hackers get a kick out of outsmarting corporate and government IT and security administrators. They thrive on making headlines and being notorious. Defeating an entity or possessing knowledge that few other people have makes them feel better about themselves, building their self-esteem. Many of these hackers feed off the instant gratification of exploiting a computer system. They become obsessed with this feeling. Some hackers can't resist the adrenaline rush they get from breaking into someone else's systems. Often, the more difficult the job is, the greater the thrill is for hackers.

It's a bit ironic, given their collective tendencies, but hackers often promote individualism — or at least the decentralization of information — because many of them believe that all information should be free. They think their attacks are different from attacks in the real world. Hackers may ignore or misunderstand their victims and the consequences of hacking. They don't think about the long-term effects of the choices they're making today. Many hackers say that they don't intend to harm or profit through their bad deeds, and this belief helps them justify their work. Others don't look for tangible payoffs; just proving a point is often a sufficient reward for them. The word *sociopath* comes to mind when describing many such people.

The knowledge that malicious attackers gain and the self-esteem boost that comes from successful hacking may become an addiction and a way of life. Some attackers want to make your life miserable, and others simply want to be seen or heard. Some common motives are revenge, bragging rights, curiosity, boredom, challenge, vandalism, theft for financial gain, sabotage, blackmail, extortion, corporate espionage, and just generally speaking out against "the man." Hackers regularly cite these motives to explain their behavior, but they tend to cite these motivations more commonly during difficult economic conditions.

Malicious users inside your network may be looking to gain information to help them with personal financial problems, to give them a leg up on a competitor, to seek revenge on their employers, to satisfy their curiosity, or to relieve boredom.

REMEMBER

Many business owners and managers — even some network and security administrators — believe that they don't have anything that a hacker wants or that hackers can't do much damage if they break in. These beliefs are sorely mistaken. This dismissive kind of thinking helps support the bad guys and promote their objectives. Hackers can compromise a seemingly unimportant system to access the network and use it as a launching pad for attacks on other systems, and many people would be none the wiser because they don't have the proper controls to prevent and detect malicious use.

Hackers often hack simply *because they can*. Some hackers go for high-profile systems, but hacking into anyone's system helps them fit into hacker circles. Hackers exploit many people's false sense of security and go for almost any system they think they can compromise. Electronic information can be in more than one place at the same time, so if hackers merely copy information from the systems they break into, it's tough to prove that hackers possess that information, and it's impossible to get the information back.

Similarly, hackers know that a simple defaced web page — however easily attacked — isn't good for someone else's business. It often takes a large-scale data breach, ransomware infection, or a phishing attack that spawns the unauthorized wire transfer of a large sum of money to get the attention of business executives. But hacked sites can often persuade management and other nonbelievers to address information threats and vulnerabilities.

Many recent studies have revealed that most security flaws are basic in nature. Consider these basic flaws the *low-hanging fruit* of the network, just waiting to be exploited. Computer breaches continue to become more common and are often easier to execute yet harder to prevent for several reasons:

>> Widespread use of networks and Internet connectivity

>> Anonymity provided by computer systems on the Internet and often on internal networks (because proper and effective logging, monitoring, and alerting rarely take place)

>> Greater number and availability of hacking tools

>> Large number of open wireless networks that help criminals cover their tracks

>> Greater complexity of networks and codebases in the applications and databases being developed today

>> Naïve yet computer-savvy children who are eager to give up privacy (which is easy because they've never experienced it) for free stuff

>> Ransoms paid by cyberinsurance policies can be huge

>> Likelihood that attackers won't be investigated or prosecuted if caught

REMEMBER

A malicious hacker needs to find only one security hole, whereas IT and security professionals and business owners must find and resolve all of them!

Although many attacks go unnoticed or unreported, criminals who are discovered may not be pursued or prosecuted. When they're caught, hackers often rationalize their services as being altruistic and a benefit to society: They're merely pointing out vulnerabilities before someone else does. Regardless, if hackers are caught and prosecuted, the "fame and glory" reward system that hackers thrive on is threatened.

The same goes for malicious users. Typically, their criminal activity goes unnoticed, but if they're caught, the security breach may be kept hush-hush in the name of protecting shareholder value or not ruffling any customer or business-partner feathers. Information security and privacy laws and regulations, however, are changing this situation, because in most cases, breach notification is required. Sometimes, the malicious user is fired or asked to resign. Although public cases of internal breaches are becoming more common (usually through breach disclosure laws), these cases don't give a full picture of what's taking place in the average organization.

Regardless of whether they want to, most executives now have to deal with all the state, federal, and international laws and regulations that require notifications of breaches or suspected breaches of sensitive information. These requirements apply to external hacks, internal breaches, and even seemingly benign things such as lost mobile devices and backup tapes. The appendix lists the information security and privacy laws and regulations that may affect your business.

HACKING IN THE NAME OF LIBERTY?

Many hackers exhibit behaviors that contradict their stated purposes. They fight for civil liberties and want to be left alone, but at the same time, they love prying into the business of others and controlling them in any way possible. Many hackers call themselves civil libertarians and claim to support the principles of personal privacy and freedom, but they contradict their words by intruding on the privacy and property of other people. They steal the property and violate the rights of others but go to great lengths to get their own rights back from anyone who threatens them. The situation is "live and let live" gone awry.

The case involving copyrighted materials and the Recording Industry Association of America (RIAA) is a classic example. Hackers have gone to great lengths to prove a point, defacing the websites of organizations that support copyrights and then sharing music and software themselves. Go figure.

Planning and Performing Attacks

Attack styles vary widely:

>> Some hackers prepare far in advance of an attack. They gather small bits of information and methodically carry out their hacks, as outlined in Book 5, Chapter 4. These hackers are the most difficult to track.

>> Other hackers — usually, inexperienced script kiddies — act before they think through the consequences. Such hackers may try, for example, to telnet directly into an organization's router without hiding their identities. Other hackers may try to launch a DoS attack against a web server without first determining the version running on the server or the installed patches. These hackers usually are caught or at least blocked.

>> Malicious users are all over the map. Some are quite savvy, based on their knowledge of the network and of how IT and security operate inside the organization. Others go poking and prodding in systems that they shouldn't be in — or shouldn't have had access to in the first place — and often do stupid things that lead security or network administrators back to them.

Although the hacker underground is a community, many hackers — especially advanced hackers — don't share information with the crowd. Most hackers do much of their work independently to remain anonymous.

TIP

Hackers who network with one another often use private message boards, anonymous email addresses, or hacker underground websites (a.k.a. the deep web or dark web). You can attempt to log in to such sites to see what hackers are doing, but it's not advisable unless you really know what you're doing. The last thing you need is to get a malware infection or lose sensitive login credentials when trying to sniff around these places.

Whatever approach they take, most malicious attackers prey on ignorance. They know the following aspects of real-world security:

>> **The majority of computer systems aren't managed properly.** The computer systems aren't properly patched, hardened, or monitored. Attackers can often fly below the radar of the average firewall or intrusion prevention system (IPS), especially malicious users whose actions aren't monitored yet who have full access to the very environment they can exploit.

>> **Most network and security administrators can't keep up with the deluge of new vulnerabilities and attack methods.** These people have too many tasks to stay on top of and too many other fires to put out. Network and

security administrators may fail to notice or respond to security events because of poor time and goal management.

>> **Information systems grow more complex every year.** This fact is yet another reason why overburdened administrators find it difficult to know what's happening across the wire and on the hard drives of all their systems. Virtualization, cloud services, and mobile devices such as laptops, tablets, and phones are the foundation of this complexity. The Internet of Things complicates everything. More recently, because so many people are working remotely and often using vulnerable personal computers to access business systems makes, complexity has grown even more.

Time is an attacker's friend, and it's almost always on their side. By attacking through computers rather than in person, hackers have more control of the timing of their attacks. Attacks are not only carried out anonymously, but they can be carried out slowly over time, making them hard to detect. Quantum computing will make these attacks that much faster.

Attacks are frequently carried out after typical business hours, often in the middle of the night and (in the case of malicious users) from home. Defenses may be weaker after hours, with less physical security and less intrusion monitoring, when the typical network administrator or security guard is sleeping.

HACKING MAGAZINES

If you want detailed information on how some hackers work or want to keep up with the latest hacker methods, several magazines are worth checking out:

- *2600 — The Hacker Quarterly* (www.2600.com)
- *(IN)SECURE* magazine (www.helpnetsecurity.com/insecuremag-archive)
- *Hackin9* (https://hakin9.org)
- *PHRACK* (www.phrack.org/archives)

Malicious attackers usually learn from their mistakes. Every mistake moves them one step closer to breaking into someone's system. They use this knowledge when carrying out future attacks. As a security professional responsible for testing the security of your environment, you need to do the same.

Maintaining Anonymity

Smart attackers want to remain as low-key as possible. Covering their tracks is a priority, and their success often depends on remaining unnoticed. They want to avoid raising suspicion so that they can come back and access the systems in the future.

Hackers often remain anonymous by using one of the following resources:

» Borrowed or stolen remote desktop and virtual private network (VPN) accounts of friends or previous employers

» Public computers at libraries, schools, or hotel business centers

» Open wireless networks

» VPN software or open proxy servers on the Internet

» Anonymous or disposable email accounts

» Open email relays

» Infected computers (also called *zombies* or *bots)* at other organizations

» Workstations or servers on the victim's own network

If hackers use enough stepping stones for their attacks, they're practically impossible to trace. Luckily, one of your biggest concerns — the malicious user — generally isn't quite as savvy unless the hacker is a network or security administrator. In that case, you've got a serious situation on your hands. Without strong oversight, there's nothing you can do to stop hackers from wreaking havoc on your network.

Chapter **3**

Developing Your Security Testing Plan

s an IT or information security professional, you must plan your security assessment efforts before you start. Making a detailed plan doesn't mean that your testing must be elaborate — just that you're clear and concise about what to do. Given the seriousness of vulnerability and penetration testing, you should make this process as structured as possible.

Even if you test only a single web application or workgroup of computers, be sure to take the critical steps of establishing your goals, defining and documenting the scope of what you'll be testing, determining your testing standards, and gathering and familiarizing yourself with the proper tools for the task. This chapter covers these steps to help you create a positive environment to set yourself up for success.

Establishing Your Goals

You can't hit a target you can't see. Your testing plan needs goals. The main goal of vulnerability and penetration testing is to find the flaws in your systems from the perspective of the bad guys so that you can make your environment more secure. Then you can take this a step further:

>> **Define more specific goals.** Align these goals with your business objectives. Specify what you and management are trying to get from this process and what performance criteria you'll use to ensure that you're getting the most out of your testing.

>> **Create a specific schedule with start and end dates and the times your testing is to take place.** These dates and times are critical components of your overall plan.

REMEMBER

Before you begin any testing, you need everything in writing and approved. Document everything, and involve management in this process. Your best ally in your testing efforts is an executive who supports what you're doing.

The following questions can start the ball rolling when you define the goals for your security testing plan:

>> Does your testing support the mission of the business and its IT and security departments?

>> What business goals are met by performing this testing? These goals may include the following:

- Working through Service Organization Control (SOC) 2 audit requirements

- Meeting federal regulations, such as the Health Insurance Portability and Accountability Act (HIPAA) and the Payment Card Industry Data Security Standard (PCI DSS)

- Meeting contractual requirements of clients or business partners

- Maintaining the company's image

- Prepping for the internationally accepted security standard of ISO/IEC 27001:2013

>> How will this testing improve security, IT, and the business as a whole?

>> What information are you protecting (such as personal health information, intellectual property, confidential client information, or employees' private information)?

» How much money, time, and effort are you and your organization willing to spend on vulnerability and penetration testing?

» What specific deliverables will there be? *Deliverables* can include anything from high-level executive reports to detailed technical reports and write-ups on what you tested, along with specific findings and recommendations. You may also want to include your tested data, such as screenshots and other information gathered to help demonstrate the findings.

» What specific outcomes do you want? Desired outcomes include the justification for hiring or outsourcing security personnel, increasing your security budget, meeting compliance requirements, or installing new security technologies.

After you know your goals, document the steps you'll take to get there. If one goal is for the business to develop a competitive advantage to keep existing customers and attract new ones, determine the answers to these questions:

» When will you start your testing?

» Will your testing approach be *blind* (aka covert testing in which you know nothing about the systems you're testing) or *knowledge-based* (aka overt testing in which you're given specific information about the systems you're testing, such as IP addresses, hostnames, usernames, and passwords)?

TIP

I recommend the latter approach. If you're testing your own systems, this approach likely makes the most sense anyway.

» Will your testing be technical in nature, involve physical security assessments, or use social engineering?

» Will you be part of a larger security testing team (sometimes called a *tiger team* or *red team*)?

» Will you notify the affected parties of what you're doing and when you're doing it? If so, how?

REMEMBER

Customer notification is a critical issue. Many customers appreciate that you're taking steps to protect their information. Just make sure that you set everyone's expectations properly.

» How will you know whether customers care about what you're doing?

» How will you notify customers that the organization is taking steps to enhance the security of their information?

» What measurements can ensure that these efforts are paying off?

DO YOU NEED INSURANCE?

If you're an independent consultant or have a business with a team of security assessment professionals, consider getting professional liability insurance (also known as errors and omissions insurance) from an agent who specializes in business insurance coverage. This kind of insurance can be expensive if something goes awry during your work, and you need protection. Many clients require insurance before they will hire you to do the work.

Establishing your goals takes time, but you won't regret setting them. These goals are your road map. If you have any concerns, refer to these goals to make sure that you stay on track. You can find additional resources on goal setting and management in the appendix.

Determining Which Systems to Test

After you've established your overall goals, decide which systems to test. You may not want — or need — to assess the security of all your systems at the same time. Assessing the security of all your systems could be quite an undertaking and might lead to problems. You should eventually assess every computer and application you have, but whenever possible, break your projects into smaller chunks to make them more manageable, especially if you're just getting started. The Pareto principle (focusing on your highest-payoff tasks) should take precedence. You might need to answer questions such as these when deciding which systems to test based on a high-level risk analysis:

>> What are your most critical systems?

>> Which systems, if accessed without authorization, would cause the most trouble or suffer the greatest losses?

>> Which systems appear to be most vulnerable to attack?

>> Which systems are undocumented, are rarely administered, or are the ones you know the least about?

The following list includes devices, systems, and applications on which you might perform vulnerability and penetration tests:

>> Routers and switches

>> Firewalls, including their associated rulebases

>> Wireless access points

>> Web applications and APIs (hosted locally or in the cloud)

>> Workstations (desktops, laptops — running locally or at users' homes)

>> Servers, including database servers, email servers, and file servers (hosted locally or in the cloud)

>> Mobile devices (such as smartphones and tablets) that store confidential information

>> Physical security cameras and building access control systems

>> Cloud security policy configurations, such as those for Amazon Web Services (AWS)

>> Supervisory control and data acquisition (SCADA) and industrial control systems

The systems you test depend on several factors. If you have a small network, you can test everything. For larger organizations, consider testing only public-facing hosts such as email and web servers and their associated applications. Assuming you meet all outside requirements, the security testing process is somewhat flexible. Based on compliance regulations or demands from business partners and customers, you should decide what makes the most business sense or what you're required to do.

Start with the most seemingly vulnerable or highest-value systems, and consider these factors:

>> Whether the computer or application resides on the network or in the cloud and what compensating security controls might already exist

>> Which operating system (OS) and application(s) the system runs

>> The amount or type of critical information stored on the system

A previous information risk assessment, vulnerability scan, or business impact analysis may have generated answers to the preceding questions. If so, that documentation can help you identify systems for further testing. Bow Tie and Failure Modes and Effects Analysis (FMEA) are additional approaches for determining what to test.

TIP

Vulnerability and penetration testing goes deeper than basic vulnerability scans and higher-level information risk assessments. With proper testing, you might start by gleaning information on all systems — including the organization as a whole — and then further assess the most vulnerable systems. Book 5, Chapter 4 discusses the vulnerability and penetration testing methodology.

Another factor that helps you decide where to start is your assessment of the systems that have the greatest visibility. It may make more sense (at least initially) to focus on a database or file server that stores critical client information than to concentrate on a firewall or web server that hosts marketing information, for example.

ATTACK-TREE ANALYSIS

Attack-tree analysis, also known as threat modeling, is the process of creating a flow-chart-type mapping of how malicious attackers would attack a system. Attack trees are used in higher-level information risk analyses; they're also used by security-savvy development teams for planning new software projects. If you want to take your security testing to the next level by thoroughly planning your attacks, working methodically, and being more professional, attack-tree analysis is the tool you need.

The only drawback is that attack trees can take considerable time to create and require a fair amount of expertise. Why sweat the process, though, when a computer can do a lot of the work for you? A commercial tool called SecurITree, by Amenaza Technologies Ltd. (www.amenaza.com), specializes in attack-tree analysis. You could also use Microsoft Visio (www.microsoft.com/en-us/microsoft-365/visio/flowchart-software)) or SmartDraw (www.smartdraw.com). The following figure shows a sample SecurITree attack-tree analysis.

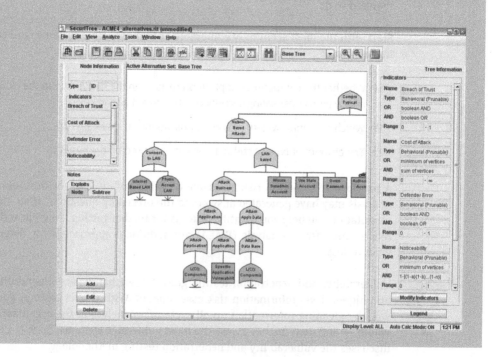

Creating Testing Standards

One miscommunication or slip-up can send systems crashing during your security testing. No one wants that to happen. To prevent mishaps, develop and document testing standards. These standards should include

» When the tests are performed, along with the overall timeline

» Which tests are performed

» How much knowledge of the systems you require in advance

» How the tests are performed and from what source IP addresses (if performed via an external source via the Internet)

» What to do when a major vulnerability is discovered

This list is general best practices; you can apply more standards for your situation. The following sections describe these best practices in more detail.

Timing your tests

They say that "it's all in the timing," especially when performing security tests. Make sure to perform tests that minimize disruption to business processes, information systems, and people. You want to avoid harmful situations such as miscommunicating the timing of tests and causing a denial of service (DoS) attack against a high-traffic e-commerce site in the middle of the day or performing password-cracking tests in the middle of the night that end up locking accounts and keeping people from logging in the next morning. It's amazing what a 12-hour time difference (2 p.m. during major production versus 2 a.m. during a slower period) can make when testing your systems. Even having people in different time zones can create issues. Everyone on the project needs to agree on a detailed timeline before you begin. Having team members' agreement puts everyone on the same page and sets correct expectations.

TIP

If required, notify your cloud service providers and hosting co-location providers of your testing. Many companies require such notification — and often approval — in advance before they allow testing. These companies have firewalls or intrusion prevention systems (IPSes) in place to detect malicious behavior. If your provider knows that you're conducting tests, it may be less likely that they block your traffic, and you'll get better results. They might even preapprove your source IP addresses, which is recommended.

Your testing timeline should include specific short-term dates and any specific milestones. You can enter your timeline in a simple spreadsheet program, a project-focused Gantt chart, or in a larger project plan. If you're testing client networks, you might list these dates and time frames in a statement of work or in a simple email. That's often all that's needed.

A timeline such as the following keeps things simple and provides a reference during testing:

Test Performed	Start Time	Projected End Time
Web application vulnerability scanning	June 1, 21:00 EST	June 2, 07:00
Network host vulnerability scanning	June 2, 10:00 EST	June 3, 02:00
Network host vulnerability analysis/ exploitation	June 3, 08:00 EST	June 6, 17:00

Running specific tests

You may have been charged with performing some general vulnerability scans, or you may want to perform specific tests such as cracking passwords or trying to gain access to a web application. You may even be performing a social engineering test or assessing Windows systems on the network. However you test, you don't necessarily need to reveal the specifics of the testing. Just high-level information should suffice. Even when your manager or client doesn't require detailed records of your tests, document what you're doing at a high level. Documenting your testing can eliminate potential miscommunication and keep you out of hot water. Also, you may need documentation as evidence if you uncover malfeasance.

TIP

Enabling logging on the systems you test along with the tools you use can provide evidence of what and when you test. Such logging may be overkill, but you could even record screen actions by using a tool such as TechSmith's Camtasia Studio (www.techsmith.com/video-editor.html).

Sometimes, you know the general tests that you perform, but if you use automated tools, it may be impossible to understand every test completely. This situation is especially true when the software you're using receives real-time vulnerability updates and patches from the vendor each time you run it. The potential for frequent updates underscores the importance of reading the documentation and readme files that come with the tools you use.

Conducting blind versus knowledge assessments

Having some knowledge of the systems you're testing is generally the best approach, but it's not required. Having a basic understanding of the systems you hack can protect you and others. Obtaining this knowledge shouldn't be difficult if you're testing your own in-house systems. If you're testing a client's systems, you may have to dig a little deeper into how the systems work so that you're familiar with them. A small number of clients may ask for a full blind assessment, but most people are scared of them. Blind assessments can be valuable, but the type of assessment you carry out depends on your needs.

The best approach is to plan on *unlimited* attacks, wherein any test is fair game, possibly even including DoS testing. (Just confirm that in advance!) The bad guys aren't poking around on your systems within a limited scope, so why should you?

Consider whether the tests should be performed so that they're undetected by network administrators and any managed security service providers or related vendors. Though not required, this practice should be considered, especially for social engineering and physical security tests. Book 5, Chapters 6 and 7 outline specific tests for those purposes.

WARNING

If too many insiders know about your testing, they might improve their habits enough to create a false sense of vigilance, which can negate the hard work you put into the testing. This is especially true for phishing testing. Still, it's almost always a good idea to inform the owner of the system, who may not be your sponsor. If you're doing this testing for clients, *always* have a main point of contact — preferably someone who has decision-making authority.

Picking your location

The tests you perform dictate where you run them from. Your goal is to test your systems from locations that malicious hackers or insiders can access. You can't predict whether you'll be attacked by someone inside or outside your network, so cover your bases as much as you can. Combine external (public Internet) tests and internal (private network) tests.

You can perform some tests, such as password cracking and network infrastructure assessments, from your office. For external tests that require network connectivity, you may have to go off-site (a good excuse to work from home), use an external proxy server, or simply use guest Wi-Fi that might have a separate Internet connection. Many security vendors' vulnerability scanners can be run from the cloud. If you can assign an available public IP address to your computer, plug into the network outside the firewall for a hacker's-eye view of your systems. Just make sure that system is secure because it will be exposed to the world!

Internal tests are easy because you need only physical access to the building and the network. Just plug right in and have at it. If you dig around from the perspective of a visitor or guest, you might find an open network port that provides full access to your network. This is often a huge vulnerability, especially if the public has full access — such as in a hospital lobby or waiting room area.

Responding to vulnerabilities you find

Determine ahead of time whether you'll stop or keep going when you find a critical security hole. You don't need to keep testing forever. Just follow the path you're on until you've met your objectives or reached your goals. When in doubt, have a specific goal in mind and stop when you meet that goal.

REMEMBER

If you don't have goals, how are you going to know when you reach your security testing destination?

If you discover a major hole, such as SQL injection on an external web application or a missing patch that provides full remote access to a critical system, contact the necessary people as soon as possible so that they can begin fixing the issue right away. The necessary people may be software developers, product or project managers, or even Chief Information Officers in charge of it all. If you wait a few hours, days, or weeks, someone may exploit the vulnerability and cause damage that could have been prevented, potentially creating bigger legal issues.

Making silly assumptions

You've heard what you make of yourself when you assume things. Even so, you make assumptions when you test your systems. Here are some examples of those assumptions:

>> All the computers, networks, applications, and people are available when you're testing. (They won't be.)

>> You have all the proper testing tools. (When you start your testing — at least early on in your journey — you'll be lucky to have half of what you actually end up needing.)

>> The testing tools you use minimize your chances of crashing the systems you test. (Nope, especially if you don't know how to use them properly.)

>> You understand the likelihood that you're going to overlook something. (You will.)

>> You know the risks of your tests. (The risks can be especially high when you don't plan properly.)

Document all assumptions and ensure all the right people are onboard. You won't regret doing that.

Selecting Security Assessment Tools

Which security assessment tools you need depend on the tests you're going to run. You can perform some security tests with a pair of sneakers, a telephone, and a basic workstation on the network, but comprehensive testing is easier when you have good, dedicated tools.

REMEMBER

The tools discussed in this book aren't malware, based on what's known of them. The tools and even their websites may be flagged as such by certain antimalware and web filtering software, but they're not malware. For example, Metasploit is often flagged as malware when it's a completely legitimate security testing tool. This book covers only legitimate tools, many of which have been in use by professionals for years. If you experience trouble downloading, installing, or running the tools covered in this book, consider configuring your system to allow them through or otherwise trust their execution. Keep in mind that this book can't make any promises. Use checksums where possible by comparing the original MD5 or SHA checksum with the one you get using a tool such as CheckSum Tool (http://sourceforge.net/projects/checksumtool). A criminal could always inject malicious code into the actual tools, so there's no guarantee of security. You knew that anyway, right?

TIP

If you're not sure what tools to use, fear not. This book introduces a wide variety of tools — free and commercial — that you can use to accomplish your tasks. Book 5, Chapter 1 provides a list of commercial, freeware, and open-source tools. The appendix contains a comprehensive list of tools.

It's important to know what each tool can and can't do, as well as how to use each one. Consider reading the manual or help files. Unfortunately, some tools have limited documentation, which can be frustrating. You can search forums and post a message if you're having trouble with a specific tool, and you may get some help.

WARNING

Security vulnerability scanning and exploit tools can be hazardous to your network's health. Be careful when you use them. Always make sure that you understand what they are capable of before you use them. Try your tools on test systems if you're not sure how to use them. Even if you're familiar with the tools, this precaution can prevent DoS conditions and data loss on your production systems.

If freeware and open-source security tools end up causing you more headaches than they're worth or don't do what you need them to do, consider purchasing commercial alternatives, which are often easier to use and typically generate much better reports. Some commercial tools are expensive, but their ease of use and functionality may justify the initial and ongoing costs. In most situations with security tools, you get what you pay for.

Chapter **4**

Hacking Methodology

Before you dive headfirst into your security testing, it's critical to have a methodology to work from. Vulnerability and penetration testing involves more than poking and prodding a system or network. Proven techniques can guide you along the hacking highway and ensure that you end up at the right destination. Using a methodology that supports your testing goals separates you from the amateurs. A methodology also helps ensure that you make the most of your time and effort.

Setting the Stage for Testing

In the past, a lot of security assessment techniques involved manual processes. Now certain vulnerability scanners automate various tasks, from testing to reporting to remediation validation (the process of determining whether a vulnerability was fixed). Some vulnerability scanners can even help you take corrective actions. These tools allow you to focus more on performing the tests and less on the specific steps involved. Following a general methodology and understanding what's going on behind the scenes will help you find the things that really matter.

Think logically — like a programmer, a radiologist, or a home inspector — to dissect and interact with all the system components to see how they work. You gather information, often in many small pieces, and assemble the pieces of the puzzle. You start at point A with several goals in mind, run your tests (repeating many steps along the way), and move closer until you discover security vulnerabilities at point B.

The process used for such testing is the same as the one that a malicious attacker would use. The primary differences lie in the goals and how you achieve them. Today's attacks can come from any angle against any system — not just from the perimeter of your network and the Internet as you may have been taught in the past. Eventually, you'll want to test every possible entry point, including partner, vendor, and customer networks, as well as home users, wireless networks, and mobile devices. Any human being, computer system, or physical component that protects your computer systems — both local and in the cloud — is fair game for attack, and it needs to be tested eventually.

TIP

When you start rolling with your testing, you may want to keep a log of the tests you perform, the tools you use, the systems you test, and your results. This information can help you do the following:

>> Track what worked in previous tests and why.

>> Prove what you did.

>> Correlate your testing with firewalls, intrusion prevention systems (IPSes), and other log files if trouble or questions arise.

>> Document your findings.

TIP

In addition to general notes, taking screen captures of your results (using Snagit, Snip & Sketch, or a similar tool) whenever possible is very helpful. These shots will come in handy later if you need to show proof of what occurred, and they'll also be useful as you generate your final report. Also, depending on the tools you use, these screen captures may be your only evidence of vulnerabilities or exploits when the time comes to write your final report. Book 5, Chapter 3 lists the general steps involved in creating and documenting a security testing plan.

Your main tasks are to find the vulnerabilities and to simulate the information gathering and system compromises carried out by someone with malicious intent — a partial attack on one computer, perhaps, or a comprehensive attack against the entire network. Generally, you look for weaknesses that malicious users and external attackers might exploit. Assess both external and internal systems (including processes and procedures that involve computers, networks, people, and physical infrastructures). Look for vulnerabilities. Check how all your systems interconnect and how private systems and information are (or aren't) protected from untrusted elements.

These steps don't include specific information on the methods that you use for social engineering and assessing physical security, but the techniques are the same. Book 5, Chapters 6 and 7 cover social engineering and physical security in more detail.

TIP

If you're performing a security assessment for a client, you may go the *blind* assessment route, which means that you start with just the company name and no other information. This blind assessment approach allows you to start from the ground up and gives you a better sense of the information and systems that malicious attackers can access publicly. Whether you choose to assess blindly (covertly) or overtly, keep in mind that the blind way of testing can take longer, and you may have an increased chance of missing some (or many) security vulnerabilities. Blind assessment isn't the ideal testing method, but some people may want it.

As a security professional, you may not have to worry about covering your tracks or evading IPSes or related security controls because everything you do is legitimate, but you may want to test systems stealthily. This book discusses techniques that hackers use to conceal their actions and outline some countermeasures for concealment techniques.

Seeing What Others See

Getting an outside look can turn up a ton of information about your organization and systems that others can see, and you do so through a process often called *footprinting.* Here's how to gather the information:

>> Use a web browser to search for information about your organization. Search engines, such as Google and Bing, are great places to start.

>> Run network scans, probe open ports, and seek out vulnerabilities to determine specific information about your systems. As an insider, you can use port scanners, network discovery tools, and vulnerability scanners (such as Nmap, SoftPerfect Network Scanner, and GFI LanGuard) to see what's accessible and to whom.

TIP

Whether you search generally or probe more technically, limit the amount of information you gather based on what's reasonable for you. You might spend an hour, a day, or a week gathering this information. How much time you spend depends on the size of your organization and the complexity of the information systems you're testing.

The amount of information you can gather about an organization's business and information systems can be staggering and often widely available. Your job is to find out what's out there. This process is often referred to as open-source intelligence (OSINT). From social media to search engines to dedicated intelligence-gathering tools, quite a bit of information is available on network and information vulnerabilities if you look in the right places. This information potentially allows malicious attackers and employees to access sensitive information and target specific areas of the organization, including systems, departments, and key people. Book 5, Chapter 5 covers information gathering in detail.

Scanning Systems

Active information gathering produces more details about your network and helps you see your systems from an attacker's perspective. You can do the following things:

>> Use the information provided by WHOIS searches to test other closely related IP addresses and host names. When you map and gather information about a network, you see how its systems are laid out. This information includes determining IP addresses, host names (typically external but occasionally internal), running protocols, open ports, available shares, and running services and applications.

>> Scan internal hosts when they're within the scope of your testing. (They really ought to be because that's where the large majority of vulnerabilities exist.) These hosts may not be visible to outsiders (you hope they're not), but you absolutely need to test them to see what rogue (or even curious or misguided) employees, other insiders, and even malware controlled by outside parties can access. A worst-case situation is that the intruder has set up shop on the inside. Just to be safe, examine your internal systems for weaknesses.

TIP

If you're not completely comfortable scanning your systems, consider using a lab with test systems or a system running virtual machine software, such as the following:

>> VMware Workstation Pro (www.vmware.com/products/workstation-pro.html)

>> VirtualBox, an open-source virtual-machine alternative (www.virtualbox.org)

Hosts

Scan and document specific hosts that are accessible from the Internet and your internal network. Start by pinging specific host names or IP addresses with one of these tools:

>> The basic ping utility that's built into your operating system (OS).

>> A third-party utility that allows you to ping multiple addresses at the same time, such as NetScanTools Pro (www.netscantools.com) for Windows and fping (http://fping.sourceforge.net) for Linux.

>> The site WhatIsMyIP.com (www.whatismyip.com) shows how your gateway IP address appears on the Internet. Just browse to that site and the public IP address of your firewall or router appears. This information gives you an idea of the outermost IP address that the world sees.

Open ports

Scan for open ports by using network scanning and analysis tools such as the following:

>> Scan network ports with NetScanTools Pro or Nmap (https://nmap.org).

>> Monitor network traffic with a network analyzer, such as Omnipeek (www.liveaction.com/products/omnipeek-network-protocol-analyzer/) or Wireshark (www.wireshark.org).

Scanning internally is easy. Simply connect your PC to the network, load the software, and fire away. Just be aware of network segmentation and internal IPSes that may impede your work.

Scanning from outside your network takes a few more steps. The easiest way to connect and get an outside-in perspective is to assign your computer a public IP address and plug that system into a switch on the public side of your firewall or router. Physically, the computer isn't on the Internet looking in, but this type of connection works the same way as long as it's outside your network perimeter. You can also do an outside-in scan from home, from a remote office, or even via a laptop connected to your cellphone hotspot.

Determining What's Running on Open Ports

As a security professional, you need to gather the things that count when scanning your systems. You can often identify the following information:

- Protocols in use, such as Domain Name System and NetBIOS
- Services running on the hosts, such as email, web, and database systems
- Available remote access services, such as Remote Desktop Protocol, telnet, and Secure Shell (SSH)
- Encrypted network services such as SSL/TLS and IPsec
- Permissions and authentication requirements for network shares

You can look for the following sample open ports (which your network scanner reports as accessible or open):

- Ping (ICMP echo) replies, showing that ICMP traffic is allowed to and from the host.
- TCP port 21, showing that FTP could be running.
- TCP port 23, showing that Telnet could be running.
- TCP ports 25 or 465 (SMTP and SMPTS), 110 or 995 (POP3 and POP3S), or 143 or 993 (IMAP and IMAPS), showing that an email server could be running.
- TCP/UDP port 53, showing that a DNS server could be running.
- TCP ports 80, 443, and 8080, showing that a web server or web proxy could be running.
- TCP/UDP ports 135, 137, 138, 139, and, especially, 445, showing that a Windows host could be running.

Thousands of ports can be open — 65,534 each for both TCP (Transmission Control Protocol) and UDP (User Datagram Protocol), to be exact. A continually updated listing of all well-known port numbers (ports 0–1023) and registered port numbers (ports 1024–49151), with their associated protocols and services, is located at www.iana.org/assignments/service-names-port-numbers/service-names-port-numbers.txt.

TIP

If a service doesn't respond on a TCP or UDP port, that result doesn't mean that the service isn't running. You may have to dig further to find out.

If you detect a web server running on the system that you test, you might be able to check the software version by using one of the following methods:

- ** Type the site's name followed by a page that you know doesn't exist, such as www.*your_domain*.com/1234.html. Many web servers return an error page showing detailed version information.

- ** Use Netcraft's What's That Site Running? search utility (https://sitereport.netcraft.com/), which connects to your server from the Internet and displays the web-server version and operating system, as shown in Figure 4-1.

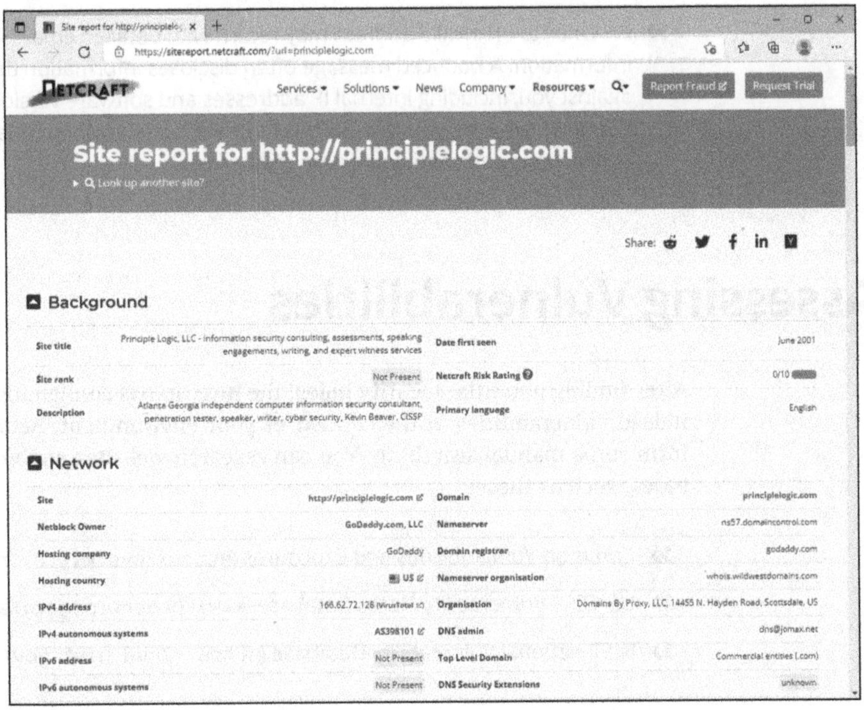

FIGURE 4-1: Netcraft's web server version utility.

You can dig deeper for more specific information on your hosts by using these tools:

- ** NMapWin (https://sourceforge.net/projects/nmapwin) can determine the system OS version.

- ** A scanning and enumeration tool such as SoftPerfect Network Scanner (www.softperfect.com/products/networkscanner) can extract users, groups, and file and share permissions directly from Windows.

>> Many systems return useful banner information when you connect to a service or application running on a port. If you Telnet to an email server on port 25 by entering **telnet mail.your_domain.com 25** at a command prompt, you may see something like this:

```
220 mail.your_domain.com ESMTP all_the_version_info_
    you_need_to_hack Ready
```

Most email servers return detailed information, such as the version and the current service pack installed. After you have this information, you (and the bad guys) can determine the vulnerabilities of the system from some of the websites listed in the next section.

>> An email to an invalid address may return with detailed email header information. A bounced message often discloses information that can be used against you, including internal IP addresses and software versions. On certain Windows systems, you can use this information to establish unauthenticated connections and sometimes even map drives.

Assessing Vulnerabilities

After finding potential security holes, the next step is confirming whether they're indeed vulnerabilities in the context of your environment. Before you test, perform some manual searching. You can research websites and vulnerability databases, such as these:

>> Common Vulnerabilities and Exposures (http://cve.mitre.org/cve)

>> US-CERT Vulnerability Notes Database (www.kb.cert.org/vuls)

>> NIST National Vulnerability Database (https://nvd.nist.gov)

These sites list known vulnerabilities — at least, the formally classified ones. Many other vulnerabilities are more generic in nature and can't easily be classified. If you can't find a vulnerability documented on one of these sites, search the vendor's site. You can also find a list of commonly exploited vulnerabilities at www.cisecurity.org/controls/. This site contains the SANS Critical Security Controls consensus list, which is compiled and updated by the SANS organization.

If you don't want to research your potential vulnerabilities and can jump right into testing, you have a couple of options:

» **Manual assessment:** You can assess the potential vulnerabilities by connecting to the ports that are exposing the service or application and poking around in these ports. You should manually assess certain systems (such as web applications). The vulnerability reports in the preceding databases often disclose how to do this, at least generally. If you have a lot of free time, manually performing these tests may work for you.

» **Automated assessment:** Manual assessments are great ways to learn, but people usually don't have time to complete most manual steps. If you're like me, you'll scan for vulnerabilities automatically when you can and dig around manually as needed.

Many great vulnerability assessment scanners test for flaws on specific platforms (such as Windows and Linux) and types of networks (wired or wireless). They test for specific system vulnerabilities and may focus on standards such as the SANS Critical Security Controls and the Open Web Application Security Project (www. owasp.org). Some scanners map the business logic within a web application; others map a view of the network; others help software developers test for code flaws. The drawback to these tools is that they find only individual vulnerabilities; they don't necessarily aggregate and correlate vulnerabilities across an entire network. This task is where your skills and the methodologies shared in this book come into play.

TIP

One of my favorite security tools is a vulnerability scanner called Nessus by Tenable (www.tenable.com/products/nessus). It's both a port scanner and vulnerability assessment tool, and it offers a great deal of help for vulnerability management. You can run one-time scans immediately or schedule scans to run on a periodic basis.

As with most good security tools, you pay for Nessus. It's one of the least expensive tools. A free version, dubbed Nessus Essentials, is available for scanning smaller networks with fewer features. Additional vulnerability scanners that work well include QualysGuard (www.qualys.com) and GFI LanGuard (http://www.gfi. com/products-and-solutions/network-security-solutions/gfi-languard).

REMEMBER

Assessing vulnerabilities with a tool such as Nessus requires follow-up expertise. You can't rely on the scanner results alone. You must validate the vulnerabilities that the tool reports. Study the reports to base your recommendations on the context and criticality of the tested systems. You'll find that higher-end vulnerability scanners provide proof and related information to help you in your validation efforts.

Penetrating the System

You can use identified security vulnerabilities to do the following:

>> Gain further information about the host and its data

>> Obtain a remote command prompt

>> Start or stop certain services or applications

>> Access other systems

>> Disable logging or other security controls

>> Capture screenshots

>> Access sensitive files

>> Send an email as the administrator

>> Perform SQL injection

>> Launch a denial of service attack

>> Upload a file or create a backdoor user account proving the exploitation of a vulnerability

Metasploit (www.metasploit.com) is great for exploiting many of the vulnerabilities you find and allows you to fully penetrate many types of systems. Ideally, you've already made your decision about whether to fully exploit the vulnerabilities you find. If you have chosen to do so, a screenshot of a remote command prompt on a vulnerable system via Metasploit is a great piece of evidence demonstrating vulnerability.

REMEMBER

If you want to delve further into best practices for vulnerability and penetration testing methodologies, check out the Open Source Security Testing Methodology Manual (www.isecom.org/research.html). The Penetration Testing Execution Standard (www.pentest-standard.org/index.php/Main_Page) and PCI DSS Penetration Testing Guidance (http://www.pcisecuritystandards.org/documents/Penetration-Testing-Guidance-v1_1.pdf) are great resources as well.

Chapter **5**

Information Gathering

One of the most important aspects in determining how your organization is at risk is finding out what information about your business and your systems is publicly available. Gathering this information is such an important part of your overall methodology that the subject deserves a dedicated chapter.

This chapter outlines some free, easy ways to see what the world sees about you and your organization. You may be tempted to bypass these Open Source Intelligence (OSINT) exercises in favor of the cooler, sexier technical security flaws, but don't skip this step! Gathering this type of information is critical and is often where many security breaches begin.

Gathering Public Information

The amount of online information you can gather about an organization's business, people, and network is staggering. To see for yourself, use the techniques outlined in the following sections to gather information about your own organization.

Social media

Social media sites are the new means for businesses to interact online. Perusing the following sites can provide untold details on any business and its people:

>> Facebook, now known as Meta (www.facebook.com)

>> LinkedIn (www.linkedin.com)

>> Twitter (twitter.com)

>> YouTube (www.youtube.com)

Employees are often very forthcoming about what they do for work, details about their business, and even what they think about their bosses — especially after throwing back a few when their social filters have gone off track! You can also find interesting insights based on what people say about their former employers via Glassdoor (www.glassdoor.com/Reviews/index.htm), Crunchbase (www.crunchbase.com), and Google and other online reviews.

Web search

Performing a web search or simply browsing your organization's website can turn up the following information:

>> Employee names and contact information

>> Important company dates

>> Incorporation filings

>> Securities and Exchange Commission (SEC) filings (for public companies)

>> Press releases about physical moves, organizational changes, and new products

>> Mergers and acquisitions

>> Patents and trademarks

>> Presentations, articles, webcasts, or webinars (which often reveal sensitive information — often ironically labeled *confidential*)

TIP

Bing (www.bing.com) and Google (www.google.com) ferret out information — in everything from word processing documents to graphics files — on any publicly accessible computer. Also, they're free. Google is my favorite. Entire books have been written about using Google for advanced searches, so expect any criminal hacker to be quite experienced in using this tool, including against you.

With Google, you can search the Internet in several ways:

>> **Typing keywords:** This kind of search often reveals hundreds and sometimes millions of pages of information — such as files, phone numbers, and addresses — that you never guessed were available.

>> **Performing advanced web searches:** Google's advanced search options can find sites that link back to your company's website. This type of search often reveals a lot of information about partners, vendors, clients, and other affiliations.

>> **Using switches to dig deeper into a website:** If you want to find a certain word or file on your website, simply enter a line like one of the following into Google:

```
site:www.your_domain.com keyword
site:www.your_domain.com filename
```

You can even do a generic file-type search across the Internet to see what turns up:

```
filetype:swf company_name
```

Use the preceding search to find Adobe Flash .swf files, which can be downloaded and decompiled to reveal sensitive information that can be used against your business.

Use the following search to hunt for PDF documents containing sensitive information that can be used against your business:

```
filetype:pdf company_name confidential
```

Shodan (www.shodan.io) is another popular tool for searching for information and systems that are exposed to the Internet and may be revealing sensitive business assets. Shodan will help uncover systems associated with your domains that you may not have known about, including top ports and Internet service organizations associated with your domains.

Web crawling

Web-crawling utilities, such as HTTrack Website Copier (www.httrack.com), can mirror your website by downloading every publicly accessible file from it, similar to the way a web vulnerability scanner crawls the website it's testing. Then you can inspect that copy of the website offline, digging into the following:

>> The website layout and configuration

>> Directories and files that may not otherwise be obvious or readily accessible

>> The HTML and script source code of web pages

>> Comment fields

Comment fields often contain useful information such as the names and email addresses of the developers and IT personnel, server names, software versions, internal IP addressing schemes, and general comments about how the code works. In case you're interested, you can prevent some types of web crawling by creating Disallow entries in your web server's robots.txt file, as outlined at www.w3.org/TR/html4/appendix/notes.html. You can even enable web tarpitting in certain firewalls and intrusion prevention systems. Tarpitting stops attacks in their tracks and prevents the bad guys from moving forward as if walking through a tar pit. Crawlers (and attackers) that are smart enough, however, can find ways around these controls.

TIP

Contact information for developers and IT personnel is great for social engineering attacks. Book 5, Chapter 6 covers social engineering.

An additional tool you can use for discovering internal emails for business is called Hunter (hunter.io). This is a great way to find contact information to use in phishing or other social engineering campaigns.

Websites

The following websites may provide specific information about an organization and its employees:

>> Try the following government and business websites:

- Detailed information about public companies can be found at www.dnb.com/products/marketing-sales/dnb-hoovers.htm and https://finance.yahoo.com.

- SEC filings of public companies can be found at www.sec.gov/edgar.shtml.

- Patent and trademark registrations can be found at www.uspto.gov.

- Patent search capabilities can be found at /https://patentscope.wipo.int/search/en/search.jsf.

- The website for your state's secretary of state or a similar organization might offer incorporation and corporate-officer information.

>> Background checks and other personal information can be found at the following locations:

- LexisNexis (www.lexisnexis.com)

- Zabasearch (www.zabasearch.com)

Mapping the Network

As part of mapping out your network, you can search public databases and resources to see what other people know about your systems.

WHOIS

The best starting point is to perform a WHOIS lookup by using any of the tools available on the Internet. In case you're not familiar with it, WHOIS is a protocol you can use to query online databases such as Domain Name System (DNS) registries to find out more about domain names and IP address blocks. You may have used WHOIS to check whether a particular Internet domain name was available.

For security testing, WHOIS provides the following information that can give a hacker a leg up in starting a social engineering attack or scanning a network:

>> Internet domain name registration information, such as contact names, phone numbers, and mailing addresses

>> DNS servers responsible for your domain

You can look up WHOIS information at the following places:

>> WHOIS.net (www.whois.net)

>> A domain registrar's site (such as www.godaddy.com)

>> Your Internet service provider's technical support page

Two of my favorite WHOIS tool websites are DNSstuff (www.dnsstuff.com) and MXToolBox (mxtoolbox.com). For example, you can run DNS queries directly from MXToolBox to do the following:

>> Display general domain registration information

>> Show which host processes email and is allowed to send emails for a domain (the Mail Exchanger [MX] record and a Sender Policy Framework [SPF] record, respectively)

>> Map the location of specific hosts

>> Determine whether hosts are listed on public blocklists

An inexpensive commercial tool called SmartWhois (www.tamos.com/products/smartwhois) is handy to use for WHOIS lookups. A great site for both free and paid Internet domain queries is www.mxtoolbox.com. Another commercial product called NetScanTools Pro (www.netscantools.com) is excellent at gathering such information, among many other things.

The following list shows various lookup sites for other categories:

>> **U.S. government:** https://domains.dotgov.gov/dotgov-web/registration/whois.xhtml?_m=3

>> **AFRINIC:** https://afrinic.net/ (Regional Internet Registry for Africa)

>> **APNIC:** www.apnic.net/about-apnic/whois_search (Regional Internet Registry for the Asia Pacific Region)

>> **ARIN:** http://whois.arin.net/ui (Regional Internet Registry for North America, a portion of the Caribbean, and subequatorial Africa)

>> **LACNIC:** lacnic.net/cgi-bin/lacnic/whois (Latin American and Caribbean Internet Addresses Registry)

>> **RIPE Network Coordination Centre:** apps.db.ripe.net/search/query.html (Europe, Central Asia, African countries north of the equator, and the Middle East)

If you're not sure where to look for a specific country, www.nro.net/list-of-country-codes-and-rirs-ordered-by-country-code/ has a reference guide.

Privacy policies

Check your website's privacy policy. A good practice is to let your site's users know what information is collected and how it's being protected but nothing more. Many privacy policies divulge a lot of technical details on security and related systems that shouldn't be made public.

WARNING

Make sure that the people who write your privacy policies (often, nontechnical lawyers) don't divulge too many details about your information security program or infrastructure. Be sure they don't reveal, for example, the brand and model of firewall you use, or any other technical information about your network and system architecture. This type of information could certainly be used against you by the bad guys — not a good idea.

Chapter **6**

Social Engineering

ocial engineering takes advantage of what's likely the weakest link in any organization's information security defenses: people. Social engineering is people hacking; it involves maliciously exploiting the trusting nature of human beings to obtain information that can be used for personal — and often political — gain.

Even with the challenges society has with expediency (wanting things now, no matter what the cost) and lack of critical thinking (or, just *not* thinking), social engineering is one of the toughest hacks to perpetrate because it takes bravado and skill to come across as trustworthy to a stranger. By far, it's also the toughest thing to protect against because, again, people are involved, and they're often making their own security decisions.

This chapter explores the consequences of social engineering, techniques for your own security testing efforts, and specific countermeasures to defend against social engineering.

Introducing Social Engineering

In a social engineering scenario, those with ill intent pose as someone else to gain information that they likely couldn't access otherwise. Then they take the information obtained from their victims and wreak havoc on network resources, steal or delete files, and even commit corporate espionage or some other form of fraud against the organization they attack. Social engineering is different from *physical security* exploits, such as shoulder surfing and dumpster diving, but the two types of hacking are related and often are used in tandem.

Here are some examples of social engineering:

>> **"Support personnel"** claiming that they need to install a patch or new version of software on a user's computer, talking the user into downloading the software, and obtaining remote control of the system.

>> **"Vendors"** claiming to need to update the organization's accounting package or phone system, asking for the administrator password, and obtaining full access.

>> **"Employees"** notifying the security desk that they have lost their access badge to the data center, receiving a set of keys from security, and obtaining unauthorized access to physical and electronic information.

>> **"Phishing emails"** sent to gather the user IDs and passwords of unsuspecting recipients or to plant malware on their computers. These attacks can be generic in nature or more targeted — something called *spearphishing* attacks. The criminals use those login credentials or malware to gain access to the network, capture intellectual property, encrypt files for ransom, and so on.

Sometimes, social engineers act like confident, knowledgeable managers or executives. At other times, they play the roles of extremely uninformed or naïve employees. They also may pose as outsiders, such as IT consultants or maintenance workers. Social engineers are great at adapting to their audience. It takes a special type of personality to pull this trick off, often resembling that of a sociopath.

REMEMBER

Effective information security — especially the security required for fighting social engineering — often begins and ends with your users. Technical controls are available that can help fight social engineering; however, never forget that basic human communications and interaction have a profound effect on the level of security in your organization at any given time. The *candy-security* analogy is "hard, crunchy outside; soft, chewy inside." The *hard, crunchy outside* is the layer of mechanisms — such as firewalls, intrusion prevention systems, and endpoint security controls — that organizations typically rely on to secure their information. The *soft, chewy inside* is the people and the processes inside the organization. If the bad guys can get past the thick outer layer, they can compromise the (mostly) defenseless inner layer.

Starting Your Social Engineering Tests

Social engineering is an art and a science. Social engineering takes great skill to perform as a security professional and is highly dependent on your personality and overall knowledge of the organization.

TIP

If social engineering isn't natural for you, consider using the information in this chapter for educational purposes to find out how to best defend against it. Don't hesitate to hire a third party to perform this testing if doing so makes the best business sense for now.

REMEMBER

Social engineering can harm people's jobs and reputations, and confidential information could be leaked, especially when phishing tests are performed. Plan things, and proceed with caution.

You can perform social engineering attacks in millions of ways. From walking through the front door purporting to be someone you're not to launching an all-out email phishing campaign, the world is your oyster. For this reason, and because training specific behaviors in a single chapter is next to impossible, this chapter doesn't provide how-to instructions for carrying out social engineering attacks. Instead, it describes specific social engineering scenarios that are known to work well. You can tailor the same tricks and techniques to your specific situation.

An outsider to the organization might perform certain social engineering techniques such as physical intrusion tests best. If you perform these tests against your own organization, acting as an outsider might be difficult if everyone knows you. This risk of recognition may not be a problem in larger organizations, but if you have a small, close-knit company, people may catch on.

REMEMBER

You can outsource social engineering testing to an outside firm or even have a trusted colleague perform the tests for you.

Knowing Why Attackers Use Social Engineering

People use social engineering to break into systems and attain information because it's often the simplest way for them to get what they're looking for. They'd much rather have someone provide login credentials or literally open the door to the organization than physically break in and risk being caught. Security technologies such as firewalls and access controls won't stop a determined social engineer.

Many social engineers perform their attacks slowly to avoid suspicion. Social engineers gather bits of information over time and use the information to create a broader picture of the organization they're trying to manipulate. Therein lies one of their greatest assets: time. They've got nothing but time and will take the proper amount necessary to ensure that their attacks are successful. Alternatively, some social engineering attacks can be performed with a quick phone call or email. The methods used depend on the attacker's style and abilities. Either way, you're at a disadvantage.

Social engineers know that many organizations don't have good patch management, full network visibility, incident response plans, or security awareness programs, and they take advantage of these weaknesses.

Social engineers often know a little about a lot of things — both inside and outside their target organizations — because this knowledge helps them in their efforts. Thanks to social media platforms such as LinkedIn, Facebook, and other online resources discussed in Book 5, Chapter 5, every tidbit of information that social engineers need is often at their disposal. The more information social engineers gain about organizations, the easier it is for them to pose as employees or other trusted insiders. Social engineers' knowledge and determination give them the upper hand over management and employees who don't recognize the value of the information that social engineers seek.

Understanding the Implications

Many organizations have enemies who want to cause trouble through social engineering. These people may be current or former employees seeking revenge, competitors wanting a leg up, or hackers trying to prove their worth.

Regardless of who causes the trouble, every organization is at risk — especially given the sprawling Internet presence of the average company. Larger companies spread across several locations are often more vulnerable given their complexity, but smaller companies can also be attacked. Everyone, from receptionists to security guards to executives to IT personnel, is a potential victim of social engineering. Help desk and call center employees are especially vulnerable because they're trained to be helpful and forthcoming with information. In today's world of so many people working from home, social engineering's impacts are even greater.

Social engineering has serious consequences. Because the objective of social engineering is to coerce someone to provide information that leads to ill-gotten gains, anything is possible. Effective social engineers can obtain the following information:

>> User passwords

>> Security badges or keys to the building and even to the computer room

>> Intellectual property such as design specifications, source code, and other research-and-development documentation

>> Confidential financial reports

>> Private and confidential employee information

>> Personally identifiable information (PII) such as health records and credit card information

>> Customer lists and sales prospects

If any of the preceding information is leaked, financial losses, lowered employee morale, decreased customer loyalty, and even legal and regulatory compliance issues could result. The possibilities are endless.

Social engineering attacks are difficult to protect against for various reasons. For one thing, they aren't well documented. For another, social engineers are limited only by their imaginations. Also, because so many methods exist, recovery and protection are difficult after the attack. Furthermore, the hard, crunchy outside of firewalls and antimalware software often creates a false sense of security, making the problem even worse.

With social engineering, you never know the next method of attack. The best things you can do are remain vigilant, understand the social engineer's motives and methodologies, and protect against the most common attacks through ongoing security awareness in your organization. I discuss how these techniques work in the rest of this chapter.

Building trust

Trust — so hard to gain, yet so easy to lose. Trust is the essence of social engineering. Most people trust others until a situation forces them not to. People want to help one another, especially if trust can be built and the request for help seems reasonable. Most people want to be team players in the workplace and don't realize what can happen if they divulge too much information to a source who shouldn't be trusted. This trust allows social engineers to accomplish their goals.

Building deep trust often takes time, but crafty social engineers can gain it within minutes or hours. How do they do it?

>> **Likability:** Who can't relate to a nice person? Everyone loves courtesy. The friendlier social engineers are — without going overboard — the better their chances are of getting what they want. Social engineers often begin to build a relationship by establishing common interests. They often use the information that they gain in the research phase to determine what the victim likes and to pretend that they like those things, too. They can phone victims or meet them in person and, based on information the social engineers have discovered about the person, start talking about local sports teams or how wonderful it is to be single again. A few low-key and well-articulated comments can be the start of a nice new relationship.

>> **Believability:** Believability is based in part on the knowledge social engineers have and how likable they are. Social engineers also use impersonation — perhaps by posing as new employees or fellow employees whom the victim hasn't met. They may even pose as vendors who do business with the organization. Often, they modestly claim authority to influence people. The most common social engineering trick is to do something nice so that the victim feels obligated to be nice in return or to be a team player for the organization.

Exploiting the relationship

After social engineers obtain the trust of their unsuspecting victims, they coax the victims into divulging more information than they should. Whammo — and then the social engineer can go in for the kill. Social engineers do this through face-to-face or electronic communication that victims feel comfortable with, or they use technology to get victims to divulge information.

Deceit through words and actions

Wily social engineers can get inside information from their victims in many ways. They're often articulate and focus on keeping their conversations moving without giving their victims much time to think about what they're saying. If they're careless or overly anxious during their social engineering attacks, however, the following tip-offs might give them away:

>> Acting overly friendly or eager

>> Dropping the names of prominent people within the organization

>> Bragging about their authority within the organization

- » Threatening reprimands if their requests aren't honored

- » Acting nervous when questioned (pursing the lips and fidgeting — especially the hands and feet, because controlling the body parts that are farther from the face requires more conscious effort)

- » Overemphasizing details

- » Experiencing physiological changes, such as dilated pupils or changes in voice pitch

- » Appearing rushed

- » Refusing to give information

- » Volunteering information and answering unasked questions

- » Knowing information that an outsider shouldn't have

- » Using insider speech or slang despite being a known outsider

- » Asking strange questions

- » Misspelling words in written communications

A good social engineer isn't obvious with the preceding actions, but these signs may indicate that malicious behavior is in the works. Of course, some social engineers may behave atypically. *Psychology For Dummies*, 3rd Edition, by Adam Cash (published by Wiley) is a good resource on complexities of the human mind.

Social engineers often do a favor for someone and then turn around and ask that person whether they mind helping them. This common social engineering trick works pretty well. Social engineers also use what's called *reverse social engineering*. They offer to help if a specific problem arises. After some time passes, the problem occurs (often at the social engineer's doing), and then the social engineer helps fix the problem. They may come across as heroes which can further their cause. Social engineers may ask an unsuspecting employee for a favor. Yes — they outright ask for a favor. Many people fall for this trap.

Impersonating an employee is easy. Social engineers can wear a similar-looking uniform, make a fake ID badge, or simply dress like real employees. People think, "Hey — that person looks and acts like me, and even hangs out at the same coffee shop, so they must be one of the good guys." Social engineers also pretend to be employees calling from an outside phone line. This trick is an especially popular way of exploiting help desk and call center personnel. Social engineers know that these employees fall into a rut easily because their tasks are repetitive, such as saying, "Hello, can I get your customer number, please?" over and over.

Deceit through technology

Technology can make things easier — and more fun — for the social engineer. Often, a malicious request for information comes from a computer or other electronic entity that the victims think they can identify. But spoofing a computer name, an email address, a fax number, or a network address is easy. Fortunately, you can take a few countermeasures against this type of attack, as described in the next section.

Hackers can deceive through technology by sending an email that asks victims for critical information. Such an email usually provides a link that directs victims to a professional, legitimate-looking website that "updates" such account information as user IDs, passwords, and Social Security numbers. They also may execute this trick on social networking sites such as Facebook and Twitter.

Many spam and phishing messages also employ this trick. Most users are inundated with so much spam and other unwanted email that they often let their guard down and open emails and attachments that they shouldn't. These emails usually look professional and believable and often dupe people into disclosing information that they should never give in exchange for a gift. These social engineering tricks can occur when a hacker who has already broken into the network sends messages or creates fake Internet pop-up windows. The same tricks have occurred through instant messaging and smartphone messaging.

In some well-publicized incidents, hackers emailed their victims a patch purporting to come from Microsoft or another well-known vendor. Users may think that the message looks like a duck and quacks like a duck — but it's not the right duck! The message is actually from a hacker who wants the user to install the patch, which installs ransomware or creates a backdoor into computers and networks. Criminals use ransomware to extort money and backdoors to hack into the organization's systems or use the victims' computers (known as *zombies*) as launchpads to attack another system. Even viruses and worms can use social engineering. The LoveBug worm, for example, told users they had secret admirers, but when the victims opened the email, it was too late. Their computers were infected. (And, perhaps worse, they didn't have secret admirers.)

Many computerized social engineering tactics can be performed anonymously through Internet proxy servers, anonymizers, remailers, and basic SMTP servers that have an open relay. When people fall for requests for confidential personal or corporate information, the sources of these social engineering attacks are often impossible to track.

Performing Social Engineering Attacks

The process of social engineering is pretty basic. Generally, social engineers discover details about people, organizational processes, and information systems to perform their attacks. With this information, they know what to pursue. Social engineering attacks typically are carried out in four simple steps:

1. Perform research.

2. Build trust.

3. Exploit relationships for information through words, actions, or technology.

4. Use the information gathered for malicious purposes.

Depending on the attack being performed, these steps can include numerous substeps and techniques.

Determining a goal

Before social engineers perform their attacks, they need a goal. This goal is the first step in these attackers' processes for social engineering and is most likely already implanted in their minds. What do they want to accomplish? What are the social engineers trying to hack, and why? Do they want intellectual property or server passwords? Is it access that they desire, or do they simply want to prove that the company's defenses can be penetrated? Perhaps they seek to push their ransomware? In your efforts as a security professional performing social engineering, determine the overall goal before you begin. Otherwise, you'll be wandering aimlessly, creating unnecessary headaches and risks for yourself and others along the way.

Seeking information

When social engineers have a goal in mind, they typically start the attack by gathering public information about their victim(s). Many social engineers acquire information slowly over time so that they don't raise suspicion. However, obvious information gathering is a tip-off. The rest of this chapter covers other warning signs to be aware of.

REMEMBER

Sometimes, criminal hackers go straight for the kill by sending out thousands of phishing messages at once. There's no preparation and no research outside of gathering email addresses. They blast off the messages and see what sticks.

Regardless of the initial research method, a criminal may only need an employee list, a few key internal phone numbers, the latest news from a social media website, or a company calendar to penetrate an organization. Book 5, Chapter 5 provides more details on information gathering, but the following techniques are worth calling out.

Using the Internet

Today's basic research medium is the Internet. A few minutes of searching on Google or other search engines using simple keywords such as the company name or specific employees' names often produces a lot of information. You can find even more information in Securities and Exchange Commission (SEC) filings at www.sec.gov and other sites such as www.dnb.com/products/marketing-sales/dnb-hoovers.htm and https://finance.yahoo.com. Many organizations — and especially their management — would be dismayed to discover the organizational information that's available online! Given the plethora of such information, especially given what is shared on social media these days, it's often enough to start a social engineering attack.

REMEMBER

Criminals can pay a few dollars for a comprehensive online background check on people, executives included. These searches turn up practically all public — and sometimes private — information about a person in minutes.

Dumpster diving

Dumpster diving is a little riskier — and certainly messy — but it's a highly effective method of obtaining information. This method involves rummaging through trash cans for information about a company.

Dumpster diving can turn up even the most confidential information because some people assume that their information is safe after it goes into the trash. Most people don't think about the potential value of the paper they throw away. Documents often contain a wealth of information that can tip-off social engineers with information needed to penetrate the organization. The astute social engineer looks for the following hard-copy documents:

>> Internal phone lists

>> Organizational charts

>> Employee handbooks (which often contain security policies)

>> Network diagrams

>> Password lists

>> Meeting notes

- Spreadsheets and reports
- Customer records
- Printouts of emails that contain confidential information

Shredding documents is effective only if the paper is cross-shredded into tiny pieces of confetti. Inexpensive shredders that shred documents only in long strips are worthless against a determined social engineer. With a little time and tape, a savvy hacker can piece a document back together if that's what they're determined to do.

TIP

Hackers often gather confidential personal and business information from others by listening in on conversations held in restaurants, coffee shops, and airports. People who speak loudly when talking on their cellphones are also great sources of sensitive information for social engineers. (Poetic justice, perhaps?) Airplanes are great places for shoulder surfing and gathering sensitive information. In public places and on airplanes, you hear and see an amazing amount of private information. You can hardly avoid it!

The bad guys also look in the trash for USB drives, DVDs, and other media. Similarly, they might just plant USB drives around your office or parking lot to lure in unsuspecting users and infect their computers once they plug the devices into their systems. See Book 5, Chapter 7 for more on trash and other physical security issues, including countermeasures for protecting against dumpster divers.

Phone systems

Attackers can obtain information by using the dial-by-name feature built into most voice mail systems. To access this feature, you usually press 0 or # after calling the company's main number or after you enter someone's voice mailbox. This trick works best after hours to ensure that no one answers.

Social engineers can find interesting bits of information at times, such as when their victims are out of town, by listening to voice mail messages. They can even study victims' voices by listening to their voice mail messages, podcasts, or webcasts so that they can learn to impersonate those people.

Attackers can protect their identities if they can hide where they call from. Here are some ways that they hide their locations:

TIP

- **Residential phones** sometimes can hide their numbers from caller ID if the user dials *67 before the phone number.

   However, this feature isn't effective when calling toll-free numbers (800, 888, 877, or 866) or 911. Likely, it will work on traditional landlines, disposable cellphones, and Voice over Internet Protocol (VoIP) services, though.

>> **Business phones** in an office using a phone switch are more difficult to spoof, but all that an attacker usually needs are the user guide and administrator password for the phone-switch software. In many switches, the attacker can enter the source number — including a falsified number, such as the victim's home phone number.

>> **VoIP servers** such as the open-source Asterisk (`www.asterisk.org`) can be configured to send any number.

Phishing emails

One of the most common and successful means of hacking is carried out via email *phishing*, wherein criminals send bogus emails to potential victims in an attempt to get them to divulge sensitive information or click malicious links that lead to malware infections. Phishing has been around for years, but it has gained greater visibility recently, given some high-profile exploits against seemingly impenetrable businesses and government agencies. Phishing's effectiveness is amazing, and the consequences are often ugly. Success rates (or failure rates, depending on how you look at it) are sometimes as high as 70 percent. A well-worded email is all it takes to glean login credentials, access sensitive information, or inject simulated malware into targeted computers.

You can perform your own phishing exercises. A rudimentary yet effective method is to set up an email account on your domain (or, ideally, a domain that looks similar to yours at a glance). Then request information or link to a website that collects information, send emails to employees or other users you want to test, and see what they do. Do they open the email, click the link, divulge information? Or, if you're lucky, do they do none of the above? The test really is as simple as that. *Security Awareness For Dummies* by Ira Winkler (published by Wiley) shows how to run a full phishing simulation campaign.

Whether the cause is today's rushed world of business, general user gullibility, or downright ignorance, it's astonishing how susceptible the average person is to phishing email exploits. A phishing email that has a great chance of being opened and responded to creates a sense of urgency and provides information that presumably only an insider would know. Many phishing emails are easy to spot, however, because they have the following characteristics:

>> Have typographical errors.

>> Contain generic salutations and email signatures.

>> Arrive in inboxes at odd times, such as in the middle of the night.

>> Ask the user to click a link, open an attachment, or provide sensitive information such as login credentials.

>> They have a sense of urgency; for instance, they encourage the user to take action by the end of the business day.

A more formal means of executing your phishing tests is to use a tool made specifically for the job. Commercial options available on the Internet include LUCY (www.lucysecurity.com) and Cofense, formerly known as Phishme (https://cofense.com). With these email phishing platforms, you have access to pre-installed email templates, the ability to *scrape* (copy pages from) live websites so you can customize your own campaign, and extensive reporting capabilities so you can track which email users are taking the bait on. They also integrate awareness and training into the system so that users can be educated about what they did after the click or sharing of information has taken place.

You can use tools like LUCY (shown in Figure 6-1) for email phishing testing. LUCY is powerful, and its support to be top-notch.

Social Engineering

FIGURE 6-1:
Using LUCY to start an email phishing campaign.

Figure 6-2 shows a sample of the various LUCY phishing campaigns you can launch, including malware simulation and SMS phishing (smishing), which is a particularly fun exercise to run.

FIGURE 6-2:
Sample email
phishing template
options in LUCY.

Social Engineering Countermeasures

You have only a few good lines of defense against social engineering. Social engineering puts your layered defenses to the true test. Even with strong security controls, a naïve or untrained user can let a social engineer into the network. Never underestimate the power of social engineers — and the gullibility of your users in helping them get their way. Heck, even well-trained IT and security professionals can and do fall for social engineering, especially phishing.

Policies

Specific policies and standards can help ward off social engineering in the long term in the following areas:

» Classifying information so that users don't have access to certain levels of information they don't need

» Setting up unique user IDs when hiring employees or contractors

» Establishing acceptable computer use that employees agree to in writing

- >> Removing user IDs for employees, contractors, and consultants who no longer work for the organization

- >> Setting and resetting strong passphrases

- >> Requiring multifactor authentication (MFA), especially for critical accounts and systems

- >> Responding quickly to security incidents, such as suspicious behavior and known malware infections

- >> Properly handling proprietary and confidential information

- >> Specifying security standards for personally owned computers that are used to access business systems

- >> Escorting guests around your building(s)

These policies must be enforceable *and* enforced for everyone within the organization. Keep them up to date, tell your users about them, and (most importantly) test them.

User awareness and training

One of the best lines of defense against social engineering is training employees to identify and respond to social engineering attacks. User awareness begins with initial training for everyone and follows with security awareness initiatives to keep social engineering defenses fresh in everyone's mind. Align training and awareness with specific security policies. You may also want to have a dedicated security training and awareness policy that outlines the specifics of your ongoing security education. For detailed information about creating and implementing security awareness programs, see Book 6.

TIP

Consider outsourcing security training to a seasoned security trainer. Employees often take training more seriously if it comes from an outsider, just as a family member or spouse may ignore what you have to say but takes the same words to heart if an outside expert says it. Outsourcing security training is worth the investment for that reason alone.

Social Engineering

Chapter **7**

Physical Security

I nformation security is more dependent on nontechnical aspects of IT, security, and the business than on the technical side of things that many people and vendors swear by. *Physical security,* which is the protection of physical property, encompasses both technical and nontechnical components, both of which must be addressed.

Physical security is an often-overlooked but critical aspect of an information security program. Your ability to secure your information depends on your ability to physically secure your office, building, or campus. This chapter covers some common physical security weaknesses as they relate to computers and information security that you must seek out and resolve. The chapter also outlines free and low-cost countermeasures you can implement to minimize your business's physical vulnerabilities.

WARNING

This book does not recommend breaking and entering, which would be necessary to *fully* test certain physical security vulnerabilities. We don't want you to get shot or go to jail! Instead, approach those areas to see how far you *can* get. Take a fresh look — from an outsider's perspective — at the physical vulnerabilities covered in this chapter. You may discover holes in your physical security that you previously overlooked.

Identifying Basic Physical Security Vulnerabilities

Regardless of your security technology, practically any breach is possible if an attacker is in your building, your data center, or even a remote user's home. That's why looking for physical security vulnerabilities and fixing them before they're exploited is so important.

In small companies, some physical security issues may not be a problem. Many physical security vulnerabilities depend on such factors as

>> Size of building

>> Number of buildings or office locations

>> Number of employees

>> Presence of a receptionist or security guard

>> Location and number of building entrance and exit points

>> Placement of server rooms, wiring closets, and data centers

Thousands of possible physical security weaknesses exist. This is doubly true today given the size of the remote workforce and vulnerabilities associated with employees' homes. The bad guys are always on the lookout for them, so you should look for these issues first. Here are some examples of physical security vulnerabilities to look for when performing security assessments:

>> No receptionist or guard to monitor who's coming and going

>> No visitor sign-in or escort required (or enforced) for building access

>> Employees being overly trusting of visitors because they wear vendor uniforms or say that they're in the building to work on the copier or computers

>> No access controls on doors or the use of traditional keys that can be duplicated with no accountability

>> Doors propped open

>> IP-based video, access control, and data center management systems accessible via the network with vendor default user IDs and passwords

>> Publicly accessible computer rooms

>> Unsecured backup media such as tapes, hard drives, and USB drives

>> Sensitive information stored in hard-copy format lying around cubicles rather than being stored in locked filing cabinets

>> Unsecured computer hardware, especially routers, switches, and unencrypted laptops

>> Lack of alarm systems, including home alarms

>> Sensitive information being thrown away in trash cans rather than being shredded or placed in a shred container

When these physical security vulnerabilities are uncovered, bad things can happen. All it takes to exploit these weaknesses is an unauthorized individual with malicious intent.

Pinpointing Physical Vulnerabilities in Your Office

Many potential physical security exploits seem unlikely, but they can occur to organizations that don't pay attention to the risks. The bad guys can exploit many such vulnerabilities, including weaknesses in a building's infrastructure, office layout, computer-room access, and design. In addition to these factors, consider the facility's proximity to local emergency assistance (police, fire, and ambulance) and the area's crime statistics (burglary, robbery, and so on) so that you can better understand what you're up against.

TIP

Those responsible for physical security are often disconnected from those in charge of IT and information security. Do what you can to facilitate better communications between you and them.

Look for the vulnerabilities discussed in the following sections when assessing your organization's physical security. This research won't take a lot of technical savvy or expensive equipment. Depending on the size of your office or facilities, these tests shouldn't take much time either. You might even consider integrating some of these items into your user awareness and training program to help ensure that their homes are properly secured. The bottom line is to determine whether the physical security controls are adequate, given what's at stake. Above all, be practical, and use common sense.

Building infrastructure

Doors, windows, and walls are critical components of a building — especially in a data center or another area where confidential information is stored.

Attack points

Criminals can exploit building infrastructure vulnerabilities. Ask yourself the following questions about some commonly overlooked attack points:

>> Are doors propped open, and if so, why?

>> Are there gaps at the bottoms of critical doors? (Gaps could allow someone to use a balloon or other device to trip a sensor inside an otherwise-secure room.)

>> Would it be easy to force doors open? (A simple kick near the doorknob is usually enough for standard doors.)

>> What is the building or data center made of (steel, wood, or concrete), and how sturdy are the walls and entryways? Determine how resilient the material is to earthquakes, tornadoes, strong winds, heavy rains, and vehicles driving into the building. Also, determine whether these disasters would leave the building exposed so that looters and others with malicious intent could gain access to the computer room or other critical areas.

>> Are any doors or windows made of glass, and is this glass clear, shatterproof, or bulletproof?

>> Do door hinges on the outside make it easy for intruders to unhook them?

>> Are doors, windows, and other entry points wired to an alarm system?

>> Does the building have drop ceilings with tiles that can be pushed up?

>> Does the building have slab-to-slab walls? (If not, someone could easily scale the walls, bypassing any door or window access controls.)

Countermeasures

Many physical security countermeasures for building vulnerabilities require other maintenance, construction, or operations experts. If building infrastructure isn't your forte, you can hire outside experts during the design, assessment, and retrofitting stages to ensure that you have adequate controls. Here are some of the best ways to solidify building security:

>> Strong doors and locks

>> Motion detectors

>> Cameras to discourage criminal activity, to catch perpetrators in real-time, or to provide evidence of what happened after the fact

>> Windowless walls around data centers

>> Signage that makes it clear what's where and who's allowed

>> A continuously monitored alarm system with network-based cameras located at all access areas

>> Lighting (especially around entry and exit points)

>> Entrances that allow only one person at a time to pass through a door

>> Fences (with barbed wire or razor wire if necessary)

REMEMBER

Some of these items can easily apply to your users' homes. Don't be afraid to encourage users who often work from home to ensure that their homes are properly secured and are, ideally, protected with alarms and cameras.

Utilities

When assessing physical security, you must consider building and data center utilities, such as power, water, generators, and fire suppression. These utilities can help you fight incidents and keep other access controls running during a power loss. You have to be careful, though, as they can also be used against you if an intruder enters the building.

Attack points

Intruders often exploit utility-related vulnerabilities. Ask yourself the following questions about some commonly overlooked attack points:

>> Is power-protection equipment in place, such as surge protectors, uninterruptible power supplies (UPSes), and generators? Also, determine how easily accessible the on/off switches on these devices are — that is, whether an intruder can walk in and flip a switch or scale a fence to cut off a simple lock and gain access to critical equipment.

>> When the power fails, do physical security mechanisms fail *open* (allow anyone through) or fail *closed* (keep everyone in or out until power is restored)?

>> Where are fire-detection and -suppression devices located — alarm sensors, extinguishers, and sprinkler systems? Determine how an intruder can abuse them. Also, determine whether they're accessible via a wireless or local network with default login credentials or over the Internet. Finally, determine whether these devices are placed where they can harm electronic equipment during a false alarm.

>> Where are water and gas shut-off valves located? Determine whether you can access them or would have to call maintenance personnel if an incident arose.

» Where are local telecom wires (both copper and fiber) that run outside the building located? If they're aboveground, someone could tap into them with telecom tools. If they're buried, digging in the area might cut them easily. If they're located on telephone poles, they may be vulnerable to traffic accidents or weather-related incidents.

Countermeasures

You may need to involve outside experts during the design, assessment, or retro-fitting stages. The key is *placement.* Be sure to consider the following:

» Ensure that major utility controls are placed behind closed and lockable doors or fenced areas and out of the sight of people passing through or nearby.

» Ensure that you have a lot of cameras with ample coverage.

» Ensure that any devices accessible over the network or Internet are tested with vulnerability scanners and other techniques outlined in this book. If the devices don't have to be network- or Internet-accessible, disable that feature or limit who can access the systems via firewall rules or a network access control list.

» Ensure that someone walking through or near the building can't access the controls to turn them on and off.

TIP

Security covers for on/off switches and thermostat controls and locks for server power buttons, USB ports, and even PCI expansion slots in workstations and servers can be effective defenses. Don't depend on them fully, however, because they can often be easily cracked open.

WARNING

When choosing a data center to host your systems, ask for a tour of their data center. If that's not possible, then ask for a copy of their latest Service Organization Control (SOC) 2 audit report to ensure there are no gaping holes in the center's physical security.

Office layout and use

Office design and use can help or hinder physical security.

Attack points

Intruders can exploit various weaknesses around the office. Ask yourself the following questions about common attack points:

» Does a receptionist or security guard monitor traffic in and out of the main doors of the building?

» Do employees have confidential information on their desks? Determine whether mail and packages lie outside someone's door — or, worse, outside the building — waiting for pickup.

» Where are trash cans and bins, recycling bins, and shredders located, and are they easily accessible? Open recycling bins and other careless handling of trash invite dumpster diving. People with ill intent often search for confidential company information and customer records in the trash, and they're often successful. Accessible trash can create many security exposures.

» How secure are the mail and copy rooms? If intruders can access these rooms, they can steal mail or company letterhead to use against you. They can also use and abuse your fax machines (assuming that you still have any!).

» Are closed-circuit television or IP-based network cameras used *and* monitored in real-time? If your setup is less proactive and more as-needed, you must be confident that you'll be able to access videos and related logs quickly when you need them.

» Have your network cameras and digital video recorders been hardened against attack, or have their default login credentials been changed at least? This security flaw is nearly 100 percent certain on practically all types of networks, in public utility companies, hospitals, manufacturing companies, and all other types of businesses.

» What access controls are on the doors: regular keys, card keys, combination locks, or biometrics? Determine who can access the keys and where they are stored. Keys and programmable keypad combinations are often shared, making accountability difficult to determine. Find out how many people share these combinations and keys.

Some organizations have unmonitored front lobbies and a Voice over Internet Protocol (VoIP) phone available for anyone to use. Anyone could enter the lobby, disconnect the VoIP phone (or use the phone's data port), plug a laptop computer into the connection, and gain full access to the organization's network with minimal chance of being detected or questioned. This type of situation is easy to prevent: Disable network connections in unmonitored areas if separate data and voice ports are used or if voice and data traffic is separated at the switch or physical network levels.

Similarly, lobbies can be very high-traffic public areas. If an organization uses the lobby as a waiting area and provides access to an open network port, all anyone has to do to get onto the organization's full corporate network environment is plug into an Ethernet port. Not only could they get access to the Internet, but they also have full access to the internal production network. This is scary stuff, especially given the vulnerabilities that exist on some internal networks! At best, this type of setup is a large-scale ransomware infection waiting to happen.

Countermeasures

Physical security is challenging because security controls are often reactive. Some controls are preventive (that is, they deter or delay indefinitely), but they're not foolproof. Putting simple measures such as the following in place can reduce your exposure to building and office-related vulnerabilities:

>> A receptionist or a security guard who monitors people coming and going is the simplest countermeasure. This person can ensure that every visitor signs in and that all new or untrusted visitors are always escorted. Make it policy and procedure for all employees to question strangers and report strange behavior in the building.

WARNING

>> *Employees Only* or *Authorized Personnel Only* signs show the bad guys where they *should* go instead of deterring them from entering. Not calling attention to critical areas may be a better approach.

>> Have single entry and exit points to a data center.

>> Place trash bins in secure areas.

>> Use cameras to monitor critical areas, including trash bins. (It's amazing how cameras can shape the behavior of would-be criminals.)

>> Dispose of hard-copy documents in cross-cut shredders or secure recycling bins.

>> Limit the numbers of keys distributed and passcode combinations that are shared and ensure that access is also logged and monitored.

TIP

Make keys and passcodes unique for each person whenever possible, or (better) don't use them at all. Instead, use electronic badges that can be better controlled and monitored.

>> Use biometric identification systems. They can be effective, but they can also be expensive and difficult to manage.

Network components and computers

After intruders obtain access to a building, they may look for the server room and other easily accessible computer and network devices.

Attack points

The keys to the kingdom are often as close as someone's desktop computer and not much farther than an unsecured computer room or wiring closet.

Intruders can do the following:

>> Obtain network access and send malicious emails as a logged-in user.

>> Crack and obtain passwords directly from the computer by booting it with a tool such as the ophcrack LiveCD (http://ophcrack.sourceforge.io).

>> Place penetration drop boxes such as those made by Pwnie Express (https://github.com/pwnieexpress) in a standard power outlet. These devices allow malicious intruders to connect to the system via a cellular connection and perform dirty deeds. This method is a really sneaky (spylike) means of intrusion that you can use as part of your own security testing.

>> Steal files from the computer by copying them to a removable storage device (such as a phone or USB drive) or by emailing them to an external address.

>> Enter unlocked computer rooms and mess around with servers, firewalls, and routers.

>> Walk out with network diagrams, contact lists, and disaster recovery plans.

>> Obtain phone numbers from analog lines and circuit IDs from T1, Metro Ethernet, and other telecom equipment to use in subsequent attacks.

Practically every bit of unencrypted information that traverses the network can be recorded for future analysis through one of the following hard-to-spot methods:

>> Connecting a computer running network analyzer software (including a tool such as Cain and Abel) to a switch on your network.

>> Installing network analyzer software on an existing computer.

How would someone access or use this information in the future? The easiest attack method is to install remote-administration software on the computer, such as VNC (www.realvnc.com). Also, a crafty hacker with enough time can bind a public IP address to the computer if the computer is outside the firewall. Hackers or malicious insiders with enough network knowledge (and time) could conceivably configure new firewall rules to do this if they have access to the firewall. Don't laugh; you can find firewalls running with default passwords, which is about as bad as security gets.

Also, ask yourself the following questions about some common physical vulnerabilities:

>> How easily can computers be accessed during regular business hours, at lunchtime, and after hours?

>> Are computers (especially laptops) secured to desks with locks, and do they have encrypted hard drives and screens that lock after a short period of nonuse?

>> Do employees typically leave their phones and tablets lying around unsecured, such as when they're traveling or working from home, hotels, or the local coffee shop?

>> Where are business laptops and related systems located in users' homes? Are they encrypted in the event of loss or theft?

>> Are passwords stored on sticky notes on computer screens, keyboards, or desks? (This practice is a long-running joke in IT circles, but it still happens.)

>> Are backup media lying around the office or data center susceptible to theft?

>> Are safes used to protect backup media, and who can access them?

Safes are often at great risk because of their size and value, and they're typically unprotected by the organization's regular security controls. Consider creating specific policies and technologies to protect them.

TIP

Safes should be specifically rated for media to keep backups from melting during a fire; examples include FireKing safes (www.fireking.com/products/safes/data-safes).

>> Are locking laptop bags required? What about power-on passwords? Encryption can solve a lot of physical security-related weaknesses.

>> How easily can someone connect to a wireless access point signal or the access point itself to join the network? Rogue access points are also important to consider.

>> Are network firewalls, routers, switches, and hubs (basically, anything with an Ethernet or console connection) easily accessible, enabling an attacker to plug into the network easily?

>> Are all cables patched through on the patch panel in the wiring closet so that all network drops are live (as in the case of the unmonitored lobbies mentioned earlier in this chapter)? At a minimum, put unused ports on a separate VLAN or, ideally, a physical network that is air-gapped from the production network environment.

REMEMBER

This setup is common but a bad idea because it allows anyone to plug into the network anywhere and gain access, as well as to spread malware.

Countermeasures

Network and computer security countermeasures are simple to implement yet difficult to enforce because they involve people's everyday actions. Here's a rundown of these countermeasures:

» Make your users aware of what to look out for so that you have extra sets of eyes and ears helping you.

» Require users to lock their screens — which takes only a few clicks or keystrokes — when they leave their computers. Better yet, set a Group Policy Object in Active Directory or local computer policy to force timeouts after a few minutes. If you use biometrics for authentication, set up the systems to lock immediately once the user steps away.

» Ensure that strong passwords are used. (Book 2, Chapter 5 covers this topic.)

» Require laptop users to lock their systems to their desks with a locking cable — especially important for remote workers and travelers, as well as employees of large companies and/or those who work in locations with a lot of foot traffic.

» Require all laptops to use full disk encryption technologies. One great option is BitLocker in Windows. Another option is WinMagic SecureDoc Full Disk Encryption (www.winmagic.com/products/full-disk-encryption-for-windows). Many modern endpoint security programs offer full disk encryption as well. FileVault built into the macOS is a good option for that growing group of computers. It's also important to consider encryption for removable media since sensitive information inevitably ends up there.

» Keep server rooms and wiring closets locked, and monitor those areas for any wrongdoing.

» Keep a current inventory of hardware and software within the organization so that it's easy to determine when extra equipment appears or goes missing — especially important in computer rooms.

» Replace traditional door locks and keys with more modern access control systems and ensure that the system does adequate logging that can be referenced in the event of a physical security event.

» Properly secure computer media during storage and transport.

» Scan for rogue wireless access points, and shut them down.

» Use cable traps and locks that prevent intruders from unplugging network cables from patch panels or computers and using those connections for their own computers.

» Use a bulk eraser on magnetic media and shred them before they're discarded.

6

Enhancing Cybersecurity Awareness

Contents at a Glance

Chapter **1**

Knowing How Security Awareness Programs Work

A successful security awareness program motivates people to behave according to defined practices that decrease risk. Creating a program that successfully changes behavior throughout an organization involves more than simply communicating a bunch of facts about security awareness. Just because people are aware of a problem doesn't mean they will act on their awareness. In other words, awareness doesn't guarantee action. (Everyone knows that fast food isn't the healthiest choice, but most people still eat it.) This chapter sets the foundation for understanding the issues and the solutions.

Understanding the Benefits of Security Awareness

The thinking behind *security awareness* is that if people are aware of a problem, they're less likely to contribute to the problem — and more likely to respond appropriately when they encounter it.

Users who are *aware* don't pick up USB drives on the street and insert them into their work computers. They're aware of their surroundings and ensure that nobody is looking over their shoulders while they're working. They don't connect to insecure Wi-Fi networks. They're less likely to fall victim to phishing attacks. Essentially, users who are aware don't initiate losses for their organizations.

Organizations typically create security awareness programs to ensure that their employees, or *users*, are aware of cybersecurity problems that are already known to the organization. Phishing messages, covered in the next section, represent the most prolific attack against users.

Reducing losses from phishing attacks

Phishing attacks are common enough these days that many people are already familiar with the term. A working definition is "an email message that intends to trick a user into taking an action that is against the user's interests." A phishing awareness program would ideally train people to properly determine how to handle incoming emails in a way that reduces the likelihood of loss. For example, if a message asks for the disclosure of information, the ideal situation is that a user knows what information they can disclose and to whom while also determining whether the sender is valid.

To appreciate the losses that a phishing attack can cause, consider these prominent attacks:

>> **Sony:** The infamous 2014 Sony hack, which was reportedly perpetrated by North Korea, began with a phishing attack. The hack resulted in the leak of information about movies, the movies themselves, and embarrassing emails. Sony reported costs of the hack to be $35 million.

>> **Target:** The 2013 Target hack, which compromised more than 110 million credit card numbers and consumer records, began with a phishing attack of a Target vendor. Target reported the resulting costs to be $162 million.

>> **OPM:** The attack on the Office of Personnel Management (OPM), discovered in 2014, which compromised the security clearance files of 20 million

U.S. government employees and contractors, began with a phishing attack against a government contractor. The costs and losses are immeasurable because this attack is considered a major intelligence success for China, the perpetrator of the attack named by the U.S. government.

>> **Colonial Pipeline:** The Colonial Pipeline ransomware attack in 2021 began with a phishing message that captured user credentials and allowed the criminals to establish a sustained presence on the network. This allowed the criminals to find the most critical systems and eventually install the ransomware, which caused Colonial Pipeline to shut down the pipeline, halting a primary oil delivery to the U.S. east coast. Colonial Pipeline paid the criminals approximately $4.4 million, but the actual costs resulting from the shutdown were tens of millions of dollars to Colonial Pipeline and an incalculable cost to the economy.

TECHNICAL STUFF

The Verizon Enterprises Solutions' Data Breach Investigations Report, commonly referred to as the DBIR, is one of the most often cited studies in the cybersecurity field. The report, which is produced annually, is drawn from data collected directly by Verizon's managed security service. The DBIR, considered a reliable overview of real-life attacks against organizations around the world, indicates that more than a whopping 85 percent of all major attacks begin by targeting users. You can access the report at www.verizon.com/business/resources/reports/dbir.

Reducing losses by reducing risk

Just as people get themselves into automobile accidents despite advances in automobile safety, even reasonably aware users may fall victim to cybersecurity attacks. All cybersecurity countermeasures will eventually fail. Countermeasures include encryption, passwords, antivirus software, multifactor authentication, and more. Perfect security doesn't exist. Your goal in establishing a security awareness program is to reduce risk by influencing user actions.

REMEMBER

Don't expect users to be perfect — risk reduction isn't about eliminating risk altogether, which is impossible. Expect your security awareness program to reduce the number and severity of incidents, thereby reducing losses from the incidents.

Also, a more aware user knows when something seems wrong and knows how to react to it. If your users sense that they might have been compromised, they start taking actions to mitigate the loss. If they accidentally email sensitive data to the wrong person, they try to stop the message or have it deleted. If they end up on a malicious website that starts serving adware, they disconnect before additional damage can occur. They know how to properly report any and all potential incidents, so your organization can begin to stop any loss or damage in progress. In the worst case, at least they can launch an investigation after the fact to find out what happened.

In the ideal situation, even when a user takes no potentially harmful action, they report the situation to the appropriate party. They report details such as whether someone tried to follow them through a door, even if they turn the person away, because they know that the person might attempt to enter through another door or follow someone else through the door. If someone detects a phishing message, they don't click on it — instead, they report the message because they realize that other, less aware users may click on it, and then the administrators can delete the message before that happens.

As you can see, awareness requires more than knowing what to be afraid of — you also have to know how to do things correctly. Too many awareness programs focus on teaching users what to be afraid of rather than on establishing policies and procedures for how to perform functions correctly, and in a way that doesn't result in loss.

REMEMBER

The goal for awareness is for users to behave according to policies and procedures. Part of the function of an awareness program is making users aware that bad guys exist and that those bad guys will attempt to do bad things. But awareness programs primarily focus on making people aware of how to behave according to procedures in potentially risky situations.

Grasping how users initiate loss

Users can cause only the amount of damage they're put in the position to cause — and then allowed to carry out. However, even after they make a potentially damaging mistake, or even if they're blatantly malicious, it doesn't mean that the system should allow the loss to be realized.

For example, a user can click on a phishing message only if the antiphishing technology used by your organization fails to filter the message. If the user clicks on a phishing message and ransomware is activated, the ransomware can destroy the system only if the user has permission to install software on the system — and then in almost all cases, you have no standard antimalware on the system.

REMEMBER

User error is a symptom of the problems with your system. Even if a user makes a mistake, or is even malicious, the resulting loss is a problem with the system providing users with potential actions and then enabling the loss.

In essence, users may initiate a chain of actions that create the loss, but the loss is a result of failings in the system as a whole.

TIP

For more information on user-initiated loss, find a copy of my book, written with Dr. Tracy Celaya Brown, *You Can Stop Stupid: Stopping Losses from Accidental and Malicious Actions* (Wiley, 2021).

Knowing How Security Awareness Programs Work

Unfortunately, there is little consistency in what is perceived to be a sufficient, organizational security awareness program. Some organizations just have *users*, or employees, sign a document. Many other awareness programs require employees to read the document once a year (or, increasingly, watch a video).

At the other end of the spectrum, organizations like the National Security Agency (NSA) are naturally much more rigorous in their screening practices, as employees must achieve the appropriate security clearance before they can even begin working. The NSA is a special case, of course — most organizations don't engage in such rigorous screening practices.

The goal of a security awareness program is to improve security-related behaviors. The goal is not to simply make people aware of an issue — the goal is to inspire people to behave appropriately to avoid the initiation of a loss and, ideally, to detect and respond to the potential for loss. Whether people understand how their actions promote security is secondary because the goal of an awareness program is to change behaviors, not just impart knowledge.

At the end of the day, a *security awareness program* is essentially a set of tools, techniques, and measurements intended to improve security-related behaviors. Book 6, Chapter 4 describes a variety of tools that you can incorporate into your program. Some tools are more popular than others; however, no tool is absolutely required. The choice depends on your needs.

Establishing and measuring goals

The ultimate goal of a security awareness program is to change and improve security-related behaviors. Security programs are created to reduce loss. As an essential part of an organization's overall information security program, security awareness should likewise reduce loss.

Book 6, Chapter 5 covers some metrics you can use to judge whether your awareness program successfully reduces loss. Many security awareness professionals talk about the likeability of their tools, the number of people who show up to their events, and the quality of their posters. These metrics and general impressions are nice to know, but they're relatively useless from a practical perspective.

GETTING THE BUDGET YOU NEED

This philosophy generally holds true in cybersecurity:

- You don't get the budget you need — you get the budget you deserve.

Security awareness teams typically compete against other teams for budget funds and other resources. For example, the team may work under the cybersecurity, human resources (HR), compliance, legal, physical security, or another department within the organization. All these teams compete for funding and other resources. Even if your cybersecurity program has sufficient resources to fully fund all teams, including the awareness program, you have to show that you deserve the budget amount you're requesting. You need to financially justify your efforts.

You can have plans for the best awareness program in the industry, but if you cannot demonstrate that you deserve the appropriate budget, you won't get the budget you need to implement it. Book 6, Chapter 5 details how to collect metrics that help you show that you deserve what you need.

A metric demonstrating that you're changing behaviors in a way that reduces loss, or preferably improves efficiency and makes the organization money, is the most useful metric to show that you're producing value. This isn't to say that it's the only possible benefit of a security awareness program. Awareness programs also often provide intangible benefits to the organization. These benefits include protecting the organization from damage to its reputation, illustrating that the organization is committed to security, generating excitement and engagement among employees, and reassuring customers that your organization is actively protecting them.

REMEMBER

If your goal is to contribute to your organization's security effort, you must identify the benefits your program will bring to the organization. These benefits can't be that the program merely provides information. The program should improve behaviors. You must be able to show how the program returns clear value to your organization, and this value should ideally return clear value to the bottom line.

Showing users how to "do things right"

For your awareness program to help create desired behaviors, the program must show people the proper way to perform job tasks, or "do things right." In other words, you provide instructions on how to do things properly by default.

When you consider most of the materials produced by vendors, and a great deal of the materials produced by organizations for internal use, these materials frequently focus on the fact that "bad people" intend to trick you. They tell you about criminals who will do harm if you fall for their tricks. This information can provide motivation, which can be worthwhile, but it's doesn't show users how to recognize suspicious situations as they encounter them.

When you teach people to focus on the ways bad people will exploit them, the training will fail when the bad people try a different trick. Expecting users to combat well-resourced, highly skilled criminals is a losing proposition. You cannot expect users to be consistently effective in thwarting such parties.

The better approach is for your awareness training to focus on the way that users can do their jobs properly. Ensure that users have an established process that they're familiar with and that they know how to follow. The process should account for the potential of bad people trying to game the system.

Consider the example of a large online gaming company that has problems with criminals calling up the support desk to duping the support personnel into changing the passwords on specific accounts so that the criminals could go into the accounts and sell the assets. A possible solution is to create a decision tree support personnel can use to authenticate callers. As long as the support personnel follow the provided guidance, no accounts will be compromised and no one has to train the support personnel to handle each and every possible scenario that bad people might try. None of those details matter. They just need to know the one way to do their job properly.

Though this strategy may not be feasible in every case, for every job function, your awareness efforts should generally focus on providing guidance in how people should do their jobs properly. This requires embedding security within job functions.

In many cases, you may find detailed procedures already defined but not well known or practiced. In this case, your job is to find those procedures and figure out how best to translate them into practice.

Recognizing the Role of Awareness within a Security Program

Awareness isn't a stand-alone program that the security team uses to deal with the *user problem*, as it's commonly called. Security awareness is a tactic, not a strategy, used to deal with the user problem.

As covered in the earlier section "Reducing losses from phishing attacks," for a phishing attack to exploit your organization, your system first has to receive the email message on your server. Your system then has to process the message and present it to the user. The user has to review the message and decide how to act on the message. If the message contains malware, the system has to allow the malware to install and execute. If the message sends the user to a malicious link, the system has to allow the user to reach the malicious web server. If the user gives up their credentials on a malicious web server, the system then has to allow the malicious party to log in from anywhere in the world.

When a phishing attack succeeds, the user action is just one link in a fairly involved chain that requires failure throughout the entire chain. This statement is true for just about any user action, whether it involves technology or not.

Here are several concepts to consider:

>> The user is not the weakest link.

>> Awareness addresses one vulnerability among many.

>> The user experience can lead the user to make better decisions — or avoid making a decision in the first place.

>> Most importantly, to stop the problem, you have to engage and coordinate with other disciplines. See Book 6, Chapter 3.

Dealing with user-initiated loss (after all, the actions can be either unintentional or malicious) requires a comprehensive strategy to deal with not just the user action but also whatever enables the user to be in the position to create a loss and then to have the loss realized. You can't blame a user for what is typically, again, a complex set of failures.

Though it's true that, as an awareness professional, you can just do your job and operate in a vacuum, doing so inevitably leads to failure. It goes against the argument that you *deserve more*. This doesn't mean that the failure wouldn't happen even if everyone cooperated, but operating in a vacuum sends the wrong message.

REMEMBER

Awareness isn't a strategy to mitigate user-initiated loss — it's a tactic within a larger security strategy.

The security awareness program isn't the sole effort responsible for mitigating user error. If you say nothing to oppose this idea, you give the impression that you agree with it. Worse, you give the impression that users are responsible for any loss resulting from harmful actions that you already anticipate they will eventually make, such as clicking on a phishing link or accidentally deleting a file.

You have a responsibility to reduce risk by encouraging secure behaviors. But you're also part of a team and you should work in concert to support that entire security team to reduce loss. In a coordinated cybersecurity department, each team determines their part in reducing losses related to user actions and takes the appropriate actions. Likewise, each team determines how best to support each other in the overall reduction of user-related losses.

As a security awareness professional, you can be the tip of the spear in coordinating a comprehensive solution to reducing user-related losses. Your primary focus is to create behavioral improvements that reduce the initiation of losses.

Disputing the Myth of the Human Firewall

The section heading might anger a lot of security awareness professionals, but the idea of the human firewall is a dangerous myth. The idea that users are your last line of defense (which is a catchphrase for many phishing simulation companies) is fundamentally *wrong*.

First, consider that users are *not* the last line of defense in any practical way. For example, if a user clicks on ransomware, the user environment can stop the user from downloading malware by not giving the user permission to install software. Even if the software is downloaded and installed, antimalware can stop the ransomware. To accept that the user is the last line of defense, you have to discount many useful technologies that are commonplace in organizations.

Michael Landewe, the CTO of Avanan, said it best:

> If a user is our last line of defense, we have failed as an industry.

Regarding the claim of creating a human firewall, in principle it sounds great, but any security professional knows that even technical firewalls will fail. Users are less reliable than technology. Creating a human firewall implies that you will create an entire organization of users who always behave appropriately and securely. That isn't possible, however. Though humans can consistently behave well, no individual (and especially no group of humans) in the history of mankind has always exhibited error-free behaviors.

Consider also that although other technologies do only what they're instructed to do, humans can have malicious intent. If you leave your users as your last line of defense and they're malicious, the results will be disastrous.

I want you to create the best security awareness programs possible, but you need to remember where you fit within the overall chain of actions. If you give the impression that the user has ultimate control of your systems, then the first time a user fails, you fail in your self-described mission, which can damage the credibility of your program. Consider that you don't even see people who manage firewalls imply that their firewalls will stop all attacks from getting in. If you spout off to management that you will create a human firewall to repel all attacks targeting humans, then the first time a user fails, your program has failed based on *your* statements. Everything else you do will be met with skepticism, including requests for budget funds, personnel, time, and other resources. Don't set yourself up for failure from the start.

The reality is that most people don't give users and security awareness programs enough credit. Every time a user avoids clicking on a phishing message, your awareness efforts are successful. Every time a user locks up sensitive information, your awareness efforts are successful. Every time a user protects their screen from shoulder surfers, your awareness efforts are successful. These successes happen all the time.

Your users are a critical part of your organization's system, and your efforts can significantly reduce loss. Aware users help organizations avoid disaster. Even when attacks are reported after the fact, aware users respond appropriately, alert the appropriate people, and significantly reduce the resulting loss.

The awareness programs you create can provide an immense return on investment. Just be sure that you set realistic expectations.

Chapter **2**

Creating a Security Awareness Strategy

uilding a security awareness program requires having *strategy*. CBT and phishing services are tactics. Before you start buying anything, you should know how you intend to use it, and how it fits within the overall strategy of your awareness program. So often, people get ahead of themselves and buy the wrong tools for their needs, and then a security awareness professional needs to work with them to figure out how to adapt these wrong tools for a job that would have been much more straightforward had they invested in proper planning.

This chapter helps you figure out how to approach users, gauge whether they are listening to your ideas (nothing works if no one listens!), and of course, find a way to pay for it all.

Identifying the Components of an Awareness Program

To create a security awareness program that works, you first need to know the three components of any successful awareness program:

» **Communications tools:** These are the methods of communication you use to promote your awareness message. The communication tools represent *how* you communicate with your target population. These can be traditional tools, such as newsletters, posters, and videos. They can also include gamification and other, more creative efforts. (Don't miss Book 6, Chapter 8, which covers the ins and outs of gamification.)

» **Topics:** Topics are *what* you communicate through the communications tools. For example, topics might include phishing prevention, physical security, and other messages.

» **Metrics:** The methods you use to measure how well you achieve your goals are called *metrics.* In the ideal world, these metrics are the tangible savings that you create with your awareness program. (You can find much more on metrics in Book 6, Chapter 5.)

TIP

Before you can bring together these communications tools, topics, and metrics, you must perform a thorough analysis of corporate culture, business driver, past incidents, and other factors to determine a strategy for your awareness program. Book 6, Chapter 3 shows how to perform such an analysis.

REMEMBER

You can implement all the tactics you want, but you can claim that your program has the potential to succeed only when you have a defined strategy that enables you to measure how well your program performs. How well you bring together the communication tools, topics, and metrics of an awareness program is a huge part of its potential success.

Choosing effective communications tools

An organization's culture tells you how the organization prefers to communicate. Keep this in mind when you choose communications tools for your awareness program. Step back and consider the organization's culture. Be strategic with your choices.

KNOWING SOME BASIC TERMINOLOGY

You may have encountered some of the terms I use in this book in other publications. Here is how I define the following terms:

- **Organization:** I use *organization* to describe the high-level business entity. I don't use the words *company* or *business* because the readers of this book might work for another type of entity, such as a government agency. So organization represents what most people consider their company as a whole.

- **Culture:** This is the organization's behavioral and communications style.

- **Subculture:** If distinct entities within an organization have a different culture from the rest of the organization, I refer to it as a *subculture*. An organization may have many subcultures. Many organizations have no distinct culture but are composed of many subcultures.

Book 6, Chapter 3 provides ideas for how you can get to know the culture of an organization, but for now, understand that organizations often have preferred communications methods that are driven by their overall culture. Many organizations have an overabundance of internal newsletters, for example, and most people who work for these organizations just delete these newsletters before reading them whenever they receive yet another newsletter.

TECHNICAL STUFF

A big difference exists between a security culture and an organization culture. The purpose of a security awareness program is to change the security culture that exists within the organizational culture. So when you choose communication tools, you're seeking to communicate in a way that people expect you to communicate. Your ultimate goal, however, is to improve or change security-related behaviors, and — ideally — attitudes. You want to *drive* the security culture, not adhere to it.

When choosing communication tools, consider also that most (if not all) organizations contain subcultures within an overall culture. Each subculture, or subgroup, within the organization has distinct business needs and communications styles. A retailer like Walmart, for example, typically has at least four subcultures: headquarters, IT, store associate, and distribution center employee. Each of these subcultures must be addressed independently. Unlike some retail items, communication styles are rarely one-size-fits-all. For more information how best to work with the subcultures within an organization, see Book 6, Chapter 3.

TIP

The easiest way to determine there is a distinct subculture is if there are unique communications styles for a given business unit — as well as distinct needs for different topics. In a retail organization, for example, the people who work in the corporate headquarters have ready access to desktop computers, perform most of their work on those computers, and regularly handle sensitive information. The retail associates are in an open store environment, have minimal access to computers, and have tactical access to information needed to assist customers and perhaps handle a financial transaction. Both groups have vastly different awareness needs and receive information in different ways.

Picking topics based on business drivers

Once you understand how to communicate effectively within an organization's culture, you need to figure out the concerns that are important to each culture within the organization (and it may have more than one). The *business drivers* are those operational concerns that the organization considers most important. When you consider topics to cover in your awareness program, ask this question:

What do people need to understand to do their jobs properly?

When you create a security awareness program for an organization where people work on personal computers and check email frequently, you clearly want to include, as a topic of your program, the proper use of computers. The business drivers differ when you're creating a program for a warehouse-based culture. In a warehouse, people probably use personal computers infrequently, so the topics you choose to cover might be geared more toward mobile device security and the importance of not sharing inventory details, which could reveal proprietary information and imply the organization's financial status.

Don't randomly choose one topic per month for 12 months to determine your awareness program content; create conscious intent for the program. As covered in Book 6, Chapter 3, be sure you tailor the content for the needs of the culture you're addressing. You may find that you need to repeat important topics and ignore others. Your goal is to provide constant relevance to your organization and not choose topics just because they're ones that everyone else thinks your program should have.

WARNING

Avoid focusing on irrelevant topics, because users may perceive it as a waste of time. The topics you present should be either obviously useful to work life or applicable to home life. Presenting topics for the sake of presenting them isn't useful — and may even create backlash. During the height of the COVID-19 pandemic, for example, travel security wasn't relevant, as no one was traveling at that time.

Knowing when you're a success

The last component of an awareness program is arguably the most important, and often the most overlooked: metrics. Metrics allow you to measure improvement, or a lack thereof.

TECHNICAL STUFF

Metrics should be collected as frequently as reasonable, given available resources and practicality. For example, if you want to use the number of malware incidents as a metric, in theory you can log in hourly to your antimalware system. The reality is that once a week might be reasonable.

Stop and consider that typical metrics involve the percentage of people who complete mandatory training. The typical metrics may also include the percentage of people who click on phishing simulations. Ensuring that everyone completes the mandatory training may hold some value for compliance efforts, but this metric doesn't tell you whether the organization has experienced an improvement in awareness or, more important, an improvement in behaviors. Likewise, phishing simulations tell you that people recognize phishing simulations, but this metric doesn't necessarily mean that people know how to recognize real-life phishing messages.

Weigh what you know about an organization's business drivers against what you know about its culture to determine which metrics are worth collecting. In terms of business drivers, pursuing important metrics that give useful results will justify support for the awareness program. An organization's culture, on the other hand, tells you what metrics can be reasonably collected. The metrics you collect should be both important and reasonable to collect, given available resources.

Awareness programs traditionally have a difficult time justifying their existence. If you can build in the justification from the start, you enhance your chances of success. Start now: Make metrics as important to your program as any communications tool you use.

TIP

Consider collecting metrics *before* you start your awareness efforts. By measuring behaviors before you implement your program, you can show how much things have (hopefully) improved due to your efforts.

Book 6, Chapter 5 discusses how to determine metrics in more detail.

Figuring Out How to Pay for It All

Though it isn't necessarily a fundamental part of an awareness program, you must proactively understand how to acquire the funding and other required resources for your program. There are countless awareness efforts you can implement, but the most limiting factor will likely be your allocated budget and supporting resources.

TIP

You probably already have an assigned budget. However, you might be able to increase that budget by cooperating with other internal efforts, such as privacy and regulatory compliance programs. A great deal of synergy typically exists across these efforts, and you might be able to share in their budgets, if you help them achieve their goals.

Other resources might include staff to support your efforts, access to corporate communications programs that distribute communication within an organization, and executive support. Try to determine the ideal awareness program, and then examine what it might cost. For example, you might want to bring in an outside speaker. If you want to invite a prominent authority from the security industry, you must be able to pay their fee. To contain costs, you may want to consider a local law enforcement officer or an internal expert. And don't forget the venue: Before you can even enlist a free speaker, you need to reserve a place for the event.

As you bring together your plans, you should at least have in mind the general range of your budget. If you have metrics that demonstrate the value of your awareness efforts, it may increase the budget and the level of support you receive. In the meantime, as the saying goes, you can't have a prince's appetite on a pauper's budget. You can, however, become creative. Book 6, Chapter 6 addresses budgeting, and potentially increasing your budget, in more detail.

Chapter **3**

Determining Culture and Business Drivers

O ften, when an awareness manager seeks help with their awareness program, they start off talking about the videos they chose. They describe how they thought the videos were funny or the right length or whatever else they considered when choosing them.

What these managers rarely consider is how specifically the videos fit their organization's culture. They don't consider, for example, which groups within the organization will watch which video.

To put together an awareness program that works for your organization, you must tailor the program — and that includes videos and any other aspects of the program — to the organization's culture and subcultures. You must understand the business drivers and how they affect the work done by each group within the organization.

Understanding Your Organization's Culture

If you want to put together an awareness program, your first step is understanding your organization to figure out what will *really* work. Even if something works for a lot of other organizations, you have little guarantee that it will work for yours. You need to understand what defines success for your organization and how to achieve it.

REMEMBER

You must consider the security culture *and* the general culture of an organization. An organization's *security* culture is how people behave with regard to security-related concerns; the *general* culture is how the organization behaves as a whole. When you create a security awareness program, you work within an organization's general culture to improve its security culture.

For example, an investment bank typically is a formal organization: People generally dress formally and act conservatively. You might assume that they would behave more securely, but frequently that isn't the case. Investment bankers often don't want to wear badges that will ruin their $5,000 suits. They don't want the aggravation of separate passwords. And they are frequently perceived as being their organization's moneymakers, so the organization typically doesn't enforce security policies on them.

Organization culture tells you how to communicate within the organization. You need to understand this point so that you know how to influence the people in an organization. If everyone in an organization religiously reads a daily newsletter put out by the CEO's office, you might try to get content published in that newsletter to ensure your ideas reach as many employees as possible.

Culture is the combined behaviors of the organization. You see how everyone behaves and communicates. If an investment bank has fine art hanging in its lobby, you don't want to put up a cheap security awareness poster. You might put posters in certain bathroom stalls, but clearly not in a prominent place.

You can generally look around to see how your organization communicates. Consider how you know how to do your job. Consider how you find out about important information. How do mandates come down? What are the *musts* in the organization, and what are the *shoulds*? How does everyone behave in general?

TIP

When choosing the communication tools for your program, consider how they're otherwise used in an organization. For example, if you're considering using videos, consider whether videos are forced on people as a mandate. Consider these questions: Do people appreciate the other videos they're required to see? Do they follow the presented guidance? As you design your awareness program, you should consider whether what you're considering using is actually used and accepted throughout the organization. Though you might hear that something is part of a typical awareness program, you need to consider how it fits within your specific organization.

Culture isn't just a matter of looking at the walls — the overall work environment is a critical driver of culture as well. For example, if you work in a factory, your methods of communicating are limited, if not defined, by the factory's environment. Employees likely have no personal computers, which therefore might eliminate the ability to use screensavers or have them watch videos. Flight attendants and pilots have a limited ability to access information at work. Unionized environments frequently limit formal training hours, so mandating awareness videos would likely require eliminating other training requirements.

Though some nuances might not be obvious, such as limitations on training, communications mechanisms and styles are clearly apparent to even the casual observer. Though you need to delve into more than what's visible, by observing how the organization conveys information, performs on-the-job training, and generally operates — and on how its managers interact with employees — you can observe how the culture passes on information. If you see that information from the security department isn't adhered to or is generally ignored, you can observe how information that is well received makes it to the population, such as in the earlier example of the CEO's daily newsletter at the investment bank.

Before choosing a communications tool to be a part of your awareness program, find out whether the organization already uses the tool. If it doesn't, ask yourself why not. If you still want to use the tool, ask yourself why you believe it will be accepted, given that your organization has no experience with the tool.

On the heels of the COVID-19 lockdown, you also need to consider whether the communications styles you see are transient or the new normal. Microsoft Teams might be the preferred communications tool for the foreseeable future, for example, or it might be a temporary solution that you can rely on only for the short term.

TIP

If your organization has a corporate communications department, someone there might be able to provide you with invaluable guidance about the best ways to communicate. This person may have a biased perspective, but if they can provide statistics about the effectiveness of different communications tools and communications methods, their guidance can be quite useful.

Determining security culture

Security culture isn't directly related to the overall culture of the organization, but you must evaluate security culture whenever you study your organization's culture. Determining security culture is often easier than determining organizational culture.

When you perform a *social engineering assessment* (by simulating a nontechnical attack to test for security awareness vulnerabilities), you can usually determine within the first 30 seconds the level of success you will have because — after taking a quick look around — you can usually determine an organization's security culture.

Do people hold the door open for strangers? Are desks left unattended with information and computers unprotected? Do people wear badges? Is any adherence to security policies apparent?

Whether or not there are policies or procedures is irrelevant. The only thing that matters is the common behaviors, or results of those behaviors, exhibited by the population as a whole. This becomes quickly obvious.

TECHNICAL STUFF

The existence of security policies, procedures, and guidelines in no way indicates that the governance is followed. The existence of documents is only useful for audits, unless the specified behaviors become a part of common practice within the organization.

As important, you find that if people are lax with certain security behaviors, they are likely lax with most, if not all, behaviors. People who leave their desks unlocked, for example, are more likely to exhibit other weak behaviors, such as using their home computers for work purposes.

Likewise, people who exhibit strong security behaviors for one aspect of security typically exhibit strong behaviors across most, if not all, aspects of security. People who lock their desks are more likely to challenge strangers they see walking around the facilities. If you see enough of these people, they will raise the security posture of the entire organization.

You can use what you learn about an organization's baseline security culture to figure out a starting point for your awareness program. Remember, though, that although you always need to know where you're starting from, how you got there likely isn't the best way to move forward. You should use what you learn about your organization's overall culture to determine the best structure for an awareness effort moving forward.

Recognizing how culture relates to business drivers

Business drivers are important to consider when examining culture. Again, culture determines your communications tools, whereas business drivers typically determine your topics. However, business drivers are frequently defined by the culture as well.

Factory workers, for example, might have limited access to computers. This implies that employees will likely have to review critical communications on their personal computing devices and, most frequently, their mobile devices. Factory workers typically have more concerns with physical security.

TIP

Consistency of business drivers across the entire organization indicates whether an organization has a single culture or multiple cultures. Knowing what you're dealing with on this front is critical to designing an awareness program.

Identifying Subcultures

No organization of more than minor size is a monolith in any regard. That is definitely true of their security and overall organizational cultures. There are clearly many unique cultures within most organizations.

Consider Walmart. At the time of this writing, Walmart is the largest company in the world, and the company is primarily a retailer. Because Walmart is generally a retailer, you might think a single awareness program is all you need in order to satisfy the company's requirements. When you look more closely, however, you can readily see that Walmart is composed of many different cultures, each of which requires its own awareness program.

The Walmart headquarters operation, for example, deals with contracts, finance, land acquisition, intellectual property, regulatory issues, and a wide variety of other fundamental and complex business concerns. The headquarters' operation has mostly desk workers with regular PC access. These desk workers have regular access to valuable data.

Walmart also has an IT team, which keeps the organization functioning. IT employees likewise have regular computer access and possibly some intellectual property. Their access facilitates the operations of computers throughout the organization and overall operations, which includes facilitating the use of sensitive information throughout the organization.

Then you have the Walmart distribution centers. Workers in those facilities have access to computers only to assist with movement of goods. These computers are likely mobile devices. These workers have limited access to sensitive information, except that what they see and do has financial implications. If these workers see that items are out of stock, for example, they have information that could reveal the financial health of the organization or suppliers.

Then you have store associates, who have limited use of computers, except to facilitate transactions and stock shelves. These devices, especially the point-of-sales (POS) systems, have limited functionality but arguably provide the most critical function of a retail business.

Each of these business units has a unique culture, which means their communications style and business drivers are distinct. Consider that each business unit has workers with distinct skill sets and varying levels of experience with computers. In addition, the demographics between business units varies, and many other distinct characteristics exist. Also consider that each business unit has different levels of employee longevity, which affects training requirements. This doesn't even include the differing geographies where the company functions, which implies different cultural considerations. Ideally, each business unit should have its own awareness program because you need to use different communications tools and address different topics to meet the needs of each individual unit.

TECHNICAL STUFF

This chapter addresses culture and the implications for communications tools. However, the presence of distinct business drivers is still critical in the determination of whether you're dealing with a distinct subculture requiring a unique awareness program.

For example, consider that the executive team of a large organization likely has similar communications tools as the IT team. They primarily work on desktop computers and communicate via electronic means as well as have in-person discussions. However, they have very different business functions. The executive team deals with sensitive information and needs to secure the information from social engineering, accidental compromise, and the maintenance of basic computer security. The IT team deals with some sensitive information, but has other sources of concern from social engineering, computer access and maintenance, and potentially authenticating users asking for support. In this case, you might use many of the same communications tools to reach each group but customize topics to match each group's business function.

Interviewing Stakeholders

Although you can easily observe an organization's culture, generally, as you look around, keep in mind that observations alone are just a starting point. Observations can go a long way, but you also need to gather information about what isn't obvious and/or might be important to the organization.

The identity of the stakeholders varies by organization, as well as the interest among the people you approach. You might find that many people you want to talk to don't believe it's a good use of their time. Some people don't believe they have anything to contribute. Others might believe that being involved is an important task and demand to have input.

TIP

People may not always be enthusiastic to meet with you, but they will usually agree to give you at least 30 minutes of their time. Should you run into difficulty having people agree to meet with you, if you believe those people are critical to the success of your program, you can appeal to the people who mandate your program to reach out on your behalf.

TIP

It's always a good idea to interview the CEO and other executives, as they make themselves available. It gives them a sense of ownership in the awareness program, which might lead to more access to other people. Most important, it makes it significantly more likely that you will receive visible support and participation from the CEO.

Visible support from the CEO will open doors for you and ensure that you find the support and access you need from departments and people throughout the organization. Ideally, this also leads to obtaining the funding you need.

Requesting stakeholder interviews

Here are some people to consider asking for interviews (you may not be the one to conduct the interview, but you can at least request it):

>> **CISO (chief information security officer):** This person is responsible for the overall security program, and likely has oversight of the awareness program.

>> **Physical security manager:** This person likely has overlapping concerns with your efforts and may have both insight and budget to contribute. The person may also agree to have security guards and other members of their team participate in your efforts, such as to post posters during their rounds.

>> **General counsel:** The general counsel likely has guidance on what is important to the organization, and may also know constraints you're not familiar with.

>> **Compliance team:** This team may be able to offer guidance to what you should include in the awareness program. They can share their experiences in promoting compliance efforts in the organization, for example, or they might even have an interest in cooperating with your efforts and have resources to contribute.

>> **Corporate communications team:** These might be the most important people to interview. In many organizations, they are the gatekeepers to the employees. They control all messaging to employees. They frequently have standards you must meet in order to have your materials distributed. They

can tell you what communications tools are most widely accepted by the organization as a whole, and they may have a regular communications venue you can contribute to. This team possibly has a graphics team that can help you create materials. These people are likely long-term partners for your awareness program. Early on, however, you need to understand their roles and requirements and determine how they want you to work with them.

>> **Human resources team:** The human resources (HR) department is critical to an awareness program. They manage personnel policies, know what type of training requirements and limitations employees may have, and maintain a general awareness of any privacy or other concerns you may not have considered previously.

>> **Training teams:** Many organizations have in-house training teams who create and manage training programs across the organization. This involves technical, compliance, and any other type of required training. They typically are involved with choosing an awareness training vendor, and likely have requirements for what type of training gets loaded into the organization's learning management system.

>> **Unions or other advocacy groups:** In some environments, there is strong union involvement in training and employment. Union contracts may limit how many hours of training employees can be required to take. Any awareness training required of employees would require removing other occupational training. You need to learn whether you face any potential limitations on your efforts, and try to win over support from people who can veto your efforts.

>> **Wellness team:** A security awareness program is essentially a behavioral change program. Though wellness programs might have different focuses for behavioral change, they likely have a great deal of experience in attempting to communicate with the employees, and they can share their experiences. They can likely tell you what has worked and what failed so that you don't have to make the same mistakes they did. An extremely competent wellness team would collect metrics to show the success of their efforts, and they might provide critical guidance to how you can prove your return on investment.

>> **Sustainability team:** Many organizations also have a team devoted to promoting recycling, conservation, and similar efforts. This team often knows the most effective ways to communicate with the organization.

>> **Safety manager:** By nature, safety programs attempt to change employee behaviors and save the organizations money. If an organization has a strong safety program in place, the safety manager likely already knows what works to influence behavior throughout the organization and has a great deal to share.

- » **Chief officers (CXOs):** Each chief officer can provide information about what can make the awareness program valuable to their operations. If you can make them believe that you can satisfy their concerns and provide a benefit to their operations, they may provide resources, support, and so much more to assist your efforts.

- » **Geographic representatives:** If your organization cuts across many geographic regions, you need to understand the differences between the regions. It may seem obvious that differences exist between North America and Asia, but even within a region, you can find *significant* cultural differences. For example, New York City and Omaha, Nebraska, are located in North America, but these locations are almost certain to have different cultures.

- » **Influencers:** Every organization has certain people who know how to influence others in the organization. You find these influencers by asking others who they are. An influencer might be a department executive, an executive assistant, an office manager, or another person in a similar role. Influencers can tell you what it would take for them to follow your guidance, as well as what you need to do convince others.

- » **Representative employees:** Ask your points of contact (POC) to arrange meetings with one or two representative users. Users, who are unafraid to speak out, frequently have input that you would never receive otherwise. They give you opinions about what will work and what won't. Make it a point to ask these folks what they think would work, and they respond with something they saw in the past that they believe had a significant impact. This can be some of the most valuable insight you can find. The representative users can provide overall attitudes about cybersecurity, describe impediments to adhering to cybersecurity guidance, and describe drivers that lead them to behave securely or insecurely, for example. In an ideal world, you stay connected with these people and use them as a focus group throughout the course of your program.

This is just a partial list of the people you may want to interview. You need to look into what is most appropriate for your organization and circumstances.

WARNING

Opinions are like noses: Everybody has one. Though you should assume the best from everyone, don't accept as the gospel truth whatever everyone else says. For example, one user told me that we should end phishing exercises because they make people feel bad if they click on a fake message. That might be true, but you cannot forego a basic component of an awareness program because one user doesn't like it (and claims that others who haven't spoken up feel the same way).

WARNING

After about ten interviews, you generally receive little new information from each additional person you interview. Collecting information isn't the only benefit to these meetings, however. You can use these interviews as meetings to win over people who wield influence within the organization. When interviews start producing an abundance of repeated information, you might consider interviewing only those people you expect to possess unique insights or influence, or who help address political considerations.

Scheduling the interviews

As a consultant who designs awareness programs, you might try to go onsite and schedule interviews to occur over two days. Schedule 30 minutes for each interview. If you have to perform interviews remotely, organizations typically schedule the interviews over a longer period. Try to limit that period to two weeks.

If you're part of an internal team, you likely have unlimited time to connect with others. Try to limit the interview window regardless so that you can eventually move the project into the design-and-implementation phase.

Creating interview content

The primary purpose of the interview is to learn about the culture and business drivers of the organization so that you can design your program. Again, this would include the communications tools, topics, and metrics. To get to those points, however, you must ask a wide-ranging set of questions.

Consider using a questionnaire going into the interview, but use the questionnaire as more of a formatted conversation starter. Some questions you include may require a simple answer; other questions may be open ended, intended to start a conversation. For example, you might ask, "What do you like most about the current awareness program? Why is that?"

TECHNICAL STUFF

Consider inviting the CISO to sit in on the meetings. The CISO can tell you how much they're learning from these interviews. Their primary purpose is to gather information that furthers the awareness program, but you can end up collecting a great deal of information that is valuable to the organization's security program as a whole.

TIP

Ask "Why?" as much as possible. The answers to why questions tell you what works and what doesn't. Things rarely work as intended. That isn't necessarily bad, as users frequently find value where none was intended.

Following are questions you should ask everyone you interview. You also need to ask questions specific to the person's job function and relationship or the influence they have to their awareness person:

>> What are the biggest problems you see?

>> What are the security strengths you see?

>> Do you have any specific concerns?

>> (If someone has been with the organization for a while) What has worked best within the company to change behaviors?

>> (If someone is new to the organization) Have you seen anything in your past organizations that you think would work here?

>> What have been the parts of the current awareness program that you like?

>> What did you not like?

>> Do you see other departments communicate well with employees? How do they do that?

>> Do you think the organization places importance on security?

>> Do you think your line manager expects certain things of you?

>> What happens if adhering to security guidelines causes you to take longer to do your job?

>> What prevents you from following good awareness practices?

>> How do you prefer to receive awareness information?

>> What information do you need?

>> What information do you want to see?

>> Can you offer any guidance to the awareness program?

Taking names

As you gather information about the organization's culture, you want to make sure that you collect the contact information of anyone who is especially critical to the success of your program. Some of these people may be responsible to distribute information, such as the primary point of contact in the corporate communications department.

TIP

The interview process is part of the analysis phase of creating an awareness program. You should already have some ideas about what you want to learn or the feedback you want before performing the interviews. Keeping these ideas in mind when you meet with people allows you to assess the feasibility and difficulty of your ideas while also proactively helping with the implementation.

You may need to work with the physical security department, for example, to distribute non-electronic information, such as administering desk drops via this department or requiring the cooperation of the cafeteria manager to put table tents in the cafeteria.

WARNING

Identify the people who control the resources you need as early in the development of your program as possible. If you wait until later, you may find that some of your ideas are impractical. If you want to plan a desk drop, for example, you need to know the resources are available to print and then distribute the materials to every desk in the organization; without this assurance, you might end up developing a concept that you can't implement.

Partnering with Other Departments

As you analyze your organization, you need to figure out which other departments you need to (or should) partner with. Many of these departments are the same as those you should consider interviewing. (Refer to the earlier section, "Interviewing Stakeholders.")

As you interview people from those departments, you need to determine which of those departments can offer you support, resources, or anything else that can further your goals. As the security awareness manager, your fundamental job is to create a communications program as well as distribute the communications. Other departments clearly have similar responsibilities in one way or another. Not only can you learn from them — they may be able to help you.

TIP

During your early conversations with the departments, try to highlight your mission and the support you have from management. This should help convince others to support you when you ask for their help.

TIP

To the best of your ability, research the efforts of other departments before you talk to them. Clearly, you won't know everything they do, but if you can at least have an idea of their efforts, you might have ideas for cooperation, the support they can provide you, and most important, the support you can provide them.

Some partnerships might be mandated. Any organization of more than trivial size generally requires that the corporate communications department distributes all information to employees. Other departments may find that you have synergistic goals and agree to help you, assuming that you will help them achieve their mission. Be aware, however, that obtaining the desired support might not be easy — and you're asking potentially overworked people to perform more work on your behalf.

Here are some types of partnerships you might consider:

>> Joint events

>> Joint communications

>> Messaging in currently available communications tools

>> Printing and manufacturing contracts and resources in place

>> Distribution resources, such as security guards doing rounds

WARNING

Partnerships are great, but be wary of relying too heavily on partners. You have no authority over the partner departments, so you have no control if they reallocate resources. Their priorities might change, or they may choose to change their programs. The more you can obtain voluntary cooperation, the better.

Chapter **4**

Choosing the Best Tools for the Job

O nce you decide on the topics you want to cover in your awareness program, you must choose how you want to communicate those topics to users. Many methods and tools are available to facilitate this communication, and your job is to determine which of those methods will work best for the organizational culture.

If an organization has people who work with desktop computers, for example, screen savers is likely one of your methods. If you're working with a manufacturing environment and the workers have morning meetings before reporting to the shop floor, you will want to supplement the content covered in those meetings with content related to your awareness program. Expect to build on the communications tools already used and, possibly, introduce brand-new tools.

This chapter describes some communications tools commonly used in awareness programs. Not all the tools covered in this chapter are used by every organization. At the same time, this chapter doesn't provide an exhaustive list of every possible tool you might use. As you read the chapter, consider which tools seem like they might work best for the various subcultures within your organization. The hope is that you discover new tools that you can add to this list. Book 6, Chapter 6 shows how to roll out the tools you choose.

Before you dive into choosing and rolling out tools, though, consider first identifying people who can perform outreach on behalf of the security team and its initiatives.

Identifying Security Ambassadors

Many awareness programs use employees from throughout their organization as an extension of their team. They find people who are willing to perform outreach on behalf of the security team to promote cybersecurity practices. These people are frequently called *champions* or *ambassadors*.

Depending on the culture of the organization, the ambassadors provide presentations and act as your local representatives. They promote your messaging. They distribute your materials. They organize local events. They take on the role that the local culture requires.

Though ambassadors may not be critical to all subcultures within an organization, having a trusted person who is a member of the local team as your representative can increase the acceptance of your program.

Finding ambassadors

Finding a team of people who already have full-time responsibilities to do the bidding of the awareness program is obviously a fairly difficult task by itself. You therefore need to be creative in your recruitment efforts.

TIP

To make your job simpler, you need to find out what's available throughout the organization's culture and see, ideally, how to piggyback on those efforts. Many organizations have local safety representatives; some organizations have local HR representatives. Sometimes the administrative assistants have an established communications channel and are willing to serve as ambassadors. Ambassadors are most useful when they have already earned respect and influence throughout their environments.

In the absence of an established group to draw from, you have to find people to recruit. They have to be willing to take on additional work, and be willing to be an enthusiastic promoter of your program. To find qualified people, you can solicit by way of internal communications channels. You might want to see whether you can offer some form of reward, such as providing bonuses or at least potential support for better raises, promotions, and evaluations.

Maintaining an ambassador program

To enjoy the benefits of having ambassadors to amplify your messaging, you have to invest in creating a communications and support infrastructure and in training the people who serve as ambassadors. You need to budget appropriately and understand that you will have to devote significant effort to maintaining the ambassador program.

WARNING

Once you find potential ambassadors, you must ensure that they have proper training. They need to be reasonably competent in overall cybersecurity awareness because they will likely be called on to make presentations and answer questions. They should also be reasonably good communicators and, hopefully, respected by their colleagues. You therefore need to create a much more detailed awareness program for your ambassadors and ensure that they score reasonably well on knowledge evaluations. This can be a major effort on its own.

Depending on the size and dispersion of your organization, you may face a major challenge to ensure the success of your ambassador program. You need to ensure that you have reliable communications and that you can, ideally, send bulk materials to ambassadors as needed. It's relatively easy to send softcopy materials via email. However, if you want your ambassadors to set up tables, sponsor giveaways, and take part in other similar initiatives, you need to ensure that they can get the materials they need when they need them.

Ideally, you will have the budget to bring your ambassadors together on an annual, if not quarterly, basis. You need to provide a consistent level of technical knowledge — consider providing training on how to give presentations and engage in overall communications. The reality is that people who volunteer to support you are well-meaning, but you have no idea about the skills they bring with them.

Again, if you have the advantage of working with an established group of people or when the organization already has a safety champion program in place (as described in Book 6 Chapter 3), you can piggyback on top of that infrastructure. In the absence of having such an infrastructure already in place, you need to create it if you want to have a viable ambassador program.

WARNING

If you want to experiment with an ambassador program, keep in mind that you're expending not just your resources but also the time of the ambassadors, who have many other responsibilities. Though you might set aside some of your own effort and budget for experimentation, if a perception exists that you're wasting the time of the ambassadors, or otherwise using them poorly, that perception will generate a great deal of pushback.

Knowing the Two Types of Communications Tools

The distinction may seem small, but you need to understand the difference between passive and active communications tools. To many, an awareness tool is just an arrow in a quiver and you pull out the one that works best. The reality, however, is that you have to be mindful that passive and active tools aren't interchangeable. They require different resources and different levels of buy-in from other parties. They require that you expend different levels of goodwill. That being said, here are the basics:

>> **Passive communications tools:** Available to, but not forced on, anyone. In short, these tools require no interruption of a user's normal activity.

>> **Active communications tools:** Require interaction from the user.

REMEMBER

The distinguishing factor for active-versus-passive communications tools is an action of some sort being required. You don't have to read a poster. If you send the poster, or its contents, via email, the user at least has to click on the email to delete it. Generally, active tools are more expensive to acquire. Probably most important, active tools require more time commitment from users, which should be considered the largest expense you incur.

The next two sections discuss how you can get the most benefit from using each type of communications tool. Both are valuable but have different types of costs associated with them. Passive tools function as subtle reminders, hopefully, at the right place and time when used in the right way. Active tools can be much more impactful and tend to immediately capture your audience's attention. They do, however, come with more costs, both related to monetary costs and, even more important, time costs.

Reminding users to take action

Passive communications tools can be reminders, but, if placed appropriately, they can function as a *nudge*, which is a tool that prompts someone to do the right thing at the right time. A common nudge is the reminder in restrooms for employees to wash their hands or a mouse pad on a desk that reminds someone to lock the computer when leaving their desk. At the National Security Agency, stickers were applied to all unclassified telephones to warn users not to talk about classified information on that phone and that the phones were monitored.

Given that passive tools require no effort on the part of the users, you can, if you're allowed to, add as many tools as is reasonable. An organization might restrict where you can place objects (imagine the aesthetics of placing a security poster next to a Picasso!). Organizations also often limit the design styles you can use. And, of course, the organization controls your budget.

REMEMBER

Design styles are typically mandated, or at least approved by, the corporate communications team. They will likely define what you can or can't do. They should guide you on the allowable "look and feel." They may also have some helpful templates and ideas for your own tools.

TIP

Consider your passive tools strategically. When you examine an organization's facilities, you'll probably see opportunities for nudges and reminders just about everywhere. Definitely consider all available options, but don't overdo it. If you take over all available space, you risk overwhelming users.

Requiring interaction from users

Active communications tools require interaction on the part of a user. With a passive communication tool, a user can choose to read a poster on a wall while doing something else in the area, such as waiting for a printer or photocopy machine. An active communications tool, such as a training video, requires focused interaction from users.

The level of commitment required by an active tool can vary greatly. If you send someone a security tip via email, they can choose to delete the email in less than a second. Reading it, however, may take three to five seconds. At the other extreme, the NSA has employees take a two-day security awareness course. You can find personal protection courses that last more than a week.

THE HIDDEN COST OF SECURITY AWARENESS

When people think of the costs of your awareness efforts, they consider the hard costs of your program that comprise your budget, such as the cost to license training or run phishing simulations. They might even consider your salary or those of your staff and consultants. These are the obvious costs for your program.

Much more costly is the cost of the time the users spend away from their job responsibilities. For example, if you create a typical program that has a monthly CBT module

(continued)

(continued)

with quizzes and a newsletter, you can estimate that users need to spend a mere 10 minutes on each module. Over a year, this totals about 120 minutes, or 2 hours of time. When the average worker, at least in the United States, works 2,000 hours a year, a couple of hours a year seem like a reasonable amount of time to devote to security awareness training.

For every 1,000 people, however, a similar calculation indicates that the equivalent of one person is devoted specifically to security awareness training. Perhaps the average compensation with benefits is $50,000. You need to determine what that figure is for your own organization. If an organization has 5,000 employees, it translates to $250,000 per year. If an organization has 100,000 employees, the cost is $5 million per year. As you can quickly calculate, the hidden cost of lost productivity can be significantly more than the hard costs of the awareness program.

Book 6, Chapter 5 discusses this hidden cost in more detail, but for this chapter, you just need to understand that active communications tools require that they provide a return on investment that justifies the time invested in the provided training.

WARNING

Active tools can be considered a nuisance. Active tools go specifically to an individual, though a passive tool isn't specifically intended for anyone. If a user already knows and practices the guidance on a poster in a public area, they can rationalize that other people may not. If you send the same content by email, the user may be insulted that you think they don't know something that they actually practice every day. You therefore should carefully consider the benefit of any active tool to the potential for aggravation on the part of the users.

When used effectively, active tools can create a positive impression of your security program as a whole. You still need to consider the hidden costs of using those tools, however, to ensure a proper return on investment. (See the nearby sidebar, "The hidden cost of security awareness.")

Exploring Your Communications Arsenal

Your "communications arsenal" contains the communications tools most commonly used in security awareness plans. With so many tools already widely in use, and more to be discovered as you gain experience, you truly have an arsenal of tools to choose from.

As you explore the descriptions of each tool, try to figure out what may or may not be applicable for your awareness plan. Consider these points as you assess each tool:

» Is the tool appropriate for the corporate culture?

» Are the resources available to implement the tool correctly?

» Will it not be overly intrusive?

Research communications tools from other types of communications programs for new ideas. Safety programs, wellness programs, compliance programs — among many other types of organizational programs that intend to modify behaviors — likely have decades of combined experience in seeing what works and what doesn't work. Listen to their experiences.

The tools described in the following sections are passive communications tools. Examples of this type of tool include posters hung by the photocopier or printer, signs posted in the breakroom, or even a sign taped inside a bathroom stall. (Whatever works.) You make these tools available to users, but you don't force them to interact with the tools.

As described in Book 6, Chapter 6, you likely will have to balance your choice of tools with budget, competition for resources among departments, and other organizational limitations, as well as a variety of concerns specific to your situation.

Knowledgebase

A knowledgebase is among the most useful passive communications tools and among the least spoken about. In short, a *knowledgebase* is a library of information regarding security topics. The library should be filled with articles related to security topics that users can search and read as they want. The articles are typically made available to the organization by way of the security team's internal website or an internal knowledge library, such as a SharePoint system. It can also be a web-based system, like Wikipedia.

One benefit of a knowledgebase is that it provides a single place users can look to find detailed information on cybersecurity related topics when they want and need it. The articles in the knowledgebase offer a reasonably deep but user-friendly description of security topics. Providing a central repository allows for a comprehensive source of information with a consistent quality. Most communications tools cover awareness topics at a very high level and with little detail; knowledgebase articles provide more practical levels of information that help users understand and apply the knowledge.

TIP

You can embed links to knowledgebase articles into your other communications tools. If you send out a newsletter, for example, you might include links to the relevant knowledgebase articles so that newsletter recipients can find more detailed information.

Here's another example: You might tell users to secure their mobile devices in your awareness program. Though you can't provide instruction for securing all potential mobile devices in a 2-minute video, you can create a series of articles that walks users through the process of securing their mobile devices. You can create as many articles as required for securing iPhones with different versions of iOS, devices with different versions of Android, and so on.

You can create articles that walk users through more practical and personal topics, such as how to secure their home Wi-Fi or how to protect their children on the Internet. Unlike other communications tools, a knowledgebase usually has few limitations, as long as you can find a hosting system. The more robust you make the knowledgebase, the more useful it becomes, and the more users access it when they need information.

WARNING

Creating a knowledgebase obviously takes a lot of work; however, you must also realize that you're committing to the work of maintaining the knowledgebase and keeping the content updated. For example, if you describe how to secure an iPhone, you have to update the content whenever iOS is updated. Though that might be required only once a year — and some topics, such as how to choose a strong password, might rarely need updating — consider also all the other technologies you need to cover.

Posters

When used for a security awareness program, a *poster* conveys information on the topic of interest, such as phishing, physical security, or password protection. Of course, posters work only if users see them. Place posters in areas where they are allowed and will be seen.

WARNING

Though posters are straightforward in purpose, you still might have to work around some limitations. In some companies, the corporate communications department specifies a particular look-and-feel for all posters — which greatly limits creativity. Likewise, though all passive materials have the potential to become background noise, where they're less likely to be noticed. Similarly, if one poster has the same look-and-feel as the next one, users are unlikely to notice when the content of posters changes. You likely want to make sure that your awareness program has consistent branding, but you must make sure that the posters you use have some noticeable distinction between them.

Hardcopy newsletters

Printed newsletters can be distributed to users throughout an organization, placed in common areas, or posted on bulletin boards or similar venues. Organizations tend to send newsletters by email in soft copy, which makes them an active tool. In environments where computers are used less prevalently, distributing printed copies is the best option.

I classify newsletters as passive because, even if a newsletter requires someone to read it, which is an active act, users can just ignore it and choose not to read it.

TECHNICAL STUFF

I find that newsletters usually have a discussion of one or more awareness topics. The discussion of a topic is typically limited to two or three paragraphs. Embedding links to relevant knowledgebase articles as they are available can be helpful. Additionally, newsletters frequently feature short news stories and tips. Newsletters should also tell users how they can contact the security team.

The general form of newsletters varies, but they're usually two or four pages long. Newsletters are usually released once per month. If you have the content and resources, however, you can consider releasing one every two weeks, if the corporate culture considers that a reasonable release schedule and if critical information needs to be conveyed.

Monitor displays

Many organizations have monitors in public and work areas and use them to provide information to passing employees. Monitors are frequently in cafeterias, in lobby areas such as elevator lobbies, and in any other place where users congregate for any period. Typically, the monitors scroll through a variety of information that relates to general organizational issues, statements from executives, promotion of wellness, and other information that organizations want to distribute to others.

TIP

Find out who controls the content that these monitors display, and see whether they will include your security content with the other scrolling content. As mentioned in Book 6, Chapter 3, you should talk to the corporate communications department, which likely controls this content, but other parties may be involved. Monitor displays are most likely of similar dimensions as any hardcopy posters you use, but in a 16×9 format. The content you can post on monitor displays is likely limited, so have a proactive plan. Consider modifying the monitor content as frequently as possible because users will stop paying attention to the content after they see it three times. Any content shown on the display can serve as a reminder, but it becomes background noise when users see it too frequently.

Screen savers

Screen savers are computer monitor displays that appear whenever a computer is locked or has been inactive for a specified period. Organizations often define the content of screen savers, which can be used to display your security awareness content. Because computer monitor sizes vary, and likely include laptops, you need to create graphics in dimensions that can work on any monitor. You also need to work with the appropriate teams to update the displays in reasonable periods.

Pamphlets

Everyone is familiar with *pamphlets* — those hardcopy materials that are frequently folded pieces of paper. Unlike posters that contain a simple and single message, a pamphlet intends to be a reference document and provides more detailed information.

As with newsletters, an active element is clearly involved in reading a pamphlet. Again, though, users can easily choose to ignore the existence of the pamphlet.

TECHNICAL STUFF

From a design perspective, pamphlets are typically standard paper held in a landscape layout and then folded in half or thirds to provide for four or six pages. Though folding into six pages results in smaller pages, that may be desirable, given the amount or categorization of the content.

As enhanced references, pamphlets typically provide detail on a single subject. This is helpful for important topics, like how to handle information according to regulatory standards or how to secure information or types of technology. You have to anticipate not just the production costs, however, but also how the pamphlets are to be distributed. You can use them as giveaways at events. You might choose to make them available in public areas. If you want to distribute pamphlets to everyone within your organization, you need to research the logistics to get that done.

Desk drops

Any awareness tool that you distribute to each and every individual — usually, by leaving it on their desk — is referred to as a *desk drop*. Typically, the desk drop is an information card or pamphlet (or is similar to a pamphlet).

Some desk drops are more elaborate. A desk drop that occurs during the Halloween season, for example, may involve a small bag of candy that also contains information employees need to know. If you choose an elaborate desk drop, remember to plan for logistical challenges.

TECHNICAL STUFF

All organizations have a mechanism to get physical information into the hands of all employees. These mechanisms are being used less frequently as electronic resources become available to both distribute information electronically and allow the provision of legal confirmation that the materials were received and acknowledged. If you can find out how to access these distribution mechanisms, you will likely need to justify the use of the resources.

Table tents

Table tents are self-standing information cards. You may imagine taking a sheet of paper in portrait layout and folding the top edge to the bottom edge. This provides for display in the two outside faces. You might find similar displays in restaurants highlighting menu items.

TIP

There are frequently other common areas with tables where people eat, take breaks, or otherwise meet. In these cases, you may be able to persuade the cafeteria workers or maintenance staff to assist with proper placement of the table tents.

One use for table tents placed in meeting rooms is as a nudge to remind users to ensure that sensitive information is not left behind in the rooms, on whiteboards, or on the meeting room computers used to display presentations.

Coffee cups or sleeves

Perhaps one of the greatest awareness opportunities companies overlook is the cups they provide for coffee. Many organizations discourage disposable coffee cups, but if your organization does use them, you can place awareness messages on the cups.

Another option is to put messages on the cardboard sleeves that slip over the hot cups to allow for easier holding (and to avoid being burned). The sleeves are less expensive than the cups themselves, but you can still print messages on them.

WARNING

Before you choose to put messages on cups, check whether the people at your organization commonly use cardboard sleeves on their cups. If they do, your messages will be covered up most of the time.

Stickers

You can create a variety of stickers to serve as nudges and short awareness messages in general. The information on the sticker should be concise and appropriate to the purpose. Stickers can be placed on computers to remind users to lock the computer when it's unattended, as well as other equipment, such as telephones.

Stickers can be created for any purpose to provide a nudge where it's needed. If the design is creative, users may want to collect them, which may increase engagement with the awareness program.

As you design your awareness program, consider where you potentially need nudges and whether stickers would be a good solution.

TIP

Mouse pads

Mouse pads with security messages make useful reminders for good security practices. The one critical issue to consider is that mouse pads aren't regularly refreshed with new messaging, so you need to ensure that any content on the mouse pad will remain valuable for an extended period.

Mouse pads work well for communicating the generic branding of the awareness program — which creates engagement. Or you might consider messaging for a problem that is common and will be a consistent problem for a length of time. The message can remind users to secure their desk, to browse the Internet safely, to be wary of phishing messages, and more.

TECHNICAL STUFF

Pens and other useful giveaways

Pens, notebooks, sticky notes, or similar objects are all common items that are given away by organizations at events and other occasions. These types of giveaways are useful reminders of your messaging. Clearly, any results generated by giveaways such as these are nearly impossible to measure, because you never know who did not initiate loss as a result of listening to the message. But if you have the resources to create these tools and make them available, you can at least generate goodwill toward the security program.

Camera covers

Perhaps one of the most useful passive tools you can provide are covers that users can place over the camera lens on laptop computers and other camera lenses. The lenses are typically slightly bigger than a pinhole, and the covers can be stickers or a slider that is permanently affixed to the computer and slides back-and-forth to open and close.

You can put a message on the cover. The message can be specific to the fact that computer cameras can be hijacked and remotely controlled, even if the light is off, or you can put other short reminders. You can even simply use the awareness program branding to provide an overarching awareness reminder.

TIP

Squishy toys and other fun giveaways

Not every communications tool has to be immediately useful. One of the most common giveaways you see at events is the squishy toy. Though the toy's initial intent is stress relief, if it's designed well, people often choose to keep it around and it can then function as a reminder of your awareness program.

You can easily find companies that sell fun objects, such as rubber ducks, and allow you to print messages on them. If you have the budget, you can potentially create small likenesses of your program mascot. Other examples of such giveaways are Frisbees, stuffed animals, small games, and other toys.

Active communications tools

Active communications tools are those tools requiring users to interact with them. A time commitment is involved with interacting with these tools. The time to interact with them likely requires users to take time away from other duties, or else it just adds to the workload.

WARNING

Many organizations do not calculate the hidden cost of time involved in required training. Some organizations, especially those with blue collar workers, are quite aware of these costs. Even if costs are irrelevant to the organization and its leaders believe that the time spent on awareness is well worth it, many employees will likely complain about being forced to participate in the training. Given the inevitability of pushback in some form, be judicious in the active tools you choose.

WARNING

Book 6, Chapter 5 discusses in detail the critical difference between engagement and effectiveness. Active tools can be engaging in that they get users involved with the awareness program. However, it doesn't necessarily translate to effective behavior change. There is clearly an intangible benefit to inspiring users to engage with your awareness program; however, don't lose sight of the fact that as a business discipline, your awareness program should create a measurable return on investment, beyond just saying that people like your efforts.

Computer based training

Computer based training (CBT) is the video training that people have grown to love or hate. It's a recorded video that may or may not offer a quiz afterward. In short, it provides a fixed body of knowledge and probably checks for an acceptable level of immediate understanding of that knowledge.

WARNING

The CBT should be integrated with the entire awareness program. It is, however, where many awareness programs default to a check-the-box effort, where the printout of the completion of CBT becomes the goal of the program and the CBT is the *de facto* awareness program. Though it will satisfy compliance requirements, it's extremely unlikely that it will create a measurable impact in the improvement of security related behaviors.

CBT comes in many formats and styles, such as extended trainings where all information fits into a single session, and it can last for an hour or more. Sometimes users are fed one or two microlearnings per month, which are typically one to five minutes long and on a specific topic. It's also common to show one full annual training that is supplemented with monthly microlearnings.

The styles of CBT vary greatly. You have animations, clip art, live action, explainer videos, and anime style, for example. There are also different styles of delivery: CBT can attempt to be funny, or it can be intentionally stodgy, or it can be short and to the point. What's important to realize is that none of these style or themes is universally right or wrong. The style has to match the culture of the organization and be effective in getting the message across.

WARNING

Most people agree that making light of important subjects, such as sexual harassment or ethics, is grossly inappropriate. You need to consider likewise whether humor makes light of critical cybersecurity issues. Humor, if used in a responsible way to get a message across, can be useful. However, you have to walk a fine line between humor for the sake of humor and humor to enhance a message.

REMEMBER

Certain themed awareness videos also follow a supposedly engaging, ongoing storyline. Engagement can have some benefits, but you need to ensure that they produce a measurable impact on changing behaviors. You don't want to provide a video series where the only benefit is that users enjoy taking time away from their normal responsibilities.

Contests

You can implement a variety of activities that encourage users to learn by way of exploration and experience. They can take many forms and are limited only by your imagination. Here are some examples:

>> **Scavenger hunts**: You give users questions that have them search for cybersecurity related information based on technology sources, such as "What does *https* stand for?" You can also have them search policies to answer questions such as, "How many characters are required for a password?"

>> **Security cubicles:** Position a cubicle in a public place, and plant common security violations inside it. Then have users try to list all the violations. Examples are a printer with materials left behind on it, a monitor that isn't locked, and a sticky note with a password written on it.

This type of event might be virtual using a picture of a workspace. Modifications can be, for example, a picture of an airport showing people exhibiting security violations, such as showing people looking at information related to workplace security within the view of others, leaving sensitive information behind, or leaving computers unattended.

» **Escape rooms:** Put users in a closed environment, and have them engage in security puzzles that they have to solve. Examples are to guess common passwords, access a cellphone by guessing a passcode, and answer questions that lead to guessing a passcode on a lock. This activity, which should be timed and solvable, can have a limited number of participants. It also involves an extensive time commitment, but it might produce some engagement and possible behavior change.

Events

An *event* is where you bring people together at a given time. And, given remote work, the event can be held remotely. Most events involve presentations of some form on security related subjects. The presentations can feature some topic of general interest, such as discussions of news related issues, or they can involve specific subjects related to your organization, such as a rollout of a new security policy. Sometimes games are associated with the event, where you award prizes to users who participate in a game of skill, such as a ring toss, or who answer security related questions.

You can find people internally who can deliver the presentations, or you can bring in outside speakers. Internal speakers are good in that they know your environment and likely your priorities. If you can persuade an executive to present, it might add the sense of importance to the event and the message. Asking for the executive's participation may also help to obtain executive buy-in to the events — and your overall efforts as well.

MANDATORY OR NOT?

When you hold an event, you have to decide whether attendance should be mandatory. Making it mandatory will obviously cause a potential impact to operations, and you will likely face some level of pushback.

WARNING

When you make attendance at an event mandatory, it has the impact of proving to the organization that they believe there is value in the event. At the same time, many users will automatically resent the event, claiming that they have obligations they absolutely cannot cancel or, if they can't, that the event will negatively impact their work schedule and/or quality. You can also expect many users to rate the event poorly by default. If you make an event mandatory, ensure that you have the support required to make it mandatory *and* that you truly expect to provide value either in content or achieving a corporate goal.

Chapter 5

Measuring Performance

A s an awareness program proceeds, no matter what the awareness program involves, security incidents will occur — you can count on it. In response, people, including the managers who determine your budget, may assume that awareness has done little to improve security. At best, the manager may keep the program going just because awareness is "nice to have."

Before you can measure whether an awareness program meets its goals, you need to do a great deal of planning: First you establish goals, and then you figure out how to measure them. Of course, some goals, such as those concerning actual behaviors, are both important and difficult to measure. Also consider that some people want metrics to be hidden, to avoid getting caught in wrongdoing.

This chapter shows how to mitigate these issues by embedding metrics into existing business processes. Accounting processes, for example, are designed to collect metrics proactively at all phases. You can — and likely will have to — work around processes already used within the organization.

THE NEXT GENERATION OF AWARENESS TOOLS

At the time of this writing, a few fledgling companies are designing awareness tools that aim to measure overall organizational behaviors. They frequently use words implying that they're changing the culture and not just providing awareness. These tools basically automate the metrics collection process described in this chapter. Be aware that many other companies that offer traditional awareness tools claim to offer similar tools and improve culture, but they do not. These companies might have concepts, but they are years away from going to market.

Because the market is in flux, and because we do not intend for you to have dependence on vendor tools, this book doesn't mention specific vendor tools. Instead, research the market and the potential vendors that claim to have implemented metrics collection and culture change tools. These vendors may be more useful than the traditional phishing and computer-based training vendors. They should at least provide ideas for how you might present your metrics.

Metrics are arguably the most critical aspect of your success as a security awareness program manager. You either figure out how to *deserve* more or you become a person whose value to the overall security effort completely depends on the personal opinion of your manager.

Knowing the Hidden Cost of Awareness Efforts

As you may imagine, awareness efforts have costs beyond the actual cost of running the program. These costs are likely higher than the cost of the program itself. Some leaders of organizations are well aware of the exponential costs of training time. These leaders usually work for organizations that employ mostly blue collar workers, where productivity is tracked by the hour. Otherwise, few people seem to consider the cost associated with the time required for users to participate in the program.

In some cases, the costs are obvious. Many hourly workers, for example, are paid specifically for their time to perform a specific job, and training time is measured in a good organization.

Many awareness professionals fail to realize that their efforts begin by costing their organization money. Most people can anticipate the immediate costs of providing CBT and phishing simulations. For one thing, collateral materials must be developed or paid to be created, and any trainers brought in must be paid. But you also must anticipate the cost of lost productive time spent by employees taking awareness training.

REMEMBER

Assuming that you're in a white collar (or another type of) environment where time can be allocated as required, you must consider that employees have to swap out time doing their actual work for time spent completing training. This training time can add up. For example, if an employee spends a brief ten minutes per month on awareness training, it equates to two hours per year. For every 1,000 employees, that equates to the equivalent of one full-time person per year devoted to awareness training. The trick is to acknowledge this calculation and to find the justification for the awareness program. You have to show the *return on investment*, or that you're reducing losses that more than justify the time users spend on your efforts.

TIP

Though few organizations I've dealt with track the time required for awareness training, you must be ready to justify it. You don't need to highlight it, but in environments where time is tracked, you need to proactively address the issue. This is where a smart manager who isn't supportive of your efforts will challenge you. The way you respond is with metrics that justify the cost through reduced losses.

Meeting Compliance Requirements

Checking the Box is my term for all the actions an organization takes to ensure that it satisfies third-party compliance requirements. Those third parties' requirements might be government regulations, industry organization standards, customer requirements, vendor requirements, or other similar requirements. To prove that your program meets compliance standards, you may need to complete a self-assessment and document it for later reference. In many cases, independent auditors will verify compliance. The penalty for failing to meet compliance can vary greatly and result in a range of penalties that may include anything from a warning to fines or demands to cease operations.

For example, employment laws require that you post information regarding employee rights. Compliance just requires that the information be posted. Safety standards generally require some type of formal training, and people only need to complete the required training.

Security standards, such as Payment Card Industry Data Security Standard (PCI DSS), among others, have *vague* awareness compliance requirements, which in one way or another state that you need to ensure that employees complete awareness training. In this case, ensuring that everyone in your organization has completed assigned training is sufficient.

KEEPING YOUR EYE ON REGULATIONS AND LAWSUITS

At the time of this writing, Check the Box means just providing some form of awareness training along with proof that users completed the training. Standards and regulation don't specify anything else, except that the training *must* exist. As major ransomware incidents and data breaches (which have the general perception of being awareness failings) become commonplace, however, it's quite possible that regulations will become more specific.

At the same time, it's possible that some future lawsuit will challenge the appropriateness of awareness training, questioning not only the existence of awareness training but also its appropriateness and effectiveness, given the threat. As a professional, you should stay abreast of policy related issues.

When an organization is merely trying to satisfy compliance requirements (Checking the Box), you may experience difficulty justifying more than the minimum budget required to provide training to employees. In many cases, auditors state that phishing simulations are best practice and require those as a condition of compliance. In these cases, phishing simulations are required.

Given the penalties at stake if an organization fails to meet compliance, you can easily justify the budget for efforts that work toward that goal. You also can use this factor to justify hidden costs associated with the time required for employees to take the training. Any awareness efforts that present a cost beyond compliance may require additional justification. To demonstrate the justification, you must use the appropriate metrics.

Collecting Engagement Metrics

Metrics that are easy to collect tend to be popular. For this reason, Checking the Box, covered in the preceding section, is probably the most popular form of metrics. The next most common metrics are *engagement* metrics — for example, you can usually see how many people show up at events by tracking how many walk away with your complimentary squishy toys or otherwise tracking attendance.

TECHNICAL STUFF

Not only are engagement metrics easy to collect, but they also can make awareness programs seem like they're working. Though there is merit to this bit of logic, and you definitely should collect these metrics, be aware that they do not show the effectiveness of awareness efforts. These types of metrics might show goodwill generated on the part of a security program as a whole, however. Then you may be able to use these impressions to motivate users to better engage with the security program as a whole.

Attendance metrics

Attendance metrics are generally straightforward. They can overlap with compliance metrics, assuming that a compliance requirement for attendance exists. How many people completed the mandatory training? How many people showed up for a given event? How many people watched an optional video? How many people opened up an emailed newsletter?

Frequently, organizations have a *learning management system (LMS)* that manages and tracks computer-based training (CBT). An LMS, which is essentially the control system for a CBT effort, provides for storage of CBTs. It provides an environment to manage and schedule the distribution to all or parts of the organization. The LMS should allow for customization of the content. LMSes create reports that can show compliance and course completion. When you're tracking compliance, you clearly need to ensure that everyone takes all required training. Metrics may also include voluntary engagement with supplemental materials, such as when a user voluntarily takes extra awareness training or attends an event. If you provide an internal knowledge base, such as on a security portal, you can measure optional views of that content.

When you provide optional training, such as when you invite a speaker to discuss a topic where attendance isn't mandatory or you send out newsletters, the attendance or viewership implies whether you're reaching your intended audience. Engagement metrics should be examined to determine whether communications tools are being consumed beyond compliance. This strategy allows you to determine which tools can be dropped or should at least be considered for better delivery. For communications tools that have poor engagement, you either want to consider improving them or refocus your efforts into other tools.

WARNING

Some materials present a challenge for determining engagement. For example, it's difficult to know how many people read a poster or monitor display. You can place QR codes on posters, but you can't be certain that people will scan the code. For this reason, you may have to resort to surveys, if you believe that gathering this engagement is worth the effort.

When considering attendance metrics, keep in mind the hidden cost of awareness training — and the fact that every minute that employees are engaged with your program can be considered a minute that they weren't performing their primary job function.

Likability metrics

I don't recommend that you rely on likability metrics, but it never hurts to have people actually like your awareness program. You can ask people what they think of your program by asking them — typically, by way of a questionnaire that's delivered soon after training — how much they enjoy the content that's presented. Frequently, likability is collected on a *Likert scale*, which typically asks people to rate how much they enjoyed the materials on a scale of 1–5.

TECHNICAL STUFF

This type of metric has varying usefulness. Though you *of course* don't want to force unlikable training on anyone, the reality is that likability doesn't equate to effectiveness of training. If you have no other metrics to provide, however, likability is at least something with a positive implication.

Knowledge metrics

Knowledge metrics can show whether users have increased their knowledge about cybersecurity. Increased knowledge doesn't mean that you're getting the behavioral changes you seek, but it can indicate whether your messaging is getting across. Testing for knowledge level usually involves a short quiz covering the relevant knowledge.

TIP

If you test people immediately after they complete training, these quizzes can test their short-term memory, as opposed to actual knowledge a person possesses and may act on. You may want to also test people periodically to see how well they retain the information.

In the ideal world, you need to determine the essential knowledge required by an individual to perform their functions properly. You then develop a quiz that best tests for that knowledge. Typically, the quizzes are multiple-choice tests, which means that accuracy is reduced by 20–25 percent, depending on the number of answers presented. Multiple choice is the best option because grading and administration can be easily automated.

Measuring Improved Behavior

The goal of an awareness program is to improve security related behaviors. Metrics that actually measure behavior improvement are therefore useful to collect. Behavior is quite different from knowledge. Just because people know something doesn't mean that they will act on it.

To measure improved behavior, you need metrics that demonstrate the actual behaviors. Awareness programs sometimes include simulations of scenarios to test whether people behave properly. Collecting actual behavioral metrics can be difficult and expensive, however. You must be creative to come up with ways to do so that are simple and inexpensive.

To test security awareness in practice, for example, a company might hire consultants to make telephone calls to its employees and entice them to divulge their passwords. This method can cost a great deal of money and cannot be performed regularly. As an alternative, you can track security related calls to the Help Desk, which can be a sign of awareness, as more aware people detect and report more incidents.

REMEMBER

Behavioral metrics are among the most useful metrics. They show actual behavioral improvement, and not just specious indications of likeability. Even better is if you can combine the improved behaviors with monetary savings resulting from those improvements for a real return on investment.

Tracking the number of incidents

A key way to measure behavior is to track the number of incidents that are the clear result of a user action. Depending on the environment, this might include the number of injuries, system outages, malware incidents on a network, lost USB drives, or data compromises, among any other type of loss that can be created by a user. The most important phrase in this paragraph is *number of*. You are counting occurrences.

OBSERVING SECURITY BEHAVIOR

If a specific security behavior is immediately observable, you can consider it as a metric. Here are some examples of security behaviors you might track:

- You can track user adoption of security technologies such as multifactor authentication (when it's optional).

- You can also run a password cracker to examine password strength, beyond your organization's password policy.

- You can look to web content filters to examine bad web browsing habits.

- DLP software might be able to tell you the number of attempts to transmit sensitive data outside the company.

(continued)

(continued)

- You can look to websites such as http://haveibeenpwned.com to see whether anyone from your organizational domains has had credentials compromised on websites around the Internet.

- If you have access to dark web services, you may be able to also check whether your users reused passwords on other sites.

- If you find a compromised password, you can test it on your own systems to see whether the password is active and you are vulnerable.

- You can observe the number of people walking around your facilities who aren't wearing badges.

- You can count the number of unsecured desks during specific periods.

Examining behavior with simulations

Simulations are something to consider when you want to examine behaviors. Some simulations are more realistic than others. You can perform USB drops, pretext phone call simulations, tailgating simulations, phishing simulations, and more. You need to track these over time to measure improvement.

Phishing simulations have become common for security awareness metrics. The one problem with this metric — and all simulations, for that matter — is that such simulations can be manipulated to mislead. You can create a false impression of tremendous success by testing first with highly complex simulations, and then later, testing with simplified simulations that make detecting phishing attempts a bit easier. Also, people sometimes learn to detect the simulations.

When you perform a simulation, you want to force a diverse sampling of your potential victims. Though phishing simulations are relatively easy to reach all users, the reality is that your limited resources mean you can test only a small percentage of your organization. You therefore need to ensure that your sampling is representative of the organization as a whole.

If you try pretext phone calls targeting only the IT staff, for example, you might (hopefully) feel a false sense of security in that they are more aware by default. Likewise, certain geographical areas are more trusting than others. Assuming that you have no experience in performing random sampling, you minimally need to be aware that you should purposefully seek out and study whether different cultures, locations, departments, and types of workers, for example, have different responses and vulnerabilities.

TURNING SIMULATIONS INTO TEACHABLE MOMENTS

It's possible to incorporate awareness into simulations. In general, a simulation is a metric. You are performing them to specifically measure behaviors. If you interrupt the simulation to tell people that it's a simulated attack, it can impact your results, because users will likely tell other people that a simulated attack is being conducted. It's just human nature. So you should consider incorporating awareness into your simulations carefully.

However, a simulation can provide quite a valuable teachable moment. Determine the most effective ways to do so and then decide whether the simulation provides the potential for rewarding people. For example, if you present tailgating simulations, you can take both red and green cards with you. If someone stops you, give them a green card indicating that your interaction is part of an awareness study — and maybe tape a $5 bill to it. If they do not stop you, give them a red card, which tells them that the interaction is part of a study and that they should have stopped you — and that, had they stopped you, you would have given them $5. Ideally, the participants will tell all their coworkers about the simulation so that word-of-mouth becomes a helpful awareness tool.

For pretext phone calls, you might attempt to persuade users to visit a would-be malicious website. If they go, they instantly receive a lesson in awareness. Again, users are likely to tell their friends about this type of experience.

When users tell others that they were duped by a simulation, it's useful info, given the available resources. Again, simulations are expensive, and if users warn others that a simulation may be occurring, more users will be more aware and more likely to report incidents, fearing that *they* are potentially the victim of a simulation.

WARNING

Simulations can be expensive, if you use an outside contractor. They can be somewhat resource intensive, if you do it with your own resources. Some phishing simulation companies provide USB simulation capabilities along with their other services. Either way, simulations, when done properly, can be useful metrics. Doing them well can be challenging, however.

Tracking behavior with gamification

Book 6, Chapter 8 shows how you can apply gamification within your security awareness program. In the truest sense of the word, *gamification* involves rewarding desired behaviors, and it can be one of the best methods for tracking behavioral change. To implement gamification, you have to identify the desired behaviors to track and set up a tracking system.

Demonstrating a Tangible Return on Investment

Demonstrating a tangible return on investment (ROI) is the most effective way to prove that you deserve more. When you can provide a specific monetary amount of loss that's reduced based on your efforts, you can use the information to demonstrate why you deserve more resources to further improve your work.

Here's an example of how you can determine the cost savings associated with behavioral changes. In the safety field, if the average injury costs the organization $50,000 and you demonstrate that your efforts have reduced the number of injuries from 20 to 10, you have saved the organization $500,000. In the security field, if you consider that the average data breach costs an organization $1.3 million, and if you can demonstrate a reduction in data breaches, you can demonstrate a significant ROI.

TECHNICAL STUFF

Though you want to see losses decrease, if your business is growing or certain types of crimes are proliferating, an increase in losses is inevitable. For example, if you increase your staff by 25 percent, you can assume that user-related incidents may go up by 25 percent. You must measure improvements in relative terms in that case. So, in this case, if user related incidents that you track increase by less than 25 percent, you are reducing losses.

TIP

Certain organizations and industries have a better understanding of measuring user related costs than others. Using Six Sigma-like methodologies, they obtain data to understand exactly what potential losses are and where they can arise. You can conceivably look into similar organizations and look at the possible costs of incidents they suffer. Depending on your field, you may be able to find readily available studies on the costs of incidents.

Recognizing Intangible Benefits of Security Awareness

Not all awareness efforts can be expected to have a clear tangible benefit. Some aspects to consider are cultural. For example, you might incorporate a security awareness knowledgebase within a corporate knowledgebase and track how many people read the phishing article. Metrics like these can serve as a critical indication of the awareness program's contribution to the organization.

TIP

Consider providing awareness training specific to home and family needs. Some organizations initially think doing so is a waste of limited resources, but people are more likely to pay attention when something impacts them personally. If they behave securely at home, they will take those behaviors to work. It also generates goodwill.

To understand what might have intangible benefits to the organization, you need to understand the organization's culture. You need to talk to stakeholders and to people running other behavioral change programs to determine what they believe is valuable, other than the obvious. In some cases, you might find that the intangible benefits are easy to achieve and are even more valuable than some tangible benefits to the organization.

In many cases, your organization might track intangible benefits and assign a value to them. For example, brand value might seem to be an intangible, but many organizations do track it. Major cybersecurity incidents, such as those at Target and Sony, significantly harmed brands and produced intangible damage — you might want to work with your corporate communications department to see whether someone can offer any guidance on intangible value.

Knowing Where You Started: Day 0 Metrics

To signal that your awareness program deserves more resources, you have to show that efforts are making a difference. What many people forget to do is collect metrics before they start implementing the awareness program — these starting metrics are known as *Day 0 metrics* (said as "day zero metrics"). If you don't know where you started, you can't determine how much you've improved. This is especially true with behavioral and ROI metrics, which are the metrics that provide the most benefit for your awareness program.

TECHNICAL STUFF

Specifically, you need to first determine which metrics you intend to collect throughout the year of the awareness program — ideally, including behavioral metrics. You then collect the metrics before initiating your program. This is the Day 0 metric.

If you already have an awareness program in place, you can use Day 0 engagement metrics to measure the improved perception of your awareness efforts. Clearly, improved engagement is a secondary concern to improved ROI, but such metrics can be useful for a variety of reasons, as described earlier in this chapter, in the section "Collecting Engagement Metrics."

By collecting Day 0 metrics, you can then determine the impact your program had on the desired behaviors. In the ideal world, this will demonstrate the ROI provided by your efforts. If there is no improvement, you can at least be alerted to that fact and make changes as quickly as possible to improve the situation.

TIP

When you collect Day 0 metrics, resist the urge to use the opportunity to promote awareness, because doing so can taint the metrics collection. If you tell someone they did or did not click on a phishing message, for example, they might warn others that phishing simulations are occurring. Though you might consider it a lost opportunity to deliver a just-in-time awareness message, a pure Day 0 metric is more than worth the lost opportunity.

If you're collecting the number of malware incidents, for example, ask the administrators who administer the antimalware software to pull statistics at almost any time. In fact, ask for the statistics before beginning any awareness efforts. Also request statistics again after completing a round of phishing simulations, and then again after completing training on safe web browsing, given that malware generally gets on a network by way of phishing and unsafe web browsing.

Chapter **6**

Assembling Your Security Awareness Program

E arlier chapters of this book describe what goes into an awareness program and explain why these programs work; this chapter shows you how to turn theory into practice.

Knowing Your Budget

In an ideal world, you would put together a program and then determine the budget you need. You would then approach management and whoever else you need in order to get the budget allocated for your program. Unfortunately, you probably will not have this luxury, especially if you're taking over an existing security awareness program or creating and managing a program from scratch. Most often, you're allocated a budget that you must work within.

Figuring out your budget involves more than simply running with a number that's been given to you, however. To determine your *actual* budget, consider these three sources:

>> **Any funding you can get from other sources,** including executive team and other departments

>> **Must-have items defined by the organization,** including existing vendor contracts and other requirements that must be met

>> **Discretionary spending,** or what's left over to spend

The following sections cover each of the preceding items in detail.

REMEMBER

If other programs underspend, or if an incident causes more money to flow into the awareness program, you may consider seeking additional funding. Keep in mind, however, that your budget was likely determined six months before the current fiscal year. You will likely have to make do with whatever you get.

BENEFITING FROM AN INCIDENT WINDFALL

Nobody enjoys when incidents occur, but here's the good news: Incidents can prompt executives to increase the security budget.

When an incident occurs, you must be proactive and claim your piece of any increase. The organization's first priority will be to mitigate the damage and clean up the computer systems. This work can be intensive and costly. Even though chances are good that such incidents are caused by awareness failings, awareness continues to be an afterthought for most organizations when allocating their budget.

Even when an organization understands that awareness must be improved, any perception that an awareness program consists of merely computer-based training (CBT) and phishing simulations can limit budget increases. You have to state specifically how you want to improve security awareness. This chapter explains that you need to be realistic about what you can afford, and focus on that. At the same time, you need to consider what you want to include and its potential cost.

Only fools and liars tell you that perfect security (often pitched as "the human firewall") is possible. Only imperfect security exists, and some form of incident will occur. Be prepared to exploit the inevitable incident. Have a business case for desired awareness efforts readily available. When people ask what could have prevented the incident and how can the next incident be prevented or limited, you will be ready to propose the additional awareness tools you want to implement, along with the required costs of doing so.

Finding additional sources for funding

Your budget might be set, but if you're creative, you may be able to find additional sources for funding. You can often find people throughout an organization who are willing to support you. You just have to know where to look.

Securing additional executive support

It's possible that if you're creative, you can go to senior management and ask for additional budget amounts. Clearly, you have to go in with a plan. You need to know what you want to say, with clear business intent. Gaining management support is covered later in this chapter (see the later section "Gaining Management Support"); for now, keep in mind that executive management may provide *additional* funding, if you can provide the right influence and if funding is available to be had.

WARNING

When you approach executive management, you must be mindful of any internal politics. You clearly need to keep members of your management chain involved when you approach their managers, or parties outside of your chain of command. Your managers may have information that can help you, such as knowledge of any hot button issues that will help to gain support for increased budget. During a recent engagement, for example, executive management expressed a major concern about ransomware, and tying a budget request specifically to preventing ransomware incidents facilitated a major budget increase. Also know that you might alienate other parties competing for budget.

Coordinating with other departments

A good security awareness program overlaps with a great deal of other organizational efforts. You should coordinate your effort with the relevant departments. If enough synergy exists across departments, you may be able to team with them on a variety of efforts.

For example, you may be able to embed your security awareness efforts within other departments' programs. Their efforts may not align perfectly with yours, but they should cost you relatively little, if any, of your budget. This can save your program a ton of money. Alternatively, if you incorporate another department's messaging into your efforts, you may be able to ask that department to contribute to your efforts.

TIP

You need to proactively determine how you want to work with the other departments and then provide them with a clear value proposition. These other departments likely have the same resource challenges that you do. If they're smart, they won't give up their resources in a way that is less effective than their currently intended plans.

You must be able to lay out specifically what you want and what you will provide. At the same time, you shouldn't make the proposal sound like a formal negotiation. The other department should feel that you see them as a friend and partner, not as a business transaction. You may encounter periodic competition for resources and attention from end-users, but the departments you partner with likely face the same problems you do. You should attempt to work with them whenever feasible.

WORKING WITH CORPORATE COMMUNICATIONS

In most organizations, the corporate communications department, or a department of a similar name, is either your greatest ally or the bane of your existence. The corporate communications department is generally responsible for the distribution for all materials to the organization. They maintain distribution lists. They create standards for materials to be distributed inside the organization. They set rules for distribution, such as types of materials that can be distributed and how frequently items can be distributed over certain channels.

This department is frequently constrained by its own resources, and would have to fit your requests into their workflow. Despite these limiting factors, however, they can significantly help your awareness program. They might have a graphics artist at their disposal. They know how to distribute your information to everyone inside the organization. They usually know which outreach efforts work and which ones don't. They know which newsletters get read and which ones do not. They often have suggestions for how best to reach various subcultures throughout the organization.

Their team can also supplement your team. They might integrate into your team and take on many of your responsibilities. Though corporate communications can be a burden to your effort, you will likely be required by your organization to work with that department and adhere to its mandates. You need to accept this fact and incorporate them into your plans.

Allocating for your musts

Having the freedom to allocate all funds from a budget that's dedicated exclusively to your awareness program is a best-case scenario. When you receive the budget for your security awareness program, however, you may find that a portion has already been allocated to other contracts. For example, your organization may have already entered into CBT and phishing simulation contracts that are charged against your budget. Also, many vendors that provide secure email gateways sometimes bundle in CBT and phishing training, so you don't have to allocate from your own budget for those tools.

When you encounter such situations, you need to adjust discretionary spending to accommodate budget constraints. If whatever software or services are already contracted overlap with any of your plans — well, at least for the short term — you don't have to spend time evaluating vendors.

You may also have regulatory or compliance standards that require you to implement a tool you didn't necessarily want to implement. For example, a standard you must meet may imply the use of CBT. In this case, you need to allocate the budget for CBT.

TIP

If a contract is already in place with a vendor that impacts your budget, you may be able to negotiate out of it to free up funding. Many vendors in the awareness field provide software and other services, such as antimalware products and secure email gateways. The awareness components of the contract are usually the least expensive part of the contract. Sometimes, you can get them to bundle awareness services with the larger contract, which can reduce or eliminate your costs for the awareness tools.

Limiting your discretionary budget

After you consider your allocated budget, all the potential funds you might receive from other sources, and then what you have already allocated, you have some idea about what you have left to spend. As you continue with the rest of the program, you can start to figure out which potential communications tools are feasible.

REMEMBER

Though you don't necessarily want to limit your imagination to just those items that cost little money, you have to be realistic about what you can accomplish. As the saying goes, you don't want to have a prince's appetite on a pauper's budget. You can be creative and possibly gain more support as time goes on, but you have what you have.

Appreciating your team as your most valuable resource

Money is an important resource, but don't forget that you need people to implement your plan. The corporate communications department might be able to supplement your efforts; however, you need to balance all your spending plans with the staff you have available to implement those plans.

TIP

If you need to bring on additional expertise (because you're short-staffed or for any other reason), you might consider outsourcing to specialists. If outsourcing is part of your plan, you have to budget for any contractors accordingly.

Without enough staff, you may have to limit efforts you can otherwise afford. Some communications tools, such as newsletters, don't generally require a significant financial or work effort to implement. Other communications tools, such as holding events, require extensive planning and logistics. Running phishing exercises, even with some of the more robust tools available, requires several days of effort. You need to plan, design the phishing messages, schedule the exercise, upload email addresses, troubleshoot problems (such as advancing messages through spam filters), interpret results, retest as required, and so on. (*Security Awareness For Dummies*, by Ira Winkler, provides a detailed look at phishing exercises and the role phishing campaigns play within a professional security awareness program.)

REMEMBER

Before you choose a communications tool, think beyond the cost — consider the manual effort that implementing the tool will require. Also consider that paying for additional support will eat into other aspects of your budget. You can implement some incredible awareness effort with the appropriate funding, but without the people to support the implementation, doing so is impractical.

Choosing to Implement One Program or Multiple Programs

Most organizations contain multiple subcultures, each with its own business drivers and communications style. Accordingly, you may find that each subculture warrants its own awareness program.

TECHNICAL STUFF

Subcultures can be classified by roles within an organization. For example, executives may be located across many geographies. Although different geographic regions often have distinct cultures, executive jobs may be similar enough across geographies to warrant a common awareness program. This might be true for many other job functions, such as researchers, factory workers, or cashiers. Many organizations therefore implement what is referred to as *role-based awareness programs*, which are designed for different job functions, such as executive or warehouse workers.

Ideally, you should consider creating multiple awareness programs so that each subculture has a program tailored to meet its needs. Unfortunately, you may barely have the resources to implement a single awareness program. Even so, you can usually find creative solutions within the scope of the available resources to meet the needs of the entire organization.

TIP

Many CBT and phishing simulation tools allow you to customize materials for various groups within an organization. You can use these tools to ensure that people who work in the accounts payable department, for example, receive phishing messages and CBT modules that have been tailored to their needs. Keep in mind that although you can use these tools to tailor content by subculture, they don't add new communications tools to those that are already available.

If you have the resources to implement multiple programs, for different regions or business units, or role-based awareness programs, you should go for it. Reaching different parts of an organization around the world with unique programs can be logistically complex. Doing so is worth the extra cost in money, effort, time, and people, however, if you can manage it. It provides for a much more targeted effort to make an impact tailored to the targeted populations.

TIP

You need to figure out how many subcultures or roles you can support. You won't have unlimited resources, and you must consider those efforts that will likely create the most benefit. Implement programs that address the greatest losses, or where the cultures differ significantly. For example, cultures may differ significantly for an organization that has teams that communicate almost exclusively by email, and teams that don't even have computers at their workstations.

Managing multiple programs

When you implement multiple awareness programs, whether implemented via subcultures or role-based, you need to design the programs *to be* independent entities. You can, however, design the programs one at a time, or simultaneously design the multiple programs.

Aspects of the programs may overlap. For example, you will likely use CBT and phishing simulations for most programs. This can allow for a more cost-effective use of materials. It also simplifies administration of the program.

Each program will also have unique aspects. Consider how the communications tools you use in the program vary depending on whether workers work primarily on a computer issued by the organization or must access email and other communications from their personal devices.

Beginning with one program

Even when you intend to implement programs unique to subcultures, consider starting by implementing a single program for the entire organization. Doing so can reduce risk while simplifying the rollout of the program.

WARNING

You always encounter issues with an initial rollout. Approvals from stakeholders come slower than expected. You encounter logistical issues when sending materials among facilities. You run into issues with suppliers. People might not read your newsletters. Promised support might not come to fruition. Now consider managing these issues while rolling out multiple programs simultaneously.

TIP

Start with the base program that encompasses the most concerns simultaneously. After seeing how things go during the first quarter, add the aspects of the program that are specialized to various subcultures and roles. To limit risk, add just one or two new subcultures per quarter, depending on the available resources.

Some subcultures warrant unique awareness programs sooner than others. This may include executives or high-risk groups, such as accounting or human resources. Even if you don't intend to implement multiple programs for multiple subcultures, you might consider separate programs just for high-risk groups. The cost of assigning special attention to these groups probably isn't so great that it can't be done.

TIP

If you want to address specific subcultures with a single awareness program, you can simply provide special components for those groups. You might create special in-person briefings for executive management on concerns specific to them. The executive security team, for example, might appreciate specific guidance on how to secure their home Wi-Fi networks and home computers. The executive managers were otherwise subject to the same awareness program as everyone else.

Gaining Support from Management

Though many awareness managers have the true support of their management and their management believes in the value of a well-implemented security awareness program, many awareness programs, unfortunately, are considered

Check-the-Box efforts. Management authorizes and funds the program like it's in place only to satisfy external requirements. If you're reading this book, you clearly believe otherwise, as do I. Whether or not your management team believes in the true value of your efforts, this section intends to gain you as much support as possible.

Perhaps the greatest indicator of the likely success or failure of your program is the level of senior management support you have for it. If senior management supports your efforts, you will get the support from the departments you need. You're more likely to get a reasonable budget. You're more likely to get management to ensure that users spend the required time on your training and other efforts. Though you can't expect to get everything, it's a big start.

If you're lucky, your senior managers see security awareness for the actual value and understand that the awareness program is a critical risk-reduction tool. Sometimes, awareness is a pet project of management. Management may support your efforts for a variety of reasons.

WARNING

You should go to management with a clearly defined plan, but be aware that this support might be limited or burdened by preconceived notions. For example, some managers might state that they think awareness is critical, but believe that awareness is specifically CBT and that phishing simulations and other efforts are not necessarily. Some executives might have heard a speaker they like and then want you to spend a large portion of your budget on bringing in that speaker. So, despite some support, you might have to fight for efforts you find more critical.

Assuming that you lack full management support of your efforts, it's worth the effort to try to increase the level of support. You might want to increase your budget — and management support can provide that increase. Even if you're satisfied with your budget, you need to ensure that you can gain the support of the other departments, as well as the guarantees that users will be required to devote the relevant length of time to your efforts. Remember, the length of time required for the awareness efforts on the part of the users is the costliest aspect of your program.

This is one aspect of culture where you definitely need to understand the organizational culture and business drivers, to ensure that you can improve the security culture. You need to understand what will allow you to obtain and keep that support. This might include any preferences or hot button issues that will attract support. The more you understand what motivates your management to support any effort, the more likely you'll know how to gain that support for your efforts, so do your research.

TIP

Here are some questions to consider when you seek support for your awareness effort:

>> Are any projects top priorities for the organization?

>> Which efforts have support, and can you associate with them?

>> If similar efforts lack support, why?

>> Do you know the managers personally?

>> Do you know their attitudes on security awareness?

>> Is a particular person more sympathetic?

>> Can you demonstrate the value of your efforts to gain further support?

>> Which incidents have occurred in recent memory?

>> Did any data breaches take place?

>> Were any fines levied? Why? How much?

>> Were the adverse audit findings?

>> Have there been studies about customer perceptions relevant to cybersecurity? What were the findings?

>> Can you align your program with the organization's stated value and mission statement, and can you demonstrate that alignment clearly?

These are just a few considerations, and your circumstances likely provide for other considerations. You can ask your coworkers, and any executives to whom you have immediate access, what might best influence other executives — or at least those managers who matter in providing support.

CREATING AN EXECUTIVE AWARENESS PROGRAM

I stated previously that a part of your awareness program might focus on the needs of executives. Depending on how much success you're having getting support for your awareness program, you might want to start with the executive team.

Normally, you want to work out the kinks in your program, before launching programs specific to executives. You want to put your best foot forward. However, if you need to increase the level of support to increase visibility, funding, access to stakeholders, and/or resources in general, you likely want to start with the executives in an attempt to impress them and demonstrate the value of your efforts.

You can potentially put together an entire program just for executives, or you can just create high-value tools. Either way, you want to pull out all the stops to demonstrate how much value a good awareness program can provide. For example, you don't have to subject executives to off-the-shelf videos on generic topics. Focus on topics and tools that are personal to the intended audience. For example, you can discuss how to protect home networks. Securing mobile devices and personal computers is likely to be of specific value. Also consider one-on-one sessions and other highly personalized experiences to ensure that the message is clear.

Phishing simulations can be a double-edged sword. If you can put together highly tailored spear phishing messages, and the executives click on it and appreciate the warning, they can become major supporters of future efforts. On the other hand, if they're offended for being "tricked," they can pull funding or other resources. Executives might appreciate simulations. This may not be universal, and as discussed earlier, you need to know your audience — especially the executives.

If you're going to create a program for executives, you need to do it well. If it's perceived to be a waste of time by the executives, you might lose the support you already have. You need to ensure that every aspect of your program is as tight as possible. If a communications tool is poor or questionable, you should strongly consider holding off on the delivery — or cancel it.

Devising a Quarterly Delivery Strategy

One of the biggest mistakes you can make in an awareness program is to design it as an annual program. Scheduling the program a year in advance is a mistake. You would think that annual planning would allow for a well-thought-out and well-rounded program, but in reality, you can't know what issues will crop up a year in advance.

Many awareness professionals are surprised to find that creating an annual schedule that you update as extraordinary events occur isn't the best approach. For example, when events such as the COVID-19 pandemic hit, many awareness topics became irrelevant and others became critical. Then there are data breaches that can impact your industry, or internal incidents. Just as important, you don't want to move off an important topic unless you know that the desired behavior change has occurred.

Here are some shortcomings of annual programs:

>> Insufficient behavior change may occur for the perceived investment.

>> Awareness failings are perceived as incidents occur throughout the year.

>> Lack of reinforcement occurs when a topic highlighted by the program changes too quickly.

>> Employee turnover causes new employees to completely miss topics that are addressed by the program before their start of employment.

>> World events can disrupt the program.

>> Missed and important topics are not revisited for more than a year.

To account for these issues and more, lay out a program only three months in advance. This short period provides for a great detail of versatility and allows you to focus your efforts. A program scheduled this way isn't a set-it-and-forget-it program, which is what many organizations seem to want.

Having a program that you adjust every quarter provides built-in versatility to adapt to changing circumstances and new requirements. It also enables you to examine improvement over the course of the program. Being creative is much easier when you put your focus into a short period with a small set of goals. You can focus on the trees instead of the forest.

Ensuring that your message sticks

A critical principle in all learning is *reinforcement*. People need to see a message several times over an extended period for it to sink in and then to become practice. The model proposed here is designed to provide enhanced reinforcement beyond what most awareness programs usually provide.

In the typical awareness program strategy, an awareness manager looks at potential topics and assigns a given topic for each of 12 months of a year. These topics are all too frequently driven by which topics are in the library of videos provided by the CBT vendor. Then the awareness manager determines the other communications tools they will distribute each month. So a person will be pushed a video and perhaps be exposed to a companion poster and newsletter for that topic. The users then watch the mandatory video, maybe they see the poster someplace, and maybe they open and read the companion newsletter. At that point, users begin to forget what they learned previously, and unfortunately, they will not be exposed to that topic again for a year or so.

An awareness program also typically has a phishing campaign that may or may not be integrated into other aspects of the awareness program. A good awareness manager usually schedules events as well. All these components form common awareness programs.

When you plan for quarterly programs, you can be more creative with how awareness materials are distributed. The most effective structure for a program, as opposed to working with one topic a month, is that you work with three topics simultaneously over three months. This way, each topic can be reinforced over the entire three months of the program.

TECHNICAL STUFF

No matter whether you manage a CBT-focused awareness program, a role-based awareness program, a multi-culture awareness program, or another type, you can implement multiple topics simultaneously. Doing so reinforces multiple topics constantly over a specific period. You can implement the delivery of multiple topics simultaneously with any format of scheduling or delivery.

Distributing topics over three months

Most traditional marketing formats flood individuals with information on a specific subject, in multiple formats, all at once. This tactic appears to make sense. Providing information in multiple formats can help reinforce memory retention. Although the information is reinforced to a certain extent, the Forgetting Curve still kicks in immediately.

Imagine if McDonald's said something to the effect of, "I had a TV commercial, a social media ad, and put up a poster along a highway for a month. We are done for the year." Clearly, that isn't how any commercial organization implements its marketing campaigns. It provides constant reinforcement of messaging, even if it's running multiple promotions.

Though many awareness professionals espouse the importance of marketing concepts, they don't implement the same methodologies as marketing professionals, which involve constant reinforcing over an extended period. Again, the concept of one topic per month is an arbitrary use of time and an implementation methodology.

All this leads me to recommend the methodology of choosing three topics and distributing information on those three topics simultaneously over three months. From a structural perspective, you choose the communications tools you want to use each month and intersperse the topics across the communications tools each month.

For example, over the three months, if you're going to use videos, newsletters, and posters, the video in Month 1 would be on Topic 1, the newsletter would be on Topic 2, and the poster would be on Topic 3. In Month 2, you can then rotate the topics across the communications tools. You then rotate the topics again in Month 3.

Figure 6-1 shows how you might intersperse topics across a quarter. The awareness program shown in the figure intends to educate people on USB drive security, social engineering prevention, and travel security. Those topics are rotated among most of the communications components listed. In addition, some active components, such as the monthly event and the roadshow, use random topics. As you see, the topics rotate and are reinforced over an extended period.

Tool	Month 1	Month 2	Month 3
Computer-based training	Social engineering	Travel security	USB security
Poster	Travel security	USB security	Social engineering
Featured article	USB security	Social engineering	Travel security
Newsletter	Social engineering	Travel security	USB security
Lunch and Learn	Travel security	USB security	Social engineering
Table tents	USB security	Social engineering	Travel security
Event	Kick-off booth	Security cubicle	Speaker
Roadshow	Human resources	Information technology	Marketing

FIGURE 6-1: A sample quarterly awareness program interspersing topics.

Figure 6-1 shows just a sample of an awareness program. You can add or delete as many communications tools as you want. The sample program shown in the figure doesn't include phishing, for example. Given resources and the likely limitation of engagement that you can have with employees, you will likely rely mostly on passive engagement tools and strategic active engagement.

REMEMBER

Your goal is to provide as much reinforcement as reasonable over the course of the program.

In the ideal world, you will develop a separate program for each subculture you're responsible for. There might be total or complete overlap between programs for different subcultures, and that's okay. You just need to remember that they're a distinct subculture when it comes to the next round and evaluation of metrics. You can also likely reuse materials between different subcultures. However, you should define programs for each subculture, even just to acknowledge that they're distinct subcultures that will require a reevaluation for each quarter.

TIP

There is typically no reason that guides you on which topic to start with in a given format. If there's a subject you want to focus on, you can choose to give it a little more exposure than the other topic. For example, you can use posters for the same topic over two or more months. You would use two distinct posters, but they can be on the same general topic.

ACCOMMODATING DELAYS WITHIN A QUARTERLY SCHEDULE

Though the ideal is to have a program execute consistently within a quarter, it's frequently difficult to have a program released exactly on that time schedule. It's admittedly tight, and you need your material created and reviewed for dissemination. A dozen or so people might have to approve the content of your program, which can take more time than you hope for.

Additionally, you might find that certain events can slow down a program, or you might want to delay part of your program. For example, in many cultures, the month of December is a bad time to try to establish engagement. Many people are away from work for a week or more, and even when people are supposedly engaged, many personal issues are distracting. People are rushing to complete work before they leave for the Christmas and New Year's holidays, because they have parties and events to plan around. If you have a critical message to share, there are times to avoid it and perhaps, just for an example, to extend content from November into December. You might also have the timing of organizational events to consider or work around.

The time to measure results and create a new program based on the findings from the previous program may also create a delay. You need to either plan ahead or work off Month 2 metrics.

For these reasons and more, you might want your quarterly programs to happen over more than three months.

Similarly, if you want to truly focus on a topic, you may just decide to use the one topic for two of the three topics you use. Just as there's no reason to focus on one topic per month, there's no reason that you can't consciously choose to have a single topic doubled up.

Deciding Whether to Include Phishing Simulations

Let me be clear: Despite what seems to be the status quo, a phishing simulation isn't a requirement for a security awareness program. Phishing is perhaps the most common attack targeting awareness failings. To a large extent, however, basic phishing attacks are filtered out by email servers, and phishing simulations don't provide perfect awareness against more advanced attacks.

Phishing simulations *can* raise general awareness, however. People may become more aware as a result that they can be hit by an attack. This is no guarantee of perfection, but any reduction in risk can be helpful.

First, you need to decide whether you want to perform regular phishing simulations. You might have access to a phishing service as a result of another service you have, such as an antimalware service. You might earn a discount for insurance if you use a particular awareness service that includes phishing simulations. So you might already have phishing services available to you.

On the other hand, incorporating these simulations into your program can be a major expense to your organization. The service might eat up most of your anticipated budget. If this is the case, strongly consider whether you want to spend that amount of money on a phishing simulation service.

WARNING

Free alternatives, such a GoPhish, are available, but you have to be technically adept to configure the software and run it yourself. Also consider the time required to create and run the simulations. A homegrown solution is possible, but these solutions have limitations and can require significant resources.

Before you sink a ton of resources into creating a phishing simulation that may not give the results you seek, check out *Security Awareness For Dummies*, by Ira Winkler (published by Wiley), to understand what goes into creating a campaign that best serves your overall awareness effort.

Planning Which Metrics to Collect and When

Metrics are as fundamental to an awareness program as videos, posters, or phishing simulations. They must be embedded within the program at every possible phase and level. *Metrics are the difference between being a valuable business function and being the unwanted appendage of the security program.*

Book 6, Chapter 5 gets into the nitty-gritty with regard to metrics. You get ideas for how to track engagement and improved behavior. The upcoming sections in this chapter focus on how you might implement metric collection within your awareness program.

Considering metrics versus topics

The natural inclination in the choice of metrics is to choose metrics that match the topics currently highlighted by your program (in a given quarter, for example). This isn't typically the most feasible way to do it. You want to track for continuous improvement, and as topics change, you want to measure something that is representative of overall awareness. For that, you need metrics that are easy to collect consistently.

TIP

Engagement metrics are relatively easy to collect, if they're available. These, again, are critical to know if you want to continue with a given communications tool. Collect these at all opportunities.

You should, however, try to collect behavioral and incident metrics that are consistent and available. Ideally, these metrics should be available throughout the course of a year, and be somewhat independent of outside influence. If they can represent common awareness, it would be ideal. Phishing simulations are one example; however, they might not be representative of actual phishing awareness.

REMEMBER

When you determine which metrics to use, don't consider as your primary question whether the metrics represent the short-term goals of your awareness program. The primary question you should ask is, "Which metrics are representative of awareness, and will I have consistent access to them?"

Choosing three behavioral metrics

After you have all the possible metrics to consider, find at least three behavioral metrics to track. These metrics can be for a variety behaviors and/or incidents. Though the more metrics you can collect provides a fuller picture, three typically provides enough to create a substantial dashboard, especially when combined with engagement metrics.

TIP

If you can easily collect more relevant metrics with little cost, such as by asking for the number of security-related calls to the help desk or the number of blocked web queries or malware incidents, for example, you should. You don't have to report all of them, but you will be able to make better decisions and provide better information.

Incorporating Day 0 metrics

I have already stated the importance of taking Day 0 metrics. This advice cannot be understated. You should begin designing your metrics collection program as part of your overall awareness program. You can collect the metrics while you're designing the program. The initial data collection doesn't have to take place immediately before the program rollout.

Scheduling periodic updates

Obviously, you need to update your metrics periodically. How frequently you update the metrics depends on their availability, the ease of collection, and the resources required to collect them.

WARNING

You should minimally attempt to collect metrics once per quarter, or during whatever period you've defined as your awareness cycle. At most, you should collect metrics once per month. If you collect them too frequently, you may find normal deviations that can give you false results. You need to see the trends *over time*.

TIP

As things change, periodically consider whether you want to change your metrics. It can be due to logistics, resources, or change in business needs, for example. A better source of metrics may arise. Just realize that you might need to change metrics and that is okay.

Biasing your metrics

When you complete penetration tests or are otherwise asked to collect metrics, if you believe that there's a need to have dramatic results, you can produce a high failure rate. In other words, you can tailor the attack so that people will fail. If you want the program to look successful, you can create easy attacks.

TECHNICAL STUFF

You might find some reason to bias results, such as showing very poor awareness on Day 0 metrics, so that you can show improvement for your program over time. For example, you can use a very high sophistication email message that will be extremely difficult to detect. If you want to show strong awareness, you can use blatant phishing messages. If you are doing a tailgating exercise, you can have someone dress like they clearly don't belong at the facility. Alternatively, you can have someone dress like a maintenance worker with a proper uniform. There are many ways to tailor the results as you see fit.

Branding Your Security Awareness Program

Awareness is a marketing effort. So, whenever you create a security awareness program, you must consider basic marketing concepts and the importance of *branding*. This involves tying a unique and recognizable identity to the program so that it's recognizable across the different components of the program.

In general, when users see something from your program, they should know it's part of your program. Successful branding makes this happen.

Creating a theme

When you work with an organization that has a mission statement and aligns many efforts with it, consider devising a theme that aligns with that organizational mission statement. Doing so will likely provide you with additional support and allow your awareness efforts to be included in other efforts that demonstrate alignment with the mission statement.

If the organization has mission statement, you can still create a theme to assist in the branding. Tie it to service to customers, employee well-being, protecting family, or whatever else suits your needs. A theme isn't required, but it can be useful to attach a higher purpose to cybersecurity.

Maintaining brand consistency

Every program should have some sort of theme and consistency to it. Though your program materials should not look so alike that they fade into each other, the materials should appear similar enough, or have some common branding, to reflect that they belong to a coordinated awareness program.

Iterations of passive materials, such as posters, need to be noticeably different from one iteration to the next while also showing consistent branding. If you put up a poster in a common area, for example, people might see it at first but, after a few visits to that common area, stop noticing it. If you then change the poster but use an overall look that is too similar to the original, people might not notice the change. Fortunately, maintaining branding can be as straightforward as using a logo or catchphrase on all your program materials.

Coming up with a catchphrase and logo

Your program should have a *catchphrase*, or slogan, that attempts to keep security concerns in people's minds. Try to come up with a catchphrase that highlights the mission of your program.

Here are some examples of catchphrases that produced results: company and me; cybersecurity is my job; securing our patients' IP is our lifeblood; it's a jungle out there. Some of these catchphrases were synergistic with other corporate efforts.

Some, at an organization's request, highlight responsibility to its customers. Some were just created because someone thought they sounded good. There's no consistent driver in themes or messaging.

A logo can also be useful to tying all the materials together. It can reflect the slogan or be used independently of one. A visually catchy logo can be quite useful.

Promoting your program with a mascot

Having a mascot can be extremely helpful in promoting your program. When used properly, a mascot creates excitement for your efforts. People frequently want to pose for a photo with the mascot. Mascots also make great giveaways — potentially, as a stuffed animal or a squishy toy.

The mascot doesn't have to be directly related to the theme for your program, although it can help. If the mascot isn't related to your theme, it should at least be endearing. If the organization already has a mascot, you may be able to get permission to use a version of the organizational mascot for your program.

Creating a mascot takes a little more creativity than your typical graphics efforts. You may therefore have to reach out to a good graphics artist who is more creative or has experience with mascots. Try to create a mascot that is reasonably well liked. Don't expect that it will be universally loved, however — some people dislike mascots altogether. A mascot can be limited to a graphic that appears in the corner of posters, or it can mean persuading someone to wear a costume. Depending on what you want to do with the mascot, it can be quite useful and versatile — and it can also be costly.

A mascot can become quite a visible symbol of your awareness program. The right mascot can greatly support your efforts. At the same time, just make sure to take your organization's culture into account because it can trivialize a program in more formal organizations.

» Securing approvals for your program materials

» Collecting Day 0 measurements

» Showcasing your progress with well-designed reports

» Assessing your program

» Planning each subsequent cycle

» Factoring in recent news and incidents

Chapter **7**

Running Your Security Awareness Program

Planning a security awareness program is pretty difficult; however, running the program is where things get real.

When you run your program, you will discover that any planning was insufficient, incomplete, idealistic, and more. Even if your planning was mostly correct, you will learn some humbling lessons when you run the program. What you thought would work, doesn't. Promises are not kept. Incidents happen. Funding can be lost. Deliverables are late. You need to be able to adapt and improve your program as circumstances dictate.

This chapter doesn't cover every possible situation you may encounter, but it describes the critical operational issues you often find when you implement an awareness program. Running an awareness program, in large part, involves general project management. Books and resources are available to find out about that discipline. Some issues may seem like common sense, depending on the common knowledge you have as part of your awareness management experience.

Nailing the Logistics

The broad term *logistics* refers to the detailed coordination of a complex operation. For an awareness program, you have to work with suppliers, distributors, partners, and a variety of other vendors. During the planning phases, you should have identified all these parties, but the reality is that you will miss a few. It's impossible to plan for all possible situations that can come up with regard to working with outside parties.

As you determine all the communications tools you intend to implement, you need to determine where you'll acquire them and their cost and required development resources. Document these resources so that you can identify any logistical issues that arise.

Determining sources or vendors

For each communications tool you use — with the term *communications tool* meaning any component of your awareness program — you should identify where you intend to get the tool. That can be from an internal source, such as a graphics department. Or you might create the tool yourself. It can also be from an external source, such as a vendor.

REMEMBER

Your organization may dictate that you use certain vendors. For example, you may have phishing and CBT contracts already available via your secure email gateway vendor. Or your organization may have a requirement that all posters be created by the internal corporate communications department. So, depending on whether the source is good or bad, you may have the blessing or curse of having a large portion of your work already accomplished.

The communications tools you choose must match the culture of your organization. A "funny" video series might be appropriate for a high-tech company, but it's likely to be inappropriate for an investment bank. Similarly, videos that feature cartoon characters aren't appropriate for all environments.

TIP

You need to determine the amount of money you have available. The budget determines which vendors you can use. You might want to create your own videos, for example, but few awareness programs have the resources to do so. Many vendors try to be competitive from a pricing perspective, but some may be more expensive than others. For example, many of the more established vendors lack competitive pricing for organizations of fewer than 1,000 people.

Scheduling resources and distribution

Remember to build in time for delivery from vendors and internal sources. Note that internal resources can be slower than external sources. Unless it's already built into your schedule, corporate communications is unlikely to have people sitting around waiting for a new project, and they have to work your requirements into their schedule.

You may also face distribution considerations. If you want to send a newsletter to all employees, you're likely competing with a variety of other efforts for such a broad distribution. A smart communications team doesn't want a constant stream of random information fed to all employees — or else it all may become background noise. A typical organization has critical human resources information to periodically distribute, wellness information, executive communications, and other necessary information. Adding in a regular security awareness communication could require waiting for an appropriate opening in the schedule. Corporate communications, assuming you have such a department, likely has guidelines on how and when you can send different types of information to different levels of distribution.

Contracting vendors

If you will deal with external vendors, find out about the organization's contracting processes before you begin to approach potential vendors. You need to know the requirements for having purchase orders issued, the criteria for potential vendors, and the forms required by your organization to initiate the onboarding of vendors and ensure that the legal department provides a timely review of contracts. After you identify the vendors you want to use, start the contracting process as soon as possible.

Recognizing the role of general project management

Running a security awareness program has as much to do with basic project management as it does with awareness. Your skills in scheduling, budgeting, tracking, negotiations, and other tasks will likely be as important, if not more so, than your security awareness skills.

You need to set your expectations properly. To improve security behaviors and reducing losses from human actions, you need a formal, well-managed awareness program.

A great event cannot be executed unless you schedule it, budget for it, ensure the availability of the appropriate resources and people, advertise for the event, arrange refreshments, and so on. The content of the event is clearly critical, but it will never have a chance to succeed if you cannot bring together the event as a whole.

TECHNICAL STUFF

It may be helpful to invest in taking a project management course or looking for people to join your team who have project management certifications, such as a PMP, or similar experience.

Getting All Required Approvals

Many organizations have a department that approves all materials released to the organization. Ask about the typical turnaround time for these approvals. The review process may seem burdensome, but it serves several purposes:

» **Quality control:** Organizations try to ensure that distributed materials properly represent the organization. Spelling and grammatical errors are not only embarrassing but can also decrease the effectiveness of the communications.

» **Legal review:** Given the litigious nature of the business environment, there's a need to review for basic concerns, such as using appropriate language and not violating labor agreements.

» **Branding standards:** Reviews help ensure that any materials you distribute meet organizational branding standards. For example, you might need to adjust content to include new logos, appropriate color schemes, and gender-inclusive wording.

WARNING

Many people believe that the review process required to secure approvals is burdensome and unnecessary, but issues of poor taste and questionable wording do come up. In December 2020, for example, GoDaddy was heavily criticized for running a phishing simulation that told employees that if they clicked on the message, they would receive a holiday bonus. In response, many people stated that they would not do business with the company in the future. Though some people claim that criminals may use such a tactic, so it's fair game to run such a simulation, the backlash from employees and customers damaged the GoDaddy brand.

TIP

Work with the team that provides reviews proactively. Typically, the first time you put content through review, you may see several rounds of requested change because you're unfamiliar with the organization's standards or requirements. Allocate twice the expected turnaround time on your first rounds of program materials. As you become familiar with the review process and the evaluation criteria, you can expect the normal turnaround time.

Getting the Most from Day 0 Metrics

You must collect Day 0 metrics (said as "day zero metrics") before you begin your program (see Book 6, Chapter 5). By this time, you should have already determined the metrics you intend to study throughout the year. You can collect those metrics at any point before you begin the program. (In my experience, it generally takes at least two months from the time you start planning an awareness program until the formal launch of the program.)

TIP

Collect Day 0 metrics as soon as possible to get a head-start on your efforts. Some metrics, such as the number of security-related calls to the help desk, may appear easy to collect, but simple tasks have a way of becoming more complicated than you anticipate.

For example, you might find that the help desk doesn't categorize calls to the level you require. You may not have authorization for some data that you wanted for some reason. With phishing simulations, you may find that your technical team is slow in implementing required allowlisting of domains. (*Allowlisting*, also called *whitelisting*, is the technical term for allowing messages through email filters that would otherwise be blocked because they appear to be phishing messages.) Certain people might not be readily available because of illness or leave.

ADAPTING PHISHING EXERCISES FOR METRICS COLLECTION

A phishing simulation is an extremely common component of a security awareness program. When you perform a phishing exercise for metrics collection, however, you need to approach the simulations a little differently.

Most phishing simulations include training messages that inform users who fall for the message that they clicked on a phishing simulation. The messages tell the user how they could have performed better. If you incorporate these training messages into a simulation intended for metric collection, you increase the odds that users will warn other users about the simulation, which undermines the usefulness of the metrics you collect.

When you're doing a metrics-only phishing simulation, such as a Day 0 metrics collection, you should not provide any training or messaging that informs users of the simulation. If the phishing message simulates sending users to a link, provide generic content or a simple 404 message stating that the web page wasn't found. If the message intends to persuade users to give up their logon credentials, allow them to enter the credentials

(continued)

Running Your Security Awareness Program

(continued)

and move on. You have an extended period to train them after you collect the metrics, and in this case, collecting accurate metrics is more important than any increase in awareness you might possibly gain.

When you examine phishing metrics, be sure to consider the percentage of people who properly report the messages. This metric is more important than the number of people who fall for the message compared with the number of people who don't. The proper response to a phishing message isn't just not to click on the message but also to report the message.

Reporting the messages is so important, in fact, that you might consider rewarding users who do so. Book 6, Chapter 9 covers this topic in more detail.

As part of your planning, you should have identified three or so metrics that you intend to track over the course of the program (see Book 6, Chapter 5). If you have the time and resources, you should collect all potential metrics reasonably available to you as part of a Day 0 effort. Collecting these metrics on an ongoing basis may be impractical, but if you have the initial metrics, you may be able to use them as a starting point to compare with metrics you collect in the future.

REMEMBER

Collect any metric that's available on Day 0. If you can collect malware incidents, do it. If you have the time to sit outside a door to see how many people, if any, stop tailgaters to ask for a badge, do it. If you want to test for yourself, try to tailgate people on their way in and count how many people stop you to ask for a badge. Walk around your facilities after hours and determine the percentage of desks that are left unsecured. If you have free time, do these things as experiments to get a feel for the overall security posture of your organization. If you later need a supportive metric, you may be able to return to these metrics.

Creating Meaningful Reports

A theme of this book is that you need to deserve more. You only truly deserve more, of course, when you can demonstrate that you deserve more to the appropriate executives in your organization. This means that you can provide metrics in a meaningful way.

You may need to create reports for your direct manager and your manager's direct manager. You need to find out what reports you need to provide, and the type of information they require. Some reports will probably be status reports to inform management how you're spending your time and budget. Management will want to see that the program is being managed well. These reports will likely be standard reports for all people running other projects in your department or another group. If your organization doesn't provide report formats, you can create whatever your management is comfortable with.

Perhaps most important is a report detailing your measurable results. This report should be simple and focus on improvements that can be attributed to your efforts. By this point, you should have chosen the metrics you want to collect and use to prove that you deserve more resources and support. Ideally, these metrics define a return on investment. If not, the metrics should define measurable improvement in behaviors. You can resort to compliance, engagement, or likability metrics, but they should imply some intangible benefits.

Presenting reports as a graphical dashboard

Reports that are to be provided to executive management should be concise. Consider presenting them as a graphical dashboard. You should have each of your three or so metrics portrayed in graphical form. The graphical format should show before-and-after metrics so that the improvement you create is clear. This can be a bar graph, line graph, percentage change, or whatever gets the job done. Your choice of display should match the data.

Figure 7-1 includes a comprehensive index score, where five metrics that were collected are normalized. It simultaneously shows all improvements in the metrics.

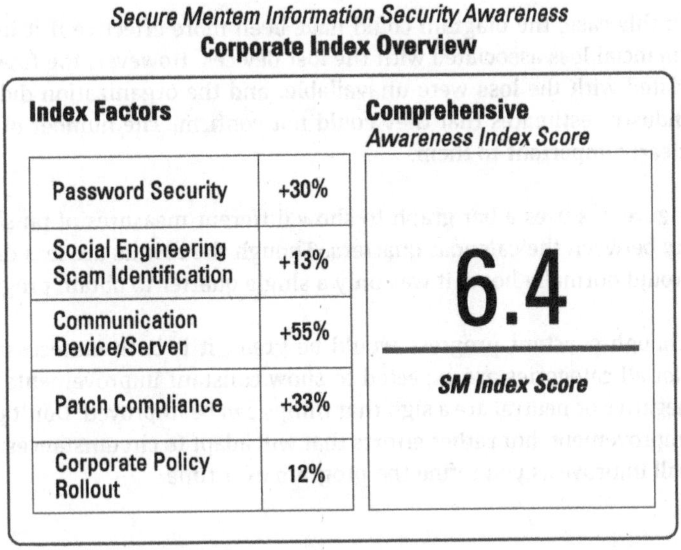

Secure Mentem Information Security Awareness
Corporate Index Overview

Index Factors		Comprehensive *Awareness Index Score*
Password Security	+30%	
Social Engineering Scam Identification	+13%	**6.4**
Communication Device/Server	+55%	
Patch Compliance	+33%	*SM Index Score*
Corporate Policy Rollout	12%	

FIGURE 7-1: Consolidated metrics dashboard.

Figure 7-2 portrays the number of lost or stolen mobile devices. In this case, a line graph is most appropriate because it allows for the depiction of the lost device over time. A note indicates when the awareness program began. In this case, increased awareness resulted in more accurate reporting on behalf of the users. Users who are more aware are likely to report concerns more frequently.

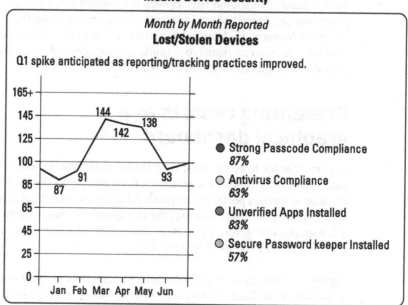

Mobile Device Security

Month by Month Reported
Lost/Stolen Devices

Q1 spike anticipated as reporting/tracking practices improved.

● Strong Passcode Compliance
87%

○ Antivirus Compliance
63%

● Unverified Apps Installed
83%

○ Secure Password keeper Installed
57%

FIGURE 7-2:
Mobile
device loss.

In this case, the diagram could have been more effective if it included the likely financial loss associated with the lost devices. However, the financial costs associated with the loss were unavailable, and the organization did not want to use industry estimates that they could not confirm. The number of lost devices was clearly important to them.

Figure 7-3 uses a bar graph to show different measures of phishing susceptibility between the calendar quarters. Though the results are less dramatic than you would normally hope, it was only a single quarter to obtain progress.

TIP

Though constant progress would be great, it is both unnecessary and unlikely. Not all categories are expected to show constant improvements. Results that are negative or neutral are a sign that things can be improved. Don't promise constant improvement, but rather efforts that will adapt to circumstances as they arise and will improve as you refine the program over time.

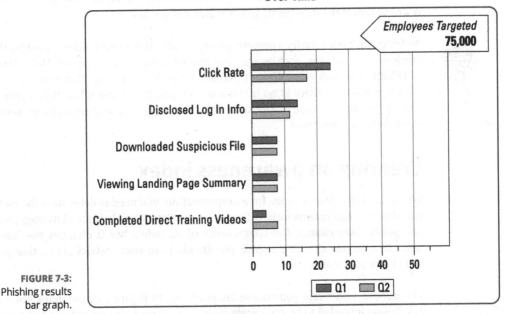

Employee Susceptibility Over Time

Employees Targeted
75,000

- Click Rate
- Disclosed Log In Info
- Downloaded Suspicious File
- Viewing Landing Page Summary
- Completed Direct Training Videos

0   10   20   30   40   50

Q1   Q2

FIGURE 7-3:
Phishing results
bar graph.

The reports you choose to provide are up to you. Different organizations have various preferences for reporting. Some organizations have established reporting templates and protocols because of quality control efforts like Six Sigma. (*Six Sigma* is a set of techniques and tools for process improvement and is a common business process that's implemented in many organizations.) Though you will likely need to provide, to different levels of management, some reports that detail the types of efforts and resources expended, be sure to create summary graphics that show some quick wins. Ideally, some low-hanging fruit will allow you to demonstrate early progress.

Adding index scores

An *index score*, such as the one shown in Figure 7-1, is essentially an average score you create that incorporates metrics. You basically create a formula that combines all the metrics into a single number. Some awareness indicators can go up. Some can go down. Others can remain neutral. Individually, it's a sign of improvement. However, an index score looks at indicators in aggregate to reflect an overall sign of improvement.

Figure 7-1 shows an index score that reflects a rating the organization could use to track their performance over time, as just showing that reduced phishing simulation click rates did not translate into an overall improvement in organizational awareness. Index scores offer a single number that can be presented on a dashboard to represent the overall security awareness effort.

TECHNICAL STUFF

An index isn't necessarily a percentage or an indication of perfection. Consider the stock market indexes, such as the Dow Jones Industrial Average, NASDAC, FTSE, or Nikkei. A perfect value doesn't necessarily exist. Though a value of 0 is possibly the minimum, there is no maximum. You just know that when this mythical value goes up, the value of stocks in general goes up. An awareness index works essentially the same way.

Creating an awareness index

To create an awareness index for an organization, you need to determine the metrics that you can consistently collect. Like the Dow Jones Industrial Average, you can periodically change the components of an index, but it changes the index score to a certain extent. To start, you should have your metrics set so that you can create your index.

The number and range you choose are arbitrary. In Figure 7-1, the index score is 6.4. It was intended to be on a scale from 1–10. It could have easily been 64 on a scale of 1–100. It seemed better not to have it appear to be a percentage at that time.

TIP

Here are the basic steps to derive an index:

1. **Give a weight to the different metrics.**

   If you have three metrics, the default would be to give each one 33.3 percent of the index value. If you think one of the metrics is more important, you might perhaps break it out as 50 percent for the most important metric and 25 percent each for the remaining two.

2. **For each metric, determine a rating system.**

   For example, for a phishing simulation, you may say that the percentage of people who didn't click on a message is the score. So, if 80 percent of the users did not respond to the metric, it would be an 8 (for a scale of 1–10). If you study unsecured desks, and 65 percent of desks are secured, that would be a 6.5. If you also want to include the people who completed awareness training, and 90 percent of people completed the training, that would be a 9.

3. **Calculate the index.**

   If you then want to create an index based on the numbers in Step 2 and you believe that all values are equal, the index score would be (8 x 0.33) + (6.5 x 0.33) + (9 x 0.33). The index score would then total to 7.755 or rounded to 7.8.

You can modify the weights for each component of the index as appropriate. As long as you collect information and perform the calculations in a similar way, the index represents an overall awareness score that takes into account fluctuations in the metrics collection process.

Reevaluating Your Program

You need to evaluate regularly how successful your program is. Though you should be collecting individual metrics as they are scheduled, you need to evaluate the entire program at predetermined intervals. If you follow my advice and implement your program in quarterly cycles, the end of every cycle is a regular checkpoint. Even if you implement your program on an annual cycle, reevaluating your program every three months is likely prudent.

REMEMBER

Metrics are the most critical aspect of your awareness program. You have to show that you deserve more — more resources, more funding, more support from management. You have to show that you're providing a return on investment. Other people will consider this, so you want to consider it first.

You should be more aware than anyone else with regard to the areas of success and failure within your program. You need to consider where you're fundamentally adding value, where you're failing, and where progress is uncertain. You need to take an honest accounting of the results of your efforts.

WARNING

If your program draws positive feedback from users, this doesn't guarantee that the program is a success. You need to find metrics that prove your efforts provide value to the organization. Try to see the less successful aspects of the program more readily than the apparent successful ones. Other people will, especially those who approve your budget.

Likeability is good. Positive comments are good. But providing metrics that state there is improved behavior and ideally a tangible return on investment is best. If all you have are likeability and participation metrics, make the most of them. You have to be able to frame these metrics in the best light possible, however.

Your goal at this point is to accept the honest metrics to determine how to better move forward. If you identify clear returns on investment, you need to continue that improvement. At the same time, find the deficiencies — and you will find deficiencies.

Running Your Security
Awareness Program

REMEMBER

Embrace your successes. Tout those successes. You do need to sell yourself and your efforts. Just be aware of the reality of the situations, both positive and negative, so that you can constantly improve your program.

Reconsidering your metrics

You should have chosen your metrics to be sustainable, reasonably easy to collect, and relevant to the organization and your program. This section applies to your first time through a program. You can, and possibly should, reconsider your metrics periodically, but for the first run of your program, you need to consider whether the metrics you chose to collect fit your purposes, and were as easy to collect as you anticipated.

Metrics that initially fit your purposes may stop working for you as circumstances change. You might lose resources to have a social engineering test performed every quarter. You may have pushback on your phishing program. You might find that responses to questionnaires are inconsistent. A change of management may cause support to fluctuate for aspects of your awareness efforts.

TIP

Here are some questions to ask when you assess your metrics:

>> Is the metric producing apparently consistent results?

>> Is there legitimate pushback to the metric?

>> Was the metric actually meaningful to the organization?

>> Was the metric as easy to collect as anticipated?

>> Is the metric producing meaningful results that aren't similar to other metrics?

>> Is there another metric that might produce more meaningful results and be easier to collect?

If you do achieve results, you may receive an increased budget, which would allow for more costly and time-consuming metrics collections. For example, you may gain the resources to add a USB drop, which can be expensive. So you can change metrics for good reasons as well as bad.

Evaluating your communications tools

Your communications tools are your awareness program. You need to consider how they're performing, in both the number of people that engage with the tool and their actual effectiveness.

In some cases, the usage is obvious. If you hold an event and it's standing room only, it's seemingly a well-attended event. If few people show up, and if you record the event and few people watch the recording, clearly the event isn't worth the effort. With newsletters, you might be able to track how many times they are read. You might be able to count clicks on links in the newsletter. Again, if there are few clicks, it likely isn't worth your efforts to continue to create the newsletter. Other forms of communications tools should have their own ways of measuring engagement with the tool.

TECHNICAL STUFF

Engagement metrics are not a great way to judge the effectiveness of an overall awareness program, but you should collect engagement metrics for the tools you use. You don't use these metrics to prove how well you're changing behaviors. You use engagement metrics to determine how to allocate your limited resources moving forward. For example, if few people read a newsletter, discontinue the newsletter and use the funding and effort on other tools that have been shown to be more accepted by the users.

TIP

While considering engagement metrics, you want to study a breakdown in demographics. Are certain regions engaging with different tools than others? Are people in given job functions engaging with certain tools? For example, you know that people who don't regularly use computers likely won't engage with computer-based tools, but is there a trend in what they do engage with? You may, for example, find that relatively few people look at your mobile device content, but it's the only content that factory workers engage with. You therefore may want to continue to use it because it's the most reliable way to reach that demographic.

Clearly, there will be cultural differences across the world. This is expected, and you want to address the cultures. You may however need to make some hard choices. You may determine that though some cultures prefer one communications method, it might not warrant the overall effort given the competing resources.

Measuring behavioral changes

As covered in Book 6, Chapter 6, in your first cycle (or whatever previous cycle you were on), you should have had three topics of focus. Those topics represent your learning goals for the cycle. As you end a cycle, you should determine whether your goals have been met.

Keep in mind that you may not know whether you have met your goals. Your metrics are unlikely to equate directly to the topics you're running in this cycle of your program. Phishing is likely to be one of those metrics, but it might not be a formal topic in your current campaign. This is okay.

Throughout a cycle, your reasonable hope should be that people pick up some information and begin to apply it. It's likely that there will be, at best, some memory of what you present and a more frequent application of that information. You cannot expect much more than that, and that is okay. Even small improvements are a start, and if you can consistently build on small improvements, you achieve major improvements over time.

If your program addresses a critical need or behavior with a properly defined metric, you can make a fair determination. For example, if ransomware is a major concern and you're collecting ransomware statistics, you can make a fair determination of your success. For a broad topic, like social engineering or mobile device security, you probably can't determine whether or how much improvement has occurred without appropriate metrics.

As you consider the success of your behavioral modification goals, you can look to your overall metrics, or you can look to small improvements in your goal. In the worst case, consider that you won't always be able to measure success.

REMEMBER

You need to determine whether behavior change differs across the various demographics throughout your organization. For a variety of reasons, some areas might have seen more success than others. IT departments will likely respond to different behaviors than others. If the awareness program is in the IT organization, for example, you will likely have more support and adherence from your own department. You may also find that you created a theme that resonates more with one age group than another.

In the end, you need to be honest with yourself about whether the topics were well addressed and you achieved the desired goals. If not, you have to examine whether there were perhaps inconsistent results across the organization. Inconsistencies are perhaps the most telling, because they can provide clues to why your program is or isn't working.

Redesigning Your Program

After you evaluate how you did (or are currently doing) in the cycle you're finishing, you can consider what you should be doing in the next cycle. Ideally, you've had reasonable success and the program flowed and executed well. If that isn't the case, you have some problems to address. Even if everything went perfectly, you can still look to make enhancements.

TECHNICAL STUFF

Awareness programs are generally evolutionary. Rarely are there radical changes. Some things are added, and others are eliminated. Even successful efforts are enhanced and improved as you learn more and can at least do things more efficiently.

Anything stand out?

There might have been something you wanted to do in the previous cycle that you didn't have the time or resources to implement. You might have wanted to start out conservatively, and add more aspirational efforts after you were comfortable that everything was going reasonably well. Now is the time to consider adding to your program.

Assuming that the resources are there, and that you have the bandwidth, you should consider adding what you can. This doesn't mean that you cannot or should not remove other communications tools that no longer fit, however.

Adding subcultures

It isn't uncommon to start your awareness program as a single program, and adding programs for subcultures is a logical stepping stone. As you become more confident in your program and abilities, it's time to consider creating unique programs for the appropriate subcultures.

REMEMBER

As covered in Book 6, Chapter 6, subcultures can be defined by geography, business role, department, function, and/or any other distinct and reasonable categorization. If you choose to create a unique program for a specific geography, you don't have to create a unique program for every geography. If you choose to create a special program for call center operators, you don't have to create a program for all other job functions.

TIP

As you consider adding subcultures, you should determine how much extra effort and other resources you have available. For example, you will likely send phishing messages to all employees. If you have unique awareness programs for some subcultures, you should create unique phishing campaigns for the subcultures and the creation, management, and reporting of unique campaigns might require significant effort. If you're using different posters in different geographies, you will still have the about the same level of effort to distribute the posters, but there is extra effort and cost in designing the posters.

You will likely be able to use a lot of your materials from your main campaign for chosen subcultures. Therefore, it isn't a linear increase in cost and resources for subcultures, though you do however have to determine what aspects will be unique to the subcultures. The goal is to determine what will make the program for the subculture more effective. Though it isn't necessarily out of the question to design a completely unique program for a given subculture, it usually isn't necessary. There should normally be overlap in the use of much, if not most, of the material used, saving you significant resources.

As you determine the subcultures you want to target, and then determine the resources required, you can identify which if any subcultures to add.

Adding, deleting, and continuing metrics

The previous section discussed metrics and how your chosen metrics might have been shown to be inappropriate for your needs. For these reasons and others, you might consider adding or deleting metrics.

TECHNICAL STUFF

If you have been using some metrics for your dashboard or incorporated into an index, you have to just accept that there is a fundamental change in the basis for the overall awareness metrics. You might need to annotate it for management when you submit the metrics for reporting. In all likelihood, you won't get a question as good management will understand the inevitability of periodic changes. There might be basic questions as to why and what will be the impact, but these are questions that are straightforward to address.

Adding and discontinuing communications tools

Based on an evaluation you perform after your running your program's first cycle, as described in the earlier section "Evaluating your communications tools," you may decide to change which communication tools you use in your program. Most likely, though, you will reuse the same tools across cycles. This section helps you plan accordingly.

TIP

I usually recommend that awareness managers start conservatively and limit what they do in the early cycles to see what works, and what doesn't, and then add things as they become comfortable enough to add more. In the planning stages, there should have been a variety tools you considered but chose not to use. During every review, consider which tools you might want to discontinue and which communications tools you want to add.

Your metrics might be able to tell you where you need more engagement from different populations. Are there additional tools that would better reach different populations? Are there tools that are apparently reaching some populations and you want to increase the usage of those tools?

If you learn that the events you held were well liked and seemed to have made an impact, you might want to hold more events. On the other hand, even if the events were reasonably well attended, you might find that the events were resource intensive. In this case, you may decide that they aren't a good use of limited resources and look to other tools that could prove a better use of your time.

The following list presents some more aspirational tools to implement as your program begins to mature. These tools require more effort, so you likely want to make sure that the basic program is running well before adding them. These tools are usually more appropriate for some subcultures. Even if you believe that they can and should be implemented throughout your entire organization, you likely want to start implementing the tool within a subculture or small part of your organization to work out any problems on a smaller scale:

>> **Gamification:** A rewards structure where you create positive consequences for desired behaviors. Gamification is a good tool to consider adding to an established program. For details on integrating gamification with your awareness program, see Book 6, Chapter 8.

>> **Experiential engagement:** Contests, security cubicles, scavenger hunts, speakers, event tables, and so on. See Book 6, Chapter 4 for more suggestions for experiential engagement.

>> **Security ambassadors:** Users you entrust to perform outreach within their own communities. They function as your local hands, eyes, and ears in their organizations, as described in Book 6, Chapter 4.

REMEMBER

You can consider which tools you're comfortable to add to the current program. Again, you want to use everything possible, but at the same time, as with all cybersecurity efforts, you have limited resources and you need to determine the best balance for your needs.

Revisiting awareness topics

The natural inclination for most awareness programs is to address 12 topics over the course of the year, changing the topic monthly. Book 6, Chapter 6 discusses why this approach is a mistake.

TIP

For every cycle, you need to determine which three topics are your most critical awareness needs. This recommendation may differ from the practice of most awareness practitioners, but consider the three current topics as potential topics to feature in the next cycle. In other words, the driver for the content of your awareness program at any given time is your business needs, as described in Book 6, Chapter 3.

This doesn't mean that you completely ignore what topics you had in the previous cycle. If it's a generic topic where you aren't necessarily collecting relevant metrics, such as travel security, you can move on to other subjects. However, if it involves common and concerning topics such as phishing, malware, or secure workspaces, you should definitely consider the topics for any cycle, even if it was used before.

If you choose to rerun a topic, you still need to create fresh content. Showing the same content from one cycle to the next makes the topic come across as background noise. With phishing, for example, you can discuss basic phishing one cycle, cover spearphishing in another cycle, choose web link safety for the next one, and so on. There are many ways to keep a topic fresh.

TECHNICAL STUFF

If you're collecting metrics regarding specific topics and the metrics come back bad, you want to rerun a topic and attack it in a different way. It should not even be an option to remove the topic until you see improvement. Again, this isn't the way many professionals approach the problem, given that they have mapped out their program a year in advance, but it should be the way you do it.

In essence, with the exception of the likely elimination of less relevant topics from the previous cycle, every topic is viable in every cycle. You then take the three topics and place them in the matrix, as described in Book 6, Chapter 6.

Considering Breaking News and Incidents

When choosing topics for the next cycle, you must consider any incident that your organization, your industry, or the general public experiences. If you have a significant phishing loss or a ransomware incident, for example, you should incorporate it into your program and address it in your program in the coming cycle.

If incidents occur in your industry and you receive warnings from relevant Industry Sharing and Analysis Centers (ISACs), you should incorporate the incident and the relevant topics into your awareness program. (There are ISACs for many industry sectors, including the financial sector, state governments, and healthcare.) For example, even cybersecurity companies were informed that North Korean hackers were targeting security researchers using what amounts to catfishing tactics via Twitter. Though it's unlikely that any random individual would be targeted, incidents such as this one make the threat real to an organization and an industry.

When a cyberattack becomes a major headline, try to make it relevant to your users. In the Twitter hack in 2020, a hacker was able to social-engineer login credentials out of a Twitter employee, and then use those credentials to change the passwords of notable Twitter users and sell access to the accounts. The lessons to promote based on this incident included social engineering, vishing (voice phishing), phishing, multifactor authentication (which is vital), password security, and many others.

Widely publicized malware incidents, such as Wannacry, which had a massive impact around the world, are a great time to promote the importance of running antimalware software and system updates, and other issues.

TECHNICAL STUFF

When COVID-19 began to have an impact around the world and created an environment where work-from-home became the default when at all possible, many awareness programs were sent into a scramble. Organizations who incorporated flexibility into their strategy had no problems adjusting to the circumstances from a strategic perspective, because they already anticipated creating a fresh program on a regular basis.

The COVID-19 pandemic presented a unique circumstance in that not only were topics affected but delivery methods were also somewhat changed. People still had email and online access to watch computer-based training. Posters, in-person events, desk drops, and the like were no longer useful. Likewise, many metrics were no longer relevant. Phishing simulations, for example, were still potentially valid, but tailgating tests and clean desk counts were no longer possible.

Chapter **8**

Implementing Gamification

Behavioral science studies indicate that consequences are four times more effective in creating desired *behaviors* than providing information via traditional awareness campaigns. Gamification is essentially a formalized process used to build meaningful consequences into your awareness program, and therefore should be four times more effective at achieving desired behavior changes than your other efforts.

It is therefore worth your time to consider putting a significant portion of your efforts into implementing gamification. It doesn't mean that you should — it means that you should consider it. However, be aware, before you continue reading this chapter, that the benefit comes with implementing actual gamification and not just a game, which is explained throughout the chapter.

Understanding Gamification

To most people, the word *gamification* implies that games will be a part of your awareness program. After all, the word gamification starts with most of the word *game*. The words, however, differ in meaning.

The definition of gamification is the application of typical elements of game play to encourage engagement with a product or service. This chapter discusses those elements later, but the important issue is that gamification isn't a game. Gamification encourages desired behaviors by providing positive consequences to those behaviors.

As an example, consider businesses that want to encourage salespeople to sell more of a particular product or service. You might think that salespeople should not need to be incentivized to sell more, because they already earn greater commissions based on how much they sell. That is true, but businesses frequently want to encourage even greater sales of certain products and services. So businesses created sales incentives. Many companies have a President's Circle for salespeople: The top salespeople receive special bonuses and trips, and people become extremely competitive to win the trips. Despite the fact that salespeople already earn commissions, enhanced rewards for selling more and selling specific types of services and products focuses them to hit targets beyond the minimum goals.

Consider, however, if these businesses did not give out trips for top salespeople and instead created a game to see who could name the features of a product. The game might be fun. Some competition might exist to be the person who knows the most about the business's products. In the end, though, while salespeople knowing more about the product "should" perhaps generate more sales, in this example, properly implemented gamification should reward and encourage sales, not knowledge. Encouraged by gamification, salespeople become even more competitive to win the trips and the acknowledgment. The game may be fun, but fun doesn't pay the bills.

TECHNICAL STUFF

Other examples of gamification include frequent flier programs, grocery store frequent shopper programs, and credit card rewards. Frequent flier programs reward customers with upgrades and preferred boarding for being a loyal customer, getting the airline-branded credit card, and other actions that increase the airline's profits. Grocery store rewards provide cheaper prices for customers who essentially allow themselves to be tracked so that the store can sell the information to vendors and better market to the customers. Credit card companies give cash-back bonuses or frequent flier miles to people who use the credit cards, which encourages people to use their credit cards more frequently.

REMEMBER

Awareness influences behaviors. Behaviors generate a consequence. Consequences then reinforce or discourage behaviors. If your gamification program quizzes people on information to encourage learning, you have a game. If your program rewards people for practicing the desired behaviors in a real environment, you have a true gamification program.

For security awareness purposes, consider a common game where you have users look at a password and determine whether the password is weak or strong. They might logically learn more details about password strength, and they can have fun doing so, but there is no indication that they will then create a password. You have essentially provided awareness, not consequences. Though it might help users lengthen the Forgetting Curve, it has no bearing on actual password strength. This is a game.

On the other hand, suppose that you run a password cracker against the master password file. You reward users who have passwords that cannot be cracked, and you force other users to change their passwords. That is gamification. It is dealing with actual passwords and reinforcing actual security behaviors. This strategy has a measurable impact on improving password strength.

Even if you consider that someone may enjoy the game so much that they're encouraged to go back to their computer and immediately change their passwords, it's a one-time event and they may or may not change their passwords back after having had to remember complex passwords for a time. Either way, everyone knows that just because someone knows what they should do, it rarely means that they will do it when there is nothing else to encourage otherwise more difficult behaviors.

Gamification, however, captures people exercising the appropriate behavior and rewards them for it. It generates positive consequences for demonstrating the desired behaviors. So a person who is rewarded for having good passwords, or who suffers a negative consequence of a weak password, is much more likely to not have weak passwords now and in the future.

REMEMBER

Gamification uses rewards to create a positive consequence that reinforces behaviors as they are demonstrated. If you're just trying to make learning information fun (providing an antecedent), that is a game, not gamification. There is some scientific proof that people might retain information slightly longer (slow the Forgetting Curve), but there is no proof that it actually creates increased and consistent behavior change, which is what actually provides value back to the business.

Identifying the Four Attributes of Gamification

Gamification is a commonly used business process. A great deal of research has been done in the field, and standardization exists for the field. This is good news because you can use defined attributes for gamification to determine whether you're implementing it properly.

Perhaps the best and most commonly referenced set of attributes are those defined by Jane McGonigal in her iconic book *Reality Is Broken* (Penguin Books, 2011). *Reality Is Broken* gives the definitive descriptions of the four attributes of gamification, but here is a quick summary:

>> **Goals are clearly defined.** You need to let users know the rules. They need to know specifically what it takes to earn the rewards at given levels. There are frequently levels or rewards that grow progressively more difficult to achieve as someone rises through the levels.

>> **Rewards are desirable to the participants.** Users should want to earn the rewards. The rewards need to be something that would be considered valuable and worthy of effort to the targeted audience.

>> **Goals are achievable.** If a person does want to achieve the goals, the time and effort to do so must be reasonable, given the potential reward. For example, if you want to reward people for reporting phishing messages, you don't want the basic reward level to require the reporting of 1,000 messages. The lowest tier might just require reporting a single message. Additionally, you would want to provide phishing simulations and counting the reporting of the simulated phishing message to ensure that the user has an opportunity to earn the rewards.

>> **Participation is voluntary.** If people don't want to actively engage in your gamification, they shouldn't have to. They might unintentionally earn rewards along the way, such as reporting a phishing message without the intent of being part of the gamification program. However, they should not be forced to intend to earn rewards. But when a person begins to earn rewards, it just might encourage them to intentionally engage with the gamification program.

To design a true gamification program, you need to incorporate each of these attributes. For the most part, it just makes sense. If nobody wants your rewards, nobody will try to achieve them. Ensure that each attribute is embedded within your gamification program.

**TECHNICAL
STUFF**

Your awareness program is attempting to reduce your overall risk related to user-initiated loss. Your efforts cannot be limited to only those who want to be made more aware. That said, you can implement gamification for everyone and let people opt in for as much of the gamification as they choose. For example, you can send phishing simulation messages to everyone, and if they report them, you can reward them per a gamification plan that rewards people for reporting potential phishing messages. You can offer points for attending events that help people increase tiers in the gamification program, but they don't have to attend. They're more likely to attend, though, if the rewards are worth it.

The purpose of security countermeasures is to reduce organizational risk. The return on investment (ROI) of any countermeasure is that it reduces more loss than it costs to implement the countermeasure. As awareness training may have minimal obvious ROI, and gamification has the potential to be four times more effective than traditional awareness, even if you have a chance to reach only 25 percent of your users, you will likely have a higher ROI with gamification.

Figuring Out Where to Gamify Awareness

Generally, when you implement gamification, you don't target the entire organization. That approach likely isn't practical. For example, if you're in a manufacturing organization, factory workers, who don't use computers as part of their jobs and rarely access corporate email, won't likely be great candidates for gamification. People who regularly use computers are better candidates.

WARNING

Gamification does take some effort to implement, and the larger the target population, the more effort it takes to implement and manage the program. Therefore, picking and choosing where to implement gamification isn't based just on where it will have impact, but rather on the level of resources you can put toward the program. You need to choose wisely which subcultures gamification is appropriate for. If you try to include too large of a group of users, it may quickly become extremely costly and labor intensive — and impractical.

When you choose a target population for gamification, you need to understand the subcultures. Which subculture within the organization is more likely to be appropriate for gamification? As important, which subculture also has business drivers that are appropriate to target via gamification and are valuable enough to implement a resource intensive program?

TIP

Those subcultures that had awareness-related losses are the primary places to consider. Because there are potentially valuable rewards and promotions at stake, cultures that have a great deal of business value can be easily compromised because of failings related to security awareness.

You can bring gamification to the entire organization, and you perhaps should, with phishing reporting, for example, but you do have to account for the resources, which includes the technology to implement and track the program, the expenses or organizational capital for the rewards, the effort to promote the rules, rewards, and successes, and the people to run the effort. This sounds almost ironic, but you need an awareness program to promote the gamification program.

Examining Some Tactical Gamification Examples

Many awareness managers are overworked with their awareness programs as is, let alone adding a resource-intensive effort that will drain funding. Many might believe that gamification sounds like a great addition to your program, but a full gamification program is too resource intensive to implement now.

The following sections cover some forms of gamification that are more tactical and can be implemented with limited resources and effort on your part. It also helps when there are limited resources for rewards. These forms of gamification can address some tactical concerns as well, such as phishing reporting or security tool adoption. They essentially create a basic reward structure for exhibiting desired behaviors, which is gamification in its purest form.

Phishing reporting

If someone reports a phishing message, you provide some form of reward. It's that simple. It goes beyond the typical sentiment "Thank you for reporting the message" or "Congratulations! You detected our phishing simulation!" Though they sound great the first time, by the second time — and especially by the third time — a user reports a phishing message, the user not only believes that they receive no benefit but also may assume that the organization doesn't even care.

You need to do something more if you want to keep encouraging reporting of possible phishing messages. You need to either give an immediate reward for every report of a phishing message or track the number of reports and reward for a specific number of reports — and, ideally, better rewards for higher tiers of reporting. Most important, you need to let the user know that their reports are being tracked and they will be rewarded.

For example, the first tier might involve a generic "Thank you." However, it also includes a message that if they report two more potential phishing messages, they might receive a certificate for a free coffee or a similar item. You should also refer to a website that documents the tiers with the number of phishing messages reported and the respective rewards. Clearly, you need a reporting mechanism and the budget for the possible rewards, but it should have an impact in reported phishing messages. You should also mention that they will receive periodic phishing simulation messages so that they know they will have an opportunity to earn rewards.

WARNING

Some users might gratuitously report nonphishing messages, just to earn the rewards. You just have to be on the lookout for potentially abusive behaviors and adjust your program accordingly — or at least know how to deal with abusive users.

REMEMBER

You want people to report anything questionable because even generic spam messages indicate a weakness in your filters. The goal of reporting phishing messages is so that you can detect threats and remove them from the inboxes of users who aren't as aware as those reporting the messages.

Clean desk drops

Many organizations have a problem with people who don't physically secure their documents and computers. As a late night exercise that can help with this issue, you might print up green and red cards and bring along bags of Hershey Kisses. The green cards might say that the security team performed a physical security assessment and found that the desk was secure and then thanks them for that and offers a Hershey's Kiss. The red cards could say that you performed a security assessment and found that the desk was insecure; you can then ask the user to please secure their desk in the future, for which they might receive a reward during the next assessment. Both cards should indicate that there will be future assessments and provide a link to a website explaining the assessment.

You can work with a team of people to walk around the targeted facilities, and examine desks together to see whether computers are turned off (or at least whether a password-protected screen saver is active), laptops are secured in or to the desk, the physical desktop is clear of sensitive documents, and the desks and associated filing cabinets are locked. If they are properly secured, drop a green card and a Hershey's Kiss. If a desk isn't properly secured, drop a red card.

Counting the cards before and after the exercise makes metrics collection simple. Though you might consider the Hershey's Kiss a reward, the true reward is the acknowledgment people feel when they pass a test. Informing users that future assessments will occur keeps them on their toes. And conducting future assessments allows for metrics tracking over time.

Be sure to provide language for responding to queries that assures people that you're not tracking individual desks, and no punishments are associated with this effort. You might informally track which departments seem especially insecure as a whole, however, and decide to distribute extra posters or other nudges, related to physical security, to those departments.

Tailgating exercises

Tailgating exercises address concerns regarding unauthorized people entering an organization's facilities.

As with desk drops (described in the preceding section), you can print green and red cards. The green cards thank people for stopping any person trying to follow them into the building and come with a reward, such as having $20 bills taped to them. The red cards inform the recipient that they should have stopped the tail-gater, asked them for their badge, and referred the person to the main entrance, if they were a visitor. Be sure to mention that they would have been given a financial reward if they had responded appropriately. You also might enlist accomplices to perform the tests at different entrances.

The goal of this gamification effort is to get the people you test to provide the awareness to others. You can perform a tailgating or other effort such as this one only so many times without people being warned. You can reasonably expect that people will tell their coworkers about the cards they received.

TIP

The number of cards you distribute at the beginning and the end of the exercise allows for you to track metrics. If you start each exercise with 20 red cards and 20 green cards and then count the number of each color remaining at the end of the exercise, you can quickly calculate the percentage of people who stop you (and your accomplices) compared to who didn't. If you gave out 7 green cards and 7 red cards, it means that you were stopped 50 percent of the time. You stand to benefit most by performing an exercise like this one several times over two months at varying times of day.

USB drop reporting

For USB drop reporting, you can commission the creation of USB drives to use as part of an assessment. Because modern computers are rarely configured to autorun software, you may need to require special-purpose USB drives that will cause an executable to run on a computer upon loading. The program can track the device and display a message that devices should have been reported to the Help desk, and request people to send them to the Help desk. You can distribute the USB devices around the parking lots, cafeterias, and other common areas.

People who returned the devices per security procedures, without opening them, receive a financial reward. The awareness program can then promote the fact that people who returned the devices received a financial reward. You can repeat this exercise on multiple occasions over time.

Reporting security incidents

This activity doesn't involve simulations, but consider establishing a program to reward the reporting of potential security incidents. When you do so, be sure to identify rewards for the reporting of varying levels of potential security concerns.

**TECHNICAL
STUFF**

This effort is primarily an outreach effort to inform people about what the security team should be alerted to, how to be sent an alert, and the potential rewards for doing so. From that point, you can either provide rewards as promised for individual incidents or track the number of reports over time.

This is simple and basic. The focus is getting people to report incidents.

Ad hoc gamification

If you put together awareness programs long enough, you will need to deal with tactical awareness concerns. These are due to incidents the organization suffered, strategic technology plans, or industry trends. For example, if an organization suffered from credential phishing attacks, there's an urgency to implement multifactor authentication. Organizations that implement Bring Your Own Device (BYOD) policies need mobile device security. Sometimes you see industry trends with targeted phishing campaigns and you need to make an emergency awareness campaign of targeted attacks. Gamification is a great strategy for these efforts.

Consider the case of a high-tech organization with a policy that they cannot implement mandates. Unfortunately, this means that the CISO can't force developers to implement security patches on their personal systems. Because this particular organization is a noted high-tech company, employees had free food already. They had unlimited time off. Their stock options were valuable enough that even monetary incentives were not impactful. One way to approach this scenario is to play to the organization's pride. Though the CISO could not force the application of patches, the CISO could at least scan the systems. You can create a gamification program that examines the proliferation of fully patched systems.

You might consider, for example, creating a contest to reward the most secure department. As part of this program, you could examine the percentage of fully patched systems for each department and create a leader board over the period of a month. You would report weekly on which department was the most secure. Department managers and teams in general wouldn't want to be identified as the least secure, so they might exert peer pressure to encourage their teammates to implement autopatching (where the operating system installs security patches automatically). Departments that achieve 100 percent compliance can receive a trophy for their efforts.

REMEMBER

Business drivers tell you what behaviors should be rewarded, and then understanding the culture tells you how to best influence the users within that culture. You can hold a contest for people who follow your guidance, implement short-term rewards, or do whatever else you think will work. Remember, though, that the rewards must be meaningful for the users.

Putting Together a Gamification Program

If you're going to put together a full-scale gamification program, your goal is to reward a variety of security-related behavior over the course of a year or longer. Gamification efforts are independent of the other awareness program efforts, such as whether you implement your awareness program in quarterly or annual cycles. Gamification can be much more difficult to implement than most traditional programs. The bad side is that it does require more planning and resources; on the good side, however, the continuous nature of the program allows for modifications and improvements as necessary.

Determining reward tiers

Reward *tiers* are the different levels a user can obtain within the scope of the gamification program. For example, frequent flier programs have levels like Basic, Silver, Gold, Platinum, and Diamond. It takes a certain threshold of miles flown and dollars spent with the airline to earn the different status levels. You need to define your own reward tiers.

Consider first laying out the high-level structure of the program — how many tiers you want to have. The more tiers, the more effort is required by you in the planning and maintenance of the program. At the same time, the more tiers, the easier it is for you to maintain engagement.

TIP

In general, having five tiers is most effective. You can make it easy for people to achieve the first tier, and reasonably easy to achieve the second tier, and then the third tier becomes more challenging, which activates people's competitive nature. Basically, you want to create it so that after people achieve a tier, they believe that the next tier, although more difficult to achieve, is reasonably attainable.

The fourth and fifth tiers are then more challenging to achieve and are there to truly distinguish people who deserve recognition and the more desirable rewards. It isn't expected that everyone achieve, or even want to engage with, these tiers. The tiers are there, however, to encourage strong security behaviors and reward those who make the effort.

HOW POKEMON GO DEALS WITH POINTS

Niantic released Pokémon Go in July 2014 and within a year achieved 60 million regular players and more than $1 billion in annual revenue. Fundamentally, Pokémon Go is a simple game: You catch Pokémon. Despite this, the game developers have created engagement by implementing challenges, especially including completing the 40 different base levels. The first 10 levels were relatively easy to obtain. To advance from Level 1 to Level 2, you essentially had to achieve 1,000 points, which is catching 2 Pokémon. To achieve Level 3, you had to earn 2,000 additional points, which is again trivial. You can probably get to Level 12 with minimal effort. However, it grows more difficult as you go along. For example, to go from Level 19 to Level 20 involves earning more points than you needed to get from Level 1 to Level 10. Going from Level 39 to Level 40 involves earning more points than going from Level 1 to Level 34. Generally for the upper levels, you had to earn about 30 percent of the total points in order to reach the next level. You can assume that by that point, however, the players are invested. Over time, enough players earned Level 40 status that Niantic had to create 10 more levels to maintain engagement.

Assigning point levels

Now that you have your tiers, you should create a basic point structure to achieve the tiers. You have time to change it before you implement the program, but you need something to work with moving forward.

You clearly don't want to implement a point system like Pokémon Go (see the nearby sidebar "How Pokémon Go deals with points"), where you need to earn millions of points, because it would seem difficult, if not unachievable. Generally, you get the best results from a structure where users have to have a total of 100, 300, 600, 1500, or 3000 points to achieve the respective tiers.

Of course, you have to assign points to tasks that make the point system reasonable. See the upcoming section, "Assigning points to behaviors."

Creating a theme

Salesforce, the major software company, created a security gamification program and used a *Star Wars* theme to name the different levels. The Salesforce CEO is widely known as an avid *Star Wars* fan, which was why this theme was chosen. It provided something for people to distinguish the tiers while recognizing the notoriety of achieving them. *Star Wars* was readily meaningful to the organization, so it was a natural fit.

TIP

Your organization might not have a natural fit, but you can find *something*. You can use a popular movie reference. If you're in the defense or intelligence industry, you can consider military ranks. In the corporate environment, you might consider security associate, security manager, security director, security vice president, or CISO. The security team might not approve, but at least you should see the theme of recognizing a title that represents the difficulty and significance of achieving a given tier.

Offering valid rewards

To have true gamification, you need to provide valid rewards. Rewards generally involve certificates, tchotchkes, monetary rewards, executive recognition, or promotion consideration.

At the lower tiers, you generally give a certificate and an inexpensive giveaway. Mouse pads, squishy toys, stickers, and other items are inexpensive and easy to have. If you create a mascot for your awareness program, some version of the mascot can make a great giveaway. If you have a sufficient budget, you can look into more expensive items like T-shirts, other clothing items, and cellphone chargers, among others. Some organizations give away gift cards for Starbucks, Amazon, or other popular vendors.

You might also consider giving away security-related tools. For example, you can give a home license for antimalware, screen filters that prevent people from looking over someone's shoulder to read the screen, cable locks that prevent theft of laptops, and similar items. These things are just practical and reinforcing of security efforts.

TIP

Some organizations have other rewards programs where they let employees and departments give away points that can be used to trade in for different merchandise. If your organization makes use of such reward programs, get points specific for your rewards program. These programs not only provide rewards but also add legitimacy for your program.

At the higher tiers, you should endeavor to get the achievement something that can have a positive impact on promotions and salary increases. If your organization awards days off, cash, and other similar rewards, you want to attempt to allocate those types of rewards for your program. If your organization already has a rewards program, attempt to have a large number of points allocated for the higher tiers.

REMEMBER

What is most important is that the rewards are reasonably desirable to achieve the higher tiers of your program. At the lower tiers, you're generally allocating rewards that are appropriate to encourage someone to spend a minimal amount of effort. Once you get past the bottom two tiers, you should look for rewards that are truly desirable and worthy of those who are investing time in your program. This requires an understanding of your culture.

Assigning points to behaviors

After you have figured out what points people need to achieve different rewards, you need to identify how you will award users those points. If you will require 100 points to achieve the first tier, you need to determine how people can reasonably earn those 100 points.

REMEMBER

Your business drivers should ideally be how you determine those points. What behaviors do you want to reward? What are the simple and basic behaviors you want to reward?

Intuitively, you want people to take your training. You want people to report your phishing messages. You want people to lock their desks. You want people to attend events, read an article, and so on. These are the low-level points.

How long do you want it to take for people to achieve a basic tier? For example, if you want them to do it within two months, you might say that watching a mandatory video is worth 50 points. Reporting a phishing message or basic security violation might likewise be worth 50 points, and people can achieve the first the tier in less than a month. The second tier can be achieved in less than three months.

TIP

Then you consider what stretch activities you might want to reward. Report security incidents. Attend a focus group. Organize a local event. Attend a formal training class. Write a summary of an article to share. Contribute to a security newsletter. You may have other ideas about what is important to your organization.

These activities might be worth 100 or 200 points. It makes achieving the third tier reachable within a reasonable period, when combined with the lower-level activities. It is possible, and even likely, for everyone to achieve the third tier by doing only the basic activities, but it will take a longer period.

At the highest level, you want people to serve as your security ambassadors. You want people to find security vulnerabilities that are critical to your organization. You want people to make a contribution to your organization's security posture. These might be worth 300 to 500 points and make the higher levels achievable over time.

REMEMBER

All these generic recommendations have no specific knowledge of your culture and business drivers. Be creative as possible in how you create your point systems. This takes a thorough understanding of both your culture and its business drivers.

Tracking users and the points they earn

Clearly, you need a system that can track your users and the points they earn. This can be accomplished by using a spreadsheet. You can create a database to track the point structure and allow for retrieval. You may also create a web page that allows users to self-report their activities.

You can find commercially available gamification tracking software. Gamification is a well-accepted business function, and many companies created software tools to facilitate the implementation of a gamification program. These tools facilitate tracking. They're usually designed for large organizations implementing sales and customer retention programs, and might require a great deal of tailoring to meet your needs. It's also likely that security awareness vendors will begin to implement some form of gamification tracking in the future. A great resource for gamification tracking and implementation tools can be found at https://technologyadvice.com/gamification.

Your tracking system may be, ironically, the most complicated aspect of your program to implement. It's something to consider well before you implement your gamification program.

Promoting the Program

It may seem like a major irony, but to implement an awareness gamification program properly and effectively, you need to promote the gamification program. For gamification to work properly, people have to voluntarily engage with the program. They have to know *how* to engage with the program. They have to know the rewards and how to achieve them.

You need to promote the existence and basic structure of the program. See Book 6, Chapter 4 to discover the best tools to promote the gamification program.

Create website that defines the gamification program as simply as possible. You can then promote the website and program via emails and other tools that are appropriate for the culture. As people earn points in the program, the system can send them emails to inform them of their status and possibly include tips on how to earn more points. Consider posters, events, and other communications tools, as appropriate, to further promote the program.

Announcing those people who have achieved different tiers, as well as some of those rewards, is possibly one of the most effective methods to promote the gamification efforts. Announcing awardees and their rewards provides social proof that your peers are engaged in the gamification program and that the awards are achievable.

Index

C

geographic representatives, 567

geotagging, 154

GFI LanGuard, 347, 505

ghosts, 256

Gibson, William, 387

Git, 367

GitHub, 360

giveaways, 584–585

Glassdoor, 508

GLBA (Gramm-Leach-Bliley Act), 458

GoDaddy, 624

Google, 508–509, 520

  credit reporting, 64

  expunged records, 65

  location tracking, 66

  Social Security numbers, 65

  undermining security questions, 66

Google Authenticator, 385

Google Chrome privacy mode, 87

Google Cloud, 316

Google Cloud Discovery Service, 315–316

Google Photos, 252

governance by design, 368

government-issued documents, 246–247

Gramm-Leach-Bliley Act (GLBA), 458

gray-hat hackers, 55–56, 455, 477

green-hat hackers, 56

H

Hackin9, 483

hacking and hackers. *See also* cyberattacks; cybercriminals

  advancements and changes that affect, 10–20

    economic, 15–16

    political, 17–20

    social, 14

    technological, 10–11, 13

  anonymity, 484

  crackers, 477–478

  defined, 454–455

  hacker mindset, 473–484

hackers for hire, 478

hacktivism and hacktivists, 18, 25, 54–55, 478

hat colors, 55–56, 455, 477

  liberty, 481

  magazines for, 483

  monetization, 56–60

  motivations of, 474, 478–481

  planning and performing attacks, 482–483

  reformed hackers, 464–465

  role in advancement of technology, 475

  skill levels, 474, 476–478

  stereotypes, 473–474, 476

  thinking like, 475–476

hacktivism and hacktivists, 18, 25, 54–55, 478

hard drive/SSD light, never seeming to turn off, 228

hard resets, 280–285

  Android devices, 284

  Apple devices, 285

  defined, 280

  Mac computers, 284–285

  Windows computers, 281–283

hard tokens, 432–433

hardware security modules (HSMs), 437–445

  cloud HSMs, 438

  cryptography, 438

  defined, 437

  DNSSEC, 442–443

  financial data security requirements, 442

  key management services, 438–441

  OpenDNSSEC, 443–444

  tamper resistance, 441

  vendors, 444–445

hardware tokens, 119, 145–146

hash attacks, 42

hashed format, 245

having security controls in place first, 354

Health Information Technology for Economic and Clinical Health (HITECH) Act, 458

Health Insurance Portability and Accountability Act (HIPAA), 112, 188, 386, 457–458

heatmaps, 327–328

wiper attacks, 27

Wireshark, 501

Wiz, 376

work information, oversharing on social media, 155–156

worms, 35

WS_FTP (Progress Win-Sock FTP), 436

X

XSS (cross-site scripting), 40, 46–47

Y

YouTube, 508

Yubiko, 435

Z

Zabasearch, 510

zero trust architecture (ZTA), 419–420

zero trust framework, 407–427

  challenges in implementing, 419–427

    agile method, 427

    business collaboration, 426–427

    change, 424

    DIY solutions, 425–426

    full visibility, 425

    integrating legacy systems, 424–425

    roadmaps for, 419–420

    step-by-step approach, 420–423

    team building, 427

    third-party solution, 426

  defined, 407

  features of, 409–419

    accountability, 414–415

    cloud security posture management, 418–419

    endpoint device management, 410–411

    end-to-end encryption, 411–412

    least privilege policy, 416

    multifactor authentication, 409–410

    Network Access Control, 417–418

    policy based access, 413–414

  shifting from perimeter security, 408

zero trust maturity model, 419–420

zero-day malware, 13, 38

zombies, 26, 484, 520

Zoom bombing, 110

ZTA (zero trust architecture), 419–420

About the Authors

Joseph Steinberg: Joseph Steinberg serves as a cybersecurity expert witness and as cybersecurity advisor to both businesses and governments around the world. He has led organizations within the cybersecurity industry for nearly 25 years, has been calculated to be one of the top three cybersecurity influencers worldwide. Steinberg is one of only a few people worldwide to hold the suite of advanced information security certifications: CISSP, ISSAP, ISSMP, and CSSLP. His cybersecurity-related inventions are cited in well over 500 U.S. patent filings. In addition to his primary work, Steinberg currently serves as a senior policy analyst at the Global Foundation for Cyber Studies and Research think tank, as a cybersecurity expert member of *Newsweek* magazine's Expert Forum, and as an advisor to the WonderKey Collective nonprofit that provides technology and related resources to underserved and underfunded communities across the United States. Steinberg also presently serves on the Cybersecurity Council of CompTIA, the world's largest technology trade association and its second-largest related certifying body.

Steinberg authored *Cybersecurity For Dummies* and other publications, including the official study guide from which many chief information security officers (CISOs) study for their certification exams.

Kevin Beaver: Kevin Beaver is an independent information security consultant, professional speaker, and writer with Atlanta-based Principle Logic, LLC. He has three and a half decades of experience in IT and has spent most of that time working in security. Kevin specializes in performing independent information security assessments for corporations, security product vendors, software developers/cloud service providers, government agencies, nonprofit organizations, among others. He also provides information security consulting services and serves as a virtual chief information security officer (CISO) for many of his clients.

Kevin authored *Cloud Security For Dummies* (Wiley). He has also authored or co-authored 12 information security books, including *Hacking Wireless Networks For Dummies*, *Implementation Strategies for Fulfilling and Maintaining IT Compliance* (Realtimepublishers.com), and *The Practical Guide to HIPAA Privacy and Security Compliance* (Taylor & Francis Group).

Ted Coombs: Ted Coombs is a consultant technologist in Appleton, Wisconsin. He has spent over 40 years as a software developer, information security expert, and forensic computer scientist. He was formerly the vice president of PivX, an information security firm in Newport Beach, California. He currently consults as a futurist, sharing backgrounds in computer technology, anthropology, molecular biology, optic and mechanical engineering, and laser physics. He is semiretired, and in his spare time he creates adventure guides for Franko Maps, writes technology books, and paints portraits.

Ted is author of *Hacking For Dummies*, 7th Edition (Wiley).

Ira Winkler: Ira Winkler, CISSP, is chief security architect for Walmart, where he focuses on behavioral cybersecurity. He is also a member of the faculty of the University of Maryland Baltimore County Center for Cybersecurity. Mr. Winkler began his career at the National Security Agency, where he served as an Intelligence and Computer Systems Analyst. He moved onto support other US and overseas government military and intelligence agencies.

Ira authored *Security Awareness For Dummies* (Wiley), as well as six other award winning and bestselling books, including *You Can Stop Stupid* (Wiley), *Advanced Persistent Security* (Syngress), *Spies Among Us* (Wiley), *Through the Eyes of the Enemy* (Regnery), *Corporate Espionage* (Prima), and *Zen and the Art of Information Security* (Syngress).

Publisher's Acknowledgments

Executive Editor: Steve Hayes
Compilation Editor: Colleen Diamond
Project Editor: Colleen Diamond
Copy Editor: Colleen Diamond

Production Editor: Tamilmani Varadharaj
Cover Image: © Skorzewiak/Shutterstock

Learn cybersecurity inside and out

This book is the one-stop reference you need to secure your data from prying eyes in the cyber universe. You get a rundown of the threats that are out there, plus straightforward advice on how to defend against them. Industry experts give easy-to-understand and actionable steps you can take now to secure business networks, cloud data, personal computers, and smart home devices. You also get insight into how cybersecurity professionals keep hackers on their toes through penetration testing and increasing cybersecurity awareness within the business culture. Put your data on lockdown with this all-in-one guide.

6 Books Inside...

- Grasping Cybersecurity Basics
- Enhancing Personal Cybersecurity
- Safeguarding a Business
- Securing the Cloud
- Testing Your Security
- Enhancing Cybersecurity Awareness

This All-in-One gathers the expertise of the leading *For Dummies* authors in the world of cybersecurity, including **Joseph Steinberg**, author of *Cybersecurity For Dummies*; **Kevin Beaver**, author of *Hacking For Dummies*; **Ted Coombs**, author of *Cloud Security For Dummies*; and **Ira Winkler**, author of *Security Awareness For Dummies*.

Cover Image: © Skorzewiak/Shutterstock

Go to Dummies.com™
for videos, step-by-step examples, how-to articles, or to shop!

Computers Security/General
$49.99 USA/$59.99 CAN/£37.99 UK

ISBN 978-1-394-15285-8

9 781394 152858

54999

for
dummies®
A Wiley Brand